CONTRIBUTIONS TO OJIBWE STUDIES

CRITICAL STUDIES IN THE
HISTORY OF ANTHROPOLOGY

Series Editors

Regna Darnell
Stephen O. Murray

A. IRVING HALLOWELL

CONTRIBUTIONS *to* OJIBWE STUDIES

Essays, 1934–1972

Edited and with introductions by
Jennifer S. H. Brown and Susan Elaine Gray

UNIVERSITY OF NEBRASKA PRESS
LINCOLN AND LONDON

Acknowledgment for the use of copyrighted
material appears on pages 607–11, which
constitute an extension of the copyright page.

Set in Arno Pro by Kim Essman.
Designed by Ashley Muehlbauer.

Library of Congress Cataloging-in-Publication Data

Hallowell, A. Irving (Alfred Irving), 1892–1974.
Contributions to Ojibwe studies : essays, 1934–1972 /
A. Irving Hallowell, edited and with introductions by
Jennifer S. H. Brown and Susan Elaine Gray.
p. cm. — (Critical studies in the history of anthropology)
Includes bibliographical references and index.
ISBN 978-0-8032-2391-2 (pbk. : alk. paper)
1. Ojibwa Indians—History. 2. Ojibwa Indians—Social life
and customs. I. Brown, Jennifer S. H. II. Gray, Susan
Elaine. III. Title.
E99.C6H257 2010
977.004'97333—dc22   2009047710

CONTENTS

ILLUSTRATIONS

SERIES EDITORS' INTRODUCTION
Regna Darnell and Stephen O. Murray

Critical Studies in the History of Anthropology was established with the intention to consolidate an emerging audience of practicing anthropologists and historians committed to tracing the effects of the past upon contemporary practice. The anthropologists among series readers are perhaps more interested in ethnographic verisimilitude than their historical colleagues, but both are committed to the enterprise of historicism in its broadest sense—that is, the framing of past persons and events in the context of their own times prior to judgment. This position is the characteristic anthropological one of cultural relativism, transposed from synchronic space to diachronic history.

Jennifer S. H. Brown has been the key figure in drawing A. Irving "Pete" Hallowell into the mainstream of history of anthropology in recent years. With Maureen Matthews she followed Hallowell's footsteps through Berens River Ojibwe country and spoke with the people who remember "their" anthropologist and continue to draw upon his work. She and Susan Elaine Gray have continued to explore the continuity from past to present and its critical importance for the Ojibwe future in the region between Hudson Bay and Lake Winnipeg. Their attention has turned from Hallowell, the ethnographer, to Chief William Berens, the consultant and confidant of a younger ethnographer who knew how much he had yet to learn. "Willie" Berens was an articulate contemporary leader of his time, a Christian with a family and cultural heritage that remained deeply enmeshed in Anishinaabeg traditional spirituality. He chose not to use his dream gifts fully, but continued to value them as belonging to his people and undergirding their identity in a rapidly changing world.

The papers themselves span almost four decades during which Hallowell pursued his increasing understanding of the Ojibwe and used that understanding to test the theory and practice of his own anthropological discipline. More than most, he was able to move with changes in disciplinary culture over the course of his career. When Regna Darnell was his student during the mid-1960s, Hallowell had moved beyond the language of culture and personality and adopted the then-contemporary rhetoric and methods of ethnoscience. In both analytic modes he sought ways to show readers from other cultural backgrounds how Ojibwe persons (and "other-than-human persons") saw the world. He understood this as a question of ontology, not merely of epistemology. Hallowell's sense of the importance of history of anthropology as an anthropological problem applied our own method of defamiliarization to the Ojibwe over time and honed from his ethnography, rife with Ojibwe voices and representative anecdotes, a trenchant mode of disciplinary critique.

Brown and Gray have divided the papers into seven thematic sections, with each proceeding in roughly chronological order. Hallowell's 1972 reflection on his own career as an anthropologist supplements their introduction of the editorial project itself. The range of audiences (interdisciplinary and popular) and the complexity of information approached from a variety of theoretical angles introduce considerable repetition. This repetition may be framed by readers of this volume in the spiral mode of Anishinaabeg pedagogy, with each iteration adding depth and complexity. Hallowell's articles, like Malinowski's books, circle around the interrelationship of cultural forms and values. Each is a cameo standing on its own terms but also very much a part of a larger vision of the Ojibwe world that almost by definition will remain partial and ongoing.

"Culture and material life" (background on northern Algonquians), "marriage and kinship" (the experimental white rats of interwar anthropology), "the patterning of experience in time and space" (Ojibwe pragmatic worldview, the "behavioral environment of the self"), "stress and anxiety, fear and aggression" (the psychic costs of Ojibwe worldview), "in sickness and in health" (the inseparability of cultural values in mental and physical well-being and the stresses of what was then called "acculturation"), "religion, dreams and the spiritual life" (the intensely personal character of Ojibwe dreams as templates for everyday behavior; specialization of spiritual practitioners), "personality, the self, and worldview" (the grand though ethnographically grounded generalizations in culture and personality terms)—Hallowell's is an oeuvre that bears revisiting. When I [Darnell] received the manuscript, I treated myself to rereading papers that have been part of my own experience of anthropology and have guided my own fieldwork among northern Algonquians, also now of four decades' duration. Having long mused about the psychic reality of Algonquian grammatical categories, I was particularly pleased to see the previously unpublished piece on "rocks and stones," which are animate grammatically and often spoken of as living beings. Other contemporary anthropologists also draw heavily on Hallowell's understandings. To cite just one example, Tim Ingold's notion of "dwelling" among circumpolar hunters and gatherers is deeply embedded in these understandings. The lexicon of Anishinaabeg terms, presented as an appendix to the volume, renders in current orthography the lexicalized culture accessible to Hallowell as a field anthropologist of the 1930s. It provides a major resource for contemporary Anishinaabeg.

Critical Studies in the History of Anthropology has published a number of biographies. These sometimes focus on matters internal to anthropology and other times on external forces shaping the discipline. But there is almost always an ethnographic component. We are the people who go away to experience alternative lifeways and return to tell about what we have learned. Hallowell is one of our classic, lasting ethnographers. Hallowell speaks for himself about his life and chooses the things he wants to emphasize. Brown and Gray cite with interest George Stocking's speculative and rather psychoanalytic interpretation of why Hallowell saw the Ojibwe as he did. To us, consistency of the ethnographic interpretation throughout Hallowell's career should take precedence over dubious attributions of motive.

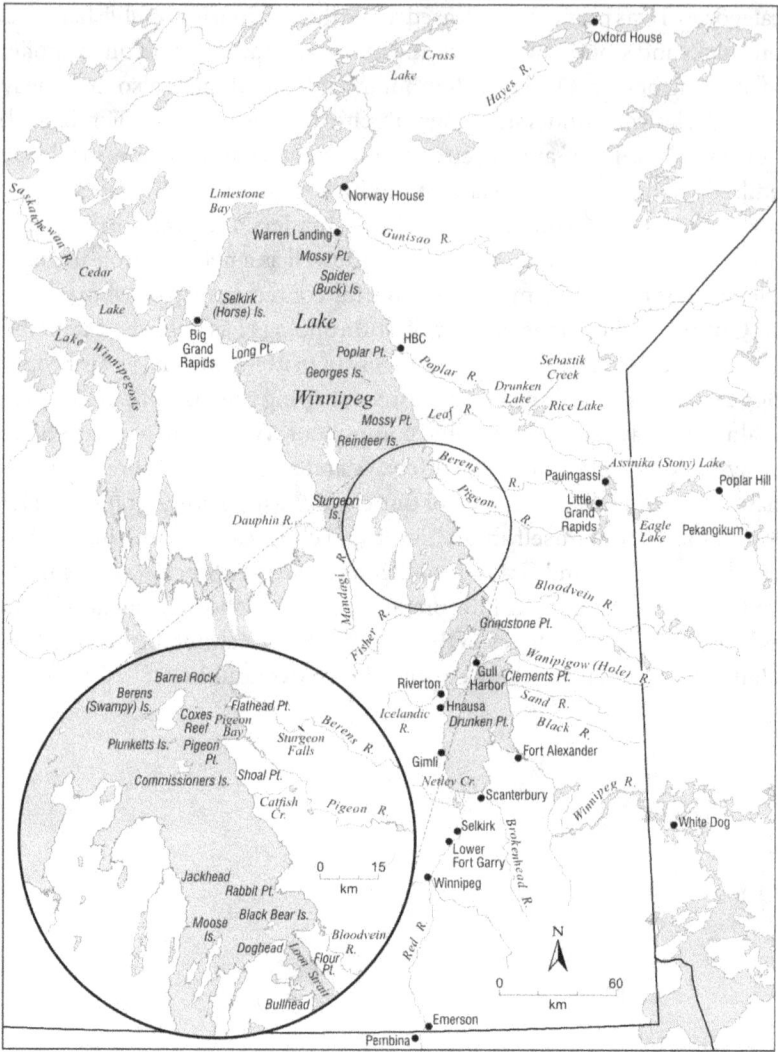

1. Berens River Area. Map created by Victor Lytwyn and Weldon Hiebert for the editors.

From 1930 to 1940 A. Irving Hallowell, a professor of anthropology at the University of Pennsylvania, made repeated summer fieldwork visits to Lake Winnipeg, Manitoba, and to the Ojibwe community of Berens River on its east side. He also traveled up that river several times to a number of other Ojibwe communities, under the guidance of William Berens, who was the treaty chief at Berens River from 1917 to 1947. Berens became Hallowell's closest collaborator, making his work possible. The two men remained friends until the chief's death in 1947.[1]

American anthropologists were fairly common sights in Canada from the late nineteenth to mid-twentieth century. Fieldwork among Canadian aboriginal people attracted them and offered opportunities to broaden their knowledge of Native North America, as anthropology became a recognized profession and a field of advanced graduate study in the United States. A good many Americans besides Hallowell built at least part of their careers on work in Canada; notable examples included Franz Boas, David G. Mandelbaum, Ruth Landes, Edward Sapir, and Frank Speck. Canada did not begin training its own graduate anthropologists until much later; it had no departments of anthropology until 1936 (at the University of Toronto), and the first Canadian PhD in anthropology was not awarded until 1956.[2]

Among the American anthropological sojourners of his time, Hallowell was unusual for the frequency of his return trips to Canada over a decade, and for the extent to which his Canadian Ojibwe work became the centerpiece of his prolific writings and his career contributions. Many different facets of Ojibwe culture, society, history, psychology, and worldview drew his attention. The articles and essays that he published on the Ojibwe over almost four decades from 1934 to 1972 appeared in close to twenty different publications that ranged across anthropology, sociology, botany, medicine, psychology, psychiatry, folklore, and religious studies. He was the first scholar to do substantial ethnological and ethnohistorical work on the Ojibwe of this region, and the research materials that he gathered (now housed at the American Philosophical Society in Philadelphia) are

1. A. Irving Hallowell and Chief William Berens at Pauingassi, Manitoba, probably in summer 1933, on Hallowell's first visit to Pauingassi. The photographer is unknown. (*Courtesy of the American Philosophical Society.*)

unique resources of immense historical value for the aboriginal people and history of Manitoba and northwestern Ontario.

THE COLLECTION

This volume presents twenty-eight of Hallowell's writings that focus entirely or to a great extent on the Ojibwe or Anishinaabeg of the Berens River region. (We regret that his major essay, "Ojibwa World View and Disease" [1963], could not be included here owing to a permission issue.) This is the first time that the great majority of Hallowell's Ojibwe essays have been gathered from their many disparate and scattered locations into one collection. Years ago, some of his most important Ojibwe papers were reprinted in two books containing his essays on numerous other subjects, but those volumes are long out of print. In any case, the wide range of topics that those books covered reduced their interest for Ojibwe readers and specialists.[3]

This collection sharpens our focus on Hallowell's Ojibwe writings as a group. It provides an in-depth view of his contributions to our knowledge and understanding of a major North American aboriginal people. As well, and at a more implicit level, the volume is a contribution to the history of North American anthropology. Hallowell's approaches to and analyses of his findings offer a window onto his role in the shifting intellectual currents in anthropology over four decades. Some of his earliest writings were empirical, concrete expositions that recalled those of his principal mentor, Frank G. Speck. Many of Hallowell's later articles were broader in scope and more theoretical; they laid out sometimes rather abstract sets of issues and problems that he would then address by using his Ojibwe findings and analyses as exemplary. Finally, in his last years Hallowell became more historically oriented in his outlook and interests. The first three chapters of his *The Ojibwa of Berens River*, written in the 1960s, offer a substantial narrative of regional Ojibwe history that was foreshadowed to an extent in his 1955 essay, "The Northern Ojibwa" (chapter 1 in this volume). His other major historical contribution (which lies beyond the scope of this book) was to the founding of the history of anthropology as a field in its own right; see especially his three essays from the 1960s that were reprinted in *Contributions to Anthropology* in 1976.[4]

The articles chosen for this book have been arranged into seven parts, each with a particular theme. Hallowell's earlier articles mainly appear in the first parts, and within each section the articles generally follow chronological order. But at any given time in his career Hallowell was writing on a range of different topics. Therefore, his writings do not divide themselves neatly into distinct periods, but are best grouped thematically even if they span two or three decades. Each part opens with a brief introduction by the editors. The prologue that follows was in fact Hallowell's last published essay (1972). Because of its autobiographical content, it serves well to set the stage for the collection in Hallowell's words. Entitled, "On Being an Anthropologist," it provides a critical and useful context in which to read the writings that follow. Its reflective and reflexive qualities offer the author's own introduction to his work and to his thoughts as he looked back over five decades in his field. Of course it does not tell the whole story. It omits the personal dimensions of his life, and particularly the little-known series of tragedies surrounding his adopted son. A recent essay on Hallowell by one of his former students, historian of anthropology George W. Stocking Jr., has suggested how these elements of personal tragedy may have influenced the trajectory of Hallowell's work from the late 1930s into the 1940s. Stocking also assesses Hallowell's place in twentieth-century anthropology, and his essay is recommended as useful background reading.[5] For a review of Stocking's and other scholars' views on Hallowell's legacy, see also the preface to William Berens, *Memories, Myths, and Dreams,* cited in note 1.

With respect to the prologue and other articles presented here, it should be noted that usage of ethnonyms (ethnic names) for the Ojibwe has shifted since Hallowell wrote. In the *Handbook of North American Indians,* vol. 6, *Subarctic* (1981) and in other writings for the last three or four decades, "Northern Ojibwa" has been used to refer to people north of the Berens River area, people who historically have been distinct from their more southerly congeners in that they lacked clans and did not practice the highly structured Midewiwin or Grand Medicine Society ceremony. In this context, then, the people of Island Lake, whom Hallowell visited in 1930, would still qualify as "Northern Ojibwa," but the Berens River people are categorized with their neighbors to the south.

Another recent shift in usage and spelling should also be noted: the term, *Ojibwe,* rather than *Ojibwa* (or *Ojibway*), is now often preferred by linguists and Native speakers as yielding better pronunciation than the sound elicited by wa, or way. Another widespread shift in the usage of ethnonyms has been the trend toward adopting people's own terms of self-designation. Many Ojibwe people now refer to themselves as Anishinaabe (plural -eg), shifting away from the use of outsiders' terms such as the French-derived name, "Saulteaux." As Hallowell's texts now qualify as historical documents, however, we have not changed his usages or spellings. One further note may be helpful for people reading this book across borders. In the United States the use of the term "Indian" remains prevalent and widely accepted, sometimes in tandem with "Native American." In Canada the usage of "Indian" has become widely discountenanced as pejorative, and in formal usage entities formerly labeled as Indian bands are described as First Nations. "Native" is commonly used in journalism, but Canadian academic writing generally favors "aboriginal" as a generic term. Terminology will doubtless continue to evolve and vary across regions and borders, as it has already done for several centuries.

Notes

1. Two basic sources for Hallowell's Berens River work and his relationship with William Berens are his *The Ojibwa of Berens River, Manitoba: Ethnography into History* (Fort Worth: Harcourt Brace Jovanovich, 1992), with introduction and afterword by Jennifer S. H. Brown, and *Memories,*

Myths and Dreams of an Ojibwe Leader by William Berens, as told to A. Irving Hallowell, ed. by Jennifer S. H. Brown and Susan Elaine Gray (Montreal: McGill-Queen's University Press, 2009).

2. Robert L. A. Hancock, "Toward a Historiography of Canadian Anthropology," in *Historicizing Canadian Anthropology*, ed. Julia Harrison and Regna Darnell, 35 (Vancouver: University of British Columbia Press, 2006).

3. See Hallowell, *Culture and Experience* (Philadelphia: University of Pennsylvania Press, 1955), reprinted by Schocken Books (New York, 1967), and Waveland Press (Prospect Heights IL, 1988); and *Contributions to Anthropology* (Chicago: University of Chicago Press, 1976).

4. We do not review Hallowell's career in depth here, as other sources already provide excellent overviews. See, for examples, the introductory material in Hallowell, *The Ojibwa of Berens River* (1992); the general introduction and section introductions by various scholars in Hallowell, *Contributions to Anthropology* (1976); and Anthony F. C. Wallace, "Alfred Irving Hallowell, December 28, 1892–October 10, 1974," *Biographical Memoirs*, vol. 51, 195–213 (Washington DC: National Academy of Sciences, 1980).

5. Stocking, "A. I. Hallowell's Boasian Evolutionism: Human Ir/rationality in Cross-Cultural, Evolutionary, and Personal Context." In *Significant Others: Interpersonal and Professional Commitments in Anthropology*, ed. Richard Handler, 196–260 (Madison: University of Wisconsin Press, 2004).

ACKNOWLEDGMENTS

The quality, richness, and depth of the essays in this volume are due in large part to A. Irving Hallowell's close relationship with his friend, interpreter, and mentor, William Berens. Several decades later, the interest and encouragement of William's son, Percy, and other descendants, such as John and Maurice Berens and Darlene Rose Overby, have bolstered our efforts to publish these revealing, informative, and sometimes challenging pieces.

We would like to thank several people who have been helpful in the preparation of this work. Roger Roulette and Rand Valentine provided invaluable help and guidance on the linguistic challenges that we faced in creating the glossary: Victor Lytwyn and Weldon Hiebert created the map of Lake Winnipeg and the Berens River area; and Anne Lindsay has always been quick and resourceful with valuable research assistance.

Thanks are also due to Gary Dunham, formerly of the University of Nebraska Press, and to our current editors at the press, Matthew Bokovoy, Elisabeth Chretien, and Kathryn Neubauer, for all their work and support. We also thank Beth Carroll-Horrocks and Martin Levitt at the American Philosophical Society Library in Philadelphia for major research assistance when Jennifer Brown researched Hallowell's papers there years ago; and, most recently, Charles B. Greifenstein and Earle Spamer of the APS, for their interest and assistance with permissions and searches for documents and photographs.

The idea for this volume arose in conversations between Jennifer Brown and Gary Dunham some years ago, when he was anthropology editor for the University of Nebraska Press. At his initiative, the necessary reprint permissions for the articles were secured from the various publishers involved. The articles were then scanned, a tedious process in itself. A hiatus followed, as Jennifer Brown had a great many commitments in hand and was not able to continue her work with the Hallowell papers and Berens River history for some years, until resources and time became available to her through being awarded a Canada Research Chair at the University of Winnipeg in a federally funded program to support research scholars at Canadian universities. In 2006 and 2007, she was able to enlist the collaboration of her research associate Dr. Susan Gray, whose position is also supported by the CRC program, and the two of us began intensive work on the book of William Berens texts, already cited, and on this volume.

As curious, unpredictable things can happen to texts in the scanning process, we have proofread all the chapters with care. We have silently corrected obvious printers' errors and typos. We have also standardized the format of citations to an extent, as various printers followed somewhat different conventions; articles now consistently appear in quotation marks, and book and journal titles are italicized. We have eliminated the use of *op. cit.* in notes, inserting instead authors' surnames and abbreviated titles. Arabic numbers have been substituted for cumbersome roman numerals in journal volume citations. Hallowell's tables and figures have been renumbered to correspond to the sequence in which they appear in this volume. A few of Hallowell's articles were published in British journals and accordingly follow British spelling conventions, which we have retained.

It has sometimes seemed helpful, or, indeed essential, to add updated references and to indicate areas in which recent research has made it necessary to qualify Hallowell's earlier statements. These added materials appear in the introductions to the various sections, or are inserted in the notes to the individual chapters, enclosed in square brackets as editorial emendations.

A major challenge was how to handle the distinctive orthography that Hallowell used for Ojibwe words. We decided to retain his orthography in the texts. The Ojibwe terms and concepts featured in Hallowell's writings, and the names of the Ojibwe people he referred to, have never before been assembled and transcribed in one place. As a remedy, Susan Gray compiled a glossary of them all, which appears at the end of this volume. As some printers handled Hallowell's orthography more carefully than others, the glossary helped achieve a standard for how he wanted the words to appear, even if that standard was not always respected in the past. The compiling of the glossary has provided a guide and a basis for standardizing the orthography throughout the book.

Susan Gray's other major undertaking was to work with Ojibwe linguists Roger Roulette, and later, Rand Valentine, to work out equivalencies to Hallowell's spellings in the orthography now most commonly used for Ojibwe, our standard being *A Concise Dictionary of Minnesota Ojibwe* (1995) by John D. Nichols and Earl Nyholm. As numerous terms recorded by Hallowell do not appear in that dictionary, the linguists' aid was essential in clarifying and verifying spellings. Their advice on meanings was also critical. Hallowell would have been the first to admit he never learned the language; he relied implicitly on the highly bilingual skills and knowledge of William Berens, even as he tried to understand key Ojibwe concepts and terms to the deepest extent possible. Hallowell's analyses stand up very well indeed and the core content of the glossary still comes from his work. But clarification and verification have still been critical steps.

The glossary makes a key contribution in another way. For the first time, it gathers all the terms that Hallowell used in his published articles, providing an overview of the functional vocabulary that he gathered and drew upon for his analyses. It also helps to document the Berens River Ojibwe language, or more specifically, the dialect spoken by Chief William Berens and his family in the 1930s, along with the Cree elements that sometimes turned up in their usage.

The preparation of this book has renewed our appreciation of the depth, scope, and quality of Hallowell's work. Now, for the first time, it is possible to survey the range of his research and scholarship in one volume, and to trace and read in a connected way all the data and understandings that he published on the Ojibwe over four decades. Not least, this volume has an index. This is the first time that any of Hallowell's collected writings have been indexed, as that feature was sadly missing from *Culture and Experience*, and from *Contributions to Anthropology*.

Today's readers will respond in various ways to Hallowell's writings or to certain aspects of them. Some will dismiss, for example, his Rorschach studies, although they were fresh and experimental in the late 1930s and 1940s as a new tool that held promise; they still stir interest and find uses in some quarters. Newer generations of readers will also pause over some of his uses of language: for example, the generic "man," subsuming woman, and the use of the term, "primitive" (which he often qualified) with reference to small, isolated communities distant from modern technology and large-scale societies. But when we disapprove, we reflect our own times and what passes for sophistication in present circles; who knows how some of our usages will be viewed in future? People of a certain time write in the language and terms available to them and accepted as standard by their peers; and usages change, as noted with respect to the ethnonyms mentioned above. Hallowell's writings have become historical documents, a fate that befalls all written texts if they survive. In that respect too, they are worth reading and rereading, as windows into Ojibwe life and into an ethnographer's prose and mindset, as he and the Berens River people met and tried to make sense of one another during and after those remarkable encounters of the 1930s.

One final point should be made about this collection. Like every other field anthropologist, Hallowell carried away a great deal of knowledge and learning from his Berens River sojourns. He made some efforts to return the fruits of his research. For example, William Berens wrote to Hallowell on July 10, 1941, "I'm thanking you very much [for] those books you send me. We like to read those." We don't know what books Hallowell sent, but they may have included an advance copy of Hallowell's *The Role of Conjuring in Saulteaux Society*, which Hallowell dedicated "To Chief William Berens whose genial companionship in camp and canoe, in fair weather and foul, never failed to enliven my task" (University of Pennsylvania Press, 1942). Hallowell also sent, or brought back to people on his return trips, copies of photographs he had taken on his visits. For example, at Pauingassi, Manitoba, in the early 1990s, Charlie George Owen, grandson of Fair Wind (Naamiwan), the old medicine man whom Hallowell met there in the 1930s, had on his living room wall a framed photograph of his grandfather taken by Hallowell. And Brother Frederic Leach, the Oblate priest whom Hallowell met at the mouth of the river, received a number of prints of Hallowell's photographs, which eventually were deposited in the Archives of Manitoba and misattributed under Leach's name.

As Hallowell never managed to return to Berens River after the summer of 1940, however, none of his further research or writing came back to the Berens River people until we began to follow his trail back to the individuals who still remembered him. As new connections were built, relatives of William Berens, and many others, too, became interested in his work. Our work has progressed in tandem with the Berens River peoples' growing interest in their own histories as local schools have developed a stronger focus on First Nations history and increasing numbers of people have plunged into researching their family histories. The publication of this volume forms another chapter in those developments. Aside from its value for the rest of its audience, it allows aboriginal scholars, students, and community members to read these works for themselves, to make of them what they will, and to draw upon them for whatever they contribute to local knowledge and to keeping alive the memories of the people whom Hallowell knew. It is an exercise in repatriation of a sort, bringing back to the communities some of the knowledge kept by past generations whose voices have long been silent, while, at the same time sharing it with the world at large.

CONTRIBUTIONS TO OJIBWE STUDIES

PROLOGUE

On Being an Anthropologist
A. Irving Hallowell

BECOMING AN ANTHROPOLOGIST

The social scientists of her sample, comments Anne Roe (1953), often show a sense of rebellion against traditional family values. I think this was true of me. Since I had no outstanding talents and evinced no special interest in any of the professions, my conservative parents assumed I would take up a business career. Therefore, after a three-year course in a manual-training high school, I was sent to the Wharton School of Finance and Commerce of the University of Pennsylvania.

In those days, before World War I, the Wharton school had a much more flexible curriculum. It was also then the home of social sciences (economics, sociology, and political science), but anthropology was in the College of Liberal Arts. The school permitted its students to take many electives in the college; so in addition to the required business-oriented courses, I sampled chemistry, history, English literature, and Italian Renaissance painting, though I did not look into anthropology. Above all, I discovered social science and took all the courses in economics and sociology that were offered. I had work with Scott Nearing, and in my senior year I was admitted to a seminar given by Simon N. Patten, a singular economist of that time who is now almost forgotten. In rebellion against classical economics, Patten attempted to deal with problems of change and evolution and tried to open up a perspective emphasizing abundance rather than scarcity (see Patten, 1924).

Soon I gave up all thought of a business career. The social sciences and ideas of social reform absorbed my interest. I wanted to go ahead with graduate studies, but because there were no family funds, and fellowships with stipends were scarce in those days, I entered social work and took some graduate courses in sociology on the side. Since I had been brought up in a protected environment, social work opened my eyes to how "the other half" lived. As a representative of the Family Society, I went into the homes of unfamiliar ethnic groups—Poles, Italians, Negroes. Casework among people with such diverse backgrounds provided me with a wide experience in interviewing.

It was also at this time—the late 1910s and early 1920s—that I was first introduced to psychoanalysis. Psychoanalysis was then a novel, exciting, and controversial topic among American intellectuals, especially in New York. A. A. Brill, the first American psychiatrist to become a member of Freud's group in Vienna, published his translation of Freud's *Interpretation of Dreams* in 1913. It almost immediately stirred up tremendous interest. Many social workers eagerly turned to psychoanalysis for a new illumination of social theory and interpersonal relations. In Philadelphia, the Pennsylvania School of Social Work engaged A. A. Goldenweiser, an anthropologist, to give a series of lectures on psychoanalytic theory. Goldenweiser was one of the first social scientists in this country to attempt to apply Freudian psychology to the elucidation of social facts. His lectures had nothing to do, however, with personality and culture studies as they subsequently developed.

During my undergraduate days I had met Frank G. Speck. We were both members of the same fraternity. At the fraternity house I had often listened to his stories about his experiences with Indians. (Speck was a gifted raconteur.) I had also dropped in to hear him lecture. Casting around for courses which were given at a time that would fit my social-work schedule, I signed up for several of his.

I found the general anthropological approach very stimulating as compared with the approach of sociology. I thought the anthropologists' rejection of a unilineal theory of cultural evolution very progressive. The idea of "culture," too, was rather new and it was not in the sociologists' kit. Anthropology opened a vista far beyond the ethnic groups in my own backyard. Abstract and theoretical social problems now had a very broad base.

Another feature that impressed me was the political attitude which characterized the anthropologists of that period. If I may use so old-fashioned a label, it was very "liberal." Perhaps this was due to the dominant influence of Franz Boas. My own attitudes were on the liberal side. I was very doubtful, for instance, about our entry into World War I, and I had socialistic inclinations.

Since I already knew Speck and since his classes were small, we quickly became well acquainted. I became a candidate for a master's degree in anthropology, dropped my courses in sociology, and decided to leave social work for a career in anthropology. At the time I thought this was a radical shift, but now I see a continuity: my move was well within the broad boundaries of the social sciences, theoretical and applied.

Speck helped me to obtain a Harrison Fellowship so that I could devote full time to graduate work. During one semester I made a weekly trip to New York to attend Boas' seminar at Columbia University. All the members of the group, which included Ruth Benedict and Melville Herskovits, were assigned books for seminar reports and discussion. My assignment consisted of Edward Westermarck's *History of Human Marriage* and John Dewey's *Human Nature and Conduct,* which had only recently been published. A group of us from Boas' seminar also met privately each week with Goldenweiser for anthropological discussions.

With my interests ranging over broad social problems, it may seem paradoxical that the people in whom I became most interested were the American Indians. But these were the primitive, aboriginal people of America—and they were Frank Speck's pets. At this time, he was engaged in "salvage anthropology" among the Indians of the eastern United States.[1] Speck's self-involvement with the study people and their problems was perhaps greater than that of other anthropologists of the period. He was always extolling the sovereign virtues of the Indians and proclaiming the intrinsic values of their culture. Current political events and problems in American life held little interest for him; he was critical in general of the values of American culture. This attitude Speck shared with other anthropologists, for these were the days of Harold Stearns' *Civilization in the United States,* to which both Robert H. Lowie and Elsie Clews Parsons contributed.[2] It was also the time when many American writers and artists were going abroad to do their work.

Speck was about as detached from American culture as one could be. He would not, for instance, buy a car, and he never read newspapers. In a sense, he was also detached from the university and its affairs. I never remember his serving on a committee; his thoughts and energies were entirely devoted to his research among Indians. And I imitated my mentor for a long while. I, too, identified myself with the Indians, and tried to avoid serving on university committees. Anthropology in all its aspects was the overarching thing and Boas was king, for Speck had been not only a student of Boas but also a deeply rooted follower. Boas had said the last word. What one strove for was to follow Boas in his ubiquitous interests—ethnology, archeology, physical anthropology, and linguistics. Anthropology, despite broad areas of specialization, was regarded as an all-embracing study of man which should be conceptualized and pursued as a whole even while the individual engaged in specialized investigations.[3]

FIELDWORK IN THE 1920S

It was in this spirit, following Speck, that I began my fieldwork among an acculturated group of Indians in eastern Canada, the St. Francis Abenaki. These Abenaki, who were related to the Penobscot of Maine whom Speck had studied intensively, lived on a reservation sixty miles east of Montreal on the south side of the St. Lawrence River. They were bilingual but they lived much as the French Canadians did who surrounded them. I set out to recover for the record the remnants of their aboriginal culture. It did not occur to me to study their "community" or any problems of "acculturation." In fact, this latter approach was not articulated in anthropology until the 1930s. These were the days when the major emphasis was on "culture traits" and "trait complexes," such information to be reconstructed from fast-disappearing native cultures (see Beals, 1953).

Thus I collected Abenaki objects of material culture for the Museum of the American Indian (Heye Foundation) in New York. There were more of these to collect than one might suppose—the last birchbark canoe, for example, and a native "slow match." I made a series of physical measurements (unpublished). I also studied the native language, which was still spoken by everyone, made a collection of loan words, and secured some folktales in text.[4] I collected information on their hunting customs and particularly on their hunting territories, a special interest of Speck's, and wrote a paper (unpublished) on the subject. I became interested in the Abenaki kinship system, and I was able to document changes unknown to the Indians themselves. This was made possible through my discovery of an eighteenth-century manuscript dictionary on the reservation. Melville Herskovits (1938) pointed out that my paper (1928) was one of the earliest attempts to demonstrate changes in a kinship system from documentary sources. (Incidentally, the Abenaki system does not belong to the Northern Algonkian pattern, which reflects cross-cousin marriage.)

Although I made quite a few brief trips to the Abenaki, this kind of fieldwork did not satisfy me. A number of years went by while I fretted for an opportunity to work in a really "primitive" culture. Meanwhile, there was the problem of a thesis, and nothing appropriate had emerged from the Abenaki investigations.

Finally, with a lead from J. G. Frazer and with Speck's encouragement, I began research in what I would later call "bear ceremonialism." In the course of studying the variety and detail of local ceremonies, I was soon led to evidence of the occurrence of related ceremonies in the Old World as well as the New. There appeared to be a nucleus of common ceremonial traits suggesting historical connections from Lapland to Labrador. If one took this finding, along with a somewhat similar distribution of other culture traits commonly shared by the peoples of Eurasia and northern North America, an old culture stratum seemed indicated (see Hatt, 1933; Lowie, 1934). With respect to antiquity, I drew attention to the peculiar disposal of bear skulls and long bones at Drachenloch, Switzerland, during paleolithic times and the crudely modeled figure of a bear in the cave of Montespan. Other archeological evidence of an ancient bear cult has since turned up. I realized that there was a local setting for bear ceremonialism everywhere—involving mythology, world view, the hunting of other animals, and so on—but I chose to be selective and to consider the geographical distribution of the associated features of bear ceremonialism in a broad cultural-historical setting.

Incidentally, Bertold Laufer at first discouraged me by questioning my ability to handle the Eurasian data. But things worked out somehow, and later he was extremely complimentary about the final product.[5] The monograph which ultimately emerged (Hallowell, 1926) has created more reverberations in Europe than anything else I have written. At first it was taken up by the Kulturkreise School. Then it helped focus further fieldwork among the Russians. More recently it has been discussed by those interested in prehistoric religion (see Campbell, 1959; Maringer, 1960; Lissner, 1961).

KINSHIP, CULTURE, AND PSYCHOLOGY

Meanwhile, my interest in kinship was further stimulated by the residence in Philadelphia of an Araucanian Indian, J. Martin Collio, with whom both Speck and I had personal contact. I obtained a set of kinship terms from him as early as 1922. At first they were very puzzling to me. Eventually, they turned out to be the Omaha pattern, an ill-defined type at the time. I hesitated to publish my information, partly because the data were obtained from a single informant, but also because I half-hoped that someday I might be able to go to South America and do fieldwork among the Araucanians. Then, stimulated by an article by A. Lesser (1929), I presented my material at a meeting of the American Anthropological Association in 1929. It met with little or no discussion so I put the paper aside. More than a decade later, in 1943, at a lecture he gave before the Philadelphia Anthropological Society, G. P. Murdock remarked that in his survey of social organization and kinship throughout the world, he was struck by the absence of the Omaha pattern in South America, although he suspected its presence among the Araucanians. So I sent my paper, in its original form, to the *American Anthropologist* and it was published (Hallowell, 1943).

Long before this, however, I had made some other excursions into the relations between kinship pattern and social behavior, which led directly to my study of the Northern Ojibwa. In Montreal, in the late 1920s, I discovered some old dictionaries which suggested that cross-cousin marriage had once existed among the North-Central Algonkians. While this finding would excite very little interest today, in the United States in the 1920s the prevailing view, supported by such influential anthropologists as Kroeber and Truman Michelson, was that kinship terms were to be considered as purely linguistic phenomena. Thus, one aspect of the problem was the traditional attitude of American anthropologists toward the study of the functional ramifications of kinship in its total sociocultural setting. At any rate, at the International Congress of Americanists in 1928, I read a paper raising the question of the existence of cross-cousin marriage among the Algonkian (Hallowell, 1930). As I recall now, I received no support for my hypothesis but a rather critical appraisal from Michelson. It was not until shortly after the congress that I learned that W. D. Strong, who had recently spent fifteen months in Labrador, reported the practice of cross-cousin marriage among the Barren Ground band of the Naskapi. So I made plans to go into the field in order to discover whether the kinship pattern together with the practice of cross-cousin marriage actually existed in any contemporary North-Central Algonkian group.

I went into the field both "functionally" and "problem-oriented." My first trip was made in 1930 to the Algonkians of the Lake Winnipeg region. Pursuing my search for cross-cousin marriage among the Ojibwa of the Berens River, I well remember an early conversation with William Berens, my closest collaborator. I hesitatingly asked him whether a man could marry a woman he called *ninam*. His reply was, "Who the hell else would he marry?" In a sense, the problem I had come to investigate was solved: the Ojibwa of the Berens River did practice cross-cousin marriage and used the appropriate terminology. The situation among the Northern Algonkians was more complicated, however, because historical circumstances had led to differential changes in terminology and social practice among different groups. Later I concluded that "Northern Algonkian kinship systems are . . . intelligible as variants of a basic pattern that has undergone modifications as the result of acculturative processes and differences in local conditions" (Hallowell, 1937).

My fieldwork among the Cree and Ojibwa of the Lake Winnipeg region had hardly begun when I was drawn into a newly emerging area of research in anthropology: the psychological interrelations of individuals and their culture. From its beginnings, anthropology has been influenced by developments within the academic tradition in psychology; but around 1920 it was psychoanalysis with its psychiatric background, its concepts of individual psychodynamics and personality, that challenged anthropologists.[6] This was another facet of the great impact of psychoanalytic theories on the thinking of the modern world, particularly on the sciences of human behavior. As I have said, I first met psychoanalysis burgeoning in social-work circles in Philadelphia. The anthropologists' interest, however, was on a directly professional level, and there was much discussion and many thoughtful reviews of the writings of Freud and other analysts. All of this interested me very much. All through the 1920s I followed the various new developments in psychoanalysis and in psychological anthropology.

Now, in the 1930s, I became directly involved in psychological anthropology through Edward Sapir. After Sapir went to Yale in 1931, we became better acquainted and had some stimulating discussions on psychoanalysis and anthropology. Sapir had long been interested in psychoanalysis. As early as 1917 he had reviewed Freud's *Delusion and Dream* and Oskar Pfister's *The Psychoanalytic Method* for *The Dial*. Any and all new ideas in the field he welcomed, so that, for example, he gave C. G. Jung's *Psychological Types* an appreciative and thoughtful review in *The Freeman* (1923). More recently he had been listening to Harry Stack Sullivan expound his ideas on the collaboration of social scientists in the testing of his interpersonal-relations theory. Sapir had also explored various methods of getting at such information in different cultures.[7] It was to be expected, therefore, that when Sapir became chairman of the Division of Anthropology and Psychology of the National Research Council he would set up a committee on "Personality in Relation to Culture." Sapir invited me to be a member. Among the others were Ruth Benedict, Harry Stack Sullivan, Adolf Meyer, and A. A. Brill.

There was strong resistance among professional anthropologists to this psychological approach. There were also many real problems, including the question of how far psychoanalytic concepts were to be used as compared to behavioristic or Gestalt concepts. Another basic question was: From what sources were psychological data, apart from ethnological data, to be derived?

The Rorschach test was relatively new at this time. It had many advantages over other psychological tests of personality: it was a subtle means of probing many of the complexities of personality and it was "culture-free." The scoring system also made comparisons possible on either an individual basis or a group basis. From the scanty literature on the Rorschach, I learned enough to be able to try my hand at administering and scoring the test. On my next trip to the Berens River I stopped in Chicago hoping to see the Rorschach expert, Samuel J. Beck, but I missed him. So on my own I collected a large sample of protocols from both adults and children.

It was after this field trip in 1937 that I met Bruno Klopfer, who became very interested in my Indian Rorschach records. We had several conferences to discuss my material and then decided to collaborate on joint papers to be presented at the 1938 meetings of the American Anthropological Association in New York (Hallowell, 1938; Klopfer, 1938). There was a great deal of curiosity (a large audience came to hear the papers), and while there was some interest, there was more derision. Who could take playing with ink blots seriously? However, I went ahead with my research in personality and culture among the Ojibwa using the Rorschach test (see Hallowell, 1956).

In recent years there has been a lessening of interest in personality and culture. Anthropologists are busy cultivating other fields, and psychologists have been critically evaluating the Rorschach test (see Lindzey, 1961). However, I should say that my own conception of psychological anthropology has always been a broad one that transcends the study of personality and culture in the narrow sense. There are many psychological areas that should be dealt with. It may surprise some when I say that I never gave a course myself under that rubric; my course was called "Culture and Psychology." Consequently, I fully agree with John Fischer's remarks and the shift he made in the 1965 *Biennial Review of Anthropology* by changing the title of his section from "Culture and Personality" to "Psychology and Anthropology."

Within this broad framework my interests expanded still further. Using my Ojibwa investigations for specific illustrations, I explored such topics as acculturation processes and personality changes (chaps. 18–19 in Hallowell, 1955), culture and perception (Hallowell, 1951), and the nature and concept of the self (chaps. 4 and 8 in Hallowell, 1955).

My Ojibwa experience in the early 1930s was a plunge into a new world and involved problems I was little prepared to face. Since Alanson Skinner's preliminary survey in 1911, nothing had been done in the area. It was an immense region and I had to choose a locale. As a matter of fact, I started with the Cree and then shifted to the Ojibwa after discovering that, while there was plenty of evidence everywhere for acculturation, up the Berens River there were some pagan Indians. These Ojibwa had retained attitudes and a world view which were "primitive," even though their tools, clothing, and diet were not. This fact involved the acculturation problem in a modified form, one quite different from the situation in eastern Canada. I think it was not until about this time, however, that I realized there were no completely unacculturated Indians in the United States and Canada. Before anthropologists were professionally trained in fieldwork, Indians everywhere had been transferred to reservations when the frontier was closed in 1890.

My original attitude toward the Indians nevertheless persisted. I deeply identified myself with the Berens River Ojibwa. To the small number of white people in the area I paid practically no attention. I never made friends with the personnel of the Hudson's Bay Company posts and became only casually acquainted with the missionaries, among whom I was more friendly with the Catholics than with the Protestants. Since I was completely oriented toward Indians and their culture rather than the total community, I did not at first realize what the basic pattern of relationship was between whites and Indians. Actually, it exemplified all the basic features of the pattern in the South between whites and Negroes; for example, the use of first names for Indians (my friend Chief Berens was "Willie"); a tabu on eating together; the use of the back door by Indians when visiting whites (missionaries included); discountenance of intermarriage; "passing." I have always regretted not making a serious study of this relationship pattern. At the time I did not think of it, for my exclusive concern was the Indians.[8]

Although the Ojibwa I worked with were not "primitives" in the sense of having a fully functioning aboriginal culture, they were closer to it than I had thought. There was a graded spectrum on the Berens River, those at the mouth of the river being the most acculturated and those inland the least. As I found out later, when I spent the summer of 1946 with a group of students on the Ojibwa reservation at Lac du Flambeau, Wisconsin, this was only one segment of a wider acculturation problem. Here I found myself in the position of being an authority for these highly acculturated Ojibwa on the really old-fashioned Ojibwa "up north."

It was the gradual realization of this broader acculturation problem that led me in the end to attempt to interpret and expound the world view of the most conservative Ojibwa (see chap. 18 in Hallowell, 1955; Hallowell, 1960). This became an excursion into ethnoscience—or ethnosemantics, if you will—for I became aware of how sharply different the Ojibwa world was from our own and of the necessity for testing the meaningfulness of familiar conceptual dichotomies, such as natural-supernatural, for example. This process meant the reintegration of ethnographic material collected under separate and quite different categories on another level. In short, it involved an attempt to see the Ojibwa world as they saw it—an *emic* as contrasted to an *etic* viewpoint. Ecologically, it led me to the concept of a behavioral environment—a concept borrowed from Gestalt psychology—an environment culturally constituted in such a way that it structures the major psychological field in which individuals act, forming their basic cognitive orientation.

THE LATER YEARS: EXPLORATIONS IN BEHAVIORAL EVOLUTION

All these investigations in psychology and culture inevitably led to a general consideration of the psychological dimension of human evolution (Hallowell, 1950; 1963; 1965). In this endeavor I assumed a more inclusive perspective than the one provided by physical anthropology and archeology alone, one that emphasizes the continuities as opposed to the discontinuities in behavioral evolution between man and the nonhominid primates. I tried to bring together as an integral whole the organic, psychological, social, and cultural dimensions of the evolutionary process as they relate to the underlying conditions necessary for human existence. As Dobzhansky (1962) has pointed out, "Human evolution cannot be understood as a purely biological process, nor can it be adequately described as a history of culture. There exists a feedback between biological and cultural processes" (see also Menaker, 1965). And, we may add, there is a feedback between specifically psychological processes and cultural ones: the emergence of ego processes, the development of self-objectification, the socialization of symbolic forms, and the rise of sociocultural systems. In this development there was no "critical point" at which culture emerged, as Kroeber maintained (see Geertz, 1964).

Beyond the world views of man, basic to his life everywhere, there is another evolutionary problem: how man has so fully assimilated subjective and unconscious experiences and integrated them with the acquisition and accumulation of pragmatic knowledge about the external world, in a manner difficult to disentangle. David Beres, a psychoanalyst, departing from the restricted meaning of the term "imaginative" as the obverse of "realistic," extends its psychological connotation to include "a process whose products are images, symbols, fantasies, dreams, ideas, thoughts and concepts." Imagination in this sense is a complex function entering into "all aspects of psychic activity—normal mentation, pathological processes, and artistic creativity." His point is that "imagination is not opposed to reality, but has as one of its most important applications, adaptation to reality." In other words, reality can best be understood, not only as a relatively indeterminate concept, but as one which is *always* infused with imaginative processes. Symbolic representations, derived from such processes, involve mediating ego functions between the external world and the inner drives of man. "To be aware of reality it becomes necessary to have two points of reference—one is the perception of the external world, the other the internal image, the mental representation."[9]

From this perspective, dreams, fantasies, myth, art, and the world views of man, as articulated in cultural traditions, may be interpreted as making positive use of psychological resources in cultural adaptation and personal adjustment. Reliable knowledge of reality in any scientific sense need not be assumed to be a necessary condition for either biological adaptation or cultural adjustment to the actualities of human existence. Man is an animal who has been able to survive by making cultural adaptations in which his own imaginative interpretations of the world have been fed back into his personal adjustment to it.

What I have tried to do in this chapter, in semi-autobiographical fashion, is to outline a personal record of my own experience in anthropology, of my changing values and problems in fieldwork. How this personal experience is related to the wider picture of the basic changes and emphases in the anthropological tradition and to changing values in the wider world, I leave to others.

Notes

"On Being an Anthropologist" was first published in Solon T. Kimball and James B. Watson, eds., *Crossing Cultural Boundaries* (New York: Chandler,

1972), 51–62, and is here reprinted from Hallowell, *Contributions to Anthropology* (Chicago: University of Chicago Press, 1976), 3–14.

1. "It was not an uncommon experience and considered quite a *coup* for a student of Boas to catch the dying gasp of an American Indian language and culture. Sapir in the field of language and Speck in that of natural history exemplify the tradition. Speck, beloved by the Indians and learned beyond most men, sometimes managed to reconstruct a society and its culture from the merest fragments, approaching the feats of psychoanalysts in his study of Delaware ceremonies, which rank among those of the first class in American ethnology" (Fenton, 1953).

2. According to Hoffman (1962), Stearns' book, "which appeared early in 1922, was a historical landmark of the post-World War I years, a curious document of disaffection, pointing to and reiterating the failure of culture, entertainment, family life, religion—of everything but science, and even it scored only a partial success in the survey of American life and institutions" (21). "The twenties were marked by a disrespect for tradition and an eager wish to try out any new suggestions regarding the nature of man—his personal beliefs, convictions, or way to salvation." (33).

3. I am writing, of course, as an American anthropologist. But see Hultkrantz (1968) and the commentaries on that article.

4. The St. Francis Abenaki dialect is still spoken today [1972] and presents some interesting problems; see Day (1964; 1967).

5. In his presidential address to the American Oriental Society, Laufer (1931) said: "We owe a model investigation to Dr. A. I. Hallowell . . . into the bear ceremonialism in northern Asia and America where the worship of the bear is widely distributed and practically alike in form and content."

6. For a historical summary of the influence of psychology on anthropology, see Hallowell (1954).

7. For a more extended discussion of the seminal influence of Edward Sapir on personality and culture studies, see Hallowell (1954, 203ff.)

8. As a matter of fact, there is a racial problem in Canada that has been little studied; see the novel by Bodsworth (1960).

9. All quotations in this paragraph are from Beres (1960a, 1960b).

References

Beals, Ralph. 1953. "Acculturation." In A. L. Kroeber, ed., *Anthropology Today: An Encyclopedic Inventory.* Chicago: University of Chicago Press.

Beres, David. 1960a. "Perception, Imagination and Reality." *International Journal of Psycho-Analysis*, vol. 41.

———. 1960b. "The Psychoanalytic Psychology of Imagination." *Journal of the American Psychoanalytic Association*, vol. 8.

Bodsworth, Fred. 1960. *The Strange One*. New York: Dodd, Mead.

Campbell, Joseph. 1959. *Masks of God: Primitive Mythology*. New York: Viking.

Day, Gordon M. 1964. "A St. Francis Abenaki Vocabulary." *International Journal of American Linguistics*, 30: 371–392.

———. 1967. "Historical Notes on New England Languages." *Contributions to Anthropology: Linguistics* I. Bulletin 214. Ottawa: National Museum of Canada.

Dobzhansky, T. 1962. *Mankind Evolving: The Evolution of the Human Species*. New Haven: Yale University Press.

Fenton, W. N. 1953. "Cultural Stability and Change in American Indian Societies." *Journal of the Royal Anthropological Institute*, 83: 169–170.

Geertz, C. 1964. "The Transition to Humanity." In Sol Tax, ed., *Horizons of Anthropology*. Chicago: Aldine.

Hallowell, A. Irving. 1926. "Bear Ceremonialism in the Northern Hemisphere." *American Anthropologist*, 28: 1–175.

———. 1928. "Recent Historical Changes in the Kinship Terminology of the St. Francis Abenaki." *Proceedings of the Twenty-second International Congress of Americanists*, 97–145. Rome.

———. 1930. "Was Cross-Cousin Marriage Practiced by the North-Central Algonkian?" *Proceedings of the Twenty-third Congress of Americanists*, 519–544. New York.

———. 1937. "Cross-Cousin Marriage in the Lake Winnipeg Area." *Twenty-fifth Anniversary Studies*, 1: 95–110. Publications of the Philadelphia Anthropological Society, ed. D. S. Davidson.

———. 1938. "An Experimental Investigation of a Series of Berens River Indians." Unpublished.

———. 1943. "Araucanian Parallels to the Omaha Kinship Pattern." *American Anthropologist*, 45: 489–491.

———. 1950. "Personality Structure and the Evolution of Man." *American Anthropologist*, 52: 159–173. (Presidential address to the American Anthropological Association, 1949; also chap. 1 of Hallowell 1955.)

———. 1951. "Cultural Factors in the Structuralization of Perception." In J. H. Rohrer and M. Sherif, eds., *Social Psychology at the Cross-Roads*. New York: Books for Libraries.

————. 1954. "Psychology and Anthropology." In John Gillin, ed., *For a Science of Social Man*. New York: Macmillan.

————. 1955. *Culture and Experience*. Philadelphia: University of Pennsylvania Press. Chap. 4, "The Self and Its Behavioral Environment"; chap. 8, "The Ojibwa Self and Its Behavioral Environment"; chap. 18, "Background for a Study of Acculturation and the Personality of the Ojibwa"; chap. 19, "Acculturation and the Personality of the Ojibwa." (Presidential address to the Society for Projective Techniques, 1950.)

————. 1956. "The Rorschach Test in Personality and Culture Studies." In Bruno Klopfer et al., eds., *Developments in the Rorschach Technique*. New York: Harcourt Brace Jovanovich. Vol. 2.

————. 1960. "Ojibwa Ontology, Behavior and World View." In S. Diamond, ed., *Culture in History*. New York: Columbia University Press.

————. 1963. "Personality, Culture and Society in Behavioral Evolution." In S. Koch, ed., *Psychology: A Study of a Science*. New York: McGraw-Hill. Vol. 6.

————. 1965. "Hominid Evolution, Cultural Adaptation and Mental Dysfunctioning." In A. V. S. de Reuck and Ruth Porter, eds., *Ciba Foundation Symposium on Transcultural Psychiatry*, London. Boston: Little, Brown.

Hatt, G. 1933. "North American and Eurasian Culture Connections." *Proceedings of the Fifth Pacific Congress*. Canada. 4: 2755–2768.

Herskovits, Melville. 1938. *Acculturation*. New York: J. J. Augustin.

Hoffman, Frederick J. 1962. *The Twenties*, rev. ed. New York: Viking.

Hultkrantz, A. 1968. "The Aims of Anthropology: A Scandinavian Point of View." *Current Anthropology* 9: 289–310.

Klopfer, Bruno. 1938. "Personality Investigation and Its Variables as Shown by Tests of Berens River Indians." Unpublished.

Laufer, Bertold. 1931. "Columbus and Cathay, and the Meaning of America to the Orientalist." *Journal of the American Oriental Society* 51: 99.

Lesser, A. 1929. "Kinship Origins in the Light of Some Distributions." *American Anthropologist*, 31: 710–730.

Lindzey, Gardner. 1961. *Projective Techniques and Cross-Cultural Research*. New York: Appleton.

Lissner, Ivar. 1961. *Man, God and Magic*. New York: Putnam.

Lowie, R. H. 1934. "Religious Ideas and Practices of the Eurasiatic and North American Areas." In E. E. Evans-Pritchard, Raymond Firth, B. Malinowski, and I. Schapera, eds., *Essays Presented to C. G. Seligman*. London: K. Paul, Trench, and Trubner.

Maringer, Johannes. 1960. *The Gods of Prehistoric Man*. New York: Knopf.
Menaker, E. and W. 1965. *Ego in Evolution*. New York: Grove.
Patten, Simon N. 1924. *Essays in Economic Theory*, ed. by R. G. Tugwell. New York: Knopf.
Roe, Anne. 1953. *The Making of a Scientist*. New York: Dodd, Mead.

1

APPROACHING OJIBWE CULTURE AND MATERIAL LIFE

Introduction

A. Irving Hallowell's chapters in this section are accessible, well-focused pieces that exemplify in different ways the concrete, strongly descriptive character of much of his writing in the 1930s. In that period, he was making sense of historical and field-based data rather than taking on some of the broader, more theoretical issues that occupied him in many later articles. Chapters 2, 3, and 4 offer cases in point. They reflect how he was still learning many basic things about Ojibwe lifeways and culture, geography, and material life; his deeper, more encompassing understanding of their cosmology and worldview (see especially chapters 22, 23, 27, this volume) came later.

Chapter 1, "The Northern Ojibwa," was written in 1955 specifically to introduce the papers on the Ojibwe that Hallowell assembled in *Culture and Experience*. It comes first in this volume, as it is his best short overview of the people and region. His description of this essay in the preface to *Culture and Experience* stated its purpose well, and may be usefully repeated here: "a brief and broad-gauged ethnohistorical account of the Ojibwa as an ethnic group with special reference to the position of the Berens River people who so constantly reappear in the chapters of this volume" (1955, ix).

In this chapter, as elsewhere, Hallowell showed a fine grasp of the relevant published primary and secondary source materials that he consulted to create this overview. He was always a careful provider of documentation and footnotes. A wide-ranging scholar, he brought together historical and ethnographic evidence; in effect, he was already doing ethnohistory when that term became current in the 1950s (the journal, *Ethnohistory*, published its first volume in 1954). His use of the term in the passage quoted above is one of its relatively few early appearances in print, aside from its use in the newly founded journal. It also reminds us that his mentor, Frank Speck, was, if anything, an early proto-ethnohistorian. Hallowell's 1951 obituary of Speck commented on this feature of his work: "Although the term "ethnohistory" appears in some of his later writings, he was always an ethnohistorian."[1]

Unlike ethnohistorians of recent years, Hallowell did not get to spend time in archives, which in any case were far less accessible and well organized during his research career than they are now. For the Berens River area, the most relevant repository of primary documents for his purposes would have been the immense Hudson's Bay Company Archives (HBCA), documenting the northern fur trade and its relations with Native people from the 1670s onward. But the HBC records were in London, England until 1974 when they moved to Winnipeg, Canada, and given the constraints of travel times and expenses, Hallowell as a field anthropologist naturally gave priority to his summer fieldwork, complemented by the references he could find in university libraries. Even if he had hoped to tap that resource, research travel of all kinds was drastically curtailed for scholars in the World War II years and their aftermath.

Chapter 2, a brief early piece entitled, "Notes on the Northern Range of *Zizania* [wild rice] in Manitoba" (1935), takes up a highly specific topic that contrasts with the scope of chapter 1, yet it has the same concrete, descriptive, well-grounded quality. It also signals Hallowell's range of interests, being his only foray into a botanical journal, *Rhodora*, the journal of the New England Botanical Club, a respected periodical that began publication in 1899. In it, Hallowell combined his own field observations with William Berens's firsthand knowledge and experience of Ojibwe wild rice growing, demonstrating that Ojibwe people successfully managed and harvested this important food source for a considerable time in areas of Manitoba rather farther to the north than had previously been recognized.

The following chapter, "Rocks and Stones," is the only essay in this book that has not been previously published. An eight-page typescript, it appears from internal evidence to have been written in 1935 or 1936, as it makes reference to Hallowell's experiences and to stories he heard during his field summer of 1934 and in some cases before. (He was not at Berens River in the summer of 1935.) It is not clear what Hallowell planned to do with this text. But it is an observant overview of a topic that also held great interest for him in some of his later writings, most notably, in "Ojibwa Ontology, Behavior, and World View" (1960, reprinted as chapter 27, this volume). Stones and their animate qualities and potentialities engaged the reflections of a number of the Ojibwe men with whom Hallowell had some of his deeper discussions along the Berens River, and the topic seemed to him to offer a window into Ojibwe thought processes that he explored on a number of occasions. A current generation of scholars has in turn picked up on the issue, and thanks to anthropologist Tim Ingold and others, Hallowell's published discussions of and stories about Ojibwe views regarding the characteristics of certain stones are among his most cited texts.[2] This text will be of interest for them as for other readers, as it clearly foreshadows some of Hallowell's later and more reflective writings on this subject.

As Hallowell footnoted this text very little, not having prepared it for publication, we have added a number of annotations that provide context and identify more fully some of the people referred to. Hallowell, in his many publications, varied in the extent to which he identified the Ojibwe people who shared information with him, but commonly, persons whom he did not identify in one essay are identified somewhere else by initials, and in still another place by name, as in this essay. William Berens, in particular, regularly received personal credit for his contributions; as Hallowell wrote in the 1960s "from the beginning of my association with him, I became historically oriented as a matter of course . . . . This enabled me to integrate data concerning the cultural present with changes in the historic past, often with reference to specific individuals."[3] In chapter 3, as elsewhere, Hallowell was often writing (ethno)history, and the specificity of his texts continues to make them valuable to and useful for the descendants of the people he met, and for the history of the region.

Chapter 4, "Notes on the Material Culture of the Island Lake Saulteaux," presents some of the most northerly Ojibwe research that Hallowell did, when he visited Island Lake, Manitoba, in July of 1930. Like some of his other writings in the 1930s, it recalls the style and interests of Frank G. Speck in its attention to material details of dwellings, clothing, tools and other artifacts, subsistence, etc. It is of interest to read this article in conjunction with Hallowell's detailed unpublished journal of his field travels that summer, which adds concrete information on travel conditions, people met, and other local observations. (We could wish that Hallowell had kept such journals on his later Berens River field trips, but he did not, beyond some brief field diaries that survive from the summers of 1931 and 1932, and one, even more telegraphic, for 1933.)

Reading this article and the diary of 1930, we begin to see the reasons why Hallowell, after that year, turned away from his initial plans for field research north of Lake Winnipeg, and towards Berens River. Norway House, Cross Lake, Island Lake, and other communities in that area had been subject to heavy fur trade and mission traffic. Hallowell, in his time there, must have been reminded, to a degree, of Frank Speck's doing of salvage ethnography among eastern Algonquian groups, as he collected numerous traditional Cree and Ojibwe artifacts for the collections of the Museum of the American Indian, Heye Foundation, in New York City and saw various changes occurring. His 1938 essay ended by noting that soon after he left Island Lake, gold was discovered there. Even though mining was abandoned after several years, he concluded that, "it is not unlikely that even the semblance of aboriginal culture I observed has been still further modified."

Further, travel to Island Lake proved arduous, consuming fifteen days from Norway House that summer, and while people appeared friendly and helpful, he found no one to equal Chief William Berens, whom he had met at Berens River on his steamer trip up Lake Winnipeg to Norway House. The two men had established an instant rapport, and Berens had encouraged Hallowell to visit him again for a few days on his way down the lake in August. Hallowell did so, and his diary records the time he spent with the chief. Their good conversations, Berens's friendly interest, and the prospect he offered of their traveling together up the river to more remote Ojibwe communities, permanently reoriented the focus of Hallowell's research and writing away from his first plan of working among the Cree. In a sense, the Island Lake trip itself helped that reorientation, however; for Hallowell found that these people were in fact more "Saulteaux" than Cree linguistically and in their connections. And since his ethnohistorical readings had already stimulated his interest in Ojibwe history and culture, the shift in emphasis came readily for several reasons.[4] Hallowell, by the end of August 1930, had found the people who would provide the focus for his research and writings for the next four decades.

Notes

1. Hallowell, 1951 ("Frank Gouldsmith Speck, 1881–1950," *American Anthropologist* 53[1]: 67–87), 68. A search of the *American Anthropologist* on www.anthrosource.net turned up a few uses of the term in the 1940s, the first being in October 1943, 637, in a footnote, as "Ethno-History."

2. See the preface to William Berens, *Memories, Myths, and Dreams of an Ojibwe Leader* (2009), which reviews Hallowell's scholarly legacies as seen by some more recent writers.

3. Hallowell, *The Ojbwa of Berens River, Manitoba: Ethnography into History* (Fort Worth: Harcourt Brace Jovanovich, 1992), 11.

4. Hallowell, *Ojibwa*, 4–6, describes this shift in interest and his meeting with Berens; see also his prologue to this volume, and the introduction to William Berens, *Memories, Myths, and Dreams* (2009).

ONE

The Northern Ojibwa

At approximately fifty-two degrees north latitude a small river that has its source almost three hundred miles to the east flows into Lake Winnipeg. To the Indians who live in this region it is still *omīmīsīpī*, Pigeon River. The reference is to the passenger pigeon (*Ectopistes migratorius*), now extinct, but formerly one of the most familiar and distinctive avian species of North America. This bird once was a source of food to the native population at the season when huge migrating flocks numbering in the thousands were said to darken the sun. On maps, however, this is the Berens River, probably named after a factor in charge of one of the trading posts of the Hudson's Bay Company more than a century ago.[1] Another small stream to the south now bears the name of Pigeon River (see fig. 1).

It is the nine hundred or more Indians of the Berens River among whom I did fieldwork during the decade 1930–40 who are referred to in many of the papers collected in this volume [*Culture and Experience*, 1955]. Locally known as *Saulteaux*, in the patterns of their speech and manner of life they belong to a much larger—and geographically widespread ethnic and linguistic group—the Ojibwa. But this larger whole, although readily identifiable, was never at any time unified in any political sense, so that it cannot properly be called a nation or, except by traditional usage, even a tribe. The Berens River Saulteaux represent a local variant of this larger unit. Furthermore, the lineal ancestors of these Indians, and of other closely related neighboring people, only a few generations ago did not occupy the area east of Lake Winnipeg—they migrated into it. It is partly due to this migration into more remote regions that these groups of Ojibwa Indians were able to conserve a great deal of their aboriginal culture during a period when armed conflicts with an expanding white population, the effects of the fur trade, and Christianization led to more rapid culture changes among the Ojibwa elsewhere.

We can be fairly certain that there were no local trading posts in the country bordering on eastern Lake Winnipeg until quite late in the eigh-

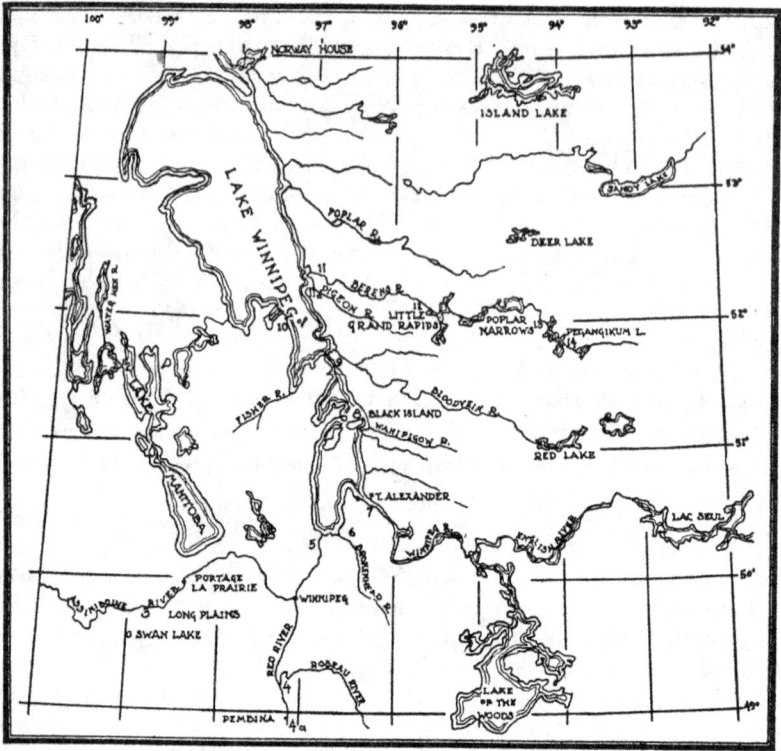

2. Lake Winnipeg Region

teenth century. The North West Company post at the mouth of the Winnipeg River, for example, was not established until 1792. While two other posts to the north (at the mouth of the Bloodvein and the Poplar River), appear on maps of 1817 and 1818, it is not likely that they were in operation prior to the last decade of the eighteenth century at the earliest. On the Berens River itself the present post of the Hudson's Bay Company dates from the early nineteenth century.[2] It is traditional among the Indians, however, that the North West Company operated a small post in the same locality prior to this, as well as one about forty miles up the river at Old Fort Rapids. Thus, while the Ojibwa of the country east of Lake Winnipeg had local facilities for trade from the late eighteenth century onward, the presence of a few isolated trading posts did not change the major culture patterns of their lives.

Efforts to Christianize the Indians of this area were extremely tardy. As late as 1854 when the Reverend John Ryerson made an inspection tour of the Wesleyan missions on Lake Superior and in the Northwest, there was no mission of any kind on the eastern shores of Lake Winnipeg between Fort Alexander at the southern end of the lake and Norway House.[3] The latter was in Cree territory, north of Lake Winnipeg, where the Reverend James Evans had opened a mission in 1840. Ryerson stopped at Berens River en route to Norway House and, although the Hudson's Bay Company factor informed him that the local Indians wished a missionary, Ryerson's conversations with them were far less encouraging. Consequently, during the early childhood of my mentor, Chief [William] Berens, who was in his late sixties when I first met him, there was no missionary in residence on the Berens River. It was his father, Jacob Berens, who was active in recruiting the first missionary, but this effort did not bear fruit until 1873.[4] It is not surprising, therefore, that while every member of the band at the mouth of the Berens River was reported as a convert by 1892, during the entire period of my investigations un-Christianized Ojibwa were still to be found inland. In the Lake Pekangikum band, which I visited in 1932, there was not a single Christian reported before 1924. A decade later the Dominion Census (1934) reports 130 Indians still adhering to "Aboriginal Beliefs" out of a total population of 891, a proportion of 14 percent.

While it is impossible to say exactly when the Berens River—a relatively tiny waterway in a labyrinthine network of greater and smaller rivers and innumerable lakes of all sizes—first became known to white men, the Lake Winnipeg area was one of the last in North America to be explored. Lake Winnipeg itself, one of the lesser great lakes of the continent, was not discovered until the explorations of Sieur de la Verendrye and his associates (1731–44). It immediately became the pivotal point in the exploration of northwestern North America, the extension of the fur trade, and the eventual discovery of the long sought "Western Sea."[5] Before the end of the eighteenth century, Lake Winnipeg had become the crossroads of a continent, traversed by the canoes of explorers, fur traders, and missionaries, whereas before there had been only those of native Indian hunters and fishermen. Its northern end was crossed by white men who either had come all the way from Hudson Bay, or had followed the route from Lake Superior that led to Lake Winnipeg through its most southerly tributary on the east, the Winnipeg River, or had entered the lake from the Red River that flowed into it directly from the south. Most of them hurried on to ascend the main water highway that led to the greater Northwest, the Saskatchewan River.

Of the Indians who lived on the rivers and lakes directly east of Lake Winnipeg before the middle of the eighteenth century, we know nothing directly. There is some evidence that in the late seventeenth or early eighteenth century some Assiniboine, a branch of the Siouan-speaking peoples whose territory once extended as far as the Lake of the Woods, were living east of Lake Winnipeg as far north as the narrows. (At least this is what some of my Indian informants told me.) But there is no doubt that up until the eighteenth century the Woods and Swampy Cree were the predominant people surrounding not only Hudson Bay but also Lake Winnipeg. Their neighbors in the prairie and wooded region to the west and south were the Assiniboine. As late as 1775 when Alexander Henry (the elder) reached the mouth of the Winnipeg River, he found a Cree village there.[6] By the beginning of the nineteenth century, however, a decided change had taken place. The Cree were no longer to be found to the east, south, and west of Lake Winnipeg. Bands of Ojibwa had displaced them and the locus of the Cree had shifted to the north. In the whole area east of Lake Winnipeg, Ojibwa—the direct ancestors of the Berens River population and of other Ojibwa now occupying the small eastern tributaries of Lake Winnipeg—had settled.

All these Indians represent migrant branches of an ethnic group which had occupied a comparatively restricted region in the seventeenth century. The Ojibwa were first reported near the Sault Ste. Marie, at the eastern end of Lake Superior, and in the Upper Peninsula of Michigan in the *Jesuit Relations* (1640).[7] This early association with the Sault is the source of one of their major ethnic appellations for over a century—*Saulteurs,* given to them by the French traders. It persists today in the Anglicized form *Saulteaux.* One of the earliest forms of the name given to them was *Baouichitigouian,* the equivalent of the modern Ojibwa *báwáctīgowinínīwak,* literally "Rapids People" or "People of the Falls or Rapids." In some other Indian languages a similar designation for them was employed, while in others they were called "Leapers" or "Jumpers," probably an incorrect rendering of *Saulteurs.* *Outchibouec,* the source of the later English *Ojibwa,* is also an early name for them. It appears as a synonym in the seventeenth century, its meaning usually being rendered as "to roast until puckered up." This refers to the puckered seam of their moccasins. *Chippewa* is actually a corruption of Ojibwa and was officially adopted in the publications of the Bureau of American Ethnology many years ago. A further synonym *Bungi* was current at the beginning of the nineteenth century and probably did not originate much earlier. In 1808, the younger Alexander Henry, who was trading near Pembina writes: "The Ogeebois are commonly called by the English Algonquins, by the Canadians Saulteurs, and by the H[udson's] B[ay] Co. servants Bungees."[8] And one of the early settlers of Lord Selkirk's Red River Colony (Manitoba) says: "In the early days of the writer the Ojibeways living in the vicinity of the Red River and Portage [La Prairie, Manitoba] Settlements were usually called Bungees, for the reason that when they asked or begged for anything, they invariably commenced their petition with the word Pungee [*pangi*], a little. The settlers noticed this and so dubbed them Bungees."[9] When referring to themselves, Ojibwa use the term *änicinábek*, men (singular, *änicinábe*). This carries a highly provincial connotation since Frenchmen, Englishmen, and Americans received generic appellations of their own—they were not *änicinábek*. Thus the Ojibwa of the Berens River, and linguistically and culturally related groups in the Province of Manitoba and elsewhere in Canada, retain a derivative of one of the old French forms of their name that still carries overtones of the rapids of the St. Mary's River, now so far away. On the other hand, Indians speaking the same language and with the same aboriginal cultural background are known in the United States as Chippewa or Ojibwa, although this designation for them is not entirely unknown in some parts of Canada.

In the United States, the Ojibwa constitute one of the largest remnants of our aboriginal population, only exceeded in numbers by the Navaho and possibly the Sioux. They occupy reservations in Minnesota (10), in Wisconsin (5), in North Dakota (1), and in Montana (1); in Michigan there are to be found several thousand non-reservation Ojibwa. In all, they possibly number 30,000 persons [1955], although all estimates are approximate and include mixed-bloods. Across the border in the Dominion of Canada, there are perhaps only 20,000 of these Indians, although the number of reservations in the provinces of Ontario, Manitoba, and Saskatchewan on which they now live outnumber those in the United States five or six to one.

An interesting sidelight on the Ojibwa is their special relation to American culture. Owing to the immense popularity of Longfellow's poem, *The Song of Hiawatha*, published in 1855, the Ojibwa have received a vicarious distinction, unique among aboriginal American tribal groups. They have achieved an enduring fame, not through wars or conquests, not because of any monuments of native art, but through the projection of an artistic image of them that has become an integral part of American literary tradition. The creation of this image came about through a peculiar combination of circumstances.

In 1839, Henry R. Schoolcraft, who took up his residence at Sault Ste.

Marie in 1822 as agent of Indian Affairs and later married an Ojibwa woman, published *Algic Researches*. These little duodecimo volumes were not only the first extensive body of Indian myths and tales collected at first hand, they were published at a time when the term "folklore" was not even known to English usage, and they were mainly Ojibwa narratives. Despite the fact that Schoolcraft says that "the value of these traditional stories appeared to depend, very much, upon their being left, as nearly as possible, in their original forms of thought and expression,"[10] he did not follow his own better judgment. He weeded out whatever he considered to be vulgar or indecent; some of the stories seemed too prolix, so he shortened and simplified them. And he could not escape the Romantic spirit of his age. The result was that despite his aim to be faithful to the spirit of the originals he reshaped the narratives in accordance with his own taste. As we know now from the comparative material that has since become available, some of the stories "are distorted almost beyond recognition."[11]

A few years later (1843) Schoolcraft published a long narrative poem *Alhalla*, based on an Indian theme. But the theme was the Creek Indian wars and in no way reflected his personal knowledge of the Ojibwa. Like a number of other poems in the same category published before *Hiawatha*, it is known to none save literary specialists. What was primarily unique about Longfellow's poem was the fact that "*Hiawatha* was the first poem of its kind in America based on Indian legend rather than on Indian history."[12] Indeed, the legends Longfellow used were necessarily those of the Ojibwa because no other comparable collection was available. He derived his inspiration from *Algic Researches* and made use of other publications of Schoolcraft. Out of a total of fifty-eight myths and tales that I have listed in my "Concordance of Ojibwa Narratives in the Published Works of Henry R. Schoolcraft," Longfellow drew upon twenty-one for the material in his famous poem.[13] He himself actually knew nothing about the Ojibwa at first hand. But he had watched Black Hawk and his braves in a powwow on Boston Common in 1837, and he had seen the remnants of the northeastern Algonkian tribes who still lived in Maine. In 1849 *Ka-ge-ga-gah-bowh* (George Copway), a famous Ojibwa Christian convert, had lectured in Boston on "The Religion, Poetry, and Eloquence of the Indian," and Longfellow had entertained him in his home.

Four thousand copies of *Hiawatha* were sold the first day of publication; a year and a half later, sales reached the 50,000 mark. Eventually, it became *the* poem of the American Indian. The picture of aboriginal life and values that emerged was shorn of a large measure of historical reality through the exercise of Schoolcraft's personal taste, in the first instance, and the subsequent refraction of the material through the poet's imagination. Nevertheless, despite some distortions of ethnographic fact, the background of the action is essentially Ojibwa.[14] Longfellow himself wrote in his notes, "The scene of the poem is among the Ojibways on the southern shore of Lake Superior." Besides, one of the special features on which the poem depends for effect is the liberal use of Ojibwa words and proper names. Even despite the choice of the name of an historic Iroquois for the hero—under the mistaken impression that it was a synonym for the quite distinct legendary *Manabozho* of Ojibwa mythology (the name Longfellow originally had in mind)[15]—and a Dakota name for the hero's mother, the Ojibwa flavor of the whole is not destroyed. In any case, the Ojibwa affiliations of the hero gradually were submerged in Hiawatha, *The Indian* of poetry,[16] a figure compounded of early nineteenth-century knowledge of the Ojibwa colored by the still persistent tradition of the Noble Savage and the Romantic spirit of the age.[17]

Prior to the conclusion of treaties with the Ojibwa and their assignment to reservations (in the United States not until after the War of 1812 and in Western Canada subsequently to the establishment of the Dominion Government in 1867), they had undergone an enormous territorial expansion. This was roughly concomitant with the spread of the fur trade in the eighteenth and early nineteenth centuries. In what became the states of Wisconsin and Minnesota they had first displaced the Fox and then the Sioux by the middle of the eighteenth century. About the same time and later, many of the Canadian Ojibwa began to move closer to Hudson Bay and westward to the region of Lake Winnipeg and beyond. As early as 1794 Ojibwa were to be found near the Pas and even a considerable distance farther up the Saskatchewan River. Some of them, coming under the cultural influence of the Assiniboine with whom they came into contact on the northern Canadian prairie adjacent to the coniferous forest and poplar parkland, later became known as the Plains Ojibwa. Most of the Ojibwa, however, did not stray outside the northern coniferous forest belt, the region in which their aboriginal hunting, fishing, and gathering culture is so thoroughly rooted. In broad terms, their native culture is essentially a variant of that characteristic of other northern peoples of Algonkian lineage whose habitat in the aboriginal period, as now, was the Eastern Sub-Arctic and the Northern Great Lakes.[18]

The ancestors of the Berens River Indians were, then, among the western Ojibwa migrants, a fact for which I have abundant evidence in extensive genealogical data. By following back the various patrilineal family lines in the contemporary population to specific ancestors, it was possible in most cases to discover something about the reputed birthplace of these individuals or the localities where they spent most or all of their lives, their movements from one locality to another, and similar information about their descendants. Thus, instead of finding that the family lines of the contemporary native population merged with other family lines of individuals who had formerly lived on the Berens River, it was discovered that the progenitors of almost every traceable patrilineal line came *to* the Berens River from some locality outside. Indeed, all the information collected turned out to be so consistent in this respect and so completely in harmony with the known facts of Ojibwa migrations that it became more and more apparent that it shed genuine light upon a local phase of the larger movement.

Since the small tributaries of eastern Lake Winnipeg north of the Winnipeg River do not connect with important lines of water travel to either Hudson Bay or Lake Superior, the Ojibwa who repopulated this region remained relatively remote from the traffic that passed through Lake Winnipeg by way of the well-known canoe routes. They were thus enabled to maintain their existence in a sheltered enclave until the seventies of the nineteenth century. Consequently, there was little intermarriage with whites, as compared with many Ojibwa elsewhere, since their only direct contacts were with the personnel of a few scattered trading posts. This probably accounts for the relatively few mixed-bloods in my genealogies. The racial picture, in fact, is the inverse of that presented by Ojibwa in the United States where it has been estimated that only 18.7 percent are *full-bloods*.[19] Among the Berens River Ojibwa, on the other hand, probably less than this number are *mixed-bloods*.

These Indians were thus able to maintain a high degree of cultural conservatism. The basic factor operative from the beginning in producing this result, and still influential in their lives (as well as in those of other northern hunting peoples), is somewhat paradoxical. While fur-trading posts were the original focal points for the mediation of changes in the technology of these Indians through their acquisition of firearms, kettles, awls, traps, etc., and in their consumptive habits by the introduction of flour, tea, tobacco, and liquor in the early days, nevertheless the demand for furs supported and encouraged the perpetuation of their aboriginal ecological adaptation—hunting. In consequence, not only was their subsistence economy retained, but the seasonal movements, institutions, attitudes, and beliefs that were closely integrated with it.

Fundamental to the Northern Ojibwa mode of hunting, for example, was the hunting-territory system. Since sons usually hunted with fathers or fathers-in-law, or brothers with brothers, rights to the usufruct of tracts of land by successive generations of male hunters was institutionalized.

Furthermore, since the trapping of furbearing animals is a pursuit carried on when snow covers the ground and the lakes and rivers are frozen, the operation of the hunting-territory system involves a biseasonal movement of the population. In the late fall there is a centrifugal movement of families that have been camping together during the summer to their winter hunting grounds (average size, ninety-three sq. miles), and when the ice breaks up in the spring a centripetal movement to the summer fishing settlements again. These latter settlements vary in size from less than fifty to 200 persons. They are always larger than the winter hunting groups, which run, on the average, from twelve to eighteen persons, with one active hunter to 3.5 other persons (1949a ["The Size of Algonkian Hunting Territories," chapter 9, this volume]). Typically, they consist of a nuclear group of at least two married couples and their children. In composition we find most frequently a man hunting with a married son, or if he has no sons, a son-in-law. Brothers, whose father is dead, may also be found together in the same winter hunting group. These patterns of seasonal movement have deep roots in the past and they largely persist today except for the fact that certain settlements, instead of being seasonal, are occupied all the year round, such as the one at the mouth of the Berens River. There the men visit their hunting grounds periodically during the winter, while their wives and children remain in the settlement.

But it is not merely the objective aspects of hunting that have persisted among these Indians; attitudes and beliefs about the nature of animals and man's relation to them are equally involved. For, to these Northern Ojibwa, hunting in the aboriginal period of their culture was not a secular occupation as it is among white men. Success depended as much upon a man's satisfactory relations with the superhuman "masters" of the different species of game and furbearing animals, as upon his technical skill as a hunter and trapper. In psychological terms these entities were among the great "givers," who bestowed extraordinary powers upon men, who acted as their "guardian spirits," and without whose "blessings" and assistance a satisfactory human life was thought to be impossible.

Thus, since the persistence of hunting cannot be separated in Ojibwa culture from beliefs about the nature of the world, the dynamic entities that function in the cosmos, and man's relation to them, it was a factor in the perpetuation of the concomitant institutions, attitudes, and beliefs with which hunting was integrated. Much of this whole complex has persisted up until the present day, and it seems reasonable to infer that despite whatever acculturation may have occurred during the fur-trade era, the integrity of the aboriginal culture must have remained essentially intact until two events, occurring after 1870, gave an impetus to the more radical modifications which reshaped the cultural picture and gave it its modern form.[20] These two events were the establishment of a resident missionary at the mouth of the Berens River in 1873 [1874] and the Treaty of the Dominion Government with all the Indians of the Lake Winnipeg area in 1875, to which the Berens River Ojibwa were a party.

The mission was established when my friend, Chief William Berens, was a boy of eight or nine years, so that within his lifetime he saw the whole process of Christianization take place. But this process is still not complete; some of the Indians in the up-river region are only now [1955] being converted. On the other hand, the Indians living at the mouth of the river, where there has been the most continuous contact with whites, have been Christians for sixty years. By the Treaty of 1875 the Indians in almost all of the area surrounding Lake Winnipeg (100,000 sq. miles) were, for the first time, brought into formal relations with the young Canadian government. It was following this treaty that reservations were assigned to different groups, and that local bands, with chiefs and councillors, were constituted. Prior to this time there were no chiefs in the modern sense, nor any formal band or tribal organization. Of institutionalized penal sanctions there were none, nor were there any juridical procedures provided in the aboriginal culture. No one, in short, was responsible for punishing crime or settling disputes. The major social sanction was the fear of misfortune and disease, an inescapable penalty for wrongdoing and one that functioned through the internal psychological mechanisms of guilt and fear, rather than shame or any kind of direct punishment that could be instituted by one's fellows. Effective leadership rested in the so-called "medicine men," those who were reputed to have gained the most power, through their dreams, from superhuman entities (*pawáganak*, dream visitors). It is significant that such individuals were frequently the first "chiefs" elected to represent the newly constituted "bands" in their dealings with the Dominion Government. Today [1955] there are three of these bands on the Berens River.

Of the two inland bands, the one whose reservation is located on Lake Pekangikum (Ontario) at a distance of some 260 miles east of Lake Winnipeg is known by that name. Approximately midway between this group and the Berens River Band, at the mouth of the river on Lake Winnipeg, is the Little Grand Rapids Band. The reservation of this inland band is about a hundred miles from the mouth of the river and, if approached by canoe, there are some fifty portages to be managed. When I first made the trip from Lake Winnipeg to Lake Pekangikum in the summer of 1932, I was much impressed with the cultural gradient as one proceeded inland. The Indians of the Berens River Band were the most acculturated while those at Lake Pekangikum were the least acculturated. The latter band was still the stronghold of those Indians who clung to their native beliefs. During the past decade [1945–1955] the situation has radically changed. Mining operations near Red Lake, not far to the south of Lake Pekangikum, have opened up a new channel of communication with the outside world; acculturation processes have been greatly accelerated. A secular school has been built by the government, and a small Catholic church has been erected on the reservation, services being held by an itinerant priest. In the summer of 1953 some Mennonites from the Chippewa country in Minnesota (Red Lake) arrived with the intention of spreading their version of the Gospel among these Indians.[21]

Because they have remained hunters and fishermen, even after Christianization and other changes in their culture, none of the Ojibwa on the Berens River live continuously within the confines of their reservations. Such confinement would make it impossible for them to make a living at all, since the nature of the country itself does not permit the raising of any crops, with the exception of a few potatoes and other garden produce. For physiographically this is a region that lies on the southwestern border of the Laurentian area (or Canadian Shield) surrounding Hudson Bay like an arc from Labrador to the Arctic Coast. It is low, with many swamps besides its myriad lakes; there is only the meagerest of soil cover for the great outcroppings of rocks striated by the glaciers that long ago scoured the surface of the whole Laurentian area. The winters are severe and the summers short. The average annual temperature ranges between a maximum of 76°[F] and a minimum of 21° below zero (mean 31°). The lakes and rivers are frozen six months during the year; the normal snowfall averages highest in November (11.1 in.), but even in March a heavy fall may be expected (av. 7.2 in.) and the annual average is 47.4 inches. As there is little to encourage white settlement the region still remains a sheltered enclave; no highways or railroads have ever been built. In summer the only means of transportation, other than a few small passenger and freight vessels that ply Lake Winnipeg, is the canoe. In winter, travel is only possible on snowshoes or by dog train. The only alternative at either season is the airplane.

The population of the region, too, remains predominantly Indian. The only whites are the fur-traders, a few trappers, a lonely member of the Canadian Mounted Police, a handful of missionaries (Protestant and Catholic) and, before the last war, an increasing number of prospectors, always eager to wrest new mineral secrets from the depths of the Canadian Shield. It is even likely that the density of population remains fairly close to what it was in aboriginal times. In the area covered by the Winnipeg Treaty of 1875, I estimated it to be 0.028 persons per square mile, a figure that coincides with the estimate Kroeber made for the Eastern Sub-Arctic area in the aboriginal period.[22]

On the Berens River itself, however, the population has been steadily increasing, especially in the up-river bands. From 1852, when the first official census figures were published, until 1934, it had almost doubled and there is reason to believe that the acceleration had started before the earlier date. This conclusion is based upon figures obtained by calculating the average number of offspring per married woman and per fruitful woman as recorded in my genealogies for three generations.[23] The women of the youngest generation, when still living, were past the child-bearing age for the most part, the women of the next ascending generation were all past menopause, when living, and those of the oldest generation were dead. In temporal terms, the oldest women of the youngest generation selected represent those whose reproductive life began within the last quarter of the nineteenth century—in the period, that is, immediately subsequent to the treaty; the child-bearing period of their grandmothers began a century ago or more. In these three generations the average number of offspring per fruitful woman was 3.8, 4.2, and 4.9, respectively, and the average number of offspring for all three generations was 4.5. It thus seems apparent that, whatever the rate of infant mortality has been, the Berens River population, in gross biological terms, is a healthy one.[24] This is also indicated by the fact that in the up-river bands during the period of my observations in the thirties the percentage of children under sixteen years averaged almost 50 percent of the total population of these bands. Up until that time there had never been a resident physician anywhere on the river and when, a couple of years before the war, a small hospital was opened by the Catholic mission at the mouth of the river, it was put in charge of nuns who were trained nurses. Aside from this, the Indians have been dependent entirely upon their own native remedies, except for the lay medical aid rendered by the local missionaries, both Protestant and Catholic.

So far as schools are concerned, these have been conducted primarily in connection with the missions, although a purely secular school, attended almost exclusively by Protestant children, has existed on the reservation of the Berens River Band for many years. Because of the seasonal dispersions of the Indians to their hunting grounds in winter, especially in the case of the inland people, education has been very sporadic in the case of most individuals. Consequently, very little English is spoken, even by the Indians of the Berens River Band who are the most acculturated.

On the Berens River Reservation there are few ostensible signs of the old culture. The Indians live in log houses all the year round; no native dances or ceremonies persist and one never hears the sound of an Indian drum. But during the period when I visited the settlements of the Little Grand Rapids Band and those farther inland, even in the groups officially listed as Christians, some flavor of old Indian life remained. In the summer months particularly, when one first caught sight of the birchbark-covered tipis of an encampment of these inland Indians, sharply defined against a background of the dark and stately spruces that line all horizons, it was easy to imagine oneself to be approaching a summer settlement of a century or more ago. But a closer view soon revealed the more ostensible results of acculturation. An iron kettle would be swinging over an open fire while in an adjoining camp a woman would be chopping wood with an iron axe, and a frying pan would be in the hands of another. All such tools and utensils, obtained from the "company" store, have been taken for granted for several generations, as have woven dress goods. Sweaters, woolen underwear, stockings, overalls are more recent, and now candy bars and chewing gum are obtainable. Flour, too, out of which bannocks are made, comes from the store as does tobacco and the inevitable tea which is as integral a part of daily consumption today as it was completely exotic in the aboriginal past.

Nevertheless, men might be beaching a canoe containing the carcass of a deer or moose, evidence of a successful hunt, and out over the lake possibly other figures bending from canoes to obtain fish from set nets that scarcely were out of the water day or night. For fish, rather than flour, is actually the "daily bread" of these Indians during the summer months. Fish drying on scaffolds in the sun, or fish being smoked, or fish being "ponasked" by the fire, is everywhere. In another part of such an encampment the women were likely to be tanning skins, making moccasins, mending nets, or stitching with spruce roots the bark covers for the tipis. And it was still their duty to chop and haul wood. Babies, snugly strapped in their cradleboards were being carried on their mothers' backs while the raw sphagnum moss—the natural absorbent and deodorant in which they nestle—was sunning in almost every camp. For a few days in midsummer the *wabanówiwin*—a ceremonial "dance"—often was to be seen or, if someone was ill, the beating of a drum resounded in one's ear night after night. A "sucking" doctor might be at work, trying to remove a material object projected by sorcery into the body of the patient. And if the patient failed to recover, the cause of the disease might be sought through conjuring. Then, after nightfall, the barrel-shaped conjuring lodge, with the medicine man inside, swayed from side to side amidst an encircling group of Indians as the moon rose and the spruces became silhouetted against the sky. All ears would be keyed to hear the voices of the spirits that the conjurer had summoned to secure hidden knowledge of the patient's illness that no human being alone could discover. Or the conjurer might be asked to consult his spirit helpers about the health or whereabouts of some absent person, or the location of some lost object.[25] In this atmosphere one could not help but feel that, despite many outward appearances, much of the core of the aboriginal thought and belief still remained.

Notes

"The Northern Ojibwa" was written specifically for the Hallowell essay collection, *Culture and Experience* (Philadelphia: University of Pennsylvania Press, 1955), where it appeared as chapter 5.

1. [Ed. note: On the name, Berens River, see Hallowell, *The Ojibwa of Berens River, Manitoba: Ethnography into History* (Fort Worth: Harcourt Brace Jovanovich, 1992), 14–15, ed. note 2.]

2. For information on the dates and locations of forts and trading posts, see the compilation of Ernest Voorhis, *Historic Forts and Trading Posts of the French Regime and of the English Fur Trading Companies* (Department of the Interior, National Development Bureau, Ottawa, Canada [1930], mimeographed); Gordon Charles Davidson, *The North-west Company* (Berkeley, 1918). [Victor P. Lytwyn, *The Fur Trade of the Little North: Indians, Pedlars, and Englishmen East of Lake Winnipeg, 1760–1821* (Winnipeg: Rupert's Land Research Centre, University of Winnipeg, 1986) is now the best available source: Eds.]

3. John Ryerson, *Hudson's Bay, or A Missionary Tour in the Territory of*

the Honorable Hudson's Bay Company (Toronto, 1855). [Ed. note: The HBC postmaster whom Ryerson met was Robert Cumming who served at Berens River 1828–1856; see Warren Sinclair's useful compilation, "Robert Cumming Research Notes 1812–1864," copy deposited at the Hudson's Bay Company Archives, Winnipeg.]

4. A reference to Jacob Berens, and an excellent photograph of him and his wife, is to be found in John Maclean, *Vanguards of Canada* (Toronto: Missionary Society of the Methodist Church, 1918), 124.

5. See Lawrence J. Burpee, *The Search for the Western Sea* (London, 1908), xxv–xxvi.

6. Elliott Coues (ed.), *New Light on the Early History of the Greater Northwest: The Manuscript Journals of Alexander Henry and David Thompson, 1799–1814* (3 vols.; New York, 1897), I, 35n.

7. See *Atlas of the Historical Geography of the United States* by Charles O. Paullin, John K. Wright, ed. Carnegie Institution of Washington and the American Geographical Society of New York, 1932. John R. Swanton, who prepared the map, "Indian Tribes and Linguistic Stocks, 1650," confines the Ojibwa of southern Canada to an area north of Lake Superior bounded by the Albany River. Immediately to the west are the Assiniboine who sweep up towards the eastern side of Lake Winnipeg as far as the Narrows and likewise appear west and south of it. Cf. Swanton, *The Indian Tribes of North America* (Bureau of American Ethnology Bulletin 145, 1952). [Ed. note: for fuller and more recent analyses of the histories, locations, and names (synonymies) of the groups referred to, see relevant articles in the *Subarctic* (vol. 6) and *Plains* (vol. 13) volumes of the *Handbook of North American Indians* (Washington DC: Smithsonian Institution, 1981 and 2001].

8. Coues, *New Light,* II, 533.

9. Reverend A. C. Garrioch, *First Furrows: A History of the Early Settlement* of *the Red River Country, including that* of *Portage la Prairie* (Winnipeg, 1923). It is obvious from the testimony of the foregoing writers, and others that could be mentioned, that the name Bungi was used in a generic sense and did not refer exclusively to any particular group of Ojibwa. Hence, the later use of it by Alanson Skinner in a specific sense ("Political Organization, Cults and Ceremonies of the Plains-Ojibwa and Plains-Cree Indians," *Anthropological Papers, American Museum of Natural History,* 11[1914], pt. 6, 477) was only confusing, especially in historic perspective. Skinner's use of Saulteaux (ibid., 9[1911], pt. 1, "Notes on the Eastern Cree and Northern Saulteaux," 117) is scarcely clarifying either. He attempted to distinguish Ojibwa, Chippewa, Northern and Southern Saulteaux, and *Plains* Saul-

teaux. The latter was another synonym for "Long Plains Ojibwa" (=Plains Ojibwa=Bungi). The Southern Saulteaux are, in his terminology, the Ojibwa of the northern shore of Lake Superior and the Northern Saulteaux an offshoot of this group. The confusing if not meaningless identification to which Skinner's terminology gave rise is illustrated in the work of that most erudite scholar, Father W. Schmidt *(Der Ursprung der Gottesidee,* II [Münster in Westfalen, 1929]), 504), who writes: "In die Gruppe der Steppen-Ojibwa rechne ich auch die Nord-Saulteaux ein. . ."

10. Henry R. Schoolcraft, *Algic Researches, Comprising Inquiries Respecting the Mental Characteristics of the North American Indians. First Series, Indian Tales and Legends* (New York, 1839), I, 43.

11. See Stith Thompson, *Tales of the North American Indians* (Cambridge, 1929), Introduction.

12. W. L. Schramm, "Hiawatha and its Predecessors," *Philological Quarterly* 11 (1932), 321–43; Stith Thompson, "The Indian Legend of Hiawatha," *Modern Language Association,* 38 (1922), 128–43.

13. The figure referred to was arrived at by collating the sources cited in Chase S. Osborn and Stellanova Osborn, *"Hiawatha" with its Original Indian Legends* (Great Lakes Edition of the Song of Hiawatha [Lancaster, Pa., 1944]) with the narratives listed in my "Concordance" (Hallowell, 1946b).

14. For the appraisal by two anthropologists see Herman F. C. Ten Kate, "The Indian in Literature," *Report of the Smithsonian Institution for 1921* (Washington, 1923), 511–12; Frank G. Speck (with Florence I. Speck), "The Ojibwa, Hiawatha's People," *Home Geographic Monthly,* II (no. 4, 1932), 7–12.

15. As Grace Lee Nute (*Lake Superior* [Indianapolis, 1944], 97) has said: "What a pity the poet substituted another name for the one first chosen! Nanabozhoo is known east, north, south, and west of Lake Superior: Hiawatha is a minor Iroquois substitute." The same mythological character is known among the Berens River Ojibwa as *wísakedják,* possibly due to Cree influence.

16. Douglas Leechman, a Canadian anthropologist ("Longfellow's Hiawatha," *Queens Quarterly, 51* [1944], 307–12), writes: "no matter how confused in origin or how far from the truth Longfellow's hero may be, there is no doubt that he is *the* Indian of poetry, just as the Fenimore Cooper Indian, despite Mark Twain's strictures, is *the* Indian of fiction."

17. Cf. the comments on Schoolcraft and Longfellow in Roy Harvey

Pearce, *The Savages of America. A Study of the Indian and the Idea of Civilization* (Baltimore, 1953).

18. See A. L. Kroeber, *Cultural and Natural Areas of Native North America* (University of California Publications in American Archeology and Ethnology, *38* [1939]); Regina Flannery, "The Culture of the Northeastern Hunters: A Descriptive Survey," and John M. Cooper, "The Culture of the Northeastern Indian Hunters: A Reconstructive Interpretation," in Frederick Johnson (ed.), *Man in Northeastern North America* (Papers of the R. S. Peabody Foundation for Archeology, Phillips Academy [Andover, 1946]). For a bibliography of the Ojibwa see George P. Murdock, *Ethnographic Bibliography of North America* (2nd ed.; New Haven, 1953).

19. Carrie A. Lyford, *The Crafts of the Ojibwa (Chippewa)*. Education Division, U.S. Office of Indian Affairs (1942), 12.

20. For examples of two different types of cultural change that have occurred, see my papers, "The Incidence, Character, and Decline of Polygyny among the Lake Winnipeg Cree and Saulteaux" (1938c) which is supported by quantitative information, and "The Passing of the Midéwi·win in the Lake Winnipeg Region" (1936c)[chapters 6, 21, this volume]. The former article contains a map indicating the boundaries of the area covered by the Winnipeg Treaty of 1875. For other cultural changes see chapter 7 on temporal orientation and for samples of folktales of European derivation see 1939c.

21. Letter from R. William Dunning (August 1953). Mr. and Mrs. Dunning have been summer school teachers at Lake Pekangikum since 1950. [The American Mennonite missionaries became based at Red Lake, Ontario; see R. W. Dunning, *Social and Economic Change among the Northern Ojibwa* (Toronto: University of Toronto Press, 1959, 17), eds.]

22. See Hallowell, 1938c, 238. ["The Incidence, Character, and Decline of Polygyny," chapter 6, this volume.]

23. Unpublished data.

24. A comparable study by Hortense Powdermaker in Melanesia showed, for example, that the average number of offspring per fruitful woman was only 2.9. See "Vital Statistics of New Ireland as Revealed in Genealogies," *Human Biology*, III (1931).

25. See Hallowell, 1942a. [*The Role of Conjuring in Saulteaux Society*. Publications of the Philadelphia Anthropological Society, vol. 2. Philadelphia.]

TWO

Notes on the Northern Range of
Zizania [wild rice] in Manitoba

In the course of an ethnological study of the Saulteaux Indians of the Berens River conducted during the past three summers, the writer has collected a considerable amount of ethno-botanical data. The river mentioned rises in Ontario, flows northwestward and empties into Lake Winnipeg at approximately 52° 20′ N. Lat. The band of Indians farthest up the river inhabits the neighborhood of Lake Pekangikum (Ontario), some 260 miles from the mouth. A second band, the Little Grand Rapids group, occupies the district midway between the Pekangikum band and the Berens River band proper, located at the mouth of the river.

Among the other items *Zizania aquatica* L., although not as important today as formerly, is a food plant well known to all of these Indians. This use of *Zizania*, paralleled by many American natives elsewhere, would scarcely be worth recording in a botanical journal were it not for the fact that data obtained on the precise localities where the plant flourishes in abundance, seems to indicate that it grows somewhat farther north than has hitherto been reported in this area. Many years ago, for example, when Prof. A. E. Jenks published his "Wild-Rice Gatherers of the Upper Lakes,"[1] he included data obtained from botanists and the botanical literature on the geographical range of *Zizania*. He stated its northern limits to be approximately 50°.[2] Even in the "Check List of Manitoba Flora" issued by the Botany Department of Manitoba Agricultural College, 1922, the only locality specified for *Zizania* is Sturgeon Creek, in the southern part of the province. Yet until recently the native Indians of various localities east of Lake Winnipeg and almost as far north as 53° have been annually harvesting the plant and utilizing it as one of their staple foods for many years.

My personal interest in the range of *Zizania* grew out of the question which arose in my mind as to whether the Indians made use of it throughout its limits. Consultation with Dr. J. M. Fogg Jr. and correspondence with Dr.

Hugh M. Raup made it seem worthwhile to record the information I had secured from the Indians, despite the fact that I have not myself observed *Zizania* in all of the localities mentioned below. My principal informant, I might add, was Chief William Berens, of the Berens River Band, an exceptionally intelligent Indian, who has travelled widely throughout the country east of Lake Winnipeg, especially between 52° and 54° N. Latitude. According to his observations, *Zizania* does not range as far north as the last mentioned degree, the latitude of Norway House. I visited this locality in 1930 and can testify that the Cree Indians of this district make no use of *Zizania*, a fact which in itself has no botanical value, although it is consistent with Chief Berens' statement. The latter also asserted that no wild rice grows on the canoe route between Norway House and Island Lake to the east, a distance of some 175 miles, at approximately the same latitude. This negative observation is also supported by my own inquiries at Island Lake in 1930 [chapter 4, this volume], which disclosed no utilization of the grain there by the Saulteaux-speaking natives.

Turning now to positive information as to the occurrence of *Zizania*, the following localities are those in which the plant grows in sufficient abundance to have made it worthwhile for the Indians to harvest the grain. Formerly, several of these were visited exclusively for this purpose, although not today. In a forthcoming publication [not found] I shall indicate these localities on a map. For the purposes of this note, approximate references to degrees of latitude and longitude will have to suffice.

1. In a number of small lakes and creeks on Chief Berens' hunting ground, none of which are named on official maps (Lat. 52° 35', Long. 96° 30') *Zizania* grows in abundance. In 1933, he said, there was sufficient wild rice to feed "three or four battalions of men."

2. A lake which, in the native tongue, is known as the "wild-rice gathering place" (Lat. 52° 35', Long. 96°) is another well-known locality. The Indians of the Poplar River band (north of Berens River) used to frequent this lake for the purpose of harvesting *Zizania* as did members of the Little Grand Rapids band of the Berens River.

3. On the Berens River itself wild rice is fairly abundant from the mouth of the river as far inland as Long Lake (Lat. 52° 10', Long. 96° 5'), a distance of some 60 miles. Long Lake is likewise the approximate boundary between the hunting grounds of the Berens River band proper and the Little Grand Rapids Indians.

4. In approximately the same general locality the Etomami River enters

the Berens River at Etomami Falls.[3] Above the falls and along the river as far as a fairly large lake *Zizania* grows in abundance. Some of the [Little] Grand Rapiders used to gather their wild rice here, since farther up the river it is said to be absent. When I visited Lake Pekangikum in 1932, I found that these Indians did not utilize *Zizania* at all, although they knew its nutritive properties. I was told that it did not grow in sufficient quantities anywhere within their habitat to enable them to exploit it economically. This negative economic fact is reflected by the absence, in their calendrical terminology, of a "wild rice gathering moon" which is to be found in the terminology of the other two bands, as well as among wild rice gatherers of the Great Lakes.

Native place-names, sometimes continued in English translation, are likewise legitimate clues to the occurrence of *Zizania*, because a Wild Rice River or Lake would not be so named by the Indians unless it had reference to the presence, and probably economic exploitation, of the plant in such a locality. I wish, therefore, to call attention to the following localities south of the Berens River which Chief Berens believed to be those exploited by the Indians of the Blood Vein and Hollow Water River bands.

5. Rice River, a small stream which enters Lake Winnipeg from the east at 51° 15′ N. Latitude.
6. Rice Lake (51° Lat., 95° 31′ Long.).

It would appear from this brief survey that, like their Ojibwa congeners to the southeast, the Saulteaux Indians east of Lake Winnipeg utilized *Zizania* whenever it occurred within their habitat and even made considerable journeys at times to harvest the grain in neighboring localities. While not enlarging the range of *Zizania* in any precise botanical detail the data presented unequivocally indicate that its limits exceed 50° N. Lat. in Manitoba and that there is legitimate doubt whether the plant occurs in any abundance, if at all, beyond 53°.[4]

Notes

Published in *Rhodora*, Journal of the New England Botanical Club, 37, no. 440 (August 1935): 302–4.

1. Albert E. Jenks, in *Nineteenth Annual Report of the Bureau of American Ethnology*, 1897–98, 2: 1013–37. Washington DC, 1900.
2. Jenks, 1028.

3. Not to be confused with the junction of the same river and the Berens River much nearer the mouth.

4. [Ed. note: Numerous writings have extended historical, cultural, and botanical perspectives on wild rice in the region. Victor P. Lytwyn's monograph, *The Fur Trade of the Little North: Indians, Pedlars, and Englishmen East of Lake Winnipeg, 1760–1821* (Winnipeg: Rupert's Land Research Centre, University of Winnipeg, 1986) cites numerous traders' references to Native reliance on and trading of wild rice in the region surrounding the Berens River and is helpful in tracing the locales mentioned by Hallowell. Also important is D. Wayne Moodie's article, "Manomin: Historical-Geographical Perspectives on the Ojibwa Production of Wild Rice," in Kerry Abel and Jean Friesen, eds., *Aboriginal Resource Use in Canada: Historical and Legal Aspects* (Winnipeg: University of Manitoba Press, 1991), 71–79. For a comprehensive study focused more on Minnesota and Wisconsin, see Thomas Vennum, Jr., *Wild Rice and the Ojibway People* (St. Paul: Minnesota Historical Society Press, 1988). On the botany of *Zizania*, see William G. Dore, *Wild-Rice* (Ottawa: Publication 1393, Research Branch, Canada Department of Agriculture), 1969. Dore cited Hallowell's article as the earliest ethnological account of wild rice in the Manitoba area, but identified the plant in question not as *Z. aquatica* but as *Zizania palustris* var. *palustris*, the most common variety found in Canada; see his distribution map of the area (p. 27). Botanist Richard Staniforth clarifies that wild rice "was formerly thought to be a single species: *Zizania aquatica*. In relatively recent years taxonomists have realized that it is a complex of several species." *Z. aquatica* does not occur in Manitoba (e-mail to Jennifer Brown, April 1, 2008).]

THREE

Rocks and Stones

Swept almost clean of any real covering of soil by the glacial ice, the Berens River country would present to the eye vast rocky wastes, labyrinthine waterways, and muskeg if the great forests of spruce, jackpine, and poplar did not exploit what little soil there is and conceal the surface contours of the Pre-Cambrian Shield from view. Only where forest fires destroyed this woody cloak is the country exposed in all its rocky nakedness. On the canoe route from the mouth of the river to Little Grand Rapids, a distance of 110 miles, there are some fifty portages to be made. Yet, except on the longer of these, one's feet seldom tread genuine soil on the entire trip. Instead, one is constantly scrambling over huge, sloping, glacier-smoothed boulders. The Indians find it practical to wear rubbers over their moccasins when travelling, not so much as a protection against moisture, but to prevent them slipping on the rocks in making landings and in carrying their loads over the portages.

Despite the fact that the general trend of their thought is so emphatically animistic, it would caricature the beliefs of these people to assert that a spirit lurks in every rock, or that they believe that every stone has a soul. They are not given to sweeping generalizations of this sort, nor do they necessarily follow through all the logical implications of their assumptions. When I bluntly asked old Alec Keeper [Kiwitc] whether *all* the rocks one could see were alive, he quietly replied, "Some are."[1] That is really what interests the Indian: The fact that "*some* are," rather than the more abstract question whether *all* are. The stones that are alive are valuable to him in terms of culturally defined purposes. These fit into his scheme of things. Whether one classes stones to have similar potentialities is a question which has little or no significance abstractly. But it remains an open question. A dream revelation, or validation through personal experience is always sufficient to settle such matters definitively.

In mythology, moreover, we have a prototype of lithic animation where Flint (piwánɑk) is personified and is born of the same mother as the winds and the Great Hare [Misabos]. As Flint sprang from her womb she was torn to pieces by his violent exit. He chose the swift current of the river as his dwelling place, while the winds, his brothers, chose the four quarters of the earth as theirs. The Great Hare avenged his mother's death by attacking Flint and destroying him bit by bit, thus reducing him to proportions which made him harmless and at the same time of some value to the Indians.[2] Today Flint is regarded as a very powerful pawágan, although his earthly fragments are no longer of any practical value.

What these Indians believe then, is that certain rocks and stones exhibit animate or magical properties under certain circumstances. The rocky escarpments along the river at certain places, large, smoothly rounded boulders, irregularly corrugated stones of considerable size and possibly of igneous origin, as well as smaller pebbles which can be held on the hand or carried in the pocket, all have been known to exhibit such properties.

In some of the rocky escarpments mentioned, live semi-human creatures called memegweciwak who will be described presently. They have been seen to disappear into the rocks toward which they paddled their canoes and human beings have visited them there. The rocks are said to have opened to admit them just like a door.[3]

The portable types of stones which evidence animate properties or magical potencies one does not acquire by a simple volitional act. Indeed, it would be worse than foolish merely to set out to look for one. It is only by means of spiritual guidance, revelation, that it is possible to find such a stone. This is the subjective selective factor which differentiates stones seen in the wabanó or in the possession of individuals from hundreds of boulders or pebbles having the same external appearance that strew the country from end to end.

Yellow Legs, the great-grandfather of Chief William Berens and leader of the midéwi·win held at the mouth of the river for many years, obtained a stone with remarkable animate properties in the following manner: In a dream the precise location of this boulder was revealed to him. It lay on a tiny island[4] in the middle of Lake Winnipeg, thirty miles south of the mouth of the Berens River. Yellow Legs did not go and get it himself, but instructed two men whom he sent to the precise spot where they should find it. He told them they would see a bear's tracks leading out of the water. These tracks, he said, would lead them directly to the stone. But as a further clue to its identification, Yellow Legs informed them that they would find a few branches broken directly above it. The men found everything as described, the bear's tracks, the broken branches, the stone itself. The latter they brought to Yellow Legs who used it in the midéwi·win. It is now in the possession of Chief Berens.[See Berens, 2009, illustration 89.]

The reputation of this particular stone, which is about the size of a bowling ball but slightly elongated rather than spherical, has travelled far beyond the mouth of the river. Chief Berens has refused to sell it, although he said both Indians and white men had made him attractive offers. He pointed out a mouth and eyes to me on the stone but I found them hard to discern, although a rough indentation undoubtedly represented the former.[5] At a certain point in the ritual of the midéwi·win Yellow Legs would tap the stone several times with a new knife. Then the mouth would open. Yellow Legs would insert his fingers in it and withdraw a small caribou-skin sack with medicine in it. After mixing some of this medicine with water he would pass the decoction around and a small sip was taken by all those present. Today the stone no longer exhibits its animate traits.

Such conceptions in regard to the animate nature of stones by no means belong to the past nor are exclusively associated with the midéwi·win. In the settlements up the river individuals still act upon this animistic hypothesis under certain circumstances.

A few years ago, one of the traders at [Little] Grand Rapids and his son were digging up their potato patch. They struck a large, smoothly rounded boulder similar to the one just described and of a type which is still used as part of the paraphernalia of the wabanówĭwin. The trader called John Duck who lives nearby and is the leader of the wabanówĭwin at [Little] Grand Rapids. The trader jokingly told John that he had found one of the stones belonging in his wábano pavilion. The latter did not seem pleased at this, but he bent down and spoke to the stone in a low voice, inquiring whether it had ever been in his pavilion. According to John the stone replied with a negative.[6]

As this incident suggests, today such stones are intimately associated with the wabanówĭwin. They are disposed in the different pavilions in various ways. Usually there are one or more of them that lie in the central axis near the upright posts. But in the pavilion at Pauingassi there is also a stone placed at the threshold of each of the four doorways. In this pavilion they are painted with certain symbols, an innovation which seems to be attributable to Namɑwin [Fair Wind]. They are always sacred objects but none of them, so far as I know, have manifested specific animate characteristics although the attitude of John Duck is sufficiently indicative of how they are regarded.

In the wábano pavilion of Asagesi at Duck Lake there were no stones exposed (1932). However, I did not see a wabanówĭwin there, only a dance being held at the pavilion at the time of my visit. In another pavilion which Asagesi had built previously at Lake Pekangekum, described in 1925, there were two large boulders east of two of the medial posts. Asagesi spoke of a large stone "underground" in telling me about his dream revelation to which the position of one of the three stones corresponds. In his Duck Lake pavilion he places a smaller stone, which he privately showed me, at the west side of the central post when the regular ceremony is being held.

A boulder similar in form to those seen in the wábano pavilions may be seen near the western end of one of the portages between Poplar Narrows and Pekangikum—kamini ` tgŭtci waŋ, water running on both sides of (the) rock. It is called "our grandfather's rock" (kimi comissab kunan) and is said to have been revealed in a dream to Pazagwi' gabau who placed it there a number of years ago. It is regarded as sacred and has become a shrine where passers-by often leave sacrifices of tobacco and other objects.[7]

Another type of sacred stone of which I have only seen two specimens is flatter in shape than those previously described and deeply corrugated. One of these lay at the foot of a medial post in the wábano pavilion at Pauingessi. It was unique among the stones there, the others being large, smoothly rounded boulders.[8] John Duck privately showed me a similar stone in his possession but it was not publicly exposed in his wábano pavilion on any of the half dozen occasions when I was present at the ceremonies held there. Only three stones were used in his pavilion and all of them were of the other type.

To the knowledge of Chief Berens, stones of the corrugated variety are extremely rare in the country. It is possible that their value as sacred objects is partially connected with this fact. However, as I shall bring out later, both Namawin [Fair Wind, at Pauingassi] and John Duck seem disposed to introduce novelties from time to time and I believe that the former is probably responsible for introducing this particular type of stone into the contemporary category of sacred lithic objects. Curiously enough, on the way down the river in 1932 while the Indians were eating lunch, I wandered a short distance away in the bush and discovered a toboggan cached there. Among the stones used to weigh it down was one of the corrugated variety. I could not discover to whom the toboggan belonged, so whether this stone had been used for its practical value alone or whether it had some sacred meaning or destination as well, I do not know.

John Duck, I might add had, in addition to the corrugated stone mentioned, several other stones of curious shapes and different sizes in his possession which he claimed had prophylactic and therapeutic attributes. These will be described later in connection with the wabanówīwin.

In 1934 I obtained from Alec Keeper a smoothly rounded pebble about two inches long and one and a half inches in diameter, which his father, who had been the leading midé up the river [see n. 7], had given him. He told me that I had better keep it in a tin box or it might "go." He, too, emphasized the fact that stones which are alive can only be found through dream revelation. Placing several objects on the floor, he said, "A person will dream that they are placed just like this, and that is how he will find them." The son of this man, Ketagas, gave me the following account of how he obtained a stone with animate properties and great medicinal value:

About four years ago I was very sick during the winter. I thought I was going to die. One night I dreamed of Pauingessi Lake, which is the deepest water in this part of the country. Miki·nă´k spoke to me in my dream. He told me to come and see him (i.e., in Pauingessi Lake). I went to where he was. Down into the water I went, where Miki·nă´k lives. He said, "Take a good look at me all over." He looked very strong. I could see no weak spot anywhere. Then he told me to go and look on a rock near my house (at [Little] Grand Rapids facing the water). "That's where you'll find me," he said. Although I was very sick, the next morning I managed to get up and go outside. I went down to the water and looked for the rock Miki·nă´k had described to me. Sticking out of a little hole on top of the rock I found a little stone in the shape of a turtle. I knew then that Miki·nă´k had kept his promise. I picked up the stone and took it into the house with me. The next day I went to the same place again. I could not find the hole in the rock in which I had found the stone lying. The rock was smooth there. There were no holes of any kind in it. This made me believe that I had been really blessed.

This stone, which Ketegas showed to me, was egg-shaped in contour but flat and less than an inch through its greatest diameter. It had some dark amorphous markings on it which Ketagas interpreted as representing his three children and himself. "You may not think this stone is alive," he said, "but it is. I can make it move." (Although he did not demonstrate this to me.) He also stated that on two occasions he had loaned the stone to sick people to keep with them during the night. Both times he found it in his pocket in the morning. He kept it in a little leather case he had made for it so that it was always kept clean. It saved his life, he said, for after securing it his health immediately improved.

At a wabanówīwin witnessed in 1934, which was held to cure a certain woman, this stone was placed in a glass sugar bowl filled with water that was put at the foot of the upright post at the east end of the ceremonial pavilion. The water in the bowl was drunk later by the patient.

Ketagas also claimed that on account of being blessed by Miki·nă´k he could at any time make the water calm by throwing tobacco into it as a sacrifice. He said that the leader of the wabanówīwin on the occasion mentioned had asked him to use the stone in the way described with the idea of keeping the day calm.

While certain stones, obtained under these various circumstances, are not believed to be animate but are regarded as sacred and sometimes have therapeutic values attributed to them, other classes of stones discovered under other conditions are regarded as having malevolent properties. John Duck, for instance, in addition to the stones already mentioned, showed me two others, one pointed (slate?) and the other a small, egg-shaped pebble about a half inch in diameter, which he said had been magically projected at him by a sorcerer who desired to kill him. These had not actually entered his body so they failed of their purpose. Once such a magic missile enters a man's body it is sure to kill him unless he is powerful enough to eject it.

Alec Keeper showed me such a stone that had been projected at his father on one occasion when the latter was conjuring. It did not kill him but fell in the conjuring tent. A cosmic parallel to this magical projection of missiles among men takes place among the various supernatural entities. One pawágan will attempt to shoot another with huge boulders. When the missile fails to hit its mark it may strike the earth. This is what sometimes causes the earth to shake. When you see a spark of fire (shooting star?) travelling between the sky and the earth, that is one of those great stones hurled by one pawágan at another. "One time when we were travelling at night," Alec went on, "we saw one of these great sparks falling towards earth. We were approaching a big ridge and it seemed that the great spark was aimed directly at it. When it hit the ground we saw sparks fly upwards and we felt the earth shake much harder than when it thunders. No one ever finds such stones nowadays."

Notes

American Philosophical Society Library, Philadelphia. Alfred Irving Hallowell Papers, 1892–1981, Ms. Coll. 26. Unpublished typescript, written ca. 1935–36 to judge by internal evidence.

1. [Alec Keeper, of the Sturgeon clan at Little Grand Rapids, was one of Hallowell's most valued consultants and was second only to William

Berens in the number of stories that he shared with Hallowell (Hallowell papers, APS, Research notes, genealogies).]

2. [See Berens, *Memories, Myths, and Dreams*, Part IV, "The Birth of the Winds, Flint, and the Great Hare".]

3. [See William Berens's account of his experience with these beings in Berens, *Memories, Myths, and Dreams*, Part III, 8.]

4. Now called Egg Island but known to the Indians as wigwasimanis, Birch Island. [See also Berens, *Memories, Myths, and Dreams*, Part III, 5, "The Medicine Stone".]

5. Cf. the anthropormorphic physiognomy of the same type of boulder figured by Frances Densmore, *Chippewa Customs* (Washington DC: Bureau of American Ethnology, Bulletin 86, 1929), pl. 37b. [Reprint: St. Paul: Minnesota Historical Society Press, 1979.]

6. [John Duck is frequently mentioned in Hallowell's writings, and in those of others. See, e.g., Luther Schuetze, *Mission to Little Grand Rapids: Life with the Anishinabe 1927–1938* (Vancouver: Creative Connections, 2001), 157–59 (in which Schuetze told of Duck [Machkojence] doing a shaking tent ceremony for Hallowell, and of his later Christian conversion on which occasion he gave his big drum to Schuetze, a missionary for the United Church of Canada. Hallowell's photograph of John Duck and his wabano pavilion appears in Hallowell, *The Ojibwa of Berens River, Manitoba: Ethnography into History* (Fort Worth: Harcourt Brace Jovanovich, 1992), 84, fig. 16. Hallowell described Duck's shaking tent ceremony in *The Role of Conjuring in Saulteaux Society* (Philadelphia: University of Pennsylvania Press, 1942), chapter 7.]

7. [This text was typed by someone else, and Hallowell did not always proofread these unpublished texts; the term for "our grandfather's rock" has been reconstructed in the glossary. It is pictured in Hallowell, *Ojibwa*, 58, fig. 8. The man who placed it there was a Midewi·win leader and medicine man, and the father of Alec Keeper, mentioned above (Hallowell papers, genealogies).]

8. [The pavilion at Pauingassi (the standard spelling of the name) was constructed for ceremonies held by Fair Wind (Naamiwan), an important spiritual leader. See Hallowell's photographs of the pavilion and of Fair Wind in Hallowell, *Ojibwa*, 75, fig. 11, and 83, fig. 15; also, Maureen Matthews and Roger Roulette, "Fair Wind's Dream: *Naamiwan Obwaajigewin*," in Jennifer S. H. Brown and Elizabeth Vibert, *Reading beyond Words: Contexts for Native History* (Peterborough ON: Broadview Press, 1996), 330–60.]

FOUR

Notes on the Material Culture
of the Island Lake Saulteaux

Island Lake (Manitoba, Canada) is located approximately 115 miles east of northern Lake Winnipeg and is within the drainage basin of the Hayes River. It is reached by a canoe route from Norway House estimated at 160–170 miles.[1] This route has only been known about thirty-five years, the earlier "trail" communicating with the lake passing through God's Lake, to the north, across a two to three miles *muskeg* (Mossy Portage) and over a height of land.[2] Even the present route is by no means easy. In fact, Dr. Grant writes: "this journey, on account of its long, numerous, and very difficult portages, no doubt merits the claim put forward for it of being perhaps the most difficult regular route that is undertaken in the north[3] at the present time." At least thirty portages[4] are necessary while seven rapids can be either "lined" or "run," depending upon the season of the year and the depth of the water. The writer made the trip in July, 1930, with Mr. E. Farrington, Game Guardian. A Cree Indian (Thomas Evans) of the Norway House Band, acted as guide. Our trip consumed fifteen days, five going in, during which weather conditions and engine trouble[5] delayed us somewhat, and a little over three days coming out, when we averaged eighteen hours or more a day of steady travel.

Although the Hudson's Bay Company first established a post at Island Lake sometime before 1824, it was abandoned twice and the post occupied at the present time was not built until 1864.[6] In fact, until the canoe route described above was opened, the Indians of this band, as compared with those at Oxford House, God's Lake, Cross Lake and Norway House were among the most isolated in this part of Manitoba, since they were not so close as were the other bands mentioned to the direct line of travel between York Factory and Norway House.[7] There was some contact with missionaries, no doubt, before 1903, but it was not until this date that the United Church of Canada began more intensive work among the natives by assigning a resident missionary to the band. This was followed twenty years later by Catholic missionary effort.

The Indians account for the many islands in the lake by an exploit of *Wísakedják,* their mythical culture hero. Many years ago he was hunting beaver and, finding a huge lodge, began to chop at it with his axe. What is now called Beaver Hill, between God's Lake and Island Lake, is all that remains today of this lodge. While *Wísakedják* was chopping, a strong wind from the north was blowing and the mud from the lodge was spattered southward and now forms the 3,642 or more islands in the lake.[8] The rest of the tale relates how the beaver dived, but was finally killed with a stone and dragged from Beaver Hill Lake over the rocks, where traces of the animal's blood can still be seen.

In summer the Indians congregate at the western end of the Lake[9] in three settlements, all of which are radial, as it were, to the Hudson's Bay Post, which they reach by water.[10] Smooth (or Flat) Rock is approximately nine miles southeast of the post. It is here that most of the Protestant Indians congregate. The Catholic Mission, which I was not able to visit, is located at "Maria" Portage (*misínigäp*),[11] almost eleven miles due south from the company. The third settlement is on the western side of Waasagomach (*wasígamak*) Bay to the northwest of Maria Portage, of which it is really an outpost. The Annual Report of the Department of Indian Affairs[12] gives the total enrollment of the band in 1929 as 713, 513 being Protestant and 200 Catholic.

Linguistically, the Island Lake natives may be characterized by calling them Saulteaux or, better perhaps, Saulteaux-Ojibwa, indicating more clearly by this hyphenated term the close relationship of their language to Ojibwa proper. Locally, they are said to speak a mixed dialect of Saulteaux and Cree This mixture is reported to be especially typical of the Maria Portage groups,[13] while the natives at Smooth Rock are reputed to speak a purer Saulteaux.[14] It may be pointed out in this connection that Cree is utilized in the United Church services and at the Catholic mission too, so that in recent years practically all of the Island Lakers have learned to understand Cree and many speak it.[15] The assimilation of Cree would consequently appear to be partly the result of Christianization and partly due to contact with the Norway House Cree since the canoe route referred to has been open. The linguistic base at Island Lake may very well be Saulteaux-Ojibwa with an overlay of Cree due to modern conditions.[16] On the other hand, it is not impossible that a much older contact with Cree-speaking peoples has affected the language much more deeply than a superficial inspection would indicate, since the Saulteaux of this region may have been marginal to Cree bands for a considerable period, because to the south and east we find only Saulteaux spoken today. Locally it is said that the unity of the band as now constituted is of relatively recent origin and that it was originally made up of people from (1) Stevenson (Deer) Lake to the west where Cree traits predominated, (2) Red Sucker Lake to the east, and (3) the Severn River district to the south.

From the cultural standpoint, the people at Island Lake closely resemble those described by Skinner[17] to the southeast, and the Berens River Saulteaux to the south whom I have studied in recent years. It is my purpose here to give in rather sketchy outline, the data on material culture I was able to secure in a short visit,[18] primarily devoted to obtaining information upon a topic I have discussed elsewhere.[19]

All of the Island Lake camps which I visited at Smooth Rock were of the same general type. A pole tipi,[20] with canvas covering, sometimes supplemented by birchbark, was flanked with two or more canvas tents.[21] This composite dwelling had a single fire, always in the center of the tipi and the hearth was usually surrounded by a few stones. There was no hoop in any of the structures which I saw but, for smoking fish and drying moccasins or clothing, a few poles (*äkwáwänakün*) were tied across the upper portion of the tipi. The floor in every dwelling was covered with spruce boughs, and iron kettles, a frying pan, perhaps, and a wooden spoon (*ämi'kwán*) or two, were to be seen not far from the fireplace. In the more remote corners crumpled bedding of various kinds was in evidence, small trunks or boxes containing personal belongings and pieces of clothing. Blood relatives or those related by marriage, occupied these composite dwellings in common. In one there lived a woman with an unmarried and a married daughter, the latter living in one of the tents with her husband, while the former slept on the opposite side of the fire with her mother. The tipi of my interpreter and chief informant, Richard Munias, was occupied by his wife and himself and their seven children, by Richard's brother and his wife and by his mother-in-law. The entrance to each dwelling is covered by a piece of canvas to which a stick is fastened at the lower end to make it fall into place. When everyone is out a spruce sapling is usually laid against the outside of the door.[22] I could not discover any recollection of a dome-shaped dwelling.[23]

The sweat-lodge (*mätutzwán*) made of willows bent in a dome-like form is known. Richard described one that he had seen his grandfather make. Stones were heated and water thrown over them. Then the lodge was covered with a rabbit-skin blanket. The only article of clothing retained was the breech cloth (*änziän*) worn between the legs and over a belt (*kinoziäp*). It was not customary to run into the water after sweating.

It is possible that the modern form of the Island Lake summer camp may represent the functional survival of an older form of multiple family dwelling constructed by erecting a ridge pole against which other poles and bark were laid on either side. Such a dwelling had a door at each end, several fireplaces and was called *càbandawan*.[24] At Sandy Lake, when a boy, Richard claimed that he saw an unusually large one. It had ten fires[25] and when used for dancing, the participants moved clockwise around the fires, to the beat of two drums.

I was told that winter camps in the "bush" are rough log shacks and that they usually contain a peculiar type of chimney and fireplace about two feet wide, constructed of mud mixed with stones or sticks. The logs used for fuel are placed on end so that they lean towards each other at the top like a tipi.[26] Formerly, it was customary in winter to cover the bark tipi with a layer of moss, about a foot in thickness. Poles were laid on top of this coating of moss. The latter would freeze solid.[27] When hunting or travelling with dogs in winter the ordinary "open-top" camp is made. A rough windbreak of brush is erected and on the lee side the snow is cleared away as much as possible. A flooring of evergreen branches is then laid down, on top of which canvas or caribou skins are thrown. Stretched out between the windbreak at their heads and a fire at their feet, the Indians spend many a winter night with nothing but the stars overhead, even when the temperature is 30° [F] or more below zero.

Matches are, of course, in everyday use for making fire. The flint and steel method is also familiar, but no information on any purely aboriginal device could be obtained.

In summer, white fish is [the] principal staple of these Indians. It is usually boiled. Pieces of fish clamped in a split stick, tied at the top and stuck in the ground at an angle may also he seen smoking by the fire. After smoking, pounded fish (*no`kahïganak*) is sometimes prepared. It can be kept months in this form without spoiling. Trout are fairly abundant in Island Lake and the losh [Fr. *loche* or burbot—eds.] is also caught. It can be said with truth that these Indians always have their gill nets in the water. Wooden floats are used with unshaped stones as sinkers. The nets themselves, made of twine purchased at the post or secured at Treaty time from the Government, are manufactured by the women. A netting needle and block gauge of wood are employed.[28] The needle, probably of European origin, is of the type found among most of the Indians of the eastern woodlands of North America.

Moose and caribou are hunted, rabbits are snared, ducks are shot and even gulls and crows are eaten. Partridges are caught with a pole snare.[29] The principal fur bearing animals trapped are fisher, otter, martin, lynx, red fox and muskrat. Beavers are scarce compared with former days. Fur is traded for clothing, ammunition, kettles, tea, tobacco, flour, etc. Tea is drunk in large quantities, despite the fact that it sells for $1.50 per pound. A native substitute, sometimes used, is the boiled leaves of *kagïgebak* (Labrador tea, *Ledum*). Bannock, made of flour, water, lard and baking powder, is part of the daily diet of white men in camp and on the trail, and is also made by the natives. It is also customary to dispose of body vermin and head lice by eating them. While sitting in one of the camps one afternoon I observed one of the women hunting the latter in the head of her daughter, a child of about eight years. Presently the mother caught one and slipped it into her mouth. After a few minutes the woman took off the brightly colored handkerchief, which so many of the women now wear over their heads, and lay at full length while the child sought out the lice in her mother's head. After a considerable search she finally caught one and ate it. In respect to the eating of dogs or dog sacrifice, no information could be obtained.[30] Although the Island Lakers are acquainted with wild rice it apparently does not flourish this far north.[31]

Woven rabbit (hare) skin garments are still made. In winter, adults formerly wore almost a complete outfit of this material, except moccasins, but at present only caps are used. For children, the hare skin coat still survives and an excellent specimen, with hood attached, was obtained. Blankets are also made of the same material. They are usually sewn into a sheet and used as bedding in winter. The technique employed in the manufacture of these articles involves the use of a wooden frame around three sides of which a strip of skin is first bound by a string. It is made into the desired fabric by means of a series of interlooping stitches, usually called "knotless netting".[32] In summer, the European style of clothing, with the exception of moose hide moccasins, decorated with beads,[33] is worn. I saw a child, however, at one of the portages, dressed in a tanned skin suit and wearing a cap with a fringe in front which fell over the infant's face. This costume was said to be especially designed to keep the child free of mosquito bites. In winter, coats of caribou skin, with hoods, are sometimes worn by the men. They may open down the front or conform to the "pull over" style. I did not see any of these but it was stated that these skin coats were never painted like those of the Naskapi. A pair of so-called "winter" or "mit" moccasins were obtained. They differ from the ordinary variety[34] in not having the seam run over the toe. The characteristic feature is a side seam starting from the heel seam and running along the outer side of the foot and around the toe. This style[35] is undecorated and is said to provide more room in the toe for the extra foot covering required in winter.

So far as I could discover snow-goggles of native manufacture are unknown, although to protect the eyes from the glare of the sun on the snow in the spring, smoked or colored glasses are purchased from the traders.

Cradle boards (*tikïnágan*) for carrying children were much in evidence. The ones I observed lacked a hoop at the top. They all had a roughly carved tooth pattern carved out along the upper edge with a border of incised geometrical designs below and some with a cut out pattern under that. The child is first bound in a kind of sack, laced across the front, practically identical with the type used in the Labrador peninsula without the board. The infant is sometimes carried about in this way. When the cradle board is used the child is held in place by a piece of cloth, attached to the "trough" of the board, which is then laced across the front with sinew or string.

Tattooing (*djïsdahótowin*)[36] is still practiced to a limited degree. My informant and his son Ewart each had a tiny mark, not more than one eighth of an inch in length, on the back of one wrist. A woman, whom I did not see, is said to have a small circle tattooed on one or both cheeks. Another woman has two parallel lines across the back of her lower forearm. The technique employed is the needle and thread method, with charcoal.

In regard to tools and implements of aboriginal manufacture, one-handed (*mï`kitàigan*) and two-handed (*päskwátcïgan*) scrapers of bone are employed in the tanning process and the crooked knife (*wagï`kuman*) is in constant use. Wooden spoons (*ämï'kwán*) are made, but wooden bowls are not. An "ice scoop" (*kwabawhán*) of wood is used in winter for removing snow and ice from the hole through which the nets are "set."[37] A plentiful supply of fish in winter is even a greater necessity than in summer because the dogs are fed upon it. Despite the fact that the bow and arrow cannot have been used as a hunting weapon in this locality for many years, boys are often seen with a bow and arrow in their hands. The release used is the Mediterranean.[38]

Information regarding four types of snowshoes was obtained and specimens of three varieties secured. (1) The ordinary man's shoe (*tcangak-*

wïwagim) appears to be identical with that used by the Cree. The birch frame is made in two pieces. These are rather sharply bent upward at the toe into a point as the term used for them indicates. Nowadays string is used for lacing the toe and heel and moose hide in the body of the shoe. The string is easier to obtain than the babiche and is also said to make the shoe lighter. (2) The second type of shoe *(inïnagim)* has a blunt, almost flat "prow" and the frames are made of a single piece of wood. Those figured were obtained from a woman but the same style may be used by men when following the dog sled, as the pointed shoes are said to get in the way. (3) The so-called "bear-paw" snowshoe *(makwátum)* is a crudely netted emergency type, the frame of which may be made of spliced branches of any sort of wood available and the netting may be of willow bark.[39] (4) The fourth variety *(mistikwagim)* is one made entirely of wood.[40] Similar snowshoes have been reported from the Caribou Eskimo and sporadically between the Great Lakes and Hudson Bay, the Labrador peninsula and from New England.[41] At Island Lake they are said to be an emergency shoe. The pair I obtained appear to have been whittled out entirely with a crooked knife. There is one crossbar on the bottom of each shoe to prevent it from slipping.[42] The origin of this type of snowshoe and its relation to the netted varieties presents a problem of interest. It is possible that it may represent the survival of an ancient form historically connected with Old World types, which preceded the netted shoe in the New World.[43]

Birchbark is said to be very scarce nowadays, partly on account of the numerous forest-fires, so that vessels made of it are not plentiful, although a few are to be seen in daily use. A fairly large storage box *(wïkwemút`)* *was* secured. It is undecorated and unbound at the rim. Two small trays were also obtained and a small round vessel which was sewn together with more precision and bound at the rim with spruce root. Another interesting article of birchbark was a "fan" *(wewsähïgan)* used to keep oneself free from mosquitoes.

No birchbark canoes are now manufactured at Island Lake, although the technical knowledge involved undoubtedly persists in the minds of the older men.[44] The canoes employed for freighting goods to and from Norway House in summer[45] and those locally used, are all of the commercial variety. Those used for freighting are usually rowed by one man while another paddles and steers. The oarlocks are of native make. A slender limb of spruce or balsam cut off a few inches from the trunk is left attached to the main body of the tree which is shaped into a block which can be detached and nailed to the side of the canoe. Thus an upright peg of great strength is formed and the short thick oars, also of native manufacture, rotate upon these oarlocks by means of leather straps fastened to the oars.[46] An improvised sail made from a "tarp" is often set up when crossing the larger bodies of water in a favorable wind.[47]

No woven textiles[48] or basketry of native make are known but in talking about the various materials used in making this and that object, my informant volunteered the information that his father had seen "pots made of mud." This was after I had met the old man, who lived some distance away, so I was not able to secure any further details, although I suspect that he meant potsherds. But the fact is of interest because. Skinner was evidently convinced that the Saulteaux made pottery "up to fairly recent times,"[49] although he was not able to find anyone who commanded the technique. While potsherds have been found by Indians and white men at various points in the bush country east of Lake Winnipeg there are no grounds for believing that the Saulteaux-Ojibwa, recent invaders in this region, made them and no one has ever attributed pottery making to the Cree. There is some evidence that points to the Assiniboine, a point I hope to discuss elsewhere. Stone pipes were made in the past but I could not find anyone who owned one. The enema syringe (*pindabawádjïgan*) made of a jack fish bladder and a bone tube is used in severe cases of constipation.[50]

For sewing bark, as has been mentioned, split spruce roots (*watap*) are used. For sewing other materials, native thread made of moose or deer sinew (*atis*) is employed. Rope is made out of braided willow (*wïgóbe`äp*). It is said to be strong enough for packing fairly heavy loads. All the pack straps in ordinary use, however, are purchased from the traders.

Of games, snow snake (*sósïman*) is sometimes played in winter and two excellent specimens of the northern form of the ring and pin game (*näpäwan*) were obtained. The holes in the leather when caught by the pin count four, each bone caught on the pin counts one, with the exception of the bone next the leather tail piece which, known as the "eye," counts twenty when speared by itself. Instead of the metacarpal bones of the deer, a small bunch of spruce twigs bound tightly together and lacking the perforated leather tail piece may be made. In this form the object of the game is to catch the point of the pin in the bunch of twigs.

Within a year after I visited Island Lake gold was discovered there [1931]. A mining enterprise was started, carried on for several years and then abandoned. Today it is not unlikely that even the semblance of aboriginal culture I observed has been still further modified.

Notes

First published in 1938 in *Journal de la Société des Américanistes de Paris*, new series, 30: 129–40. Hallowell's detailed diary account of his trip to Island Lake is in his field notebook of July-August 1930, in the Hallowell Papers, Ms. Coll. 26, American Philosophical Society, Philadelphia.

1. J. F. Wright, *Island Lake Area, Manitoba.* Summary Report, 1927, Part B, Canada Dept. of Mines (1928), 55B gives 160 miles; S. J. C. Cumming in an article on the Island Lake Post in *The Beaver* (periodical of the Hudson's Bay Company), Dec. 1928, gives 170 miles.

2. J. C. Boileau Grant. *Anthropometry of the Cree and Saulteaux Indians in Northeastern Manitoba.* Bulletin 59, Canada Dept. of Mines (Ottawa 1929), 4. I was told that the York boats were, at one time, dragged across this portage, although in more recent years it was the practice to make Mossy Portage a relay point and to transfer the freight to canoe crews who came up from Island Lake.

3. I.e. in this region of Manitoba.

4. The longest of these are two of the Ponask portages over the first height of land. They measure 6,200 and 6,500 feet respectively and cross "rocky, hilly country with wet swamps in the depressions." Over a second height of land, just before reaching Island Lake, there are two other fairly long "carries" of 1,650 and 4,300 feet. See Wright, *Island Lake Area,* 55B.

5. The Johnson detachable outboard motor is a recent innovation which is now utilized by most of the white men and many of the Indians in this part of the country.

6. Cf. Cumming, "Island Lake Post."

7. Cf. Grant, *Anthropometry,* 4, in respect to this point.

8. Counted by some industrious soul, on the map published in the National Topographical Series, based on aerial photographs of this region. It is the only map which gives any adequate notion of the topography.

9. The Lake itself is 75 miles in length by 50 miles at its widest point (Cumming, "Island Lake Post") but the islands are so numerous that one scarcely gets a glimpse of the mainland or any very great expanse of water.

10. These settlements are on Indian Reserve 22 and the Band itself is one of those belonging to the Norway House agency.

11. This place name has reference to the Losh *(Lota maculosa),* a species of fish locally known as "maria." The livers of these fishes are considered a great delicacy. [See William Fox on the loche or burbot, at *http://www*

.adamsheritage.com/articles/fox/fishstory/long_point.htm accessed 21 March 2008: eds.]

12. Ottawa, 1930.

13. Cf. the statement of Father Dubeau, the missionary at Maria Portage, quoted in Grant, 1.

14. Since I only came into personal contact with the natives at Smooth Rock, I have no comparative data to offer on this point, but a short text I recorded is certainly Ojibwa, rather than Cree, although the list of kinship terms I obtained shows a decided mixture of Cree and Ojibwa forms. [Ed. note: H. Christoph Wolfart ("Boundary Maintenance in Algonquian: A Linguistic Study of Island Lake, Manitoba," *American Anthropologist* 75[5], 1973, 1305–1323) concluded on the basis of field studies that his data showed that "the speech of Island Lake is Ojibwa with an admixture of Cree." He expressed agreement with Hallowell's "cautious statement" about the language being "Saulteaux-Ojibwa with an overlay of Cree" (1973, 1317).]

15. On the other hand, the Cree Indians who freight goods into the Lake during the summer months do not, as a rule, speak or understand Saulteaux, and in fact, often avoid spending even a night at Island Lake.

16. Cf. the opinion of Mr. Fred Disbrow, whose mother is a Saulteaux of the Berens River band, Grant, *Anthropometry*, 1.

1817. *Notes on the Eastern Cree and Northern Saulteaux.* Anthropological Papers of the American Museum of Natural History. New York, t. IX, pt. 1 (1911).

18. A collection was made for the Museum of the American Indian (Heye Foundation), New York. [Ed. note: 105 items from Hallowell's 1930 trip to Norway House, Grand Rapids, Cross Lake, and Island Lake were catalogued by the museum as 17/6819 to 17/6924. Despite Hallowell's caveat about the Saulteaux (Ojibwe) aspect of the Island Lake people and language, all these items were listed as "Swampy Cree." It is also curious that, while this article indicates that Hallowell definitely acquired some items at Island Lake, the catalogue did not list any of them as coming from there. The collection is now at the new Museum of the American Indian in Washington DC.]

19. I.e. cross-cousin marriage, an investigation supported by a grant-in-aid from the Social Science Research Council, NY. See "Cross-Cousin Marriage in the Lake Winnipeg Area," in D.S. Davidson, ed., *Twenty-fifth Anniversary Studies*, 95–110. Philadelphia Anthropological Society, 1937. [Reprinted as chapter 5, this volume.]

20. The poles forming this part of the dwelling are not moved when a change in camp is made, since others are so easily obtained. In former days

when birch bark was used more exclusively for the tipi covering it was the practice to carry specially prepared rolls of bark from place to place. A bark roll of this kind (reduced in scale) and sewn with spruce root was obtained. Cf. Skinner, *Notes on Eastern Cree*, 119; Frances Densmore, *Use of Plants by the Chippewa Indians*, 44th Annual Report of the Bureau of American Ethnology, Washington, 1928, 389–90.

21. In the summer of 1907 at Fort Resolution (Great Slave Lake) E. T. Seton, *The Arctic Prairies*, 1911, see sketch c, 149) observed a similar arrangement among the Athabascans camped there. "Chief Squirrel" he says, "lives in a lodge that is an admirable combination of the white man's tent with its weather-proof roof and the Indian *teepee* with its cosy fire."

22. In this connection it is interesting to quote a passage from Drage, *An Account of a Voyage for the Discovery of a Northwest Passage*, etc. (London, 1748–49), vol. I, 184, in which he is describing the dwellings of the Cree of that period. "You enter the Tents by turning a Piece of Skin", he says, "to which there is a stick fastened on the Inside of it, to make it flap and close; they have no Bolts or Locks; the Tent Door is never made fast but when they are all out, and then it is by laying Logs of Wood against it, seemingly to keep out the Dogs more than for any other Purpose."

23. Which according to K. Birket-Smith (*The Caribou Eskimos*, Report of the Fifth Thule Expedition, V, vol. II, 136–37) is "an ancient element in North America," although in historic times it occurs only in the eastern part of the continent "in a curve from Labrador along by the ocean and south about the Great Lakes, depositing themselves along the periphery of the great sub-arctic region where the later, conical tent prevails."

24. Among the linguistically and culturally related Saulteaux farther south at Berens River this form of dwelling was only recently abandoned. See also F. Densmore, *Chippewa Customs*, Bulletin 86, Bureau of American Ethnology. Washington, 1929, 26–27.

25. Chief W. Berens of the Berens River band told me that in former times he recalls as many as six families living in such a dwelling. Skinner, *Notes on Eastern Cree*, 120, refers to a four-family swelling evidently similar in construction to the type described to me.

26. Mr. Clark, who was formerly in charge of the Hudson's Bay post at Island Lake told me that this type of chimney is of Scotch origin and that the position of the logs gives a greater amount of light than the ordinary arrangement. [Ed. note: This was probably Alexander Cooper Clark, from Aberdeen, who served the HBC in the area, 1914 to 1932: see Hudson's Bay Company Archives Biographical Sheets].

27. A tipi-like structure of *logs* covered with earth and moss is known and used on the Berens River. For a photograph of such a dwelling, for which the locale is unfortunately lacking, see P.H. Godsell, "The Ojibwa Indian," *Canadian Geographical Journal*, Jan. 1932, 55. Birket-Smith (*The Caribou Eskimos*, 133) calls attention to the fact that the Cree and Chipewyan commonly "cover the lowest part of their conical tent with snow."

28. Cf. Densmore, *Chippewa Customs*, pl. 59, b.

29. Densmore, *Chippewa Customs*, 131 and pl. 45, e.

30. The Midewi·win is not known this far north. See A. I. Hallowell, "The Passing of the Midewi·win in the Lake Winnipeg Region." *American Anthropologist* 38 (1935), 302–304. [Chapter 21, this volume.]

31. See A. I. Hallowell, "Notes on the Northern Range of Zizania in Manitoba." *Rhodora* 37 (1935), 302–304. [Chapter 2, this volume.]

32. D.S. Davidson, "Knotless Netting in America and Oceania." *American Anthropologist* 37 (1935), 117–34. See sketch, 120 (type I) and distribution, 123.

33. I was told that beadwork had only been done at Island Lake since about 1925 and from the specimens obtained the work is not as carefully done as on the articles from Trout Lake and Norway House. Beadwork replaced silk embroidery which, again, is said to have been done better at Norway House.

34. Which corresponds to Wissler's three-piece pattern (Type B). For distribution see Wissler, *The Relation of Nature to Man in Aboriginal America*, 1926, 24 and 26. Several varieties are found in Asia, as well as in North America.

35. Corresponds to Wissler's two-piece pattern (Type C), 23–24. Since it is also known on the Berens River the line on his map may be extended to include the region east of Lake Winnipeg. Cf. G. Hatt, *Mocassins and their Relation to Arctic Footwear*, Memoirs of the American Anthropological Assocation, vol. 3, 3, 1916, 179 seq. For more recent distributional data see Isabel T. Kelly, *Ethnography of the Surprise Valley Paiute*, University of California Publications in American Archaeology and Ethnology. Berkeley, vol. 31, 1932, 110–113.

36. This term, literally "squirting," has a dual connotation, the other reference being sexual.

37. It may be remarked that the form of this implement is similar to the Cree "snow shovel" figured by Skinner (51) but both are quite dissimilar from the Caribou Eskimo "snow shovel" illustrated in Birket-Smith, *The

Caribou Eskimos. In vol. 2, Tables B56 and 57, snow shovels and "ice scoops" are segregated. This distinction, it seems to me, is apt to cause confusion, unless data on both form and function are given in each case, especially since Dr. F. G. Speck tells me that the Montagnais sometimes use their wooden "snow shovels" (similar in form to the Island Lake ice-scoop) as "ice-scoops" although they usually manufacture a typical form of ice-scoop.

38. Wissler's distribution of this form of release as given on pp. 35 and 39, can be extended southward to include all of the area around Hudson Bay and Lake Winnipeg.

39. Cf. Skinner, *Notes on Eastern Cree,* fig. 54 and p. 146. Also Densmore, *Chippewa Customs,* pl. 54, c, d.

40. Cf. Skinner, and Densmore, *Chippewa Customs,* pl. 54a and p. 148.

41. For distribution see D. S. Davidson, *Snowshoes,* Memoirs of the American Philosophical Society, vol. 6, 1937, 140, fig. 54.

42. Davidson figures them 141, fig. 55 c, and another pair of the same type I obtained from the Cree of Cross Lake, Manitoba.

43. See Davidson., *Snowshoes,* chap 8.

44. E.g., Peter Munias, the father of my informant, was a noted canoe maker.

45. A great many Indians from Norway House and Island Lake are employed in transporting supplies and furs to and from these points for the Hudson's Bay Company, Hyers, and other traders. The rate paid is $15.00 per 100 lbs. A canoe manned by two Indians usually carries 1,000 lbs.

46. Some canoes are provided with two pairs of oars.

47. The use of a sail by the aborigines of this region of Canada dates back to the earliest contacts with the Whites.

48. Except the rabbit skin robes mentioned, and these are not "woven" in the narrow sense of the term, since a true warp and weft is not present.

49. Skinner, *Notes on the Eastern Cree,* 130. Cf. also Densmore, 162, who attributes pottery found on a site on Lake Winnipegosis to the Saulteaux, despite the fact that this branch of the Ojibwa did not reach this part of Canada until late in the 18th century and none of the modern Saulteaux of Manitoba have any knowledge or tradition of pottery making. [Ed. note: For more recent archaeological studies citing a ceramic tradition in the region, see Kevin Brownlee and E. Leigh Syms, *Kayasochi Kikawenow: Our Mother from Long Ago, An Early Cree Woman and her Personal Belongings from Nagami Bay, Southern Indian Lake* (Winnipeg: Manitoba Museum of Man and Nature, 1999), 5, 37; James V. Wright, "Prehistory of the Canadian

Shield," *Handbook of North American Indians*, vol. 6, *Subarctic* (Washington DC: Smithsonian Institution, 1981, 92–93), on the widely distributed Selkirk ceramic complex, ca. AD 800–1600.]

50. Skinner, 161, also records the use of this article. Cf. A. I. Hallowell, "The Bulbed Enema Syringe in North America." *American Anthropologist*, new series, 37 (1935), 708–710.

2

MARRIAGE AND KINSHIP

Introduction

The two articles in Part II date from 1937 and 1938 respectively, and are Hallowell's most detailed publications on Ojibwe marriage and kinship. The first article, "Cross-Cousin Marriage in the Lake Winnipeg Area" (chapter 5), presents some of the research that originally brought Hallowell to Manitoba in the summer of 1930 and integrates it with his later observations on cross-cousin marriage from his Berens River fieldwork in following summers. The second article (1938, chapter 6) is an overview and analysis of the patterns of polygyny that he found in tracing the families and genealogies of the Lake Winnipeg area.

In 1972, Hallowell reflected on how he was first drawn into kinship studies in the 1920s (prologue, this volume, "On Being an Anthropologist"). In examining kin terms recorded in early dictionaries of Algonquian languages, he proposed that they offered evidence for the presence of cross-cousin marriage as a widespread older Algonquian pattern that had faded in many areas under outside pressures. His research with Ojibwe at Island Lake, Manitoba, and at Berens River and with individuals from other Lake Winnipeg communities reinforced this view, leading to the conclusions presented in his 1937 article. As he recalled in his 1972 essay, many anthropologists of the 1920s took the view "that kinship terms were to be considered as purely linguistic phenomena." He found, however, that they had great importance for social relations and behavior, and as indices of change. Chief William Berens, vividly quoted in the prologue on the subject of marrying one's cross-cousin (*ninam* for a male speaker in Ojibwe, and also translated as "sweetheart"), emphasized how basic the category was in determining whom one could marry, and also taught Hallowell about its implications for behavior and the structuring of kin ties.

In brief, the term, "cross-cousin," is a classificatory term applied by anthropologists to a kinship category that in its simplest form comprises father's sisters' children and mother's brothers' children, that is, children of siblings of the opposite sex. Children of same-sex siblings, in contrast, are termed parallel cousins, and the kin terms applied to them are the same as those for brother and sister, connoting the fact that they are subject to an incest tabu and cannot marry. Many societies around the world classify cousins in this way. In English-language usage, however, all these cousins are simply classed as first cousins, and the distinction is lost. The spread of English and other European languages, and of church and mission pressures against first-cousin marriages, has tended to displace indigenous categorizations and the prescriptions and behavior that accompanied them. Hallowell in his article noted examples of these changes when he talked with a descendant of Chief Peguis with roots in the St. Peter's reserve on the Red River in southern Manitoba, where missionaries had long been active and the English language was prominent.

The Ojibwe term for cross-cousin also subsumes other relatives descended from siblings of the opposite sex who, in English usage, would be lumped with, for example, second and third parallel cousins. And it applies to other kin who in English would be distinguished in other ways, as Hallowell's article demonstrates. The critical factors are that people identified as cross-cousins are of the same generation, and that owing to the cross-sex distinction in ascending generations, they also belong to different patrilineal clans ("sibs" in Hallowell's terms). Clans are exogamous, unilineal descent groups; one does not marry within one's own clan (and parallel cousins are of course clan mates). But outside the clan, as Hallowell found, a wide range of people were potential marriage mates whose relationship allowed a certain license in behavior. Men and women of any age who were cross-cousins were entitled and expected to follow a script of joking and bawdy teasing that even their own spouses would enjoy and find hilarious (see, for example, William Berens's personal story on this theme in Berens, *Memories, Myths, and Dreams*, III, 14).

Hallowell's 1938 article "The Incidence, Character, and Decline of Polygyny among the Lake Winnipeg Cree and Saulteaux" (chapter 6), explores another marital practice upon which Christian teachings had a considerable impact. As in the preceding article, Hallowell gathered as much concrete data as he could, combining the study of Treaty 5 payment records with fieldwork to go beyond impressionistic generalizations. Through studying actual cases of men who had multiple wives, he assessed the frequency of the custom, the positions and roles of the men practicing it, and the numbers of women involved and their relationships, e.g., as sisters in some instances. Although numbers of important men were monogamous, the older men with multiple wives whose names Hallowell found in the records, and whom he heard about from Chief William Berens and others, included some of the most influential and powerful leaders remembered by the Native people of the region in the 1930s.

Hallowell concluded that the spread of Christian missions correlated strongly with the decline of both cross-cousin marriage and polygyny from the late 1800s onward. In particular, missionaries applied direct pressures on polygynists to set aside all but one wife before they could be baptized, though as Hallowell showed, some clergy also took seriously the situation of displaced wives and of their maintenance. On cousin marriage, the clergy discouraged any marriage between persons they viewed as close relatives, i.e., first and second cousins, but since they might not even grasp the cross/parallel distinction, the fading of cross-cousin marriage may have resulted from more indirect pressure and from the rising dominance of English and its kin categories among those Ojibwe people most exposed to outside pressures.

In the years in which these two articles appeared, another anthropologist, Ruth Landes, published her first major works on the Ojibwe, based on her 1932 summer fieldwork at Manitou Rapids on the Rainy River, Ontario, and on some follow-up visits and correspondence with her prime informant, Maggie Wilson. Her perspectives on cousin marriage contrast with Hallowell's in some notable respects. In 1937, she acknowledged the importance of the cross-cousin relationship and associated behavior in the Ontario region where she worked, but reported that at Manitou, "there is a blanket tabu on marriage between all relatives, which means that cross-cousin marriage, also, is forbidden." Like Hallowell, she came to see this as a recent development, but suggested, without explanation, that it may have been "a consequence of contact with the Dakota Sioux"; she did not explore the question of mission influence.[1]

On polygyny, too, Landes took a rather different tack than Hallowell. In *The Ojibwa Woman* (1938), she wrote, "The pretentious marriage form is polygyny. It is usually the shamans . . . who are distinguished by polygyny. Plural marriage is a sumptuary display on the part of men . . . .the possession of plural wives is a tacit boast of some force."[2] In "The Ojibwa of Canada" (1937), she stated, "Plural marriage . . . is not a cooperative arrangement but a difficult concession to a man's desire to display his individual superiority."[3] As her biographer, Sally Cole, notes, Landes brought a feminist perspective to her interpretations, and was also doubtless influenced by the views of Maggie Wilson, herself a strong and critical person on matters of gender relations.

In 1938, Hallowell wrote a warm review of *The Ojibwa Woman* in the

American Sociological Review, crediting Landes's success in bringing forward women's viewpoints and roles.[4] Certainly her work deserves to be read in tandem with Hallowell's and adds a different angle of vision. But he had an advantage in that he spent considerably more time around Lake Winnipeg and along the Berens River than she did at Manitou. The close ties that he developed with William Berens and others allowed the gathering, over time, of familial and genealogical histories covering several generations. The two articles that follow are rich sources for the ethnohistory of the region and are also illuminating in their own ways on gender relations.

Notes

1. Landes, "The Ojibwa of Canada," in Margaret Mead, ed., *Cooperation and Competition among Primitive Peoples* (Boston: Beacon Press, 1961 [first published 1937], 104). In August 1932, one month into her fieldwork at Manitou, Landes wrote to Ruth Benedict that three different old people had told her that cross-cousin marriages "have been discountenanced since the beginning of time" and that when they did occur they represented a "relaxation of the old ways" (Sally Cole, *Ruth Landes: A Life in Anthropology* [Lincoln: University of Nebraska Press, 2003], 72). As a newcomer boarding with the local Indian Affairs farm instructor, Landes may have been told, at first, only what the local Ojibwe people thought she should hear.

2. *The Ojibwa Woman* (Lincoln: University of Nebraska Press, reprint, 1997), 66.

3. "The Ojibwa of Canada," 106. She added that polygyny was "of no economic aid to an Ojibwa man, but an economic drain" (a point that could be argued).

4. Quoted in Cole, *Ruth Landes*, 102.

FIVE

Cross-Cousin Marriage in the Lake Winnipeg Area

In a paper read at the International Congress of Americanists in 1928,[1] I pointed out that Ojibwa, Ottawa, and Algonkin kinship terms recorded in early documents reflected cross-cousin marriage so positively, that it seemed reasonable to infer that this form of mating had formerly been practised. Up until that time no ethnologist had reported this custom from any Algonkian people,[2] although two statements by early nineteenth-century observers (H. Y. Hind and Duncan Cameron) apparently referred to the practice of cross-cousin marriage by some of the Saulteaux-Ojibwa bands between Lake Nipigon and Lake Winnipeg.[3]

I attributed the contemporary absence of the custom to the transformation of native marriage institutions under white influences, and pointed to evidence which showed that the contemporary relationship terms of several bands in the linguistic groups under discussion were variants of an older pattern which harmonized with cross-cousin marriage. As a correlative and better documented instance of modern changes in Algonkian relationship terms under changing conditions, I referred to my study of the St. Francis Abenaki kinship system.[4]

Shortly after the Congress I met William Duncan Strong. He had just returned from northern Labrador and told me of his discovery that cross-cousin marriage was practised by the Barren Ground Band of the Naskapi and that this custom was clearly reflected by their kinship system.[5]

With Strong's data as a basis I undertook a comparative study of Cree-Montagnais-Naskapi terms, using both published sources and two manuscripts of the seventeenth century. It was possible to show that throughout this linguistic group there were not only consistent lexical indications of cross-cousin marriage, but a striking equivalence between the terms used and those employed by the Ojibwa-Ottawa-Algonkin.[6] In the meantime Speck had secured positive evidence regarding the practice of cross-cousin marriage by the Mistassini band of Montagnais and to a certain extent at Lake St. John.[7]

Wishing to pursue the possible distribution of the custom to the west, I was fortunate enough to receive a grant-in-aid from the Social Science Research Council in support of field work in the environs of Lake Winnipeg. Just before leaving Philadelphia in June, 1930, I received a publication by J. C. Boileau Grant, on the somatology of several Cree and Saulteaux bands in the region I planned to visit.[8] He had made his observations in the summer of 1927. One of the bands measured, a group I was later to visit, made their summer headquarters at Island Lake, 115 miles east of northern Lake Winnipeg. In some prefatory remarks under the caption "marriage" Grant wrote, *"though for the most part it is the custom of these Indians to marry their cousins, they nevertheless adhere to the tradition of not marrying into their own totem."* Not being an ethnologist, Grant did not realize the significance of his statement in regard to cousin-marriage, nor did he explain that cross-cousins were meant.

Although I was not aware of it at the time, E. S. Curtis in his summary account of the western Woods Cree, published in 1928, had already referred to their practice of cross-cousin marriage and its connection with their kinship structure.[9] Consequently, Curtis must be credited with the earliest published reference to cross-cousin marriage as a going concern among a contemporary Algonkian people. And, in the summer of 1927 when on the Upper Albany River, J. M. Cooper met an Anglican minister, himself a Saskatchewan Cree, who told him, quite unsolicited, that cross-cousin marriage was permitted in this Algonkian group.[10]

Thus while encouraged by the observations of Strong, Speck, and Grant, I did not know of these other independent reports of cross-cousin marriage among the western Cree when I started my own field inquiries in the Lake Winnipeg region.

During the course of the summer I visited three bands of Swampy Cree (Grand Rapids,[11] Norway House, Cross Lake) and two groups of Saulteaux-Ojibwa (Island Lake, Berens River). In the summers of 1931 and 1932 short visits were made to the Saulteaux bands at Wanipigow River and Poplar River. Since that time I have made a more detailed study of the social organization and general ethnography of the three bands on the Berens River. Other investigators such as D. Jenness,[12] Regina Flannery,[13] J. M. Cooper,[14] T. Michelson,[15] and Ruth Landes[16] have also reported the occurrence of cross-cousin marriage elsewhere among Cree, Ojibwa, and Montagnais speaking peoples.

The positive generalizations which can be made from the data already secured in the Lake Winnipeg area are the following:

1. The kinship pattern of all of the bands visited and of those about which I have information is of the "bifurcate collateral" type,[17] the generation principle is paramount and since there are no specific terms for relatives by marriage, the characteristic equations that occur are the following:

a. mother-in-law = father's sister = mother's brother's wife.
b. father-in-law = mother's brother = father's sister's husband.
c. son-in-law = cross nephew = husband of parallel niece.
d. daughter-in-law = cross niece = wife of parallel nephew.
e. woman's sister-in-law = woman's female cross-cousin.
f. man's brother-in-law = man's male cross-cousin.
g. sibling-in-law of opposite sex = cross-cousin of opposite sex.
h. The term for "sweetheart" is identical with the last mentioned term or a derivative of it.

2. Inquiry revealed that the mating of cross-cousins was recognized as a traditional form of marriage, that a certain proportion of married individuals now living were of this relationship, and that unions of this sort were still contracted.

When I asked an English-speaking Indian (Alfred Settie) at Norway House whether it was possible to marry *ki·tim*, he replied, "You bet your life. That's what they all do here!" The United Church missionary, Rev. S. D. Gaudin, who speaks Cree fluently and at that time had been in missionary work forty years, said that sixty percent of the Indians of this band were married to their cousins.[18] He added that the percentage was higher farther to the north but that nowadays, at Norway House, since parents no longer arranged matches for their children, the custom was dying out. Rev. S. D. Gaudin began his missionary work among the Cree of the Nelson House Band in 1891, where he remained fifteen years. Native customs were in full swing when he went there, and he said that the degree of inbreeding was much higher than it is now or in the Norway House band.

In addition to securing kinship terms, sample genealogies and other information in the Cree and Saulteaux bands personally visited, data obtained from Indians belonging to other groups, or whose parents or relatives belonged to these bands, is sufficient to include, tentatively, the following bands in our generalizations:

Cree: Norway House, Cross Lake, Grand Rapids, Nelson House, Split Lake, Oxford House, God's Lake.[19]

	FIRST CROSS-COUSINS				SECOND CROSS-COUSINS								
MARRIAGES (numbers to left, husbands; to right; wives) (1)	*mother's brother's daughter*	*father's sister's daughter*	*mother's half brother's daughter*	*father's half sister's daughter*	*mother's mother's brother's daughter's daughter*	*mother's mother's sister's son's daughter*	*mother's father's brother's son's daughter*	*mother's father's sister's daughter's daughter*	*father's father's brother's daughter's daughter*	*father's father's sister's son's daughter*	*father's mother's brother's son's daughter*	*father's mother's sister's daughter's daughter*	*Number of Relationships*
GENERATION III													
14\7	X												1
6\13		X											1
21\28	X	X											1
16\10	X												1
19\27	X												1
17\30	X												1
GENERATION IV													
39\ {132, 133, 134}	X	X						X		X			4
44\36	X	X			X					X			4
45\37		X								X			2
46\38		X								X			2
32\40	X										X		2
22\29	X										X		2
33\41	X										X		2
34\42	X										X		2
53\50		X								X			2
48\51	X										X		2
49\52	X										X		2
GENERATION V													
147\144	X									X	X		3
137\152				X						X	X		2
157\114	X	X			X			X		X	X		6
169\124		X	X		X			X			X		5
98\94	X			X	X					X	X		5
91\84	X			X	X					X	X		5
93\86		X									X		2
107\101	X										X		2
95\118	X	X						X			X		4
81\88	X										X		2
83\90							X				X		2
110\104									X	X			2
87\80					X	X	X		X	X			5
92\85									X	X			2
Totals	20	10	1	3	6	1	2	4	3	13	16	0	79

(1) These are the numbers that appear on genealogical charts in the possession of the author, which may later be published.

1. Relationship of Island Lake Wives to Husbands

Saulteaux: All of the bands bordering on eastern Lake Winnipeg from Poplar River on the north to Wanipigow River on the south, and in the interior those at Little Grand Rapids,[20] Pekangikum, Sandy Lake, Deer Lake and Island Lake.[21]

3. What are the fundamental principles of cross-cousin marriage among these Cree and Saulteaux peoples? How does it work? In the first place, their kinship pattern defines the social status of individuals in such a way that only persons of the same generation are potential mates.[22] Secondly, in one's own generation, there is a dual classification of relatives of the opposite sex: (a) full (or half) siblings, parallel cousins of the first degree and more remote cousins, or other individuals who fall into the terminological category of "siblings"; (b) cross-cousins of the first degree, siblings-in-law of opposite sex, second "cross-cousins,"and other related persons who fall into the terminological category of "cross-cousin of opposite sex."

Since kinship terms are widely extended in usage, individuals actually *unrelated* by blood may fall into either of these two groups. If two unrelated men, for instance, marry sisters they will adopt the term "brother" for each other, while unrelated women who marry brothers will call each other "sister." In the case of the Saulteaux, who have a sib [clan] organization, a man visiting a strange camp will call all of the girls of his approximate age group "cousin," except those belonging to his own sib, those whom he can classify as "sisters," through some known blood connection, or those whom he can 'place' through the terminology he knows that his parents apply to their parents.

In a community with a kinship pattern of this sort it is inevitable that persons who call each other "cousin" should marry, not through the compulsion of precept, but because of the prohibition of sibling marriage.[23] But the actual *degree* of blood relationship that exists between the members of these unions may vary from zero to that between first cousins. The marriage of cross-cousins in this latter, narrow sense cannot be viewed as an independent custom or unit trait, but rather as an integral part of the operation of the social system as a whole.

If such a social system, ideally conceived, is thought of as operating in face-to-face groups, where everyone addresses everyone else by a kinship term and no one marries outside the group, then *all* marriages would occur between individuals who previously called each other by a "cousin" term. Furthermore, if the population in which such a marital situation operated were not replenished by new family lines, through the marriage of outsiders into it or the migration to it of new family units, the original family lines would inevitably become more and more highly linked. While this is, of course, a theoretical rather than a realistic picture of conditions either today or in the past among the Lake Winnipeg bands, it nevertheless has been very closely approached in some instances. For the real density of population has always been low in this area and there is every reason to believe that marriages in the past have been intra-group (or intra-local) rather than inter-group (inter-local) affairs.[24]

In view of these general conditions, the collection of genealogical data is the only possible means of obtaining any precise notion of the extent of inbreeding or information in respect to the presence or absence of actual blood relationship, between married persons. At Island Lake I was lucky enough to secure as informant, a man (Richard Munias) who not only spoke English but who happened to be a member of the Sturgeon sib, whose family had intermarried with a family of the Sucker sib over a number of generations. In his father's generation, for example, six marriages between first cross-cousins had occurred. These were the total number possible between the children of two brothers and a sister. In the genealogical material obtained, which included 188 individuals all told (chiefly lineal and collateral relatives of my informant) the number of married individuals in four generations is 152. Of these, sixty-four persons (thirty-one men and thirty-three women) married first or second cousins (thirty marriages being monogamous and one polygamous), all but four of these marriages being between relatives of the former class. Among these, there are twice as many cases (20) in which a man is married to his mother's brother's daughter, as those (10) in which he is married to his father's sister's daughter. It is a striking fact that a number of the wives are not only related to their spouses as *double* first cousins, but that *all* of the individuals of generations IV and V (see table) who are related to their spouses as first cousins are related to them as second cousins, too. My informant's wife, for instance (no. 114) in addition to being his double cross-cousin of the first degree (mother's brother's daughter *and* father's sister's daughter) is related to him as second cousin in four other ways (mother's mother's brother's daughter's daughter, mother's father's sister's daughter's daughter, father's father's sister's son's daughter, father's mother's brother's son's daughter). All of the women, moreover, who are related to their husbands *only* as second cousins are related to them in more than one way.

In this connection, Radcliffe-Brown's differentiation of Australian kinship systems into Type I (Kariera) and Type II (Arunta) comes to mind.[25] "The Kariera kinship system," he says, "is based on and implies the existence of the form of marriage known as cross-cousin marriage" (p. 15). "A man may only marry a woman to whom he applies the same term of relationship that he does to his own mother's brother's daughter. If it is possible for him to marry the daughter of an actual brother of his own mother he normally does so, but of course this only happens in a limited number of instances" (p. 17). "The Aranda system (Type II) divides the female relatives whom a man may marry in the Kariera system into two parts, from one of which he must now choose his wife while those of the other are forbidden to him" (p. 21). This system "also requires a special marriage rule, by which a man marries his mother's mother's brother's daughter's daughter or some relative who is classified with her and denoted by the same term of relationship" (p. 20).

Putting matters in another way we may say that Type II is a system in which the marriage of *first* cross-cousins has been suppressed and the marriage of second or more remote cross-cousins encouraged. But both types are actually based upon cross-cousin marriage, unless we think of the latter in the narrowest terms.[26] In the Island Lake genealogy the four marriages of second cousins would be typical examples of those which occur in kinship systems of Type II in Australia. But sociologically among the Saulteaux they are undifferentiated from those of first cousins. In one sense the biological basis of any such differentiation is more apparent than real. In a population where marriages of first cross-cousins occur with any frequency, and particularly where these marriages are unrestricted (i.e., of the bilateral type) as in the case of both the Saulteaux and the Kariera, the inbreeding that results progressively reduces the number of ancestors of the individuals of succeeding generations.[27] Consequently, as I have already pointed out, individuals become related as *both* first and second cousins. If more information were available about the ascendants of Generation III (table) the same thing would probably be true for them. In Australia, where the density of population is low and comparable to that of the Lake Winnipeg groups and where there are likewise economic similarities[28] it seems to me that among the Kariera and other bands with Type I marriage comparable inbreeding must occur. A proportion of marriages must at the same time be those of first and second cross cousins, while others are unions of second cousins (Type II). Viewed from this standpoint Type II represents a cross-cousin marriage system of a restricted kind but based upon the same principles as Type I. It limits the degree of possible inbreeding.[29]

In the social system of the Island Lake Saulteaux and other groups of the Lake Winnipeg region then, marriages between the children of full brothers and sisters occur (i.e., cross-cousin marriage in the narrowest sense) and in addition there are marriages of second cross-cousins, who are the children of parallel cousins (i.e., *terminological* brothers and sisters).

How far the magnitude of inbreeding in the Island Lake genealogy cited is a fair sample of inbreeding in the band as a whole, which numbered a little over 700 at the time, I do not know. I was able to spend only a few days there and have never returned since.

My genealogical study of the Berens River Bands, which have the same kinship organization and social customs as the Island Lake Saulteaux, supports the general observations stated above and makes it possible to make a further point, although my analysis of the relationships of the individuals involved in about 200 marriages is not yet completed. This analysis, when finished, will give the relative incidence of first and second cross-cousin marriages during several generations for the entire native population of the river as well as data on other kinds of blood relationship among married individuals or the absence of it and the social classification of these from the native viewpoint.

In one case, for instance, a man married his mother's co-wife's brother's daughter. Now a co-wife is terminologically equated with mother's sister and therefore the co-wife's brother's daughter is in turn classified with a cross-cousin. Biologically the individuals involved in this marriage were not related at all. But since the parents of these individuals used "brother" and "sister" terms for each other, the marriage is a cross-cousin marriage from the native standpoint and likewise falls into this category if the objective criterion be a marriage of the children of siblings (in the extended sense) of the opposite sex.

Of considerable frequency is another type of cross-cousin marriage in which the individuals may not be either related by blood, nor the children of terminological brothers and sisters. Such cases are those in which a man may marry his brother's wife's sister, or a woman her brother's wife's brother (or equivalent marriages of siblings-in-law). On account of the fact that the term for "siblings-in-law of opposite sex" (*nīnam*) is the same as that for a cross-cousin, such marriages, from the native standpoint, fall into the same class as the cross-cousin marriages described above. I may add that the reason these marriages occur quite frequently is because on the Berens River and elsewhere in this region it is considered desirable for the brothers of one family to marry a series of sisters in another. At Poplar River there is one such instance in which six brothers married six sisters, the two families being unrelated when the *original* marriage took place, which is not, of course, to be classified as a cross-cousin marriage.

But when unrelated individuals marry there is a special term (*ndindawa*) adopted between their parents that binds the latter together in much the same fashion *as if* they were related as siblings and siblings-in-law to each other. It is obvious, too, that a social system that permits or encourages cross-cousin marriage will also involve the marriages of a series of siblings of one family with a series of siblings in another family, even aside from cases such as those referred to above. Consequently it may be assumed, I think, that regardless of blood relationship or the terminology employed by parents, such marriages are actually an integral part of the social system considered as a whole. Marriages of fraternities and sororities are also mentioned in the mythology.

From the standpoint of native culture, therefore, it is impossible to define cross-cousin marriage (1) in terms of *one* specific biological relationship (i.e., first cousins), or (2), a more inclusive degree of biological relationship (i.e., second or more remote cousins) or (3) even with exclusive reference to the use of "sibling" terms by the parents of individuals to the union. The actual formula is very simple. All marriages between persons who are *nīnam* (the Saulteaux term) to each other are cross-cousin marriages in terms of the social system in actual operation and in the thought of the Indians themselves.[30]

While in the past, as I have suggested above, a large proportion of marriages must have been cross-cousin marriages in the widest sense, this is not to be understood as equivalent to the assertion that *all* marriages fell into this category. I have many marriages in my Berens River genealogies of several generations ago that according to the characterization of the Indians themselves were not between *nīnamak. A* good many of these, I may say, seem to have been inter-group (local or band) marriages.

Without genealogically supported evidence of the incidence of various classes of marriage between blood kin, and without an understanding of how cross-cousin marriage works in terms of the social system considered as a whole, intertribal comparisons cannot mean very much. Nor do I see how historical problems can be intelligently formulated. Cross-cousin marriage among the Lake Winnipeg Cree and Saulteaux is certainly something different from cross-cousin marriage among the Miwok and other California groups, or from that occurring on the Northwest coast, or elsewhere.[31] To discuss it as a "culture trait" divorced from the social context of which it is a part and in terms of which it is integrated with other traits in different ways among different peoples, can only lead to superficial and inept comparisons, if it does not involve an actual distortion of fact.

4. If the fundamental principles of the kinship system and marital practices of the Algonkian bands of the Lake Winnipeg area, as outlined above, are correct, then certain problems of cultural dynamics can be more adequately formulated with reference to this type of aboriginal social organization as a datum line.

As already pointed out, my personal contacts have been principally with the Indians living in the bush country on the eastern shore of Lake Winnipeg and inland,[32] where an aboriginal social organization of the type described remains essentially intact.[33] On the western side of the lake the penetration of the country by roads and railroads, and the suitability of its soil for farming have led to incursions by white settlers and, in the course of time to more radical transformations in the economic life, the religious beliefs, and the social organization of Indians whose native languages and culture were originally identical with those across the lake. Moreover, in earlier times, as well as now, some visiting back and forth occurred. The history of the Midéwi·win shows how close the connections were only a few decades ago[34] and there is blood relationship through intermarriage and the migration of families. Members of the Moose sib, for example, at the mouth of the Berens River are descendants in the male line of an ancestor [Yellow Legs] born on the west side of Lake Winnipeg, some of whose lineal and collateral descendants still live there. Several men of the Berens River band were also born across the lake.

Under these general conditions I think we may assume that any differences in kinship terminologies, kinship patterns, or marital practices that the Indians west of Lake Winnipeg exhibit, are the result of modern local conditions or, putting it another way, variants under specific circumstances of the master pattern of social organization once common to all the Indians of this region.

While I have not investigated this problem in detail, a single instance that came to my attention will illustrate its importance. At Fisher River today there are domiciled[35] most of the remnants of the Saulteaux that formerly constituted the St. Peter's band.[36] In 1907 they surrendered their lands and were moved from their old reserve on the Red River, near Selkirk. The old St. Peter's Indians were among the first to come in contact with the white settlers on the Red River and as early as 1875 the Deputy Superintendent of Indian Affairs characterized them as "the best settled and most progressive of all the Bands which have been a party to Treaty No. 1."[37] There is said to be a very high percentage of white blood in the Saulteaux division of the Fisher River Band today;[38] many of these Indians are farmers and consequently lead a more sedentary life than the hunters and fishermen of the eastern side of the Lake and they may still be considered as "progressive" when compared with most of the bands of the area.

In this group, according to my informant,[39] first cousins of neither type marry and blood relationship in itself is considered a bar to marriage. So far as the usage of kinship terms is concerned, what seems to have happened is this: the old terms neither have been outmoded nor become recrystallized into a distinctively new pattern of usage. Their application simply has become more fluid through synonymous usages that do not occur in the bands which have retained the aboriginal social system. Thus Anglicized synonyms for "my mother" (*nimama*) and "my father" (*nipapa*) have come into vogue,[40] descriptive terms occur for "father's brother," "father's sister," and "mother's sister," the term for "mother's brother" (= father-in-law) may be likewise used for "father's brother" and the term for "father's brother" (= stepfather) for "mother's brother,""[41] but the term for "mother-in-law," on the other hand, has become restricted and no longer is equivalent to "father's sister." In the first descending generation from Ego the term for cross-nephew (=son-in-law) or cross-niece (=daughter-in-law) may be used for parallel nephew and niece respectively, and in one's own generation the distinction between parallel and cross-cousin is no longer rigidly maintained, the tendency being to group these together as against full brothers and sisters. *Ní·nam* can therefore be used for cousins in the English sense as well as for sibling-in-law of the opposite sex. Only the diminutive of this term conveys the sense of "sweetheart." Evidence of such a radical change in kinship pattern and marital practice, controlled as it is by specific data on the aboriginal social systems of related Saulteaux groups of the same region, suggests a broader problem.

5. If, as now seems more likely than a few years ago, it can be assumed that the fundamental social organization of the Algonkian peoples north of the Great Lakes and the St. Lawrence River was once essentially similar to that in the Lake Winnipeg area, then the problem of contemporary variants in northern Algonkian kinship systems and marital practices may profitably be attacked in terms of this hypothesis. Only recently Fred Eggan[42] has admirably and conclusively demonstrated that the confusing and hitherto sometimes irreconcilable data on the kinship system of the Indians of the Gulf States can be understood as variants, under different conditions of acculturation, of the Crow pattern that underlies them. It seems to me that northern Algonkian kinship systems are likewise intelligible as variants of a basic pattern that has undergone modification as the result of acculturative processes and differences in local conditions.

Notes

Published in 1937 in D. S. Davidson, ed., *Twenty-fifth Anniversary Studies* (Philadelphia Anthropological Society), 95–110; reprinted in Hallowell, *Contributions to Anthropology* (Chicago: University of Chicago Press, 1976).

1. Was Cross-cousin Marriage Practiced by the North-Central Algonkian? *Proceedings, Twenty-third International Congress of Americanists [ICA]*, New York, 1928, 519–44.

2. R.H. Lowie, *Primitive Society*, 1920, 27, wrote, "While relatively rare in America, this usage is reported from the northern coast of British Columbia, from central California and Nicaragua; and the fact that in South America Chibcha women have a single word for husband and father's sister's son suggests that they too, frequently mated with cross-cousins."

3. Hallowell, "Was Cross-cousin Marriage Practiced," 522.

4. Recent Changes in the Kinship Terminology of the St. Francis Abenaki. *Proceedings, ICA*, 22, Rome, 1928, vol. 2, 97–145.

5. See W. D. Strong, Cross-cousin Marriage and the Culture of the Northeastern Algonkian. *American Anthropologist* 31: 277–88 (1929).

6. A. I. Hallowell, Kinship Terms and Cross-Cousin Marriage of the Montagnais-Naskapi and the Cree. *American Anthropologist* 34:171–99 (1932).

7. F. G. Speck, Mistassini Notes, *Indian Notes* (Museum of the American Indian, Heye Foundation), vol. 7, no. 4 (1930), 421–424.

8. J. C. Boileau Grant, Anthropometry of the Cree and Saulteaux Indians in Northeastern Manitoba. *Bulletin* 59, Canada Dept. of Mines, Ottawa, 1929.

9. E. S. Curtis, *The North American Indians*, vol. 18: 70–71 and 156.

10. Personal communication, Dr. Cooper, Feb., 1937.

11. Mouth of the Saskatchewan River. [Not to be confused with Little Grand Rapids on the Berens River.]

12. The Ojibwa Indians of Parry Sound, their Social and Religious Life. *Bulletin* 78, Canada Dept. of Mines, 1935, 98.

13. Found in 1933, 1935 among Eastmain and Rupert House Montagnais. MS. Field notes.

14. Definitely established in 1932 among Ft. George Montagnais, in 1933 among Albany Cree, in 1934 among Neoskweskaw (formerly Nitcikun), Montagnais. As regards Moose Factory Cree and Rupert House Montagnais, Dr. Cooper writes me (Feb. 14, 1937), "I have statements (1932, 1933, 1934) from one or more informants from each of these groups that permissive

or preferential cross-cousin marriage obtained but other informants were hazy or in certain cases denied its occurrence." In all these instances the information refers to first cross-cousins.

15. First hand information from Great Whale River and Albany River, where bilateral cross-cousin marriage occurs, and from Moose Factory and Attawapiskat, where the typical marriage is between a man and his father's sister's daughter. At Weenusk [Winisk], the kinship system favors cross-cousin marriage but "both types apparently are forbidden" ([Michelson] personal information—Feb. 12, 1937).

16. *Ojibwa Sociology*, Columbia University Contributions to Anthropology, NY, 1937. Chapters II and IV.

17. See R. H. Lowie, Relationship Terms, *Ency. Brit.*, 14th ed. 1929, vol. 19: 85. It should be noted, however, that in the kinship terminology "father's brother" = "step father" so that while formally the pattern is bifurcate collateral, psychologically and sociologically it is equivalent to the bifurcate merging pattern, as an example of which Lowie cites the Ojibwa proper.

18. At first he said 75 percent, but I am inclined to think that even 60 percent is too high. I mention this estimate rather as an indication of the common occurrence of the custom than as an accurate measure of its magnitude. Genealogical data are the necessary basis for any quantitative statements of incidence. [Ed. note: Hallowell in his 1930 field diary spelled "Settie" as "Settee," which is the more usual spelling of this Cree surname.]

19. Dr. Michelson offers corroboration from another source in his letter, n. 16, above: "From a physical anthropologist I know it (cross-cousin marriage) occurs at Oxford House and God's Lake."

20. On the Berens River.

21. The latter are on the borderline between Cree and Ojibwa (Saulteaux) speaking peoples.

22. There are cases where this formal impediment has been overcome but it is unnecessary to consider them here.

23. This rule is supported by the fear that its infringement will result in sickness.

24. My Berens River genealogies offer definite evidence on this point.

25. A. R. Radcliffe-Brown, The Social Organization of Australian Tribes, *Oceania*, Monograph No. 1, 1934.

26. When Tylor first called attention to the marriage of cross-cousins (On a Method of Investigating the Development of Institutions, *JAI* (1889), 18: 245–69), he spoke only of *first cousins*, and in other definitions given since and discussions of the subject it is not always clear how far the writer

has taken the occurrence of the marriage of second cousins or individuals terminologically classified as cross-cousins into account. In *Notes and Queries on Anthropology* (5th ed. 1929), 56, the implication of the definition given there ("Cousins of which the mother of one is sister to the father of the other are called cross-cousins") suggests a highly restricted usage.

27. In an unpublished manuscript. I have dealt with the magnitude of inbreeding in the Island Lake genealogy as measured by Raymond Pearl's Coefficients of Inbreeding and Relationship.

28. See Radcliffe-Brown, Social Organization, 35, for data on Kariera.

29. Inquiry among the Plains Cree and Plains Ojibwa (Saulteaux) in the summer of 1931 leads me to infer that marriages of first cross-cousins are infrequent, but that marriages of second cross-cousins have a fairly high incidence in some groups. Father Moulin, who, at the time, had been at the Hobbema Reserve (Alberta) for twenty-eight years, stated that the marriage of first cousins was extremely rare among these Cree. On the other hand, the tendency for the grandchildren of a brother and sister to marry was so pronounced that it necessitated that he obtain special dispensation in about fifty percent of the marriages he performed. He believed that these marriages were usually those of second cross-cousins. He also thought that formerly, when the bands were smaller and the Indians separated during the hunting season, the marriage of first cousins must have occurred. Besides there must have been inbreeding, since all the Indians here are descendents of a few families. I have no information to show that this suppression of first-cousin marriages, however, has affected the fundamental principle of the kinship system of the Plains Cree and Ojibwa, which is essentially that of their Woodland relatives. But it would be interesting to know whether this restriction, if it could be genealogically substantiated, is a result of their association with the peoples of Plains culture, where cousin marriages are tabu, or is explicable in some other fashion, such as the influence of the missionaries.

30. As I worked out the blood connections between certain individuals in my genealogies it often happened that I was able to point to distant relationships that these individuals themselves were only partially aware of. They had not made precise blood connection a matter of reflection.

31. Perhaps this is one of the reasons why the various theories, advanced from time to time as "historical" explanations of cross-cousin marriage *per se*, have only seemed plausible with respect to specific conditions. As Paul Kirchhoff has pointed out (Verwandtschaftsbezeichnungen und Verwandtenheirat, Zeitschrift für Ethnologie, Band 64, 1932, 64), all these explanations work either on the basis of pre-suppositions seldom realized,

or they explain too little. But I do not find any evidence in the case of these Algonkian peoples that would support his general principle that marriage with cross-cousins evolved from older forms of kin marriage, particularly those between individuals of different generations.

32. Except for a brief visit to the Cree of Grand Rapids (mouth of Saskatchewan) in 1930 and to the Saulteaux of Jack Head in 1936.

33. The basin of Lake Winnipeg lies along the western contact zone between the rocks of the Pre-Cambrian Shield and the Paleozoic limestones so that the terrain east of it is of fundamentally different geological origin than that to the west of it.

34. See A. I. Hallowell, The Passing of the Midéwi·win in the Lake Winnipeg Region. *American Anthropologist* 38: 32–51 (1936). [Chap. 21, this volume.]

35. Along with some Cree, originally from Norway House. [Ed. note: Hallowell does not clearly distinguish the Fisher River reserve (established for and by Cree from Norway House), from the adjacent Peguis reserve, created by the highly problematic displacement of the St. Peter's Ojibwe from their reserve near Selkirk.]

36. This band was a party to Treaty No. 1 (1871).

37. See *Annual Report*, Canadian Department of Indian Affairs, 1875, 38.

38. More than half was reported to be mixed bloods in the Annual Report of 1875.

39. The grandson of Red Eagle [Mis-koo-kee-new (Henry Prince)]who signed the Treaty of 1871, who in turn was the son of the famous Pegwis [Peguis] who previously negotiated with Lord Selkirk. [Ed. note: This informant was A. E. Prince, whom Hallowell met at Berens River on August 18, 1930. He was a minister of the Church of Christ from the Fisher River reserve. The kin terms Hallowell got from him "show how Saulteaux breaks down under English influence," Hallowell wrote that day. He added that Prince was married to a daughter of English-born Frederick Disbrowe, Hudson's Bay Company post manager at Berens River for many years, and his first Ojibwe wife. (Hallowell field notes, Hallowell papers, Ms. Coll. 26, American Philosophical Society, Philadelphia.)]

40. A development that has likewise occurred in a number of bands on the eastern side of the Lake.

41. Both of which usages are contrary to a bifurcate collateral pattern.

42. Historical Changes in the Choctaw Kinship System. *American Anthropologist* 39: 34–52 (1937).

SIX

The Incidence, Character, and Decline of Polygyny among the Lake Winnipeg Cree and Saulteaux

Depending upon the number of individuals involved and their sex, it has long been customary to differentiate marital unions as monogamous, polygynous, and polyandrous. These terms have likewise been used more or less systematically to characterize familial institutions, and surveys have been undertaken to establish the occurrence of the different forms of marriage prevailing at this or that period or place in the history of mankind. Cases of polyandry still remain something of a collector's item. Yet how much do we know about how polyandry actually works, even in the societies where it is known to occur? The fact is that, without further analysis, such broad characterizations, when applied to any particular people, are insufficient to evoke a precise or realistic picture of actual marital conditions. Simply to assert that such and such a people are polygynous really does no more than make us aware that a certain type of plural marriage is permitted. In one society polygynous men may, at the most, have two or three wives, in another the average number of wives may be twice this number or more. The sororate may act selectively with respect to the choice of the second wife here, while there, some other agency is influential. Polygyny, too, may be a caste or class prerogative in one society and not in another; household and general domestic arrangements will differ, and so on.

Among the factual data necessary for a realistic account of polygyny in any given society, information on the actual incidence of polygynous marriages and the number of wives each man has, is basic. Yet this is a type of information often difficult or impossible to obtain among the aboriginal peoples of the contemporary world. Among North American Indians of today, for example, it is practically impossible to secure such information. Polygynous marriages are known to have existed in the past, but they have long since disappeared under the moral pressure exerted by the missionaries as well as through the operation of other factors. As a basis for estimating their former incidence we usually are forced to rely upon retrospective generalizations of the natives themselves, or statements of contemporary observers. In a few instances, genealogical data are available which, while never penetrating very far into the past, provide the basis for more precise quantitative inferences.

SOURCE MATERIAL

A few years ago I was fortunate enough to come into possession of some documentary material that furnishes reliable information, over a period of seven years, on the *actual* incidence of polygyny among Cree and Saulteaux bands of the Lake Winnipeg region. These documents comprise two Treaty Books. They contain the original entries of annuities paid to Indians who were parties to Treaty No. 5. This Winnipeg Treaty, as it is often called, was negotiated in 1875 and the entries are for that year and each succeeding year until 1881. By the terms of this treaty, the Dominion Government obligated itself, in return for the claims relinquished by the aborigines, to pay each Indian $5.00 annually in perpetuity. Consequently the records of these payments, year by year, are as accurate a measure as can be obtained of the native population. And since the entries are made in columns headed *Men, Women* (wives), *Boys, Girls, Other Relatives,* to the left of which appears the name of some particular male individual, a certain amount of statistical information can be compiled from them. In addition, a gossipy note or two is occasionally entered opposite the name of an individual which provides a colorful touch and sometimes a clue to personal events in their lives. With the exception of the initial year of the treaty period when all of the Indians within the geographical limits defined were not present to receive their annuity, or did not fully understand the conditions imposed, there is no reason to suppose that, during the succeeding years, any eligible native failed to collect the amount promised for himself, his wife or wives, children, and other relatives.

ETHNIC GROUPS

The geographical boundaries officially delimited by the Winnipeg Treaty embraced an area estimated at 100,000 square miles.[1] Linguistically, the native population belonged to the Algonkian stock. Occupying the eastern border of Lake Winnipeg and inland to the Height of Land[2] were the Saulteaux (Ojibwa) speaking peoples. From south to north, beginning at the Winnipeg River,[3] they comprised: (a) the so-called Island bands,[4] i.e.,

Indians living east of Lake Winnipeg in the region of the Manigotagan (Bad Throat) River, the Blood Vein River, and those in the neighborhood of Dog Head and, on the western side of the lake the band at Jack Head, and a few nomadic families from White Mud (now Icelandic) River that really belonged to the St. Peter's band on the Red River; and (b) the Berens River bands (i.e., the band at the mouth of this river and the people farther inland for 250 miles, now divided into two additional bands, [Little] Grand Rapids and Lake Pekangikum, as well as the Indians on the Poplar River to the north). In 1876 these Saulteaux Indians, as represented by treaty payments, numbered 668 persons.

To the north of them, surrounding northern Lake Winnipeg and extending up the Saskatchewan River to the west, were Cree speaking bands that made up the remaining adherents to the Winnipeg Treaty. They comprised the following bands: Norway House, Cross Lake (sixty miles north of Norway House), Grand Rapids (mouth of the Saskatchewan), Moose Lake, The Pas, Cumberland Lake [House]. The Indians of these Cree bands who received treaty payments in 1876 numbered 2,185. Adding the population of the Saulteaux bands to them, we get a total of 2,853 individuals. For the territory embraced by the Winnipeg Treaty this gives an areal density of 0.028 persons per square mile.[5]

All of these Indians were hunters, trappers, and fishermen and, except for the fact that the Saulteaux had sibs, while the Cree did not, their basic social organization was identical.[6] Other aspects of their culture only differed in details that are irrelevant to the topic under discussion.

REGIONAL PREVALENCE OF POLYGYNY

At the time that the Winnipeg Treaty was made, however, there were essential differences in the above mentioned bands with respect to the degree to which Christianity had been embraced. Significantly enough, this aspect of the acculturative process exhibits a definite correlation with the presence or absence of polygyny. Polygyny is absent in all of the Cree groups with the exception of the bands at Cross Lake and Moose Lake. That this fact is connected with missionary efforts there is no reason to doubt. In 1840, with Norway House selected as the base of operations and Rev. James Evans in charge, the British Wesleyan Missionary Committee inaugurated the first attempt to Christianize the native Cree in the neighborhood of northern Lake Winnipeg.[7] In the forties missionaries were also sent to Cumberland and The Pas and later to Grand Rapids.[8] Some of these Cree bands, then, had

had missionaries in residence for as much as thirty-five years. The two bands mentioned were not among these, however, and despite their proximity to Norway House, the Cross Lake Cree are referred to by Commissioner Morris at the time of the treaty as the "Wood or Pagan Indians of Cross Lake."[9] The chief [Täpästä`nɑm], he says, had just been baptized.

In contrast with the Cree, the Saulteaux east of Lake Winnipeg had remained unchristianized much longer. As late as 1854 when Rev. J. Ryerson made an inspection tour of Wesleyan missions on Lake Superior and in the "northwest," there were no missions of any kind on the eastern shores of Lake Winnipeg between Fort Alexander and Norway House[10]. The first mission to be established there was at Berens River. But this was not until 1873, only two years before the treaty[11] was signed.

As of the year 1876, when the first representative census derived from annuity payments is available, the bands in which polygynous marriages recur comprise only 39 percent of the native population within the boundaries delimited by the Winnipeg Treaty. In the remainder of the Indian population of this area, polygyny was even then an institution of the past, although it is possible that sporadic cases were kept under cover and the annuity payment collected under the guise of "other relatives,"[12] in the communities under direct missionary influence. In view of what has been said above, however, with respect to the relatively late influence exerted by the missionaries in the Saulteaux bands, it is significant that polygyny is reported in all of them. But numerically, the Saulteaux comprised less than a quarter (23 percent) of the entire native population of the treaty area at this time.

LOCAL INCIDENCE OF POLYGYNY

I have summarized the information on the local incidence of polygyny for the period 1873 to 1881 in the accompanying table. It exhibits the total number of married men, the number of wives reported for each man, the percentage of polygynous marriages, and the percentage of men with *more* than two wives. The Moose Lake Cree have not been included because, for some reason unknown to me, the entries are limited to the years 1876 to 1878. In 1876 there were six men with two wives apiece out of a total of forty-three married men, a percentage that falls within the range exhibited by the other bands.

Table 2 also indicates correlative information on the total population of the several bands and on the sex ratio for adults and for minors.[13] It will be seen that among the minors, with few exceptions, males predominate,

Year	Band	Population	Adults		Minors		Married Men*						
			M.	F.	M.	F.	Total	With 1 wife	With 2 wives	With 3 wives	With 4 wives	Percent polygynous	Percent with more than 2 wives
1875	Berens River	201	39	53	58	51	34	29	3	2	0	15	6
	Island Bands	28	8	10	5	5	5	4	1	0	0	20	0
	Cross Lake	161	35	42	38	46	29	23	6	0	0	20	0
	Total	390	82	105	101	102	68	56	10	2	0	17.6	3.6
1876	Berens River	392	75	102	120	95	69	58	9	1	1	19	3
	Island Bands	276	59	67	86	64	47	44	1	2	0	6	4
	Cross Lake	185	38	48	41	58	33	25	8	0	0	24	0
	Total	853	172	217	247	217	145	127	18	3	1	15.2	2.8
1877	Berens River	410	84	106	123	97	75	65	8	1	1	13	3
	Island Bands	236	47	60	76	53	38	36	0	2	0	5	5
	Cross Lake	207	46	51	47	63	36	30	6	0	0	16	0
	Total	853	177	217	246	213	149	131	14	3	1	12.1	2.7
1878	Berens River	439	91	111	137	100	81	71	8	2	0	12	2
	Island Bands	241	47	62	76	56	39	36	1	2	0	8	5
	Cross Lake	207	52	54	46	55	40	35	5	0	0	12	0
	Total	887	190	227	259	211	160	142	14	4	0	11.3	2.5
1879	Berens River	474	93	115	156	110	83	73	8	2	0	12	1
	Island Bands	244	50	63	73	58	41	38	1	2	0	7	5
	Cross Lake	216	53	59	51	53	44	40	4	0	0	9	0
	Total	934	196	237	280	221	168	151	13	4	0	10.1	2.4
1880	Berens River	480	88	113	163	116	79	70	8	1	0	11	1
	Island Bands	243	45	62	73	63	40	37	1	2	0	7	5
	Cross Lake	225	52	61	57	55	44	40	4	0	0	9	0
	Total	948	185	236	293	234	163	147	13	3	0	9.8	1.8
1881	Berens River	497	95	114	168	120	78	69	8	1	0	12	1
	Island Bands	253	50	65	77	61	45	42	2	1	0	7	2
	Cross Lake	231	48	65	60	58	44	42	2	0	0	5	0
	Total	981	193	244	305	239	167	153	12	2	0	8.4	1.2

* With spouses living.

2. Local Incidence of Polygyny

and among the adults, women. While these ratios are necessarily crude, I see no reason to doubt the relative proportion of the sexes as indicated. Indeed, it is a striking fact that the population figures compiled by Alexander Henry at the beginning of the nineteenth century, which contain an entry for the natives of "Lake Winnipic," exhibit a comparable sex ratio for adults.[14] Wissler, moreover, who has compiled the most elaborate data we have on sex ratios among the Canadian Indians from Canadian Government records comparable to those I have used, finds low ratios for adults under non-reservation conditions[15] Among the Woods Cree, in particular, he found a striking excess of females.[16]

While I do not believe that it is legitimate to argue from the Lake Winnipeg population statistics that a surplus of women, under aboriginal conditions, was a primary causal factor in the prevalence of polygyny, it is evident that such ratios as those exhibited in table 2 constitute a favorable condition for polygyny, whereas this would not be the case if there were a surplus of men. I would also like to point out that the band figures taken separately, rather than the totals for each year, are probably of the most sociological significance, since intra-band, rather than inter-band marriages were the rule. It will be seen from an inspection of these figures (table 2) that the percentage of polygynous men ranges from five to twenty-four, the percentage of men with more than two wives from zero to six.[17]

On the whole I am convinced that the quantitative data tabulated are not only a reliable measure of polygyny in these particular bands but that the maximum percentages approximate the maximum incidence of polygynous marriages in the general cultural and ecological conditions under which the native population lived. If so, our data are not merely an adequate sample of the former incidence of polygyny under older aboriginal conditions in this area, which the Berens River Saulteaux and Cross Lake Cree undoubtedly approximated at the period immediately following the treaty. They are a measure of the extent to which polygyny occurred among Cree and Ojibwa peoples generally at still *earlier* periods. A glance at some of the statements made by traders, missionaries, and travelers who came into contact with these Indians in the 18th and early nineteenth centuries will be instructive in this connection, supplemented by the later observations of ethnologists in the twentieth century.

COMPARATIVE INCIDENCE OF POLYGYNY

Some of the early observers of the Cree and Ojibwa (Saulteaux) simply assert that polygyny is permitted, while a few statements are couched in terms that lead one to suppose that almost every man had more than one wife. Alexander Henry the Younger [the Elder], for instance, asserts that "the Cristinaux have *usually* two wives each, and often three" (italics ours).[18] We do have statements, however, which are probably more exact. Franklin (Richardson), for example, referring to 120 Indian hunters (Cree) who frequented Cumberland House in the early nineteenth century says, "Of these a few have several wives, but the majority have only one . . . ."[19] Ballantyne,[20] too, remarks that a single wife is the rule. Hence Skinner's categorical statement for the Eastern Cree that "polygamy was once common but, has now been given up,"[21] is an extremely loose statement for an ethnographer to make. But he is equally incautious in respect to the Northern Saulteaux, among whom he finds polygyny not only to be common but *only limited by a man's means to maintain a harem*" (italics ours).[22] This statement, however, can be balanced by that of [Peter] Grant[23] who says that these Indians are generally content with one wife.

While these estimates of the number of wives retained by polygynous men vary somewhat, they indicate a general trend of agreement in respect to the small number of spouses in plural marriages. For the Cree two or three are mentioned by Henry[24] and Drage[25] ("a number which they seldom exceed"). Ballantyne[26] states that it is "looked upon as neither unusual nor improper to take two or even three wives," while a very good hunter may have four; and Robson says "they generally content themselves with two."[27] Here again Skinner overtops the estimate of others on this point in his assertion that the number of wives in polygynous marriages "varied from four to five."[28] In individual cases of course this may have been true. La Verendrye[29] reports a Cree "chief" (La Marte blanche) with five wives, Grant refers to a similar case,[30] and Keating to an Ojibwa chief with nine wives.[31] But these figures can scarcely be taken as an average in view of other statements quoted. Observers of the Ojibwa (Saulteaux), moreover, are in agreement with those referring to the Cree. Grant says a good hunter may have two or three wives.[32] Kohl states that they "rarely have more than three wives."[33] Cameron writes that they "seldom take more than four."[34] Densmore[35] adheres to an estimate of two or three as usual in polygynous marriages, but says that a Canadian Chippewa stated that many Indians had two and that in olden times some men had five. It is all the more amazing then to read Skinner's statement that among the Saulteaux, "men having thirteen wives are still remembered though five to seven were more *common*" (italics ours).[36] One cannot help wondering whether Skinner was completely unaware of the fact that Indian informants, like ourselves, may sometimes exhibit the common human trait of projecting their own personal fantasies into statements made about by-gone days.

In my own genealogical data from the Berens River, including reliable information on some 200 marriages, I have recorded a single instance in which a man had six wives. This is the same individual who appears in the treaty records of 1876 with four wives, two of his spouses having already died. So far back as the memories of the Berens River Indians go, this man holds the polygynous record. They never heard of anyone having more wives than Cɛnawágwaskang.

I think that it is clear from the foregoing statements by persons who had a much better opportunity to observe native habits under aboriginal conditions than any contemporary ethnologist, that their assertions both in regard to the prevalence of polygyny and the number of wives most common in plural marriages, are in general accord with the statistical data presented. They bear out its reliability as an accurate quantitative index of polygyny under aboriginal conditions.[37] This consonance is particularly significant, it seems to me, with respect to the small proportion of men who had more than two wives.

SORORAL POLYGYNY

Only a few early observers tell us whether the wives of polygynous men were ever sisters, and if so, how frequently this was the case. Nevertheless we have some specific statements.[38] Referring primarily to the Cumberland House Cree, Franklin[39] states that a man's "second wife is for the most part the sister of the first; but not necessarily so, for the Indian of another family often presses his daughter upon a hunter whom he knows to be capable of maintaining her well."

For the Saulteaux we have Cameron's assertion[40] that plural wives were "sometimes all sisters" and Peter Jones' general comment for the Ojibwa proper that men making polygynous marriages generally chose sisters.[41] Skinner[42], referring to both the Cree and Saulteaux, likewise stresses the occurrence of sororal polygyny. For the former he asserts that a man "marrying the eldest of a group of sisters, usually if he married again, took the younger sisters as they became old enough."

In view of the many non-quantitative statements about the prevalence of sororal polygyny throughout ethnological literature, it is unfortunate that the more exact information on the occurrence of polygyny in the Lake Winnipeg region does not also permit a quantitative answer to this further question. It is impossible, however, to tell from the Treaty Books how many of the men who made polygynous marriages took sisters for their wives.[43] I can only turn to the information contained in my Berens River genealogies as a reliable sample of Saulteaux, if not Cree, practice. I also obtained some positive information in respect to Poplar River polygynists. According to this data it appears that the wives of polygynous men were often, but by no means always, either blood or classificatory sisters.

Eight polygynous marriages appear in my genealogies. In six of these marriages the husband had two blood sisters as wives. In one of the remaining instances, the man[44] had six wives, three of whom belonged to the same sib. I was told quite positively, however, that these women were not blood sisters. But they fall into the social category of sisters because of their common sib membership. In the remaining case, the wives were neither sisters nor members of the same sib.

Of the five polygynous men from Poplar River who appear in the treaty records it is certain that three of them did not have blood sisters as wives and it is probable that the others did not. Whether any of the wives of these men were classificatory sisters I cannot say.

This factual evidence, numerically slight as it is, proves that on the Berens and Poplar Rivers at least, the marriage of sisters, whether blood or classificatory, was not an inevitable correlate of polygyny. In the former region it is particularly impressive that Cɛnawágwaskɑng had no blood sisters among his six wives and that Pɑzɑgwí·gabau, one of the most noted leaders of the Midéwi·win, took both his wives from different families and different sibs. These instances are important because both these men were outstanding personalities of the aboriginal regime.

Why did men who had more than one wife often choose sisters? Personally, I do not think that there is any categorical answer to this question. I have not run across any information in the field or in the older literature that suggests a clearly defined customary motivation.[45] Nor does the evidence cited above suggest any formal rule.[46] The reason the natives now advance for the sororal polygyny of the past is that sisters were supposed to get along better together than women of different families. The same motivation is reported by some of the earlier observers of the Cree and Saulteaux,[47] and it is likewise familiar in ethnological literature at large. So far as the Lake Winnipeg Algonkian are concerned, it is a rationalization that may symbolize the "solidarity of sisters" as a cultural ideal and need not be taken as a literal statement of fact.[48] In terms of the functioning of the aboriginal social organization of these peoples,[49] it was probably inevitable that, in some instances, sisters would be taken as wives. At any rate, it seems to me that under the caption "sororate," sororal polygyny has too often been treated as if it were an independent variable or even a possible "cause" of other social phenomena. A familiar verbal label has made it only too easy to point up one facet of plural marriage. Hence the importance of sororal polygyny may be overemphasized, if its actual incidence and the role that it plays in the social order as a whole is not taken into account.

While certainly an item worthy of note among the Lake Winnipeg Cree and Saulteaux, it probably was a great deal less than momentous in the total operation of their social life.

RANK OF PLURAL WIVES

Statements in the literature are contradictory in respect to differences in the rank of wives. For the Cree, Drage specifically states that there were no distinctions in rank,[50] while Franklin,[51] on the other hand says, "the first wife always remains the mistress of the tent, and assumes an authority over the others, which is not in every case quietly submitted to." In the case of the Saulteaux, Grant[52] writes that the first wife "claims a certain superiority over the others and is generally considered by the husband as chief mistress of the family." Kohl says, "the first wife, however, always remains at the head of affairs."[53] Among the Berens River Saulteaux I did not secure any positive information that suggested evidence of any different ranking among the wives, except that the first wife was said usually to "boss" the others. I do not believe, however, that such a status could have been very highly formalized among these northern people. Presumably, the first wife would be older than the others, which would in itself be a socially recognized token of a certain degree of authority, especially within the household. For among both Cree and Saulteaux a man and his wives constituted a single household group.[54] Plural wives never had separate wigwams.

OFFSPRING OF POLYGYNOUS MARRIAGES

As might be expected, the number of offspring of polygynous unions were often, but not always, larger than those produced by monogamous unions. Table 3 gives the distribution of dependent living children by monogamous and polygynous marriages for the years 1876, 1878, and 1881, which years have been arbitrarily selected as samples. An inspection will indicate that the largest number of offspring in each year are those of polygynous marriages. Since the average number of children per fruitful woman, calculated from my Berens River genealogies is 4.5, it may be assumed perhaps that, at any one time, it was not likely that there were more than seven or eight dependent children present in a family, as the age of marriage for both sexes was early. It will be noted in the table that nine, ten, or eleven children only occur in polygynous families. The fact that a notable proportion of monogamous marriages appear without issue probably is to be explained by the fact that year to year records include a considerable number of unions that have been

Year	Number of Children	0	1	2	3	4	5	6	7	8	9	10	11	Total
1876	Number of monogamous marriages	15	35	25	16	20	13	1	1	1	0	0	0	127
	Polygynous marriages	0	1	3	2	3	2	2	4	2	1	1	1	22
	Total	15	36	28	18	23	15	3	5	3	1	1	1	149
1878	Monogamous marriages	28	28	26	24	20	12	1	0	3	0	0	0	142
	Polygynous marriages	0	1	0	5	1	1	2	3	2	2	1	0	18
	Total	28	29	26	29	21	13	3	3	5	2	1	0	160
1881	Monogamous marriages	26	28	30	27	22	12	4	4	0	0	0	0	153
	Polygynous marriages	0	1	1	0	2	2	3	0	1	3	1	0	14
	Total	26	29	31	27	24	14	7	4	1	3	1	0	167

* Appearing in the column headed "Boys and Girls" in the Treaty Books.

3. Distribution of Dependent Living Children by Monogamous and Polygynous Marriages

freshly contracted. On the other hand, the polygynous marriages recorded for these years are those of individuals of middle age or older.

In respect to the *total* number of offspring in polygynous, as compared with monogamous, unions, no satisfactory quantitative data are available.[55] The only information I have on this question comes from a handful of polygynous unions that occur in my Berens River genealogies. Five of the eleven polygynous men of the Berens River Bands who received treaty payments in 1876 (table 2) appear in my records,[56] but I lack full information on the children of one of them. In table 4, I have summarized my information in respect to the total offspring of the other four men in the treaty records and of Ogáwapwan, whose name does not appear in these records. If miscarriages and stillbirths were included, the number of children in each case

Name of man	Number of children by wife						Total	Dependent children 1876
	1	2	3	4	5	6		
1. Cenawágwaskaŋg	5	4	2	5	4	0	20	7
2. Kepegíʹjiʹkweäs*	8	10					18	8
3. Tetabaiyábin†	8	9					17	6
4. Pazagwíʹgabo	8	5					13	6
5. Ogáwapwan	4	4					8	?

* Oldest son of Cenawágwaskaŋg.
† Son of Pazagwíʹgabo.

4. Total Number of Children by Polygynous Marriages of Berens River Men

would be higher. I tried to obtain information in regard to the number of children who died in infancy, but it is unlikely that the cases entered are all that occurred. In connection with these figures, I may say that the range in the number of offspring of married women for the three generations in my genealogies for which I have the most complete information, is from zero to thirteen. Only one woman bore thirteen children, none twelve, and only two women gave birth to eleven offspring. In view of these data the number of offspring of the first four polygynous marriages listed in table 4 is obviously due to the fact that they *are* polygynous unions. However, the average number of children born to these eleven child-bearing wives of four polygynous men is six, which is higher than the average for child-bearing women of the Berens River as a whole.

WHO WERE THE POLYGYNOUS MEN?

If the data summarized in table 2 are a reliable index of the incidence of polygyny under aboriginal conditions, the relatively small percentage of polygynous men raises further questions. Who were these men? What were their personal characteristics and life histories? Why were these particular men, rather than others, polygynous? What role did their rank or personal achievements play in the situation? Did polygyny give them a higher social status?

While it will be impossible to answer all these questions satisfactorily they are among the questions that need to be answered in order to understand the functioning of polygyny in Cree and Saulteaux culture. By synthesizing the information contained in the Treaty Books with that obtained by local inquiry among the Berens River Saulteaux and the earlier observations on culturally and linguistically related peoples outside the Lake Winnipeg region, it is possible to obtain some insight into the dynamic factors at work.

If we include six men of the Moose Lake band (Cree), the actual number of polygynous men whose names occur in the Treaty Books is twenty-nine. Detailed biographical information about all of these particular men would, of course, throw a great deal of light upon the polygyny of this region as a going concern. Since information of this character is unavailable, I will take the polygynous men of the Berens River as a point of departure. The information which I obtained about them, while not as full or detailed as might be desired, comes directly from their immediate descendants and offers some clues that make intelligible the more fragmentary facts concerning polygynous individuals elsewhere.

Of the twenty-nine polygynous men recorded in the Treaty Books, twelve appear on the rolls of the Berens River bands during the seven years covered by the records. Five of these latter are men already mentioned as living on the Poplar River. Another man is listed solely for the year 1875, and afterwards appears on the roll of the Blood Vein River division of the Island bands. I have no information about him. Of the six men remaining, all of whom lived on the Berens River itself, I can identify only five in my genealogies. In addition there are the three polygynous men who appear in my records but not in the Treaty Books.[57]

Cenawágwaskang, the most notorious of the Berens River polygynists, was a noted hunter and also the most famous conjurer of his time. He had gained prestige, that is to say, in the two most important aspects of life—the economic and the magico-religious.

Pazagwí·gabau and later, his son, Tetabaiyábin, were successively headmen of the Midéwi·win, this being the supreme position of magico-religious importance in Saulteaux society. While it required no little ambition, persistence, and intelligence to secure and fulfill the exacting requirements of this role, these men were respected and feared chiefly because of the magical power they were believed to have at their command. In addition, Pazagwí·gabau was a conjurer and practiced ni'baki'win, a special curative technique by which material objects, magically projected into a person's body in order to cause illness or death, were removed.

Without further elaboration it is obvious that these men were among the most important in a society which lacked any institutionalized leadership of a purely *secular* kind. No one was formally charged with executive, legislative, judicial, or penal functions. It was precisely for this reason that the individuals who exercised magico-religious, curative, or clairvoyant functions became the real leaders in effect, even in spheres outside of their immediate specialties. Men of this type then were prominent among the polygynists.

The same situation appears to have existed among the Poplar River Saulteaux. For according to what information I have, two of the five polygynists there were prominent "medicine men."

On the Blood Vein River to the south a similar correlation holds in the case of the one man about whom I have positive information. He was known to my Berens River informant as Wagi·békwan, Crooked Back. Although he does not appear in the Treaty Book under this name he was undoubtedly one of the two men with three wives recorded for the Island bands. I was told that at first he had two blood sisters as wives. When one of these women fell ill, his parents-in-law promised Crooked Back another one of their daughters if he was successful in curing the one who was ill. He did cure the latter and then took the third sister as a wife. A custom similar in principle was once in vogue among the Berens River Saulteaux and is reported for the Ojibwa by Ruth Landes. She writes,[58] "If a shaman had cured a girl of a dangerous illness, had 'given life to her' through the power of his guardian spirits, he might receive her in payment for his priceless services." The Blood Vein case involves the application of this idea indirectly and it is easy to see how such a prerogative exercised by those engaged in professional curing could operate in building up a series of plural wives.

Further evidence in respect to the status of the Berens River men mentioned comes from another angle. It was formerly the custom, during the period when the competition for fur was keener than it is now, for the factor at the local post to make one or more of the best Indian hunters or leading men his unofficial agents.[59] These Indians were counted upon to exercise sufficient control over their fellows so that the fur the latter caught would be taken to the Company and not to a rival trader. The "Barter Chiefs" usually received a new suit of clothes annually, a little rum, tobacco, and sometimes a red feather to wear in their hats.[60] Thus the fact that Cɛnawágwaskang and Tetabaiyábin were "Barter Chiefs" in their time is additional evidence that they were leaders, as well as excellent hunters.

It is clear then that among the Saulteaux east of Lake Winnipeg the polygynous man was often, if not inevitably, out of the common run. He must have been an exceptionally good hunter[61] and often he was a leader by virtue of the reputation he had built up as the possessor of magico-religious, curative, or clairvoyant powers. Thus while we cannot say that polygyny was a prerogative of rank in a formal sense, in effect, it often amounted to this, and consequently became a tangible sign of social prestige.

The two other Berens River polygynists who appear in table 4 (nos. 2 and 5) were said to have been excellent hunters, but so far as I know, they were not noted for any magico-religious powers. I do not think that this fact contradicts the correlation pointed out above in the case of the other men in view of the extremely individualistic character of Saulteaux society and the fact that polygyny was not a formally recognized prerogative. While a good hunter might or might not be a polygynist, there was a greater expectation that a man who, in addition, was noted for his possession of magico-religious powers and hence stood out as a leader among his fellows, would be a polygynist.

A few casual statements by early observers support the correlation between leadership and polygyny, and personally I would assume that magico-religious powers were the supporting base upon which the fact of leadership rested. The three most striking examples have already been cited—a Cree "chief" with five wives (La Verendrye), a Saulteaux chief with the same number (Grant), and an Ojibwa chief with nine (Keating)— because the number of wives these men had was above the average. Although it is impossible to identify the tribes Carver[62] refers to, it is worth while to call attention to a passage in which he stresses the fact that chiefs have the most wives. At the same time he points out that polygyny is not limited by rank.

In the Lake Winnipeg region the fragmentary evidence we have indicates that the correlation between magico-religious functions, leadership, and polygyny was carried over into the treaty period. The pagan bands, in particular, when asked to elect chiefs and councillors by the commissioners, often chose the "medicine men" who had been their unelected leaders under the aboriginal regime. Täpästä`nam, of the Cross Lake band, was one of these, and Sagatcíweäs, leader of the Midéwi·win, was elected by the Island bands. These two men were not among the polygynists but two of the councillors of the Island bands were. One of these was Thickfoot, the leader of the band from Dog Head, who sulked because he was not made chief; the other was the leader of the band across Lake Winnipeg at Jack Head. The leader of the [Little] Grand Rapids band on the Berens River, who also became a councillor under the head chief of all the bands,

Jacob Berens, was also a polygynist. At Moose Lake, too, a councillor was polygynous. If we had more detailed information I feel sure that these fragmentary correlations would be upheld with evidence that would demonstrate the selective influence of characteristic cultural values upon the incidence of polygyny. The deeper lying personality factors must, of course, remain obscure.

DECLINE OF POLYGYNY

Perhaps the most striking feature of the statistical data presented in table 2, when the total figures for all of the bands together are inspected, is the progressive annual decline in the percentage of polygynous men as a whole, and of those having more than two wives.

As already pointed out, polygyny once flourished in the population of the whole area delimited by the Winnipeg Treaty. By 1876 it was already extinct in the bands representing 61 percent of the Indian population. The decline observable in our sample thus represents a continuation of this process of extinction, under conditions of acculturation that were spreading to the bands previously unaffected. The most effective factor leading to decline was undoubtedly the hostile attitude that the missionaries assumed towards polygyny. Everywhere they went they took vigorous measures to stamp it out.

Behind the bare statistical data revealed in the Treaty Books, it is possible to discern some details of the processes at work. With a single exception,[63] no new names of polygynous men appear in these records after 1876. This means, of course, that fresh polygynous unions were not being contracted. Although I have no way of proving it, I judge that most of the polygynous men were of middle age or older at the time the treaty was signed. Such was the case with respect to those belonging to the Berens River bands and several others who were known by reputation to my Berens River informants.

Secondly, some names of polygynous men disappear from the Treaty Books as the years go by. I think we may assume that death accounts for their absence from the record rather than removal to some other locality. If the latter were the case, they would appear on the roll of some other band unless they moved to a section of the country outside of the borders of the Winnipeg Treaty. In a few instances the wives and children of the polygynists of one year can be identified in successive years. In these cases it is quite obvious that death removed the husband.[64]

In the third place, one or more of the wives of several polygynous men died during the period covered by the records. Cɛnawágwaskang for instance, had only three wives left by 1878, but he still falls into the polygynous category. But in cases where a man had only two wives to begin with and lost one of them, I have henceforth counted him as monogamous.

Finally there is evidence of separation. The second wife of a Cross Lake bigamist, for instance, is entered under her own name in 1881, as "abandoned wife No. 2 of Andrew O—." Whether this abandonment was due to the increasing adoption of the Christian ideal of monogamous marriage that was permeating this band at the time, I do not know. But this process was at work and together with the other causes mentioned, helps to account for the decline in polygynous unions. The evidence in the case of the Cross Lake band in particular is clear because in 1879 the second wives of two polygynous men are given separate entries and marked "put away."[65] One of these women had evidently taken her children with her, since the former husband is paid for wife number one and five children that year, while wife number two is paid the usual amount for herself and *two children.* One may well speculate upon the human effects of these early attempts at stamping out polygyny since in this particular case we get a glimpse behind the scenes. In 1881 this woman received treaty payments for *three children* but no husband appears on the record either in that year or the previous one. Nevertheless, the fact that polygynous men actually were putting away their wives indicates the process of acculturation that was occurring. Christian attitudes were being substituted for native ones and polygyny as an approved form of marriage was being broken up.

Fortunately enough, we have the personal testimony of Egerton R. Young,[66] who was a missionary at Norway House prior to the Winnipeg Treaty (1868–1873), in respect to his handling of particular cases. Since this was the same individual who later started the first mission in the heart of the pagan Saulteaux, east of Lake Winnipeg,[67] we can assume that he utilized the same tactics there during the early part of the period represented in table 2.

Reverend Young clearly recognized how difficult it was for polygynous men to give up their wives:

> To have several wives is considered a great honour in some of the tribes. For a man to separate from all but one is to expose himself to ridicule from his pagan friends, and also to the danger of incurring the hostility of the relations of the discarded wives. Some of the most perplexing

and trying duties of my missionary life have been in connection with this matter of re-organising, on a Christian basis, the families of once heathen polygamists, who desirous to do what was right, have left the matter entirely in my hands.

At first Reverend Young thought that he could apply the rule that the first wife should always remain with her husband. But he said that this idea had to be modified. In one case that he mentions, the first wife had no children. The second wife had several small ones. So the man was advised to "put away" the first wife in this instance. Another case seems to have been decided on a purely quantitative basis. Two wives wished to become Christians. One had five children and the other four by their common husband. After asking "divine guidance" the wife with five children was told to stay with her husband, after certain of the family effects had been equally divided between them.

In another instance an old man with four wives wanted to be baptized. He was willing to give up three of them—all old women with grown sons. But when he announced his decision to his family, "there was a 'row.' The women began to wail, and the sons, who generally treated their mothers with neglect and indifference, now declared, with a good deal of emphasis, that their mothers should not be sent away, and thus degraded in the eyes of the people." The sons picked up their guns and went to see the missionary. The case was finally settled by having the old man remain with the wife who had no children and by having the sons of the other wives set their mothers up in separate wigwams.

Thus, the increasing moral pressure exerted by the missionaries, which probably made the contraction of new polygynous marriages impossible, and the insistence upon the abandonment of all wives but one in the case of individuals who desired to become full fledged Christians, combined with the death of polygynous men or their wives, led to the extinction of a form of marriage that had once been a feature of the aboriginal mode of life among the Lake Winnipeg Cree and Saulteaux.

Notes

Published in *American Anthropologist* 40 (1938): 235–56.

1. Alexander Morris, *The Treaties of Canada with the Indians of Manitoba and the Northwest Territories* (Toronto, 1880), 143. For the territorial boundaries described in the treaty itself, see p. 344. A map showing the

boundaries of Treaties 1 to 7 is to be found in George G. F. Stanley, *The Birth of Western Canada* (London, 1936), 210.

2. The topographical feature providing the eastern boundary specified in the treaty.

3. But not including the Fort Alexander band.

4. The generic designation that appears in the Treaty Books and the government documents of the period. Cf. Morris, *Treaties*, 350. Only those at Dog Head were paid in 1875, the others not being rounded up until the following year when the commissioners had some difficulty in persuading them to elect and recognize a common chief. See Morris, *Treaties*, 154 *seq.* Since that time the Indians comprising the Island bands have been subdivided into three groups.

5. The estimate given by A. L. Kroeber for the eastern sub-arctic area (Native American Population, *American Anthropologist* 36 (1934): 1–25, 5) is precisely the same. For the northern Plains a higher figure is reported, a density of 0.3+ persons per square mile calculated by Clark Wissler (*Changes in Population Profiles among the Northern Plains Indians,* Anthropological Papers, American Museum of Natural History, vol. 36, Pt. 1, 1936, 36) from Alexander Henry's [the Younger's] population data collected at the beginning of the 19th century.

6. See A. I. Hallowell, Cross-Cousin Marriage in the Lake Winnipeg Area (*Twenty-fifth Anniversary Studies*, Philadelphia Anthropological Society, 1937). [Chapter 5, this volume.]

7. See (Mrs.) F. C. Stephenson, *One Hundred Years of Canadian Methodist Missions* (2 vols., Toronto, 1925).

8. At the time the treaty was signed Morris (*Treaties*) refers to a church, school, and parsonage at The Pas (161) and similar equipment at Cumberland (163), while at Grand Rapids there was a building that served as a church and school (160–63).

9. Morris, *Treaties*, 148.

10. *Hudson's Bay, or a Missionary Tour in the Territory of the Honorable Hudson's Bay Co.* (Toronto, 1855), 80.

11. Rev. Egerton R. Young, who had been stationed at Norway House since 1868, was the first missionary. [His residence at Berens River began in spring 1874—eds.] See his *By Canoe and Dog-Train among the Cree and Salteaux Indians* (New York, 1890), 46, 252. Later, upon leaving the Berens River Mission, Rev. Young's heart rejoices at the results of his efforts "among such a wicked and degraded tribe as were these Saulteaux, so dif-

ferent from the more peaceful Crees" (265). Cf. Stephenson, *One Hundred Years*, 114, 118.

12. Some actual instances of this will be referred to later.

13. Entries in the Treaty Books under the heading "Other Relatives" have been allocated to age and sexual categories. The margin of error is small because the book containing the entries from 1879 to 1881 distinguishes male and female under "Other Relatives." This makes sex certain for these years. Both books contain notations in almost every case that indicate who the "Other relatives" are. These notes make sex differentiation possible for the years 1875–1878 and are the basis of age distinctions for the total series of years.

14. See Wissler, *Changes in Population Profiles*, 43.

15. Ibid., 38 (General Summary). In respect to the sex ratio of minors, Wissler found an approximate equality among the Cree, Assiniboine, and Blood; female minors slightly in the minority among the Blackfoot and the tribes of British Columbia (18).

16. Wissler, *The Excess of Females among the Cree Indians* (Proceedings, National Academy of Sciences, vol. 22, 51–153, 1936).

17. This latter figure would have been raised to eight percent if a man with four wives who lived up the Berens River had applied for his treaty money in 1875. As it was, he does not appear on the rolls until 1876.

18. [Ed. note: Hallowell here cites in error, E. Coues (ed.) *New Light on the Early History of the Greater North West. The Manuscript Journals of Alexander Henry and David Thompson, 1799–1814*, vol. 1, 249. The quote is from Alexander Henry [the Elder], *Travels and Adventures in Canada and the Indian Territories between the Years 1760 and 1776*, ed. James Bain (New York: Burt Franklin, 1901 [1809]), 248.]

19. John Franklin, *Narrative of a Journey to the Shores of the Polar Sea in the Years 1819, 20, 21, 22* (Philadelphia, 1824), 53.

20. R. M. Ballantyne, *Hudson's Bay* (London, 1848), 78–79.

21. A. Skinner, *Notes on the Eastern Cree and Northern Saulteaux* (Anthropological Papers, American Museum of Natural History, vol. 9, Pt 1, 1911), 57.

22. Skinner, *Notes*, 151.

23. Grant in L. R. Masson, ed., *Les Bourgeois de la Compagnie du Nord-Ouest* (2 vols., Quebec, 1889), vol. 2, 320–21.

24. [Ed. note: Alexander Henry the Elder, *Travels*, 248. See corrected citation, n. 18.]

25. T.S. Drage, *An Account of a Voyage for the Discovery of a North-West*

Passage . . . by the Clerk of the California (2 vols., London, 1748–49), vol. 1, 208.

26. Ballantyne, *Hudson's Bay*, 78–79.

27. Joseph Robson, *Account of Six Years' Residence in Hudson's Bay, 1733–36 and 1744–47* (London, 1752), 52.

28. Skinner, *Notes*, 151.

29. *Journals and Letters of Pierre Gaultier de Varennes de la Verendrye and his Sons* (Champlain Society, L. J. Burpee, ed., vol. 16, 1927), 164.

30. "Kakegameg the late chief of Lac La pluie, had not less than 5 wives" (Peter Grant in Masson, ed., *Les Bourgeois*, vol. 2, 320).

31. W. H. Keating, *Narrative of an Expedition to the Source of St. Peter's River, etc.* (2 vols., London, 1825), vol. 2, 151.

32. In Masson, ed., *Les Bourgeois*, vol. 2, 320.

33. Johann Georg Kohl, *Kitchi-Gami: Life among the Lake Superior Ojibway* (London, 1860), 111.

34. Duncan Cameron in Masson, ed., *Les Bourgeois*, vol. 2, 252.

35. *Chippewa Customs* (Bulletin, Bureau of American Ethnology, No. 86, 1929), 73.

36. Skinner, *Notes*, 151.

37. Comparisons further afield might be made. The following observations are particularly worthy of note. For the Potawatomi early in the 19th century, we have the statement of Dr. Thomas P. Hall, a surgeon in the United States Army, that "polygamy exists in proportion of 25 percent, that some men had 3, 4 or 5 wives, and one man was known to have eight." See Keating, *Narrative*, vol. 1, 92–93. K. Birket-Smith, basing his statement on quantitative information for two Caribou Eskimo groups, says that 25 percent of the men had two wives (*The Caribou Eskimo*, Report, Fifth Thule Expedition, vol. 5, pt. 1, Copenhagen, 1929), 294.

38. Early writers, of course, did not distinguish between blood sisters and classificatory sisters. When they refer to sisters we may assume that the former are meant.

39. Franklin, *Narrative*, 63.

40. Cameron in Masson, ed., *Les Bourgeois*, 252.

41. Peter Jones, *History of the Ojibway Indians* (London, 1861), 81. Cf. Kohl, *Kitchi-Gami*, 111: "Usually they take their wives from one family— frequently a whole row of sisters."

42. *Notes*, 151.

43. But I have no doubt that this information could even now [1938] be obtained locally if inquiry were made.

44. No. 1 in table 4. Only five polygynous marriages are listed in this table because information on the number of offspring in the other three cases is not full enough. Of the men in this table Nos. 2, 3, and 5 married sisters.

45. Cf., however, the statement of Sol Tax (The Social Organization of the Fox Indians, in *Social Anthropology of North American Tribes*, F. Eggan, ed., Chicago, 1937, 273–74) that in the old days the sororate was "almost compulsory."

46. Alexander Mackenzie (*Voyages from Montreal, etc. in the Years 1789 and 1793*, New York, 1803) speaking of the Cree (p. 67) says that "When a man loses his wife, it is considered as a *duty* to marry her sister if she has one" (italics ours). It will be unnecessary to go into this aspect of the sororate here, but it may be worth noting that Berens River informants took the contrary attitude. One man said that it would be better to marry them both together, otherwise it "looks as if you had been after her all along." In my genealogies there are surprisingly few cases of marriage with a deceased wife's sister.

47. E.g., Jones, *History of the Ojibway Indians*, 81.

48. R. Briffault (*The Mothers*, 3 vols., 1927, vol. 1, 626) points out in his discussion of the "reason" so often given for sororal polygyny, that "usages and customs do not generally owe their origins to the careful 'a priori' weighing of fine points of psychology," and that, by and large, there is evidence of *dissension* among sisters and *harmony* among polygynous wives who are *not* sisters.

49. See Hallowell, Cross-Cousin Marriage.

50. Drage, *Account of a Voyage*, 208.

51. Franklin, *Narrative*, 63.

52. Peter Grant in Masson, ed., *Les Bourgeois*, vol. 2, 320–21.

53. Kohl, *Kitchi-Gami*, 111.

54. Among the Berens River Saulteaux, the ca'bandawan, a rectangular structure in ground plan and prismatic in form, was the typical multiple family abode of the aboriginal regime. There was a door at either end and several fires along the central axis. A polygynous family usually occupied such a dwelling. I do not know whether this was also true of the Cree.

55. But it is worth noting that Keating, writing of the Ojibwa, says (*Narrative*, 152) that the average number of children is four; "they seldom have as many as seven, unless they have many wives."

56. Two others that appear in my genealogies probably died before 1876, and a third man, Ogáwapwan, I cannot identify in the Treaty Books. Four others in the Treaty records belonged to the Poplar River band.

57. I regret that my notes do not contain full information on the entire series.

58. Ruth Landes, The Ojibwa of Canada (in *Cooperation and Competition among Primitive Peoples*, Margaret Mead, ed., 1937), 106.

59. Atawágani·ogimakan, barter chief.

60. Local information.

61. From the native point of view this was attributable to magico-religious powers rather than to personal skill, as such. References to being a good hunter as a prerequisite to polygyny are to be found in Drage, Robson, Grant, and Ballantyne.

62. Jonathan Carver, *Travels through the Interior Parts of North America, in the Years 1766, 1767, and 1768* (London, 1778), 260.

63. A Saulteaux from Jack Head who received an annuity for one wife in 1876 and 1877, and for two wives in 1878 and three years thereafter.

64. Since I have made *married men with spouses living* the basis of enumeration, I have not counted such cases as polygynous unions. For example, the three wives and children of a deceased man of the Poplar River band (Berens River bands) drew their Treaty money in 1880 and 1881. This case was counted as a polygynous marriage from 1875 until 1879.

65. The same process had evidently begun at Moose Lake as early as 1877 for in that year three women are listed under "other relatives" along with the notation "formerly a wife." In the same year, too, the second wife of Thickfoot, leader of the Dog Head division of the Island bands, is given a separate entry with similar notation. It is interesting to note that in 1878 there is the entry that the annuity due the wife was paid to Thickfoot.

66. Young, *By Canoe and Dog-Train*, 223 *seq.*

67. At Berens River in 1873 [1874].

3

THE PATTERNING
OF EXPERIENCE
IN TIME AND SPACE

Introduction

Hallowell published the four articles in this section between the late 1930s and 1955. The first three appeared in the *American Anthropologist* in 1937, 1942, and 1949 respectively, and the first two of them (chapters 7 and 8, this volume) were reprinted in *Culture and Experience* (Hallowell, 1955). "Cultural Factors in Spatial Orientation" (chapter 10, this volume) was written specifically for *Culture and Experience*.

These articles reflect Hallowell's great interest in how people's views and concepts of space and time are suited to and reflect the cultural and material contexts and the requirements and limitations of their environments. Although in his older writings he sometimes resorted to a "modern"/"primitive" dichotomy (as in chapter 7), he was careful, here as elsewhere, to qualify his use of the latter term as not implying inferiority or lower intelligence. The differences between, for example, Western and Ojibwe temporal orientations, he emphasized, "are not functions of primitive mentality or racial makeup. They are a function of culturally constituted experience" (conclusion, chapter 7).

Near the beginning of chapter 7, Hallowell gave some insight into how he was drawn early into the mindset of the Ojibwe people around him: "From personal experience I can say that 'regression' to temporal norms less elaborate than our own is an entirely painless and not unpleasant process." On his first journey up the Berens River in July of 1932, his watch stopped, and since he had no calendar, he lost track of dates. The experience brought home "the relativity and provinciality of Western time concepts," and as he traveled upriver with his Ojibwe guides, he found it a "very simple matter to make their temporal reference points my own."

Hallowell's field diary for that journey did not mention his lack of watch or calendar. But it did show his growing interest in Ojibwe reference points both temporal and spatial. He recorded some terms for sun and stars, and also the Ojibwe names of the numerous falls and rapids encountered on the way to Little Grand Rapids, and their translations, which he later listed more completely, all the way to Pikangkum. "Cultural Factors in Spatial

Orientation" (chapter 10) discussed how the names served as landmarks and anticipatory signs or reminders of what travelers could expect to encounter as they moved—in sum, mnemonic devices. And in chapter 7, he elaborated in fine detail on Ojibwe terms for the movements of the sun, moon, and stars.

Chapter 8, "Some Psychological Aspects of Measurement among the Saulteaux," shows how Ojibwe people had their own developed techniques for assessing length, size, volume, and such in a relative way. Lacking objective measuring tools with arbitrary, abstracted units of measurement, they operated by comparing the familiar with the unfamiliar, or matching parts of the body such as feet or forearms with other entities to be measured. As for land, what mattered most for the Ojibwe were the distribution and frequency of animal and plant resources on the land (and along the waterways); the measuring of areas in abstract spatial terms was not a useful or relevant exercise. British-Canadian efforts to measure land in square miles and acres, from the Selkirk Treaty of 1817 onward, required interpretation as Hallowell pointed out in chapter 8, retelling the story of how the Ojibwe and Cree at the Selkirk Treaty were led to grasp the meaning of a two-mile-wide strip of land by scanning the distance to the horizon under the belly of a horse.

Chapter 9, "The Size of Algonkian Hunting Territories: A Function of Ecological Adjustment" (1949) has less overtly to do with measurement or spatial perceptions. Rather, it highlights the variable sizes of Northern Algonquian hunting grounds, and the variable numbers of hunters using those grounds, comparing the Berens River Ojibwe with the Ottawa of Grand Lake Victoria (Quebec). Just as Algonquians had no reason to measure off tracts of land, neither did they have motivation to hold land or enlarge their territories as such to enhance wealth or prestige. Rather, the key factors were the abundance of game (which varied spatially and over time, what with climatic, fur trade, and other pressures) and, for the Ottawa in Quebec, the incursions of white trappers in the early 1900s.

Hallowell accordingly cautioned against generalizations and assumptions, noting the need to go beyond "the bare ethnographic facts of land tenure," attending to ecological as well as cultural factors. It may be useful to read this chapter in conjunction with another, later piece not published in his lifetime, "Northern Ojibwa Ecological Adaptation and Social Organization," which appeared in 1976 in his posthumous collection of essays, *Contributions to Anthropology* (University of Chicago Press), and as chapter 4 in *The Ojibwa of Berens River, Manitoba: Ethnography into History* (Fort

Worth: Harcourt Brace Jovanovich, 1992). This text, not reprinted here, richly relates the ecological dynamics of Berens River winter hunting and summer fishing settlements to kinship patterns and behavior.

In part 3, as elsewhere, it has seemed helpful to arrange Hallowell's articles on certain themes more or less chronologically in order to provide a view of the development of his thoughts and analyses of various central topics. Here as elsewhere his earlier works were grounded in his fresh ethnographic work of the 1930s, while his later writings usually expanded his frames of reference and comparison, delved more deeply into the knowledge he gained in the field and afterwards, and presented a broader network of understanding and interpretation.

SEVEN

Temporal Orientation in Western Civilization and in a Preliterate Society

CULTURAL FACTORS IN TEMPORAL EXPERIENCE

In all human societies we find that certain classes of events have become established as formalized reference points[1] to which it is customary to relate past, present, and future occurrences, or in terms of which temporal intervals of greater or less duration may be expressed. Calendars, of course, immediately come to mind. Yet unsystematized, but no less customary, points of reference such as "a sleep"[2] are employed by many preliterate peoples as units in estimations of temporal length. Events in the life history of individuals—birth, marriage, or other significant occurrences—are constantly evoked to which other events may be related. Even in Western civilization, despite the fact that our cultural heritage provides us with the alternative of employing exact dates for all such events, similar unformalized reference points are in use.

Whether formalized or not, the characteristic reference points employed by the individuals of different human societies are relevant to a full understanding of the functioning of temporal concepts. They are basic cultural phenomena of the utmost importance in the ordering and coordination of human activities. It is impossible to picture any human society without them. In terms of individual experience, they are orientational. The individual's temporal concepts are built up in terms of them; he gets his temporal bearings by means of them, and his temporal perceptions function under their influence. It is impossible to assume that man is born with any innate "temporal sense." His temporal concepts are always culturally constituted.

Like other cultural phenomena, temporal frames of reference vary profoundly from society to society. This fact is as important psychologically as it is culturally. Thus Dagobert Fry[3] in a study of spatial and temporal concepts of the Middle Ages and the Renaissance asserts that no two peoples live conceptually in precisely the same kind of space and time. For those of us reared in contemporary Western civilization: "the dazzled but hospitable mind of twentieth-century man is offered a vast array of new discoveries, new theories, new intuitions having to do with the temporal in all its aspects, [for] not until the present era does there seem to have converged upon the problem in all its ramifications such varied and intense interest—philosophical, psychological, logical, and scientific."[4]

This paramount interest in Time is explicable on cultural-historical grounds. We moderns are habituated to a uniquely elaborated scheme of temporal norms that impinge upon our lives at every point. We not only possess a scientifically adjusted calendar, subdivided into months, weeks, days, and hours;[5] since the middle of the fourteenth century the hours of the day have been subdivided into sixty units of equal length and these units again subdivided, a development which became of more and more practical importance as clocks and watches became common.[6] By means of these devices, as well as a highly systematized calendrical scheme, individuals are enabled to maintain as exact a temporal orientation as is desired. And because it has become customary to "time" so many human activities and events with precision, a high level of *conscious* temporal orientation is inescapable. Consequently, as Parkhurst states: "That experience, that increased pervasive awareness of time as a super-sensible medium or container, as a stream, or an infinitely extended warp upon which the woof of human happenings is woven, is without question a notable characteristic of present-day consciousness."[7]

Time extends beyond the range of our personal observation and experience, or that of the life span of any one generation of human beings. Through the device of successively numbering the years that have elapsed before and since the assumed birth of Christ, it is possible to "date" events in the remote past and to conceptualize the past history of humanity in units of comparable length (years, centuries, millennia) and likewise the history of the earth and the solar system. Not only the past, the future is likewise part of the same temporal continuum. This structuralization of future time permits the exercise of foresight by individuals, or even nations, in planning and coordinating all kinds of future activities in detail, a possibility excluded for societies with time systems of a less developed order. Intervals on this time-scale can be measured and quantitatively expressed in orders of any magnitude.

This modern notion of time is also the matrix of derivative concepts that characterize Western civilization: "When one thinks of time, not as a sequence of experiences, but as a collection of hours, minutes and seconds, the habits of adding time and saving time come into existence. Time took on the character of an enclosed space: it could be divided, it could be filled up, it could even be expanded by the invention of labor-saving instruments."[8]

Time, in short, became reified to a considerable degree. It came to assume a commodity value.[9] To "waste time" is still almost a heinous sin unless confined to sacred days, holidays, vacations, or other formally defined periods.[10]

The use of a graduated scale of *small* temporal units, moreover, and the quantitative measurement of temporal intervals made other characteristic developments possible. Human activities could be accurately rated in terms of *speed*. Thus speed itself has risen into prominence as a value of Western society and functions as an important factor in the motivation of individuals. The cultural matrix, and hence the psychical relativity of speed as an incentive in behavior is not always recognized as a derivative of our own temporal concepts. Psychological tests, standardized with respect to speed in performance, have been given to native peoples without due regard for the simple fact that speed does not have the same value for them.[11] No wonder, then, that their scores rate lower than those of individuals reared in Western culture. Yet the results of such tests have been interpreted as an indication of *racial* rather than cultural differences.

In Western civilization, too, we find an approach to an apotheosis of Time typified by its elevation to a position of supreme importance in certain philosophical systems. Bergson, for example, who took issue with the Newtonian idea of time, has been celebrated as the first philosopher of our day "to take Time seriously,"[12] as one "who finds in Time conceived as *durée* [i.e., as a process, rather than as a mechanical succession of separate instants] in distinction from Time as measured by the clock, *the animating principle of the universe*."[13] Time has even been called the "Mind of Space."[14] It is hardly surprising then to find a *tour de force* written by Wyndham Lewis[15] in which he links such philosophers with Spengler and with literary figures such as Gertrude Stein and James Joyce, and characterizes them as typical representatives of a twentieth century Time Cult.

The psychological significance of time-consciousness in Western civilization also emerges with great clarity when we consider pathological cases of temporal disorientation. A person so disoriented as to be unable to give the year, month, or day of the week is almost sure to be a case of amentia, senility, or some psychotic disorder. Thus temporal orientation is of diagnostic value in mental disorders,[16] although the cultural nature and consequently the relativity of the reference points used as a standard are not always recognized as such. In other societies the disorientation of individuals would have to be judged by different temporal norms.

From personal experience I can say that "regression" to temporal norms less elaborate than our own is an entirely painless and not unpleasant process. During the summer of 1932 when I spent most of my time up the Berens River with the Pekangikum Indians, I lost track of the days of the month, since I did not have a calendar with me; the days of the week became meaningless, since, in two settlements, there were no missionaries and hence no Sunday observance or other activities that differentiated one day from another, and, as my watch stopped running, I had no way of keeping track of the hours of the day. My "disorientation," of course, was only such relative to the reference points of Western civilization to which I was habituated. Once the usual mechanical and institutional aids to these were removed, the relativity and provinciality of Western time concepts became obvious. But the significant fact is that since I remained associated with human beings it was a very simple matter to make their temporal reference points my own. My re-orientation simply involved the substitution of new, less elaborate but no less culturally determined, reference points for the old.

Ella Winter[17] gives an example of the relative ease with which it is possible to adapt oneself to a new frame of temporal reference. On her second day in Russia she was invited to a party "on the sixth." She asked what *day* of the week it was but the reply was, "I don't know. They've abolished the week and we never think about the names of days any more." The author insisted that since she was not a Russian she must know. "No American," she comments, "could forget the names of the days of the week[18] just because the Russians had introduced the five-day week and abolished Sunday." But a month later when the author was asked to tea by an American friend—"next Wednesday"—almost unthinkingly she inquired, "What date is that?" The Russians have simplified our scheme of temporal references by omitting one item.

Individuals, of course, ultimately acquire the temporal frames of reference characteristic of their society along with the rest of their cultural heritage. But this acquisition is a process, not a mechanical transference of temporal concepts from one generation to another. Binet noted this many years ago, and Sturt carried out an investigation designed to throw light upon the genetic development of some temporal concepts of children in different age groups.[19] Detailed studies of individual children, such as those made by the Sterns, and Decroly and Degand, indicate how gradually the time-concepts of Western civilization are acquired. A summary quotation based on the work of the observers mentioned illustrates this:

> Recognition that *yesterday, today*, and *tomorrow* had reference to certain days was gradually developed during the fourth year by both Hilde and Suzanne, but a clear grasp of the relationship symbolized by these terms was still confused and only *became established in the fifth year*. The correct use of *yesterday, today*, and *tomorrow* as names of days, and a fixed order of seven days making a week, involves abstract chronological schemata which first become fixed late in the pre-school period or in the early school grades. These words, to be sure, appear in the vocabulary much earlier, but they are used indiscriminately or with reference to continuous undefined past as such, continuous present, or continuous future.[20]

In some American Indian languages the terms for day-before-yesterday and day-after-tomorrow are the same.[21] It would be interesting to know how children in these societies learn to employ these words with different temporal meaning.

Once we step outside of our own society and examine the frames of reference that are relevant to the temporal orientation of other peoples, the cultural constituents of human temporal experience are thrown into even greater relief. Astronomical events, as Sherif points out, "furnish us with very convenient and stable frames of reference for a calendar. Nevertheless, we must not think that there is absolute necessity for using astronomical events as reference points for time-reckoning."[22]

Other objects, events, and activities can be and have been used. The Andamanese furnish a striking example of this: as Radcliffe-Brown writes, "In the jungles of Andamans it is possible to recognize a distinct succession of odours during a considerable part of the year as one after another the commoner trees and leaves come into flower .... The Andamanese have therefore adopted an original method of marking the different periods of the year by means of the odoriferous flowers that are in bloom at different times. Their calendar is a calendar of scents."[23]

In certain parts of the Pacific torches have been utilized as time-reckoning devices.[24] In some places market days or sacred days which occur at regular intervals have defined temporal periods similar in principle to our "week."[25] Various other human activities, the appearance of certain animals at regular seasons of the year, or meteorological changes,[26] have elsewhere been used as traditional reference points for temporal orientation. Beyond the immediate observation and experience of individuals mythology may express chronological relations between past events or even outline a definite evolutionary sequence in the development of natural objects and man.[27]

THE TEMPORAL ORIENTATION OF THE SAULTEAUX

In what follows it is my purpose to examine in some detail the cultural constituents of temporal orientation among the Berens River Saulteaux.

Movements of the Sun

According to Saulteaux belief the earth is flat and each day the sun travels from east to west above it. This is the period of daylight constituting a temporal unit for which the native term is *pezagógījik*, "one day." When the sun disappears behind the western edge of the earth, it travels eastward beneath the land, to reappear at dawn. It is during this part of the sun's journey that darkness reigns. This period is recognized as another temporal unit, *pezagwátabik*, "one night."

Strictly speaking, there are no standardized *durational* units of these alternating periods of light and darkness which, at the latitude 52° N., vary greatly in length at different seasons of the year. For the period of daylight a succession of discrete moments is recognized. These are crystallized in more or less standardized phrases that indicate the position of the sun,[28] or refer to the relation of its light to discernible objects. At the beginning of the day some very fine distinctions are drawn. The intervals between the discrete points recognized vary enormously in temporal length as measured on our absolute time scale. But this is irrelevant to the Saulteaux and, of course, it is possible to employ the intervals between any two of the points recognized as a crude measure of temporal length.

When streaks of light, distinguishable in the east, announce the first signs of coming day, although darkness still reigns on the earth, this is *pītában*, "dawn." When darkness is dispelled so that one can discern terrestrial objects at some distance, but the sun has not yet risen above the treetops, it is *tcībwaságàtik*, "before coming out from the trees (the sun)" Soon the light from the rising sun reddens the treetops. This point of time in the new day is called *miskwanagáte*, "red shining (reflected) light." In addition, there are two other expressions that refer to the position of the sun before it emerges into full view. One of these connotes the point in time when the sun is still behind the treetops, literally, "beneath trees when hangs (the) sun," *änämatikèpī ágotcing gizis;* the other, when it reaches the tops of the trees, "tops of trees when hangs (the) sun," *ékwanákak épī ` ágotcinggizis.*

Once above the trees but still low enough in the eastern sky for its position to be judged with reference to them, there are two further expressions used that involve rudimentary units of *spatial* measurement. The first refers to the fact that the sun "hangs" in the sky "the breadth of my hand" above the trees, *nīoníndjépī ` tagotcing.* The second, that it hangs *pezagwákwagan èpīápi ` tagotcing,* a thumb-middle-finger-stretch above the treetops, a distance of about twice that of a hand-breadth.

The position of the sun in the sky during the remainder of the day is differentiated with respect to much larger temporal intervals and in a less refined fashion. The following expressions are used: *eànīkketcī skīobakwit,* "as high as it goes up"; *eàptagīzigak,* "half-day (midday)"; *eàptawīnazit,* "half-way to setting"; *pangīciman gīzis,* "falling (out of sight) (the) sun" [sunset]; *poni ` animīgījigan,* "disappearing underneath day." The last term applies when a band of light still rims the horizon, after the sun itself has disappeared. For dusk, which in summer is especially prolonged at this latitude, the term *nänītaga* is used.

Movements of the Stars

While the Saulteaux do not have a highly elaborated star-lore they have names for a number of the constellations and they have observed the movements of these during the night. The appearance of the morning star, *wábanänang,* is also noticed. They know Polaris and they have noticed the rotation of the circumpolar stars, particularly Ursa Major, which they call *k` tcīotcīganang,* Great Fisher. They have also observed that from December to May the Belt of Orion (*odádawaämok,* three young men) comes up from the horizon, mounts in the sky and disappears before dawn. From the position of the former constellation in summer and the latter in winter a rough temporal orientation is obtained, but the only term that I know of which expresses any particular point during the night is *kegáeapi ` tatabíkak,* "nearly half (the) night" [midnight]. Night, therefore, lacks the *formalized* points of reference established for the daylight period,[29] but direct observation of stellar movements makes possible unformalized nocturnal orientation.

Night and day, then, are distinct temporal units,[30] formally subdivided by traditionally established discrete points of reference, but not reckoned in standardized units of duration. "Nights" or "sleeps," rather than days, are customarily used as measures of temporal length and of *distance.* A man leaving camp will tell his wife that he will return after a certain number of "sleeps" or he may express the distance to a certain point in terms of "sleeps" or "nights." This rendering of distance in temporal units reminds us of the astronomer who finds it convenient to make the vast distances beyond experience intelligible by translating them into the language of time, i.e., light-years.

Timed Daily Activities and Special Events

It seems likely that sleep has proved a convenient point of reference because of its periodic and regular recurrence. In summer, the camps quiet down at dusk, unless there is some unusual event in progress, and the relatively short period of darkness is equivalent to the period of sleep. If any of the women or girls have been visiting, one sees them making for their own dwellings as darkness approaches and the men and boys soon follow them. This pattern of returning to one's own camp before nightfall is so well established even among the Indians at the mouth of the river that, on several occasions, the family with whom I lived thought that I must be lost in the bush when I did not show up at the expected time. In winter, of course, different conditions prevail. The men are out on their trap lines or hunting long before daybreak and often do not return until after darkness has fallen.

In Western urban culture, eating at regular intervals has come to be an established pattern that in itself provides unformalized reference points in our temporal orientation. Being hunters and fishermen, the sources of food supply among the Saulteaux are precarious and meals are irregular. Hence eating cannot function, like sleeping, as a relatively stable reference point in daily activities. Since my own day in the field was organized on a routine three-meal basis, I sometimes arranged to have one informant come to my tent in the "morning" and another in the "afternoon." But it happened more than once that an informant would come so late in the morning that it was almost time for the noon meal, and on one occasion the man expected in the afternoon showed up a few minutes after the one scheduled for the morning session arrived. Neither informant, of course, had any sense of being "late" or "early," and I could not have said to either one, "come to see me as soon as you have eaten." The lack of common reference points made it difficult to coordinate our activities efficiently.

Since almost all the Indians in the upriver settlements set their nets at night and lift them in the morning, what I did say to the informants expected in the forenoon was, "Come over as soon as you have lifted your nets."

On the whole, however, there are no set times for daily activities. Their rhythm is elastic in the extreme and except when motivated by hunger or necessity they are dictated to a large degree by external circumstances and by whim.

With respect to such activities as conjuring, dances, and ceremonies, however, there is a definite temporal patterning. Conjuring, for example, is always done after dark. The Wabanówīwin, too, was formerly held at night but nowadays it takes place only during the day. As soon as night falls the dancing stops, to begin again the following morning. The giveaway dance (*mändáitīwin*), no longer performed, was also held at night. Today the only dance held after dark is the *potáte*; it is the most purely social affair that the Indians up the river have. The Midéwi·win was the ceremony with the most exactly defined temporal limits. The lodge was entered at sunrise as a song with the words, "the one that's going to rise, I'll travel with him," was chanted. And it closed at sunset with a salute to the sun.

The day set for the Midéwi·win was, of course, decided beforehand by the leader and word sent to his assistants. This likewise occurs today in the case of the Wabanówīwin, which may be held on one to four successive "days." But the time of day when it starts is not set. When the leader is ready he starts to sing and drum. Those wishing to attend come whenever they are inclined. Even the singers that the leader has asked to help him do not all come at once. They dribble in one by one. If the leader has begun in the morning all of them may not have arrived until afternoon.

In the case of the *potáte* dance, which is "owned" by several different men of the [Little] Grand Rapids settlement, and may be started by any one of them with the help of four singer-drummers, the signal for attendance is the drumming itself, begun at dusk. The songs are recognized and so everyone knows what is going on. If only a few people come the dance may cease. I was present once when this occurred.

Acculturation of Timepieces, Named Days, and the Week

Contact with traders for a hundred years and the advent of missionaries at the mouth of the river in 1873 have been the chief sources of profound changes in certain aspects of the life of the Berens River Indians. But so far as time reckoning is concerned these influences have had little effect on daily life, except at the mouth of the river. On the reserve in this locality, e.g., there are both Protestant and Catholic missions, both of which include day schools in their program. The bell of the Catholic mission rings regularly at six a.m., noon, and six p.m., so that the Indians have come to recognize these hours as punctuating certain divisions of the day. School bells also summon the children to their lessons and adults to church services on Sunday. (But Mr. C. D. Street, the Protestant schoolmaster, told me that even in the coldest weather a dozen or more pupils are on hand an hour before school starts. They are not guided by the bell, or by time-pieces, but set out for school as soon as they have had breakfast.) A similar situation obtains, however, in only one of the five settlements up the river. There are no other occasions when the collective attendance of any group of individuals is demanded at a certain hour. For, as we have already pointed out, the attendance at native ceremonies is much more flexible in this regard.

While clocks are not a novelty at the mouth of the river, where the children are taught to tell time in school, by no means every household owns one, and up the river I remember seeing only two or three. At Lake Pekangikum one family had recently purchased an alarm clock, the deferred ting-a-ling of which seemed to fascinate them, rather than its utility as a time-reckoning mechanism. There are perhaps a dozen men at the mouth of the river who own watches. But they seldom carry them about, to say nothing of using them in the regulation of daily activities. I remember, too, the pride with which a young fellow of the pagan Duck Lake settlement showed me his recently-acquired gold-filled watch that contrasted more than favorably with my Ingersoll. And in 1936 I found that a young girl [Shabwan] at [Little] Grand Rapids had acquired a wrist watch. The chief of the Berens River Band [William Berens], however, constantly carries a watch and frequently consults it.

In the aboriginal cultural pattern, "days" and "nights" are not grouped in any temporal unit of a higher order. There is no "week." Nor are there any named "days," although there are special terms for yesterday, day before yesterday, tomorrow, and day after tomorrow. Under missionary influence, however, the emphasis upon the Sabbath as a day of rest and religious ob-servance (*aiyamayegījigan*, praying day) made it necessary to instruct the Indians in the calculation of its periodic recurrence. Consequently, the week is now recognized as a unit of time among the Christianized natives and there is a term for it. It is interesting to observe, however, that this temporal unit was assimilated as part of a new *religious* orientation, rather than as a secular temporal concept as such. Sabbath observance is such a tangible and fundamental tenet of Protestant Christianity that it was one of the first things taught to the Indians by the missionaries. Egerton R. Young, the first resident missionary on the Berens River, tells of a visit he once received in the summer from an Indian woman who lived some distance inland. She had heard of the "Great Book" and had come for information.

"Before she left," says Rev. Young,[31] "I gave her a sheet of foolscap paper, and a long lead pencil, and showed her how to keep her reckoning as to the Sabbath day. I had, among many other lessons, described the Sabbath as one day in seven for rest and worship; and she had become very much interested and promised to try to keep it." The following winter he visited the woman's camp. During the course of a meal which he took in her wigwam, the old woman, "inserting one of her greasy hands in the bosom of her dress . . . pulled out a large piece of soiled paper, and unfolding it before me, she began in excited tones to tell me how she had kept the tally of the 'praying days,' for thus they style the Sabbath. . . . Imagine my great delight to find that through the long months which had passed since I had given her that paper and pencil, she had not once missed her record. This day was Thursday, and thus she had marked it. Her plan had been to make six short marks, and then a longer one for Sunday. 'Missionary [she said], sometimes it seemed as though I would fail. There were many times when the ducks or geese came very near, and I felt like taking my gun and firing. Then I remembered that it was the praying day, and so I only put down the long mark and rested. I have not set a net, or caught a fish, or fired a gun, on the praying day since I heard about it at your house so far away.'" [Nowadays nets are lifted if people are short of food; otherwise not.]

An Indian family I once visited in the Pauingessi settlement was keeping a similar record of the days of the week and their account was likewise accurate. But I fear that I did not exhibit the enthusiasm of Reverend Young when I verified it for them. Today, no one ever sets out on a journey from the mouth of the river on Sunday and even the Christian Indians at [Little] Grand Rapids have become so completely acculturated to this periodic holy day that on one occasion when a gold strike was reported nearby, and on a Sunday the missionary made a visit to the spot to look it over with a view to staking a claim, he was subjected to open criticism on this account.

The spread of Christianity, then, has been responsible for creating the basis for a new temporal unit in the minds of the Indians. But even so the concept of the week as such does not seem to function very significantly in their life and thought. It is the periodicity of the Sabbath, signalized by going to church and abstaining from certain secular activities, that is the important reference point in their lives.

Following the establishment of this reference point, the day-naming pattern, with which we are so familiar, developed. But the Indians did not attempt a rendering of English names for the days of the week. Consequently their series of names has a quality all its own. Monday is literally "cease praying day" (*pónīaiyàmayegíjigan*), Tuesday is two days "after" (*nijogíjigan*), Wednesday is "half (week) gone" (*api'taúwase*), Thursday, the "great half gone" (*k`tcíapi`taúwase*), Friday, "approaching day" (*enīogijigan*), and Saturday, *pakwéjigangíjigan*, "flour (bread) day." This last designation, so I was told, arose from the fact that it was the custom of the Hudson's Bay Company to pay their employees in kind on Saturday.

These terms have been in use at least fifty years at the mouth of the river. At [Little] Grand Rapids they are known but not commonly used. Farther up the river, especially in the pagan settlements where Sunday is not observed, they would, of course, have no meaning.

It seems to me that one can observe in the naming process that has accompanied the acculturation of new features, the fundamental pattern of native temporal orientation. I refer to the emphasis upon particular concrete events as basic reference points. Thus Sunday becomes characterized as "praying day" and Saturday as "ration day," while the other days relative to these are neutral in character, because they are signalized by no outstanding events. But the whole psychological focus of the day names is obviously Sunday. A religious event colors the whole series, with the exception of Saturday, in which case an event of economic importance overshadows it.

The same underlying principle is reflected in the native nomenclature of the next highest order of temporal unit—the "moon."

Lunar Changes

As in the case of the day, a "moon" is not a division of continuous time, it is a recurring event. The period when the moon is visible, and its changing appearance as it waxes and wanes is a "moon." Twelve named lunations form a loosely coordinated succession with which no day count is integrated. The moons are differentiated by names which refer to such non-celestial phenomena as the appearance in the country of certain birds, the condition of plant life, the rutting of animals, human economic activities, etc. These are all seasonal periodicities, subject to considerable variation, that are loosely coordinated with particular lunations. There is an interesting episode in one of the myths in which an attempt to identify a moon by trying to catch sight of an eagle beguiles an old cannibal to his death. The latter is asked what moon it is and replies, "Midwinter moon." "No, you're wrong. This is Eagle Moon. Look! There is an eagle now passing behind you." (Eagle Moon is the one following Midwinter Moon.) When the old man turned to look, his throat was cut and his murderer remarks, "Did you expect to see an eagle at this season?"[32]

This episode reflects both the chronological uncertainty connected with the aboriginal lunar calendar and the court of appeal in case of doubt. Since in any solar year there are more than twelve and less than thirteen lunations, a seasonal dislocation arises which the Saulteaux correct by adding an unnamed moon to the series.[33]

Thus the lunar calendar itself is intrinsically flexible because its real emphasis is less upon the successive waxing and waning of the moon, than upon non-celestial phenomena. The succession of events of the latter class provides the real temporal guide. But the correlation of non-celestial phenomena with lunar periodicities by means of a conventional nomenclature defines *limits* of elastic, yet standardized, divisions of time which the mere observation of the arrival of different species of birds in the spring, the ripening of berries, etc., would not in themselves be sufficient to establish.

Although a nuclear group of characteristic names for the lunations seems to typify the Ojibwa-speaking peoples, the other names employed show considerable variation.[34] The calendrical nomenclature, as might be expected, is closely connected with local conditions and varies accordingly. Of the nuclear group of names, one referring to the appearance of vegetation, usually the blossoming of flowers, is always to be found, one or more that have reference to the ripening or gathering of berries, others that indicate the appearance of certain birds, especially the wild goose, etc. On the Berens River, for example, three lunations are named for birds which make their local appearance at that time of year. Roughly, these lunations correspond to our months of March (*migazīwīgīzis*, Eagle Moon), April (*ni`kīgīzis*, Goose Moon), and May (*mángogīzis*, Loon Moon). The periodic reappearance of the geese in April is attested by the records kept for a series of years by the Natural History Society of Manitoba.[35] They usually appear during the first week of this month and are to be seen only until the second week in May. They do not reappear until August, after which they are seen no more until the following April.

Most of the moon names, as might be expected, are identical among all the Berens River bands. But it is noteworthy that not all of them are. The following differ. For the sake of convenience they have been correlated with our series of month names to which they roughly correspond. The letters in parentheses preceding each native name indicates the band in which its use is found: B.R., Berens River Band; G.R., [Little] Grand Rapids Band; P., Pekangikum Band). January: (B.R.) *kictcopabīwatakinam;* (G.R.) *kagīnwasīgetgīzis,* Long Moon; February: (B.R.) *api`tapībungīzis,* Half-winter Moon; (P.) *kījégīzis,* Kind Moon (so-called because the winter is beginning to moderate); July: (B.R.) *ati`ktemini`kawīgīzis,* Ripe-berries-gathering Moon; (G.R.) *wabagwanīwīgīzis,* Blossom Moon; September: (B.R.) *mänómini`kawīgīzis,* Wild-rice-gathering Moon; (P.) *ämanozówīgīzis,* Rutting Moon; December: (B.R.) *opa`piwatcagenazis;* (G.R.) *pitcībabunwīgīzis,* Early Winter Moon.

It will be noted that although different names are used, the terms for both July moons refer to the condition of plant life which is likewise reflected in the name for the June moon (*sagībagauwīgīzis,* Leaves-coming-forth Moon). The reappearance of vegetation at this season of the year after the disappearance of snow and ice transforms the external aspects of the country so radically that it would seem to be an almost inescapable standard of reference in any scheme of temporal divisions based on the general pattern characteristic of the Saulteaux. July marks the peak of vegetation development.

On the other hand, there are marked local variations in the occurrence of wild rice in sufficient quantities to make it worth harvesting.[36] This is the explanation of the difference in nomenclature for the September moon at the mouth of the river and at [Little] Grand Rapids, as compared with Pekangikum. Within the habitat of the latter band wild rice is so scarce that it is never harvested. Hence, one would hardly expect to find it in their calendrical scheme since, as I have pointed out, the nomenclature of the lunations is intrinsically elastic, and likewise pragmatic. It may also be remarked in passing that there are no sugar maples in this country so that, as compared with other Ojibwa peoples in whose calendar a "sugar-making moon" is found, the Berens River Saulteaux lack a lunation of this name.

Ceremonies are not standardized with respect to performance in particular moons and while some individuals know the moon in which they were born, others do not. At the mouth of the river English month names are known and utilized to some extent so that the aboriginal calendar, as such, is being supplanted. Children in school are taught the English names of the months. Mr. Street said: "They always prize a calendar and follow it studiously at home. Some homes use our names altogether; others never."

Within each lunation discrete points are recognized, but these are not conceptualized as periods of temporal duration. In principle they parallel the points recognized in the changing position of the sun during the course of the day. But in the case of the moon, reference is made to differences in its size as it waxes and wanes. The following terminology is employed: *eoskagotcing,* newly hanging; *eanimitcapikizazit,* bigger; *eàptawàbkizit,* half; *kegáewáwīezit,* nearly round; *èwáwīezit,* round; *epákwezit,* going; *eáptawàbkizit,* half (-gone); *eagasabikizit,* getting small; *emetasīget,* it is going.

Seasonal Changes

Observable changes in temperature, vegetation, and other natural phenomena define the seasons for the Saulteaux. Six are recognized. The names of these differ from those of the lunations in being nondescriptive terms. The Indians cannot translate them. But chosen natural phenomena define the limits of each season quite specifically and no intercalation is ever necessary. It is recognized, too, that the moons fall into seasonal units. This is quite possibly the chief conceptual mechanism by means of which they are kept adjusted to the solar year.

The passing of winter, for example, is signalized by the appearance of the migratory birds, the first of which are seen in March. Now the moons that correspond to our months of March, April, and May are those with bird names and these three lunations together constitute the season called *äsígwan,* the spring season of the Saulteaux. The following season, *nībín,* equivalent to our summer, does not begin until the ice has completely disappeared from the lakes and rivers and there is no more snow to be seen on the ground. Since slightly over one inch of snow is to be expected at this latitude in May, *nībín* normally begins in June and continues through August and into early September. It is significant that the June lunation, the first moon of the summer season, bears a name that refers to the reappearance of leaves on the deciduous trees and that up the river July is called the "moon of blossoms." It is in this latter month that the highest mean annual temperature occurs.

The next season recognized, *tagwágin,* begins when the leaves of the poplars and birches start to fall. It is a short season, never longer than a "moon." It is immediately followed by another short but named interval, *pīgī `kánaan,* defined by the fact that, although the trees have lost their leaves, the winter has not yet set in. This is also the period of so-called "Indian summer" after which "freeze up" occurs and the first heavy snows of the winter are due. These normally do not occur until November, the term for which, "freezing moon," indicates that the winter, *bībún,* has actually set in, to continue through three additional moons. Two sub-season winter units comprising two moons each are named. The first part of the winter season is called *askībibun,* "new, fresh, winter"; the latter and most severe half, when the temperature drops the lowest, is called *megwábībun.*

Ceremonies like the Midéwi·win, the Wabanówīwin, the "give-away" dance, etc., were always held during the summer season. This was the period when the Indians congregated in their summer fishing settlements. With the falling of the leaves began the dispersal to their hunting grounds.

Seasonal names occur in the mythology and, in the myth accounting for the origin of summer, it is explained how it came about that winter was reduced to only five moons (*sic*) in length. In one myth, too, the *passage of time* is conveyed not with reference to nights or moons but in terms of seasonal change. Miki·nă 'k (the Great Turtle) chases a moose and, although there is snow on the ground when he starts the pursuit, he does not catch up with the animal until open water. Length of time is of importance in this story because it is one of the contributing factors to the humor of the tale.

In conversation that has reference to past events, seasonal names, too, appear to be more frequently employed than "moon" names. Although less exact, these larger units are sufficiently precise and they function in much the same way among ourselves. Despite the instrumental value of our exact time scale, for certain purposes constant references to month, day, and hour of past events would appear pedantic even in our society.

Annual Cycle

As Cope, speaking of the Indians in general, says,[37] "the year may be regarded as the *interval* between recurrent events, since no attempt is made to compute its length in days,[38] and since the number of moons is somewhat uncertain in the native mind."

In native Saulteaux thought the concept of such an interval, reckoned with reference to the recurrence of winter, but not conceived as the sum of a series of smaller divisions of time, is undoubtedly present. But this concept is by no means identical with our concept of the year as a temporal unit of continuous duration reducible to smaller measurable units which we conceive to have a precise beginning and ending reckoned from the stroke of midnight on December thirty-first. When asked to name the "moons," for example, the Saulteaux will begin almost anywhere in the series but usually with the current "moon." Consequently the question whether the Indians, in the absence of such a concept of temporal continuity, actually reckon a beginning or ending of their annual cycle is irrelevant.[39] What is significant is whether some recurring solar event, like a solstice or some terrestrial occurrence, is traditionally recognized as a discrete point of reference with respect to some temporal interval that is of a higher order of magnitude than the lunation or the season. Such an interval was an integral part of the temporal concepts of the native Saulteaux but was of little practical importance. Yet its recognition explains why at present the Indians often employ the term "winter" in reckoning their ages or to place events in a supra-annual time scale. "Winter," as a recurrent annual event can be used to symbolize a "year," if reckoning in such terms becomes of interest. And if one wishes to say, as Cope does in interpreting the calendrical schemes of other northern peoples, that winter signalizes the "beginning" of the "year," such a statement is also intelligible since it is the recurrence of this season that has received formal emphasis with reference to an annual cycle.

Today the Saulteaux of the Berens River Band proper are familiar, as I have said, with the white man's mode of temporal reckoning. And they use the term *pezigoa`ki*, "one earth," for one year. But I think this is a new term, a judgment that receives correlary support from the fact that Baraga [*A Dictionary of the Ojibway Language*] makes "year" and "winter" synonyms.

Although winter is the formalized reference for computing yearly intervals in the aboriginal conceptual scheme, the recurrence of the other seasons provides unformalized points of reference that punctuate equivalent intervals. And among human activities the annual performance of the Midéwi·win was once prominent. Today, the payment of annuities each year by the Dominion Government is another regular occurrence and at the mouth of the river the Indians know that there are legal holidays, like Dominion Day and Labor Day, that recur annually.

Reckoning of Past Events

The recognition of a yearly interval by no means implies that the year as a temporal unit functions very actively in native life and thought. In terms of aboriginal life, in fact, there was little, if anything, that demanded calculation in annual units of time. Consequently I believe that Cope rightly emphasizes the fact that

> although it is often loosely stated the Indian could tell his age by the expression "so many winters had passed over his head," or that he was so many winters old, this expression is no doubt developed through contact with civilized peoples. The expression more in keeping with the Indian calendric systems is that found in so many tribes: "I was so

large when a certain event happened." This event may be a year of famine, a year of some epidemic, the growth of a particular tree or grove, or some remarkable exploit . . . .Such vague statements or references as these are probably as near as the Indian, of himself, ever came to considering his age.[40]

Among the Saulteaux, so far as age is concerned, instead of a chronological year count, the life cycle of individuals was divided into a number of terminologically distinguished age grades corresponding to maturation stages. The generic term for child, *apīnondjī,* includes the viable fetus within its connotation, while the infant from birth until it begins to walk is called *ockapīnondjī,* fresh (new, young) child. Sexual differentiation is expressed in the terms *i`kwézes,* little girl, and *kwīwīzes,* little boy, applied to children under puberty. The next age-grade terminologically recognized is what may be called youth. After puberty and before marriage a male is *ockīnīge* and a female *ockinīgi`kwe.* For mature individuals there are only terms for married man, *onabemīmä,* and married woman, *wīwīmän.* Bachelors and spinsters are rare and it is interesting to note that the words used for such unmarried individuals are the youth terms with a prefix, *keté-,* meaning "old" (*ketéockīnīga,* "old young man," and *ketéockīnīkwe,* "old young woman") a kind of temporal paradox. For succeeding periods of maturation there are no terms with a chronological connotation used until old age is reached (*mintímoye,* "old woman," *ákīwezi,* "old man"). To indicate extreme old age the augmentative prefix *k'tchi-* may be added to these terms.

Such terms, correlated with references to occurrences extrinsic to the individual, such as the signing of the Treaty, the advent of the missionaries in different settlements, the tenure of Hudson's Bay Company post managers, and the Great War (because several Berens River Indians enlisted) or events in the life history of individuals—marriage, journeys, former hunting grounds, customary camping sites—are sufficiently exact, though unformalized, points of reference for purposes of native temporal orientation. They occur again and again in conversation and in the personal reminiscences I have collected. It is in the use of such unformalized reference points that the Saulteaux are most like ourselves,[41] the difference being, of course, that they lack the more exact frame of temporal reference that we possess which permits time measurement in precisely defined units and temporal comparisons of a more accurate order.

Events in the past are also frequently correlated with the life-span of certain deceased relatives of the living or other deceased persons. So long as the names, personal characteristics, and activities of deceased individuals are carried in the memories of living persons a useful, although non-quantitative and unformalized, frame of reference for past events is maintained. The collection of extensive genealogical information has convinced me of the accuracy of the knowledge that is the basis of this human frame of reference. Through the assimilation of a considerable portion of it myself, I found that I was able to use the information acquired in relation to the temporal sequence of certain events much as the Indians themselves do. But in quantitative temporal terms retrospective genealogical information of this sort completely fades out in less than two centuries. One hundred and fifty years is the outside limit of any genuine historic past so far as the Berens River Indians are concerned. Events attributed to so distant a past that they cannot be connected with any known generation of human individuals are simply described as having taken place "long ago." Consequently we are plunged into a bottomless mythological epoch that lacks temporal guideposts of any conventional sort. As a matter of fact, it would be more accurate to assert that once we enter the mythological world of Saulteaux belief, temporal concepts actually lose most, if not all, chronological significance.

One of the reasons for this is the fact that the most prominent anthropomorphic characters of mythology like Wísakedják and Tcakabec are not only living beings, they are conceived as immortal. They were alive when the earth was young and they assisted the Indians then. They are still alive today and continue to aid mankind, this latter fact receiving empirical demonstration in dreams and by the manifestation of the presence of such beings in the conjuring lodge. The conventional pattern of dream revelation and the conjuring lodge are, then, institutional means of keeping mythological beings and spiritual entities of other classes constantly contemporary with each new generation of individuals, despite the passage of "time." Such spiritual entities, in fact, are actually more "real" than distant human ancestors no longer remembered. Mythology itself sometimes reflects this emphasis on the contemporaneity of such beings by incorporating episodes with modern trimmings in narratives that contain nuclear elements not only found among the Saulteaux but over wide areas in North America.

It is true, nevertheless, that certain episodes in the mythological narratives provide a basis for certain broad temporal inferences. And independently of immediate mythological references, I found that the Indians entertain similar chronological notions. It is noteworthy, for example, that in many of the mythological narratives, the form of the name given to familiar animals contains the augmentative prefix. There are references to the Great Snake, the Great Mosquito, the Great Beaver, the Great Trout, etc. This has a temporal significance. Formerly the earth was inhabited by many of these monster species now only represented by smaller varieties of their kind. In the myths there are likewise accounts of how certain of these great animals became extinct (the Great Mosquito) or how the familiar variety of the species came into being (as, e.g., small snakes).[42] It was explained to me that the mythological characters had power enough to overcome the monster fauna but that ordinary human beings would be constantly harassed if they had to live on the earth with such creatures today. Nevertheless, a few such species still survive according to the firm conviction of the Indians. There are Indians now living, in fact, who have seen them. But the events in the myths which involve the monster animals are conceptualized as occurring in a far-distant past. They took place "long ago" in a period when the earth was "new." Consequently a temporal distinction is recognized between those days and the present.

Another temporal clue is afforded by the transformation in the appearance of certain animals by Wísakedják. The latter made the kingfisher much prettier than he once was, shortened the tail of the muskrat, gave the weasel a white coat in winter, etc.[43] Here again a temporal inference lies in the fact there was once an epoch far distant in the past when the familiar animals of today had not assumed their contemporary characteristics.

Human beings, too, were not always like they are now, either in appearance or knowledge. Until Tcakabec, after being in the belly of a fish, was scraped clean by his sister, all human beings were covered with hair.[44] All women once had toothed vaginas. And until Wísakedják by accident discovered the pleasure of sexual intercourse no one knew about it.[45]

The myth of the theft of summer likewise contains the assertion that at one time winter lasted all the year round.

The flood episode in one of the narratives of the Wísakedják cycle also has chronological implications since Wisakedjak and the animals previously inhabited an earlier land mass.[46] But the Indians themselves do not appear to follow through such temporal implications with reference to their mythological corpus as a whole. I found that they were not willing to commit themselves to any chronological relationship of the "flood," for example, and the adventures of Tcakabec, although they agreed to the obvious fact that the birth of the winds must have preceded the contest between the North and South Wind that appears in another myth.[47] As a rule, however, the temporal sequence intrinsic to the events of each narrative is accepted without reference to the temporal sequences of any other narrative. Even the narratives of the Wísakedják cycle are not systematized chronologically. But I have received the impression that the narratives with anthropomorphic heroes like Kaiánwe and Aásī are conceptualized as occurring on the earth in the post-fluvial epoch.[48]

On the whole, then, events that are believed to have taken place "long ago" are not systematically correlated with each other in any well-defined temporal schema. They are discrete happenings, often unconnected and sometimes contradictory. Yet the past and the present are part of a whole because they are bound together by the persistence and contemporary reality of mythological characters not even now grown old.

CONCLUSION

For the Saulteaux, as we have seen, temporal orientation depends upon the recurrence and succession of concrete events in their qualitative aspects— events, moreover, which are indications, preparatory symbols and guides for those extremely vital activities through which the Saulteaux obtain a living from the country which they inhabit.

Durations, too, are interwoven with, and experienced as, events in all their individuality. Night is darkness, the stars and their movements, sleep, quietness. Day is the light, the journey of the sun across the sky, the round of domestic duties. A "moon" is the waxing and waning of the moon which occurs when, for instance, the wild rice is being gathered, when activities spanning a number of days are pursued. Any comparison of such durations must be by metaphors and not by exact measures.

Ideas of speed and magnitude necessarily belong to the same category. The Saulteaux are confined to gross time estimates and relatively simple qualitative judgments about speed based upon the observation and comparison of objects in their immediate environment. It would be impossible for them to measure the rate of moving objects at all. Any idea of length of time must be confined to extremely narrow limits. Just as they will reply to the query: "How many children have you?" by naming them, a direct request for the number of "moons" will result in the naming of them one after another. An answer to: "How long ago?" becomes: When I was a child; when my father was young, and so on.

All these means of temporal orientation are *local*, limited in their application to the immediate future, the recent past, immediate activities, phenomena known and dealt with in their own environment. Beyond these all is vague and loosely coordinated temporally.

In Western civilization similar, undifferentiated experience of time remains, but it is also transcended by abstract quantitative measures which enable us to think far differently about it. We can think in terms of abstract units of temporal duration: of a day in terms of hours, detached from the phenomena themselves, or of a month as a variable unit of time made up of a certain number of days.

Time conceived in this abstract fashion, in continuous and quantitatively defined units, is the basis of an intellectual order of temporal concepts available for use as a standard of reference, or measurement, for all classes of events. Time assumes for us an autonomous character and we are free to manipulate temporal concepts instrumentally, without constant reference to specific events. Thus we can think of it as infinitely divisible, a means for coordinating activities of all sorts with great precision. It likewise makes possible the measurement of exact temporal intervals and the rate and speed of moving objects.

These contrasting differences in the temporal orientation of Saulteaux culture and of Western civilization undoubtedly imply profound differences in the psychological outlook which is constituted by them. Such differences are not functions of primitive mentality or racial makeup. They are a function of culturally constituted experience. In these terms our temporal orientation in Western civilization is likewise a function of experience in a cultural tradition with radically distinct patterns and entirely different historical roots.

Notes

Published in *American Anthropologist* 39 (1937): 647–70. Reprinted in Hallowell, *Culture and Experience* (Philadelphia: University of Pennsylvania Press, 1955), 216–35.

1. See M. Sherif, *The Psychology of Social Norms* (New York, 1936), Chap. 3.

2. Cf. M. P. Nilsson, *Primitive Time-Reckoning* (Lund, 1920), 15.

3. Fry, *Gotik und Renaissance als Grundlagen der Modernen Weltanschauung* (Augsburg, 1929).

4. Helen Huss Parkhurst, "The Cult of Chronology," *Essays in Honor of John Dewey* (New York, 1929), 293.

5. Despite the solar basis of our calendar, however, the temporal divisions of the day as conventionally adjusted in terms of Standard Time, adopted by U.S. railroads in 1875 (see Lewis Mumford, *Technics and Civilization*,

New York, 1934, 198) and Daylight Saving Time transcend "sun-time" and symbolize the importance of the cultural factor in our temporal frame of reference.

6. Mumford, *Technics*, 16. This author maintains (14 ff.) that "the clock, not the steam engine, is the key-machine of the modern industrial age." For an historical resume of time-keeping devices, see A. P. Usher, A *History of Mechanical Inventions* (New York, 1929), Chaps. 6, 10, and Bibliography, 379–80.

7. Parkhurst, "The Cult," 293.

8. Mumford, *Technics*, 17.

9. Mumford, *Technics*, 270. "Under capitalism time-keeping is not merely a means of coordinating and inter-relating complicated functions; it is also like money, an independent commodity with a value of its own."

10. Those "masters of regimentation," as Mumford (42) calls the new bourgeoisie of the seventeenth century, "reduced life to a careful, uninterrupted routine: so long for business; so long for dinner; so long for pleasure—all carefully measured out, as methodical as the sexual intercourse of Tristram Shandy's father, which coincided, symbolically, with the monthly winding of the clock. Timed payments; timed contracts; timed work; timed meals; from this period on nothing was quite free from the stamp of the calendar or the clock. Waste of time became for Protestant religious preachers, like Richard Baxter, one of the most heinous sins. To spend time in mere sociability, or even in sleep, was reprehensible."

11. Cf. O. Klineberg, *Race Differences* (New York, 1935), 159–61. This author points out that "the large majority of tests of intelligence depend at least to some extent upon speed." He also stresses the fact that "indifference to speed is cultural and not innate," a conclusion that is supported on the one hand by the absence of any "physiological basis for a racial difference in speed of reaction" and on the other by the fact that "American Indian children who have lived a long time among Whites or who attend a busy and progressive school show a definite tendency to approximate White behavior in this respect."

12. S. Alexander, *Space, Time and Deity* (London, 1927), vol. 1, 44.

13. Alexander, *Space*, 36. Italics ours.

14. Wyndham Lewis, *Time and Western Man* (New York, 1928), Preface, xi.

15. Lewis, *Time*.

16. See George H. Kirby, *Guides for History Taking and Clinical Examination of Psychiatric Cases* (Utica, 1921), 69. For abnormalities in the judgment

of temporal intervals see P. Schilder, "Psychopathology of Time," *Journal of Nervous and Mental Disorders,* 83 (1936), 530–46; N. Israeli, *Abnormal Personality and Time* (New York, 1936).

17. Winter, *Red Virtue* (New York, 1933), 171–72.

18. "The word Saturday is still used, but means not a definite day of the week, but any one of his free days the worker gives to additional voluntary work" (Winter, 172).

19. Mary Sturt, *The Psychology of Time* (London, 1925). A questionnaire method was employed.

20. F. Lorimer, *The Growth of Reason* (New York, 1929), 114.

21. L. Cope, *Calendars of the Indians North of Mexico* (University of California Publications in American Archaeology and Ethnology, vol. 16 [1919], 125.

22. Sherif, *Psychology,* 11.

23. A. Radcliffe-Brown, *The Andaman Islanders* (Cambridge, England, 1922), 311 ff.

24. W. Hough, "Time Keeping by Light and Fire," *American Anthropologist,* 6 (1893), 207.

25. H. Webster, *Rest Days* (New York, 1916), 193 ff.

26. B. Malinowski, "Lunar and Seasonal Calendar in the Trobriands," *Journal of the Royal Anthropological Institute,* 57 (1927).

27. As in Polynesian mythology. See R. B. Dixon, *Mythology of All Races,* IX. *Oceanic* (Boston, 1916).

28. The term *gizis is* applicable to both sun and moon. Generically therefore, it may be translated "luminary." In actual use it is defined by its context so that in the English rendering of terms I have used sun or moon. The Saulteaux themselves sometimes use a term which means "night luminary" for the moon. The translations of native words embody the meanings understood by the Indians. They are not based on refined etymological analysis.

29. In the Southwest, on the other hand, nocturnal points of reference are elaborated, as certain songs are customarily sung at certain intervals during the course of ceremonies held at night (Cope, *Calendars,* 126).

30. Our "day" of twenty-four hours is a conventional unit for which we have no specific term. By calling it a "day" we employ the principle of *pars pro toto.* Cf. Nilsson, *Primitive Time-Reckoning,* 11 *et seq.* But this author is mistaken when he asserts that reckoning in "nights" among primitive peoples involves the same principle. Since they do not entertain the concept of a day-night period as a unit, "night" cannot be regarded as a symbol

of the whole, but simply as a discrete recurring phenomenon that can be counted.

31. Egerton R. Young, By *Canoe and Dog-Train Among the Cree and Salteaux Indians* (New York, 1890), 263–64.

32. [Ed. note: Hallowell is referring to a myth that William Berens told him, "Wémtigóze." See Berens, *Memories, Myths, and Dreams* (2009) Part IV.]

33. Cf. J. G. Kohl, *Kitchi-gami* (London, 1860), 120: "they add every now and then a thirteenth nameless moon in order to get right with the sun again," and "it is often comical to listen to the old men disputing as to what moon they are in." Cf. Cope, *Calendars*, 131, 137–39.

34. See the compilations in Cope, *Calendars*, 165–66, where seven series of names for the lunations are given.

35. *Bird Calendar,* designed and compiled from the records of A. G. Lawrence, Ornithological Secretary.

37. Hallowell, "Notes on the Northern Range of *Zizania* in Manitoba." *Rhodora* 36, 302–04. [Chapter 2, this volume.]

37. Cope, *Calendars*, 136. Italics ours.

38. It is hard to say, of course, whether such practice as notching a stick for every day of the year, carried out by the father of one of Densmore's informants, was a native custom or one suggested by contact with the whites. See Frances Densmore, *Chippewa Customs* (Bulletin, Bureau of American Ethnology, No. 86, 1929), 119.

39. Cf. Cope, *Calendars*, map 2, where the "beginning of the year" among various peoples of native North America is indicated. Cf. Nilsson, *Primitive Time-Reckoning*, 267 et seq., for a further discussion of this question.

40. Cope, *Calendars*, 136–37.

41. Cf. Nilsson, *Primitive Time-Reckoning*, 105: "Whoever looks back over his past life sees chiefly the more important events, not the dates of the years, and to these he joins the more peripheral events and so finds his way in the labyrinth of memory."

42. [Ed. note: For example, in 1933 William Berens told Hallowell the myth of the Big Mosquito (k`tcizagimé). See Berens, *Memories, Myths, and Dreams,* Part IV.]

43. [Ed. note: Hallowell is referring to the myth, "Wísakedják and the Water Lions" that William Berens told him in 1933. See Berens, *Memories, Myths, and Dreams,* Part IV.]

44. Tcakabec was a tiny but powerful man who lived with his wise sister. The two had been orphaned at an early age. Tcakabek was ever-curious and

continually disobeyed his sister's advice and instructions. This landed him in some serious predicaments, such as the one to which Hallowell refers here. For a Swampy Cree rendition of this myth see Louis Bird and Susan Elaine Gray, *The Spirit Lives in the Mind: Omushkego Stories, Lives, and Dreams* (Montreal: McGill-Queen's University Press, 2007) 23–29.]

45. [Ed. note: See "Wísakedják Discovers Women," told by Berens to Hallowell in 1933. Berens, *Memories, Myths, and Dreams*, Part IV.]

46. [Ed. note: "Wísakedják and the Water Lions." Berens, *Memories, Myths, and Dreams*, Part IV.]

47. [Ed. note: Berens told Hallowell "The Birth of the Winds, Flint and the Great Hare: from a girl who is magically impregnated," and also narrated, "South Wind Enters a Contest with the North Wind" in the summer of 1933. See Berens, *Memories, Myths, and Dreams*, Part IV.]

48. [Ed. note: See Berens, *Memories, Myths, and Dreams*, Part IV for these myths, "Kaiánwe," and "Aásī," which Berens told Hallowell.]

EIGHT

Some Psychological Aspects of
Measurement among the Saulteaux

We cannot investigate measurement among aboriginal peoples upon the assumption that they explicitly recognize and fully abstract those attributes of things which we think of in quantitative terms. Nor can we assume that differences in magnitude, expressed in numerical terms, are particularly interesting to them. The problem, rather, is to discover what attributes of things are measured, how the operation of measurement is carried out, the purposes for which it is used, and the extent to which the results are expressed in numerical terms.

An attempt will be made here to show how such spatial attributes as distance, length, and area are handled by the Saulteaux and the extent to which their culture implements, but at the same time limits, the measurement of these attributes.

In the first place, observation and experience are sufficient to enable any adult human being to make crude estimates of distance, length, and area. Among the Saulteaux, as among us, such perceptual discriminations as "far" and "near," "long" and "short," "large" and "small" are made constantly and receive linguistic expression in connection with all sorts of activities in daily life. This is what may be characterized as the level of "contrast-comparison." Functionally, it is grounded in acquaintance with the qualities and relations of things derived from direct experience. This level of discrimination is undoubtedly a generic human trait. And for many purposes it is all that is needed. Such crude discriminations are useful enough for making comparisons within a given class of objects, but their scope is practically limited to such comparisons. A "big" tree, a "big" man, and a "big" lake simply are not commensurable in such terms. There is no translatability between such groups or kinds. There is no standard against which just the height of a man and the height of a tree can be measured.

Any intercomparisons must be expressed as similes or metaphors such as, "a *wíndigo* (cannibal giant) is as tall as, or taller than, the trees."

It is out of this crude phase of perceptual discrimination, however, that the measurement of spatial magnitude has arisen. Measurement in this sense[1] is a refinement of such naive comparisons. It cannot be viewed as categorically distinct because in its most elementary form it remains qualitative rather than numerical; only in its developed phases does measurement carried to the point of numerical determination become equivalent to quantitative statement. What measurement implies is simply this: For estimates of magnitude based upon naive discrimination it substitutes the operation of *matching* as a determinative technique.[2]

The simplest form of this operation occurs when we determine by *direct matching* that string *x* is longer, shorter, or equal in length to string *y* by the juxtaposition of the two. Or we can determine (i.e., measure) the length of an object of another class by matching it against string *x*. But since direct matching necessarily has such a limited scope as a means of measurement, it being impossible to use it when two objects cannot be juxtaposed, another procedure must be adopted. By using string *x* we can match *indirectly* two logs of wood that are not easily manipulable. String *x* then becomes an informal standard of measure in such a procedure. If we standardize its length, it becomes a *unit of measure* by means of which we determine the length of a variety of objects and express their magnitudes in terms of the standard unit chosen.

Of course the units chosen as standards of measure may be extremely varied in character. They may be concrete or abstract, dynamic or static. They may be customarily employed without being highly formalized or part of an integrated system of measures. And they may vary from culture to culture. Their fundamental significance lies in the nature of the operation that is performed by means of them, not in their intrinsic character. For this reason it is more important to investigate the circumstances under which primitive people perform the operation of genuine measurement and the extent to which they use it, than it is to determine the fact that they employ this or that customary unit of measurement.

Furthermore, measurement as a particular kind of operation is more widely prevalent than the use of conventional units of measure. In a given society we can no more infer the actual extent and character of measurement as an operation from the use of standardized measures alone than we can infer the extent of numerical operations from a minimum vocabulary of number words. In certain circumstances empirically derived units of measure or a process of direct matching are adequate means for the ends to be achieved. In so far as this is the case, they are no less important for an understanding of measurement than the use of the more conventional units of measure.

It is the fundamental principle involved in the process of measurement that also enables us to gain further insight into the conditions under which differential units of measure must have arisen. For it would appear that under the cultural conditions found in most primitive societies there could have been no demand for the refined operational techniques of a culture like our own and the accompanying units of measure that they require. The technique of direct matching was sufficient for many purposes, and in many spheres of activity, measurement was not demanded at all. Since there was no cultural motivation to this end, there was no incentive for the invention of new operational techniques in the measuring process. Even in occidental culture today there is no need under many circumstances for the measurement of spatial attributes in terms of the most refined units of measurement that are part of our heritage. In everyday life we, too, resort to naive discriminations and often employ the simpler matching operations in so far as these are sufficient to the ends we have in view. But the psychological implications are quite different for ourselves, on the one hand, and the Saulteaux, on the other. We are able to choose from a variety of means provided by our culture and adapt them to our ends; the Saulteaux are limited to very simple means. Differential cultural factors, then, connected with the operation of measuring, have refined our perceptions of spatial magnitude, whereas individuals in Saulteaux society have been confined to a stage of spatial perception in which such refinements play only a minor role.

DISTANCE

Among the Saulteaux, as among ourselves, it is possible to answer the question "how far" in a purely relative way. The Saulteaux employ two contrasting terms for this purpose, one meaning "near" or "close by," the other "a great way off." Actual measurement is not involved here; the question is answered by indicating the relative position in space of the object or place referred to with reference to the speaker.[3]

In linear measurement, however, it is necessary to emphasize a basic difference between the Saulteaux and ourselves that penetrates to the very roots of both cultures. For us, distance-away, distance-apart, and length are all brought under the same conceptual system of measures. A linear dimension of any kind can be quantitatively expressed in terms of a single scale of graduated standardized units, the smallest and largest of which can only be arrived at by complicated instrumental means. The very existence of such a scale in occidental culture is, of course, a unique, as well as recent development. It likewise typifies the means which our culture provides for dealing with spatial attributes and the level of objectivity, refinement, and organization which our spatial concepts have attained.

Primitive peoples like the Saulteaux not only lack such refinements; they do not even have any common units which are applicable to *all* classes of linear measurement, to say nothing of a graduated scale of such units. This means that such measures as they employ for different kinds of linear distances are not comparable, nor is it possible to convert measures of a lower order into those of a higher order and vice versa. Consequently, distance-away, or distance-apart, when thought of in terms of places or objects in space, is an entirely different thing from the length of a manipulable object of some sort like a canoe or a piece of string. There is no means of bringing linear concepts of all kinds into a single unified category of spatial attributes because the units of measure expressing the distance traveled on a journey, for example, are categorically distinct from those applied to the length of a piece of string.

Although some of the Berens River Indians today estimate distances in terms of miles, this is simply one of the results of acculturation processes which have been occurring for about a generation. An incident which occurred in July 1817 when Lord Selkirk made his treaty with the Cree and Saulteaux in the neighborhood of what is now the city of Winnipeg, illustrates the culturally constituted barriers faced by the natives in situations where some comprehension of distance magnitudes was required. In this case the problem was solved on the spot by one of the chiefs who, not being able to fall back upon any units of measurement provided by his own culture, devised nevertheless a means whereby the miles of the white man were translated into a concrete and immediately perceptible datum that was comprehensible to his fellow Indians.

The settlers were to possess the land for two miles back from the western bank of the Red River according to the terms of the treaty, but the Indians wanted to know how far two miles was. Even though Mr. [Peter] Fidler, the surveyor, produced his chains and measured off the mileage this did not quite satisfy the Indians. Then one of the chiefs is said to have had an inspiration. There happened to be some horses grazing out on the plain close to the spot the surveyor's man had reached with his measuring chains. Noticing these horses the chief announced that two miles was as far as a man could see daylight under the belly of a horse. All the Indians "puckered their eyes to the western glare, the setting sun" and were satisfied that they knew what two miles meant.[4]

Natively, distance is measured in units of activity.[5] In respect to a journey, for example, this is customarily expressed by saying how many times one has slept or will sleep en route. Such a unit is concrete and qualitative. It is processual in character in contrast to an abstract static unit like a mile. A concrete, recurring process within the larger activity, the journey is abstracted and matched against the latter, instead of an abstract linear measure, the mile. Similarly, instead of "sleeps" the linear distance to a place may be measured by "nights" on the road. In this case the concrete recurring event utilized is darkness. Since all measurement involves some kind of matching operation, the underlying principle is the same despite the choice of categorically distinct units. The same principle is applied by the Saulteaux to the "length" of a journey that may take less than a day. The question "how far" is answered by reference to the position of the sun in the sky, i.e., the process of walking from one point to another is measured by matching it against a natural process, the course of the sun through the heavens.

For the life economy of the Saulteaux, *when* one returns, *when* we shall expect to meet are more important than the distance traveled. For provisioning, too, the number of days consumed in the journey is the important thing. Such judgments can never depend upon linear distance predominantly: weather conditions, high or low water, the number of individuals paddling a canoe, or the size of the load, all are contributing factors to the rate of travel in summer. In winter the roughness of the going, the quality of the snow, or the flatness of the country must be considered. Thus the qualitative units employed by the Saulteaux as a measure of distance are extremely crude and variable. In terms of their system of calculation the distance between points traveled by water has been considerably reduced in recent years with the introduction of the outboard motor among them. And in effect this is quite true because the actual linear distance is inconsequential for them. Their terms of measurement, crude as they are, prove eminently satisfactory under the conditions of life which their culture imposes.

The intrinsic limitations of such units for accurately measuring distance are equally obvious. They are a contributing factor to the vague concepts of space beyond the experience of individuals. Their qualitative character makes it impossible for the Indians to conceptualize distance in abstract numerical terms.

Unable, for example, to communicate the idea of distance in quantitative terms to the people up the river (particularly the Pekangikum Indians who are the least acculturated of any group), I do not believe that I ever succeeded in conveying to them any realistic notion of the distance I had traveled to reach their country. Matters were further complicated by the fact that my *rate* of travel in different kinds of conveyances was not the sort of knowledge that could be taken for granted. Consequently, my attempt to convert distance into the concrete qualitative units intelligible to them (i.e., sleeps) made my home only twice the distance the mouth of the river lay from Lake Pekangikum, about 260 miles. Actually it was more than six times that distance. The difficulty lay in the fact that I spent the same number of nights on the train and the boat between Philadelphia and the mouth of the Berens River as I spent ascending the river. The differential factor, of course, was the speed of the train. This mode of conveyance was known to them only by hearsay. The only mode of travel within their observation that could be used analogically to give them an idea of the speed of the train was the airplane, familiar through use in the Forestry Service and by prospectors who fly over the country to many inland points.

MANIPULABLE LENGTH

As I have already said, measuring always makes use of the principle of matching. Consequently, in measuring what may be called "manipulable lengths," this principle may be applied without the use of any standardized units of measure. The following are illustrations:

One man told me, for instance, that in constructing a deadfall for bear, his father made the preliminary measurements in the following manner: After the bedlog[6] of the trap was in place he knelt upon it, bent forward, and keeping his back horizontal with the ground, extended his hands forward as far as they would reach. Where they touched the ground defined the limits of the "pen." The fall-log would then be sure to strike the right part of the bear's spine. To judge the height of the notch in the upright post where the outer end of the lever rests, he would elevate a knee. In this case the matching of the trap to fit the bear is mediated through the close correspondence in size between the bears of the country and a man.

Matching is also used in making moccasins[7] where the length of the foot is measured by a piece of string, or nowadays by drawing the outline of the foot on a piece of paper.[8] The same principle sometimes was used in the manufacture of a birchbark canoe. An old canoe was set upright and stakes driven into the ground at intervals around the outside of it in order to outline the size and shape of the new canoe to be built.

In dealing with manipulable length the Saulteaux likewise make use of various parts of the body as semistandardized units. The right forearm with the elbow as a base is one extremely convenient "yardstick" and variable lengths may be marked off on it by the side of the left hand, or the distance between the elbow and the tip of the forefinger may be used as a unit.[9] A man may say, for example, that he tracked a bear with footprints "as long as this," indicating the length by putting the right elbow on the ground, extending his arm, and marking the limit with his left hand placed across wrist or knuckles. The same kind of measure is used when reporting the size of the footprints reputedly made by a *wíndīgo*. In making a birchbark canoe the two crossbars fore and aft were made equivalent in height to the distance between a man's elbow and wrist, while the middle bars were of a height corresponding to the distance between the elbow and the tip of the forefinger or this dimension plus one thumb-first-finger-spread.

In addition to the use of the full spread of these, the thumb and forefinger may be used to indicate smaller dimensions. I recall a discussion of how much the water had risen at Little Grand Rapids. One man spread his thumb and first finger apart to indicate this. All the other men agreed that he was right. In our scale it was about three inches.

Another unit of length in which the fingers are employed is the spread of the thumb and middle finger (*pejiwákwagan,* one finger stretch). The width of three or four fingers, or even of all five digits (hand), was another type of unit used. Canoe ribs almost always were three fingers in width, whether used in small or large canoes.

To measure greater lengths the fist with outstretched thumb is used. Both hands are laid on the object with the tips of the thumbs touching. Together they cover two units. If the left fist with the thumb extended is now crossed over the right, a third unit is covered, and if the right fist is now withdrawn from under the left and the extended thumb touched to the left thumb, a fourth unit is measured, and so on.

The dimensions between the tips of the fingers when both arms are stretched out (fathom) constitute another unit (*pejīgonik,* one arm-stretch); half of this is equal to the distance from the breast bone to the fingertips of one hand. When birchbark canoes were manufactured, they were spoken of as two or three "stretches" in length, half a "stretch," and so on.

"Steps" or paces as units of length likewise are known to the Saulteaux. The length of a log house may be thought of in terms of "steps" and the logs measured off accordingly. The *wábano* pavilion of John Duck at Little Grand Rapids was said to be fourteen steps long and six steps wide. When measured, this pavilion was approximately forty feet by fifteen feet. This makes the Saulteaux "step" about two and a half feet which is very close to our "pace," usually set at three feet.

All these units of measure are completely independent of one another. They are not part of a system of measures and cannot be expressed in terms of each other. But in contrast to the traditional inadequacies which beset them in dealing with linear dimensions of any considerable magnitude, the Saulteaux by the use of direct matching and of conventional units of measure are able to deal more accurately with the linear dimensions of the objects whose manipulation is important in their daily lives.

They have no measuring tools in the more literal sense, i.e., detached objects like a foot-rule, which embody standardized units of measure that are the same for any and every operation of measuring no matter who performs it. The integration of these more accurate forms of measurement with industrial processes is not accidental. The possession and use of such devices is also of inestimable importance from a psychological point of view. In dealing with space relations they refine perceptions to a degree impossible without them. In recent years the more sophisticated Saulteaux at the mouth of the Berens River have learned to use our measuring tools, especially in building houses. When using a foot-rule they also employ English terms for numerical values, as "three and a half" or "two and a quarter inches."

AREA

The limitations imposed upon the Saulteaux with respect to the measurement of non-manipulable length naturally restrict the accurate measurement of non-manipulable areas. Their judgments of differences in areas of any considerable magnitude can only be based upon the most elementary kinds of perceptual discrimination.

Since their country is studded with innumerable lakes of different sizes, the Saulteaux recognize proportional difference in the areas covered by these bodies of water. But in the absence of any means of measurement, area as an abstract spatial attribute, cannot be mentally manipulated in an accurate fashion. Instead of being abstracted, area to the Saulteaux mind is only comprehended as a concept that remains closely linked with "region" or "place"; it retains all the character of a particular locality. If a region has natural boundaries, a lake for instance, that set it off from the surrounding country, it is easily comprehended in semi-abstract areal terms, and belongs more to the category of "thing" or "object" having shape and size and perceptible surface extensity. Otherwise it may never even be thought of in this way at all.

An interesting question arises here. The Saulteaux, like other Algonkian peoples, break up during the winter into hunting groups. The average number of persons per group is 14.9. Each hunting group is associated with a different locality. Related individuals in a paternal family line frequently occupy the same hunting ground for more than a generation. Hunting rights in such regions are socially sanctioned in native law and trespass resented.

In the course of collecting information in regard to the geographical aspects of this native economic system, Indians have been asked by the investigator to delineate the boundaries of their hunting territories on a map; or the investigator has done it himself under their supervision. Although I have used the same procedure in securing data on the geographical locale of Saulteaux hunting territories, I believe, nevertheless, that a false impression is created if the inference is drawn that the natives themselves conceptualize their hunting grounds in abstract areal terms.[10] It is my impression that the contrary is the case, despite the fact that these hunting territories may vary greatly in size, from 13 to 212 square miles. [See chapter 9, "The Size of Algonkian Hunting Territories," this volume.]

I believe that the reason why the Saulteaux do not make areal abstractions and comparisons of their hunting territories is not due simply to the lack of any accurate measures; it is, rather, explained by the absence of cultural values that would motivate such an abstraction on their part. If we consider for a moment how deeply the concrete details of the terrain over which they hunt must be embedded in their personal experience and their lack of knowledge of other districts than their own, it is difficult to see why judgments in abstract spatial terms should occur without an extremely forceful motivation as a leverage. And it is just this sort of motivation that we search for in vain.

In the first place, there is nothing in Saulteaux culture that motivates the possession of land for land's sake. Usufruct, rather than the land itself, is an economic value and land is never rented or sold. The use of the land and its products are a source of wealth rather than land ownership itself. There is no prestige whatsoever that accrues to the man who hunts over a large area. Nor is there any direct correlation between the size of the winter hunting group and the area of the hunting ground they occupy.[11] This is to be explained, perhaps, by the sectional variability in the incidence of the fur-bearing animals, differences in hunting skill, and maybe other variables. Finally, what is even more important is the fact that a smaller hunting territory may afford a living equal to, or even better than, a larger one. Consequently, it is impossible for the Saulteaux to measure areas in units of productivity (e.g., skins of animals trapped) as we find to be the case among some agricultural peoples (e.g., how much barley or rice can be grown).[12]

Under these conditions, why should an abstract concept of area arise, or comparisons of hunting territories in terms of size be made? Such a concept has no functional value for the Saulteaux, no more than has abstract distance.

In actual life then, the Saulteaux simply employ such generic terms as "large," "small," "big enough." But in a myth that accounts for the origin of the "island" (that is, the earth) on which man now dwells, it is interesting to find the area *measured* in a unique fashion. Wísakedják and a few animals have survived a flood by building a raft. They are floating about and do not know what to do. Finally Wísakedják sets his animal companions diving for earth. They fail. But at last muskrat secures a tiny quantity. This is magically expanded when Wísakedják blows upon it. They land on the island created and then Wísakedják calls a caribou to him. He tells the animal to run around the newly formed island. The caribou soon comes back and says, "It's pretty small yet." So Wísakedják keeps blowing upon the earth. After a bit he says to another young caribou, "You run around now." So this caribou runs around. When he gets back he is old, he has lost some of his teeth. Wísakedják is not yet satisfied with the size of the earth, so he blows some more. Then he directs a third caribou to run around the "island." This one never comes back. So Wísakedják says, "it is big enough." (That is, "big enough for people to live on.")[13]

Measurement in this case is based on the principle already described. Two kinds of processual units are employed: (1) the maturational changes in an animal, (2) the procedure of running around the island. It is impossible, of course, to obtain any idea of area in absolute spatial terms from the application of such units. Under the conditions described in the myth, a comparison of the differences in the area of the earth at subsequent periods was inferred from the relative time occupied by the animals in making the circuit. But any comparisons outside these conditions would be impossible unless the units employed were standardized in some way.

If we now turn to manipulable areas, we find that the Saulteaux deal with them more effectively. But their approach is pragmatic rather than abstract. There are several reasons for this. In the first place, elementary processes of perception are more adequate as a basis for making discriminations in the size of manipulable areas than in the case of those of greater magnitude. And through experience in handling materials and objects of various kinds, excellent quantitative judgments can be made. In the second place, the Saulteaux are compelled to deal with simple problems of proportion in order to convert raw materials such as hides and bark into objects of domestic use. In making a bark container, for example, its proportions must be adequately controlled from start to finish. But in these relatively simple manufacturing processes, area never has to be handled in a purely quantitative, abstract way. The size, shape, and proportions of the object being produced are all inseparable. Initially, of course, the question "is this piece of skin 'big enough' to make a pair of moccasins" or "is this piece of bark 'big enough' to make a rogan," does arise. But it can be answered in terms of an estimate based on experience, how it "looks," without resort to actual measurement. Once the process of manufacture itself is started further judgments become chiefly relevant to the interrelations of size, shape, and proportions which the finished product will have. Measurement is not in terms of any standardized unit; the basic unit chosen is some part of the object itself or a series of them.

Of course, in the past the flat patterns for such manufactured objects were developed through cutting and fitting directly. Perhaps when a new one was needed, the old one was taken apart and thus the flat pattern shape exposed. With this as guide the outline of a new one could be traced on the material. Today these patterns may mediate the judgments of whether the material is "enough." The "key unit" will be judged against the actual object (for example, the length of the foot in the case of a moccasin) and the rest of the pattern adjusted to keep the shape and proportions constant.

The manufacture of a bark container, a rogan, may be taken as an example (fig. 1). In this case the bottom is the basic unit, although of course, the total overall size of the finished product is the initial guiding judgment. (In this account I am paraphrasing the observations of my colleague, Dr. Dorothy M. Spencer, who collected the information under my direction.)

1. To begin with, a rectangular piece of bark is chosen; it must be roughly shaped by a crooked knife and rough spots are smoothed off. Its size is

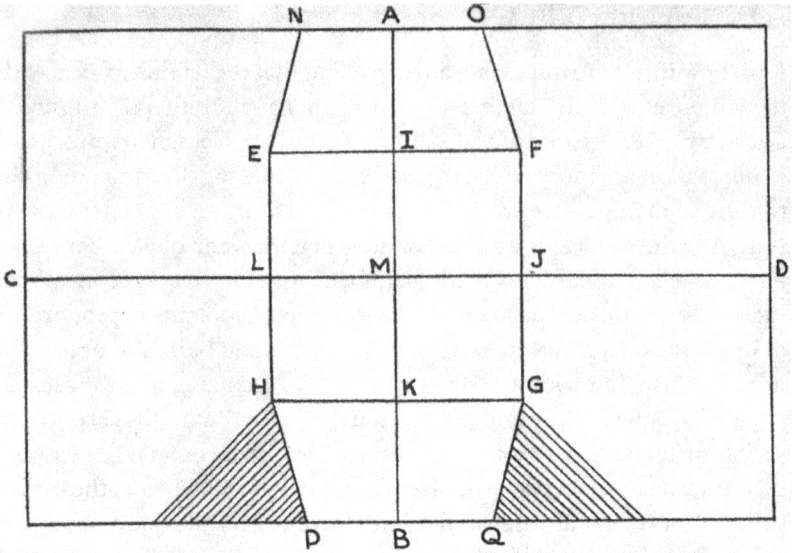

1. Pattern for Rogan

a matter of judgment based on the experience of the woman undertaking the task. (See diagram.)

2. The median point (A, B, C, D) on each edge of the rectangle is determined by folding the bark upon itself.

3. The median points on opposite edges of the rectangle are now joined by lines made lightly with a knife.

4. The next step is to measure off the area that will form the bottom of the container (E, F, G, H). This area may be square or rectangular. In the example given it is square. Its size is not measured by any conventional quantitative unit but is arrived at by a process of proportional measurement in the following way:

   A small strip of bark, judged to be half the length of the bottom of the rogan is prepared (the worker usually experiments a little first before adopting a length). With this piece of bark the distance from the center M to points I, J, K, L are measured and marked on the bark; then the distance from L to E, L to H and so on. In this way the corners of the bottom, E, F, G, H, are defined. Small holes are punched in the bark at these points with an awl.

5. The points N, O, P, Q are not determined by measurement; they are a

matter of "shape judgment." When marked, a line is drawn from the corners of the bottom of the rogan to them.

6. The lines referred to above serve as guides for cutting. This is now done and the pieces left free are folded up along the lines EF and HG.

7. The remainder of the bark sheet is now folded to form the sides of the container in such a way that the shaded parts appear on the outside of the bottom. The corners of these are temporarily tied together with string, and where the other pieces of bark overlap at the sides, they are held together with wooden pins until the sewing is complete. (This step and the treatment of the rim need not concern us here.)

8. The lid is made of two pieces of bark, one circular, the other a long rectangular strip. These are sewn together so that the edge of the strip is perpendicular to the surface of the circular piece and fits into the container. The area of the circular piece is determined by direct matching with the top of the container after its completion: it is cut round more or less the right size, tried against the top, and trimmed to fit.[14]

CONCLUSIONS

In this paper I have pointed out that measurement, as such, is a refinement of naive discrimination mediated by some sort of matching process and I have described the kind of measurements that the Saulteaux use in dealing with such spatial attributes as distance, length, and area. Among these Indians there is relatively little interest in or use of measurement on a fully developed quantitative level. Yet their possession of certain conventional units of measure permits simple quantification, as in the estimation of distance in terms of a certain number of "sleeps." By and large, however, measurement among the Saulteaux remains on the most elementary level except in those instances where white influences are apparent. But this is thoroughly consonant with the type of culture they possess and the kind of life they lead. In such a simply organized and individualistic society where articles are manufactured only for domestic use and not for sale, there is no demand for the application of *standard* measurements to any article produced. The variableness of units of measure (as e.g., body parts) consequently does not matter. Each person constructs for himself and measures for himself or other members of his immediate household group. No truly objective standard is necessary. In each situation the individual solves in his own terms problems of measurement that may arise.

The low level of abstraction that we find in respect to distance, length, and area is connected both with the relative absence of quantification and with general cultural conditions. There is no need to develop any traditional devices for rising to a higher level of abstraction because the processes of measurement already known are adequate to meet the simple problems to be solved. Consequently, we cannot point to any socially derived incentives that might lead to progressive changes in the methods of measurement. In fact, the traditional press of the culture fosters conservatism. This is illustrated specifically by the factors which would seem to discourage the emergence of any abstract notions of area in connection with the use of hunting territories. The only influences which are now at work in the opposite direction are those which come from increasing contacts with white people and new educational opportunities.

Comparative data from other primitive societies would, I believe, lend support to the conclusion that the level of abstraction utilized in dealing with certain spatial attributes is not a simple function of maturation or intellectual capacity on the part of individuals. It is a function of the status of the cultural heritage as well. For the cultural heritage of a people limits or promotes the manner in which and the terms in which the individual deals with the spatial attributes of the world about him. If a culture does not provide the terms and concepts, spatial attributes cannot even be talked about with precision. Individuals are left to fend for themselves, as it were, on the level of elementary discriminatory reactions. This limits the possibilities for the mental manipulation of more refined and developed concepts that require symbolic representation in some form. Without such instruments in the cultural heritage certain areas of action are excluded and the solution of many practical problems impossible.

Thus, an analysis of processes of measurement is one angle of approach to the problem of how individuals deal with the spatial attributes of things under different cultural conditions. It is also possible to throw some light on the concepts of space that are held. The relation of these questions to wider and more fundamental problems is evident—problems in which both psychologists and anthropologists find a common field of interest. A great deal more needs to be known about how the spatialization of the world arises in the experience of a human being; the kinds of discriminations that are made; the degree of refinement to which they are carried; how these are related to motility, the manipulation of objects, and the concepts of space that are held. It seems to me that anthropologists can contribute a great deal to the solution of such problems by analyzing the cultural constituents of the spatially coordinated behavior of individuals in different human societies.

Notes

Published in *American Anthropologist* 44 (1942): 62–77; reprinted in Hallowell, *Culture and Experience* (Philadelphia: University of Pennsylvania Press, 1955), 203–15.

1. Cf. Victor F. Lenzen, "Procedures of Empirical Science," *International Encyclopedia of Unified Science*, I (no. 5, 1938), 9, who says that, "Measurement is the general procedure of assigning numbers to the properties of objects. A measurable property is usually called a magnitude, but the term quantity is also used."

2. John Dewey, *Logic, the Theory of Inquiry* (New York, 1938), 202, 204, 213.

3. Another way of answering the question "how far" without the use of any units of measurement is illustrated by the experience of Dr. Dorothy Spencer in Fiji. She says, "When I asked how far, or, is it far, to a certain place I would be told it is near to *x*—meaning it is *near* from here to *x* (or nearer to *x*, than *y*), so that I having been to *x* would know that I would have a longer journey to *y*. When I left this time to go from Namalomulo to Nasauoko, Nambuma said, 'It was a *good* path to Bukuya' and I understood her to mean, and rightly, that the journey I was about to undertake would be worse than the one to Bukuya."

4. See Frederick Niven, *Mine Inheritance* (New York, 1940), 380. The source material is cited in the bibliography of this excellent historical novel of the founding of the Red River Colony. [Ed. note: see Alexander Morris's account in, *The Treaties of Canada with the Indians of Manitoba and the North-West Territories* (Toronto, 1880), 15, which in turn derives from Joseph James Hargrave, *Red* River (1871), 77.]

5. Processual units of various kinds as measures of distance are very common. Cf. Max Wertheimer, "Über das Denken der Naturvölker," *Zeitschrift für Psychologie* 60 (1912), 375. Some instances he cites are "a cigarette distant," a "pipe of tobacco away."

6. I am following the terminology of J. M. Cooper in his *Snares, Deadfalls and Other Traps of the Northern Algonquins and Northern Athapaskans* (Anthropological Series 5, Catholic University of America [1938]), 50 et seq.

7. "A shoemaker of old Pekin makes shoes with no unit of measure and no measuring scale. A strip of blank paper and his thumb nail are his measuring

tools. He transfers the foot measures to his paper slip using his thumb nail as a marker. Skilfully he transmutes these measures into perfectly fitting shoes without a unit of length." H.D. Hubbard, "The Romance of Measurement," *Scientific Monthly* 33 (1931), 356–57.

8. An interesting application of the same principle is to be found in Beatrice Blackwood, *Both Sides of Buka Passage* (Oxford, 1935), 228. In building a ceremonial structure used in connection with the initiation of boys, certain portions of it were provided by villages other than the one in which it was erected. Special importance is attached to the horizontal ridgepoles supporting the roof, which must run the full length of the building. In order to have them absolutely correct in length, a fibre string of the proper linear dimensions is sent to the village which is to supply the poles. In this case it measured 65'8".

9. I.e., a cubit, in English measure 18 inches.

10. Cf. A.L. Kroeber, *Handbook of the Indians of California* (Bulletin 78, Bureau of American Ethnology [1925]), 160–61, Yuki: "The native did not think, like modern civilized man, of his people owning an area circumscribed by a definite line, in which there might happen to be one or many water courses. This would have been viewing the land through a map, whether drawn or mental; and such an attitude was foreign to his habit. What he did know was that the little town at which he was born and where he expected to die lay on a certain river or branch of a river; and that this stream, or a certain stretch of it, and all the creeks flowing into it, and all the land on or between these creeks, belong to his people; whereas below, or above, or across certain hills, were other streams and tributaries, where other people lived, with whom he might be on visiting terms or intermarried, but who had proprietary rights of their own."

11. The same may be said for Algonkians generally. See my article, "The Size of Algonkian Hunting Territories; A Function of Ecological Adjustment." [Chapter 9, this volume.]

12. Hogben, *Mathematics for the Million* (New York, 1937), 64. I was informed of another method of areal measurement by Ann Fuller (private communication): Among the peasants in Palestine the measure is "enough land to plant 200 vines." This is a more accurate measure than produce since it actually involves *spacing*. A very ancient method of measuring land in the Old World which survived into modern times was based upon the *quantity* of grain required to plant it. These are the so-called "seed-measures." See Edward Nicholson, *Men and Measures: A History of Weights and Measures Ancient and Modern* (London, 1912) 65–66, 90–92, 256–58. Hallock and

Wade, *Outlines of the Evolution of Weights and Measures and of the Metric System* (1906), observe, 15, that: "Babylonians, in common with other Asiatic nations, also employed for measuring land the amount of seed required to sow a field and statements based on this idea are found in many old Assyrian documents." And p. 20, "For the measurement of area the Hebrews employed generally the amount of seed required to sow the land, or the amount of ground that could be ploughed by a yoke of oxen, the latter unit being the zemed, which in the *Old Testament* is translated by Acre (*1 Samuel* XIV, 14; *Isaiah* V, 10)."

All these methods of measuring area, it should be noted, are only characteristic of agricultural peoples; it would be impossible for hunters and gatherers to develop them. Hence one would not expect any progress in the development of measures of area among hunting peoples. This appears to correspond with historical facts.

13. [Ed. note: See the myth "Wísɑkedják and the Water Lions" which William Berens told Hallowell in 1933. William Berens, *Memories, Myths, and Dreams of an Ojibwe Leader* (2009), Part IV.]

14. Methods of measurement analogous in principle are described by Ruth Bunzel, *The Pueblo Potter* (New York 1929), 50. In this case the problem is to adjust the proportions of the designs to be executed to the size of the area to be painted. "All potters measure the surfaces of their jars in one way or another," although "there is a considerable individual variation in the amount of measuring that is done." One customary measure is the distance between the thumb and the tip of the middle finger when spread apart. The procedure of one expert pottery maker is described as follows: "First she studied carefully for some minutes the undecorated form, turning it around in her hands. Then she measured hastily with her thumb and middle finger the greatest circumference of the jar. Then she drew in the outlines of the first design, which was to be used four times around the jar. After the first element was completed, she measured it and the remaining space and drew in the second element. The two together occupied a little more than half the space, so the remaining two had to be slightly crowded, but this was hardly perceptible in the finished product." One informant commented: "If I start to paint before it is all measured, then I get nervous that it may not come out right."

NINE

The Size of Algonkian Hunting Territories
A Function of Ecological Adjustment

A new note has recently crept into the now familiar discussions of the hunting territory system of the Northern Algonkians. First, there was the initial period of description, begun by Speck more than thirty years ago.[1] At that time, when the crude evolutionary theories of cultural development that prevailed in the 19th century were being outgrown, there was even a certain novelty in the idea that, instead of communal ownership, there were hunting peoples who maintained a system of ownership in severalty.[2] Soon, the geographical distribution of the hunting-territory system among Algonkian peoples was well under way and the land-tenure systems of other hunting peoples in North America and elsewhere were drawn into the discussion.[3] Following this, and in keeping with the intellectual climate of the period, the question of historical depth arose: How far was the observed system of land tenure among the Algonkians completely aboriginal? Despite a few dissident voices, the weight of evidence, when systematically marshalled and analyzed by Cooper (1939),[4] lent support to the aboriginal thesis, at least in so far as certain nuclear features of the institution were concerned. Cooper even went further and advanced the hypothesis that such a system might be a "tarriant" phenomenon from very ancient times, among the marginal peoples of the world.[5] More recently, however, Cooper has expressed doubt about his own hypothesis. He says, "It looks as if land tenure among hunting peoples is delicately responsive to ecology, especially to the fauna exploited as the staple food supply. It looks likewise as if such tenure can and does adapt and change readily and swiftly in accordance with changing local ecological conditions."[6]

Thus a new note has been struck in the discussion of land tenure among the Northern Algonkians, similar overtones being clearly perceptible in a previously published article by Speck and Eiseley.[7]

To my mind this ecological hypothesis has some important methodological implications. It calls for a more dynamic type of analysis than has been previously undertaken. Instead of concentrating upon cultural description, the facts of geographical distribution and problems of historical depth and continuity, the major question becomes in effect: What are the *actual* determinants or controlling factors involved? Once this question has been broached, the level of inquiry is shifted from the plane of description and chronological reconstruction to that of process and the structural dynamics of human adjustment. It involves a more detailed examination of all the conditions under which a given human population makes its fundamental ecological adjustments in a specific locale. Within this frame of reference, however, we are forced to take new data into account, data of a *non-cultural* nature. For we can hardly pursue an ecological hypothesis without giving due weight to relevant demographic facts, as well as those pertaining to the character, incidence and fluctuations of fauna or other pertinent information. Perhaps in this case, as well as in others, our very devotion to cultural description and historical explanation, on the implicit, if not explicit, assumption that culture is a phenomenon, *sui generis*, has blinded us to the relevance of some of the very data that are needed if the actual dynamics of the hunting-territory system is to be fully understood or explained. Furthermore, if we begin to ask questions about the controlling factors of the hunting-territory system it is not likely that we shall arrive at a satisfactory explanation if we operate exclusively with generically descriptive traits that purport to characterize the normative aspects of the institution considered as a whole. We need more precise information about the variabilities and constancies that are found in the actual operation of the hunting-territory system under given conditions. If we had more inclusive data at our disposal from different localities, we might then be able to discover some of the factors responsible for the variable and constant features of the system and thus illuminate its basic dynamics. In this paper I have selected only a single variable—the size of Algonkian hunting grounds—as a concrete illustration of the more general problem.

What precise information do we have about this attribute of Algonkian hunting territories that would enable us to state the factors responsible for its great variability? All we can say is that this feature not only varies greatly in magnitude, when we consider band conditions, but even more so when the mean variation reported for different ethno-linguistic groups is taken into account. At one extreme we have the Newfoundland Micmac, the average size of whose hunting territories Speck estimated to be 2,000 square miles,[8] while on the other hand we have an estimate of eight to ten square miles for the White Earth Ojibwa.[9] But even these figures cannot be said to be typical of the ethno-linguistic units referred to, since the Ojibwa elsewhere are known to have much *larger* hunting grounds and other Micmac groups are reported to have much *smaller* territories (Cape Breton Island 400, Nova Scotia 200 square miles). Since this is the case, it is impossible to make any satisfactory statement about the mean size of Algonkian hunting territories in general, particularly in view of the fact that it is doubtful if we actually have on record an adequate sample of the mean size of the hunting grounds of Algonkian peoples throughout their habitat.[10] It is indeed somewhat paradoxical that while many descriptive generalizations have been made about the Algonkian hunting-territory system, mean size is not among them. This is analogous to describing all the morphological characteristics of an animal like the elephant without reference to the size of the creature. The explanation, of course, lies partly in the phenomenon of variability itself. Nevertheless, this variability must have its limits as well as its determinants. And where we have the most precise information, the range of variability *does* seem to have characteristic limits in different localities.

The size and composition of the winter hunting groups that are associated with the hunting territories present another interesting variable. So far as composition is concerned, the small biological family (unmarried children and parents) cannot be taken as typical, and consequently there is a considerable range in size, even within the same locality. If we have data on both the size of hunting territories and the size of hunting groups we can, of course, discover whether the size of the latter varies concomitantly with the former or in some other way. We also have the necessary information for stating the density of population among one people as compared with another. And if we likewise know whether the population in increasing or decreasing, we may gain some insight into the relation between population dynamics and the functioning of the land tenure system under such conditions.

Another problem of focal interest is the ratio of active hunters to other persons in different locales. How variable or constant is this ratio? If it should turn out to be relatively constant in different regions, despite variations in the size of hunting territories, the size of hunting groups or fluctuations in fauna, it would then appear that we have a ratio that perhaps defines some primary unit in ecological adjustment.

If, in addition to such demographic data as I have mentioned, we also had adequate information about the incidence of the various fur bearers and other animals in given regions, I believe that we could obtain some significant answers to questions of ecological adjustment.[11] It might then be possible to advance a hypothesis, empirically grounded in the structural dynamics of the ecological adjustment of specific groups, that would throw further light upon questions of historical depth and continuity. For we know that, even if such an institution as the hunting-territory system has persisted in time, it has not done so in an ecological vacuum. There must be conditions present that either re-enforce its continuance or lead to change.[12]

So far as the Northern Algonkians are concerned, one of the conditions of such continuity is the fact that they have lived in the same faunal and climatic zone and no faunal catastrophe has occurred as in the case of the Sioux. And it is true, as Kroeber has pointed out[13] with respect to both Algonkians and Athabascans, that as a result of the demand for furs, "the long-run effect of Caucasian contacts was to entrench these peoples more firmly in their occupation as hunters." Nevertheless, the Algonkians have undergone many demographic and cultural readjustments. Today they exhibit various levels of acculturation. It is hard to believe, therefore, that all these processes of readjustment have left their land tenure system *completely* unaffected. If a closer study of the hunting-territory system as it operates today can give us an insight into the actual factors that control its variable features, it should be possible to deduce some of the necessary and sufficient conditions that underlie stability as well as change. It might even be possible to explain such variant and less characteristic patterns of ownership in severalty as the allotment system as an emergent practice that arose under specific local conditions.

By way of illustrating some of the possibilities that an ecological approach suggests, I wish now to present some concrete data from two localities within the habitat of the Northern Algonkians. I shall confine my discussion to the one major variable mentioned above—the mean size of their hunting grounds, some correlative demographic data, and the controlling factors that may be involved.

The two groups chosen belong to the same ethno-linguistic unit—the Ojibwa-Ottawa Algonkian.[14] One group is the Grand Lake Victoria Indians, located in the Province of Quebec; the other is the Berens River Indians in Manitoba. These Indians not only have the same linguistic and cultural background, they live in the same faunal zone, hunt the same animals with the same technological equipment, dispose of their fur in a market controlled by commercial companies operating throughout the Dominion of Canada, and have approximately the same standard of living. Any local differences, therefore, must be viewed against the broad background of linguistic, cultural, technological and other uniformities.

Davidson collected the data on the Grand Lake Victoria group in 1926;[15] I collected the material on the Berens River Indians between 1932 and 1934.[16] These data comprise, among other things, detailed information on seventy-four winter hunting groups, thirty-one representing the Grand Lake Victoria Band and forty-three the Berens River Saulteaux (Northern Ojibwa). Only those winter hunting-groups are included for which reliable information in respect to the size of the hunting territory and the number of persons in the hunting groups has been recorded. Consequently a few groups have been omitted, but there are so few that the sample used is thoroughly representative.

I have calculated the areas of the hunting grounds in square miles by the use of a planimeter applied to the original maps on which the boundaries were drawn. These boundaries were outlined in most cases by the Indians themselves or by the investigator under the immediate instruction of the Indians. They represent approximations subject to errors dependent upon the scale of the maps employed and the ability of the Indians to recognize familiar landmarks. In the case of the Berens River people large-scale maps of the National Topographic Series were used. These permitted somewhat greater accuracy than in the case of the smaller-scale maps which Davidson was compelled to use. The resulting figures as a whole offer a sound quantitative basis for a comparison of the mean size of the hunting grounds for the two groups. So far as I know these are the only two groups where we have figures compiled on the basis of direct planimetric measurement.

Quantitative information on the size of hunting grounds, the size of winter hunting-groups, density of population and the ration of hunters to other persons for the two groups under discussion has been tabulated below.

The mean size of the hunting grounds in the two localities is remarkably different. Those of the Grand Lake Victoria group average more than three times those of the Berens River Indians. *A priori* one might suppose that this difference might be a simple function of the size of the hunting groups. But this is not the case. In fact, the size of the hunting groups in the localities compared bears an inverse relation to the size of the hunting grounds. For the winter hunting-groups of the Berens River Indians are *three times as large* as the hunting groups of the Grand Lake Victoria Indians. And when we calculate the mean density of the population the contrast is even more striking. While the picture exhibited by the Berens River Indians is one person to 6.2 square miles, among the Grand Lake Victoria Indians it is

Name of Group	Size of Hunting Grounds			Size of Hunting Groups		Density of Population	
	No.	Range (sq. mi.)	Av. (sq. mi.)	Range (no. persons)	Av. (no. persons)	Range (sq. mi. per person)	Av.
Grand Lake Victoria	31	64–1716	316[18]	2–17	5.6[19]	13–146	55.6
Berens River	43	13–212	93	4–49	14.9	1–24.5	6.2

Name of Group	Ratio of Active Hunters to Other Persons					
	Active Hunters		Other Persons		Ratio	
	Range	Av.	Range	Av.	Range	Av.
Grand Lake Victoria	1–3	1.3	1–14	4.3	1:0.5–1:65	1:3.1
Berens River	1–10	3.3	2–39	11.6	1:1–1:8	1:3.5

5. Grand Lake Victoria and Berens River Hunting Grounds. Note: Twice the figure of the area (100–150 sq. mi.) attributed to Australian hordes of 20–50 persons. See Steward. The Tete de Boule (Davidson, 1928b) also average 5.6 but no group numbered more than 13 persons. My own unpublished data on the St. Francis Abenaki, while not quite so precise, approximate the same figure.

one person to 55.6 square miles. The former figure, incidentally, is a little higher than Kroeber's estimate of the aboriginal density of the population north of the Great Lakes (one person per 5.3 square miles) while the latter shows an even greater sparsity than Kroeber's estimate of one person per 34.6 square miles in the eastern sub-arctic.[17]

When we turn to the ratio of active hunters to other persons, however, we get a different picture. The ratio is approximately identical, being one hunter to 3.1 non-hunters in the case of the Grand Lake Victoria Indians, and one active hunter to 3.5 non-hunters in the Berens River group. This fact is even more interesting when the composition of the hunting groups in the two localities is compared, for the mean number of active hunters per hunting group is 1.3 at Grand Lake Victoria while it is 3.3 among the Berens River Indians. This is explained by the fact that since the Grand Lake Victoria hunting groups are small there is only a single hunter in the large majority of them (70.9 percent). The reverse is true of the hunting groups in the Berens River region; only eleven percent of them operate with a single active hunter.[18]

Two important inferences can be made from the analysis of the data just presented. (1) The constancy in the ratio between hunters and non-hunters appears to be independent of either variability in the size of the hunting territories or of the size of the hunting groups. If such a ratio should be supported by information from other groups it would be a basic fact in the ecological adjustment of these northern hunters. When thought of in terms of group composition it is equivalent to a small family consisting of a hunter, his wife and two children. (2) The second inference that can be made on the basis of the data from the two groups compared is that the size of the hunting territories is in no sense a simple function of the size of the hunting group that makes use of them.

What then are the controlling factors in the size of hunting territories? In the first place it may be pointed out that there is nothing in the economic culture of these people to motivate the accumulation of large tracts of land. The products of the land are a primary source of wealth rather than the ownership of land in the sense of "real estate." For land has no value in exchange. Referring to intra-band variations in the size of hunting grounds Davidson remarks:[19] "It will be noted that some individuals own exceptionally large tracts of land . . . such conditions, however, are not the result of willful endeavors on the part of the respective owners to acquire property and wealth. It may be said in this respect that no lust for territory larger than that necessary to insure a reasonable bounty of fur, is at all present in the minds of these people." I can only add that, among all the Algonkian people with whom I have been acquainted, there is also no prestige whatsoever that accrues to the man who hunts over a large tract of land as compared with the man who traps over a smaller area. So we must conclude that so far as intra-band factors are concerned, economic competition is not a controlling factor in the size of hunting grounds; nor can variability be connected with any ranking system or the functioning of prestige.

Nor do I think that the size of hunting tracts is in any sense a function of inheritance rules that tend to stabilize rigid boundaries over the generations. While I cannot give the evidence here I can only say that my own data from the Berens River indicate great flexibility in this regard. The hunting territory boundaries of one generation are not *precisely* those that prevail in the next generation.

It seems difficult, therefore, to explain variations in the size of hunting territories in terms of purely cultural factors.

If we now turn to non-cultural influences that might possibly be control-ling factors in the size of hunting grounds, one factor that conceivably might influence the situation is to be sought in population dynamics. Assuming that migration from the region does not take place, what effect does either increase or decrease of population have upon the size of hunting territories? In the two areas from which I have cited data, we have contrasting pictures in this respect. The Grand Lake Victoria Indians in the period prior to and succeeding Davidson's study show a decline in population (252 in 1912 to 85 in 1929),[20] whereas between 1902 and 1934 the Berens River population increased sixty-nine percent (527 to 891). While it might appear that the smaller size of the Berens River hunting territories could be explained as a result of population pressure within a limited habitat, I must confess that I see no actual evidence for this. My mapping shows that the boundaries of hunting grounds could be extended but this has not taken place. All I can say is that there seems no economic advantage in doing so, since their needs are met just as well by hunting in more restricted areas. In other words, the decisive factor may be the relative abundance of game and fur-bearing animals available within a given area. Davidson made this general observa-tion twenty years ago.[21] He pointed out that "physically it is possible for a man to cover only so much trapline. His catch for the year, therefore, is not limited by the amount of distance covered but rather by the number of game animals in his district. A normal territory, therefore, would be one which would annually produce the yearly catch of the trapper. *Such a tract would thus depend in size more upon the abundance of game than upon its extent in miles. Given this normal territory, additional lands would be useless to a hunter.*" (Italics ours.) This seems to me a sufficient explanation of the situation observed among the Berens River Indians. But the same principle may be invoked to explain the *larger* hunting territories of the Grand Lake Victoria Indians. That is to say, if it were known that game was less abundant in the region hunted over by the Grand Lake Victoria Indians, then it may have been *necessary* for them to range over *larger* areas in order to make a living. Since we know that the ratio of hunters to non-hunters is the same in both areas and that the standard of living is approximately the same, this provides an attractive ecological hypothesis. Unfortunately, I have not been able to secure the necessary data on the relative abundance of fauna in the two regions that would be required to prove that such a differential factor is the crucial determinant of the size of hunting territories.[22]

The situation is complicated by another factor which is present in the Grand Lake Victoria region and absent in the Berens River area. This factor is the direct competition with white trappers for fur-bearing animals among the Grand Lake Victoria Indians. Davidson is quite explicit about this. He says: "Throughout the domain of the Grand Lake Victoria and Lake Barriere Indians, the trapping operations of the white men are yearly becoming more serious. The alarm felt by the Indians may well be realized when we learn from one hunter that as many as twelve white men were trapping on his own territory in the winter of 1925–26. Other Indians report the presence of any number between two and six, and *not one* Indian reported that his territory has not been invaded some time during the season."[23]

From an ecological point of view this means that the actual hunter-game ratio is quite different than is the case if we consider the Indians alone. It also means, of course, that there is less game available to the Indian trappers. Even if we ignore a possible differential in the incidence of the economically valuable fauna in the two regions, the presence of white trappers introduces a new factor whose influence has to be evaluated in the case of the Grand Lake Victoria people. Since this influence has not been studied it is impossible to draw any conclusions. It may even be considered an open question as to whether the factor of white competition bears any relation to the size of the hunting territories in this region. But it cannot be denied that the situation as described is part of the modern ecological picture. At any rate, I must let the solution of this particular problem rest.

It has been the major purpose of this paper to call attention to the need for a type of investigation which goes beyond the bare ethnographic facts of land tenure rather than to give any final solution to particular problems. On the basis of the concrete material presented it has been shown that a number of possible explanations of the mean difference in the size of the hunting territories in these two localities must be rejected. On the other hand, certain factors that appear to be of determinative importance have been pointed out. If investigations based on sound ecological hypotheses were carried through rigorously and systematically on the basis of an inclusive body of relevant facts, I believe that we could arrive at an explanation of the actual factors that control the size of Algonkian hunting grounds as well as the basic dynamics of the hunting territory system as a whole.

Notes

Paper read at American Anthropological Association meetings, Albuquerque NM, December, 1947; reprinted from *American Anthropologist* 51 (1949): 35–45.

1. Speck's initial paper, based on a lecture delivered at the University of Pennsylvania, was entitled, "Basis of American Indian Ownership of the Land." It was printed in the *Old Penn Weekly Review*, vol. 13, no. 16, 1915.

2. Lewis H. Morgan, e.g., in his characterization of the stage of Savagery, had written, "Lands, as yet hardly a subject of property, were owned by the tribes in common." (*Ancient Society*, 537)

3. Speck's "Family Hunting Territories and Social Life of Various Algonkian Bands of the Ottawa Valley," with maps showing the actual boundaries of the hunting grounds of the Timaggami, Timiskaming, Kipawa and Dumoine bands, was published in 1915. A preliminary world-wide survey of similar systems of land ownership appeared in the *Proceedings of the 22nd International Congress of Americanists* (1928). The contributions of Cooper, Davidson, and myself to this phase of the problem can be easily located in the literature cited and need not be referred to here. But attention needs to be called to Cooper's discussion of the three major forms of ownership in severalty, since this important contribution is somewhat disguised under the generic title "Land Tenure among the Indians of Eastern and Northern North America" and it appeared in a relatively obscure source.

4. "Is the Algonkian Family Hunting-Ground System Pre-Columbian?" The world distribution of the family hunting-ground and related systems is brought up to date in this article. For additional bibliographical items see Cooper, 1941, note 87, 57.

5. Cooper, 1939, 84–85.

6. Cooper, 1946, 294. Cf. the same author's discussion of the factors that he deems "responsible in large part for the system of tenure in *severalty*," observable among marginal peoples in his *Temporal Sequence*, 1941, 59–60.

7. Speck and Eiseley, 1942.

8. Speck, 1922, 196.

9. Speck, 1917, 89.

10. In his first paper, Speck wrote: "The districts among the Algonkians seem to average between two and four hundred square miles to each family in the main habitat, while on the tribal frontiers they may average from two to four times as large." This estimate of the range of the mean size of Algonkian hunting territories is repeated word for word in Speck, 1928, except that the phrase "nearer the central range of the tribes" is inserted after "habitat." The need for more precise information is illustrated by the fact that, while one of the groups discussed in this paper falls within the range indicated, the Berens River Ojibwa do not.

11. Cooper, 1941, 59, already has suggested the determinative weight of

"migratory or markedly nomadic, and/or gregarious habits of the fauna," upon the prevalence of a *communal* type of land tenure and the contrasting influence of "non-migratory and/or non-gregarious fauna, or fauna of a relatively restricted home range," upon systems of tenure in *severalty*. Both groups of Indians discussed below primarily exploit animals of the latter category and are characterized by ownership in severalty. However, the question of the relative *incidence* of the staple game animals in different localities is another variable of possible weight in the determination of the *size* of hunting grounds.

12. Cf. the statement of Cooper, 1946, 293, that "these various considerations and points of evidence suggest that the family hunting-ground system, as found among the various discontinuously distributed hunting peoples in the coniferous belt of North America and Eurasia, is of multiple rather than of unitary origin, representing local adaptation to differing ecologies and subsistence quests, and that it is not integral to taiga economy as such in the sense that it developed and spread uniformly with this economy." Such a statement is a far cry from the not-too-distant debates in cultural anthropology about diffusion *versus* independent development. It will no doubt become increasingly evident in our studies that any crude choice between such polarities, unless the crucial evidence is available, actually leaves us high and dry so far as the complex realities of the historic process are concerned.

13. Kroeber, 1939, 96.

14. Voegelin, 1941, has pointed out the linguistic unity. To my mind there can be no doubt about a parallel ethnic unity.

15. Davidson, 1926. [Ed. note: 1928a? 1926 not in references.]

16. Hallowell, unpublished Ms.

17. See Steward, 338, for these figures. Kroeber's (1934 and 1939) are expressed in number of persons per 100 km^2. It is also worth noting that the latter's density figure for the Ojibwa north of the Great Lakes, 9.54 persons per 100 km^2 (1939, 141), which is the equivalent of one person per 6.51 square miles, is practically identical with the figure given above for the Berens River Ojibwa.

18. Of the thirty-one hunting groups of the Grand Lake Victoria Indians, twenty-two have one active hunter; six others have two, while the remaining three have the maximum of three active hunters. In contrast, only five of the forty-three winter hunting-groups of the Berens River Ojibwa have a single hunter, while fifteen have three, six have five, and the two largest groups of all have ten active hunters each.

19. Davidson, 1928a, 87.

20. Figures from census (Dominion of Canada). The influenza epidemic of 1918 decimated the band approximately 25 percent.

21. Davidson, 1928a, 88.

22. Speck and Eiseley, 1942, 221, point out that "we are greatly in need . . . of a more detailed knowledge of the animal and human inter-relationships of the whole Canadian region. An approach to this aspect of the dove-tailing cycles of human and animal fluctuation in number will be a future step in the method of treatment of the economic problems of the area, under ecological conditions."

23. Davidson, 1928a, 73–74.

References

Cooper, John M.

1938   Land Tenure Among the Indians of Eastern and Northern North America. *Pennsylvania Archeologist,* 8: 55–59.

1939   Is the Algonquian Family Hunting Ground System Pre-Columbian? *American Anthropologist,* 41: 66–90.

1941   *Temporal Sequence and the Marginal Cultures.* Catholic University of America, Anth. Series, no. 10, Washington.

1946   The Culture of the Northeastern Indian Hunters: A Reconstructive Interpretation. In *Man in Northeastern North America.* Papers of the R. S. Peabody Foundation for Archeology, vol. 3, 272–305.

Davidson, D. S.

1928a   The Family-Hunting Territories of the Grand Lake Victoria Indians. *Atti del XXII Congresso Internaz. degli Americanisti,* Rome, 1926, 69–95.

1928b   Notes on Tete de Boule Ethnology. *American Anthropologist,* 30:18–45.

Hallowell, A. Irving

[n.d.]   The Hunting Customs and the Hunting Territories of the St. Francis Abenaki. Unpublished manuscript.

[n.d.]   Winter Hunting Groups, Hunting Territories, and Inheritance Rules among the Berens River Saulteaux (northern Ojibwa). Unpublished manuscript.

Kroeber, A. L.

1934   Native American Population. *American Anthropologist,* 36: 1–25.

1939   Cultural and Natural Areas of Native North America. *University of*

California Publications in American Archeology and Ethnology, vol. 38.

Morgan, Lewis H.

1878　*Ancient Society, or Researches in the Line of Human Progress from Savagery through Barbarism to Civilization*. Henry Holt & Co., New York. (Ed. Chas. Kerr & Co., Chicago, 1907.)

Speck, Frank G.

1915a　Basis of American Indian Ownership of the Land. *Old Penn Weekly Review,* 13: 181–196

1915b　*Family Hunting Territories and Social Life of Various Algonkian Bands of the Ottawa Valley*. Memoir 70, Anth. Series, no. 8, Geological Survey of Canada.

1917　Social Structure of the Northern Algonkian. Publications of the American Sociological Society, vol. 12.

1922　*Beothuk and Micmac*. Indian Notes and Monographs, Museum of the American Indian, Heye Foundation, New York.

1928　Land Ownership among Hunting Peoples in Primitive America and the World's Marginal Areas. *Atti del XXII Congresso Internaz. delgi Americanisti*, Rome, 1926, 323–32.

Speck, Frank G., and Loren C. Eiseley

1939　Significance of Hunting Territory Systems of the Algonkian in Social Theory. *American Anthropologist,* 41: 269–80.

1942　Montagnais-Naskapi Bands and Family Hunting Districts of the Central and Southeastern Labrador Peninsula. *Proceedings American Philosophical Society,* 85: 215–42.

Steward, Julian H.

1936　The Economic and Social Basis of Primitive Bands. In *Essays in Anthropology in Honor of Alfred Louis Kroeber*. University of California Press, Berkeley.

Voegelin, C. F.

1941　North American Indian Languages Still Spoken and Their Genetic Relationships. In *Language, Culture and Personality, Essays in Memory of Edward Sapir*. Sapir Memorial Publication Fund, Menasha, Wisconsin.

TEN

Cultural Factors in Spatial Orientation

Spatially, like temporally, coordinated patterns of behavior are basic to the personal adjustment of all human beings. They involve fundamental dimensions of experience and are a necessary condition of psychological maturity and social living. Without the capacity for space perception, spatial orientation and the manipulation of spatial concepts, the human being would be incapable of effective locomotion, to say nothing of being unable to coordinate other aspects of his behavior with that of his fellows in a common social life.[1] In addition to the psychophysical and psychophysiological conditions of human space perception, we know that variations occur, between one culture and another, with respect to the selective emphasis given to the spatial relations and attributes of things, the degree of refinement that occurs in the concepts employed, and the reference points that are selected for spatial orientation. The human individual is always provided with some culturally constituted means that are among the conditions which enable him to participate with his fellows in a world whose spatial attributes are, in part, conceptualized and expressed in common terms. Ontogenetically, self-orientation, object-orientation, and spatio-temporal orientation are concomitantly developed during the process of socialization.

Long ago Poincaré pointed out that the notion of space must be understood as a function of objects and all their relations. There is no such thing as space independent of objects. Relations among objects and the movements of objects are a necessary condition of space perception. More recently, James J. Gibson, approaching the problem from the standpoint of psychophysics, has developed the hypothesis "that space is constituted of the same variables as things . . . that surfaces and margins are what we see, not air. Space must be filled to be visible; empty space is an abstraction."[2] This author distinguishes problems concerned with (a) "the perception of the substantial or spatial world," "the world of colors, textures, surfaces, edges, slopes, shapes, and interspaces," what he calls *literal* perception; from

(b) "the perception of the world of useful and significant things to which we ordinarily attend." He calls the latter *schematic* perception.[3]

While it remains an open question how far the purely psychophysical dimensions of perception may be influenced by culturally constituted experiential factors, schematic perception, involving the meaningful aspects of experience, can hardly be understood without reference to an articulated world of objects whose relations and attributes become meaningful for the individual, not simply through the innate psychological potentialities he brings to experience but, above all, through the significance for experience that the development, patterning, transmission, and accumulation of past experience, in the form of a cultural heritage, have come to imply. The question: Is space perception native or acquired? though once hotly debated, is in actuality a pseudo-problem.[4] What Gibson argues against is an extreme form of perceptual relativism: "that perception is inevitably a constructive process which creates the world to suit the perceiver; that we see things not as they are but as we are." While "it is perfectly true," he says, "that perception can be fluid, subjective, creative, and inexact . . . it can also be literal . . . the student of human nature and society needs to remember this when he is in danger of assuming that men are the passive victims of their stereotypes and perceptual customs."[5]

Psychologists repeatedly have emphasized that unlike other aspects of experience (e.g., color and sound), which are mediated through highly specialized sense organs, perception of space requires the participation of several sense modalities including, for instance, tactual-kinesthetic components. There is no "spatial sense," equivalent to vision and hearing, by means of which we perceive such attributes of space as extension, shape, size, direction, locality, and distance. Such experience is "intersensory" by its very nature; yet it is as primary as experience mediated by specialized sensory modalities.[6] Furthermore, the role that differential linguistic and cultural factors play in the processes through which the spatial attributes of things become abstracted, conceptualized, expressed in traditional forms of speech, and made the basis of action cannot be overlooked in this case any more than it can be in the functioning of perception mediated through specialized sense modalities.

There is an additional factor, however, that has been neglected in discussions of space perception and spatial orientation. This is the peculiarly human capacity of achieving a level of psychological organization that makes possible the perception of the self as an object in a world of objects other than self. In addition to reference points anchored in the objective world, the human being constantly makes use of himself as a reference point. "Perceiving the world has an obverse aspect, perceiving oneself."[7] While we may, perhaps, assume this, it should not be forgotten that self-awareness as a universal psychological attribute of man is no more given at birth than the traditional schema of reference points to be found in a culture or the vocabulary of spatial reference. Self-identification and the perception of self as an object in relation to other objects is the result of a long socialization process, just as the skills underlying the achievement of a "sense of direction" only emerge from a complicated learning process. (See Hallowell, "The Ojibwa Self and its Behavioral Environment" [chapter 26, this volume].)

Furthermore, in order to be spatially oriented in the widest sense, that is, beyond the field of immediate perception, the individual must not only be aware of himself but of his own position in some *spatial schema*. At the same time he must be capable of maintaining awareness of his own changes in position, and be able to assume the position of others in the schema with reference to himself. What spatial orientation in man actually involves is a constant awareness of varying relations between the self and other objects in a spatial schema of traditionally defined reference points. If I have a destination beyond my limited field of vision, for example, I not only have to know where I am going but I have to know where I am now in relation to my goal and, as I move toward it, I have to be aware of the changing relations involved. In order to reach my goal and return to my starting point, I have to make use of formal or informal reference points. I may be guided, in part, by a "mental" map. But in any case, I have to maintain some kind of topographical or astronomical,[8] if not directional, orientation in which my own changing position must be appraised. Gibson points out that this type of locomotion—that is, "the act of going to an object or place beyond the range of vision—represents a much higher and more complicated level of mobility than that confined to a spatial field where optical stimulation yields all the necessary cues because the goal-object lies within it."[9] What we take for granted, without a close analysis of all the necessary conditions involved, is that the human individual will necessarily advance from the simpler to the more complicated level of finding his way about during the course of ontogenetic development. Yet this is certainly one of the vital points where the cultural factors that are an integral part of the spatialization of the world of man play an outstanding role. The human being not only advances from a rudimentary to a more complex level of spatial orientation and mobility; the possibility is opened to him through various kinds of symbolic means to become oriented in a spatial world that transcends his personal experience. Place naming, star naming, maps, myth and tale, the orientation of buildings, the spatial implications in dances and ceremonies, all facilitate the construction and maintenance of the spatial patterns of the world in which the individual must live and act.

While striking cultural variations occur, possible universals should be looked for. Is there any culture, for instance, in which there are *no* names for places and topographical features in the environment of the people? From the standpoint of human mobility and spatial orientation, this practice would appear to have a generic human function. When integrated with individual knowledge and experience of the terrain it affords a schema of reference points for topographical orientation. Such points are not only a guide to action but, once known, can be mentally manipulated and organized in the form of "mental maps," and the spatial schema inherent in them communicated.[10] Maps among nonliterate peoples are, of course, the projection in the form of graphic symbols of space relations abstracted from knowledge already available in these "mental maps" rather than the outcome of such sophisticated techniques as surveying, serial photography, etc.[11] It is amazing how accurate such maps can be.[12] While maps are of limited occurrence among nonliterate peoples, names of topographical features and places appear to be universal.

Perhaps the most striking feature of man's spatialization of his world is the fact that it never appears to be exclusively limited to the pragmatic level of action and perceptual experience.[13] Places and objects of various classes are conceptualized as having a real existence in distant regions. Even though the individual never experiences any direct perceptual knowledge of them—since information must be mediated through some symbolic means (the spoken or written word, graphic representation)—such regions are, nevertheless, an integral part of the total spatial world to which he is oriented by his culture. For man everywhere has cosmic concepts; he is oriented in a universe that has spatial dimensions. The individual not only has heard about other groups of human beings he may not have seen; they are given a *locale*. He knows *where* the land of the dead is and something about it even though he has not yet visited it. Gods and spirits are given an abode and mobility in space; they not only exist but they exist *somewhere*; they may be "here" now and later "there." Likewise in Western culture world explorations and science have accustomed us to accept as reliable all sorts of information about the location of distant peoples, about natural phenomena of various kinds, the location and contours of the land masses of the earth, and so on, all beyond our direct perceptual experience. Astronomers, too, tell us about the spatial relations of bodies in the far-flung stellar universe. We assume, of course, that our knowledge of distant regions is more dependable than that of the primitive peoples we study, and this is undoubtedly true. At the same time it should not be forgotten that it is acquired by most individuals through symbolic mediation and that the qualitative differences of this knowledge are extremely recent in our own culture. We need only to compare the spatial orientation and knowledge of medieval man in Europe with our modern outlook to appreciate this. In *The Other World*, Howard R. Patch devotes a chapter to "Journeys to Paradise," many descriptive accounts of which are to be found in medieval literature. This author points out that "The Garden of Eden was universally believed to exist, and, although cut off from ordinary approach, was supposed still to be waiting for the saints before their ascent to Heaven. Medieval maps often showed its location."[14] In other words, it was a *place* located on the earth that might be visited by travelers, "even if they had to have recourse to supernatural means."[15] Even subsequent to medieval times there are references to such journeys and the author notes that, "when Christopher Columbus discovered the New World, he thought he was close to the Garden of Eden."[16] Today the Garden of Eden has disappeared from our universe; it has no spatial existence. Similarly, Dante could present to his readers an intelligible image of hell "pictured as a huge funnel-shaped pit, situated beneath the Northern Hemisphere and running down to the centre of the earth."[17] If we now ask, *where* is hell, what answer can we give if the cosmographic picture of our universe, defined on the basis of scientific knowledge, is accepted? As *places* heaven and hell in this universe are "nowhere."

What appears to be particularly significant in our human adjustment to the world is that over and above pragmatic needs for orientation and without any pretense to reliable knowledge of regions of space outside their personal experience, human beings in all cultures have built up a frame of spatial reference that has included the farther as well as the more proximal, the spiritual as well as the mundane, regions of their universe. What the recent history of Western culture demonstrates is the revolutionary challenge offered to the spatial orientation embedded in an older tradition when more reliable knowledge of distant regions, combined with the development of abstract mathematical concepts of space, established the foundations of the qualitatively different type of spatial orientation that is now possible for us.

The unique combination of factors that account for the distinctive mode of human spatial orientation has not always been clearly recognized. For a long period, dating back to the late eighteenth century when the idea of the Noble Savage had such a vogue, the problem was obscured because of the widespread notion that savages, as compared with civilized man, had an innate sense of direction. This notion was based to some extent on the exaggeration, if not misrepresentation, of the observations of early travelers and missionaries. Pierre Jaccard, in a book which should be better known,[18] calls attention to the excellent observations of Père Lafitau (1724) on the Iroquois. Their later distortion by Charlevoix, he thinks, gave rise to "la legende de l'instinct d'orientation des sauvages." In the nineteenth century, after the concept of biological evolution took hold, one of the prevailing ideas was that the "senses" of primitive man were more acute than those of civilized man, even though he might be intellectually inferior. Indeed, "savages" and the lower animals were thought by some to be alike in many respects. Haeckel (1868) in his *Natural History of Creation* observed that if one compared African Negroes, Bushmen, and the Andamanese with apes, dogs, and elephants, on the one hand, and with civilized man, on the other, one would be compelled to make a distinction, not between man and animal, but between civilized peoples on the one side, and savages and animals on the other. The question then of an innate, or special, sense of direction in primitive peoples became entangled with the more general question whether "primitive" mind and "civilized" mind represented psychological categories that had an evolutionary significance. Jaccard concludes:

> Si tous les sauvages possédaient des facultés de direction, inconnues de nous, on pourrait peut-être accepter provisoirement l'hypothèse d'une différence de nature entre leur psychologie et la nôtre. Mais cette supposition n'est plus même permise aujourd'hui: il est en effet démontré que la plupart des non-civilisés sont tout aussi embarrassés que nous lorsqu'ils se trouvent dans une région dépourvue de repères, loin des horizons familiers de leur pays natal... loin de montrer la bestialité des sauvages, les faits d'orientation lointaine témoignent de l'excellence des pouvoirs d'attention, de memoire et d'observation des plus intelligents d'entre eux... c'est de reconnaitre que les sauvages et les civilisés possèdent a des degres divers une même aptitude, plus ou moins développée chez les différents individus, selon les circonstances... l'hypothèse d'un sens particulier de la direction, affiné chez le sauvage et émoussé chez le civilisé, par suite des conditions d'existence, n'est pas plus soutenable que les

interprétations basées sur une opposition entre l'intelligence et l'instinct. Aucune différence appreciable n'apparait entre les capacités sensorielles et les fonctions mentales élémentaires des diverses races humaines: ce fait seul suffit à démontrer l'erreur de toutes les théories attribuant aux sauvages des facultés d'orientation inconnues des civilisés.[19]

We now know, of course, that even in studying animal behavior, the concept of "instinct" is too categorical and affords us no help at all in explaining how animals find their way about. Despite the fact that we are still in the dark on many frontiers of this area of investigation, great progress has been made in our detailed knowledge of some of these determinants in vertebrates and insects.[20] Astonishing as the performance of some of these creatures is with respect to their mobility, we can be certain that the crucial determinants are of a different order than those in human spatial orientation. Consequently, although at a very rudimentary perceptual level, there certainly is some overlapping in the spatial world of ourselves and other animals, the phenomenological differences must be very great indeed no matter what local cultural variables are among the human factors involved.[21]

THE SPATIAL ORIENTATION OF THE SAULTEAUX
Directional Orientation

From an abstract point of view it might appear that the basic directional orientation of the Saulteaux is equivalent to that of occidental culture, since they recognize four cardinal directions as fundamental reference points which can be roughly equated with north, south, east, and west. Actually, the equivalence is not only historically fortuitous; it differs from our own directional orientation qualitatively and functionally in important respects.

The occidental directional schema is based on scientific knowledge that the Saulteaux do not possess. In our schema "true" north is taken as an absolute reference point; it is determined precisely by mechanical means, and instrumental correction for possible error is made under certain circumstances. Furthermore, the possession of a magnetic compass and the knowledge of how to use it enable us to check our directional orientation exactly at any time.

The Saulteaux, on the other hand, rely exclusively upon the direct observation of natural phenomena in order to maintain their directional orientation. Their most inclusive reference points are the North Star, the movements of the sun, and the "homes" of the four winds. Sometimes to these are added "straight up" (zenith), and "down" (nadir). The standardized and linguistically formulated cardinal directions of their culture, however, refer only to the four winds. It is through the traditional emphasis upon these that the wider aspects of their spatial universe are defined.

In their mythology the winds are anthropomorphic beings, each associated with a complementary direction. The winds are brothers who at birth enunciate their personal relations to humanity. The firstborn was East Wind, who said, "I shall be fairly kind to human beings." The next was South Wind, who said, "I'll be very good and treat human beings well, as long as any exist on this earth." The third child born spoke and said, "Human beings shall call me West Wind. I'll be a little rough on them but I'll never be wicked." "Be easy on our mother," he went on as another boy popped out. This one said, "Human beings shall call me North Wind. I'll have no mercy on any human being. I'll treat him just the same as the animals." At this remark his brothers asked, "How do you expect human beings to exist if you are going to treat them like that?" (But no answer is given in the myth.) Shortly after this the brothers decided that they could not remain together any longer. The East Wind said, "I'll go to live in the east." The West Wind said, "I'll sit opposite you at the other end of the earth." The South Wind said, "I'll go to the southern end of the earth," and the North Wind said, "I'll go to the northern end."[22]

In another myth North Wind invites his brother South Wind to a trial of strength, but is unable to worst him. Then the South Wind invites his brother North Wind to come south for a return contest. All the South Wind did was to blow on him. After the first couple of days North Wind could hardly hold his head up. One of his eyes drooped, and then the other. Finally, on the sixth day he had to give up; he was beaten. The South Wind said, "Now you know you're not the boss of everything." "And we know he is not the boss," added the narrator, "for, if he were, we would never have any summer."[23]

For the Saulteaux, direction is only partially abstracted from *place*. That is, their conception has more the meaning "in the direction of such and such a place," "toward *x*." What we refer to abstractly as the cardinal directions are to them the *homes* of the winds, the places they come from. Similarly, east is thought of as the place where the sun rises; west, the place where it sets; south is the place to which the souls of the dead travel, and the place from which the summer birds come. In a myth summer is stolen from a place in the south. Indeed, the Saulteaux equivalents for north, south, east, and west are *place names* in a very real sense, rather than abstract terms for direction. They are far, distant, it is true, but in myths at least, people have been there. They define the periphery of the Saulteaux world, being the "farthest" places, although not different except in generality of direction, from places in the immediate environment. Such a connotation exists in Western civilization side by side with the highly abstract one expressed in terms of angles and their measurement used in science. We say, "He lives in the West," or "The South grows cotton." The terms "Occident" and "Orient" are also used as nouns denoting places or regions. The latter arose at a period when, like the Saulteaux, the people employing them thought that the earth was flat.

I do not mean to imply that the Saulteaux terms are never used abstractly. But the degree to which this occurs is a function of the social situation. Abstraction is at its highest level when directional terms are employed in finding one's way about or in constructing a ceremonial pavilion. This may happen similarly with direction toward any place: a place, *x*, may be defined as "on the way to" *y*.

Thus it is inevitable that the directional orientation of these Indians is more flexible and less exact than our own, and that they must rely upon cues from several different classes of natural phenomena. Such limitations are intrinsic to the traditional means with which their culture provides them for ascertaining directional orientation. There are many instances of these limitations. I have heard Indians refer to the Milky Way, which is considered the path the Summer Birds follow flying north, as running north and south. This is not the case, but the approximate direction satisfies them. Another example is to be found on a map of Eagle Lake drawn by Adam Keeper, an Indian at [Little] Grand Rapids. On it he marked the four directions, but he was not aware of the discrepancy between his directional orientation and the measured directions of our schema. This is demonstrated by the fact that while he included a neatly ruled line representing the boundary between the provinces of Manitoba and Ontario, he made no use of it as one of his directional coordinates. Every Indian knows this line because it is actually cut out through the woods for miles and miles, and it runs exactly north and south. The fact that Adam ignored this cue shows the extent to which he has clung to his culturally constituted orientation in drawing the map, and the extent to which the local spatial interrelations of landmarks and contours predominated for him.

We can be certain, then, that the north of the Saulteaux is not our exact north and that the other directions they recognize are likewise approximate, more inclusive, than ours. For example, east means "in the general direction of east" and is closer to our everyday usage when exact reckoning is unnecessary. If an Indian is asked where the east is he will point to where the sun rises. From his point of view it is unnecessary to take into account the variations in the sun's positions at different seasons of the year and to arrive at a measured point on the horizon designated "due" east. What the range of their margin of error may be I do not know; but it is obvious that for the Saulteaux directions, unlike our own, are not fixed coordinates.

Qualitatively and functionally therefore, the existence of a four-directional schema in Western culture, on the one hand, and in Saulteaux culture, on the other, presents only a superficial resemblance. The behavioral implications in the two societies are quite different. Western man has been freed from the direct observation of nature in so far as he depends upon mechanical instruments for the determination of direction, or does not need to maintain his orientation with respect to compass points at all so far as the pursuit of daily life is concerned. The latter is particularly true of urban populations where such directional orientation may be almost completely ignored. [24]

The Saulteaux, however, constantly maintain a directional orientation. Traveling in the open as they do at all seasons of the year, across lakes and through a network of waterways in the summer and over snowclad wastes in winter, the direction of the wind in particular is always noticed and their practical activities adjusted accordingly.

Knowledge of Terrain

This culturally defined framework of directional orientation, with its customary reference points in certain natural phenomena, exposes the basic and most inclusive schema through which the Saulteaux orient themselves in a world of space. Closely integrated with it, and overshadowing it in importance, is the direct knowledge through experience of the topography of the country and the relations in space of one locality to another.

This direct experiential knowledge, however, varies greatly among individuals. Most of the Berens River Indians have never traveled any considerable distance from the locality in which they were born. There is also a marked sexual dichotomy in direct knowledge of the country. Women travel far less than men. There are certainly few, if any, women of the Pekangikum Band who have been to the mouth of the river and most of them have not been as far as [Little] Grand Rapids, halfway there. In contrast to this, most of the men of the Pekangikum Band have been both to the mouth of the river and [Little] Grand Rapids.[25] At any rate, it would be erroneous to assume that a first-hand, detailed knowledge of all parts of the river and its environs is possessed by any single individual. The terrain which is most familiar to these Indians is their winter hunting ground and the region surrounding the fishing settlement in which they live during the summer months. They are, in short, bound in their direct knowledge and experience to the areas with which their major economic activities are connected, a narrowly circumscribed spatial world which, even under modern conditions, has expanded very little. But within these limits the individual often possesses a phenomenally rich knowledge of the details of the terrain that contrasts sharply with his ignorance of parts of the country about which he has no direct knowledge[26] and of the still wider spatial world regarding which he sometimes entertains fantastic ideas.

In functional terms, it is not only the direct experience of the terrain which assists the individual in building up his spatial world; language crystallizes this knowledge through the customary use of place names. These in turn act as geographical reference points by means of which localities of various classes may be organized in spatial terms. This is not to imply that in Saulteaux culture the range of their application is coextensive with the total number of lakes, islands, points, rivers, and streams that might be named. Place names function integrally with the geographical knowledge and experience of the individual. Consequently, the local place names referring to topographical features within the radius of a particular summer settlement[27] are not known to the Indians of other settlements and the same applies to those attached to the geographical features of the winter hunting grounds. On the other hand, the place names of the major lakes, rivers, etc., and a general knowledge of their directions from their home and vague distances such as "long journey," of the environs of the Berens River as a whole are known to every Indian, regardless of whether he has ever traveled them or not. Correlated with the directions, these reference points define the wider limits of the geographical environment in which these Indians think and act, just as the place names for more circumscribed localities serve to organize the space relations of their local environment.

Beyond the Berens River itself, and peripheral to it, only a few geographical localities are at all familiar to the average Indian. On the west side of Lake Winnipeg the names of the larger lakes are known and a few Indian reserves and trading posts. To the north, trading posts such as Norway House, Oxford [House], God's Lake, stand out, and such geographical points as Deer Lake and Island Lake. Of course, every Berens River Indian has heard of Hudson Bay and the rivers that flow into it. To the southeast, Lake Seul is well known because long ago a number of Berens River families came from there. To the south there are a number of rivers that are familiar, particularly the Red River which flows north to Lake Winnipeg. Cities like Selkirk and Winnipeg are known, and Ottawa because the government is there. But no Indian has been to all these places, and I am sure that their location with respect to one another and to the Berens River district is not understood.

If any of these places is thought of spatially I am certain that it is only as the context of the reference requires it. Any idea of its relation to other places in a spatial schema that is conceived as a geographical continuation of the Berens River region itself is totally foreign to the minds of these people. This seems to indicate that without some graphic means as an aid, place names are only effective in organizing one's spatial knowledge within the limits of one's direct experience or through a limited extension to regions immediately peripheral to such experience. Outside of this they tend to become disparate and unorganized, verbally known places.

Native Maps

Within a familiar terrain, however, such as the part of the country which he has known since childhood, or his hunting ground, an individual clearly grasps the precise location and has some idea of the relative distances of every significant detail of the topography in relation to every other. When integrated with some inclusive directional orientation such knowledge needs only graphic projection, and we have a rudimentary *map*. It is significant, nevertheless, that this organization of the spatial perceptions of the individual into a coordinated whole, a "mental map,"[28] applies only within the narrow limits indicated. It is deeply imbedded in the "active" experience of the individual.

That such a well-integrated organization of the spatial relations of certain parts of their geographical environment exists in some terms in the minds of some individuals may be inferred in several ways. I had in my possession maps of the National Topographical Series which are based on airplane photographs and on which the smallest lakes, rivers, and creeks are represented. In the first place, a number of Indians who had never seen a detailed map of the part of the country with which they were most familiar almost immediately grasped the geographical relations on these once a few landmarks had been identified. But it was necessary to orient the map in relation to the observer. The Indians could not adapt themselves to looking at it in the conventional manner familiar to us with north at the top. They always had to have north on the map matched with north as it actually was from their point of view at the moment. Once they were fully oriented, it appeared as if they rediscovered on the map what was already organized in their minds. Some of them felt so much at home that often when I was trying to get them to delineate their trap lines or the boundaries of their hunting territories on the map, they would delay the process by side conversations with other Indians present, pointing to the outlet of some little creek where a moose had been killed or where some other event of interest to them had taken place.

Still more convincing evidence of the organization of the details of geographical relations in the mind of the individual was demonstrated by the objectification of such information in the form of maps which certain individuals drew for me. I secured five of these from three different men. That there is considerable individual variation in the ability to project such knowledge in graphic form is suggested by the admiration of other Indians for these maps. They said that it would have been impossible for them to perform such a task. The making of maps, however, was known in aboriginal days.

These aboriginal maps were intended to guide the individual using them through territory unknown to him. Their purpose was not to delineate a section of the country as such, but to indicate a route to be followed, and the emphasis was upon a succession of landmarks roughly indicated in their relations to one another and with only such other details of the topography as were necessary for the identification of the landmarks of primary interest. This is a very rudimentary form of map which does not require the refined abstract coordination of place, direction, distance, area, and contour that we expect. Areas and distances might be only relatively proportional, for instance, and yet such a crude delineation would serve its purpose.[29] The graphic emphasis upon a succession of landmarks is worth noting because it bears a close correspondence to the actual method of traveling about, just as the very limited geographical region for which detailed special knowledge is organized in the minds of individuals.[30] As might be expected, the narrow geographical limits of such organized positive knowledge bears an inverse relation to the ignorance of the terrain outside of the experience of the individual.[31] In this connection it is well to remind ourselves that without maps it would likewise be impossible for us to obtain any exact comprehension of geographical relations outside our experience.[32]

A startling illustration of this intrinsic limitation upon realistic spatial concepts of an unknown region is illustrated by the following episode. All the Indians were interested in a series of photographs I had taken of them, and some of them also were intrigued by the large-scale maps of their country to which I have already referred. So, when one old man asked me to send him a *photograph* of the United States, I thought my interpreter had misunderstood him and that what he referred to was a map. But no! What he wanted was a photograph of the United States. Evidently the United States was to him a place regarding which he had only the vaguest idea and no notion whatsoever of its spatial extensity.

Travel

There still remains the practical question: How *do* the Saulteaux find their way about and what cues do they employ? The answer is a simple one: by means of the directional cues already described, combined with the constant use of all the relevant knowledge of the topography of the country they possess.

In addition to standardized reference points, i.e., named places and named directions, this includes a mass of impressions undiscriminated in speech but immensely important nevertheless. The characteristic manner of their procedure at all seasons, and whether traveling on land or water, can be reduced to a common principle. They always move from one point to another, rather than in a given direction toward a goal.[33] Directional orientation usually functions as the wider frame of reference to facilitate the step by step procedure.

In principle, this step by step procedure emerges in certain mythological narratives where it takes the following form: The protagonist is directed from point to point in a strange country by a series of old women. The first old woman he encounters not only directs him on his way, she tells him what to look out for, how to avoid obstacles to his progress, and so on. And finally, she tells him that he will come upon another old woman on whom he can depend for directional advice for the next stage of his journey. Of course, events occur as anticipated; the second old woman is reached who directs him to a third. The analogy to actual travel should be clear. Familiar landmarks in a journey correspond to the old women; they mark the nodal points in a geographical progression in space and while they fail to give advice in a literal sense, they are anticipatory signs of the particular features of the country in the ensuing segment of the journey that must be mentally prepared for before they are encountered.[34]

A commonplace illustration of ordinary procedure is illustrated by the ascent of the Berens River from its mouth to [Little] Grand Rapids, a hundred miles inland from Lake Winnipeg. The river is not in its entire length the natural road we usually think a river to be, for in places it opens into lakes. On this portion of it there are approximately fifty rapids, all named, which function as the nodal points in the journey. It is these geographical items which are checked off, as it were, in traveling up and down the stream, and one's position on the river at any time, particularly when eating and sleeping, is always talked about with reference to this schema of rapids. They also function as anticipatory signs of the features of the country to be encountered between them. No wonder then that the local Indians thought it curious and even hazardous when some white men a few years ago ascended the river without a guide. They were probably equipped with the excellent maps that are available. To the Indians they would have no anticipatory signs to guide them; they would not know what to expect.

A journey I once made across Lake Winnipeg in a skiff with an improvised sail illustrates the step by step principle in terms of another mode of travel. It also happened that the early part of the trip was made in a heavy fog which obscured the ordinary visual cues. My guides were, of course, very familiar with the directions of landmarks. Leaving the reserve early in the morning we rowed along the shore to Flathead Point where we disembarked to eat breakfast. Pigeon Point was not visible, but we headed in that direction rowing all the way. The wind was from the northwest. We set sail for Commissioner's Island, which we reached about two and a half hours later. The fog having lifted somewhat in the meantime, we were able to sight the island some distance away and adjust our course accordingly.[35] From there we made for Sandhill Island, which we reached in an hour and a half. We spent the night there. The next morning it was easy to reach Stony Point and then to follow the shore south to Jack Head.

An analogous principle of travel in winter is set up under quite different circumstances when an Indian lays his trap line and makes his rounds periodically. The relation of the traps to each other, to certain topographical features of the country, and to his camp, define a spatial order in which he regularly moves from point to point.

In winter, however, during long journeys on snowshoes or with a dogsled, when darkness obscures familiar landmarks and a storm makes even the stars invisible, then directional orientation inferred from the wind must be depended upon as the main cue. Under these conditions one has no choice but to proceed in a given direction; it is impossible to follow the visible cues provided by a series of landmarks, and it is possible to lose one's way badly. If directional orientation by means of the wind fails, there is nothing to do but make camp and wait until weather conditions change and the usual cues can be picked up again.

Topographical cues are, in fact, so important that if masked by snow an individual may lose his way even on familiar ground. An Indian once told me of such an experience which he considered very humorous because the trail was one frequently traveled by everyone—I had often used it myself in summer. But my friend missed his way one winter night when the drifted snow had radically distorted cues familiar even at that season of the year. On the other hand, there are well-known general patterns in the topography of their country which are used by the Indians as cues. The rocky ridges as well as the muskegs east of Lake Winnipeg, for instance, run east to west like the rivers so that whether it is cloudy or misty, night or day, a general orientation is possible. This pattern also can be used as a cue in winter when snow is on the ground. A Berens River Indian once went to fight a forest fire on the west side of the lake. He got lost because he was not familiar with local topographical landmarks and the muskegs had a different directional pattern. Not being aware of this latter fact, he relied on the muskegs and became disoriented. To an outsider, general topographical patterns would not be obvious so that without any explanation of the actual clues being used it might appear somewhat mysterious how the Indians familiar with the country did find their way about in stormy or snowy weather and without a compass.

In connection with this dependence upon topographical cues it is interesting to recall the predicament of Wísakedják, the culture hero of the Saulteaux, told in a myth. Wísakedják had been temporarily deprived of his sight by getting his head encased in a bear skull, and the method he employed to find his way about was to ask each tree he bumped into what its name was. Wísakedják wished to reach a lake since he thought he might find some people there, and he accomplished this by differentiating between trees that grew near the water and those that did not, adjusting his course accordingly.[36]

If, as sometimes is the case in winter, there is a well-marked trail in the snow to be followed, then travel is greatly simplified. Under such conditions the Indian participates in one of the amenities of Western culture, the road, which we take for granted and which so enormously facilitates our movements from place to place. Neither directional orientation nor the use of such cues as the Saulteaux are compelled to employ are necessary in following a modern road. The contrast between this method of getting about and the other procedures described brings into sharp relief a basic difference in the pragmatic aspects of spatial orientation as demanded by Saulteaux culture on the one hand and Western culture, on the other.

Fear of Disorientation

The sharp contrast between the extremely intimate knowledge of a familiar terrain and the very hazy ideas which are entertained about other regions is sufficient, I believe, to account for a certain timidity on the part of these Indians in venturing into unknown territory unless accompanied by someone who is already acquainted with the region. While directional orientation can be maintained in unknown regions, the lack of all the well-known landmarks inevitably must lead to a certain amount of spatial disorientation. And there is always the possibility that one may really become lost. Hence, there is rational ground for apprehension.

A feeling of satisfactory spatial orientation, then, probably is one of the basic ties that bind the individual to familiar territory. The Indian would not analyze or express his feelings in such terms, but I think that it is a legitimate inference we are enabled to make from the very nature and character of his spatial orientation. It is likewise consistent with the basic role played by spatial orientation in all human behavior. For we, too, feel some sense of spatial disorientation in a strange city or country, even when such orientation is less vital to our activities than to those of the Saulteaux and under cultural conditions which offer an opportunity for a more immediate and adequate reorientation. Furthermore, the feeling of the Saulteaux themselves about the loss of an adequate spatial orientation was illustrated in their concern when on one occasion I had difficulty in finding my way back to our camp, and their admonitions on others to be careful and not to lose my way when I went about by myself. Since I never was lost and their concern at times seemed a bit silly to me, I think that their attitude in these situations is quite revealing.[37]

The same apprehension on their part can be demonstrated in another way by the story of the Indian who found his way back home from a strange part of the country. Early in the nineteenth century, when the Hudson's Bay Company reigned supreme in western Canada, some Indians raided a post at Sandy Narrows, in order to obtain knives, powder, etc. The leader of the party was a man called Brimmed Hat [Tcɑsämän]. After he was apprehended it was planned to send him to England where he could observe for himself the power and magnitude of the white man's civilization. On the way to York Factory where he was to be put on a ship, Brimmed Hat escaped. This was near White Mud Falls on the Hayes River. Later he showed up again at Sandy Narrows, a distance of approximately three hundred miles as the crow flies. To the Indians such a journey was miraculous, and they believe he must have had the aid of supernatural helpers. First of all, he could not proceed in the usual way from one known point to another in a strange country. From our standpoint a correct directional orientation might have been a sufficient guide to him, combined, perhaps, with some general knowledge of the watersheds since Hayes River drains into Hudson Bay and the Berens River is on a shed from which the rivers empty into Lake Winnipeg. Besides this, he had no gun, not even a knife, and no way to secure skins to make new moccasins.[38]

Cosmic Space

The apprehension with which the Saulteaux individual views excursions into strange regions, combined with his lack of experience in any but a circumscribed environment, and the limitations imposed by his culture upon the acquisition of accurate knowledge of distant regions, offers him no critical basis for an evaluation of what is beyond his experience. It is no wonder, then, that the traditional dogmas of his native culture in regard to the wider reaches of the universe are so thoroughly reified and uncritically accepted as part of his spatial world.

There is the Land of the Dead, for instance, far to the south. There is a road which leads directly to it which deceased souls follow, and a few individuals are known to have visited the Land of the Dead and afterwards returned to their homes. They have given accounts of their journey and of what they saw there. (See Hallowell, "Spirits of the Dead in Saulteaux Life and Thought" [chapter 22, this volume]. I remember that my interpreter once told an old Indian that I came from the south and that the United States lay in that direction. The old man simply laughed in a wise way and made no comment.

The earth itself, according to Saulteaux belief, is flat, a notion that is, of course, supported rather than contradicted by the naive observation and experience of all human beings. No Indian can be convinced that the earth is spherical. According to Saulteaux dogma the earth is also an island, and there is an account in mythology (the earth-diver motif) of how this island came into existence. Contacts with the whites and, in certain cases, acquaintance with maps in the geography texts of their children have strengthened rather than undermined this dogma. For many Indians have been told, and others have seen it indicated on the maps of the world, that the western hemisphere is surrounded by water.

A stratification of worlds within the cosmos is another item of Saulteaux dogma that defines certain space relations in their conceptual universe. Since the earth is flat, it is easy to understand how this additional feature fits the general scheme. While this idea of the stratification of worlds is developed in considerable detail in other parts of America and even among related Algonkian peoples,[39] the Saulteaux emphasize only the lower world immediately below this one, although they assert that there are other worlds farther down as well as one or two above "the central plane" on which they live.

The world that lies just below is called *pitawákamik*. It is also peopled by *änicinábek*, Indians. These lower world people only differ from those living on this earth by being immortal. When they grow old, they then become young again. This underworld was once visited by some Berens River Indians. They went out hunting and saw some strangers whom they followed to the lower world. At first the people living there wanted to kill them. But when the lower world people found that the Berens River Indians were so much like themselves, their lives were spared. The same species of animals and plants are found in *pitawákamik* as up here, but when it is night there it is day here and vice versa.

I have never heard of a corresponding upper world inhabited by human beings. However, the idea of strata in the universe is exemplified in the account in one of the myths in which the youngest brother of Mätcīkīwis climbs up a tree to Thunder Bird Land. Here the Thunder Birds appear in human guise. When the daughters of the "boss" of these creatures come to earth they appear as women and marry human beings.[40]

Within this cosmic scheme certain spiritual entities are given a specific location. To some extent such cosmic positions are correlated with observable natural phenomena. Since thunder is heard only in the summer and usually towards the south, the Thunder Birds are associated with the south as the spiritual controllers of the summer birds and are believed to inhabit one of the upper strata of the universe. On the other hand, the controllers of the fur-bearing animals are given a northern position in the cosmic space.

In other cases the cosmic position of certain entities seems arbitrary, and some have no determinate location.

From the standpoint of the Saulteaux themselves, these concepts of cosmic space and the position of the various spiritual entities and other inhabitants within it, all are articulated as parts of an integral whole. It is in terms of the full sweep of this schema that we must endeavor to comprehend the qualitative characteristics of the farther reaches of their spatial world, as well as the relevant features of the proximate geographical environment in which they live.

Directional Orientation in Ceremonialism

Directional orientation, however, is not altogether confined to situations in which individuals are moving from place to place. The lodge erected for the Midéwi·win, rectangular in ground plan, was always built on an east-west axis, as are the Wábano pavilions seen today. The entrance to both types of structure is at the east although two or more doors are made. The "place of honor" where the leader or leaders sit in both cases is on the south side near the east entrance. Another ceremony I witnessed, which had no superstructure, took place within a square bounded by stakes. The sides of the square were deliberately oriented in the four directions. In this case the entrance used was on the north side and at the close of the ceremony everyone left by the south "door." Graves are likewise oriented north and south as a rule; the deceased faces the south, which is the Land of the Dead. Elsie Clews Parsons reported that the Pueblo Indians usually avoid sleeping with the head in the orientation given the dead in burial. It never occurred to me to make inquiry on this point.[41]

Dancing always has a conventional direction. It is what we call "clockwise," but the Indians think of it in directional terms, i.e., from east to south to west to north to east. This is likewise the order of birth of the four winds in the myth cited. In the smoking of a ceremonial pipe the leader turns the stem in a clockwise direction and sometimes pauses when the stem has faced in each direction. The symbolism of this act lies in the fact that by including all the directions, all of the spiritual entities in the entire universe are the recipients of the smoke offering.[42]

The pavilion is a structural representation, in one sense, of the directions so that the *opposites*, north-south, east-west, and the *order* about the horizon may be recognized, but no further use is made of this.

The directional ordering of the Saulteaux spatial universe, therefore, is one that penetrates religious as well as secular life. And it is obvious that it has psychological implications qualitatively different from directional orientation in Western culture. The build-up of associations of north, south, east, and west with symbolic and mythological meanings makes the directions meaningful places. It further integrates other aspects of the culture and behavior so that a "living in" the world is experienced which has its own peculiar character. In other cultures directional orientation may deeply penetrate still other spheres of life and give the spatial orientation of the people a distinctive psychological caste.[43]

CONCLUSIONS

The development of man's mastery of space and the abstract concepts that have evolved along with it cannot be explained in any psychological terms which ignore the cultural factors involved. Human space perception is biologically rooted, but the level at which it functions in the individual is not reducible to innate capacities or maturational development. The process of socialization contributes experiential components that must be considered. Some of these acquired components of space perception are a function of the cultural milieu in which the individual has been reared. The cultural patterns of different societies offer different means by which spatial perceptions are developed, refined, and ordered. The spatial concepts of different societies also vary with respect to the degree of abstraction attained. There is also inter- and intra-societal variation in the utilization of different degrees of refinement of spatial perception in connection with different life activities. The variability is correlated with the fact that one set of conditions may demand very little in the way of spatial discriminations of a certain order (e.g., measurement), but considerable refinement in other respects (e.g., directional orientation).

Such considerations point to a wider historical question: How have the cultural means themselves developed? This is a matter for actual investigation, but our analysis of Saulteaux culture is suggestive in a negative respect. The point was stressed that the Saulteaux culture provided no incentive that would lead to the development of an abstract concept of area. On the other hand, they did draw crude maps in aboriginal days. The motive here was a very simple one: to provide a guide for the traveler in a strange country. There was a demand for maps for this purpose.

If we could illuminate the conditions and purposes in any given society which are relevant to the refinement and development of space perception, we would approach an answer to the historical question.

Notes

Reprinted from *Culture and Experience* (Philadelphia: University of Pennsylvania Press, 1955), 184–202.

1. In the Preface to his *Perception of the Visual World* (Boston, 1950), James J. Gibson remarks (vii) that, "The perception of what has been called space is the basic problem of all perception. We perceive a world whose fundamental variables are spatial and temporal—a world which extends and endures. Space perception (from which time is inseparable) is not, therefore, a division of the subject matter of perception but the first problem to be considered, without a solution for which other problems remain unclear. That a solution is lacking, most psychologists would agree. The existing theories to account for the spatial and temporal character of our perceptions are not very satisfactory."

2. Gibson, *Perception*, 228.

3. Gibson, *Perception*, 10.

4. See, e.g., M. D. Vernon, *Visual Perception* (Cambridge, England, 1937), who says (64), "The problem, however, which today appears to us of greater importance is concerned with the relative importance of the various types of perceptual and ideational data which subserve spatial perception, and their mutual relationships and coordination."

5. Gibson, *Perception*, 210, 211. Cf. Preface, viii: "For many years, experimental evidence has accumulated about the effect of the observers' attitude on perception, the influence of culture on perception, and the roles of past experience and of sensory organization in perception. All of these experiments, however revealing, leave out of account the simple question of the relation of the stimulus to perception. Until this question is settled the other evidence will be hard to evaluate."

6. See, e.g., William Stern, *General Psychology from the Personalistic Standpoint* (New York, 1938), who likewise points out (99) that, "The fact that sense perception happens to be constituted under different 'modalities' has led to the practice of cutting up the investigation of dimensions and treating visual space, tactual space, auditory space, etc., as independent. These special forms of psychological space are artificial fictions; indeed, they are misrepresentations of the true nature of mind. In so far as the individual experiences space in general, this is the *one* space of his personal existence and world; specific sensory constituents of vision, touch, etc., contribute materially to this experiential structure of space, but they remain submerged and interdependent aspects."

7. Gibson, *Perception*, 225, "... perceiving the environment includes the ego as part of the total process. In order to localize any object there must be a point of reference. An impression of 'there' implies an impression of 'here,' and neither could exist without the other."

8. See, for example, Ward H. Goodenough, "Native Astronomy in the Central Carolines," *Museum Monographs* (Philadelphia, 1953).

9. Cf. Gibson, *Perception*, 229–30.

10. "The capacity of men for forming correct mental maps is very great," write the authors of *Psychology for the Armed Services* (E. G. Boring [ed.], *The Infantry Journal* [Washington, 1945], 158), "although most persons do not use their capacities to the limit. Roads and streets and signs are enough to get them around in civilized familiar regions, and they do not feel a constant need to put everything into precise spatial relation. If they had more need for constant orientation, they would practice more on the building of their mental maps, would more easily find new and better ways of getting to old familiar places, would learn more rapidly to find their way around in new regions." The stress laid here upon the absence of the need for orientation only serves to highlight the positive motivation that is found in many nonliterate cultures.

11. The most comprehensive work on such maps is in Russian: B. F. Adler, *Maps of Primitive Peoples* (Bulletin of the Imperial Society of Students of Natural History, Anthropology and Ethnography, 119 [St. Petersburg, 1910] approx. 350 quarto pp.). An English resume by H. D. Hutorowicz is to be found in the *Bulletin of the American Geographical Society*, 42 (1911), 669–79. Adler's work is based on 55 maps from Asia, 15 from America, 3 from Africa, 40 from Australia and Oceania, and 2 from the East Indies. There is an earlier but less significant work (a doctoral dissertation) by W. Drober, *Kartographie bei der Naturvölkern*, 1903 (90 pp.).

12. Dr. E. S. Carpenter has called my attention to the maps obtained from Ookpuktowk and Amaulik Audlanat, two Eskimo of Southampton Island by George M. Sutton ("The Exploration of Southampton Island, Hudson Bay," *Memoirs of the Carnegie Museum*, 12 [1936], 45–47). Sutton obtained these in 1929 when no accurate maps of the island were available. More than a decade later a modern map, prepared from aerial photographs, was made. It was then possible to make a comparison between the native maps and the one made with the use of modern facilities. Although I cannot reproduce the three maps here, the level of accuracy is certainly high in the Eskimo maps. Dr. Carpenter says: "Certain digressions, often shared, are immediately apparent, particularly in the shape of the Bell Peninsula.

But the striking feature is certainly accuracy, especially in the details of the shoreline." [Ed. note: On the dynamics of Inuit mapping, see also Renée Fossett, "Mapping Inuktut: Inuit Views of the Real World," in Jennifer S.H. Brown and Elizabeth Vibert, eds., *Reading beyond Words: Contexts for Native History* (Peterborough, ON: Broadview Press, 1996)].

13. Ernst Cassirer in *The Philosophy of Symbolic Forms. I. Language* (New Haven, 1953) discusses the expression of space and spatial relations in language in brilliant fashion, and in *An Essay on Man* (New Haven, 1944) he devotes a chapter to "The Human World of Space and Time." In this chapter Cassirer differentiates (1) organic space, (2) perceptual space, (3) symbolic space, (4) abstract space. *Organic* space he conceives of as the "space of action," a level of spatial orientation that is nonideational and, in effect, is confined to animals who "seem to be led by bodily impulses of a special kind," creatures who "have no mental picture or idea of space, no prospectus of spatial relations" (43). *Perceptual* space is more complex in nature; it involves "elements of all the different kinds of sense experience— optical, tactual, acoustic, and kinesthetic" (43). When we reach the level of *symbolic* space, we are on the borderline between the human and animal worlds. At a still higher level of human reflection and experience *abstract* space, i.e., mathematical or geometric space (44) emerges, but only after many intermediate stages. "In primitive life and under the conditions of primitive society," Cassirer says, "we find scarcely any trace of the idea of an abstract space. Primitive space is a space of action; and the action is centered around immediate practical needs and interests. So far as we can speak of a primitive 'conception' of space, this conception is not of a purely theoretical character." While this latter point is true enough, the very fact that the cosmic aspects of the world views of primitive peoples involve spatial concepts, is sufficient to show that "practical needs and interests" are actually transcended.

14. Howard R. Patch, *The Other World According to Descriptions in Medieval Literature* (Cambridge, 1950), 134.

15. Patch, *The Other World*, 153.

16. Patch, *The Other World*, 173.

17. *The Divine Comedy I: Hell*, translated by Dorothy L. Sayers (Harmondsworth, 1949), 68 and diagram, 70.

18. Pierre Jaccard, *Le sens de la direction et l'orientation lointaine chez l'homme* (Paris, 1932), a doctoral dissertation done under the direction of Edouard Claparède.

19. Jaccard, *Le sens*, 330–31.

20. See, e.g., William J. Beecher, "The Unexplained Direction Sense of Vertebrates," *Scientific Monthly* (July 1952); Albert Wolfson, "Day Length, Migration and Breeding Cycles in Birds," *Scientific Monthly* (April 1952); Charles M. Bogert, "Why the Homing Toad 'Comes Home,'" *Natural History* (September 1948); Karl Von Frisch, *Bees* (Ithaca, 1950).

21. G. Revez ("The Problem of Space with Particular Emphasis on Specific Sensory Space," *American Journal of Psychology,* I [1937]), 434n, expresses the opinion that: "Although the experience of space and perception of objects of animals seem to agree with that of our own, the theory of a general phenomenal agreement between animal and human perception is highly disputable from a logical and theoretical angle. . . . Because of the lack of language and ideas, all animals must have a different space concept . . . and order than ours . . . This must be the case regardless of their particular stage of evolutionary development and their biological relationship to man."

22. [Ed. note: See "The Birth of the Winds, Flint and the Great Hare." William Berens told this myth to Hallowell in the summer of 1933. See Berens, *Memories, Myths, and Dreams of an Ojibwe Leader* (2009), Part IV].

23. [Ed. note: William Berens told this myth, "South Wind Enters a Contest with the North Wind," to Hallowell in the summer of 1933. See Berens, *Memories, Myths, and Dreams,* Part IV].

24. Jaccard, *Le sens,* 224–25, refers to a Malagasy who, traveling in Europe, was profoundly impressed with the ignorance of directional orientation he found. In contrast, he himself constantly endeavored to maintain his orientation.

25. These remarks refer to the period of my investigations (1930–1940).

26. Explorers frequently give excellent testimony on this point by their reference to the need for changing guides in the course of their journey. Cf. Jaccard, *Le sens,* 217–19. Foureau, for example, who made the first journey from North Africa to the Congo via the Sahara and Lake Chad, complained that his high-priced guides "ne conaissaient pas le pays au delà de quelques journées de marche. Les uns après les autres, arrivés a la limite, cherchaient des indigènes pour les remplacer."

27. I possess an outline map of the Poplar Narrows settlement made by a local Indian which gives all the place names in the environs of this settlement.

28. Cf. Jaccard, *Le sens,* 213.

29. H. D. Hutorowicz says ([see note 12] 671), "Of course the fundamental

purpose of all these primitive maps is to show routes to hunting grounds, fisheries, settlements, etc." The maps of primitive people are oriented in various ways. The Tungus do not employ the cardinal points but use the prevailing direction of a major waterway. The Turkoman peoples use the main direction of the mountain ranges. The comments of V. Stefansson on Eskimo maps are pertinent here. "These Eskimo maps are likely to be good if you interpret them rightly. Here are some of the points. They are more likely to have the right number of curves in a river and the right shape of the curves than the proper distance scale. They are most likely to emphasize the things that are of more importance to themselves; for instance, portages they have to cross are of more significance to them than mountains that stand to one side . . . Primitive men are likely to confuse the time scale with the mileage scale—after a ten-day journey of say six hours each day, they are likely to dot these camps at equal intervals, although, because of better going, they may have made twice the average distance one day and half the average another." See E. Raisz, *General Cartography* (New York, 1938), 9. [Ed. note: See Fossett, cited in note 12, on the temporal dimension as integral to Inuit mapping rather than as confusion].

30. Hutorowicz [see note 11], 672: "Like all maps of primitive or ancient peoples, a Tungus map is truest of the region best known to the map-maker, and this region is usually shown in the central part of his map, so that nearer the border, distances and surface features are likely to be less accurately shown." The comparison of an early Roman map (677), made in the reign of Augustus (the *Tabula Pentigernana*) with the maps of primitive peoples is interesting. "They differ greatly in the fact that the Roman map attempts to show the whole world as then known, while primitive map-makers confine themselves to regions with which they are acquainted; but both are alike in having no degree nets, and in being little more than sketches of routes; and in both cases, the author tries to present the information of greatest importance to himself, other facts being almost ignored."

31. This may explain perhaps, the geographical ignorance of the natives in certain parts of Malekula referred to by Tom Harrison, "Living with the People of Malekula," *Geographical Journal*, 80 (1936), 100. "This difficulty of the natives not knowing a name or direction for any point a few miles away, this complete geographical ignorance of the Malekula (much less marked in Santo) is a handicap in travel, and particularly in taking a census. It means that one must cover all the ground oneself, and accept no negative statement as to the absence of villages."

32. Raisz, *General Cartography*, 1, quotes a neat analogy of the geogra-

pher P. E. James who, speaking of the individual's direct knowledge of the earth's surface, writes: "Like an ant upon a rug he may know very exactly the nature of the fabric nearby, but the general design is beyond his range of vision. In order to reduce the larger patterns of the face of the Earth to such proportions that they can be comprehended in a single view, the geographer makes use of a map." From a psychological as well as from an historical point of view the last sentence of this quotation is of particular significance. Maps, by abstracting and transforming such spatial attributes as distance, direction, area, and contour into symbolic forms that are easily perceptible in all their spatial relations, not only enable the individual to comprehend these relations more abstractly; they enable him to make measurements and calculations and plan his practical activities in a wider spatial sphere. And in travel he need have no fear of disorientation. The importance of maps as basic instruments for a realistic mastery of space by man cannot be exaggerated.

33. Cf. H. St. J. B. Philby, *The Empty Quarter* (London, 1933), 173, who describes the surprise of his Arab guides that he could march south on a compass course towards nothing, then turn due west and hit off the main camp that had been left the day before on a northeast course. Such a feat implies, of course, a developed geometry and abstract space concepts.

34. [Ed. note: Hallowell is referring to the myth, "Aásī," which William Berens narrated. See Berens, *Memories, Myths, and Dreams*, Part IV.]

35. Ordinarily the crossing between these two points would have been made without getting out of sight of land, and bearings would have been constantly taken. Wherever there has been little knowledge of the science of navigation sailors have depended upon such landmarks. Cf. B. Malinowski, *Argonauts of the Western Pacific* (London, 1922), 224: "In journeying across Pilolu," the enormous basin of Lousancay Lagoon, the largest coral atoll in the world, "the natives never go out of sight of land, and in the event of mist or rain, they can always take sufficient bearings to enable them to make for the nearest sand bank or island. This is never more than some six miles off, a distance which, should the wind have dropped, may even be reached by paddling." Even the early Greeks proceeded in much the same manner. Cf. W. H. Heidel, *The Heroic Age of Science* (Carnegie Institution of Washington, Publication No. 442 [1933]), 123: "We also read of sailors guiding their course by the stars, though in general they skirted the shore line."

36. [Ed. note: "Wísakedják Becomes Encased in a Bear Skull" was told to Hallowell in 1936 by Levique, a band councilor at Little Grand Rapids. He was the son of Flatstone, who was active in the midéwi·win. APS,

A. Irving Hallowell Papers, Series V, Saulteaux Indians, Myths and Tales, Fieldnotes.]

37. Jane Belo has emphasized the severe anxiety experienced by the Balinese when, for whatever reason, they became disoriented. They have a special term for the sensation of being spatially disoriented. "To be *pal-ing*, they say, is 'not to know where North is'; in other words, he is *paling* who has lost his sense of direction, or who has lost the sense of his own position in relation to the geography of his world. One man whom I knew was taken for a trip in a motor car. He fell asleep during the ride. When the car stopped he awoke, and leaping out, looked about desperately, cry-ing 'Where's North, where's North? I'm *paling*." ("The Balinese Temper," *Character and Personality*, 4 [1935], reprinted in *Personal Character and Cultural Milieu: A Collection of Readings*, compiled by Douglas G. Haring [Syracuse, 1949]).

38. [Ed. note: Hallowell elaborated on this episode in his unpublished manuscript, "Pigeon River People," section I, Explorers and Fur Traders, 9 (Hallowell papers, APS). Hudson's Bay Company traders also recorded it from their side, dating it to October 1834. Brimmed Hat or Tcasämän, of the Pelican clan, and some other men raided the Sandy Narrows HBC post on Stout Lake. The man in charge, William Harper, then left the post by canoe and was later found drowned on the upper Berens River. The *Aboriginal Archives Guide*, Occasional Paper No. 8, 5–7 (Ottawa: Associa-tion of Canadian Archivists and the Canadian Church Historical Society, 2007) cites this story to show how archival and oral sources complement each other and offer differing perspectives; thanks to Warren Sinclair who found the archival references and authored this section of the guide].

39. Cf. H.B. Alexander, *Mythology of all Races*, X, *North America* (Boston, 1916), 275.

40. [Ed. note: See "Mätcīkīwis," a myth narrated to Hallowell by William Berens. Berens, *Memories, Myths, and Dreams*, Part IV.]

41. Elsie Clews Parsons, *Pueblo Indian Religion* (2 vols., Chicago, 1939), I, 98–99.

42. Cf. H.B. Alexander, *Mythology*, 286–87, speaks of smoke offerings of this type as "constituting a kind of ritualistic definition of the Indians' cosmos."

43. Parsons, *Pueblo Indian Religion*, 99, states that "the order of the car-dinal directions establishes the conventional circuit which is the counter-sunwise or sinistral, whether in coiling baskets (Hopi second mesa) or in pottery design or in dancing, although now and again the sunwise circuit

is followed. A striking illustration of how the circuit may be read into life is the view, held at Zuni, that eagles nest successively in four places and then repeat their nesting round."

In China categorical-symbolical thinking as applied to space and time has deep implications for all sorts of actual behavior. (Cf. Marcel Granet, *La Pensee chinoise* [Paris, 1934], 86–114.) Derk Bodde states in "Types of Chinese Categorical Thinking," *Journal of the American Oriental Society,* 59 (1939), 201, that the Chinese are constantly made aware of directional orientation not only by the "layout of city streets along north-to-south and east-to-west axes," but by habitually thinking of the relations of household objects in terms of the directions. "When in China, for example, one wishes to have a table moved to a different part of one's room, one does not tell the servant to shift it to his right or his left, but to 'move it a little east' or west, or whatever the direction may be, even if it is a matter of only two or three inches."

Such a custom is so strange to Western thinking that some years ago when a twelve-year old boy was discovered who appeared to possess an unusual sense of directional orientation, the question arose whether this might not be an innate ability (H.R. deSilva, "A Case of a Boy Possessing an Automatic Directional Orientation," *Science,* 73 [1931], 393–94). Investigation of his personal history, however, gave the proper cue. The child's mother was left-handed and found it more convenient to substitute the cardinal directions for left and right in giving the boy directions about the locations of objects in the house. Consequently, he was brought up from babyhood to respond to such orders as, "Get me the brush on the north side of the dresser; go sit on the chair on the east side of the porch," etc. Experiment showed that the child's ability depended altogether on the correct initial visual orientation. He was easily disoriented when rotated a few times in a dark room.

4

STRESS AND ANXIETY, FEAR AND AGGRESSION

Introduction

The six articles in Part IV all have a psychological focus. They appeared in the space of five years (1936–1941), three of them (chapters 12, 13, and 14) within the same year, 1938. As George Stocking has pointed out, this was the period in which Hallowell was most drawn to psychological analysis. In 1935, Edward Sapir, who pioneered the study of "culture and personality" in anthropology, invited Hallowell to join a "Committee on Personality in Relation to Culture," which was organized under the U.S. National Research Council's division of psychology and anthropology. Hallowell chaired a subcommittee that prepared a "handbook of psychological leads for ethnological fieldwork," which was circulated in mimeographed form. His introduction to the text, written in 1936, laid down several guiding principles that reappear in his writings on the Ojibwe. He emphasized, for example, the extent to which people of different cultures inhabit different "meaningful universes" with their own "concepts of time and space." Personality development, Hallowell proposed, was best viewed "in terms of variability around a culturally patterned norm," although as Stocking noted, Hallowell took this stance while still retaining an attachment to Freudian theory[1] (most visibly in chapter 13).

In "Psychic Stresses and Culture Patterns" (chapter 11, 1936), Hallowell reflected on how concepts of "normal" behavior vary across cultures, influence the stresses that people experience, and shape their means of dealing with stress. The Berens River Ojibwe, as he had learned during four summers of fieldwork, privileged dreams as means of achieving direct contact with spiritual beings. Everyone accepted that such beings could confer great blessings and powers, for example, to "conjure" (perform the shaking tent ceremony). But if a man falsely claimed such powers he would suffer (Hallowell's Case 1 in this article). In this instance and others, past misdeeds (which people often linked to physical and mental ailments they were suffering in the present) could be remedied, in their frame of reference, by confession (public, not private as to a priest), once they or a conjuror whom they consulted had identified the problem. Cases 4 and 6 in this article both came from the direct experience of Chief William Berens, Hallowell's collaborator. In the first, a powerful conjuror had afflicted Berens in his youth, sending a threatening dream and subsequent illness because he had insulted the man's son. In the second, a dangerous spiritual being, the Great Lynx, repeatedly visited Berens in his dreams, causing him great fear that he would lose a child who was critically ill.[2] Berens's firsthand accounts of these threats and of how he dealt with them, along with the other cases detailed in this article, also informed Hallowell's later, more developed analyses of Ojibwe views of illness and of dreams (Part V and chapter 23).[3]

Two years later in 1938, Hallowell published "Fear and Anxiety as Cultural and Individual Variables in a Primitive Society" (chapter 12). Through his own observations and the stories told to him, he situated Ojibwe people's responses to alarming or stressful stimuli in cultural context, and then explored various factors that led some individuals to respond much more strongly than others to these stressors. For example, Ojibwe people generally, given their beliefs surrounding certain animals, reacted strongly against incursions of toads, frogs, or snakes into their personal space. But William Berens was especially sensitive to the presence of toads and frogs, and for good reason, given a childhood experience, and also the fact that as a Christian, he had assisted Hallowell by braving the Ojibwe taboo on telling myths in summer, the penalty for which was that toads would "crawl up one's clothes."

Hallowell went on to explore Ojibwe responses to unusual illness, and to windigo cannibals who might be seen or heard as monstrous beings or appear as humans. In both instances, cultural beliefs grounded in dreams and stories about prior experiences provided means of explaining the threats and coping with them, except in the case of one man, John Duck, a leading conjuror, whose phobias and anxieties lay outside the normal range and were highly individualized. We do not yet find in these articles Hallowell's later expansion of the concept of "person" to encompass other-than-human persons such as animals and spirit beings as part of the Ojibwe social and explanatory universe, but that idea resided implicitly in the stories he recounted.

The following two chapters, 13 and 14, both written in 1938, exhibit Hallowell's application, at the time, of psychological frameworks to his observations. Both relate to his fieldwork at Little Grand Rapids in the summer of 1936, on his fourth trip up the Berens River to that community. "Freudian Symbolism in the Dream of a Saulteaux Indian" lies beyond the range of

Hallowell's usual writings; he was never this Freudian in any other piece he published on the Ojibwe. Only two pages long and probably quickly written, it may have been an experiment, testing how far he could carry this line of analysis. The topic was a dream that William Berens told him about, which Berens took to mean that he (Berens) would receive good money for a fox he was going to trap the next winter. Hallowell, applying Freud, read it very differently, and personally. The article expresses Hallowell's intellectual stance at the time, but also reveals his doubts and insecurities about his relationship with William Berens and his fear of overworking this older man, the guide, collaborator, and friend of whom he had asked so much.

"Shabwán: A Dissocial Indian Girl" (chapter 14) also has a personal quality. In the summer of 1936, some Little Grand Rapids people asked Hallowell to help treat a teenaged girl who appeared deranged, sometimes raving and violent, and was being held down so she would not run away. Hallowell determined that she was not psychotic, and initiated a restrained and calming course of action, relieving tension, walking with her, assuring her she would get better, and so on. His interactions with her and her family went on for some days, during which she began to call him her "sweetheart." This, in Ojibwe, is the same term as that used for cross-cousin or eligible marriage mate (see chapter 5), although Hallowell did not mention the equivalency in this article. His detailed account, more forthcoming than much of his writing, recounts his psychological approach to her condition and describes the Ojibwe curing techniques that were tried; it also reveals how he was drawn into a complex personal situation of uncertain outcome. In any event, when Hallowell left the community he was thanked and credited with a cure.

Chapter 15, "Aggression in Saulteaux Society" (1940), outlines what Hallowell came to see as the darker sides of Ojibwe personality, underlying an apparent harmony, peace, self-control, and avoidance of conflict in personal relations. Living with scarce resources, in small communities where everyone was some sort of relative, people needed to cooperate, share, and control anger and emotion so that relations could be maintained. Hostilities, then, were covert; but they found expression in two ways: in gossip, and more markedly, in acts of sorcery or bad medicine, or in people's belief that others were using such practices. Bad things that happened to one were commonly attributed to personalized rather than natural causes. In turn, they could result from some earlier action of the victim, sometimes acknowledged, but often unrecognized until its consequences were felt. Protection from these forms of aggression depended greatly on the assistance and powers that a man gained from his spirit helpers during his dream fast as a youth. But it also depended on avoidance of offending others whose spirit helpers might in fact be stronger, again emphasizing the need for restraint, circumspection, and the dangers of giving offense.

In "The Social Function of Anxiety in a Primitive Society" (1941), the final chapter in this set, Hallowell explored Freud's distinction between "real" anxiety in the face of known danger, and "neurotic" anxiety regarding dangers unknown. He then went beyond Freud, placing anxiety in a cultural context and observing that "reality" is what people believe and act upon, as in the Ojibwe belief that serious illness signals that some wrong has been done. In the Ojibwe context, he observed, anxiety about disease sanctions performed "a distinct social function," motivating people to avoid bad conduct. Of course it also made them fearful, or in Freud's terms, even neurotic in extreme cases, as in the case of John Duck. If, however, the cause of the illness or disorder was identified and made public, then stress was reduced and a cure could begin. In turn, social values were reinforced as the consequences of wrongdoing were revealed. From a psychological perspective (which, as Hallowell noted, was not how the Ojibwe saw it), anxiety served as "a psychic mechanism that acts as a reinforcing agent in upholding the social code."

To an extent, these articles have a common theme. They look at some dark sides of Ojibwe lives and worldviews, in their focus on stress, fear, anxiety, and aggression. Hallowell's observations and analyses of these topics were well grounded in his fieldwork. But George Stocking's biographical study of Hallowell, cited above, also supplies a personal context that may help to explain the attention that he paid to these subjects and to psychological analysis at this point in his career. In the late 1930s, Hallowell's adopted only son was developing serious difficulties with truancy from school and had been involved in several burglaries; and in 1939, a "running battle" with police led to a charge of "assault with intent to kill" and a reformatory sentence. Hallowell's first wife, from whom he separated in this period, was a child psychologist specializing in adoption issues. Both she and Hallowell must have been seeking answers from psychology in the situations they were facing with their son, whose later murder record as an adult (1947, and again in 1973) was to bear out their worst fears.[4] Stocking's article helps elucidate this phase of Hallowell's career. We can only imagine the fears and anxieties he may have felt. At some level, Ojibwe therapeutic methods may have interested him for personal as well as scholarly reasons.

Notes

1. George W. Stocking Jr., "A. I. Hallowell's Boasian Evolutionism: Human Ir/rationality in Cross-Cultural, Evolutionary, and Personal Context." In *Significant Others: Interpersonal and Professional Commitments in Anthropology*, Richard Handler, ed. (Madison: University of Wisconsin Press, 2004), 207–8.

2. See also these stories as told by William Berens in Berens, *Memories, Myths, and Dreams of an Ojibwe Leader* (2009),Part III, 2 and 9.

3. Two early insights that Hallowell mentioned as asides in this article also deserve note, as they are not well recognized. In note 12, Hallowell pointed out that in the conjuring lodge, the spirits speak to, not through, the shaking tent operator; this is not spirit possession such as is widely found in Asia. And in part IV of the text his analysis of the windigo cannibalism case recorded by fur trader David Thompson reminds readers that as of 1934, he had questioned the appropriateness of the term "windigo psychosis" as a unitary mental disorder and suggested that the windgo pattern probably "functions as a cloak for a variety of mental processes."

4. Stocking, "A. I. Hallowell's Boasian Evolutionism," 222–29. In 1973, fifteen months before Hallowell's death, his adoptive son killed Hallowell's first wife (the son's adoptive mother) in a robbery.

ELEVEN

Psychic Stresses and Culture Patterns

A thorough understanding of the incidence, etiology, symptomatology, and forms of certain classes of mental disorder requires a serious attempt to evaluate the influence of non-organic factors, the relevance of which is thrown into sharp relief once the data of history and ethnology are taken into account, in addition to clinical observations. When a *human* perspective is substituted for the more narrowly circumscribed outlook that implicitly identifies human behavior with the *characteristic* behavior of man in contemporary Western civilization, it becomes evident that mental disorders exhibit variations which cannot altogether be attributed to organic factors alone. Fenichel,[1] for instance, refers to

> the demands of present day civilization with its contemporary manifestations which we find in the neurotic patients of today who come to seek treatment. So far as we know, other civilizations had produced neuroses, but these differed from the neuroses of today, because these civilizations demanded different instinctual privations. The taboo which we now designate 'compulsion neurosis' is normal in civilizations other than ours; a 'devil neurosis of the seventeenth century,' once studied by Freud could not be fitted into our present diagnostic scheme. Indeed we are able to observe how the clinical pictures presented by the neuroses of today are changing, obviously parallel with changes in society and morality. It is the morality which prevails at the time which is directed against instinct in individuals, and morality is a relative power the nature of which depends on the structure of society. It is at this point that the psychologist must admit his inadequacy and agree that the problem of the etiology of neuroses is not a purely individual medical problem and that it needs supplementary sociological considerations.

To the anthropologist, at least, it is a commonplace that, despite the phylogenetic unity of man and the specific identity of contemporary races of our kind, the acquired behavior patterns that characterize the human species show an amazing diversity of forms. Transmitted from generation to generation in the form of the folkways, mores, customs, beliefs, and techniques of particular groups of mankind, they comprise the cultural as opposed to the organic heritage of Man. Broadly viewed, the extremely varied character of human culture patterns, when considered in connection with the fundamental organic unity of mankind, presents a phenomenon unique among living things. Man's behavior is everywhere canalized, restricted, and defined by customary procedures that are imposed upon each new generation of human individuals in accordance with the demands of different culture patterns. Verbal communication is patterned by conventional linguistic forms. Beliefs, among other things, offer a standardized interpretation of the meaning of physical phenomena of the outer world, often a reification of mythological beings. Interpersonal relations are guided by the traditional forms of the social and economic order. Even perception itself and mental imagery is not free from the influence of culture patterns, nor are motor habits, gestures, the expression of the emotions and the motivations of the individual.

It seems likely then, that as a result of differences in the social pressures imposed by varying cultural configurations, qualitative differences in cultural values bear *some* relation to the incidence and character of psychic stresses in different human societies, quite additional to situational and organic factors. We are not yet in a position to elucidate these relations in any precise detail, but the hypothesis is one that poses an important problem for investigation.

So far as the gross incidence of clinically recognized mental disorders is concerned, it has been casually asserted from time to time that there is an increase in mental disease as a marked symptom of the stress and strain of modern life in Western civilization, in contrast to a relatively low incidence of such disorders among so-called primitive peoples. In view of the fact, however, that reliable information is not available on the incidence of mental diseases in primitive societies, such a sweeping statement is unwarranted. White[2] queried it a number of years ago, and on the basis of Mead's observations on functional disorders in Samoa, it has more recently been challenged by Winston.[3] Nevertheless, it may very well be that gross incidence of mental disorders will be found to vary in different culture provinces, if sufficiently reliable information is obtained upon which to base comparisons.

The consideration of differences in the forms and symptoms of mental disorders in various societies, in the same society at different periods, and in different contemporary classes of the population of a given society, would seem to offer a more tangible approach to possible relations between these disorders and prevalent culture terns.

There is one intrinsic difficulty, however, which makes the diagnosis of mental disorder in societies other than our own anything but a simple matter. If "normal" behavior, as defined in our culture, is taken as an absolute standard of reference and the behavior of individuals conditioned to the values of another culture are compared with it, then of course it is even possible to speak of "group psychoses and neuroses" as manifested by the individuals of the exotic society. If, however, we acquaint ourselves with the modal behavior of individuals in a series of totally different cultures and develop norms based on such a standard of reference, we discover that there always are individuals deviant from the norm in every society, and some of these exhibit definite pathological symptoms. This procedure offers a genuine parallel to the study of personality deviation in our own society because it takes account of the cultural forces which mould the normal individual in the society. "Cultural anthropology," as Sapir has said, "has the healthiest of all scepticisms about the validity of the concept 'normal behavior.' It cannot deny the useful tyranny of the normal in a given society but it believes the external form of normal adjustment to be an exceedingly elastic thing. . . .

"It is valuable because it is constantly rediscovering the normal. For the psychiatrist and for the student of personality in general, it is of the greatest importance, for personalities are not conditioned by a generalized process of adjustment to the 'normal' but by the necessity of adjusting to the greatest possible variety of idea and action patterns according to the accidents of birth and biography."[4]

The reification of dream or vision experiences, for example, is not in accord with the culture patterns of contemporary Western civilization. Individuals who interpret dreams in this manner may therefore be characterized as aberrant. But among the Saulteaux Indians with whom I have been in personal contact, as well as among many other native Americans, the deviant individual would be one to whom certain dream experiences were *not* believed to bring one into direct contact with spiritual entities of the cosmos. Without a knowledge of the cultural background of an individual the psychological significance of dream reification in terms of "normality" or "abnormality" has little or no meaning.

Thus, while the beliefs of an individual are always relevant to an understanding of his behavior, the *source* of these beliefs is of great importance.

It is chiefly in reference to the beliefs regarding the nature of the external world and the normality of interpersonal relationships that are engendered by certain traditions in our culture that the belief systems of primitive peoples appear to be "flights from reality," comparable with the delusional systems of psychotic individuals in our society. But can the concept of "reality" itself be regarded as having any absolute content? Just as the psychotic person acts as if his delusional system constituted reality (as it truly does for him), so the individuals inculcated with the belief systems of primitive societies act *as if* such beliefs were true. But whereas the psychotic reifies a specific personal version of reality, the normal individual of a primitive society reifies the generic beliefs typical of the cultural heritage to which he has been subjected. Thus, while there are many *analogies* between the delusional systems of psychotics and the beliefs of some of the so-called primitive peoples, the *sources* of these beliefs are very decidedly to be distinguished. The reality of the psychotic is a unique, subjective, and highly personal configuration, the meaning and psychological significance of which is often unintelligible, or even incommunicable to, his fellows. The reality, on the other hand, that is *culturally* defined, embodying meanings and values which are shared *in common* by whole series of individuals, has been communicated to the person along with many other ideas and behavior patterns as part of a unified cultural heritage. The delusional system of an individual of a primitive society must be evaluated with reference to the definition of "reality" characteristic of his culture and not that of some other.

Once reality is intellectually accepted as a relative term, the meaning and content of which is to be sought in culturally defined terms, considerable insight is obtained into the behavior of individuals acculturated to different reality patterns. The paradox seems to be that the deflation of reality in an absolute sense of the term offers a *genuine* realistic approach to problems of both normal and abnormal behavior. Reality for the Bushmen of South Africa is not the equivalent of reality for the Navajo any more than medieval cosmology and demonology are accredited realities in Western civilization today. And the reality of the psychotic of our culture is not the equivalent of any of these.

Science in our culture aims at an interpretation of celestial, meteorological, terrestrial, biotic, and psychological phenomena which is more definitive in an absolute sense than anything ever known before in human history. At the same time, the scientific point of view looks with equanimity upon a changing interpretation of phenomena. It is authoritative without being finalistic. Hypotheses are tested and retested and new interpretations emerge.

Yet even in Western culture, scientifically defined reality has not completely displaced some aspects, at least, of the older and more tenacious traditional versions of reality deeply rooted in the ideology and mores of our society. The recurrent "conflict between religion and science" is symptomatic of this lag. Among individuals of the educated classes, the mental habit of viewing the external objects of what we call the natural world in terms of established scientific knowledge about them, has so completely divorced our minds from other possible attitudes that we are even apt to attribute our point of view to innate intelligence or common sense, instead of to a traditionally acquired mode of thought. Hence the charge of stupidity, childishness or naïveté, sometime flung at primitive man, is a boomerang that may some day be found at our own feet. Whatever the ultimate status of scientifically defined reality may prove to be, the psychological fact remains that just as we act in accordance with this pattern of reality, or its derivatives, so primitive man acts with respect to *his* concepts of reality.[5] If we seek to understand the determinants of human behavior, this must be recognized as one of the psychological imponderables the specific weight of which can hardly be challenged. Moreover, its specific influence in concrete forms of individual behavior can readily be observed, once we establish the proper frame of reference.

When we recognize that the traditional culture patterns of any specific group of human beings provides a frame of reference that not only defines the phenomenal universe but delimits the ambit of interpersonal relations, we see that some psychic stresses which result in "abnormal" behavior of the individual are to be viewed as resultants of inner psychic forces and social pressures productive of aberrant, instead of modal, behavior. The differential factors involved in such cases are, of course, the crux of the matter. Before these factors are to be envisaged, however, one must consider the correlative, if not primary, question as to the relation between specific culture patterns and the *modal* forms of personality structure and character traits which these seem to favor. Certainly, quite aside from mental disorder, character traits inculcated by one culture may seem deviant or abnormal to persons of another culture, a fact usually thrown into relief when even individuals of different cultures are brought into more or less intimate contact.

Ever since the westward movement of Ojibwa speaking peoples into Manitoba in the eighteenth century, one of the names by which they have been known is Bungi. Etymologically, this name seems to have been derived from a native term meaning *a little of something*. The Indians were always asking the whites for a little of this and a little of that; pangi tobacco, pangi tea, pangi flour, etc. In short, from the point of view of the white man, they were persistent and annoying beggars. If we were to render the name by which the Indians became known into an English metaphor, beggar would best convey its meaning. To the whites, the outstanding character trait of the Indian was begging. And I have often heard them reviled for this same characteristic today. In my opinion, the relation of this trait to the cultural background of the Indians is quite clear. It is simply the obverse side of the positive emphasis laid in their native culture upon giving. Food, articles of clothing, pipes, and other items circulate freely among those who need them. If children are given food or candy, for instance, they will share it at once with their playmates. Among adults, those who have anything always share what they have with the "have nots." It is not surprising that the Indians should have carried over their culturally determined habits in their social intercourse with traders, missionaries, and settlers. How could they have done otherwise, particularly in view of the fact that they found themselves in the "have not" class with respect to so many novelties that the white man possessed. So to the white man, with quite different institutional patterns of distributing commodities, and hence a different evaluation of the character trait exhibited by the Saulteaux, they became Bungi—Beggars.

Benedict,[6] considering cultures as integrated wholes, has shown how they operate with gross selectivity in respect to the encouragement of certain human temperaments and psychological trends, and the consequent discouragement of others.[7] All cultures, indeed, because of their very emphasis on characteristic sets of values, must inevitably generate psychic stress in the individuals who from temperament, experience, or by reason of some inner conflict, find such values uncongenial. There are societies in which homosexuality has been culturally integrated, others in which it is tolerated, and others in which it is suppressed with vigor. We know cultures in which dissociative psychic states or hysteria have been one qualification for religious leadership[8] or even sainthood; and with the latter, we might contrast societies where there are no culturally approved channels for the expression of such psychic phenomena outside of a mental hospital.

Knowing so little about the genetic processes of cultural conditioning and personal symbolisms, to say nothing of the conflicting inner forces that the psychoanalysts emphasize, we encounter enormous difficulties in elucidating the relationship of psychic stresses to culture patterns in complex and stratified societies where the relationship of individuals to a variety of cultural patterns is so intricate. I should like to make the point, however, that *pari passu* with the investigation either of generic culture configurations which in one society may permit, or even exploit, what in another may be regarded as pathological manifestations, or of the relation of cultural configurations to the problem of mental disorder in any society, there must also be considered the role which specific culture patterns may play in bringing about psychic stresses of a much less spectacular sort.

It seems to me that the elucidation of these less serious forms of psychic stress, especially in the simpler and culturally homogeneous societies, should be of some value in throwing light on the fundamental mechanisms involved in both the genesis and resolution of such states of mind under varying conditions, as well as offering the possibility of testing some of the psychological concepts and interpretations advanced to explain the behavior of individuals habituated to the culture patterns of Western civilization.[9]

I shall attempt to demonstrate this by the analysis of some case material that shows how some characteristic culture patterns of the Berens River Saulteaux[10] seem to have functioned in relation to the psychic stresses of certain individuals. For the most part, only minor tensions are involved, although a few of these cases might possibly be considered to verge on clinically recognizable disorders. It would seem that the creation, as well as the resolution, of the psychic stress in these cases is connected with specific culture patterns. It would certainly be difficult to comprehend them except in terms of the particular values and attitudes characteristic of Saulteaux culture. On the other hand, the psychological interpretation in each case is sheer guesswork on my part, for which I crave as much indulgence as seems permissible. I did not make a detailed study of any of these individuals; in fact for the most part, I have depended on hearsay evidence. One of the individuals is dead; another, I never met. The case material suffers accordingly; it can hardly be considered a contribution towards the solution of the problem I have stated, but it does illustrate one angle of attack which a more systematic, detailed investigation might take. Its value can best be judged if this fact is borne in mind.

I. INSTITUTIONALIZED CONFESSION AS A MEANS OF RELIEVING PSYCHIC STRESS[11]

Back of confession itself lies one facet of the Saulteaux theory of disease. The relief from psychic tension that the confession affords is actually a by-product of the conscious desire on the part of some individual to cure himself or a member of his family of an illness. This follows from the belief held that disease may be the result of some moral transgression such as murder, incest, or deception.

This last mentioned transgression specifically means the offering of professional services under false pretenses, that is, without supernatural validation. Specialists in certain methods of curing disease, and in clairvoyance and sorcery, for instance, are only able to pursue these vocations because they have been blessed by certain supernatural entities. Their letters patent were obtained in a dream revelation. To practice any special vocation, such as sucking out disease entities or conjuring *without* supernatural sanction, mediated through dreams, is a form of criminal deception. Sickness is sure to follow. Apparently nervous diseases, no less recalcitrant to Saulteaux pharmacology than to Western medicine, are frequently accounted for in this way. One old man, who had a stroke during the summer of 1934, was no sooner stricken than the river began to buzz with gossip to effect that his illness was due to deception. But retribution, in the form of sickness, may fall not only on oneself; the sins of the fathers are sometimes visited upon the children—to how many generations, I do not know. There is even a native term for sickness attributable to the wrongdoing of parents. Confession of the crime is the only possible method of cure in such cases.

Case 1: Confession of Deception in the Case of a Man Who Suffered from a Phobia

This Indian was a conjurer. Power to exercise this particular vocation requires not a single dream revelation but four of them. In this way conjuring is supernaturally inspired. The details of the conjuring lodge itself, such as the particular kind of trees to be used, and other matters, are all conveyed to the human individual in these dreams. When the lodge is entered by the conjurer it begins at once to tremble and later sways from side to side while the voices of the conjurer's guardian spirits issue from it. These spirits do not enter his body and speak *through* him, but sit on the lodge poles and speak *to* him.[12] They give information about lost articles, the welfare of people at a distance, and so on. It is equivalent to a mediumistic performance in our culture. To those of us not spiritualistically inclined by faith, it can be assumed that the voices are not actually those of spiritual beings and that the conjurer himself makes the structure move, but even at this late date, the actual technique of the manipulation of the tent is in doubt. The contemporary Saulteaux, moreover, while maintaining, one and all, a vital belief in the essentially supernatural character of conjuring, admit cases of imposture. It was in this connection that I was told about the case of William Goosehead. A few years ago he could not go into the woods alone, not even for 200 yards. One can readily comprehend how abnormal this is for a man brought up in the Canadian wilderness. Finally, Goosehead confessed that he had been shaking the conjuring tent illegitimately. He had been deceiving his public. A short time after this he is said to have completely recovered from his phobia. I do not know whether there was any real connection between his confession and his recovery, but it is apparent on the face of things, that he must have labored under a considerable sense of guilt, else he would not have confessed. From the native viewpoint, confession was a possible remedy and it appears to have worked.

But if tent shaking is all hocus pocus, why should this man have felt any sense of guilt about doing what other conjurers did? I was told, for instance, that he admitted shaking the lodge with his own hands. Still, I do not believe that this is the core of the matter. I would assume that, in this culture, dream validation of conjuring is not merely a theory; it actually involves real dream experiences of the required pattern, interpreted as divine revelation. The mechanical means employed to shake the tent may then be looked upon as a sort of necessary materialistic evil. Since everyone accepts the supernatural origin of significant dreams, the sincere conjurer is supported by this common tenet of belief, as well as by his private experience. Within such a cultural context, surely this must be convincing enough to make most individuals feel that their efforts are supernaturally inspired. The native charlatan then is a man who has *not* experienced the stereotyped dreams demanded by the culture pattern yet, motivated by a desire for prestige or the material compensation involved, undertakes to conjure. I would guess that W. Goosehead was one such man. It is even conceivable that his specific fears *were* actually connected with some personal version of supernatural retribution that made him dread going into the woods alone on account of some danger from this particular source.

Case 2: Confession of Some Secret Sin as a Means
of Helping to Cure One's Offspring From an Illness

Sickness due to this cause, as I have said, is designated by a special term. Although I was not able to secure the details of it, one case of this sort did arise in the summer of 1934. In this instance, as in others of its kind, the diagnosis of the illness as due to some moral transgression on the part of a parent, was obtained by conjuring. The father of the youth who was taken ill was supposed to have confessed to the conjurer. What his crime had been, I was unable to find out. His son suffered from spells of unconsciousness and whether the boy finally recovered I do not know. But since everyone can find some hidden deed that troubles him, the illness of the child furnishes, in Saulteaux culture, the occasion, and the confession the means, for the release of a psychic tension and for the cure of an illness at the same time. Of course the transgression must be a serious one and likewise conform to the panel of Saulteaux crimes.

II. AN APPEAL TO LOVE MAGIC TO RELIEVE SHAME, EMBARRASSMENT, AND PERHAPS UNCONSCIOUS GUILT, AS WELL AS TO COMBAT A SOCIAL ATTITUDE OF RIDICULE

Case 3

A young man was discovered sleeping with an old woman. Everyone teased him about it and made him very much ashamed. No one in his proper senses, according to my informant, would ever have thought of sleeping with the old woman in question. Besides, the young man was in no way cut off from younger women. Consequently, the fact seems established that the old woman was the young man's choice, or, in psychological terms, a genuine compulsion. This was likewise the level on which the young man explained his conduct. He said that he had once insulted the old woman and that, in revenge, she had lured him to her by love medicine. He remembered nothing from leaving his tent until he found himself at the old woman's side at day-break. My informant was convinced by this explanation and offered the anecdote as convincing proof of the effectiveness of love magic. The other Indians were probably as well satisfied with the boy's personal defense; the terms of rationalization chosen by him were effective. Since the belief in love magic is strongly entrenched, even among the contemporary Saulteaux, his psychic stress could be most satisfactorily resolved by this particular explanation. In terms of native belief he became volitionally absolved in the opinion of others and possibly to himself, because it is quite possible that the old woman was actually a mother surrogate. Assuming this to have been the case, and that he actually had insulted her, the act might have been an overt defense reaction to only partially repressed inclinations towards the intimate relations which finally took place. The sexual act itself would then be a symbol of incest, the compulsion towards which he was no longer able to suppress. In these premises, his claim that the old woman had employed love magic was doubly appropriate; it not only protected him from the ridicule of his fellows, but also protected his own ego from knowledge of his unconscious desires.

III. THE ROLE OF DREAMS IN THE RESOLUTION OF PSYCHIC STRESS

A. Dreams of having one's soul kidnapped and escaping from a conjuring lodge, as symbols of self-punishment and release from some specific guilt and fear.

According to native theory, a conjurer with malevolent intent may abduct the soul of a sleeping victim. To be able to accomplish this, he must have a conjuring lodge set up somewhere, enter it, and summon his spiritual helpers to his aid. With their assistance, the soul of the sleeping individual is brought into the conjuring lodge. It may be killed there, and if this happens, the person from whom it was abducted will be found dead the next morning. On the other hand, the soul may sometimes find a way to escape from the conjuring lodge and return to the body of the sleeper. In this case the victim may suffer illness, but not death. The conjurer has missed his chance.

The testimony of individuals who have interpreted dreams of soul abduction as real experiences is accepted by the Indians as proof of the powers of the conjurers. In each of the two following cases, I wish to emphasize the connection of the dream with a previous experience of the individual which engendered a feeling of guilt and, in the first case, actual fear that a particular conjurer would take some malevolent action.

Case 4

"I was just about 16 years old when someone tried to kill me. This is what happened. We boys were playing ball one day and I got one of them mad. I guess it was my fault. He was a 'humpy' and his father was a conjurer. The 'humpy' looked so funny when he ran that I ran the same way to tease him. All the boys laughed but he got mad and said to me, 'You'll remember this.' This happened in the summer and I soon forgot all about it. I was too young to understand what he meant. The next winter, in March (Eagle Moon), we were camped about four miles up the river and all ready to pull out the next day. Everybody was well. That night after I had gone to sleep I saw someone coming from the north directly towards the camp. It was a young man. He came and stood at my feet as I lay sleeping. He spoke to me: 'You are wanted over there,' motioning with his lips towards the north. I got up and started off with him. I found that we were traveling through the air, not along the ground. I looked up and saw a river ahead of us and just one bark covered tipi. I could see the kind of trees growing there. There were lots of very straight Jack pine on the north side of the river. Now we came down to the ground near another kind of 'tent.' I walked into it. There was humpy's father in the center. I could see no end to the tent, it stretched out as far as I could see and it was full of all kinds of people. I knew then that I was inside a conjuring lodge. 'I'm going out,' I said. But the old man said, 'No. You can't go.' Then I saw my own head rolling about and the 'people' in the lodge were trying to catch it. I thought to myself that if only I could catch my own head everything would be all right. So I tried to grab it when it rolled near me and finally I caught it. As soon as I got hold of it I could see my way out and I left. Then I woke up and I could not move my legs or my arms. Only my fingers, I could move. But finally I managed to speak. I called out to my mother to make a light. I told her I was sick. I could not manage to move my head. When morning came I was still sick. I told my father about what had happened. He knew at once that someone had done something to me and that I had really been in a conjuring lodge. All that day and the next I lay sick. Then I got better. It was my soul that the conjurer had drawn away while I was asleep. If it had not found its way back to my body, I would have been found dead in the morning."[13]

That both guilt and fear were involved in this case, is, I think, plain; guilt, because the boy's deliberate mimicry was evidently in disharmony with the demands of his conscience, and fear, because of the implied threat of subsequent harm, coupled with the fact that the hunchback's father was a conjurer. The induction of fear arose from the native belief in the malevolent powers of conjurers, typical of this culture. A similar interpersonal situation, involving individuals of a different cultural context, would not have caused the same emotional precipitate. The striking fact is that the cultural pattern of the society in which this situation seems to have created inner tensions in an individual, also provided a means for their resolution. In gross psychological terms, the manifest content of the dream not only met the cultural requirements in regard to a type of vengeance that the conjurer might be expected to take, but also it functioned unconsciously as a means of self-punishment, in this latter respect doubtless meeting what were inner psychic demands. By so doing, it resolved the psychic tensions which had arisen. It may also be surmised in this case that the physical symptoms were also involved. I do not mean that they necessarily were psychogenic; they may have been seized upon, let us say, by the super-ego and exploited concomitantly with the dream, as a convenient means at hand for ego punishment. Since in the account as given, the individual was quite certain that he had successfully escaped the conjurer's clutches, it would seem that an equilibrium was achieved and that his ego had sloughed off both guilt and fear as a result of the dream experience and subsequent illness.

Case 5

I was told of another Indian who had a similar dream experience, but I was unable to secure his own account of it. Here again it is significant that several months prior to this particular dream, he had committed an act of defilement which, if I understand the attitude of these Indians aright, might well have continued to trouble his conscience.

This youth was out hunting with some other young fellows. They came upon some traps belonging to the Indians of an adjoining band. The youth had to defecate. His companions dared him, as we would say, to defecate on one of the traps. He did so and sprung the trap so that a piece of the excrement was left sticking out. Now this sort of defilement was not only an insult to the owner of the trap, it was also a deterrent to any animal that might prowl that way, and worse still, it was an affront to the "spiritual" owner of any animal species. This latter was the worst offense of all. No wonder then, that this youth needed absolution. There came a dream in which his soul was abducted, but managed to escape from a conjuring lodge. I find one detail in my notes which seems to clinch the connection: The young man dreamed that his soul was taken into the lodge of a conjurer of the same band as that of the man whose trap he had defiled.

B. A dream of self-reassurance that a son would recover from an illness that also was a token of semi-emancipation from pagan beliefs.

Case 6

W. B., who is the Chief of the Berens River Band today, was about ten years old when the first Christian missionary came to live on the Berens River. His father [Jacob Berens], chief before him, was the first Christian convert on the river and was married to a white woman. The paternal grandfather of W. B., however, was a thorough-going pagan, who lived to be a very old man and seems to have been greatly admired by his grandson. W. B. spent a good deal of time with him and thus was subjected to typical aboriginal beliefs along with the Christian aspirations of his parents. An old man today, W. B. is consequently the product of mixed Saulteaux and Christian traditions.

In order to understand the possible significance of one of the dreams of W. B., one needs information on the native beliefs in regard to *mīcīpījiu* (the Great Lynx),[14] a semimythical animal, and on the attitude of the Saulteaux towards dream visitations of this creature. It must be understood, of course, that the Great Lynx is held to have a real existence. But unlike almost all other spiritual entities that appear to man in dreams, this *pawágan*[15] brings misfortune. The Great Lynx will appear to a boy as an attractive woman inviting seduction, and to a girl in a male guise. To become involved in such a relationship provokes the unremitting jealousy of this being. If the individual who experiences such dreams later marries, his or her spouse will die or the children of the marriage will sicken and die. Consequently, it is the native dogma that individuals who have dreamed of the Great Lynx should avoid marriage. If such a person should want to risk it, their prospective spouse, if an inkling of such a dream leaks out, will not go through with it. How potent the belief has been in actually deterring the marriages of thorough-going pagans, I do not know. But there are extremely few unmarried individuals among the Saulteaux. Nevertheless, it may be assumed that the belief is likely to be a source of latent fear in such individuals as do run the risk of marriage subsequent to dreams of the Great Lynx. That this was actually so in the case of W. B., despite the fact that he was a Christian, is proved by a significant coincidence.

W. B. had several such dreams, but he was not inhibited from marrying. A few years after his marriage, one of his sons became critically ill. While the boy was sick, W. B. again had a dream visitation from the Great Lynx. He was thoroughly alarmed, thought his son was going to die, and consulted a conjurer about the matter. (I failed to ask him whether he prayed about it, too.) The conjurer promised to help overcome the Great Lynx. The next night W. B. received another visit from this *pawágan*. On this occasion they had a terrific fight. W. B. was completely victorious. He escaped without a scratch. This, he said, was because his own guardian spirits came to his aid as well as those of the conjurer. When the latter learned of the outcome, he assured W. B. that everything would be all right. And the sick boy did recover.[16]

This dream exposes another facet of the linkage of theories of disease and its cure in Saulteaux culture patterns. The dream victory of W. B. over the Great Lynx relieved the immediate stress caused by his concern over the son's illness. But I think that it may also have symbolized the inner conflicts of W. B. with respect to the mixed authority of pagan and Christian beliefs which he held simultaneously. Today at least, while outwardly adhering to the Christian faith, W. B. is profoundly convinced of the truth of many pagan beliefs. Yet, he has had more contact with the whites than any man on the river. His conscious aspirations are focused in many respects towards the culture patterns of the white man, but at the level of belief, he is much less emancipated from aboriginal patterns than are his wife and children. While his dream is of a culturally stereotyped pattern relevant to the son's illness, it may likewise have symbolized, in a more personal unconscious sense, the desire of W. B. to be still further freed from the influence of native beliefs. Since he was victorious over the Great Lynx and his son recovered, the dream may have given him unconscious assurance that he had at least freed himself from one native belief with impunity.

C. Supernatural dream revelation as a means of validating the gratification of an incestuous desire, tabooed by custom and under a disease sanction.

Case 7

All the incest taboos among the Saulteaux are upheld by a disease sanction. Marriages of certain classes of near kin are believed to be followed by the sickness and death of offspring. Specific cases are cited to prove the inevitability of these consequences. The genealogical data show that incest taboos are actually in operation. Sib exogamy is sometimes broken, but usually such sib mates are not blood kin, since distinct family lines may have the same totemic name. Marriage of any close blood relative, on the other hand, except a cross-cousin, is extremely rare, although I have recorded a few cases. No case of father-daughter or mother-son marriage has ever been heard of, and the case of full brother-sister marriage I wish to discuss is unique, an outstanding psychological achievement for the man who undertook it. It involves the overcoming of a severe brother-sister taboo which embraces parallel cousins and other individuals to whom the sibling terms are applied in daily life. The taboos between siblings of opposite sex not only forbid sex relations but also restrict their social intercourse. From a psychological point of view, it might well be expected, in view of these systematic repressions, that deviant individuals might appear from time to time to challenge their authority. At any rate it may safely be assumed that there was considerable psychic stress engendered in this individual who did so. Such a man was Sagaski. It is significant that he was no common mortal but a man reputed to possess unusually strong magical powers, and to have many supernatural helpers at his command. On this account, he was in the best strategic position possible to do as he pleased. This is probably an objective judgment rather than one which assumes the point of view of the Saulteaux themselves. For Sagaski did not do simply as he pleased. He did not live with his sister until he let it be known that one of his guardian spirits—the spiritual "owner" of the beaver—*commanded* him to take his sister as a wife, in short, to follow the beaver mating pattern instead of the human. Now since dreams are believed to be the medium of communication among the Saulteaux between man and the supernatural world, Sagaski did nothing less than invoke the highest authority possible for his marriage—a supernatural one. Furthermore, it is believed to be a sin not to follow the instruction received in dream revelations. In terms of Saulteaux theory, then, Sagaski had a perfect case. And I have no doubt, moreover, that he actually dreamed the dream he reported. Considering the psychological function of a dream theory such as that to which the Saulteaux adhere, it seems to me that their dreams should serve them in this way. At any rate, it is easy to understand how Sagaski's marriage to his sister was validated in the most effective terms which the culture itself, although tabooing incest, could offer. But there is another chapter to the story.

Evidently the guilt feelings experienced by Sagaski were not quelled even by the supernatural sanction he invoked. Perhaps his culture was too elastic, and perhaps there were deeper psychic involvements which only some means of ego punishment, not supplied by the prevalent culture patterns, could balance. At any rate, many years later, after he had had three children, he tried to induce one of them, a son, to marry his sister. But the boy refused. It would seem that this behavior of Sagaski may have represented the still latent need to justify his own previous conduct. It may even have been in response to a need to circumvent incestuous desires for his own daughter. This latter possibility receives some measure of support from a few details about the family. Sagaski's sister-wife died and only one of the children of this incestuous marriage now survives. This daughter never married and neither did two daughters by a second marriage. This is most unusual among the Saulteaux. Moreover, Sagaski trained his daughters to do many of the tasks men usually perform and guarded them much more closely than Saulteaux fathers ordinarily do. In summer, he used to camp with his family on an island and would never let the young men passing up and down the river put up their tents there even for a single night.

It would also be interesting to know how individuals in other societies, with different culture patterns, have managed to win sufficient social approval to enable them to break such a universal incest prohibition. In a recent article, C. M. Garber[17] refers to genealogical data he had collected on an Eskimo family on the Kuskokwim River. He stresses the inbreeding that he found. This includes cousin marriages and he adds, "it is not extremely rare that brother married sister." He also recorded four cases in which a father married his daughter. One cannot but wonder, what was the attitude towards these marriages? Were they casually undertaken and socially accepted like other marriages? Were the individuals concerned subject to no resulting psychic stress, or were they, like Sagaski, forced to resort to some established cultural means in order to justify and support their conduct?

In human history, supernatural sanctions of various kinds seem to have been an almost constant factor in the support of established cultural institutions. It is less frequently emphasized that they have been likewise the court of appeal for the deviant behavior of the individual. The double role which this sort of authority has played is of very considerable psychological importance. Hallucinations, delusions, visions and dreams, as culturally interpreted, have provided the individual with possible ways of adjustment to psychic stresses and to accepted social values. These individual adjustments must of necessity depend upon specific culture patterns. Without the values and the attitudes integrated with them and shared by one's fellows, one becomes isolated in a subjective world. If one cannot communicate with others through the medium of common cultural values, it is not possible to make one's deviant behavior plausible to one's fellows. It is quite possible that the decline of supernaturalism in Western civilization has forever undermined the status of a generic culture pattern which, in a multitude of forms, has been an effective, although to us naive authority, previously available to the individual as a means of resolving various forms of psychic stress. At the same time, certainly, one must not forget the potent role that supernaturalism has played in causing psychic stress.

IV. INTRA-PSYCHIC CONFLICT IN THE GUISE OF TRANSFORMATION INTO A WINDIGO (CANNIBAL)

Finally, I should like to draw attention to a brief account by David Thompson of one of those numerous cases of *cannibalistic desires (the so-called "windigo psychoses")*, which occur so typically among Cree and Ojibwa Indians. Whether all such cases can be regarded as some form of mental disorder with a culturally patterned symptomatology, is a question which Cooper and I have discussed elsewhere.[18] Let me quote the case reported by Thompson[19] as an instance in which cannibalistic desires on the part of a young man may possibly have been the culturally determined disguise of unconsciously activated incestuous desires. The youth concerned expressed a desire to eat his sister.

The episode took place in an Ojibwa summer encampment on the Lake of the Woods in 1798. Thompson says:

One morning a young man of about twenty years of age on getting up, said he felt a strong inclination to eat his sister; as he was a steady young man, and a promising hunter, no notice was taken of this expression; the next morning he said the same and repeated the same several times in the day for a few days. His parents attempted to reason him out of this horrid inclination he was silent and gave them no answer; his sister and her husband became alarmed, left the place and went to another camp. He became aware of it and then said he must have human flesh to eat, and would have it; in other respects, his behavior was cool, calm, and quiet. His father and relations were much grieved; argument had no effect on him, and he made them no answer to their questions. The camp became alarmed, for it was doubtful who would be his victim. His father called the men to a council, where the state of the young man was discussed, and their decision was, that an evil spirit had entered into him, and was in full possession of him to make him become a Man Eater (a Weetego). The father was found fault with for not having called to his assistance a Medicine Man, who by sweating and his songs to the tambour and rattle might have driven away the evil spirit, before it was too late. Sentence of death was passed on him, which was to be done by his father. The young man was called. . . . [and]. . . . informed of the resolution taken, to which he said "I am willing to die"; the unhappy father arose, and placing a cord about his neck strangled him, to which he was quite passive; after about two hours, the body was carried to a large fire, and burned to ashes, not the least bit of bone remaining. This was carefully done to prevent his soul and evil spirit which possessed him from returning to this world and appearing at his grave; as they believe the souls those who are buried can, and may do, as having a claim to the bones of their bodies. It may be thought that the council acted a cruel part in ordering the father to put his son to death, when they could have ordered it by the hands of another person. This was done, to prevent the law of retaliation; which had it been done by the hands of another person, might have been made pretext of revenge by those who were not the friends of the person who put him to death. Such is the state of society where there are no positive laws to direct mankind.

The other reported cases of the *wíndīgo* psychoses that have come to my attention are not detailed as to the person or persons towards whom the cannibalistic desires were directed. In those of which I had an opportunity to inquire, I have not succeeded in securing this particular information. The conviction has grown in me, however, that we have a particularly significant field for exploration here. Psychiatrists have reported data suggestive of a relation of the act of eating and the sex act, and have inferred a generalized symbolic relationship. Be this inference warranted or otherwise, it certainly offers an intelligible hypothesis in the case reported by Thompson, which in turn is an illustration how an unconscious symbol may become reified in the terms of a specific culture pattern. I have elsewhere[20] questioned whether the "*wíndīgo* psychosis" is to be regarded as a unitary type of mental disorder, and have suggested that further investigation will probably reveal that the cannibalistic pattern functions as a cloak for a variety of mental processes. They would seem, however, in every case to be particularly well worth detailed study to elucidate the relation between psychic stresses and culture patterns in the individual.

In conclusion, let me make due apology for the fragmentary nature of my facts, and the extended inferences that I have drawn from them. The purpose of this paper is not the solving of problems, but the pointing out of the relevance of anthropological field data to investigations in the relations of culture and personality. It seems that the anthropologist, if he were aided in formulating his problems by the psychiatrist sensitive to the implications of culture, might well collect data on the behavior of individuals in societies with culture patterns different from our own that would be of real significance to psychiatry. The relation of psychic stresses to the patterns of our own culture may perhaps best be attacked by way of the pseudo-experimental setups that are available for study elsewhere in the world.

Notes

Published in *American Journal of Psychiatry* 92 (1936): 1291–1310.

1. O. Fenichel, *Outline of clinical psychoanalysis*, 1934, 3–4.
2. William A. White, *Outlines of psychiatry*, 10th ed., 1924, 45–46.

3. Ella Winston, "The alleged lack of mental disease among primitive groups," *American Anthropologist*, 36, 1934.

4. Edward Sapir, "Cultural anthropology and psychiatry." *Journal of Abnormal and Social Psychology*, 27 [3], 1932, 235. Cf. Ruth Benedict, "Anthropology and the abnormal," *Journal of General Psychology*, 10, 1934.

5. For which the individuals who entertain these concepts find plentiful support in their actual experience. See Hallowell, "Some empirical aspects of Northern Saulteaux religion," *American Anthropologist*, 36, 1934. [Chapter 20, this volume.]

6. Ruth Benedict, *Patterns of Culture*, 1934.

7. In "The problem of feminine masochism," *Psychoanalytic Review*, 22, 1935, Karen Horney discusses the relative weight of anatomico-physiological components as contrasted with cultural factors and concludes that feminine masochism cannot be related to the former alone "but must be considered as importantly conditioned by the culture-complex or social organization in which the particular masochistic woman has developed."

8. Cf. Brenda Z. Seligman, "The part of the unconscious in social heritage." (*Essays presented to C. G. Seligman*, 1934.)

9. Cf. M. J. Herskovits, "Freudian mechanisms in primitive negro psychology." (*Essays presented to C. G. Seligman*, 1934.)

10. These Indians represent a typical segment of the contemporary native population of the woodland region of the Province of Manitoba, Canada. The river on which they live flows into Lake Winnipeg at approximately 52° N. Lat. They speak an Ojibwa dialect, and a portion of those living up the river are still un-christianized.

11. Confession in varying culture contexts is very widespread among the so-called primitive peoples, especially in America and Africa. See the survey by R. Pettazzoni, *La Confession des Péchés*, Paris, 1931.

12. Possession, i.e., the belief that a spirit (evil or otherwise) may enter the body of a human being and control his behavior, is as foreign to the ideology of most New World cultures as it is conspicuous in those of the Old World. Cf. Franz Boas, "America and the Old World" (Proceedings, International Congress of Americanists, Göteborg, 1925), 27; T. K. Oesterreich, *Possession, Demoniacal and Other* (NY, 1930), 292–3.

13. [William Berens's telling of this story is also in William Berens, *Memories, Myths, and Dreams of an Ojibwe Leader* (2009), Part III.]

14. Conceptually modeled upon the cougar or mountain lion (Felis Couguar) which was once found practically all over North America as far north as the Great Lakes.

15. I.e., dream visitor.

16. [See William Berens's telling of this experience in Berens, *Memories, Myths, and Dreams*, Part III.]

17. Marriage and Sex Customs of the Western Eskimo. *Scientific Monthly*, vol. 41, September 1935.

18. Hallowell, "Culture and Mental Disorder," *Journal of Abnormal and Social Psychology*, 29 (1), 1934, 1–9; J. M. Cooper, "Mental Disease Situations in Certain Cultures," *Journal of Abnormal Psychology*, 29(1). *Cf.* also Cooper, "The Cree Witiko Psychosis," *Primitive Man*, 6, 1933.

19. J. B. Tyrrell (ed.), *David Thompson's Narrative of his Explorations in Western America (1784–1812)*, Champlain Society, 1916, 259 ff.

20. "Culture and Mental Disorder," *Journal of Abnormal Psychology*, 29(1), 1934, 1–9.

TWELVE

Fear and Anxiety as Cultural and
Individual Variables in a Primitive Society

Many years ago Dewey pointed out some of the inadequacies of a simple stimulus-response concept in psychology.

> That which is, or operates as, a stimulus, turns out to be a function, in a mathematical sense, of behavior in its serial character. Something, not yet a stimulus, breaks in upon an activity already going on and *becomes* a stimulus in virtue of the relations it sustains to what is going on in this continuing activity. . . . It *becomes* the stimulus in virtue of what the organism is already preoccupied with. To call it, to think of it, as a stimulus without taking into account the behavior that is already going on is so arbitrary as to be nonsensical. Even in the case of abrupt changes, such as a clap of thunder when one is engrossed in reading, the *particular* force of that noise, its property as stimulus, is determined by what the organism is already doing in interaction with a particular environment.[1]

The general principle implied in these remarks suggests a further inference. The *effects* of stimuli cannot be predicted solely from their intrinsic properties. This conclusion is borne out by some recent experiments.[2] These indicate that inferences in regard to the emotional experience of individuals cannot wholly be based upon an account of immediate stimuli and bodily responses. In addition, knowledge is required of what the individual actually experiences. In the experiments referred to,

> the stimulus-situation was identical: adrenaline chloride was intra-muscularly injected. The physiological or bodily response was identical: certain phenomena of sweating, shivering, etc., were produced. But the individual mental processes were remarkably different. One person had no emotion—the emotion was "cold" and impersonal; another had a *pseudo* or *quasi emotion*, reminiscent of another occasion when he had

experienced a similar set of symptoms, but not an emotion in the present; and a third individual really felt the complete emotion of fear.[3]

The differential factors in these cases must lie, of course, in the constitution or personal history of the individuals concerned. If we seek them in the latter sphere the problem is further complicated by the universal and primary importance of learned or acquired experience in the broadest sense of the term. In life situations in particular, as contrasted with the more highly controlled experimental setup of the laboratory, the relevance of factors of this order, while extremely complex and difficult to evaluate with precision, cannot be ignored. It is hardly surprising, then, to find that C. Landis, at the close of a recent survey of experimental data, stresses the need for further investigation of the relation between learning processes and affective experience. He writes:

> The question of nature *versus* nurture is as marked in emotions as in any other type of human behavior. It is customary to speak of emotion as a natural reaction; one which is little varied by experience. Certainly this is a very inexact concept. What the natural emotional life of an individual might be like is an unknown territory. Emotional life is modified more rigorously in the growth and education of an individual than perhaps any other variety of human experience. The reason for the statement so frequently made that emotion is a natural reaction, unmodified by learning, is that emotional reactions occur in such large units of physiological disturbances that they frequently swamp the mental life of the individual. [Consequently] the most important line of future research is that of the nature of the relation existing between emotion and learning in the broadest sense of each term.[4]

If we consider this problem not only with respect to the affective experience of individuals in Western society, but from the standpoint of humanity as a whole, a fresh angle of attack is indicated. It is possible to investigate, analyze, and compare the factors that influence the typical or commonly experienced affects of individuals in human societies with widely different cultural traditions, as well as the factors that are involved in the affective experience of individuals who deviate from the collective norms of these societies. Factors of the former order I shall call *cultural variables*.

Since culture includes the content of socially transmitted experience, to which each new individual born into a society is exposed, it provides the primary frame of reference to which all varieties of learned behavior may be related. With respect to the emotions, culture defines: *(a)* the situations that will arouse certain emotional responses and not others; *(b)* the degree to which the response is supported by custom or inhibitions demanded; *(c)* the particular forms which emotional expression may take.[5] It is to these norms that the individual will learn to accommodate his behavior and in terms of which his affective experience will function.

The Saulteaux Indians whose fears and anxieties I wish to discuss live on the Berens River in Canada. I think that the relation between some of the characteristic fears experienced by these people and their traditional system of beliefs will become sufficiently clear if I discuss the former with reference to the situations in which they occur. Some of these situations, such as illness, are common to human life everywhere. Yet they do not give rise to equivalent affects. The psychological differentia, I believe, are to be sought in the content of the beliefs that are part of the cultural heritage of these Indians. These beliefs not only define each situation for the individual in a typical manner, they structuralize it emotionally. But at the same time it is interesting to note that there are usually traditional means available for the alleviation of culturally constituted fears. The individual is not altogether left at loose ends; he may obtain some relief and reassurance through the utilization of institutionalized defenses.

ENCOUNTERS WITH ANIMALS

The traditional attitude of the Berens River Indians towards animal life must be distinguished from our own. Animals, like men, have a body and a soul. (See chap. 11) [*Culture and Experience;* "Temporal Orientation," chapter 7, this volume]. Each species is controlled by a spiritual boss or owner that is of the nature of a transcendental being. Guns and traps are of no avail if this spiritual boss of the species is offended and does not wish human beings to obtain his underlings. Consequently, wild animals as a whole must be treated with respect lest their bosses be offended.

While this general attitude is characteristic, the affective responses of the Indians to different animals is not uniform. It would be impossible, however, to make any a priori judgment, based upon our attitude towards wild life, as to which animals are feared and which are not. Wolves and bears, for instance, are common in this region, but the Indians are never afraid of them. The creatures they fear most are snakes, toads, and frogs, animals that are actually among the most harmless in their environment. Indeed, the only species of snake that occurs is a small variety of garter snake.

The attitude of these Indians towards snakes was brought home to me by a striking occurrence. Once when I was traveling with a small party, one of the Indians sighted a snake, perhaps eight inches long, swimming in the water near the rock where we were eating lunch. The Indian picked up his gun and took a shot at it, missed, and shot again, and missed. The snake started to swim towards the shore, and as it began to wriggle up the rock, another man picked up a paddle and with a few hard strokes, managed to kill it. But that was not enough. They built a small fire and burned the harmless creature to a crisp.

While this episode may appear to be a trivial one, it was no trifling matter to the Indians. Even objectively considered it suggests an exaggerated affective response to an animal of this sort. To say the least, there was nothing intrinsic to the situation as such that demanded the immolation of a harmless garter snake on a pyre. It is partially intelligible, however, if reference is made to mythology. Once the earth was inhabited by many monster snakes and some of these persist today. A few individuals claim to have seen them and they are much feared. It is the identification of actual snakes with the mythical variety that accounts in part for the attitude of the Indians toward the former. But on the occasion described there was more involved than this: The snake was burnt because its approach to our camp was interpreted as having a meaning that aroused apprehension and consequently demanded the treatment received.

Wild animals, of course, habitually avoid the dwellings of men so that we might suppose that the Indian would "naturally" be startled to find a bear or snake near his wigwam, or to find a bird or squirrel inside of it. The fear that some people in our society experience when a bat flies in their bedroom at night might be thought to be comparable to the emotions which the Indians experience. But this is not the case. The beliefs of the Indians make the affect a qualitatively different thing. For to them the approach of a wild animal of any sort to their camp or habitation is an ill omen. It is a sign that someone is trying to bewitch them. The animal is thought to be the malevolent agent of a sorcerer.

In one case a man had been ill. He had taken lots of medicine but it seemed to do him no good. Then he noticed that a bear kept coming to his camp almost every night after dark. Once it would have gotten into his wigwam if he had not been warned in a dream. Since an evilly disposed medicine man may sometimes disguise himself as a bear, the sick man's anxiety rapidly increased. He became convinced that a certain man had bewitched him. Finally, when the bear appeared one night, he got up, went outdoors, and shouted to the animal that he knew what it was trying to do. He also threatened to retaliate with dire results to the suspected witch, if the bear ever returned. The animal ran off and never came back. (See also chap. 8.) [*Culture and Experience*; chapter 26, this volume.]

Even if birds alight on a dwelling, it is considered an evil omen. It is still more serious if wild animals actually enter a human habitation. On such occasions, the animal may not only be killed but burnt, as was the snake, since this is the appropriate institutionalized procedure. This act serves to dispel the fear engendered as it is thought to be the safest way of disposing of malevolent agents of this kind.

One night after settling down to sleep in our tent, my traveling companion, an Indian about sixty-five years of age, found a toad hopping towards him. He became so panic stricken that it was difficult for him to kill it. But he finally managed to do so. Then he went outside the tent with a flashlight in order to discover if there were any more toads about. He killed several with a stone. Then he collected a number of large stones and, after carefully examining all sides of the tent, weighted down the canvas here and there so that there was no possibility of any more of them crawling in. He slept hardly at all the rest of the night. After this experience, W. B. always took special pains to see that the front of the tent was closed at night and weighted snugly to the ground with a line of stones.[6] We jokingly called this our "toad dam." It must be emphasized that this man had spent most of his life in the bush, was an excellent hunter and accustomed to handling all sorts of animals. What then were the determinants of his phobia? In the first place, toads are not simply "loathsome creatures" to these Indians. They are associated with evil forces, certain parts of the animal being used in malevolent magic. Hence they are to be avoided and even their presence bodes no good for the reason I have stated. But there were more complex determinants in the fear response of W. B. It is said that if the taboo upon narrating myths in summer is broken, toads will come and crawl up one's clothes. Now my friend W. B. had been telling me native stories from time to time so that the visits of the toads were good empirical evidence of the truth of the native belief. But since W. B. was a Christian and believed himself to be emancipated from native "superstition" (although, of course, this was not actually the case) it may be inferred that the conflict engendered was somewhat disturbing to him. There were then several etiological factors at work: (*a*) the generalized belief in the malevolent attributes of toads; (*b*) the notion that their presence in a dwelling was an ill omen; (*c*) the fact that a taboo had been broken, specifically indicated by the presence of the toads; and (*d*) the conflict engendered by the semi-emancipated attitude of W. B. towards these notions.

In addition, however, there was another factor peculiar to the personal history of W. B. When a young boy, a toad had crawled up his pants and he had crushed it against his bare skin. This experience would appear to be an important differential factor which may account to some extent for the *exaggerated* fear reactions of W. B. to toads as compared with that of the other Indians. This difference was objectively proved on one occasion when I saw another Indian deliberately pick up a toad and put it near W. B. to tease him. Judged by strength of affect, W. B. was abnormal in comparison with the other Indians observed. But etiologically viewed, his phobia cannot be fully explained by reference to his personal history alone. It needs to be related to the native beliefs in regard to toads and the situational factors already mentioned.

The generalized fear of toads and frogs among these Indians is fostered by another fact. Monster species are reputed still to inhabit the country, the tracks of which are sometimes seen.

A few years ago several Indians were traveling across Lake Winnipeg in a sailboat. They pulled in at Birch Island. While a fire was being built and some food cooked, the man who told me this story [William Berens] took his gun and went off to shoot ducks. He came across some fresh tracks near the shore. They were about the size of a man's hand and formed exactly like the tracks of a frog. They indicated a jump of approximately six feet. The Indian who made this discovery hurried back to his companions. They went and examined the tracks, and agreed with him that they were those of the giant frog. The narrator said that he wanted to follow the tracks inland but his companions were so frightened that they insisted upon leaving the island at once.[7]

The psychological significance of this anecdote can best be appreciated by emphasizing two points. First, these Indians are expert hunters and accustomed to recognizing the tracks of all the animals in their environment; second, they were armed. We can only conclude that their misidentification of the tracks was a result of the mental-set which their belief in the reality of monster frogs imposed and that their fears cannot be dissociated from the malevolent attributes reputed to creatures against whom even guns might not be adequate protection. If we take these factors into account, they evidenced a normal response to a danger situation as defined for them in cultural terms.

Since disease situations occur and recur among all peoples, they provide excellent material for the investigation of the cultural differentia that may influence the individual's attitude towards his own illness and the quality of the anxieties that his relatives and friends may experience. Different human groups have different traditional theories of disease causation and when an individual falls ill, his emotional attitudes and those of his associates are intimately related to the theories held.

Among the Berens River Indians, broken limbs, colds, constipation, toothache, and other minor ailments are considered fortuitous in origin and do not arouse any marked affective states. But a prolonged illness, which has not responded to ordinary methods of treatment, a sudden illness, or one that is characterized by symptoms that are considered in any way peculiar, arouses apprehension or even fear. Why? Because of the belief that the person may have been bewitched. The individual believes that some one is trying to kill him. He becomes more and more worried and begins to reflect on his past activities and associations in order to recollect who it is that may wish him out of the way. In such a situation institutionalized means of protection are readily available. A conjurer or seer may be hired to discover the person responsible and measures taken to counteract the evil influence. Jealousy is often the motive attributed to the witch, frequently arising out of rivalry situations.

In 1876 when the Treaty with the Dominion Government was signed and an elective chieftainship first established, J. B. [Jacob Berens] and a powerful medicine man named Sag-a-tcīweäs [Peter Stoney] were rivals for the new office. J. B. won. The next day he put on his new uniform and felt fine. But that night he was suddenly taken ill. It was inferred that Sag-a-tcīweäs was responsible. Later he developed a recurrent skin disease that did not respond to native drugs. This was likewise attributed to the powerful medicine man he defeated. In this case the usual apprehension typical in such a situation was balanced by the powerful ego of J. B. and the confidence he had in his ability to withstand the malevolent intention of his rival. J. B. asserted more than once that he would outlive Sag-a-tcīweäs, and he did.

The special form of sorcery that causes the most fear is based on the theory that material objects can be magically projected into the body of the victim. Sebaceous cysts, lumps of any kind, and other symptoms are evidence of the presence of such objects. They are removable by a pseudo-surgical technique in which certain medicine men specialize. It involves the withdrawal of the object by sucking. These men, of course, produce actual objects that they claim to have removed from their patients' bodies. This serves to allay the latters' fears and in cases where a recovery is made, empirical support is given to the native theory of disease causation. Examples of such disease-causing objects are magic shells, dogs' teeth, bits of metal, and stones. One Indian showed me a series of such projectiles that had been "sent" him. His body was strong enough to resist them and they fell at his side where he found them.

Feelings of guilt for past moral transgressions are also the source of apprehension in a disease situation, since these Indians believe that sickness may be the result of such transgressions. Again, it is the fact that an individual does not respond to the usual drug remedies that precipitates apprehension. The transgressions that fall in the panel of traditional sins are murder, incest, deceit, and sexual practices such as masturbation, fellatio, the use of parts of animals as artificial phalli and bestiality. Confession is the necessary preliminary to cure when it is thought that sickness is connected with sin. An interesting aspect of their theory, however, is the belief that such sins on the part of parents may be the source of illness in their children. Consequently the anxieties aroused in disease situations where some transgression is believed to be back of the illness; are not confined to the patient. His parents are likewise suspected and they may confess sins committed in childhood or adolescence. In a series of fifteen cases illustrating the transgressions confessed, twelve were those in which sexual sins were involved (1939a). [Hallowell, "Sin, Sex and Sickness," chapter 17, this volume.]

ENCOUNTERS WITH CANNIBALS

The most intense fears the Berens River Indians experience are generated in situations that are emotionally structured by their beliefs concerning *windigowak*, cannibals.[8] They believe that human beings may be transformed into cannibals by sorcery, that cannibal monsters can be created "out of a dream" by a sorcerer and sent into the world to perform malevolent acts and that cannibal giants roam the woods, particularly in the spring. Consequently, when some human individual is reputed to be turning into a cannibal, the Indians become terror stricken. They are similarly affected when it is reported that a cannibal, created by magic, is approaching their encampment, or when some individual traveling in the bush discovers traces of a cannibal or claims that he has seen one.

Gastric symptoms are among those that the Indians interpret as evidence of incipient cannibalism on the part of human beings. When a person refuses to eat ordinary food or is chronically nauseated or cannot retain the food he ingests, suspicion is at once aroused. Even the individual so affected will develop anxiety and make the same inference. He may even ask to be killed at once. For this is the inevitable fate of reputed cannibals according to native custom. Usually they are strangled and their bodies burnt, not buried.

The last case of this sort to occur on the Berens River was in 1876 when three men killed their mother, built a pyre, and burnt her body. Since that time similar cases have occurred farther north. In 1906 two men from Sandy Lake were arrested for murder by the Mounted Police, because they had participated in the disposal of a woman reputed to be a *wíndīgo*. From the standpoint of native customary law, the strangling of a cannibal obviously is not illegal. It is a communally sanctioned defensive act, rationally justified in the circumstances.

Another type of situation is illustrated by the behavior of the Indians when it is reported that a cannibal monster is headed in their direction. One midwinter night at Poplar River, when a terrific gale was blowing, word got around that a *wíndīgo* would likely pass that way. All the Indians on the north side of the river left their homes at once and congregated in a house across the river. In order to protect themselves they engaged one of the leading shamans to conjure all through the night in order to divert the *wíndīgo* from his reputed path. The Indians firmly believed that the cannibal passed without harming them and part of the evidence they adduced was the fury of the wind, which was interpreted as a sign of his presence. Similar episodes are said to have occurred in the past and mythology recounts terrific fights between strong shamans and cannibal giants in which the former are always successful. To these Indians such monsters are quite as real, quite as much a part of the environment as the giant animals already mentioned, or, in our culture, God, angels, and the Devil.

It is not surprising then to discover individuals who claim to have seen the kind of cannibal that is reputed to roam the woods, or to have been pursued by one. Such illusions are particularly interesting in view of the fact that these Indians are expert woodsmen, who not only have spent all their lives in the bush, but are familiar with the detailed topography of their country to an amazing degree, as well as with all the various species of fauna and flora. Consequently it might be expected that the whole gamut of possible sights and sounds would be so well known to them that they would be insulated against false perception of any kind. I know from personal experience, at least, that many sounds that have startled me from time to time have always been explained by my Indian companions in the most naturalistic manner. It is all the more significant then to discover cases in which the perceptions of individuals have been so thoroughly: molded by traditional dogma that the most intense fears are aroused by objectively innocuous stimuli. It is the culturally derived *Einstellung*, rather than the stimuli themselves, that explains their behavior.

One old man, for instance, narrated the following experience.

Once in the spring of the year I was hunting muskrats. The lake was still frozen, only the river was open, but there was lots of ice along the shore. When it began to get dark I put ashore and made a fire close to the water edge to cook my supper. While I was sitting there I heard someone passing across the river. I could hear the branches cracking. I went to my canoe and jumped in. I paddled as hard as I could to get away from the noise. Where the river got a little wider I came to a point that has lots of poplars growing on it. I was paddling quite a distance from the shore when I came opposite to this point. Just then I heard a sound as if something was passing through the air. A big stick had been thrown out at me but it did not strike me. I kept on going and paddled towards the opposite side of the river. Before I got to that side he was across the river already and heading me off. I paddled towards the other side again. But he went back and headed me off in that direction. This was in the spring of the year when the nights are not so long. He kept after me all night. I was scared to go ashore. Towards morning I reached a place where there is a high rock. I camped there and when it was light I went to set a bear trap. Later that day I came back to the river again. I started out again in my canoe. Late in the evening, after the sun had set, there was a place where I had to portage my canoe over to a lake. I left my canoe and went to see whether the lake was open. There were some open places so I went back to get my canoe. Then I heard him again. I carried my canoe over to the lake—it was a big one—and paddled off as fast as I could. When I got to the other end of the lake it was almost daylight. I did not hear him while I was traveling. I went ashore and made a fire. After this I heard something again. I was scared. "How am I going to get away from him," I thought. I decided to make for the other side of an island in the lake. I was sitting by my canoe and I heard him coming closer. I was mad now. He had chased me long enough. I said to myself,

"The number of my days has been given me already." So I picked up my axe and my gun and went in the direction of the sounds I had heard. As soon as I got closer to him he made a break for it. I could hear him crashing through the trees. Between the shore and the island there was a place where the water was not frozen. He was headed in this direction. I kept after him. I could hear him on the weak ice. Then he fell in and I heard a terrific yell. I turned back then and I can't say whether he managed to get out or not. I killed some ducks and went back to my canoe. I was getting pretty weak by this time so I made for a camp I thought was close by. But the people had left. I found out later that they had heard him and were so scared that they moved away.[9]

In the situations thus far passed in review I have attempted to indicate the cultural constituents of the fears of individuals and the institutionalized means available for their alleviation. In societies with different culture patterns the same situations would be emotionally structured in a different way, the affects of individuals would be qualitatively if not quantitatively different, and other traditional defenses would be invoked.

To an outsider the fears of the Berens River Indians, and those of other primitive peoples, appear to be "neurotic," in the sense that they occur in situations where no actual danger threatens and for the reason that the sources of some of these fears are of the nature of fantasies. Can we speak, then, of "cultural neuroses" that are characteristic of whole populations? I think not. If we do so, as Karen Horney[10] has pointed out, "we should be yielding to an impression based on a lack of understanding" as well as being guilty of a fallacy in reasoning.

In the first place, the Berens River Indian *is* responding to a *real* danger when he flees from a cannibal monster or murders a human being who is turning into a *wíndigo,* or when he becomes apprehensive in a certain disease situation. To act or feel otherwise would stamp an individual either as a fool or as a phenomenal example of intellectual emancipation. Furthermore, the Indians themselves are able to point out plenty of tangible empirical evidence that supports the interpretation of the realities that their culture imposes upon their minds (1934a). [Hallowell, "Some Empirical Aspects," chapter 20, this volume.] They are naive empiricists but not naively irrational.

Once we relegate commonly motivated fears to their proper frame of reference—cultural tradition—a fundamental etiological distinction can be made between fears of this category and those which arise in individuals from conditions primarily relevant to the circumstances of their own personal history. The *genuine* neurotic, in addition to sharing the culturally constituted fears of his fellows, as Horney says, "has fears which in quantity or quality deviate from those of the cultural pattern." Any comparison, then, between the fears and defenses of such individuals and the culturally constituted fears and institutionalized defenses of whole human societies is not only superficial; it is actually misleading, since no account is taken of differences in etiological factors. Primitive peoples are sometimes accused of the logical fallacy that results from an inference that two phenomena are identical if one or more elements are shared in common. To seriously maintain that the culturally constituted fears and defenses of primitive peoples are evidence of "cultural neuroses" which are of the same order as the neurosis of individuals in Western civilization is just such a fallacy. Manifest surface analogies are compared whereas the underlying differences in the dynamic factors that produced them are ignored.

A further differentiation between the genuine neurotic and the person experiencing the "normal" fears of his culture is important. The former is inevitably a suffering individual; the latter is not. "Thus the normal person," writes Horney,

> though having to undergo the fears and defenses of his culture, will in general be quite capable of living up to his potentialities and of enjoying what life has to offer him. The normal person is capable of making the best of the possibilities given in his culture. Expressing it negatively, he does not suffer more than is unavoidable in his culture. The neurotic person, on the other hand; suffers invariably more than the average person. He invariably has to pay an exorbitant price for his defenses, consisting in an impairment in vitality and expansiveness, or more specifically, in an impairment of his capacities for achievement and enjoyment, resulting in the discrepancy I have mentioned. In fact, the neurotic is invariably a suffering person.[11]

This distinction, so clearly elucidated by Horney, is demonstrable among the Berens River Indians. There are individuals in this society who manifest phobias that are quantitatively or qualitatively deviant from those of the other Indians. These persons are among the genuine neurotics. I have already mentioned W. B. whose toad phobia was quantitatively distinguishable from that of the other natives. Further differential factors in this case, as I have pointed out, have to be sought in his personal history. It is not without interest in the present connection to add that this old man, who is of mixed white and Indian blood and an outstanding leader among his people, also manifests a marked fear of thunder and lightning (which has no cultural sanction), a periodical stutter under emotional stress, a mild echolalia at times, and an identification with his father who was chief before him. He is far less provincial in his general outlook than the other Indians on account of his many intimate contacts with white people over a long period of years and the opportunities he has had to see a little of the "outside" world at first hand. Besides, he is a man of superior intelligence and mental alertness, with a rich sense of humor and fine physical vitality. Consequently his personality traits, considered as a whole, approach those of the white man more closely than most of the other Indians of the river and to the casual observer present an essentially "normal" picture. Yet were a deeper analysis of his personality possible, I dare say that W. B. would prove to be an example of a neurotic fairly well adapted to the conditions under which his life has been lived. I also suspect, as pointed out above and also in connection with one of his dreams (1936a) [Hallowell, "Psychic Stresses," chapter 11, this volume], that an etiological factor of importance lies in a deep-seated conflict between W. B.'s ostensible acceptance of Christianity and the very profound importance which many native beliefs have had for him. The cogency of this hypothesis is suggested by the widely different attitudes taken by W. B.'s parents and grandparents towards Christianity during the early decades of missionary efforts. For W. B. was only a boy of ten years when the first resident missionary arrived on the Berens River. W. B.'s mother [Mary McKay], being white, was a thorough-going advocate of Christianity, and his father, with some personal reservations no doubt, reputedly was instrumental in obtaining a local missionary for his band. On the other hand, W. B.'s paternal grandfather [Bear or Makwa] with whom he was very intimately associated in his upbringing immersed him in native beliefs. That W. B. has been exposed to some inner conflict in consequences of these varying attitudes is evidenced by the fact that he has frequently remarked to me that as he has grown older, and as a result of discussions engendered by my ethnological investigations, during which he has served more as a collaborator than interpreter, the truth of native beliefs has more and more impressed him. He has contrasted this with the more "superior" and critical attitude he assumed when he was a young man. While it is true that all of the Indians of his generation were undoubtedly exposed to the same general conflicts in belief, the fact that W. B.'s mother was a white woman presents a unique circumstance which, combined with the extreme pagan views to which W. B. was subjected in the same family circle (household group) may have affected both the quantitative and qualitative aspects of his early identifications.

In contrast to W. B, other Berens River Indians exhibit such marked qualitative deviations from the established culture patterns of their society that there is no obvious connection between certain of their phobias and traditional beliefs. In addition to being afraid of witches, mythical animals, cannibals, etc., these individuals suffer from anxiety as distinguished from fear. (See chap. 14 [*Culture and Experience*, 1955].) Their phobias are personal and have no culturally phrased causes. Individuals subject to such phobias often rationalize them in terms of whatever beliefs seem appropriate. The most striking fact that characterizes phobias of this category is this: they occur in situations that easily can be distinguished from those that are emotionally structured by common beliefs.

One man, for example, who had hunted and trapped all his life, found himself beset by anxiety whenever he attempted to go any distance into the woods alone. He happened to be a conjuror and rationalized his anxiety by confessing that he had practiced his profession without the proper supernatural sanction (1936a) [Hallowell, "Psychic Stresses," chapter 11, this volume].

Another man could go nowhere unaccompanied by one or more companions. When alone he would always keep within sight of human habitations or people. This was the rule even when he had to urinate or defecate. If he had to relieve himself at night his wife would always get up and go with him. Sometimes his companions would tease him by stealing out of sight. As soon as he discovered this he would start to call for them and run frantically in the direction where he thought they were. One winter when he was traveling with a party of men and found himself alone in the woods he threw off his hat and mitts in his frenzy and yelled until his companions came back. Once when he was hired by the Hudson's Bay Company to cut wood he induced some small boys to go along for the ride and walk back with him while he ran ahead of the team of oxen. He rationalized his anxiety by saying that he once dreamed that a jackfish would swallow him, if this creature found him alone.[12]

A third man, whom I know personally, lives a hundred miles up the Berens River at [Little] Grand Rapids. The Indians of this band are only superficially Christianized and live much in the purely native fashion. J. D. [John Duck (Machkojence)] has spent all his life here. His children are all married and he is now about sixty years of age. He is a tall, sparsely built individual, energetic in speech and movement and an exceptionally fine singer and drummer. But he has suffered from phobias all his life. Darkness disturbs him profoundly. "Ask J. D. to go and fetch a kettle of water for you some night," one of the Indians said to me, "you'll find that he will refuse, even if you offer to pay him well for it." Once when J. D. was traveling in winter with some other men they were attempting to reach their camp late at night because they had no blankets or bedding with them. Before darkness fell, J. D. insisted that they help him collect birchbark so that they could make torches to carry with them during the rest of their journey. They did this, but every now and then the wind would blow them out. When this happened and they were plunged in darkness J. D. would fall to the ground and writhe and scream like a "crazy" man. The situation described is one which may be contrasted with those referred to earlier in this paper. J. D.'s fears are unsupported culturally. They are unique and his behavior sharply deviates from that of other individuals in the same situation. When it is understood, moreover, that the winter months are those in which these Indians are most active, since this is the trapping season, and that at the latitude at which they live the days are shortest then, so that there is constant necessity for moving about when it is dark, the abnormality from which J. D. suffers is thrown into even greater relief.

J. D. also suffers from a kind of agoraphobia [hydrophobia?]. He usually skirts the shore when he goes out alone in his canoe on the lake. In fact, he never will head directly across any extensive body of water if he can avoid doing so.

The case of J. D., however, transcends in interest the fact that he exhibits such obvious neurotic symptoms. He is a well-known conjurer (seer), doctor, and the "owner" of one of the four Wábano pavilions up the river, in which the most important native ceremony that still survives is held. According to Indian dogma the "ownership" and hence the leadership in this particular ceremony is a supernatural blessing, mediated in a dream. The details of the structure erected by different leaders thus differ in minor ways and so do the procedure followed and the content of the dream validation itself. But superficially there is adherence to a common pattern and the prophylactic and therapeutic purpose of the ceremony is common to all.

Since a man who is both a conjurer and Wábano leader is reputed to be an extremely powerful individual because he has been "blessed" by many supernatural guardian spirits, it would appear that the exhibition of such deviant fears as J. D. manifests would prove to be not only inconsistent but a definite liability. Consequently it was of some interest to discover that J. D. has long been the subject of comment for just this reason. "If he is such a strong man as he claims to be," one old Indian remarked to me, "and he has so many *pawáganak* (guardian spirits), why is he afraid to do so many things?" This commentator went on to say that while some of the people had faith in J. D. he himself had none. Because these Indians are extremely individualistic and pragmatic a wide range of judgments in respect to the abilities of any person who essays to conjure or cure is possible. Consequently the expression of a skeptical attitude towards J. D. is not in itself significant. These Indians are genuinely tolerant because they are always ready to have an individual demonstrate his professed abilities, while at the same time they never "pull their punches" if they find some flaws in his claims. In former days it is even possible that any expression of skepticism whatsoever was rarer. For the traditional attitude towards great medicine men was typically one of prodigious respect verging on fear. No one would have dared tease such a person nor challenge his authority unless he considered himself equally powerful.

In view of J.D.'s neurotic traits, which are not, of course, classified as pathological by his fellows, it is all the more interesting to note the expression of skepticism referred to above and also a lack of respect, which I found to be fairly widespread. But even this would be less significant were it not for the fact that no such attitude was manifest towards the three other Wábano leaders on the river. One of these even shared the distinction accorded the medicine man of a generation ago in being somewhat feared because he was reputed to have done away with several Indians by magical means. So far as J. D. is concerned, I was told that on one occasion when he was conjuring, members of the audience quietly stole away without his knowledge while the performance was in progress. Since seership is one of the functions of a conjurer this put J. D. on the spot. For, as people said, his guardian spirits could not be much good if they did not immediately tell him what had happened right in the neighborhood of the conjuring lodge itself. On two other occasions that I know of, some of the younger men deliberately stimulated J. D.'s fears in order to tease him. Once when he was making a speech in his Wábano pavilion during the course of a ceremony, a toy mechanical snake was released on the earthen path. It was headed for J. D. who stamped around in a panic when he saw it coming and finally ran out. Another time a young fellow obtained a firecracker and set it off at J. D.'s side while he was singing and drumming. On this occasion J. D. was so frightened that he not only ran away, he failed to come back for his drum (an extremely sacred object) until the next day. Amusing as they are, these episodes sufficiently indicate in themselves the profoundly personal character and depth of J. D.'s anxiety. They also document the attitude which many of the Indians hold towards J. D.

Although I know practically nothing about the details of J. D.'s personal life, I suspect that his conjuring, doctoring, and Wábano leadership are intimately bound up with his neurosis. They probably screen repressed aggression and somewhat compensate his deep feelings of insecurity. There is some evidence, at least, that this may be the case. J. D. assumes a domineering attitude towards others that is frequently a matter of comment. It was J. D., too, who showed me the magically projected objects that symbolized a half-dozen futile attempts to kill him. It is possible that the discovery and personal interpretation he attributed to those objects may represent the projection of his own repressed hostility towards others. At any rate, the culture of these Indians, containing as it does a theory of "disease-object" intrusion, provides an institutionalized background against which projective mechanisms in individuals can readily function. J. D.'s propensity to impress others is also so very evident that, together with the other features mentioned, it may be taken as evidence of a fundamental insecurity, connected with his anxiety. In recent years, for example, he has incorporated in his Wabanówīwin certain features of the defunct Midéwi·win, the curative ceremony that once ranked highest in prestige not only among the Berens River Indians, but elsewhere among Algonkian peoples. He has even gone so far as to coin a new term, *wábano midéwi·win,* for his ceremony. To further enhance his prestige he has also borrowed features, originally found in some of the other Wabanówīwin. Almost every year he makes some new innovation while the other Wabanó leaders do not. He was the only Wabanó owner, moreover, who tried to sell himself to me as an informant, when I first visited [Little] Grand Rapids. This made me mistrustful as I was aware that such information is traditionally sacred and esoteric. In fact, previously I had been able to obtain the information I wanted from a Wabanó leader farther up the river only with the greatest difficulty. The last time I was at [Little] Grand Rapids, J. D. said he had much more to tell me but I soon found out that all he was able to do was to repeat himself with minor variations. One summer he asked me to send him a flag with an eagle (associated with the mythical Thunder Bird) on it from the United States. He wished to fly it over his Wabanó pavilion. I was told later that upon receiving the flag J. D. called a number of the old men together. Exhibiting it to them he baldly pointed out that whereas some of the Indians had no faith in him, here was a token of the regard of a white man who had journeyed all the way from the United States to obtain medicine and information. As might be expected,

J. D. is also extremely sensitive to real or fancied slights. Once when he had planned to hold his Wabanówĩwin for three days, I attended the first day but spent the whole of the second day with an informant a couple of miles across the lake. J. D. was much annoyed, despite the fact that my contribution of tea, flour, and tobacco had practically subsidized his ceremony. On another occasion he got angry because only a few Indians attended the third day and he was forced to close the ceremony earlier than he intended. He once berated his sister, too, when he heard she had been giving me some personal reminiscences that included information about his father. J. D. evidently considered this his prerogative, a fact partially explained by the position of women among these Indians and the marked sexual dichotomy in social, economic, and religious life. But I doubt very much whether any other Indian would have become quite so emotionally upset over a matter of this sort. By and large, it would thus appear that, unfortunately for J. D., the institutions of his society that have offered compensatory defenses for his inner conflicts have not been sufficiently adequate to his needs. He remains not only a suffering individual but a deviant one, even from the standpoint of native culture itself.[13]

It would be highly desirable, of course, to know a great deal more about the four individuals discussed above. In order to demonstrate the *actual* etiological factors at work a psychiatric or psychoanalytic study of each case would have to be made. I have only attempted to indicate that the manifest behavior of these individuals suggests that the causes of their anxieties are of a different order than the culturally constituted fears of the general run of the population. In contrast with the latter, the situations that provoke the fears of these individuals are emotionally structured by highly subjective meanings that are personal and unconscious.

This differentiation, it seems to me, is of general significance. It indicates that a comprehensive account of the determining factors in the affective experience of individuals must include on the one hand an analysis of the influence of cultural patterns and, on the other, an investigation of the factors that determine quantitative or qualitative individual variations from a given cultural norm. In any particular society these two aspects of the problem are inseparable. But in Western civilization a great deal of attention has been paid to factors thought to be relevant to individual deviation without reference to the influence of the characteristic culture patterns that mold the ideologies and affects of individuals in a common manner.

In clinical practice, cases have turned up more than once that necessitate an evaluation of such factors. Some years ago a Negro committed to a mental hospital and thought to be suffering from private delusions was discovered by a psychiatrist to belong to a local religious cult of which his ideology was characteristic.[14]

It is only through the study of affective experience in a number of different human societies that the role of cultural variables can be thoroughly understood. Comparative data of this sort may also indicate that individual deviations themselves take on characteristic forms in different societies. But while the typical conflicts engendered by different cultures may vary and the symptomatology of individuals may reflect the traditions of their society, from an etiological standpoint genuine neurotics will remain comparable in so far as we can account for their behavior in terms of common dynamic processes.

Notes

First published in *Journal of Social Psychology* 9 (1938): 25–47, and reprinted in Hallowell, *Culture and Experience* (Philadelphia: University of Pennsylvania Press, 1955), 250–65.

1. John Dewey, "Conduct and Experience," in C. Murchison (ed.), *Psychologies of 1930* (Worcester, 1930).

2. Hadley Cantril and W. A. Hunt, "Emotional Effects Produced by the Injection of Adrenalin," *American Journal of Psychology*, 44, 1932, 300–7; Carney Landis and W. A. Hunt, "Adrenalin and Emotion," *Psychological Review*, 39, 1932, 467–85.

3. C. A. Ruckmick, "Psychology Tomorrow," *Psychological Review*, 44, 1937, 138–57.

4. Carney Landis, "The Expression of Emotions," in C. Murchison (ed.), *Handbook of General Experimental Psychology* (Worcester, 1934).

5. Otto Klineberg, *Race Differences* (New York, 1935).

6. [Ed. note: W. B. was William Berens. Ojibwe myths were to be told only during winter; to recite them during the summer risked bringing on a plague of toads as noted below. Berens, however, told myths to Hallowell who could only visit in summer. His Christian faith may have somewhat assuaged his fears of repercussions, but his taking that risk also shows the closeness of his relationship with Hallowell. See Berens, *Memories, Myths, and Dreams of an Ojibwe Leader* (2009).]

7. [See William Berens's telling of this incident in Berens, *Memories, Myths, and Dreams*, Part III.]

8. [See Berens, *Memories, Myths, and Dreams*, Part III, for windigo incidents related by William Berens.]

9. So far as tradition is concerned, experiences of this sort are not uncommon. But only a relatively few living individuals seem to have undergone them. In the last analysis, of course, selective factors that involve the personal history of such individuals must be taken into account as well as cultural tradition. Personality differences of this order suggest further problems that need detailed investigation. Cf. W. Morgan, *Human-Wolves among the Navaho* (Yale University Publications in Anthropology, no. 11, 1936), 3. "But Navaho, even within a family, differ so much as individuals that there is no such thing as a uniform fear of these human-wolves. Many of the stories feature a human wolf climbing upon the adobe roof of the Navaho hogans and looking down through the smoke hole in order to find his victim. Invariably, he knocks some earth loose and it may be heard by those inside the hogan as it rolls off and drops to the ground. When this occurs, it has twice been my experience that a Navaho who is apprehensive about human-wolves will hurry through the door to look around outside. But the man beside him may show little or no interest. This man may have few fears and few worries; or he may have considerable nervous tension but his anxieties have focused upon some other cultural pattern such as fears of the spirits of the dead. In either case, he will stay where he is sitting or lying on his sheepskins."

10. Karen Horney, *The Neurotic Personality of Our Time* (New York, 1937).

11. Horney.

12. Since dream experiences are believed to be the source of supernatural blessings and esoteric knowledge, such a rationalization is fully acceptable to other members of this society. Presumably the giant jack fish, not the ordinary variety, is meant.

13. In August, 1937, I received a letter from one of my Indian informants [William Berens]. He said that J.D. had been "very sick," that some people said he was crazy and that there was talk of sending him to "the hospital or to the asylum." My correspondent added that *he* did not believe J.D. was crazy but that some of the people were afraid of him. "I don't think that the poor man was looked after right," he added. [Ed. note: see glossary for a short sketch of John Duck.]

14. Information, Dr. H. S. Sullivan.

THIRTEEN

Freudian Symbolism in the Dream of a Saulteaux Indian

Sir

In his Huxley Memorial Lecture, *Anthropological Perspective and Psychological Theory*, J. R. A. I. 62 (1932), 215, Prof. Seligman pointed out that we already have "hints indicating that certain substances and objects have the same value in the unconscious of savages as the psychoanalysts attribute to them in Europeans."[1] The example he cited was the association of fæces and money among Melanesians and West Africans; to which J. S. Lincoln, *The Dream in Primitive Cultures*, 1935, 107–8, added additional cases from other parts of the world. A striking instance of an identical association, in which money is unconsciously identified with fæces, occurs in the dream of a Saulteaux Indian.

Last summer [1936], in the course of a field trip to the Berens River Saulteaux (Manitoba, Canada), I was traveling up the river to a small fishing settlement, located about 100 miles east of Lake Winnipeg. One morning I asked W. B. [William Berens] whether he had dreamed anything the night before.[2] The dream he reported was as follows: "I dreamed I was walking on snow shoes. It must have been spring because there was not much snow on the ground. I was traveling with a boy. I sighted a camp but there was on one in sight. Then I heard the sound of chopping in the bush. As we came closer a man appeared. This man handed me some money, over one hundred dollars in bills. I could see an x on some of them. But the bills were the colour of that (pointing to my sleeping bag, which was yellow-brown in hue). This man also gave me some silver and I gave some of it to the boy. I asked whether this was all right and the man said 'yes'"

I asked W. B. what the dream meant. He said it might indicate that he would catch a fox the next winter. He inferred this from the colour of the bills, which he thought was so inexplicable.

The Freudian symbolism in this dream is so transparent that it needs no further comment. On account of the colour of my sleeping bag it could hardly have been more forcibly emphasized. Moreover, the importance of the *colour* of the bills in the mind of the dreamer was further demonstrated by (a) the fact that he seized upon it immediately as the basis of his own interpretation of the dream's meaning, in which case the fox skin of the same colour as the bills in the dream means money (in exchange), and (b) his reiterated comment that it was so strange that the bills were not of the ordinary (green) colour.

I may add that the dreamer could not identify either the man or the boy in the dream. The latter, he said, was about eleven years of age. When I explained the Freudian symbolism, he seemed in no way resistant to the idea.

A possible interpretation of the general tenor of the dream as a whole might be this: W. B., who is about seventy years of age, has been my interpreter and mentor during several summers of fieldwork. He has become rather tired of the work, however, and rationalizes this by telling me that I have already written down all I need to know. Here he was then starting off on another trip, though it was to be a relatively short one. This dream is probably the expression of repressed aggression towards me. I was the man he failed to recognize, a possibility that was further precluded by transposing the season to winter. I gave him the money, which approximated the amount he would earn, but this money was also fæces, metaphorically speaking. I have more than once heard him use the vernacular term in respect to tasks he disliked performing. At the same time, since we have been close friends, he could not turn me down, and he needed the money, as well. But he was not anticipating a pleasurable trip, because internally he very much resisted going. Besides, the journey up the river is not an easy one. There are fifty portages in 100 miles and W. B. has been accustomed to do his share of the carrying, besides the cooking. Then when we are encamped there are (to him) the endless inquiries and hours of translating what other people have to say. Thus while the interpretation I have given may be regarded as tentative, the use of the Freudian symbolism does make the dream intelligible in terms of the circumstances in which it occurred. No doubt it had further meanings as well, which would require more expertness and detailed associational data to unravel.

Notes

Published in *Man* 38 (1938): 47–48.

1. [Ed. note: C. G. Seligman's essay was published in *The Journal of the Royal Anthropological Institute of Great Britain and Ireland*, 62, July-December 1932, 193–228.]

2. [Ed. note: See William Berens's telling of this dream in Berens, *Memories, Myths, and Dreams of an Ojibwe Leader* (2009), Part III.]

FOURTEEN

Shabwán

A Dissocial Indian Girl

East of Lake Winnipeg, in a country of labyrinthine waterways, swamps, glacier smoothed rocks, and unbroken forests, a scattered population of native Indians, who make their living by hunting, fishing, and trapping, are still to be found. No white settlements exist in this vast area; the only white men to be seen are a few trappers in winter, an increasing number of prospectors in summer, here and there a lone missionary and his family, and, at points a hundred or more miles apart, the post managers of the Hudson's Bay Company or independent traders.

On the Berens River, about 100 miles inland from Lake Winnipeg, there is a summer fishing settlement of a small group of these Indians. Like other natives of this region, they are locally known as Saulteaux, although they are actually a branch of the Ojibwa nation. The population of the settlement referred to, located near the foot of the largest rapids on the river, is about 200. Together with a smaller group of Indians that fish several miles north [Pauingassi], they form what is known officially as the [Little] Grand Rapids Band. In the fall the families making up the band scatter to their hunting grounds, to return the following spring to their fishing settlements. Near the [Little] Grand Rapids there is a Hudson's Bay Company post, an opposition trader and a Protestant missionary.[1] The latter also conducts a day school for as many pupils as it is possible to attract. Although a few of the younger Indians understand some English, only their native language is spoken in daily life.

To the superficial observer, a great deal of the color of native life is gone. These Indians wear no native costume, they use iron tools and steel traps which they purchase from the traders, as well as flour, tea, and tobacco. Even birchbark canoes are no longer made, those in use today being of the commercial variety. On the other hand, native dwellings covered with birchbark are still to be seen in summer, certain dance ceremonies persist, as do aboriginal hunting methods, the use of native drugs, other methods of curing disease, conjuring, etc. Above all, aboriginal beliefs still flourish with great vigor and are a constant incentive to action. Consequently the vital core of native psychology remains intact to a considerable degree. Aboriginal culture has not yet been destroyed through contact with whites. One may say, rather, that in certain respects it has been modified and in others reintegrated, as a result of changing conditions.

My first contact with the Indians of [Little] Grand Rapids was in the summer of 1932. I have visited their settlement three times since, the last visit being in the summer of 1936, when the events narrated below took place. While one of my objectives has been the collection of material for an ethnological account of the Berens River Indians as a whole, I have been concerned with certain psychological problems as a more specialized line of inquiry.[2]

In this paper I wish to give an account of what happened to Shabwán, a dissocial adolescent girl of the Grand Rapids settlement. Although these Indians do not know the exact year of their birth, she was probably between fifteen and sixteen years of age at the time. Despite the basic differences in the cultural patterns of Saulteaux society and our own, to which so much of the specific attitudes and behavior of the girl, her parents and the other Indians may be referred, there can be discerned, I believe, the operation of underlying psychological mechanisms and impulses that are familiar in comparable cases of revolt against parental authority in Western civilization.

I was drawn into the situation as a participant observer because the Indians believed Shabwán to be insane. They were terrified, because mental derangement is usually attributed to witchcraft. Their attitude towards Shabwán was constituted on the one hand by apprehension lest this be true,[3] and on the other, by their traditional notions concerning normality and abnormality in behavior. Hence the methods used in restraining Shabwán and the diagnostic and remedial measures undertaken were determined by culturally molded premises. It is this angle of the case that exhibits Saulteaux psychology in some of its most distinctive and characteristic aspects. It is an excellent illustration of the pragmatic implications of traditional beliefs and culturally phrased concepts.

Once plunged into the situation, the discovery that Shabwán was not psychotic led me to pursue the course of action described, in which it was necessary that I take respectful cognizance of native attitudes and beliefs. At the same time I sought to exploit the latter, to some extent, with remedial ends in view. To the Indians, however, my invasion of the situation was casual and as unprofessional as it will appear to the reader. The result was that I found myself exercising a genuine influence in the situation with only the barest minimum of any formally recognized therapeutic control. Evidence that such was the case is to be seen, for instance, in the fact that a week after my initial interviews with the girl, she was treated by native methods in a native ceremony. I fancy that this was somewhat of the nature of a "cultural compulsive," since my "treatment" had none of the earmarks of native therapeutics[4] and there continued to be a latent apprehensiveness that the girl would revert into "madness." Consequently there is no real paradox in the fact that before I left the members of her family openly acknowledged that I had exerted a remedial influence, and later in the summer I was embarrassed by reports filtering down the river that I had cured an insane girl!

I first heard of Shabwán one Saturday night when the chief of the Grand Rapids Band came over to our camp to ask my guide and interpreter[5] [William Berens] what had best be done with her.[6] Everyone was saying that Shabwán had gone crazy (kīwaskwe). She was violent, moaned, yelled, laughed, and talked in a silly fashion. It was necessary to watch her every minute and to forcibly hold her down most of the time.[7] The previous night Shabwán had told her parents that she was going to sleep with some other girls in another wigwam. Her mother was suspicious and later went to see if she were there. But Shabwán was not there. Neither could she be found in any of the other wigwams on the small island where her parents were camped. After some frantic searching she was discovered by herself on the bank of the island near the water. She was forcibly taken back to the family dwelling and then the trouble began. She had gotten better during the day but as night approached she had begun to rave again.

After a great deal of talking the Grand Rapids chief decided to write to the Mounted Policeman who was stationed 100 miles away at the mouth of the river and to send the letter down as soon as possible by the Indians who were making periodic trips for the Hudson's Bay Company's freight. Another plan discussed was to send Shabwán down the river at once by canoe and turn her over to the Mounted Police. Since an aeroplane was expected almost any day with an inspector of the Hudson's Bay Company, an alternative plan considered was whether the pilot could be induced to fly her out to the Mental Hospital at Selkirk (Manitoba).[8] At this time I took the statements of the Indians at their face value and decided to secure further information the next day and perhaps pay a visit to the island where Shabwán was living.

The following morning (Sunday) G., the son of the opposition trader, dropped in for a chat. When he casually remarked that he had been over to the island to witness a conjuring performance[9] the night before, I expressed disappointment that he had not told me about it. I asked him whether he had seen the "crazy" girl over there. He said that the conjuring lodge had been set up close by the wigwam of the parents of Shabwán and that the conjurer had attempted to discover the cause of her condition, without coming to any satisfactory conclusion. Before he entered the lodge the conjurer had said to Shabwán, "I'm going to try to make you better." But the girl had been overheard to say, "He can't make me better."[10] She went on to say that she wanted to see a white man.[11] Someone then drew her attention to G. and Shabwán turned to him and said in English "Aren't you J's boy?" "Yes," G. replied. "Well, you are a good boy," Shabwán went on, "your father treats the Indians right."[12] Up until this time according to G.'s account, two young Indian men were holding the arms of Shabwán. Now she asked G. to take the place of one of them. When the latter let go, G. said her fingers closed into a fist and her arms bent upwards convulsively. She closed her eyes when this happened and lost consciousness. G.'s impression was that she had no control over these movements. This was the reason that the Indians were afraid she might act in a harmful fashion and injure herself or others. So they insisted that someone keep hold of her constantly. Sometimes when an attempt was made to straighten out her arms, Shabwán would start to yell or even laugh. While he was holding her, G. said that Shabwán began to sing in Indian. He asked her father what the song was. The latter replied that it was a hymn she had learned in church.[13] All during this time the conjuring was continuing; the lodge was shaking violently and different guardian spirits of the conjurer were announcing themselves and singing their songs. After G. had been holding Shabwán's arm for half an hour or so, she started talking about two young girls whom he and an Indian lad had been "running after" the previous spring. This embarrassed G.[14] and, as it was already getting late and he was tired, he said he had to go. Shabwán tried to persuade him to stay but another young man took his place and he left. The conjuring was still in progress.

After this conversation with G., I heard no more of Shabwán until about four o'clock in the afternoon when my interpreter and I received a request to come over to the island. Shabwán was no better and her father and mother thought that perhaps I (a white man) could do something. The family[15] was living in a hemispherical shaped wigwam, typical of the summer dwellings many of these Indians now use. It was an extremely hot day and, to catch a slight breeze that swept the treeless knoll on which the Indians were camped, the canvas covering of the dwelling had been raised all around. The wigwam of the girl's grandparents was only a short distance away, as well as the dwelling of another family. Besides Shabwán, her parents and grandparents there were at least a dozen other people in the wigwam. Their faces were as gravely apprehensive as any I have ever seen.[16] As soon as we arrived a few other Indians, seeing our approach, came up and stood outside.[17]

Shabwán was lying down, her head to one side and her eyes apparently closed, and with a boy on either side holding her arms. Without saying anything I sat down near her. My interpreter began talking with the other Indians but I kept my attention fixed upon Shabwán. The first thing I noticed was that she raised her right arm a couple of times in what seemed to be a perfectly normal manner. There was not a sign of any convulsive contracture. Shortly after this she told one of the boys to release her right arm. Looking a bit apprehensive, he did so and she calmly scratched her nose. Then she told him to take hold of her arm again. I asked her parents about physical symptoms prior to her attack. She had complained of nothing it seems, no headaches or pains of any kind. She had been eating normally and her bowels had moved regularly. Turning my attention to Shabwán again I told the young fellows at her side to release her arms. They did and there were no contractures of either hands or arms. Then I took hold of Shabwán's arms myself and called her by name. She had her head turned in the other direction and I asked her to look at me. Her eyes were closed and she was groaning rhythmically. She had done this periodically when the boys were holding her, but while I was talking to her parents I also noticed that she had freed one hand and snapped the arm band of one of them in a playful manner. So I accused her of being a tease. At first she hid her face and would not look in my direction. Then there was a suppressed giggle and a shy glance. I smiled at her and she at me. Her facial expression was entirely normal. In order to test her orientation I asked her (through my interpreter) what day of the week it was, which person was her father, her mother, and her grandfather—all of which questions she answered correctly. Since she wore a wristwatch[18] I got her to compare the time with mine, which she did. This comparison of watches really seemed to arouse her interest. It was obvious that she was not disoriented in the least. I was smoking and offered her a cigarette. She took it and her mother interjected the remark at this point that Shabwán had never smoked one.[19] So I took several more cigarettes from my pack and threw them in her lap. Still holding her hand I told her that she was going to get better and that she would not be sent away.[20] After talking playfully a little longer, Shabwán sat up of her own accord, picked up a comb and started to comb her hair. Then she pulled a silk handkerchief out of her sack and twisted it about her head. The expression on her parents' faces and on those of the other Indians had undergone a change by this time. The psychic atmosphere was far less tense than when we arrived. Although her mother still seemed apprehensive I told Shabwán to get up and we would take a little walk. I took her arm and we circled the wigwam a couple of times. While we were walking I repeated what I had said about her recovery and added that I hoped to see her dancing in the wábano pavilion the following day.[21] When we returned to the wigwam the Indians were talking about what they thought was an almost miraculous change in Shabwán. After we had seated ourselves once more Shabwán showed me some of her school books and exercises. I told her that if she still felt well in the morning she was to send me a note written and signed by herself and that I would send her a can of pears.[22] She promised to do this. I was thinking of taking my leave at this point when Shabwán put her hand on her leg and said that she felt a swelling there. Almost immediately someone exclaimed, "It has gone into her legs."[23] In a moment Shabwán's mother was at her side feeling all around the girl's leg below the knee. She was extremely grave once more when she said that she could feel a lump there. Another Indian felt the same spot and said, yes, he felt something too. Then I examined her leg. There was not even the suggestion of a lump. So I almost pulled the girl to her feet again, saying, "Come with me. We will take another walk. That will do you good." When we returned nothing more was said about the lump by anyone. The suggestion had lost its potency.

When I left the wigwam Shabwán's grandfather, an old man whom I had visited several times before, shook my hand and thanked me heartily for what he thought I had done for his granddaughter. I advised the girl's parents not to restrain her physically. But when we reached the waterside, I looked back and saw Shabwán's mother and another woman tightly holding her as they made off into some bushes.[24] One of the councillors of the band,[25] who had formerly participated in the Midéwi·win[26] was present during the interview. He left with us and inquired whether I thought that Shabwán should be sent to the mental hospital in Selkirk. He said that the Chief had already written to the "Mountie." I told him that I thought it wise to wait for a few days and see how Shabwán behaved. After we had returned to our camp and had a chance to talk things over I was interested to discover that my interpreter did not think that the girl was "crazy." He suggested that she may have deliberately gone "crazy" to cover up a rendezvous she had in the woods the night her parents could not find her. Despite her parents' precautions he thought it quite possible that Shabwán had already had sex experience[27] and now wanted to "run loose."

After we had eaten our supper a messenger arrived from the island. Shabwán was raving again! We paddled over and found the girl lying on her back in the wigwam with two boys holding her as before. She may have been "raving" before we got there but at the time we arrived she was singing hymns at the top of her lungs! She would pay no attention to me at first, although I repeated her name several times and tried to engage her attention in other ways. Her father said that Shabwán had gotten worse when her sister lost her pencil. Shabwán had struck her sister and this act had apparently been sufficient to precipitate the latent apprehension of the entire family. They had restrained her at once. It was apparent, however, that the boys were not actually holding her down against her will. I was frankly amused this time when I noticed that, when one of them let go her arm for a moment, she almost immediately reached for his hand again. But Shabwán evidently did not wish to talk to me. Finally I discovered her giggling again and we both laughed. Meanwhile, I had told the boys to release her and they had left the wigwam. While I was talking to her, Shabwán started to get up. I made no restraining move, but her mother darted at her like a cat after a mouse. Shabwán was too quick for her and slipped out of the side of the wigwam, between the poles. Shabwán was laughing but her mother called for help and the girl's grandmother and another woman joined the chase, as the girl darted here and there. It is doubtful if they would have caught her as easily as they did were it not for the fact that Shabwán's bloomers began to slip down her legs. She stopped to pull them up and the older women captured her. I told my interpreter that I could not very well order the whole family about so we kept our places while all this was going on. After Shabwán was brought back to the tent I asked her whether she did not wish to get better. As might be expected, her answer was "No." She was evidently getting too much pleasure, at the moment, out of her rebellious mood. After lying down for awhile very quietly, while the rest of us engaged in some general conversation, Shabwán sat up again and the same thing happened as before. Her mother tried to stop her leaving the wigwam but Shabwán got away and after an even merrier chase the women fairly dragged her back into the wigwam, feet first, amidst her peals of laughter. It was even more evident this time how successfully she was malingering.

But it must not be forgotten that the older people were exceedingly grave about the whole business. They were evidently more convinced than ever that she was "crazy." There was even a third chase that night when I took Shabwán for another walk, and she broke away from me and started to go in the opposite direction. I stood still but the women started after her. This time Shabwán ran to her grandmother's wigwam. When they brought her back she was laughing again.

After this occurred I said I would go. Then Shabwán said she did not want to have me go. She asked to see my wristwatch again. I showed it to her and she asked me how much it cost. She said she wanted it, that I was rich and could spare it. On the assumption that she was malingering, I promised to trade wristwatches with her if she ceased running about, disobeying her parents and "got well." I also told her that the promise of the pears still held good. Then I left.

Early the next morning (Monday) I received a fairly legible note saying, "Me Shabwán better," with her English name signed to it and written after the latter, "Little Grand Rapids girl." I sent over the pears at once with the messenger, who said that Shabwán had been quiet all night.

About 2 o'clock in the afternoon Shabwán, her parents, and the two younger siblings put in an appearance at the cabin I used as an "office." Shabwán's mother was all smiles. She said Shabwán has slept quietly all through the night. I gave the children some candy and the mother some rolled oats. The father then went outside and started talking with some other Indians who were there. I got out my photograph album and Shabwán and her mother spent considerable time looking at the pictures.[28] We could hear the drumming in the wábano pavilion and I asked Shabwán's mother whether they were going over there. She said, "No." The mother and my interpreter engaged in conversation while I took Shabwán outside and photographed her. When we returned Shabwán sat quietly without saying anything to anyone. She seemed sleepy and let her head drop on her knees. Then she got up, stood at the door and looked out. Her mother, who was sitting on the floor Indian fashion, got up at once. Shabwán sat down again and her mother did the same. A little later Shabwán said it was too hot inside the cabin, that she was going out. Her mother got up and followed her outside, but without any attempt at physical restraint or any negative verbal command. Shabwán walked over to where her father was sitting and threw herself on the ground. Her mother, my interpreter, and I followed. It was very hot and although the Indians kept up a continual chatter I almost fell asleep. Shabwán pelted me with some little sticks[29] as

I lay stretched on the ground, and everyone laughed. I teased her in return but otherwise paid no attention to her. Several times Shabwán's mother suggested that they return to the island but Shabwán refused to go. Finally I got up and said I was going to the *wabanówĭwin*. At this remark Shabwán said she wanted to go, too. So we all started off, Indian file. Shabwán followed me, her mother came next with the younger children, and her father and my interpreter brought up the rear. Arrived at the wábano pavilion,[30] Shabwán found a seat inside next to her grandfather who was one of the drummers. I sat down on the opposite side and when I caught her eye, she giggled. During the next couple of hours Shabwán danced with the rest of the Indians several times and evidenced no abnormal behavior of any sort. Neither did she attract attention to herself in any other way. My impression was that the Indians took her presence there as a matter of course, although I did notice that several of them scrutinized her very closely. Before leaving the *wabanówĭwin* I called Shabwán's grandfather aside and gave him an American quarter.[31] I told him to give it to Shabwán and to tell her I wanted her to keep it on her person day and night until I asked for it again. She was to look at this talisman if she felt herself getting "sick" again.

The next day (Tuesday) Shabwán came over and danced in the *wabanówĭwin* again. I paid no attention to her but during one dance she shyly beckoned me in and I joined the line of dancers. This was the last day of the ceremony.

Despite Shabwán's normal behavior at the *wabanówĭwin* and at home, she evidently remained a subject of conjecture throughout the community because on Wednesday afternoon, while I was working with an informant some distance from the camp, news reached us that the Mounted Policeman had arrived to take Shabwán in charge. I hurried back to camp at once only to find that the rumor was false. As we were eating supper, Shabwán and her family paid us another visit. Before they left, Shabwán asked me about the "trade" I had promised to make. I told her I was not ready to make it just yet, that it would depend on whether she continued to keep well. After she had gone, I noticed a small folded square of paper on the floor near my chair. On opening it I found that Shabwán had torn a couple of sheets from her copybook on which she had written her name several times and some phrases, both in Saulteaux and in English. It was evidently a note intended for me. She asked for some cakes, said she was "butter" (better), that she was my girl and my "sweethard." [See *nīnam*, in glossary.]

On Friday, two days later, I learned through G. that Shabwán had acted "crazy" the previous night. There was a *potáte* dance being held on the island and she wanted to go.[32] Her parents forbade her to do so and Shabwán "raved" and tore up her sleeping net. She had to be forcibly prevented from leaving the wigwam. Finally her father picked up a rope and threatened to beat her. Then she quieted down.[33]

On Saturday, Kīwítc [Alec Keeper], one of the oldest Indians at Grand Rapids, opened a special ceremonial dance of which he is the "owner."[34] It began in the morning and continued until nightfall. Shabwán and her parents were not in attendance during the day, but they put in an appearance early in the evening. Shabwán was very neatly dressed and had colored her cheeks with two big spots of rouge. Dancing was in progress when they arrived and Shabwán joined the line almost at once. She beckoned me in but I did not go. This ceremonial dance was continued on Monday. Like the *wabanówīwin*[35] it is believed to be generically prophylactic for all those participating and, as in the case of the *wabanówīwin*, individuals are sometimes given special therapeutic attention. Kétegas, the son of the leader and his executive assistant, had hinted to me on Saturday that I might witness such a procedure, but I did not know then that the subject of the treatment would be Shabwán. But early on Monday evening when I saw her father talking earnestly in private to Kétegas, I suspected that such was the case. A little later Kétegas took a double-headed rattle in his hand and joined the dancers, gesturing with the rattle as he went[36] in the direction of the men, women, and children who, some sitting, squatting or stretching at full length on the grass, lined the inside of the enclosure. Then he shook the rattle over each drummer in turn. Next he circled the dance ground counter-clockwise with a shirt in his hand, rattling constantly as the Indians at the drum beat out the dance rhythm and sang in unison. There was a continuous line of dancers who kept circling clockwise around the drummers at the same time and the rhythm of their movements was accentuated by the bells which two of the best male dancers had attached to their legs. The shirt was a "sacrifice," the consecrated part of the payment that Shabwán's family had made for the remedial treatment that was to take place. Shabwán joined Kétegas at this point and he handed the shirt to her. She carried it in outstretched hands before her as she now circled the dance ground in a counter-clockwise direction, Kétegas following and actively shaking his rattle. A clean white cloth was then spread on the ground on the west side of the drum, Shabwán squatted on this while Kétegas rattled over her. Next the shirt was placed on her shoulders and there was more rattling. This part of the procedure was concluded by having Shabwán hold out her hands, palms upwards, while Kétegas rattled over them. Then rising to her feet, she carried the shirt over to Kīwítc, the leader, and laid it on the ground before him. "*Mīgwétc, mīgwétc.*" (Thank you, thank you), he said. After this Shabwán joined the line of dancers again, who had paid little or no attention to the procedure I have just described. After a little more vigorous dancing the ceremony ended.

The next day (Tuesday) about noon, one of the young men from the island brought me a small paper packet. It contained three more pages from Shabwán's copybook, folded and refolded, and tied up with purple silk thread. As before, some of the writing was in English, some in Indian and the Cree syllabary was also used. "My sweethard" was written on many lines, as in an exercise book. She also asked me to come and see her. I did not go, but I wrapped up some candy and sent it back with the messenger.

I heard from various sources during the next few days that Shabwán was behaving quite like herself, but I did not see her again until a week later, the day before I left. On this occasion I retrieved my talisman and we exchanged watches. This seemed to make her very happy. I took down an interesting story that her grandfather told me on the same visit. The old man had a fine sense of humor and my interpreter was very fond of him. Although it may appear a bit paradoxical, in view of the native treatment Shabwán received in the ceremonial dance, her grandfather and her parents expressed their thanks for what *I* had done. Everyone was in such good humor that I recalled to them the old custom that makes it the prerogative of a medicine man who has cured a woman, to take her in payment as his wife or mistress.[37] The old grandfather nodded his head at this and said that I was quite right. While I do not know whether Shabwán herself was consciously aware of this aboriginal prerogative, it remains a latent cultural fact that might have influenced her attitude towards me unconsciously and, since she appeared to be interested in white men from the start, facilitated a transfer, once I entered the situation. Against this item in the cultural background, her overt expressions towards me also seem somewhat more conventional and consequently less personal than they might otherwise appear.

Before I left I saw the councillor who was present at my initial interview with Shabwán. As I have already mentioned he was one of the former sub-heads of the Midéwi·win, along with Shabwán's grandfather. He told me that the day after the girl was taken "ill," the family sent for him and they discussed holding the Midéwi·win for her. He demanded ten articles[38] but they said they were too poor to provide them.[39] Later when Shabwán got worse they sent for him again but he refused to go. Now it is very doubtful whether this man could have revived the Midéwi·win for Shabwán, even if the "articles" he demanded had been forthcoming. It is a complicated ceremony with hundreds of songs and the councillor had never acted as the leader, although he had assisted his father. Besides, a number of other men who knew the ins and outs of the Midéwi·win would have had to participate. It is doubtful if these could have been secured. Nevertheless, the fact that this possibility was discussed at all, indicates better than anything I have previously said, the seriousness with which Shabwán's case was viewed by the Indians. For the Midéwi·win was the curative ceremony par excellence of the aboriginal regime. Curative features of the other ceremonial dances referred to, have only arisen since the Midéwi·win died out, and they inspire much less confidence.

When I arrived at the mouth of the river the "mountie" told me that he had received the Chief's letter about Shabwán but that he had been waiting for verification from some other sources before he acted. He suspected, in fact, that the case might not be as serious as the letter indicated. About a month later the lay brother attached to the Catholic Mission at the mouth of the river paid a visit to Grand Rapids. He was in charge of medical work so that he was much interested in my account of Shabwán, particularly since he had known her since early childhood. When he returned from his trip, he told me that she had not relapsed into her "crazy" state.[40]

Notes

Published in *American Journal of Orthopsychiatry* 8 (1938): 329–40.

1. [The Rev. Luther Schuetze served the United Church of Canada as a missionary at Little Grand Rapids from 1927 to 1938. See his memoir, *Mission to Little Grand Rapids* (Vancouver: Creative Connections, 2001).]

2. Embodied in the following papers: (a) "Some Empirical Aspects of Northern Saulteaux Religion" [chapter 20, this volume]; (b) "Culture and Mental Disorder," *Journal of Abnormal and Social Psychology*, 19, 1934, 1–9; (c) "Psychic Stresses and Culture Patterns" [chapter 11, this volume]; (d) "Sin, Sex and Sickness in Saulteaux Belief" [chapter 17, this volume]; (e) "Temporal Orientation in Western Civilization and in a Preliterate Society" [chapter 7, this volume]; (f) "Fear and Anxiety as Cultural and Individual Variables in a Primitive Society" [chapter 12, this volume]; (g) "Freudian Symbolism in the Dream of a Saulteaux Indian Man" [chapter 13, this volume].

3. If it were, she might turn into a cannibal (*wíndīgo*), and menace the whole community. In former days, persons believed to be turning into

cannibals were strangled, even though they gave no overt evidence of aggressive impulses. Consult Hallowell (b), (c), (f) [see note 2, above] for further information on *wíndīgo* beliefs. Prof. Frank G. Speck has pointed out to me a possible analogy between the term that the Saulteaux use for a demented person, *kīwaskwe* and *kiwáckwe*, the Penobscot word for cannibal giant. It is quite possible that there was a latent or expressed fear that the girl might become *wíndīgo*, but I did not hear of it.

4. Particularly the payment feature, the *sine qua non* in the treatment of disease. A noted medicine man usually will not undertake to treat his own child but will hire someone else. Gifts are always tendered the doctor *before* he initiates his curative procedure.

5. The chief of the band at the mouth of the river, a man of about 70 years, known and respected by all the Berens River people.

6. The missionary would probably have been consulted at this point had he not been away at the time. Although not medically trained he was the dispenser of medical supplies and drugs supplied by the Dominion Government.

7. In this account I am following the serial order of events as I recorded them in my daily notes written down at the time.

8. It was assumed that the Dominion Government would foot the bill, if this were done.

9. A barrel-like structure of poles is erected, which is then covered with birch bark or canvas. The people who attend the performance squat on the ground in a circle around it. When the conjurer enters, the lodge begins to shake and strange voices issue from it. These latter are believed to be the voices of the supernatural helpers of the conjurer and the structure is kept swaying by the spirits of the winds. Clairvoyance is one of the functions of the conjurer and such performances are frequently held to determine the causes of obscure symptoms of disease or to obtain information in regard to the proper methods of cure. I had previously seen several performances of this kind.

10. G. speaks and understands the native tongue.

11. In view of later developments this statement, although ambiguous, may seem of some importance. I regret to say that it appears in my notes without further elaboration.

12. G. was much impressed by the girl's use of English as well as the fact that she spoke to him so directly. G. knew all the girls extremely well and although he had never had any personal contact with Shabwán, his previous impression was that she was extremely shy (a characteristic surface trait

of the personality of most Indian girls). Shabwán's response to G., on the other hand, possibly the result of previous fantasy, seems psychologically significant because his pursuit of the girls of this community was notorious. She could well be bold with him.

13. G. was a Roman Catholic so was not familiar with Protestant hymns.

14. While in this society premarital continence is the avowed ideal, the social contacts of post-pubertal boys and girls are sexually focused in the fullest sense of the term. This type of association is given a distinctive character, however, owing to the fact that the culture of these people does not provide any conventional forms of recreational association between individuals of opposite sex. Boys and girls of this age do not play games together, go swimming or go canoeing or walking in pairs. In the native dances-in which the performers circle the singers and drummers-the boys and men from one continuous line and the women and girls another. The obverse of this strict sexual dichotomy in outward social life is a premium on secret rendezvous in the bush for purposes of sexual gratification alone. Consequently the pursuit of any girl or woman by a man has an obvious connotation. This is probably the reason why G. was embarrassed. Shabwán's remarks were the equivalent of a public exposé that he did not relish. The physical contacts with young men obtained by Shabwán through being "held down" are likewise of significance in this connection.

15. Besides Shabwán there were three other children, an older brother, and a younger brother and sister. Four other children had died.

16. These Indians as I have known them are seldom grave, even when they have scarcely enough to eat. Ordinarily they laugh at the slightest provocation and peals of merriment often are heard in their camps. But in the face of sickness and, above all, any hint of "craziness," they become almost terrified.

17. There is little privacy anywhere in an Indian camp and overt curiosity is seldom suppressed.

18. Very few of the Berens River Indians carry watches or own clocks. Shabwán had obtained her watch from the son of a half breed who had been to boarding school. Had I not known that Shabwán herself had attended school it would have been useless to expect her to know how to tell time. Cf. Hallowell, "Temporal Orientation"[chapter 7, this volume].

19. Both boys and girls begin to smoke at an early age. Pipes are more commonly used than cigarettes. The latter are a luxury.

20. Gossip travels so quickly through these communities that I assumed

that Shabwán may have heard already that some such measure might be taken.

21. The *wabanówīwin* is a ceremonial affair that we would call a dance. It is only held a few times a year and usually lasts several days. While superficially it is a social affair, participation is both prophylactic and curative according to Indian belief.

22. These Indians gather berries in season, but they never taste other fresh or canned fruit.

23. The concept back of this remark involves a belief in magical projection of material objects into a person's body by means of witchcraft. Such objects may be the cause of physical or mental symptoms and often they are believed to cause death. As I have already pointed out, witchcraft as a possible cause of Shabwán's behavior lurked in the background, although it was never specifically mentioned, as far as I know.

24. Evidently they had not permitted her either to defecate or urinate alone since the trouble began.

25. An elective office that has only existed since the Government made a treaty with these Indians in 1875. Every band, as now organized, has a chief and one or more councillors.

26. Often called the Grand Medicine Lodge in English. It was the most potent curative ceremony of the aboriginal regime. It has not been given at Grand Rapids form some years. See Hallowell, "The Passing of the Midéwi·win in the Lake Winnipeg Region," *American Anthropologist*, 38, 1936, 32–51 [chapter 21, this volume].

27. Personally, I am very much inclined to doubt this. While many of the girls of this community do carry on secret love affairs, prepubertal girls are not pursued and I do not believe that Shabwán was old enough to have aroused much sexual interest. G. had enjoyed such wide experience that I am sure that he would have heard about it if she had, for such matters are frequently an open secret among the younger people.

28. It contained all the photographs I had taken of the Berens River Indians and always proved diverting to visitors. [Ed. note: Hallowell's photograph of Shabwán has not been identified in his papers in the APS, Philadelphia.]

29. Trivial as this incident may appear, it was quite openly flirtatious according to Saulteaux customs. Consequently it may be viewed as the first overt sign of a positive transference. In this connection it is of interest to find the following description of courtship preliminaries written by an early 19th century observer of the Saulteaux. "Their manner of making love is not only singular, but rude and indecent, according to our ideas of good

breeding. The lover begins his first addresses by gently pelting his mistress with bits of clay, snowballs, small sticks, or anything he may happen to have in his hand; if she returns the compliment, he is encouraged to continue the farce and repeat it for a considerable time. After these preliminaries, some significant smiles and witticisms are exchanged, but of such a nature as would make our more delicate fair ones blush." See L. R. Masson, *Les Bourgeois de la Campagnie du Nord-ouest*, vol. 2 (Quebec, 1889). Account of the Saulteaux by Grant, 319.

30. A structure made of bent poles with no covering. This particular one was 40 x 15 x 8 feet. Along the central axis there are several sacred posts and stones. A beaten path around these is the dance trail. The singers and drummers sit at regular intervals outside this trail, with their backs against the inside wall of the pavilion. In the same line sit men, women and children. There are usually many other people standing or sitting outside the pavilion.

31. These Indians handle very little cash except when they receive their annuity from the Government. Few, if any of them, have seen American money.

32. This type of dance is largely a social affair, although no dances of these Indians are purely secular. It is the only one that takes place after dark and for this reason it is specially popular with the young people because there are so often opportunities for rendezvous.

33. Indian parents are usually very indulgent with their children and very, very seldom resort to corporal punishment. It is important to bear this in mind with respect to the physical restraint to which Shabwán had been subjected as well as in relation to the incident just described. This threat of her father to beat her indicates an important change in attitude on his part. It was an overt admission, although he probably was not conscious of the fact, that she was not just 'crazy.' It likewise had a salutary effect, since Shabwán submitted to his control without the threat being carried into action.

34. Leadership of the *wabanówīwin* and the *potáte* [see glossary] as well as this ceremonial dance is validated by a dream "blessing" in which the dreamer is visited by supernatural beings and given certain instructions. These ceremonial dances thus become a kind of personal property. The one in question was held in a square dance ground defined by a series of upright stakes. There was a large drum in the center hung from specially made posts. Four drummers, who sang as they drummed, sat facing each one at the cardinal points. The dancers circled about them clockwise.

35. But unlike the *potáte*.

36. Equivalent to a "blessing."

37. Cf. Ruth Landes, "The Ojibwas of Canada," in Margaret Mead (ed.), *Cooperation and Competition among Primitive Peoples* (1937), 106. "If a shaman had cured a girl of a dangerous illness, had 'given life to her' through the power of his guardian spirits, he might receive her in payment of his priceless services."

38. The conventional number, including a gun, blanket, kettle, etc.

39. It would probably have cost them over $100.

40. I received the same information during the winter of 1938 from an Indian informant.

FIFTEEN

Aggression in Saulteaux Society

This paper might have been given the paradoxical title "aggression among a patient, placid, peace-loving, preliterate people." For among the aborigines of North America the Algonkians of the northern woodlands, in contrast with Indians like the Iroquois or the Sioux, have long enjoyed the reputation of being as mild-mannered and overtly *unaggressive* a people as could be found anywhere among the native tribes of this continent. Indeed, the statement made by Speck that among the Montagnais-Naskapi of the Labrador Peninsula, "strife is scarcely present; violence strenuously avoided; competition even courteously disdained"[1] is just as outwardly true of that other branch of the Algonkians, the Saulteaux, whom I shall discuss.

Yet Father Le Jeune, a Jesuit missionary who lived among the Montagnais-Naskapi in the early part of the seventeenth century, qualified this idyllic picture of outward harmony by an astute observation. "It is strange," he wrote, "to see how these people agree so well outwardly, and how they hate each other within. They do not often get angry and fight with one another, but in the depths of their hearts they intend a great deal of harm. I do not understand how this can be consistent with the kindness and assistance that they offer one another."[2]

What interested me when I stumbled across this characterization not long ago was the fact that it could be applied with equal validity to the Saulteaux. In my opinion, it goes to the very heart of the characterological problem presented by them. What I propose to do in this paper is to offer an explanation of what to Le Jeune was a psychological paradox, by examining the conditions under which ambivalent traits similar to those noted by him are molded. While my explanation applies primarily to the Berens River Saulteaux, there are many analogies to my observations in Le Jeune's account of seventeenth-century Montagnais society.

To the casual observer, cooperation, laughter, harmony, patience, and self-control appear to be the keynotes of Saulteaux interpersonal relations.

These people have never engaged in war with the whites or with other Indian tribes. There are no official records of murder; suicide is unknown; and theft is extremely rare. Open expressions of anger or quarrels ending in physical assault seldom occur. A spirit of mutual helpfulness is manifest in the sharing of economic goods and there is every evidence of cooperation in all sorts of economically productive tasks. No one, in fact, is much better off than his neighbor. Dependence upon hunting, fishing, and trapping for a living is precarious at best and it is impossible to accumulate food for the inevitable rainy day. If I have more than I need I share it with you today because I know that you, in turn, will share your surplus with me tomorrow.

This is the superficial picture that the Saulteaux present to the observer and it could be reinforced by a detailed description of the functioning of their economic and social institutions. But it is not a complete or fully realistic portrait. It does not expose the deeper psychological realities of Saulteaux life. While at first glance there seems to be no manifest evidence of aggression and while I myself did not at first sense the undercurrents of hostility that actually exist, on more intimate acquaintance I was forced to correct my earlier impressions.[3] Furthermore, I came to the conclusion that in all probability the undercurrents of aggression that I shall describe were even stronger in the past when native beliefs flourished in full strength and acculturative influences had not set in.

I shall attempt to show how, under the cultural conditions imposed by Saulteaux society, aggressive impulses are both stimulated and channeled; what the range of behavior is that has aggressive meaning for them and the behavior considered appropriate to combat it; and what are the effective reinforcements of these patterns of behavior from other sources. I believe that the cultural molding of such impulses provides a definite clue to the psychological sources of certain personality traits which are typical of these Indians. These traits are, in part, a function of dealing with people in terms of certain culturally imposed modes of behavior. Saulteaux patterns of social behavior create a fundamental ambivalence in the interpersonal relations of individuals. My hypothesis is that the outwardly mild and placid traits of character which they exhibit, and the patience and self-restraint they exercise in overt personal relations are a socially constituted façade that often masks the hostile feelings of the individual. If some of the basic beliefs and concepts of these people were changed their aggressive impulses would be reconstellated and the personality traits referred to would no longer assume their characteristic forms.

This absence of overt aggression in face-to-face situations is an outstanding feature of interpersonal relations in Saulteaux society. While in other preliterate societies unformalized or even formalized modes of open aggression frequently are found, among the Saulteaux behavior of this kind is not sanctioned, except in the mildest form.[4] The joking relationship between cross-cousins of opposite sex[5] and the exchange of belittling remarks between men of different sibs are the only formalized patterns of such behavior that I can think of. Aside from these, hostility in face-to-face situations seldom occurs. Consequently, when expressions of hostility *do* break through in the form of verbal threats, gestures, or physical assault, they are taken more seriously than is the case in societies where such modes of behavior are commoner because they are socially sanctioned. I have never observed boys or girls in exchange of blows. At the mouth of the river I know of a case where a man gave his brother a severe beating because he believed that the latter had attempted to seduce his wife. One couple is said to quarrel frequently and even to beat each other occasionally. Parents, I may add, seldom inflict corporal punishment upon their children.

Insulting remarks, direct rebuke or expressions of disapproval, open contradiction, sneering, or calling a person names are avoided by the Saulteaux. Swearing, in the sense of blasphemy, is not a problem because their language is inadequate in this respect.[6] Gestures that suggest an approach to physical assault, like shaking one's fist in a person's face, are a deadly insult. It immediately suggests extreme hostility. Even pointing one's finger at a person, accompanied by an angry facial expression or insulting words, may be interpreted as a serious threat against one's life. Actual physical assault is only legitimate in self-defense. In the past, individuals who, according to native belief, were judged to be cannibals—*wíndigowak*—were killed. But since such individuals were thought to be a menace to the lives of others, public opinion sanctioned their execution. (See chap. 13) [*Culture and Experience*; chapter 12, this volume.]

Saulteaux society functions in terms of primary group relations and in certain respects the kinship structure buttresses the discouragement of open aggression, just as the struggle to make a living may be partly responsible for food sharing and outward cooperation in economic tasks. The Saulteaux kinship system is centripetal in tendency in the sense that everyone with whom one comes in social contact not only falls within the category of a relative, but a blood relative, through the extension in usage of a few primary terms. There are no distinct terms for persons that in English we classify as relatives-in-law. This means that from the standpoint of a man, for example, all other men will fall into the following categories: grandfather, father, step-father (father's brother), mother's brother (father-in-law), brother, cross-cousin (brother-in-law), son, step-son (brother's son), sister's son (son-in-law), grandson.[7] Thus open quarrels would be tantamount, in terms of the formal kinship structure, to the expression of hostility between relatives. But since there are many other societies in which the same situation exists, I do not believe that the kinship structure as such is the basic factor in the discouragement of open aggression. There is no intrinsic reason, moreover, why relatives should not quarrel.

However, certain specific attitudes and behavior patterns that characterize certain classes of relationship among the Saulteaux do tend to discourage *open* hostility and thereby fortify self-restraint. There is considerable emphasis laid, for instance, upon the solidarity of brothers and, in fact, of all relatives in the male line. This means that quarrels between brothers or other closely related males are more shocking than those between cross-cousins. And since the relation between a man and his mother's brother (=father-in-law) is a highly formalized one requiring at all times a display of respect and even continence of speech, this type of habitual attitude and conduct in itself inhibits open aggression.[8]

At any rate, in Saulteaux society the inhibition of openly expressed aggression in face-to-face situations is not only a socially sanctioned ideal, in actual fact it seldom breaks down. What Duncan Cameron said of the Lake Nipigon Saulteaux more than a century ago is true of the Berens River people. He remarked that "Indians, in fact, seldom quarrel when sober, even if they happen to hate each other." It will be noticed that Cameron's last phrase echoes the note of aggression struck by Le Jeune. The Indians whom both these men knew were by no means devoid of aggressive impulses, but they were observed to exercise restraint in the open expression of them.

The same is true of the Berens River Saulteaux. The problem, therefore, is to discover how individuals in this society dispose of their aggressive impulses. For it must not be supposed that in situations where any open display of hostility has been suppressed that this is the end of the matter. In fact, complete inhibition of such hostile emotions is neither expected nor demanded.

Broadly speaking, the culturally sanctioned channels for hostility are of two kinds. The first is typified by all the unformalized ways and means that may be utilized in any human society for the *indirect* discharge of aggression. Gossip is as rife among the Saulteaux as among any other people and many unpleasant and even scandalous things are said behind a person's back that no one would utter in a face-to-face situation. Even serious threats are made that may never be carried out.

The chief of one of the Berens River bands has been in office for many years.[9] Again and again some of the Indians of his band have used devious means to remove him from his office, principally by accusations in anonymous letters sent to Ottawa or circulated locally by word of mouth. But when the band has met formally no one has dared to accuse him openly of the things said behind his back. All sorts of accusations were made against a missionary up the river a few years ago and from what I could gather a great many of them were true. But when a meeting was held to air the whole matter it came to nothing because the Indians would not state their grievances to his face. This is typical. An example of another kind of covert unformalized aggression is the following:

Some years ago several Berens River Indians who were out hunting came upon the traps of an Indian of the Sandy Lake Band. There is no love lost between the people of the Berens River and the Sandy Lake Indians; in fact, no marriages occur between the two groups. One of the hunters, egged on by his companions, defecated on one of the traps. Then he sprung the trap so that a piece of feces was left sticking out. Such an act was an insult to the owner of the trap and a deterrent to any animal that might approach it. It was a doubly aggressive act because, in addition to insulting the owner, it interfered with the purpose for which the trap was set and consequently menaced his making a living. That the Indian who did it recognized the nature of his act is proved by the fact that he later dreamed that a conjurer of the Sandy Lake Band tried to kill him by sorcery.

This leads us to the second channel for the expression of aggression-sorcery and magic.[10] This society does not actually say, "Thou shalt love thy neighbor." What it does say is, "if I hate my neighbor it is better that I should not openly quarrel with him." On the one hand, that is to say, the open display of aggression is not socially sanctioned while on the other, unformalized types of *covert* aggression are tolerated and in *addition* institutionalized means of covert aggression are provided. The use of these not only enables me to injure my neighbor, but they permit the accomplishment of my ends without his knowledge. He can only suspect, but never be quite certain, that I am using sorcery and magic against him. It is this obverse side of the discouragement of open aggression that gives a potentially ambivalent aspect to all forms of cooperative effort and harmonious interpersonal relations among these people. For the availability of sorcery and magic in this society may just as truly be said to foster *covert* aggression as the cultural norms requiring self-control in face-to-face situations may be said to discourage overt aggression. With sorcery and magic at my disposal, in fact, I can vent my anger with greater effectiveness than would be possible by verbal insult or even a physical assault, short of murder. I can make a person suffer a lingering illness, interfere with his economically productive activities and thus menace his living; I can also make his children ill or lure his wife away by love magic; I can even kill him if I wish. But when I meet him face to face I will give no evidence of my hostility by gesture, word, or deed. I may even act with perfect suavity and kindness toward him and share the products of my hunt with him. Of course he may suspect that I hate him or am angry, but even if he goes so far as to accuse me openly of using sorcery and magic I will not admit it. To do so would be tantamount to an open threat. And since he suspects me it would do no good to deny hostile intentions because he probably would not believe me anyway. So I may not answer him at all, but just turn and walk away.

It can now be understood that, while there are no *official* records of murder among the Saulteaux, this does not correspond with the psychological realities of this society. Within their behavioral world, murder has occurred again and again but always as the result of sorcery, not of overt physical aggression.[11] These Indians will not only name individuals who have met their death by sorcery, they will also name their reputed murderers. And they will go on to mention an even larger number of cases in which illness or failure in hunting have been caused by the malevolent action of human beings.

But the use of sorcery and magic as instruments of covert aggression is two-edged: whether an individual himself uses them or not, the threat that other individuals may be using them against him constantly lurks in the background of his daily life. In addition to the personal friction and unconscious hostilities that arise in all human relations[12] these people are dogged by anxieties and fears arising from the belief that human beings may do them positive harm in this covert way.

Such fears have very deep and wide ramifications in view of the fact that human vicissitudes of all sorts may be interpreted as due to magic or sorcery. Such emotions are precipitated under circumstances where the cultural definition of a situation weights the explanation of events in favor of sorcery or magic. Whereas we might attribute such inevitable hazards of life as illness, misfortune, or death to chance or impersonal causes of one sort or another, the individual in Saulteaux society is bound to consider magic or sorcery as a possible cause; in fact he is forced to do so because of the character and limits of the explanation of phenomena his culture offers him as alternatives. Consequently, it is inevitable that this explanation of events will be applied under appropriate circumstances and that these cases, in turn, will later be adduced as evidence of the reality of sorcery. This vicious circle cannot be broken without radical cultural changes. The type of knowledge accessible to the Saulteaux is primarily a function of their culturally constituted attitudes towards the nature of the phenomenal world. It is impossible for them to think in terms of our category of natural causation, without utilizing the premises which have been built up in occidental culture as the result of the accumulation of scientifically acquired knowledge.

At the present day, as a result of acculturation processes, the explanation of events in terms of sorcery and magic appears to have been somewhat relaxed and diminished in range, especially in the band of Indians at the mouth of the river. But it has by no means died out. Individuals, for example, still suffer from *änicinábewápine*, "Indian sickness." This is a modern term which shows that the contemporary Saulteaux clearly recognize a distinction between the diseases known to the whites and those which are peculiar to them. Indian sickness occupies an autonomous etiological category because it is "sent by someone," as they put it. More specifically, it is based upon the idea that some material object can be projected by sorcery into a person's body in order to cause illness. White doctors cannot cure this kind of disease, so native doctors still flourish who are prepared to treat it by removing the object. Illness or even death also may be caused by an attempt on the part of a conjurer to steal one's soul during sleep.

An examination of cases of illness attributed to both these types of sorcery indicates how this explanation extends the range of personal hostilities upon a thoroughly irrational and nonrealistic plane. For in such instances suspicion usually falls upon some particular person. In fact, if an aggressor is not immediately identified a conjurer may be employed to discover him by clairvoyant means. The reason for this is that countermeasures may have to be instituted in order to save the patient.[13] The chief point of psychological interest here is what determines the selection of an aggressor? In many cases I have found that the determining factor is the belief held by the victim that he has offended the suspected aggressor in some way. In other words, the sick person is apprehensive because he feels that he has aroused another person's hostility by some act of his and that the offended person has retaliated by making him sick. This measure-for-measure philosophy is very deep-seated among the Saulteaux, pervading many aspects of their social and economic life,[14] so that it is not strange to find it operating in connection with aggressive patterns of behavior. Le Jeune, referring to the Montagnais, gives an amusing application of it which is psychologically diagnostic as well. He says, "They eat the lice they find upon themselves, not that they like the taste of them, but because they want to bite those that bite them."[15] Once we understand that the Saulteaux always think and act in terms of this same principle it is not difficult to see why an individual who thinks he may have offended another is quite ready to believe that he has been bewitched by the person he has offended. One case already mentioned illustrates this. The Indian who defecated on a trap thought that the owner of the trap had identified him because he dreamed that a conjurer of the Sandy Lake Band was attempting to steal his soul.

I have another account of a dream experience which was interpreted by the dreamer in the same way. In this instance the dreamer was a boy [William Berens] who had made fun of a hunchback by imitating the way the cripple walked. The boy believed that the father of this cripple, a conjurer, attempted to retaliate by trying to steal his soul. The next day he was ill. He soon recovered, but he considered it a close call. In other words, both these men were threatened with death because of what they had done. In another case a young man suffered from Indian disease. It was thought that the man who had sent it was angry because the victim had beaten him in a dog team race. In this instance the young fellow died despite the efforts of a native doctor who tried to "suck out" the malignant object. From a native point of view this was a clear case of murder.[16]

In all these cases we would consider the reputed retaliation—attempted murder—entirely disproportionate to the offenses committed if we considered them to be serious at all. But within the context of Saulteaux society it is obvious that their evaluation is quite different. They were considered sufficient grounds for the counter-aggressive actions that menaced the lives of their perpetrators. In this respect they are excellent psychological clues to the kind of behavioral world in which these people live and act. If individuals believe that such actions of theirs are sufficient to arouse such extreme forms of retaliation, we can only conclude that they, in turn, might be offended by acts of a similar nature. It seems reasonable to infer, therefore, that these Indians are extremely sensitive to the slightest trace of aggression.[17] There is also the concomitant inference that individuals must be constantly on their guard lest they give offense to others.

An informant once told me that his father had cautioned him thus: "Don't laugh at old people. Don't say to anyone that he is ugly. If that person is *mändáuwīzī*—has magic power—he will make you so." It is obvious from the phrasing of this statement that no abstract ethical ideal was involved. Avoidance of offense is clearly a matter of self-defense.

The cases cited also illustrate another point of psychological interest. It is apparent that it is the prevalent belief in sorcery that is of prime importance, not its actual practice. I do not mean to imply by this that no one really uses magic or sorcery to gain his ends. Quite the contrary is true. But from the standpoint of the individual who interprets his illness or misfortune as due to sorcery, it makes little difference whether in actual fact someone has gone through certain procedures or not. Such procedures in any case are secret and no one can be sure. The point is that the psychological effects are the same. This is why sorcery and magic are real to the Saulteaux. Everyone acts as if they were and they thus become effective constituents of thought and feeling. From an objective point of view, the belief system of the Saulteaux thus fosters fantasy situations in which aggressive impulses become easily entangled with interpersonal relations in ways that may engender deep and irrational consequences. I may be easily led to believe that you are hostile to me and have bewitched me when this is not true at all. Yet there is no way of coming to grips with the situation in a realistic fashion. The following story illustrates this point, and since I happen to know one of the participants well I can speak with some assurance about his feelings in the matter.

About fifteen years ago at Treaty time [ca. 1925], representatives of a number of the Berens River bands and some men from Deer Lake were camped at the mouth of the river. Joe, a young man of the Berens River Band, and Wabɑdjesi, a man from Deer Lake, were wrestling. They were having lots of fun and a crowd gathered about them. But Joe was getting the better of Wabɑdjesi. The latter became irritated at this. Since there was such a crowd of men present evidently his pride was hurt. "If you throw me to the ground," he said to Joe, "you will see sparks of fire." The narrator commented that he did this to scare Joe who knew Wabɑdjesi had the reputation of being a powerful shaman. "There won't be any sparks from the ground," Joe retorted, "but when you hit the ground you'll see plenty," and with that he let Wabɑdjesi go. But Wabɑdjesi was really mad by this time and said, "Watch out for me the first part of the winter. Then you'll know something about a Crane [his totem]." To this Joe replied, "And you'll know something about a Cree." Parenthetically it is stated that Joe was joking. He was not a Cree but his mother was. People began to talk about this exchange of open threats between the two men. Some of them even felt sorry for Joe, because Wabɑdjesi had such a big reputation as a man who was known to use sorcery and magic. Joe, on the other hand, had been to boarding school, was a Christian, and was entirely innocent of any malevolent intent.

The following winter the man who told me this story went trapping with Joe. They left the settlement in October. The first night out, just at dusk, they made camp in the shelter of a tall white spruce. They had hardly gotten settled when they heard what appeared to be the voice of a bird coming from the tree. They could not catch sight of it; neither could they identify its cry which kept sounding almost every ten minutes until midnight. They thought it strange but were not disturbed. The next morning they started off and continuing from that day throughout the winter, no matter where they went a pygmy owl seemed to be accompanying them. This was an untoward sign because sorcerers sometimes use the birds to accomplish evil ends. But neither man was ill.

In the spring after returning to the mouth of the river, they received news that Wabɑdjesi was very sick, in fact, that he was not expected to live. This made some people think that perhaps Joe really "was something." One man who had been present at the exchange of threats the previous summer even went so far as to say to him half jokingly, "you almost killed Wabɑdjesi." "I did not intend to kill him," Joe replied in the same mood; "I had pity on his two boys."

This anecdote shows how, under certain circumstances, it is possible for an individual to be accused of using sorcery when in fact he has not done so. In this case I know that Joe did not entertain hostile feelings of any sort against Wabɑdjesi. Yet if Wabɑdjesi had died as a result of his illness, I think there is no doubt that people would have believed that Joe killed him. It certainly would have been the interpretation of the Deer Lake Indians who are much less acculturated than those of the Berens River Band. For it must be noted, among other things, that Joe *did* return Wabɑdjesi's threat. At the same time it is interesting to observe that Joe on his part was a bit apprehensive during the winter. Had he been a pagan, however, he would no doubt have suffered more severely. Furthermore, I am convinced that if Joe *had* been taken ill he would have blamed Wabɑdjesi, and if he had then followed the native pattern of behavior he would have been fully justified in retaliating by some covert means. As it was, there is no doubt that

Wabadjesi, on his side, believed that Joe had taken some aggressive action against him. He could hardly think otherwise since he openly threatened Joe in the first place.

Another explanation offered me was that Wabadjesi undoubtedly tried to injure Joe but that for some reason or other, as sometimes happens, his magic turned upon him and caused the same sickness in him that he tried to project toward his victim.

One has only to multiply such episodes imaginatively to gain an idea of the extent to which the fantasies arising out of such situations can insinuate themselves into the fabric of Saulteaux society, engendering antagonisms that affect the interpersonal relations of individuals in various ways.

It is possible to cite other cases in which it can be shown how repressed—unconscious—aggressions of individuals are caught up and put into social circulation, as it were, through mechanisms of projection, displacement, and rationalization. Some frustrating experience of mine may release repressed aggression toward an associate or some other person who is in no way the cause of my frustration nor even hostile to me. But the prevalent belief in magic and sorcery enables me to rationalize my own projected aggression as hostility directed toward myself emanating from the person I have unconsciously chosen. These are familiar dynamisms, but among the Saulteaux we can discern them operating in a cultural milieu that facilitates rather than nullifies or offsets the canalizing of unconscious hostilities through them.

In one instance that I know of, G. accused two of his brothers-in-law (cross-cousins) with whom he was hunting of using magic to attract animals to their traps. This is an aggressive act because magic should only be used when hunting alone. It is so powerful that there is no chance for my hunting partner to catch any fur if I use it. Consequently, the use of hunting magic by one man of a group is tantamount to depriving the others of part of their living. G. felt frustrated because for a month and a half no animals came to his traps. "Not even a weasel," he said. Yet often he saw tracks circling them. All during this time his brothers-in-law were quite successful in their catch. G. told me about the whole affair himself and in this case there was no mention of any offense he may have committed against them. He was simply infuriated and vowed that the next time he went hunting with them he would use plenty of medicine.

Why was G. so ready to accuse his brothers-in-law of hostility? I happen to know G. quite well and, without going into detail, I will merely state that I believe there is plenty of evidence in his personal history and behavior in general to suggest that he has constant difficulty in disposing of unconscious aggression. G. is often at swords points with his father and he is the man I mentioned previously who gave his brother a severe beating. This brother, moreover, is his mother's favorite among the sons so that the source of G.'s aggression probably is very old and deep. For another thing, I strongly suspect that G. has a considerable amount of repressed hostility toward his wife. The hunting episode I believe to be thoroughly symptomatic of G. and my guess is that it involves the displacement of some of his aggression toward his wife upon her relatives. He has given additional evidence of this and it is facilitated by the fact that whereas G. is a militant Protestant, his wife and her people are strong Catholics.

On the hunting trip referred to, G. had not only accused his brothers-in-law of using magic, he had gone on to insult them as Catholics by hinting that the local priests had sexual intercourse with the local nuns. I do not believe that it is accidental either that he launched into a tirade against X, one of his brothers-in-law, and his father-in-law as well. G.'s sister is married to X and G. told me the way he got her was by love magic—that is, unfairly. Then he went on to say that he believed that his own wife had only had one child because her father had given her medicine to prevent her impregnation. G.'s wife is an attractive girl and had many suitors before her marriage, among them G.'s brother. It was a forced marriage following the girl's pregnancy. For some time G. has suffered from the suspicion that his wife has been unfaithful. While he has discovered no proof, I happen to know that his suspicions are by no means groundless and that G.'s brother is involved. G. feels disadvantaged in many other ways and seems unable to adjust himself. It is not surprising, therefore, to find G. utilizing the beliefs of his culture to screen his own repressed hostilities. This permits a plausible defense against their emergence into his conscious life.

In still another case, Kiwetin, an old man, told me about a dream he had had in which one of his spiritual helpers informed him that a neighbor of his, a middle-aged woman, was using sorcery against him. Kiwetin had been sick and this was the explanation he finally adopted when the medicine he took did no good. The woman was married, in fact she was notorious for her many husbands, her dynamic personality, and her reputed knowledge of sorcery. One of the interesting points about this case is the fact that Kiwetin emphasized the woman's outward display of kindness and amiability toward him. He was a widower and lived alone and he said she often invited him into her house to have something to eat. But he always refused. He also said that she smiled pleasantly at him, but he knew this was put on, "it was only on her face, not in her mind."[18] In other words, Kiwetin's suspicions made any genuine friendliness with this neighbor impossible. I suspect there were unconscious involvements here but I know nothing about this old man's personal history in any detail.

In this case, however, there was another psychological factor involved which I have not yet touched upon. It requires emphasis in order to round out the analysis of the strains and stresses to which a belief in magic and sorcery subjects individuals in Saulteaux society. Kiwetin was a man who, in his earlier days, was one of the leaders of the Midéwi·win, an institution which offered curative services for payment. The leaders of the Midéwi·win also possessed a great deal of information about magic of various kinds which they dispensed at a price. So in Kiwetin's account of the woman who he thought had bewitched him he made it quite clear that he felt secure against any measures she might take. In his dream he even turned down the offer of one of his spiritual helpers to injure her. Kiwetin was fully confident that he could protect himself. His sense of security sprang from his belief in the power of his *own* supernatural helpers. In this respect he was in a different situation than G. The latter was a much younger man who had been brought up during a period of fairly rapid acculturation. He did not claim to have any spiritual helpers. Consequently he lacked the inner security of members of the older generation who believed that they had powerful guardian spirits to help them. Hence, G.'s belief that magic was being used against him made him feel the full impact of the hostility of others because he was exposed to it without protection.

It is important to recognize, then, that native belief does provide a means for protection against the covert hostility of others even though from our point of view this is likewise on a fantasy level. Up until recent years every boy at the age of puberty or a little before was sent out to fast in the forest. It was then that he secured the blessings of supernaturals who were to be his guardian spirits through life. While there was no formalized fast of this kind for girls, they were not debarred in native theory from the acquisition of supernatural helpers. In Saulteaux society the belief in the power of one's guardian spirits provides the ultimate basis for a sense of security in the individual. Nevertheless, the supernatural protection thus afforded varies greatly from individual to individual. Some persons are thought to have a great deal of power derived from this source, others little. And, following the extremely individualistic patterns of this society, no one knows how strong an individual is until he exercises his power. A few individuals are known to have considerable power because they utilize it in connection with conjuring, curing, or in other professional ways. It is also possible to add to the power one acquires at puberty by purchasing a knowledge of magic from others. This is what the midé men did, thereby enhancing their prestige.

In the give and take of social life, therefore, the apprehension of aggression varied concomitantly with the reputed power of the aggressor. And the ambivalence I have referred to reached its apex in the attitude toward the midé men and conjurers whom everyone knew to be the most powerful men of all. They were greatly feared and highly respected at the same time. Outwardly they were treated with the utmost show of deference. Only an individual supremely confident of his own powers would run the risk of offending an individual of this class.[19] But one could be less certain about others because there might be no reason for a man to exhibit or exercise his powers until he was in a tight place. It is also true that the midé men and conjurers often took advantage of the reputation they enjoyed. They were the ones who were sometimes openly aggressive in situations where other men would fear to be.[20] In fact, the Indians say that formerly such individuals were constantly trying each other out.

An instance of this is the following story told to me by the son of the man called Owl.

Pazagwigabau, the one who provoked the duel by sorcery, was the arrogant leader of the Midéwi·win.[21] He is reputed to have killed many persons by sorcery, and one informant described him as "savage looking in the eyes." The father of this informant warned him as a child never to play near Pazagwigabau's camp. Owl, on the other hand, was a quiet-mannered man, small in stature and said to be kind to everyone. He was not a midé, but he had the reputation of being an excellent doctor and he was a noted conjurer. These two men belonged to different local groups and seldom came into personal contact. But on the occasion to be described Pazagwigabau had come down the river to the Hudson's Bay Co. post and found Owl sitting on the platform of the store with a lot of other Indians.

Pazagwigabau went up to Owl and said, "You think you are a great man. But do you know that you are no good? When you want to save lives you always bring that stone along. I don't believe it's good for anything." To this Owl replied, "Pazagwigabau, leave me alone. I have never bothered you."

"You are not worth leaving alone," the midé said, and with this he grabbed Owl by the front part of his hair and threw him down. Owl simply got up and said, "Leave me alone." But Pαzαgwigabau grabbed his hair a second time and when Owl made no resistance, he did it for a third time. Then Owl said, "Are you looking for trouble?"

"That's what I want," said Pαzαgwigabau, "I want you to get mad. That's why I did this." So Owl replied, "All right. I know you have been looking for it for a long time. I know you think you are a great midé. You are nothing. If I point my finger at you, you will be a dead man. But now I'll tell you something. Don't you do anything to my wife or my child. Do it to me and I'll do the same."

"Ho! Ho! Thanks, thanks," said Pαzαgwigabau. "Expect me at *kījégīzis* [kind moon, February]. I'll give you a chance to do what you like to me."

Sure enough, during *kijégīzis* Owl was taken sick. He got the shell[22] all right, but of course he brought it out. But Owl was not sick long; he easily recovered. Shortly after this, news came down the river that Pαzαgwigabau was sick. He was unable to walk. News spread that he was getting worse and worse. Every once in a while Owl was heard to say, "Huh! Huh! I guess I nearly killed him. I did not mean to, I was only playing with him." When the *ni`kīgīzis* (goose moon, April) appeared Pαzαgwigabau was only barely able to walk about. At the beginning of the summer Pαzαgwigabau came down the river again with some other members of his band. They camped near Little Grand Rapids where Owl lived. When Owl saw the old midé he walked right up to him and said, "You know who Owl is now! I was only playing with you this time. I did not intend to kill you. But I never want to hear again what you said in this place. And I don't expect you to do again what you did here. Don't think you are such a great midé!"

Of course this story may be a biased version of the events that actually occurred. We do not know what Pαzαgwigabau had to say. But as it stands it is a beautiful illustration of how overt aggression, even when it occurs, is almost immediately displaced to the level of sorcery (fantasy) for a show-down. It also exhibits in dramatic fashion the confidence of both men in their own powers. In a situation where their very lives were in imminent danger, this made each of them courageous. Although men of lesser power might have suffered greater apprehension in such a situation, every Saulteaux has a modicum of spiritual armor because of the blessings from the supernaturals that he has secured in his puberty fast. He is not completely at the mercy of hostile forces. A consciousness of this fact is the balancing factor in the total situation. One might even say that *some* confidence in one's ability to ward off possible aggression is in the nature of a psychological necessity. Otherwise, the apprehension and fears of individuals in this society might drift too easily into a paralyzing terror. In principle, confidence in one's ability to face the hostility of others, or to match hostility against hostility might be said to give a realistic, healthy tone to situations where the warp and woof are so frequently constructed of fantasies.

However, apprehension and fear cannot be totally eliminated. This is not due entirely to the fact that a belief in sorcery and magic fosters such emotions. There is always the possibility that another man's power may be greater than my own. To provoke him to exercise it by offending him is always a gamble. What may happen if I do suffer from delusions of grandeur is well illustrated by Pazagwigabo. And still another aspect of the use of sorcery and magic has been referred to that may make me hesitate to use them at all: the possibility that if they fail to work for any reason, or my victim is stronger than I, they may be retroactive in effect. Instead of accomplishing my ends I may fall ill or die by my own sorcery. But in such matters it is not possible to be wise before the event. One has to risk defeat in attempting to achieve the ends desired. Thus both for the man who is confident of his powers, as well as for the common man, the best defense is to avoid offense if one seeks what the Saulteaux call *pīmädazīwin*—life in the fullest sense.

Notes

Published in *Psychiatry: Journal of the Biology and Pathology* of *Interpersonal Relations* 3 (1940): 395–407; reprinted in *Culture and Experience* (1955), 277–90.

1. Frank G. Speck, "Ethical Attributes of the Labrador Indians," *American Anthropologist,* 35, 1933, 559–594.

2. This and many other psychological observations of Father Le Jeune on the Montagnais-Naskapi that parallel my own observations on the Saulteaux in this paper are to be found in Chapter 6, "Some Psychological Characteristics of the Northeastern Indians." (*Culture and Experience* [chapter 25, this volume].)

3. Ruth Landes, writing of the Ojibwa of the Rainy River district—"The Ojibwa of Canada," in Margaret Mead (ed.), *Cooperation and Competition Among Primitive Peoples* (New York, 1937) 102—says: "Ojibwa life may

be thought of as resting on three orders of hostility. All Ojibwa-speaking persons feel a major hostility towards those of alien speech, epitomized by the Dakota-Sioux. Next in order is the hostility that exists between different local groups of Ojibwa, and the third is the hostility felt by any household toward another whether or not of the same village. Thus the group feeling foisted upon a village by the fact of its separateness from other villages is constantly threatened by the latent hostilities of its constituent households." Landes goes on to emphasize the "atomism" of Ojibwa society by saying that although functionally the household is the irreducible unit, in thought the person is actually the unit. I do not think that Landes sufficiently analyzes the basis for local group and household hostility. On the Berens River, at least, the generalizations made would not hold. Whenever there is hostility between these large units I believe it can be reduced to specific events which have affected the lives of the component individuals. But Lands is quite right in her emphasis upon the individualistic pattern of Ojibwa society. There is a similar "atomism" in the fundamental life patterns of the closely related Saulteaux.

4. Jeannette Mirsky, for example, in her summary of data on the Eskimo of East Greenland in Mead ed., *Cooperation and Competition* (70) writes: "Murder is of frequent occurrence. The lack of social forms makes it possible for a man to murder within the group without having any punishment visited on him. There is no blood feud, no retaliatory act, either physical or magical, no substitutive procedure, no purification rite, nothing. The man remains within the group and people are careful not to provoke so powerful a person." Among the Eskimo, too, we find the famous "drum matches" which provide a sanctioned vehicle for the exchange of insults or the settlement of disputes (68–69). Outlets for aggression in Ashanti society are discussed in John Dollard and others [ed. note: Neal E. Miller, Leonard W. Doob, O. H. Mowrer, and Robert R. Sears, *Frustration and Aggression* (New Haven, 1939), 183 ff.] Among other means provided in this culture "there is a peculiar ceremony, held once a year, whose function seems almost entirely that of permitting the expression of aggression. During the ceremony everyone is permitted to tell anyone else, including the king himself, what he thinks of him."

5. Ruth Landes, "The Ojibwa of Canada," in Mead ed., 103: "Despite the prescribed friendship and affection existing between households of cross-cousins, a strong feeling of self-consciousness and even hostility exists. For when cross-cousins meet, they must try to embarrass one another. They 'joke' one another, making the most vulgar allegations, by their standards as well as

ours. But being 'kind' relatives, no one can take offense. Cross-cousins who do not joke in this way are considered boorish, as not playing the game."

6. Henry R. Schoolcraft pointed out long ago (*History of the Indian Tribes of the United States* [Philadelphia, 1857], Part VI, 682) that "The Algonquin language has no words for the expression of oaths; an Algonquin can neither swear nor blaspheme." My own impression of the St. Francis Abenaki is expressed by J. A. Maurault who, on page 15 of the *Histoire des Abenaki* (Sorel, P. Q., 1866) writes that "they . . . were not wont to show their discontent or hatred by oaths or blasphemies. The same thing may still be noticed among them. They have the greatest horror of imprecations and blasphemies; and there are no words in their language to express these, so often uttered by Canadians."

7. For a summary description of the Saulteaux kinship system see Hallowell, "Cross-Cousin Marriage" [chapter 5, this volume.]

8. Ruth Landes, "The Ojibwa of Canada," 103: "a person's behavior toward his prospective parents-in-law is characterized by the most painstaking respect, the most punctilious diffidence and the greatest efforts to avoid giving offense. And a person behaves in the same way towards his prospective child-in-law (cross-niece and cross-nephew)." See L. R. Masson, *Les Bourgeois de la Compagnie du Nord-Ouest* (Quebec, 1890), II, 262. Cameron's observations are dated 1804.

9. [Ed. note: A reference to William Berens.]

10. Formerly native games of chance and skill undoubtedly offered a channel for the expression of aggression. But all such games have died out on the Berens River. Landes, "The Ojibwa of Canada," 115–116, stresses the fact that competitive games may turn into duels between individuals. "When a pair reaches the private duelling stage, they are no longer competing as lacrosse or racing rivals."

In aboriginal days out-group aggression—that is, war—must have been an important institutionalized channel for the displacement and discharge of the suppressed aggressions of individuals. Perhaps this may even explain the ferocity in war exhibited in some cases by the outwardly pacific Algonkians of the northern woodlands, although I have no data on the Saulteaux in this regard. In this connection attention may be called to John Dollard's hypothesis ("Hostility and Fear in Social Life," *Social Forces*, 17, 1938, 19): in "direct aggression there is always some displaced aggression accompanying it and adding additional force to the rational attack. Justifiable aggressive responses seem to break the way for irrational and unjustifiable hostilities. This fact is illustrated in any war and probably accounts for the damnable character of the image of the enemy who is hated, and therefore feared with disproportionate intensity."

What I have termed magic always involves some kind of material substance or "medicine" among the Saulteaux. In fact the term *mackīkī* is applied both to the material substance one uses to catch animals or a girl, as well as to plant drugs taken to cure a stomach ache. So far as I know, any substances with genuine poisonous properties are unknown to these Indians. Sorcery covers procedures in which *mackīkī* is not involved.

11. Ruth Landes ("The Ojibwa of Canada," 109): "Outright murder does not appear to be common. Slashings frequently [*sic*] result from summer hostilities, but do not culminate in murder. Grievances are nursed by one or both individuals and avenged shamanistically, by sending bad medicine omens, winter starvation, and attacks of paralysis. When a person dies of winter starvation, or of some insanity, the suspected sorcerer is alleged to be the murderer. Murder might also result from trespass upon trapping grounds."

12. John Dollard, "Hostility and Fear in Social Life," 183.

13. Le Jeune, *Jesuit Relations and Allied Documents*, R. G. Thwaites ed., 73 vols. (Cleveland, 1937), VIII, relates the story of a young man who was very ill whom he had been called to see. His father had despaired of his conversion and baptism; now, as a last resort, he was converted, but he died. When Le Jeune questioned him about his illness he replied, "'It is . . . a wicked Algonquian who has given me this disease which sticks in my body, because I was angry at him; and his fear that I would kill him induced him to bargain for my death with the Manitou.' 'And how dost thou know that?' 'I have had the Manitou consulted, and he told me I should make haste and give presents to the Manitousiouekhi,'—these are the jugglers,—'and that he would forestall my enemy, taking his life, and that thus I would be cured; but my misfortune is that I have nothing more,—I have given my Porcelain and my Beavers; and because I cannot continue these presents, I must die'" (273.)

14. Le Jeune (*Jesuit Relations*, V, 179) says, "Although the Savages will give you something for a 'thank you'—this is a word they have learned from the French—you must make them some return for another 'thank you' otherwise you will be looked upon as ungrateful. They are willing enough to receive without giving; but they do not know what it is to give without receiving. It is true that, if you will follow them into the woods, they will feed you without asking anything of you, if they think that you

have nothing. But if they see that you have something, and they want it, they will not stop asking you for it until you have given it."

15. Le Jeune, *Jesuit Relations*, VI, 245; V, 31.

16. [Ed. note: See William Berens, *Memories, Myths, and Dreams of an Ojibwe* Leader (2009), Part III, for Berens's telling of the first incident. The second incident involved Berens's son, Jacob. Decades after Hallowell published this essay Percy Berens (Jacob's brother) spoke with Susan Gray about this tragedy. See Susan Elaine Gray, "*I Will Fear No Evil*": *Ojibwa-Missionary Encounters Along the Berens River, 1875–1940* (Calgary: University of Calgary Press, 2006), 38.]

17. Consequently the ground is well prepared in this society for the development of paranoid or pseudo-paranoid trends in individuals. And the genuine paranoid would, no doubt, find it relatively easy to build up a plausible structure of delusions. See the account of J. D. [ed. note: John Duck] in "Fear and Anxiety as Cultural and Individual Variables in a Primitive Society" (chap. 13) [*Culture and Experience*; chapter 12, this volume].

18. Another old man once told me that as a boy he had been warned against persons who cover up their motives by laughing in your face while at the same time they are ready to take some action against you.

19. Ruth Landes ("The Ojibwa of Canada," 113–14), writing of the Manitou Rapids Ojibwa of Ontario says: "Influential persons who are known or suspected to be sorcerers are recognized in more general ways than in being deferred to professionally. People cower physically before them, shrink away, hush their talk, straighten their faces lest the shaman suspect some intended offense in their behavior. Once a girl and her mother were walking along a road and passed close to where a shaman lay dozing in the grass. They were joking and talking. Yet because of their laughter the shaman became furious and muttered, 'I'll get you! I'll get you!' and the woman soon showed the effects of evil medicine; her mouth became 'twisted' and she became incontinent of urine. One boy became paralyzed shortly after the shaman chose to be offended by his careless laugh. It is perfectly consistent with this attitude that laughing, particularly on the part of women, is not loud but light. Paralysis, incontinence, twisted mouth, and the windigo insanity are sent by shamans who have been offended by casual behavior . . . . The shaman's exquisite sensitiveness to slights, real or imaginary, is intelligible to the people because it is only an accentuation of the sensitiveness felt by every person."

20. Ruth Landes ("The Ojibwa of Canada", 112) says of Chief George of the Manitou Rapids Band, "he was so feared that few shamans dared to

enter shamanistic combat with him when he insulted them with slighting remarks."

21. For further details about this man and the Midéwi·win in this area see Hallowell, "The Passing of the Midewi·win" [chapter 21, this volume].

22. I.e., a *mĭgis*. These shells are objects associated with the Midéwi·win. Their projection into a person usually is sufficient to cause death. In the ceremony of the Midéwi·win their lethal effects are demonstrated as well as the power of the midé men to revive victims. A midé would be expected to use such deadly shells in a sorcery duel. Owl's own power was sufficient to counteract the effect of Paᴢagwigabau's magical weapon and even to eject the shell from his body.

SIXTEEN

The Social Function of Anxiety in a Primitive Society

In his discussion of anxiety, Freud emphasizes the fact that it is essentially an affective reaction to danger.[1] The relationship of anxiety to danger is anticipatory, the affect is a signal: "one feels anxiety *lest* something occur."[2] Anxiety is not confined to the human species. Freud states that it "is a reaction characteristic of probably all organisms, certainly of all of the higher ones."[3] He further suggests that since it has an indispensable biological function, anxiety may have developed differently in different organisms.[4] Freud does not elaborate the point, but I think it follows from the biological role he assigns to anxiety that it must be conceived as a function of the particular danger situations that the organism faces. These vary from species to species. What is dangerous for one species of animal would not necessarily be equivalent for another species, and danger situations in the human species may differ again from those faced by infrahuman animals. For the human species itself, Freud stresses another variable. Danger situations vary ontogenetically[5] and the birth process is the "prototype of anxiety in man."[6]

What Freud does not explicitly recognize is that the occurrence of anxiety in the human species is further complicated by another variable that I shall call "cultural." However, his assumption that anxiety reactions in man are based on experience and are in that sense learned,[7] leaves the door open for an evaluation of such variables within the framework of psychoanalytic principles. These cultural variables operate through the socialization process that all human beings undergo and result in the definition of situations as dangerous in one society which, in another, may be viewed as less dangerous or not dangerous at all. This means that individuals may manifest anxiety reactions that are appropriate in a particular culture but not in another.

Such cultural variables are of importance with respect to two problems: first, the basic question in which Freud himself was particularly interested, viz., the relation between anxiety and neurosis; secondly, the *positive* role of anxiety. This social function of anxiety is definitely linked, in principle, with the biological role which Freud stresses as a generic function of anxiety. I mean that an affective reaction to danger situations, as culturally defined, may motivate behavior on the part of individuals which is as significant in terms of societal values as comparable reactions are valuable in terms of biological utility. Anxiety-preparedness in the face of any danger is a very adaptive reaction.[8]

Before discussing this second problem, however, I wish to return to the first one, the relation between anxiety and neurosis. In this connection, Freud asks, "why it is that not all anxiety reactions are neurotic, why we recognize so many of them as normal," and he emphasizes the need for distinguishing between true anxiety (*Realangst*) and neurotic anxiety.[9] The conclusion to which he comes is this:

> A *real* danger is a danger which we know, a true anxiety the anxiety in regard to such a known danger. Neurotic anxiety is anxiety in regard to a danger which we do not know. The neurotic danger must first be sought, therefore: Analysis has taught us that it is an instinctual danger. [That is, fear of the intensity of one's own impulses].[10]

This differentiation led to the terminological distinction often made between fear, i.e., real or objective anxiety, and neurotic anxiety. I shall continue to use anxiety in its widest connotation, qualifying it with the adjectives "neurotic" or "objective" according to the meaning intended. In fact, I think there is a considerable conceptual advantage in considering fear-anxiety reactions as a broad affective continuum and not attempting to make categorical distinctions except in terms of known etiological factors, since what may seem to be instances of "pure" objective anxiety actually may have neurotic involvements when all the facts are known. On the other hand, as will appear later, there may be analogies to neurotic involvements in anxiety-laden situations which, in a particular culture, may present real objective dangers to the individual concerned.

Let us turn now to the second problem, the positive role of anxiety. I wish to show how anxiety is instigated and reduced among the Saulteaux through the operation of cultural factors (beliefs and institutionalized procedures) which define certain situations as dangerous, how the motivations of individuals are affected, and how the resulting behavior is related to the maintenance of the approved social code. The beliefs relevant to our discussion still flourish today and the more recent changes in their social system have not essentially affected their functioning.

One of the striking features of Saulteaux society is the anxiety with which certain disease situations are invested.[11] In order to understand w*hy* such situations are the focus of so much affect, we have to know something about native theories of disease. These theories reflect traditional notions. They represent an ideology which is culturally derived and they involve fundamental assumptions about the nature of the universe. From the standpoint of the Saulteaux themselves, such assumptions are taken a priori and are unchallengeable. They not only represent beliefs but are also a basis for action. The affect which arises in certain disease situations is a product of reflection upon the symptoms observed in the patient and the cause of the illness interpreted in terms of the native notions of disease causation. Thus, the anxiety aroused is intimately connected with a cultural variable.

There is a correlative fact, however, which gives *social* significance to the affect generated. Disease situations of any seriousness carry the implication that something wrong has been done. Illness is the penalty. Consequently, it is easy to see why illness tends to precipitate an affective reaction to a culturally defined danger situation. Furthermore, a closer examination of the dynamics of Saulteaux society reveals the fact that fear of disease is the major social sanction operative among these Indians. In this society, certain classes of sexual behavior[12] (incest, the so-called perversions in heterosexual intercourse, homosexuality, autoerotism, bestiality), various kinds of aggressive behavior (cruelty to animals, homicide, cruelty toward human beings, the use of bad medicine to cause suffering, rough or inconsiderate treatment of the dead, theft, and a number of ego injuries like insult and ridicule, failure to share freely, etc.), behavior prescribed by guardian spirits, the acquisition of power to render specialized services to others (i.e., curing or clairvoyance), all fall under a disease sanction.

This leads us directly to the heart of one of the basic problems in the social sciences, viz., the determination of the specific conditions under which social codes are maintained and the means by which they operate under different cultural frames of reference. For despite the widest cultural variability in *homo sapiens*, we observe that all human societies are characterized by norms of conduct which, in MacIver's words, "assure some regularity, uniformity and predictability of behavior on the part of the members of a community."[13] Sheer anarchy, or literal rampant individualism, is unknown.

But this problem is not wholly a sociological one. It has important and far-reaching psychological implications, particularly in view of the fact that in many nonliterate societies, the institutions we associate with the maintenance of "law and order" are unelaborated or even absent. In the case of the Saulteaux, e.g., there were no chiefs nor any kind of political organization in aboriginal days. Nor were there any institutionalized juridical procedures or jails.

The psychological aspects of social control become evident when we examine the relation between the social sanctions operative in a given society and the motivations of individuals instigated by the prevailing sanctions. As Radcliffe-Brown has pointed out,[14] "the sanctions existing in a community constitute motives in the individual for the regulation of his conduct in conformity with usage." Hence, there is an integral, inextricable relationship between sociological and psychological factors.

In Saulteaux society, it is not fear of the gods or fear of punishment by the state that is the major sanction: it is the fear of disease.[15] Or, putting it in the terminology already employed, the motivating factor is the affect connected with certain disease situations. Individuals in Saulteaux society are highly sensitized to anxiety as an emotional reaction to a danger signal, the precipitating cause being illness interpreted as punishment. The manifest danger to which the anxiety is directed is the direct threat to someone's well-being or even life. But there is also a menace to the social code which is implied because some dissocial act has been committed. Insofar as individuals are motivated to avoid such acts through fear of disease, anxiety performs a distinct social function.

With this thesis in mind I should now like to analyze in more detail how disease operates as a social sanction in Saulteaux society in connection with anxiety-laden situations. (See also chap. 13 [*Culture and Experience*; "Fear and Anxiety," chapter 12, this volume.])

In the first place, health and a long life are very positive values to the Saulteaux. *Pīmädazīwin*, life in the fullest sense, is stressed again and again in their ceremonies. The supernaturals are asked for it. It is a prime value. In psychological terms, it is a major goal response. Disease interferes with achieving this goal. Ordinary cases of illness, however, colds, headaches, etc., do not arouse anxiety among the Saulteaux any more than they do among ourselves. They are not danger situations. But the nature of disease is such that it may become a threat to life itself, may be a real danger to the human organism. Real or "normal" anxiety is appropriate in such circumstances.[16]

A comparable affect under equivalent circumstances is found among the Saulteaux and ourselves. In both cases, the danger threatened is met with what are thought to be appropriate measures. Most disease situations

among the Saulteaux, however, do not conform to this type. They correspond either to the nondangerous variety or they rapidly pass from this
type into situations where the anxiety level is not only high, but where the
quality of the affect suggests neurotic anxiety without its actually being so.
What are the conditions that bring this about? It is here that native beliefs
about disease causation enter the picture.

In Saulteaux belief, one of the major causes of illness arises from what
they term "bad conduct" madjīijīwé bazīwin). "Because a person does bad
things, that is where sickness *(ákwazīwin)* starts," is the way one informant
phrased it. In other words, a person may fall ill because of some transgression
he has committed in the past. It is also possible that an individual may be
suffering because of the bad conduct of his parents. "When a man is young
he may do something to cause his children trouble. They will suffer for
this." Illness derived from this source is designated by a special native term
(*odjineaúwaso*). Consequently, if a child falls seriously ill, it is often attributed to the transgression of a parent. It is easy to see the anxiety-provoking
possibilities in this theory of disease causation. In addition to the normal
anxiety that the objective factors of the disease situation may stimulate, a
sense of guilt may be aroused in one or both parents. They are bound to
reflect upon what they may have done to cause their child's suffering, or
even death. Their own acts are entangled with the disease situation.

Another cause of illness is witchcraft, the hostile action of some other
human being. The significant fact to be observed in cases of this class is that
the sick person almost always believes that his sickness is due to revenge.
Some previous act of *his* has provoked retaliation in this form. Here the
patient's own impulses, previously expressed in some form of dissocial
behavior, are projected into the situation just as they are in those instances
where disease is thought to have resulted from "bad conduct." In cases
of witchcraft, the penalty that threatens has acted in a mediate fashion
instead of automatically as in the instances where bad conduct is thought
to be the source.

An illuminating clue to the psychological significance of disease situations interpreted as a result of the causes just cited is obtained if we follow
Freud's differentiation of what he terms a *traumatic* situation from a simple
danger situation. He introduces this distinction by asking what the kernel
of the danger situation is.[17] He finds that it revolves about the estimation of
our strength in relation to the danger. If we feel a sense of helplessness in the
face of it, an inability to cope with it, then he calls the situation *traumatic*.
This is precisely the differentiation that applies to those disease situations

among the Saulteaux where the cause of the illness is uncertain and obscure. In these situations, the quality of the anxiety aroused is different from that where illness is faced in the same way any danger situation is faced. It is disease situations of this *traumatic* type that operate as a social sanction.

The qualitative aspects of the anxiety aroused emerge from the combination of two determinants. The first is purely objective; ordinary medical treatment of the sick person has failed to produce improvement. The symptoms persist or the person gets worse. It is at this point that the situation becomes serious. Prior to this, the illness may not even have been considered dangerous, but when the medicine does not work, the situation rapidly becomes traumatic. This is because the suspicion is aroused in the patient or his associates that the cause of the illness is hidden. It may be a penalty for something done in the past. It may be due to "bad conduct" or witchcraft. But who knows? Yet if this is so, his very life is in jeopardy. Consequently, a feeling of helplessness arises which can only be alleviated if the precise cause of the sickness is discovered. Otherwise, appropriate measures cannot be undertaken. Meanwhile, the source of the danger remains uncertain and obscure; further suffering, even death, menaces the patient.

Thus, while from an objective point of view we often may have displayed what seems to be a "disproportionality of affect" in disease situations, at the same time the definition of such situations in terms of Saulteaux beliefs presents dangers that are not comparable to those we would recognize in similar situations. This is an important qualitative difference. The affective reactions of the Saulteaux are a function of this difference.[18]

It would also appear that there are some analogies, although by no means an identity, between the anxiety created in some of these traumatic disease situations among the Saulteaux and neurotic anxiety. This is true, at least, in the cases where the danger that threatens is believed to have arisen out of the patient's own acts, so there is the closest integral relation between inner and outer danger as in neurotic anxiety, but there are no substitute formations in the individual which project the danger outwards, as in animal phobias, while the real source of danger remains unknown. Nevertheless, it is true that the impulses of the individual become the *sine qua non* of the external danger, just as in neurotic anxiety. Consequently, these impulses are the ultimate source of the danger itself. The disease is not considered to be impersonal and objective in origin and for this reason it cannot be faced in the same terms as other kinds of illness or other objective hazards of life. The real source of danger is from within and, like neurotic anxiety, it is connected with forbidden acts.

Take the case of an Indian who believes himself bewitched, for example. At the first appearance of his illness, he may not have been worried because he may have thought that there was some other cause of his trouble, but as soon as he believes he is the victim of a hostile attack, he gets anxious. Why? Because he believes his illness is in retaliation for some previous act of aggression he has perpetrated. The assertion of these aggressive impulses on his part has led to a feeling of guilt and the illness from which he is suffering has aroused anxiety because he senses danger. His very life may be threatened. What this man fears is that he had endangered his life by acting as he did. He is afraid of the consequences of his own impulses. The source of the outwardly sensed danger lies in his own hostile impulses.

So far I have tried to explain how anxiety is integrated in disease situations among the Saulteaux and why it is that the emotion generated has qualitative features which suggest neurotic anxiety. I hope that I have made it clear, however, that these features are only analogies deduced from the manner in which the belief system of the Saulteaux compels the individual to interpret the objective aspects of disease situations under certain conditions. What we actually appear to have exhibited in these cases is an affective reaction on a fear-anxiety continuum that lies somewhere between true objective anxiety and real neurotic anxiety.[19] That this is indeed the case is supported by the fact that, on the one hand, we can point to occurrences of real anxiety in danger situations among the Saulteaux and, on the other, to cases of neurotic anxiety. An instance of the latter is the behavior of a man I have described at some length in chapter 13 [*Culture and Experience*; "Fear and Anxiety," chapter 12, this volume]. Among other things he had severe phobic symptoms, a kind of agoraphobia [hydrophobia?] and fear of the dark.

The point I wish to emphasize particularly is that at both extremes of the fear-anxiety continuum the main function of the affect has reference to the individual alone. This is true whether he runs away from some objective danger or develops phobias which are reaction formations in self-defense against some instinctual danger. The anxiety associated with disease situations among the Saulteaux, on the other hand, has a social function insofar as it motivates individuals to avoid the danger (disease) by conforming to the dictates of the social code. This is accomplished by forcing the individual to reflect upon disapproved acts under the stress of the anxiety aroused by a disease situation or to anticipate possible discomfort through a knowledge of the experience of others. In either case, the disease sanction encourages the individual to be responsible for his own conduct.

The full implications of the social function of anxiety in Saulteaux society can best be exposed, however, if we return to the traumatic disease situation and inquire what steps are taken to reduce anxiety in the individual. I have already pointed out that, in such situations, the cause of the disease is at first problematical though the suspicion is aroused that the patient himself or some other person is responsible for the illness. This means that the true cause of the trouble must be sought before the disease can be alleviated. Once the cause of the illness is discovered, the disease situation loses some of its traumatic quality because the danger can be squarely faced like any other danger and some action taken to meet it. The therapeutic measures employed can be looked upon as anxiety-reducing devices.

Now one of the distinctive features of the Saulteaux belief system is this: if one who is ill because of "bad conduct" *confesses* his transgression, the medicine will then do its work and the patient will recover. This notion is the most typical feature of the operation of the disease sanction in cases where the penalty threatened is automatically induced. In fact, it adds considerable force to the sanction so far as the individual is concerned. It means that deviant conduct may not only lead to subsequent illness but that in order to get well one has to suffer the shame of self-exposure involved in confession. This is part of the punishment. Since it is also believed that the medicine man's guardian spirits (*pawáganak*) will inform him of the cause of the trouble, there is no use withholding anything.[20] At the same time, confession provides the means of alleviating the guilt and anxiety of the individual, because, if a feeling of helplessness or being "trapped" is an intrinsic factor in these traumatic situations (or in any severe anxiety situation), confession provides a method of escape according to both Saulteaux belief and sound psychological principle.

From the standpoint of Saulteaux society as a whole, confession is also a means by which knowledge of confessed transgressions is put into social circulation. Confession among the Saulteaux is not equivalent to confession to a priest, a friend, or a psychoanalyst in Western culture. In our society, it is assumed that what is exposed will be held in absolute confidence,[21] but among these Indians the notion is held that the very secrecy of the transgressions is one of the things that makes them particularly bad. This explains why it is that when one person confesses a sexual transgression in which he or she has participated with a second person, the latter will not become ill subsequently or have to confess. Once the transgression has been publicized, it is washed away or, as the Saulteaux phrase it, "bad conduct will not follow you any more."

Perhaps this attitude towards what is secret is connected with the lack of privacy that is intrinsic to the manner in which these people live. Anything that smacks of secrecy is always suspect. There is even an aura of potential menace about such things, fortified no doubt by the covert practice of magic and sorcery. Consequently, in disease situations where any hidden transgression is thought to be the cause of the trouble, what is in effect a public exposure is a necessary step to regaining health.

In actual practice, this works out in a very simple way. When anyone is sick, there is no isolation of the patient; on the contrary, the wigwam is always full of people. Any statement on the part of the patient, although it may be made to the doctor, is not only public but also very quickly may become a matter of common gossip. Where conjuring is resorted to, in cases where all other efforts have failed to reveal the hidden cause of the malady,[22] almost the whole community may be present en masse. Under these conditions, to confess a transgression is to reveal publicly a secret "sin." Consequently, the resistance to self-exposure is very great and the shame experienced by the individual extremely poignant. In terms of our own society it is as if the transgressions committed were exposed in open court or published in the newspapers so that everyone knew that Jerry had slept with his sister or that Kate had murdered her child. Among the Saulteaux, however, it is only after such a confession is made that the usual medicine can do its work and the patient can recover. In one case, three children of a married couple were all suffering from a discharge of mucus through the nose and mouth. They had been treated by a native doctor who was also a conjurer but his medicine had done no good. Finally, a conjuring performance was held. Despite the fact that the woman's husband, who was present, had threatened her with death if she ever told, she broke down in a flood of tears and confessed to everyone that he had forced fellatio upon her.

This public aspect of confession is one of the channels through which individuals growing up in Saulteaux society and overhearing the gossip of their elders *sense*, even though they may fail to understand fully, the general typology of disapproved patterns of behavior. Children do not have to be taught a concrete panel of transgressions in Saulteaux society any more than in our own. Nor does it have to be assumed that they have been present on numerous occasions when transgressions have been confessed. Even if they are present, they may not always understand what is meant. Yet some feeling is gained of the *kind* of conduct that is disapproved. The informant who told me about the case of fellatio was present at the conjuring performance when this was confessed. She was about ten years old at the time and did not understand what was meant until later when her stepmother enlightened her.

In actual operation, the disease sanction among the Saulteaux does not completely deter individuals from committing socially disapproved acts but it functions as a brake by arousing anxiety at the very thought of such conduct. Functionally viewed, a society can well tolerate a few breaches of the rules if, through some means such as confession, a knowledge of dissocial conduct is publicized with the result that a large majority of individuals follow the approved types of behavior.

These deductions are by no means theoretical. That individuals in Saulteaux society actually are deterred from acting in forbidden ways by the disease sanction is illustrated by the following story.[23] In this case, illness did not follow incestuous intercourse. Perhaps this was because it occurred only once. In fact, this may be the moral of the story from the point of view of the Saulteaux themselves. At any rate, it gives a very clear picture of the conscious conflict between the impulses of the individual and socially sanctioned modes of conduct.

An unmarried woman had "adopted" her brother's son, a boy who was already a fairly good hunter.[24] They were camping by themselves alone in the bush. The boy had shot some meat and they were drying it. One night after they both lay down to sleep, he began to think about his *kīsagwas*.[25] After awhile he spoke to her. "How's chances?" he said.[26] "Are you crazy," she replied, "to talk like that? You are my brother's son." "Nothing will happen to us," the boy said. "Yes, there will," said his aunt, "we might suffer." "No we won't. Nothing will happen," her nephew replied.

Then he got up, went over to where she was lying and managed to get what he wanted. After he had finished, he went back to his own place and lay down again. He could not go to sleep. He began to worry about what he had done to his father's sister.

In the morning he said to her, "I'm going now." "Where?" she asked. "I'm going to live somewhere else, I'm ashamed of what I did. I'm going away. If I starve to death, all right." "No! No! Don't go," said his aunt. "If you leave who is going to make a living for me? I'll starve to death. It's not the first time people did what we did. It has happened elsewhere."

But the young man was much worried and determined to go. "No, you can't leave me," said his aunt. "I've brought you up and you must stay here." "I'll go for awhile, anyway," the boy said. "All right," said his aunt, "just for a short time. No one knows and I'll never tell anyone. There might come a time to say it, but not now."

So the young fellow went off. He came to a high rock and sat down there. He thought over what he had done. He was sorry that he did it. He pulled out his penis and looked at it. He found a hair. He said to himself, "This is *nīsagwas,* her hair." He threw it away.

That night he camped by himself, half thinking all the time that he would go back to his aunt. In the morning, he did go back to where they had their camp. He arrived at sundown.

All during the night he was away his aunt had been crying. She was so very glad to see him now. He said to her, "I wonder if it would be all right if we lived together, just as if we were man and wife." "I don't think so," the woman said. "It would not look right if we did that. If you want a woman you better get one for yourself and if I want a man I better get one."

The trouble was this young man had tasted something new and he wanted more of it. He found a girl and got married in the spring. He and his wife lived with his aunt. Later his aunt got married, too.

The narrator commented that the boy's aunt was a sensible woman. They just made one slip and then stopped. This may explain why nothing happened to them, i.e., neither one got sick and had to confess.

Among the Saulteaux, then, desire for *pīmädazīwin* can be assumed to be a major goal response. Everyone wants to be healthy, to live long, and to enjoy life as much as possible. In order to achieve this aim, certain kinds of conduct should be avoided, not only for one's own sake, but for the sake of one's children. If one does commit transgressions and then falls ill, or if one's children become ill, it is better to suffer shame than more suffering or even death. This is the setting of confession and its individual motivation.[27] Confession, in turn, by making public the transgression committed, permits the individual to recover. This is its ostensible purpose. But confession has a wider social function. It makes others aware of disapproved types of conduct which act as a warning to them. At the same time, since patients who confess usually recover, the publicity given to such cases supports both the native theory of disease causation on which the sanction rests, and the efficacy of confession itself. So while most individuals are motivated to avoid the risk of illness, there is consolation in the fact that even if one's sins find one out, there still is a means of regaining health.

In some traumatic disease situations where witchcraft is thought to be the cause of the illness, the anxiety of the patient and his associates is relieved by the removal of a material object from the patient's body by the doctor. This type of therapy is based upon the belief that it is possible to project material objects into the body of a person that will cause illness. Once the object is removed the patient is supposed to recover. The socio-psychological reverberations of cases diagnosed as due to witchcraft are much the same, however, as those in which confession has occurred. This follows because the same factors are involved: (a) a disease situation that requires explanation in terms of some previous behavior, on the part of the patient; (b) the selection, perhaps with the help of the doctor, of some offensive act that is brought forward because the patient feels guilty about it; (c) the dissemination of the cause of the illness through gossip about the case; (d) the resulting publicity given to socially disapproved types of conduct that act as a warning to others.

We can see, then, how the therapeutic measures utilized by these Indians in traumatic disease situations have the social function of anxiety-reduction, although this is not their ostensible purpose from the standpoint of the Saulteaux themselves. We can likewise understand how it is that in a society where so much anxiety is associated with disease, the persons who special-ize in curative methods are individuals who enjoy the highest prestige. In psychological terms, this prestige accrues to those who are instrumental in reducing anxiety.

It is impossible to discuss here all the further ramifications of the function-al aspects of anxiety, but we may point out that the whole magico-religious apparatus of the Saulteaux is a complex anxiety-reducing device.[28]

In summary, the thesis developed here is that, by its very nature, disease may arouse "normal" or objective anxiety, but among the Saulteaux, na-tive theories of disease causation invest certain disease situations with a traumatic quality which is a function of the beliefs held rather than of the actual danger threatened by the illness itself. The quality of the anxiety precipitated in the individuals affected by such situations suggests neurotic rather than objective anxiety because the ultimate cause of the disease is attributed to the expression of dissocial impulses. The illness is viewed as a punishment for such acts and the anxiety is a danger signal that heralds the imminence of this penalty. Insofar as individuals are motivated to avoid dissocial acts because of the penalty anticipated, the pseudoneurotic anxiety aroused in disease situations has a positive social function. It is a psychic mechanism that acts as a reinforcing agent in upholding the social code. Thus, in a society with such a relatively simple culture and one in which formalized institutions and devices for penalizing the individual for dissocial conduct are absent, the utilization of anxiety in connection with disease is an extremely effective means for supporting the patterns of interpersonal behavior that make Saulteaux society a going concern.

Finally, I should like to point out that this role of anxiety in Saulteaux society is consonant with the results that are emerging from certain researches in contemporary experimental psychology.[29] It has been found possible, in Mowrer's view, to recast the Freudian theory of anxiety in stimulus-response terms and to set up hypotheses which can be tested. In this paper, I have attempted to show how such a hypothesis is useful in interpreting observations made in a primitive society.

Notes

Published in *American Sociological Review* 7 (1941): 869–81, reprinted in *Culture and Experience* (1955), 266–76. The essay in this volume is the second version; Hallowell made some minor editorial changes to the earlier article in preparation for its republication in *Culture and Experience*.

1. S[igmund] Freud, *The Problem of Anxiety*, trans. H. A. Bunker (New York, 1936), 94, 121.

2. *Anxiety*, 147.

3. *Anxiety*, 93.

4. *Anxiety*, 94.

5. *Anxiety*, 116. Cf. 108, "Psychic helplessness is the danger which is consonant with the period of immaturity of the ego, as object loss is the danger appertaining to the state of dependence of early childhood, the danger of castration to the phallic phase, and dread of the superego to the latency period. And yet all these danger situations and anxiety determinants may persist alongside one another and cause the ego to react with anxiety at a later period also than the appropriate one; or several of them may become operative simultaneously."

6. *Anxiety*, 94. But Freud rejects O. Rank's theory "that those persons become neurotic who on account of the severity of the birth trauma have never succeeded in abreacting it completely" (123).

7. Cf. O. H. Mowrer, "A Stimulus-Response Analysis of Anxiety and Its Role as a Reinforcing Agent," *Psychological Review*, 46 (1939), 554 n.

8. Mowrer, "A Stimulus-Response Analysis," 563. "Anxiety is thus basically anticipatory in nature and has great biological utility in that it adaptively motivates living organisms to deal with (prepare for or flee from) traumatic events in advance of their actual occurrence, thereby diminishing

their harmful effects." According to Mowrer, anxiety may be viewed as "the conditioned form of the pain reaction" (555).

9. Freud, *Anxiety*, 147.

10. Freud, *Anxiety*, 147. In this paper, reference is made throughout to Freud's revised theory of anxiety. A discussion of the difference between his first and second theories will be found in Chap. 4, *New Introductory Lectures on Psycho-Analysis* (New York, 1933).

11. In chap. 13 [*Culture and Experience*; "Fear and Anxiety," chapter 12, this volume], I called attention to this affective differential as an explicit example of how cultural variables not only define situations for the individual but structuralize them emotionally.

12. Cf. Hallowell, 1939a. [Chapter 17, this volume.]

13. R. M. MacIver, *Society, its Structure and Changes* (New York. 1931), 248.

14. A. R. Radcliffe-Brown, "Sanctions," *Encyclopedia of the Social Sciences*: "What is called conscience is thus in the widest sense the reflex in the individual of the sanctions of the society."

15. In Radcliffe-Brown's terminology, disease is an example of a diffuse, negative sanction. Curiously enough, he does not mention disease at all in his article, despite the fact that it operates to some degree in many societies. Systematic attention has not been given to it as a sanction.

On the basis of the sketch of the Ojibwa given by Ruth Landes in *Cooperation and Competition among Primitive Peoples* (New York, 1937), Margaret Mead concludes (468) that. "Although they know of-and sometimes act in reference to concepts of social behavior characteristic of adjacent societies with higher integrations, they [the Ojibwa] lack effective sanctions to enforce any rule, either in mourning obligations or against incest or murder." Although Landes described Ojibwa in a different locale, the belief system and institutional setup is equivalent to that of the Saulteaux. Mead's statement is, to my mind, completely misleading. A closer analysis would show, I think, that the disease sanction is both important and effective among all Ojibwa peoples.

16. Cf. Joseph C. Yaskin, "The Psychobiology of Anxiety," *Psychoanalytic Review*, 24, 1937, Supplement 53.

17. Freud, *Anxiety*, 149.

18. Cf. Mowrer, "A Stimulus-Response Analysis," 563–64, who points out that "experienced anxiety does not always vary in direct proportion to the objective danger in a given situation, with the result that living organisms, and human beings in particular, show tendencies to behave 'irrationally,'

i.e., to have anxiety in situations that are not dangerous or to have no anxiety in situations that are dangerous. Such a 'disproportionality of affect' may come about for a variety of reasons, and the analysis of these reasons throws light upon such diverse phenomena as magic, superstition, social exploitation, and the psychoneuroses."

19. While not offered in direct support of our contention, the following remarks of Freud (*Anxiety*, 148) seem worth citing: "There are cases in which the attributes of true and of neurotic anxiety are intermingled. The danger is known and of the real type, but the anxiety in regard to it is disproportionately great, greater than in our judgment it ought to be. It is by this excess that the neurotic element stands revealed. But these cases contribute nothing which is new in principle. Analysis shows that involved with the known reality danger is an unrecognized instinctual danger."

20. There seems no doubt that this belief also opens the door wide to the use of suggestion on the part of the native doctor.

21. R. Pettazzoni, reviewing the ethnography of confession (*La Confession des Péchés* (Paris, 1931), makes the point that "la confession des primitifs en général n'est pas secrète," 128 ff.

22. Conjuring involves appeal to supernatural entities. The "bad conduct" of a parent may be discovered by this means and sometimes the spirits of the dead may be invoked for consultation if this seems relevant. Cf. Hallowell 1942a, [(*The Role of Conjuring in Saulteaux Society* (Philadelphia, 1942)] and chap. 7 [*Culture and Experience*; "Spirits of the Dead," chapter 22, this volume].

23. Cf. Mowrer, "A Stimulus-Response Analysis," 558. "This capacity to be made uncomfortable by the mere prospect of traumatic experiences, in advance of their actual occurrence (or recurrence), and to be motivated thereby to take realistic precautions against them, is unquestionably a tremendously important and useful psychological mechanism, and the fact that the forward-looking, anxiety arousing propensity of the human mind is more highly developed than it is in lower animals probably accounts for many of man's unique accomplishments. But it also accounts for some of his most conspicuous failures."

24. Probably seventeen or eighteen years of age. His aunt was not an "old" woman, I was told.

25. The term for father's sister and also for mother-in-law. Because of mother-in-law avoidance there was a double barrier to any erotic behavior.

26. The local English vernacular.

27. Among the Saulteaux there is absolutely no connection between confession and the Supreme Being, so that the disease sanction is not in any sense religious. Attention is drawn to this fact because of P. W. Schmidt's categorical interpretation of certain religious aspects of the *Urkulturen* to which, in his opinion, the Northern Algonkian peoples belong. Cf. Pettazzoni, *La Confession*, 151–52, who discusses this problem. He stresses the dissociation of confession from supreme deities or supernaturals of lesser rank except in a few cases. After referring to these, he goes on to say that, "dans le reste des cas dont nous avons connaissance—c'est-à-dire le plus souvent—la confession a lieu en dehors de toute intervention directe ou indirecte d'êtres divins."

28. Cf. R. R. Willoughby, "Magic and Cognate Phenomena: An Hypothesis," in A *Handbook of Social Psychology,* Carl Murchison ed. (Worcester, 1935).

29. Cf. O. H. Mowrer, "A Stimulus-Response Analysis," 564, and his "Preparatory Set (Expectancy): Some Methods of Measurement," *Psychological Monographs,* 52[2], 1940, 1–2, 39; and "Preparatory Set (Expectancy): A Determinant in Motivation and Learning," *Psychological Review,* 45, 1938, 62–91.

5

IN SICKNESS AND IN HEALTH

Introduction

Part V begins with two fairly short, specific articles focused on sexual behavior and its psychological ramifications (chapters 17 and 18, written in 1939 and 1949 respectively). In chapter 19, written in 1950, Hallowell looked at Ojibwe people's views of and means for coping with mental and physical illness and health in the context of his evolving understanding of their culture and worldview. Spanning just over a decade, the articles work through information that he gathered along the Berens River in the 1930s, and during brief fieldwork in the 1940s at Lac du Flambeau, Wisconsin. As the final chapter in Part V, we had planned to include Hallowell's major, seminal article, "Ojibwa World View and Disease," which appeared in *Man's Image in Medicine and Anthropology*, edited by Iago Galdston (New York: International Universities Press, 1963), but permissions issues made its inclusion impossible. It was reprinted in Hallowell, *Contributions to Anthropology* (1976), but that volume is out of print. Nonetheless, Hallowell's other writings presented here are still very rich sources on Ojibwe views of disease, and make visible his main lines of thought and analysis.

Writing for different venues and audiences, Hallowell sometimes repeated information and story elements in varying amounts of detail. His tendency in his later pieces, however, was to cast his data in a wider framework, often muting the psychological emphases of some of his earlier articles—a trend that may also be detected in the articles gathered in Parts VI and VII.

In his introduction to "Sin, Sex, and Sickness in Saulteaux Belief," Hallowell noted that his original fieldwork aim in this area was simply to gather information on "native theories of disease." He quickly discovered, however, that the people's own explanations of serious illness strongly emphasized sexual transgressions as causal in many cases. Missionaries and others often found the Ojibwe to be rather unrestrained in their behavior, what with premarital sex, flexible divorce patterns, and cross-cousin joking. But the stories of both men's and women's transgressions, which were confessed publicly as a fundamental part of Ojibwe therapy, mapped out firm standards of behavior illustrating an Ojibwe value system that was strongly self-reinforcing. The fear of illness as punishment and the public confession of sexual misdeeds maintained the norms, without external coercion or police. The existence of the violations showed that, as in any society, some people tested or broke the rules that usually prevailed. But penalties pursued them. At the same time, as Hallowell also noted in chapter 16, confession itself could mitigate the consequences of the transgressions, reducing the risk of illness or assisting a cure.

Hallowell mentioned in note 1 of chapter 17 that he gathered the case material for this paper after he had published the article in chapter 11 ("Psychic Stresses," 1936). That is, the data came from his 1938 fieldwork at Little Grand Rapids and Berens River, places he was then visiting for the fifth or sixth time. The resident missionaries in those communities lived there longer and got to know them better in certain respects. But the stories and concrete information that the people shared with Hallowell on these topics go far beyond what the clergy or other outsiders would have heard. With the help of William Berens and others, he worked to understand the Ojibwe on their own terms. (Given that aim, the use of "sin" in the article title, although alliterative, seems a problematic choice, given its baggage of Christian associations.)

Ten years later, Hallowell published "Psychosexual Adjustment, Personality and the Good Life in a Non-Literate Culture" (chapter 18). This was 1949, the year after the publication of the Kinsey-Pomeroy-Martin report, *Sexual Behavior in the Human Male*, which Hallowell cited, and his audience was the American Psychopathological Association. His aim was to explain Ojibwe kinship and sexual behavior in cultural context, explaining their disease sanction and confessional therapy. He then went on to describe male and female "modal patterns of sex behavior" in considerable detail, in courtship and other spheres, and to discuss briefly how those patterns were reinforced, for example by stories and in myth. He drew no explicit comparisons with the Kinsey report, but concluded with an overview of Ojibwe male (and female) personality structure. His Ojibwe friends might have recognized themselves to an extent in his words, but his rather abstracted characterization would have resonated more with his psychologist listeners than with them.

"Values, Acculturation, and Mental Health" (chapter 19) appeared a year later, in 1950. Acculturation as a theoretical and explanatory framework drew Hallowell's attention in the 1940s and 1950s, as he sought to organize and interpret both his Berens River data and the information that he and a number of graduate students gathered from the Ojibwe community at

Lac du Flambeau, Wisconsin, in the late 1940s. When this article was re-printed in his *Culture and Experience* (1955) it appeared with three others in a section entitled "The Psychological Dimension in Culture Change." Those pieces are not reprinted as their Ojibwe content repeats materials published here, or is rather slight or remote from Berens River, Hallowell's main research focus.

Chapter 19 outlines the four levels of acculturation that Hallowell iden-tified from fieldwork on the Berens River and at Lac du Flambeau. They ranged from the old Ojibwe culture and modal personality that he found far up the Berens River, to the more "acculturated" people who lived closer to or on the shore of Lake Winnipeg, to Flambeau, where he identified a "psychological impasse" in that the old belief system and the focus on the dream quest and spiritual helpers had faded amid poverty and economic pressures, with no viable substitutes being provided by Western culture—a problem especially serious for Ojibwe men whose traditional livelihoods had also been lost. By comparison, the Berens River folk, even the most acculturated "Lakeside" people near Lake Winnipeg, seemed "quite well adjusted," their mental health sustained by enduring values, even if fears and anxieties about disease and bad medicine were always present.

It should be noted that Hallowell qualified his own conclusions about the extent and depth of acculturation. Various evidence, he argued, includ-ing results of Rorschach and Thematic Apperception (TAT) psychological tests showed the persistence of an Ojibwe "personality constellation"; the people of all these communities "are still Indians in a psychological sense, whatever the clothes they wear, whatever their occupation, whether they speak English or not, and regardless of race mixture." The problem for the Flambeau people, he felt, was that while seen from outside, they appeared highly acculturated, "their level of psychological adjustment falls for below the optimum," as signaled especially in the men by expressions of overt aggression, crimes against property, drinking, and lack of self-regard.

A difficulty with the acculturational line of analysis, however, even when qualified, was that it implied a progressive (or regressive) continuum, an irreversible declension and loss of indigenous culture in the face of pres-sures from the dominant society. It paralleled the popular image of the Vanishing Indian that dominated public perceptions from the late 1800s to the mid or late 1900s; and of course the rural poverty and distress on many reserves in Canada and reservations in the United States confirmed the gloom. If, however, Hallowell could come back to Flambeau in this century or could observe the revitalization of North American aboriginal leadership, cultures, and values in our times, even in the face of immense obstacles, he might qualify his use of the acculturation construct even further.[1] In fact, the concept was rather muted in his last writings. He closed his 1972 autobiographical essay (prologue, this volume) on an optimistic note, observing how humans make "positive use of psychological resources in cultural adaptation and personal adjustment"; they find new ways to survive in changing circumstances.

"Ojibwa World View and Disease" (1963) was one of Hallowell's most important late pieces, along with his "Ojibwa Ontology, Behavior, and World View" (chapter 27) and "The Role of Dreams in Ojibwa Culture" (chapter 23), and as noted, we regret the absence of that article from this collection. In the 1960s, Hallowell's views and understandings of Ojibwe culture and thought matured and deepened as he reflected on materials gathered and stories and insights heard twenty to thirty years earlier. Here he developed his thoughts on Ojibwe world view, on the Ojibwe expanded concept of "persons" as including other-than-human beings as well as humans, and on their related tendency to attribute major events, illness, etc., to personalized causes, the agency of persons, whether human (or in human form), or not. His vocabulary also shifted. Whereas in his earliest writings, he referred to the Ojibwe spiritual beings who appeared in myths and dreams as "supernatural," he emphasized in this article that "neither 'natural' nor 'supernatural' are terms appropriate for describing [Ojibwe] world outlook. Instead of any fundamental dichotomy, there is, rather, a basic metaphysical unity in the ground of being" (1963, 267).

Perhaps thinking of the largely medical readership of the book in which this essay appeared, Hallowell concluded his long and sympathetic discourse on Ojibwe world view with a passage that contrasted Western scientific perspectives with the cognitive orientation of the Ojibwe.[2] Of Ojibwe disease causation theory, he wrote that the Ojibwe "are ignorant of the fact that disease is an independent variable when considered in relation to the social life of man, and human moral values," even though he credited "the psychological validity of channelling personal conduct in accordance with social imperatives by motivations rooted in anxiety and guilt" (1963, 311). Many thinkers today might be less ready to dichotomize to this extent or to see disease as so independent a variable, and we cannot say whether Hallowell's own stance might have shifted in later years. But his work in this field still stands as remarkable for its empathy, insights, and the quality of the ethnography underlying it.

Notes

1. From the late 1900s on, Lac du Flambeau, for example, became a center of political activism around issues of treaty rights and the continuance of traditional spearfishing, and the community's history and heritage have been retrieved and revived. See Larry Nesper, *The Walleye War: The Struggle for Ojibwe Spearfishing and Treaty Rights* (Lincoln: University of Nebraska Press, 2002); and Leon Valliere Jr., ed. by Elizabeth M. Tornes, *Memories of Lac du Flambeau Elders* (Madison WI: Center for the Study of Upper Midwestern Cultures, 2004).

2. As noted, this text was first published in *Man's Image in Medicine and Anthropology*, edited by Iago Galdston, a psychiatrist at the New York Medical Academy. But Galdston himself questioned the limits of Western scientism; see his "Job, Jung, and Freud: An Essay on the Meaning of Life" (*Bulletin of the New York Academy of Medicine* 34 [12] [1958]: 769–84).

SEVENTEEN

Sin, Sex, and Sickness in Saulteaux Belief

Among the Berens River Saulteaux[1] sickness is believed to result from a variety of causes. These fall into four major categories: (1) fortuitous circumstances which may result in broken limbs, cuts, wounds, colds, and minor ailments; (2) dream visits from certain spiritual entities; (3) sorcery; (4) transgression of several kinds, either on the part of the sick persons or of their parents.

Disease believed to have resulted from transgressions, in turn, involves the relation of the individuals to (a) supernatural entities, (b) the use of magical procedures, and (c) to the moral imperatives which should govern one's own conduct and one's relations to other human beings. Murder, for example, according to the aboriginal code, results in subsequent illness for one's self or one's children. So does deceit which, as specifically defined in this context, means offering professional services, such as curing and conjuring, under false pretences, that is, without the validation which a dream revelation gives. Sexual transgressions of certain kinds also fall within this last-mentioned group (c), and it is a series of these cases that I wish to discuss here. Before doing so it should be understood that, according to Saulteaux doctrines, the only effective curative procedure in all cases of illness which are the result of a transgression of any kind, is confession of the wrong one has done.[2] As compared with drugs, therefore, confession becomes a secondary therapeutic means that is used as a last resort when the patient does not respond to other methods of treatment. Once a confession is elicited, however, it is believed that ordinary medicine will produce its reputed curative effects.

Altogether I have recorded fifteen cases in which some transgression was reputed to be the source of sickness. Of these, two patients were believed to be ill because of the wrongdoing of their parents, for which class of cases, I may add, the Saulteaux have a special term. The remainder had their own personal conduct to blame. In ten instances the confession was elicited under pressure exerted by a native doctor, in two cases it occurred at a conjuring performance, and in three instances a person spontaneously confessed when suffering from sickness because of the fear that otherwise he might not recover. While there is no formalized demand that confession shall be a public rather than a private act, the character of native social life makes all confession public in effect. For in all cases of illness close relatives, if not other persons, are inevitably present. Confessed sins thus become an open secret rather than something confidential and strictly private.

The striking fact about the total series, collected, it should be emphasized, with reference to native theories of disease and with no intention of probing into sexual behaviour, is the overwhelming preponderance of sexual transgressions. There are twelve of these cases. Of the remainder, one was a case of murder (infanticide), one involved deceit, and one was that of a man who had treated too roughly a corpse he was helping to prepare for burial.[3]

The case material involving sexual sins was obtained from the following sources:

(a) A. B., an old man of the Grand Rapids Band, whose father, although not a leader of the Midéwi·win, was one of the most widely known and respected native doctors of his generation. The cases involving confession, narrated to me by his son, represent part of a total series describing other methods of treatment.[4]

(b) F. F., an old man living at the mouth of the river who occasionally practises nibakīwin[5] as well as other therapeutic methods.

(c) A. F., a man about forty-five years of age, the son of F. F., who periodically essays to cure disease, principally by herbal drugs.

(d) W. B. [William Berens], one of the oldest members of the Berens River Band.

Since the father of A. B. treated individuals as far inland as Lake Pekangikum, the cases cited, if geographically viewed, come from the entire length of the river and include instances from all three of the contemporary bands. And in time span, at least three generations are represented.

For convenience in classification, the cases are grouped under autoerotism, homosexuality, heterosexuality, and bestiality, under one or more of which appear such practices as masturbation (including the use of an artificial phallus), fellatio, and incest.[6]

(1a) A young fellow when he had to portage heavy loads would sometimes be unable to straighten himself up again. He came to my father
for medicine. My father gave him medicine but it did the man no
good. Finally my father said to him, "Do you ever bother yourself?"
The man said, "Yes." Then my father told him to stop it if he wished
to get well and be healthy like other men. He gave him more medicine
and he was all right.

(2c) The wife of T. B. had a very sick daughter. She confessed to the Indian
who was trying to cure the latter that once when she was a young
girl she had cut off the penis of a caribou and pushed half of it up
her vagina. "She allowed it to remain there all night. The next morning she took it out and looked at it. Half of it had become red.[7] She
was that hot." It was because she did this that her daughter was sick
between her legs.

HOMOSEXUALITY

(3a) A sick man was brought to my father when we were camping at Eagle
Lake. He was married and had two children. He gave my father a trap,
a blanket, a pair of pants, and a piece of cloth. The man's neck was
swollen all the way down to his chest. My father sat and looked at
this man for quite a long while. Then he took a sweat bath. After he
got through he came back in the wigwam and picked up his rattle.
He told me to raise the man up a little and to get the pan he used
when he practised nibakïwin. Then he told me to take off the rabbit-
skin blanket under which the sick man was lying. My father ordinarily used bones,[8] but this time he took a "gun worm." This did not
seem to work, so he took his bones. But he could not draw anything
from the sick man. Finally he said to the man, "You brought this
sickness on yourself. You did something wrong." After a while the
sick man spoke. "Yes," he said, "long ago when I was travelling with
another young man he made me suck his penis." After this he drew
what looked like clear soup from the sick man, and put it in the pan.
"You will get well now," he said, and after a few days the man left for
his own camp. My father used to sing a song he got from a wolf when
he was curing. That is why no one could hide anything from him.

(4a) My father cured a woman at Lake Pekangikum. She was an unmarried woman, and when he first saw her she could not move. But he

had the people put fresh brush in the wigwam and when night came he started to doctor her. She got no better, although he gave her good medicine. So finally he said, "You must have done something to bring this sickness on yourself. What was it?" The woman said that she and another girl had played with each other. After this the young woman got better because the medicine could do its work.

(5a) Another unmarried sick girl could not move her arms. She had been doctored by several other Indians before she came to my father, but no medicine had helped her. She gave my father a gun and a trap. He ordered the *pi'kogan* [9] to be cleaned up and new brush laid down. Then the girl was carried in on a blanket. He took up his rattle and began to sing. But he soon found out that she was not suffering from some ordinary sickness, something else was back of her illness. "Don't try and hide anything from me," he said to her. "If you tell me what you are hiding then you will get better." But it was a long while before the girl could remember anything. So my father said, "Those water animals (i.e., fish), did you ever do anything with them? (He said this to draw her mind towards what may have happened, my informant commented.) I mean a sucker." The girl remembered now. "After we became women, another girl and I used to be together all the time. She used to get on top of me like a man and use a sucker bladder."[10] After the girl had mentioned these things she got better. In two days she was eating regularly and on the third day she was able to walk. After treating this girl my father got her relatives to prepare a sweat bath for him so as to purify himself.[11]

HETEROSEXUALITY

(6b) A couple of years ago I was asked to doctor a girl. Her abdomen was all swelled up. I gave her some medicine but it did no good. I went back to my house and slept. The next day I told the girl's mother that she had done something which was keeping her daughter from getting well. Then she told me that when she was a young girl she had come across a drunken man lying in the woods. She had unbuttoned his pants and masturbated him.

(7c) W. could not pass his urine freely. He had been treated by a conjurer but the medicine he had been taking did not help him. When he heard that this Indian was going to conjure, W. asked him to try and find out why he did not get better. At the séance W.'s mother, a woman past sixty years, was sitting at his side. After the performance had been going on for some time and a number of *pawágans* had manifested themselves, one of these supernatural beings said, "How is the sick Indian feeling tonight?" W. replied, "Not very good." Then the *pawágan, memengwécī*, sang a song. After this was finished *memengwécī* spoke again. "It is some of my medicine that 'my grandson' (i,e. the conjurer) has been giving away. I don't know why it should not do its work. Perhaps some of the old people did something wrong. I'd like to know if I am right about that." At this one of the men in the audience said, "Why don't you speak?" He was sitting near W's mother who asked, "Are you speaking to me?" "Yes," said the other Indian. Then the old lady remained silent for a little while. Finally she spoke: "I don't know. Perhaps it is true. A long, long while ago there were four of us playing together—two boys and two girls. I was only a little girl then. We had made a little wigwam and we were playing that we were camping like the old folks. Of course I did not know that I was doing anything wrong. I had a little thimble belonging to my mother and I was sewing. One of the little boys was lying down and I was lying down, too. His little penis *(wi·nák)* was standing erect. I took the thimble and shoved it on the end of his penis. Then I told him to go and piss. He said, 'I can't, I can't. It's too tight. It hurts.' Then he started to cry a little. So I took the thimble off and we told him not to tell."

   After this recital the conjurer said, in his own voice, "I thought there was something that stopped the medicine from working."

(8d) A woman confessed when she was ill that her brother had had sexual intercourse with her. It was really accidental. This is how it happened. Her brother was courting a girl (who later became his wife). The woman had acted as a 'go-between,' and sometimes the girl would come and stay over night so that her brother could have sexual relations with her. On these nights the woman usually slept on the inside of a bed, next to the wall, and her brother's sweetheart slept on the outside of the bed. One night the brother made an unexpected visit to the bed. Both girls were asleep. His sister had changed places with his sweetheart on this particular night so that she was sleeping on the outside of the bed. She said her brother was in her before she was fully awake and realized who it was. She did not wish to make an outcry when she found out because their parents were also sleeping in the same room. So she said she kept quiet and let him finish.[12]

(9a) A married woman asked my father to doctor her. She complained of pains in her abdomen. He gave her medicine but she could not hold it on her stomach. "You must have a very bad sickness," he told her. Now my father knew that the husband of this woman did not treat her right. So he said to her, "Don't hide anything from me. Don't be ashamed to tell me what you may have done. You know this sickness is hard on you and the medicine I have given you has done you no good. Do you remember anything you did in the wrong way?" Then this woman told my father what had happened. "Shortly after we started to live together my husband used my mouth instead of my vagina," she said. "It used to make me sick at my stomach." After the woman had mentioned these things the medicine began to work and my father cured her sickness.

(10c) A man came to me to see if I could do anything for him. He could not pass his urine easily. He had already gotten medicine from Indians and from a white doctor, too, but he was no better. I dreamed that this man had done something wrong and that this was why the medicine he had taken did him no good. So I said to him, "You did something wrong with a woman, not your wife, and with a four-footed animal. Do you want me to tell you more or will you tell me what you know you have done?" He was silent at first and would not answer me. Finally he said, "I'll tell you. I did do two things. I put my penis in a woman's mouth and I had intercourse with a bitch." After a while this man got better.

BESTIALITY

(10c) Cf. above.

(11c) A woman was sick between her legs. No medicine helped her. J. J. treated her. She confessed that she had had connexion with a large dog and that she had difficulty in freeing herself from the animal.

(12c) When he was sick on one occasion, an old man confessed (without anyone asking him) that he "had often had sexual connexions with female moose and sometimes bear that he had shot, before the animals got cold. He maintained that a young female bear was closest to a young girl.[13]

The moral attitude of the Saulteaux towards the sexual behaviour occurring in the foregoing cases is sufficiently plain. Such classes of behaviour are sins; they are not crimes. No harm befalls the community as a result of such transgressions,[14] but individuals, or their descendants, suffer a penalty in the form of sickness. It is interesting to note that neither the absence of volition (in the incest case, and in that of the woman whose husband forced fellatio upon her) nor the immaturity of the individuals concerned (cases 2, 3, 4, 5, 7) are extenuating factors. In native theory the penalty inevitably follows the act, and the sins of the fathers may be visited upon their children. This temporal latitude is an important detail of the theory from a functional point of view, because it widens the base from which empirical evidence in its favour may be inferred.

With respect to the incidence in the native population of the classes of sexual behaviour that appear in these confessions I have no data. Personally, I do not see how it is possible to obtain such information, since, in my own experience, direct inquiry led to almost totally negative results. Yet I do not see how one is to escape the inference that at least certain forms of the sexual behaviour described must be fairly prevalent. If this were not the case, how could these confessions of sexual sin be so readily elicited by native doctors? And, in terms of the ideology of the people themselves, how could the native theory of the aetiological influence of sexual sins receive such convincing support? Furthermore, from what is known of human sexual proclivities at large, the practices described are by no means novel, and a fairly widespread incidence of them in any population is probably to be expected. If we can make some such generic assumption, then the specific ideology of Saulteaux culture provides the necessary lever which, in the hands of a skilful doctor, becomes an instrument that can be readily applied in cases where drugs prove ineffective. In terms of such a hypothesis, the desire to be cured of an illness is a sufficient motivation to induce individuals to probe their past experiences and produce some sexual episode which, while falling within the panel of Saulteaux sins is, nevertheless, generically human—or even primate. Of course the confession elicited provides, in turn, evidence which supports the aetiological aspect of the native theory of disease. But the act of confession itself has psychic implications for the sick individual that must not be overlooked.

Since the traditional moral imperatives discountenance sexual behaviour of the types confessed, the suppression of such experiences by individuals must occasion some degree of psychic tension. When a serious illness which fails to respond to the usual treatment occurs, a context arises in which confession as a therapeutic aid is likely to be invoked. If the individual is motivated by a desire to get well, confession affords the conscious means to that end. It likewise functions as a conscious or unconscious means for the relief of psychic stress,[15] on account of the prevalent moral attitude towards the sexual content of the confession. The conviction that at last the root of the trouble has been discovered and removed must also be of positive psychological value to the patient.

It is possible, of course, that this catharsis, in some instances, may be of genuine therapeutic value as well, and that certain bodily processes of the individual may subsequently function better, thus facilitating a cure. While I would not argue that this was the fact in any of the cases cited, I do not think such a hypothesis should be ignored. One would have to know a great deal more about the personal history of the individuals concerned, as well as possess more detailed information in respect to what they said to the doctor. At any rate, the context is appropriate for obtaining positive effects from a crude psychic catharsis, which, together with the ever-present natural recuperative powers of the organism, would be sufficient, in certain cases, to lend plausibility to the therapeutic aspects of native theory among the Saulteaux themselves.

Finally, I should like to discuss briefly the relation of the Saulteaux theory of disease to the *mores* which it sanctions. In the absence of information with respect to the intimate details of the sexual life of these Indians, or even with the case material reviewed, the generalized statement that all individuals deviating from the accepted norms of sexual behaviour are courting illness in the future for themselves or for their children, might suggest that the fear engendered by this prospect would be an effective barrier to such behaviour. And such an assumption could be supported by the constantly articulated desire of the Saulteaux for *pīmädazīwin*, well being, Life with a capital *L*. In view of the facts, however, a more realistic interpretation is possible, which incidentally illuminates the manner in which much of culture functions in human life. When functionally viewed with respect to individual behaviour, this Saulteaux theory of disease appears to act as a deterrent to the *habitual practice, possible spread, and culturally phrased approval* of certain sexual practices, rather than as a mechanically operating barrier, which altogether *prevents* their occurrence. It tends to create a nice balance, in fact, between the somewhat variable manifestations of the sexual urges of individuals and the ideal norm of sexual behaviour, traditionally imposed by culturally determined values. This equilibrium is achieved by making confession an effective means by which individuals can mitigate the consequences of indulgence in subcultural proclivities which are in conflict with the *mores* and believed to be subject to the fateful penalty of disease. If one cannot altogether escape the inevitability of sickness, it is possible to regain one's health through confession.

In this society then, while norms of sexual conduct are culturally defined, and deviations are discouraged through the fear of incurring disease, it would appear that deviations do occur with considerable frequency, but the reputed penalty for them is tempered by means of confession. This balance between the instinctual forces and cultural tradition functions through the characteristic integration of sin, sex, and sickness in Saulteaux belief.

Notes

First published in *British Journal of Medical Psychology* 18 (1939): 191–97.

1. A hunting people of Ojibwa derivation, some 900 in number, living in the forested region east of Lake Winnipeg. The easternmost band, localized in the neighbourhood of Lake Pekangikum, Ontario, is largely pagan, while those at the mouth of the river, constituting the Berens River Band proper, are Christianized and less aboriginal in their contemporary manner of life. The mid-river band at [Little] Grand Rapids may be characterized as intermediary, so far as the progress of acculturation is concerned.

2. For a general survey of confession among primitive peoples see R. Pettazzoni, *La Confession des Péchés*, 1931.

3. He had pulled the dead Indian's belt too tight.

4. [Ed. note: A.B. was Adam Bigmouth, who lived at Little Grand Rapids. Bigmouth was over 70 when Hallowell met him in the summer of 1938. See APS, Series V, Saulteaux Indians, Myths and Tales, file 25.]

5. The removal of substances or material objects from the body of the patient whose presence is attributed to sorcery.

6. The letter after each case number keys the source from which the information was obtained; thus all cases obtained from A.B. are indicated by *a*, those from F. F. by *b*, etc.

7. The penis of the caribou is white.

8. These bones or their equivalent are in the form of tubes about 2 in. long and are part of the material paraphernalia of all native doctors of this class. They are employed in the attempt to draw the 'disease entity' from the patient.

9. Bark-covered tipi.

10. A sucker's bladder is comparable in size and shape to a man's penis.

11. I was told of another case, unconnected with illness, in which a young mink was used as an artificial phallus. In this instance it was employed by a man preliminary to heterosexual relations.

12. It is worth recording the fact that before my informant learned the

details of this occurrence the brother of the girl once remarked to him that sexual intercourse with a close relative was more enjoyable than any other kind. Evidently he had found his sister an eminently satisfactory bedfellow.

13. Another man is reputed to have asserted that bear and caribou were unsatisfactory sexual objects. He maintained that he himself had used beaver and, by means of a special technique, porcupine!

14. As, for example, scarcity of game, a belief which among the Iglulik Eskimo may occasion the public confession of any breach of tabus by all members of the community (K.Rasmussen, "Intellectual Culture of the Iglulik Eskimos," *Fifth Thule Expedition*, 8 1921 123–9).

15. Cf. Hallowell, "Psychic stresses and culture patterns" [chapter 11, this volume]. The case material in the present paper was collected subsequent to the publication of the article cited, and more fully documents the very brief discussion of confession given there.

EIGHTEEN

Psychosexual Adjustment, Personality,
and the Good Life in a Nonliterate Culture

INTRODUCTION

An adequate understanding of human psychosexual adjustment calls for
more than a taxonomic study of actual sexual behavior. For sexual adjustment in man, as compared with that of other animals, is psychologically
unique, whatever his overt behavior may be. One primary key to the nature
of man's peculiar adjustment arises from the fact that his sexual activity is
everywhere drenched with moral evaluations. In addition to the biologically rooted and intrinsically rewarding values of sexual stimulation and
gratification, human beings respond to culturally phrased negative sanctions
if approved sexual objects are not chosen, and traditionally recognized
patterns of expression are not followed. Fully rewarded sexual behavior
involves an inevitable compromise between instinctual impulses and the
moral appraisal of their expression that is characteristic of a particular society. This compromise is not conscious or rational. It is a necessary part
of the socialization process, begun in infancy, by means of which the psychosexual development of the individual becomes an integral part of his
total personality organization. Consequently man's sexual behavior cannot
be fully explained as a function of purely biologic factors such as zoologic
status, level of maturation, etc., although such factors cannot, of course,
be ignored. Neither can human sexual behavior be fully understood as the
result of a relatively simple learning process in which the individual is more
or less passively moulded to the prevailing cultural norms and values of
his society. An examination of actual behavior may reveal wide variations
from the culturally phrased ideal. The Kinsey-Pomeroy-Martin report has
made this clear, so far as American males are concerned.[1] Knowledge of
individual adjustment and the resulting psychologic structuralization of
the personality is necessary to an adequate understanding of the dynamics
of the process. Once we turn to this aspect of the problem, the psychologic

derivatives of the ubiquitous moral evaluation of human sexual behavior become apparent. Psychosexual adjustment is fraught with anxiety, guilt, shame, frustration, and other affects which influence and color the qualitative aspects of human psychosexual adjustment. For man, as compared with other animals, has the unique capacity of becoming an object to himself. He not only acts but is aware of his acts and is judged to bear some responsibility for what he does. Man's autism also makes him aware of his impulses and desires, even if they do not eventuate in action. As a social being, in constant interpersonal relations with his fellows and groomed to take account of the culturally constituted goals and values of his society, man is induced to contemplate his sexual fantasies[2] and his sexual acts, to react affectively toward them, and to evaluate them. Impulses, as well as overt behavior, may be felt, or judged, to be good or bad. At the same time, human beings are subject to the institutionalized rewards and punishments that overt human behavior provokes. Thus the process of psychosexual adjustment is fraught with all sorts of possibilities for conflict. But some resolution is also demanded. The actual balance that eventuates between biologic determinants, cultural standards, and the effects of social sanctions is intimately related to societal organization and personality structure. The anthropologist can best contribute to an understanding of human psychosexual adjustment by taking account of *all* the relevant factors in the societies that he studies.

This paper aims to give an integral picture, in outline form, of the factors relevant to psychosexual adjustment among a relatively unacculturated group of Indians. These people are a northern branch of the Ojibwa and live on the Berens River in Manitoba (Canada). Locally they are known as Saulteaux and number about nine hundred. They are part of an aboriginal hunting population of northern North America and still follow this occupation. I have studied them at first hand over a number of years. The primary data on which statements in this paper are based comprise systematic ethnographic inquiry, personal interviews, participant observation, and a Rorschach sample of the population (adults and children of all age groups and both sexes). Space will permit only illustrative documentation.

CULTURAL EVALUATION OF SEX
BEHAVIOR AND SOCIAL ORGANIZATION

Among the Northern Ojibwa all sexual behavior is evaluated from two points of view: First, with respect to the persons who may properly become sexual objects, and second, with respect to the technics of sexual stimulation and gratification that may be used. The emphasis upon *both* these categories of moral evaluation is so fundamental that even if sexually appropriate partners are married, an *improper mode* of gratification subjects them to the same negative sanction that applies in cases of incest. Evaluations of the first category are closely integrated with the structuralization of the social world of these Indians viewed in terms of personal interaction and, in particular, with their kinship system.[3] Kinship terms are used in a widely extended sense and are not indices to actual blood relationship, except in the case of father and mother. They function as direct guides to interpersonal relations, since customary attitudes and patterns of social behavior are implied in the use of them. So far as sexual activity is concerned moral values are intrinsic to the system, since only a single term *(nīnam)* indicates sexual potentialities between the persons who use it. All other terms carry the connotation of sexual avoidance.

Such avoidance is accentuated in the case of (a) persons who fall into the class of siblings of opposite sex (classificatory or real), (b) persons in the relationship (classificatory or real) of "father's sister"-"brother's son" and "mother's brother"-"sister's daughter." In the Ojibwa social structure such persons are also in the potential, or actual, relationship of "mother-in-law"-"son-in-law" and "father-in-law"-"daughter-in-law" since there are no special terms for relatives by marriage. All social interaction between persons in these categories is hedged about with elaborated restrictions which makes them extremely self-conscious of the social distance that must be maintained between them. Among other things, all verbal references to sexual matters must be strictly avoided when such persons are in the presence of each other. This pattern of avoidance is the antithesis of the verbal freedom that is permissible between individuals who use the term *nīnam.*

Sexually approved behavior, then, is defined in terms of the position which individuals occupy in the social structure and between whom a certain term is used. These potential mates are of the same generation in the kinship system. They include one type of actual blood kin, cross-cousins. Since kinship terms are extended throughout the social world of the individual there are no equivocal cases. These Indians have patrilineal clans but the rule of clan exogamy automatically follows when a mate is selected from the proper kinship class.

Stated so abstractly, the culturally phrased evaluation of an approved class of sexual objects looks very simple. In order to bring into sharper relief the actual nature of the sexual values this society stresses, I wish to call specific attention to the categories of sexual objects that are logically excluded.

(a) Persons of the same sex do not use the term that defines permissible sex relations, so homosexuality is ruled out.
(b) All persons in the usual incestuous categories are also ruled out, as well as many individuals *not* related by blood. Since *nīnam* is only applicable between people of the same kinship generation, this fact alone makes legitimate sex relations between persons of different generations impossible. The tabu on sexual relations between close blood relatives is actually a function of the operation of the social system considered as a whole.
(c) Bestiality is *a priori* ruled out.

Turning now to the evaluation of sexual stimulation and gratification we find

(a) That kissing, manipulation of the breasts and oral contact with them, and coital variations involving genital contacts, are *neutrally* evaluated.
(b) That masturbation[4] (self or mutual), oral-genital contacts, the use of artificial phalli of any kind, and anal intercourse are *negatively* evaluated, and subject to sanction.

It is quite apparent that in this category of sexual behavior, genital gratification alone is positively evaluated. Consequently, in this society, sexual activity is only approved between persons of opposite sex, occupying a defined position in the social structure, who use a reciprocal kinship term, and only genital gratification receives full moral sanction.

CULTURAL SANCTIONS AND THE GOOD LIFE

The social and psychologic significance of these fundamental evaluations of erotic behavior cannot be fully understood unless a word is said about what constitutes the Good Life, the main sanction that is exploited to uphold it and the responsibility that devolves upon the individual for the consequences of "bad conduct" (*madjīijīwébazīwin*).

The central concept of the good life and the highest value is *pīmädazīwin*, life in the fullest sense; life in the sense of health, longevity and well-being, not only for one's self, but one's family. *Pīmädazīwin* is a word heard again and again in ceremonies. And the supernaturals are petitioned for it. It is made possible primarily only through supernatural help, by "blessings" from guardian spirits. "Bad conduct" interferes with achieving this desired goal. And one of the principal categories of "bad conduct" is some kind of sexual transgression.[5] "Because a person does bad things, that is where sickness starts," is the way one informant phrased it. So illness becomes the sign of "bad conduct." Since there are no organized penal sanctions and, in fact, no adult has any authority to impose any sort of penalty upon another person and since openly expressed moral disapproval is avoided because it may be taken as a sign of hostility, fear of disease may be said to be the major social sanction.

Consequently it is believed that any departure from culturally evaluated sex behavior provokes its own penalty—disease and sometimes death. The significant thing is that the supernaturals have nothing directly to do with this.[6] There are other obligations one owes them. The universe is simply constituted in such a way that disease automatically and inevitably follows sexual transgression. This means that ultimately, no one can escape moral responsibility for his sexual conduct. He must contemplate it in that light. It is also possible that an individual may suffer illness because of the "bad conduct" of his parents. The latter may thus be responsible for the sickness or death of their children. When serious illness occurs and the life of the patient may even be threatened, there is only one thing to do—confess the "bad conduct." If this is done there is a good chance that the patient may recover. "Bad conduct will not follow him any more" is the way the Indians phrase it; material medicine will then be effective. Consequently there is the strongest incentive for individuals to reflect upon their past sexual conduct when they fall ill and to confess what to them appears to be immoral behavior. This involves public self indictment, and often an agony of shame, since when a person is ill he is not isolated, but is constantly surrounded by relatives and neighbors. The transgressions confessed are, of course, those that the individual feels most guilty about; at the same time they correspond to conduct that is culturally disapproved.

NATURE OF SEXUAL MISCONDUCT CONFESSED

Under the first category (disapproved sexual objects) fall cases of homosexuality, incest, and bestiality. I have collected instances of all of these.[7] Women as well as men were partners in homosexual relations. It is perhaps worth noting that all of these individuals were unmarried.[8] All varieties of incest occur. Although I have no quantitative data for society as a whole, based on systematic interviews, in my sample of twenty-four cases, there are eight cases of parent-child incest (four mother-son; three father-daughter and one instance in which a marriage occurred between a man and his step-daughter)[9] and ten instances of brother-sister incest. Of these there was one actual marriage between a brother and a sister and three instances in which the persons were classificatory siblings (parallel cousins). In addition, there were three cases in which the severe tabu upon sex relations between individuals in the kinship category father's sister—brother's son was violated and one in which the parallel relationship between mother's brother—sister's daughter was breached. Only a single case of incest between a man and his mother's sister was recorded and one involving a grandfather and granddaughter. Bestiality includes reputed relations of men with the following animals: dog, moose, bear, beaver, caribou, and porcupine, and a woman with a dog.

Under the second category, forbidden types of technics of gratification, my cases include: masturbation (self and mutual), fellatio, the use of a sucker's bladder,[10] a caribou penis, and a mink as artificial phalli, and anal intercourse.

Mutual masturbation is found in a homosexual context, fellatio in both heterosexual and homosexual contexts; the artificial phalli in both, but anal intercourse in a heterosexual context alone.

MODAL PATTERNS OF SEX BEHAVIOR

A rather sharply defined sexual dichotomy is characteristic of Northern Ojibwa society. This is not only apparent in the division of labor found in economic tasks; it applies to prerogatives of all kinds. Leadership of ceremonies and specialized services, like curing and conjuring, that require supernatural validation, all fall to the men. In aboriginal days boys were sent out in the woods to fast before they reached puberty in order to obtain blessings from supernatural spirits; girls were isolated at menarche but this isolation was not connected with the acquisition of guardian spirits. Men were the approved mediators between the supernatural world and mankind.

Male dominance is culturally supported in this society. This is made evident throughout a wide range of attitudes and behavior. Women are supposed to be self-effacing. Self-assertion and mastery are reputed to be male characteristics. Yet it should be noted that the women chop and haul wood the year round, take entire charge of the building of wigwams, and carry infants, bound to heavy cradle boards upon their backs, in addition to performing all other domestic tasks. Physically, they are as strong and robust as the men.

Yet so far as sex is concerned they play an almost completely passive role in the sexual act itself. As one Indian, who had had some experience with white women expressed it to me, "An Indian woman never helps you." The passive role of women in sexual activity is likewise indicated by the fact that the verb applied to the hunting of animals is commonly used by men when speaking of the pursuit of a girl. And this association between animal and woman appears in one of the dreams I collected. A hunter dreamed of a beautiful girl approaching him. Waking up, he interpreted this dream as meaning that an animal had been caught in one of his dead falls. He went to the trap and, sure enough, he found a female fisher.[11]

With this preliminary characterization of the culturally defined relations of men and women in mind I wish briefly to describe in more concrete detail, the modal aspects of sex behavior.

Nothing of a sexual nature is systematically concealed from children as they grow up. The sexual side of life is an open book. Some of the myths and tales that are told over and over again lave a decided Rabelaisian flavor. Indeed, it is impossible for children living in such close proximity to their parents, either in the old fashioned wigwam or the more modern log cabin, to escape being aware of the "primal scene." While I do not have sufficient information from which to generalize about the incidence of sex play among prepubescent children, there is no doubt that it occurs. Nonetheless, some phases of it are considered wrong. This is clearly indicated by a case in which the old mother of a grown man who was ill because he could not urinate freely, confessed that years before when she was a little girl, "we had made a little wigwam and we were playing that we were camping like the old folks. Of course I did not know that I was doing anything wrong. I had a little thimble belonging to my mother and I had been sewing. One of the little boys was lying down and I was lying down, too. His little penis was standing erect. I took the thimble and shoved it on the end of his penis. Then I told him to go and piss. He said, 'I can't, I can't. It's too tight. It hurts.' Then he started to cry a little. So I took the thimble off and we told him not to tell."[12]

Boys and girls soon learn to differentiate individuals of the *ni·nam* class from siblings of the opposite sex and to differentiate their behavior accordingly. The possibility of bawdy verbal exchange between *ninamak* is soon learned too. There are no polite synonyms in Ojibwa, so sexual references always go unmasked. So far as these verbal references are concerned they are not merely permitted, but encouraged. And they continue throughout life, even if no sexual relations actually occur. On one occasion when old Chief Berens and I were making a trip together, we had barely stepped out of the canoe at one encampment when he began bantering an old woman about sneaking into her tent at night. She was one of his *nīnamak* whom he had not seen for perhaps twenty-five years. On another occasion, a married woman much younger than himself said to him, "Do you think you can make your way through?" The answer was, "The older you get the stiffer the horn." I have heard such talk again and again, by people of all ages. Between pre-adolescents of the *nīnamak* category horse-play and practical jokes may occur that are discouraged between siblings of opposite sex. This continues between *nīnamak* that are married. A man told me that very early one cold winter morning he arrived at a camp where everyone was asleep. He saw one of his *nīnamak* lying under a rabbit skin blanket. Her husband lay nearby and there were other relatives in the same wigwam. My friend said he quietly stole in, threw himself at her side and put his arms around her. She woke up and began to laugh. So did her husband and everyone else. Later he used to joke about "being under the blankets" with her. She would deny it; he would insist and everyone would have a good laugh.[13]

In former days, as I have said, all boys were sent out for a vigil. If the boy was not "pure" (*pékīze*) in the sense of having avoided all contact with girls, he stood no chance of obtaining the blessings that were essential to every man's career. From all accounts, the older Indians were very strict about this and I believe that the motivation was strong enough to have reduced overt sexual behavior in the pre-vigil period to a minimum.

Once puberty was reached marriage was in the offing, so that it is possible that, with a reduction in the length of the pre-marital period, there was actually less sexual activity between the unmarried than is true today. Nevertheless it occurred and, as now, the reputed "hunting" of girls by boys, if viewed realistically, indicates that the girls did not run "to get away," but rather to be pursued—and caught! In the initiation of sexual activity Ojibwa girls and women often play anything but a passive role.

Old Josie Josie, who lived a generation ago, used to tease the girls by telling them how his grandmother proceeded to get her man. On a fine afternoon, she would put on clean clothes, comb her hair well, take her axe and walk past the wigwams of several girls of her own age declaring loudly she was going out to cut wood. Of course they were delighted to go, too. And immediately some of the boys, who overheard all this, would begin preparations to go out hunting small birds and mammals with their bows and arrows. The girls would then go off together and, as they were engaged in chopping wood, one of them would notice that an arrow hit a tree nearby or even whizzed close by her head. This made them all laugh because they knew the party of boys was not far away. But none of them would give any outward indication of this. The next thing that might happen would be the breaking of some branches as a boy or two appeared. Then the girls would "run for their lives" (each in a separate direction). If a boy managed to catch up with her she would brandish her axe, but in a moment the boy would grab it away from her. Then the girl would be likely to trip over a root or fallen tree and there she would lie on the ground. The boy would soon have his arms around her and he would not find her an unwilling partner in his desires. Chief [William] Berens once said to me, "Don't let anyone ever tell you that an Indian girl is ever raped. There may be such a thing among the whites, but not among us."

On the other hand, if a particular young man was too avid in his pursuit of girls, they might get "mad." In one case it is said that after luring a young fellow into the bush, a half dozen of them set upon him. They tore off his clothes, threw him to the ground and one of them urinated on his naked belly, while the others held him. "You know what women are like now," they said. He became a laughing stock after this and for a long time none of the girls would have anything to do with him.

Rendezvous of the unmarried may take place on the outskirts of dances held at night, on the way home at dusk when everyone, in summer, begins to settle down for the night. Sexual contacts may be initiated in a very casual manner. As one informant put it "If you feel like having it you may say 'let's go this way' (off the path). She will go if she wants you. If not, she won't. She knows what you are after." Sometimes a young man may be encouraged to seek a girl out in her wigwam during the night, leaving at dawn. But he must be careful to know just where she sleeps! In one case a boy entered the wrong side of the wigwam and his sweetheart's grandmother hit him with a frying pan. Another informant, recounting many of his youthful escapades, described all sorts of ruses which might be used. More than once he obtained entrance to a wigwam after a dance by donning a shawl, thus disguising himself as a "girl friend" of his sweetheart.

During the pre-marital period, in fact, secret rendezvous are practically the only means of social contact between boys and girls. No opportunity occurs for genuine companionship. Their economic activities segregate them, there are few games in which both sexes participate, in dances the sexes are separated and no boy openly walks with a girl, is seen in a canoe alone with a girl, or even talking to one. But *groups* of boys and girls are constantly seen together. Consequently any kind of isolation of a girl and a boy has an aura of sex about it.

No Indian girl is surprised if asked to make a rendezvous. But if it is somewhere in the bush or anywhere but in her wigwam, another girl usually goes along, even if no "double date" is in prospect. The friend sees to it that the lovers are not surprised because it is desired to keep such affairs as secret as possible. Yet, just because a friend is taken along they often become open secrets. Fore-play is not elaborated in these affairs. In fact heterosexual petting, as defined by Kinsey, is practically non-existent. In the first place, kissing and especially deep kissing, is not customary, although there is no tabu against it. Nor are female breasts an object of erotic interest to men. I can well imagine an Indian dismissing such an idea as mouth-breast contact in the same terms as those used by lower level American males, viz., "As something that only a baby does."[14] So far as manual manipulation of the genitalia is concerned there may be some by the boy, but seldom any by the girl. And I have already referred to the fact that oral-genital contacts can only be indulged in the face of the disease sanction. The idea of oral contact with a woman's genitalia is particularly disgusting to the Ojibwa. In this connection it is worthy of note that the verbal reference to a woman's genitals is the most obscene reference that can be made. All in all then, the culturally constituted incentives are all weighted in the direction of genital contacts rather than in the direction of elaborated petting. And, as Kinsey points out, in American culture, elaborated petting is *not* characteristic of lower level sex behavior where genital intercourse is accepted but is "to some extent ... the outcome of the upper level's attempt to *avoid* pre-marital intercourse" (Italics ours). If, as Kinsey says, lower level Americans are astonished at the elaborated petting technics of higher level Americans, I am sure that the Ojibwa would be amazed and shocked beyond measure. Among them genital intercourse is highly typical of pre-marital sexual behavior, and it usually takes place with great dispatch.

A missionary friend of mine once characterized the pre-marital sexual conduct of these Indians as *amoral*. This, I think is essentially correct. For if the partners are in the correct kinship category and no forbidden modes of stimulation or gratification occur, there is no negative sanction of any generalized sort that applies. Consequently, the missionaries have found such behavior hard to modify because no pangs of conscience are involved. At the same time it must be recognized that *verbal* disapproval is often expressed by parents, particularly with respect to their daughters' behavior. And the girls may be punished if caught. There is also the risk of pregnancy, but since a girl who bears an illegitimate child is in no way socially ostracized, this possibility is hardly an effective sanction. Perhaps this pre-marital sex behavior may best be characterized as tolerated, much in the same way as comparable behavior is accepted by lower level Americans.

Because of the cultural support of male dominance and the sexual accessibility of women, the male ego is peculiarly sensitive to *rejection*. To turn a man down too abruptly, for example, may be tantamount to a personal insult. This applies both to a request for a rendezvous and an offer of marriage. Aggression is easily aroused in men under such circumstances. Sometimes, there may be a resort to love magic which is reputed to make the victim infatuated with the person using it. Or, the girl may be made ill through sorcery as a means of retaliation. Put in bald terms this means that if a girl rejects a man she may expect him to get "mad." I have information on several cases where illness was thought to be due to sorcery, employed as retaliation for sexual frustration. In one of these the woman was able to use counter sorcery and worsted her former suitor. But although her *life* had been threatened she did not kill him, although she had the power to do so. This outcome is significant when considered in relation to the dominant role of men in this culture. What seems to be implied is the assumption that men have potential sexual *rights* over women that must always be respected. This is one of the less consciously articulated but, none the less, basic facets of male dominance. There is a myth which supports the same idea. A girl refused man after man. She was very proud. Finally, a handsome youth appeared in her camp. She wanted to marry him. But he was *Dung-man*.[15] As she followed him he melted away in the sun. There is also an anecdote about some medicine men who considered a certain girl much too proud because she refused to marry anyone. They lured her out in the bush and had serial intercourse with her. Such narratives are fairly obvious warning to women of what men expect of them.

Since every woman and every man is *expected* to marry and rear a family, and because this expectation is closely approximated in fact, marital intercourse becomes the modal form of sexual outlet. It is so extremely unusual not to marry that cases of bachelorhood and spinsterhood that do occur receive an explanation that really transcends any personal choice in the matter. There is a belief that such persons have dreamed of *mīcīpijìu* (Great Lynx) one of the few superhuman entities that is given a purely malevolent character. This spirit may appear to the dreamer as a beautiful young woman or man and intercourse may take place. After this, the true character of the Great Lynx is revealed. This spirit is extremely jealous and if a person does later marry, misfortune, disease and even death may follow. One man who dreamed of the Great Lynx did marry. Once when a child of his was sick he had a dream in which he fought the Great Lynx and won! His child recovered and he felt himself released from any further menace.[16] Thus individuals who dream of the Great Lynx are fearful of marriage lest their spouses and children as well as themselves suffer misfortune. The only unmarried man of middle age that I have knowledge of was probably a homosexual.

Not long ago polygyny was still practiced. The range in number of wives was two to six, the latter figure being unique. In the seventies and eighties of the last century the percentage of polygynous men in various bands in the region studied ranged from five to twenty-four, the percentage of men with more than two wives from zero to six. One selective factor in polygyny was skill in hunting. Only very good hunters could support several wives and their children. Sometimes plural wives were sisters and occasionally a man married his deceased brother's wife.[17]

I found that neither impotence nor frigidity were understood by these Indians. I have no statistics, but my guess would be that impotence is less frequent than among us. At any rate it is expected that potency will continue until late in life. A tottering old man was once pointed out to me. Gossip had it that recently he had met a woman on a lonely path and that she had resisted his advances and had run away. I took this as a joke but the Indians took it seriously.

High frequency of intercourse is expected; nightly by the younger men. Since women are realistic about sex, if a man does not have intercourse with his wife she may suspect him of other affairs. The physiology of conception is not thoroughly understood. Most of these Indians do not appreciate the fact that a single act of intercourse may result in conception. Kinsey points out[18] that restraint of the wife constantly lowers the frequency of marital intercourse in all segments of our population, but chiefly among the educated groups. Despite the fact that I have no frequency figures it can be asserted that no such factor operates among the northern Ojibwa. When he was a young man, my friend, Chief Berens often had several climaxes in one night, particularly when he had been off hunting for a period, and had just returned home. Intercourse is avoided during the menses and then sometimes during the later phases of pregnancy. It is resumed a month or so after the birth of a child.

There is certainly no attempt on the part of the men to delay orgasm or any self-consciousness about achieving simultaneous climax. The women experience a relatively passive type of orgasm. Any tendency to bite, or any other sadistic manifestations, seemed strange to the men I talked to. Intercourse usually takes place at night. Since these people have no night clothes and seldom, if ever, completely undress for any purpose whatsoever, nudity in intercourse is almost unheard of. Nevertheless, I did record an anecdote about an orphan girl who was sent to live with her grandfather and became his mistress. In the story *she* takes the initiative, strips off her clothing and offers herself to him. The initiative taken, the incest and the nudity make this story a treble shocker. But the extremely deviant behavior of this girl highlights morally approved behavior at the same time.

Foreplay in marital intercourse is not elaborate for reasons already referred to in the discussion of pre-marital sex behavior. One of the cases of fellatio, however, involved a married couple as did the use of a mink as an artificial phallus. Two cases of anal intercourse involved married pairs. One of the women claimed that her husband forced it upon her and that once she fainted. All the women are "scared" of it, I was told. And one informant said, "if a girl bothers you, tell her you will do it that way and she will be sure to keep away from you."

Kinsey observes that "there has been an insistence under our English-American codes that the simpler and more direct a sexual relation, the more completely it is confined to genital coitus, and the less the variation which enters into the performance of the act, the more acceptable the relationship is morally." This corresponds to the Ojibwa ideal and also general practice. The further statement that "For most of the population, the satisfaction to be secured in orgasm is the goal of the sexual act, and the more quickly that satisfaction is attained, the more effective the performance is adjudged to be,"[19] can also be applied to these Indians.

Extra-marital intercourse has a high incidence among the Northern Ojibwa, but I have no figures. Like pre-marital sexual activity it does not fall under the disease sanction that applies to the improper choice of a sexual partner and improper technics in sex relations. One of my informants pointed out that it was too prevalent to be punished by illness. Like pre-marital sex relations it is tolerated rather than culturally approved. For faithfulness in marriage *is* verbally upheld as an ideal and certain women are often cited as being good women and good wives, because they have been virtuous.

Extra-marital affairs are carried on by secret rendezvous and, like pre-marital affairs, are usually casual. I know of only one case of a long continued liaison. This was between a married man with quite a large family of children, and a widow with two children. A married woman may take a companion with her to a rendezvous, as do unmarried girls. There is the same danger of being exposed, of the spreading of gossip, and in addition, the possibility that, if caught, a woman may be beaten by her husband.

THE REINFORCEMENT OF MODAL PATTERNS

If a sufficient number of deviant cases were to set up an accumulative trend, changes might be anticipated in the social organization of a group like the Northern Ojibwa and some reorganization in their value system might be also expected. Personally, I see no evidence of this in my data. In fact I should like to emphasize that the publicity given cases of "bad conduct" through confession actually *reinforces* the basic sexual evaluations of their society. For the confessions made in disease situations are never kept secret. There is no analogy to the confession booth of the Catholic Church or the confidence of a physician's office. Confession, indeed, is one of the channels through which children growing up in Ojibwa society and overhearing the gossip of their elders at first *sense*, even though they may only later understand, the typology of disapproved patterns of sexual behavior. Children do not have to be explicitly taught a concrete panel of transgressions in this society any more than in our own. Furthermore, since many people hear about what has happened to those who have transgressed the mores, this serves to validate the inevitability of the punishment for "bad conduct." At the same time, the right kind of conduct, if one wishes *pīmädazīwin, is* accentuated. Functionally viewed, a society can well tolerate a few breaches of the rules if a knowledge of such cases is a constant reminder to live the Good Life and thereby avoid illness and possibly death. The only real danger to the social order would stem from an accumulative trend, in a deviant direction, of actual conduct or, from a direct challenge to prime values that might influence actual conduct.

The one case of actual brother-sister marriage is particularly interesting in this connection. In the first place it obviously runs directly counter to the sanctioned rules of sex relationship in or out of marriage, and it was not a casual affair, as are all other cases of incest of which I have knowledge. But there was no action that could be taken about it. *Sagaskī* went on living with his sister, had three children by her and, when she died, married again. Of course, it was said that the death of his first wife and one or two of his children was a penalty for bad conduct. But if we stopped here, the much deeper significance of this case for an understanding of the operation of Ojibwa society and the psychosexual adjustment of individuals in it, would be lost. In the first place, *Sagaskī* was a well known medicine man and therefore someone noted for his power and feared because of it. Since power in this society means supernaturally derived power *Sagaskī* was in the strongest possible position to flout the mores. From one point of view this is exactly what he did. But this is not the whole story. While he flouted the mores he did not challenge their traditional validity in any way. What he actually did is extremely interesting. He claimed he had a dream, in which one of his guardian spirits, the "master of the Beaver" *commanded* him to do as the beaver did, that is, mate with his sister. *Sagaskī*, in short, felt just as guilty about his incestuous impulses as any one else, but he rationalized them in culturally approved terms by appealing to the highest authority in his society—the spirit helpers of mankind. And I have no doubt that he actually dreamed what he said he dreamed. However, a man who felt less confident of his own power might never have dared to do what *Sagaskī* did, because of a fear, among other things, of the ubiquitous disease sanction. But in *Sagaskī's* case we have a man who was undoubtedly involved in the deepest kind of libido struggle and the unconscious forces at work were scarcely under his control. This is indicated by two things. First, he is said to have urged his son to follow his incestuous example, but the son refused. Secondly, he always camped by himself—in summer on a little island, and would never allow any boys to court his daughters. Two of them never married, although one had an illegitimate child. The case of *Sagaskī*, then, was not viewed by anyone, and certainly not by himself, as a challenge to the established sexual code. In fact this case is still pointed to as an example of what *not* to do. So cases of sexual deviation may, in actual fact, lend support to modal sex behavior, and the primary values of the society.

SEX BEHAVIOR, MYTH AND TALE

Only incidental mention has been made of the treatment accorded sexual activities in myth, tale, and anecdote. If space permitted it would be interesting to examine more thoroughly the sexual interaction of the characters in myth and tale and the implicit values expressed in them with reference to actual behavior. For such traditional narratives, which are told and retold, constitute symbolic material of prime importance for a deeper psychologic understanding of the people.[20] In this society oral narratives are not regarded as fiction. They are believed to be true stories, accounts of actual events. In the myths, which are the sacred stories, the major characters are spiritual entities of one sort and another. Myth narration is equivalent to talking about these existent entities and invoking their presence. In the tales, the characters are human beings. The complex relations that exist between these traditional narratives, the kind of universe they depict, the values expressed in them and the characterologic structure and behavior of the Indians cannot be profitably discussed except in considerable detail.[21] But a few indications of the nature of these relations may be given.

So far as the evaluation of sexual conduct is concerned some of the narratives clearly support the established mores in the same way that confession on the part of individuals does. Characters who are guilty of sexual, or other "bad conduct," instead of achieving *pīmädazīwin,* come to a bad end. Transvestitism, combined with overt homosexuality, for instance, is the theme of one naturalistic tale. A woman leaves her husband and children, disguises herself as a man and takes a "wife." In order to avoid the usual masculine role in intercourse she rubs the genitals of her partner with her fingers. The "wife" is dissatisfied with this, whereupon the "husband" makes an insulting remark about her vulva as an excuse for not inserting "his" penis. Since masturbation is likewise disapproved, this tale is full of forbidden sexual conduct. Finally, the heroine is discovered and killed by her real husband. This denouement points to a moral consistent with the values assumed in actual conduct. The heroine is bad not only because of her sexual transgressions. She had deceived her husband and other people and deserted her own children, so her fate is thoroughly deserved as a penalty for "bad conduct."

The occurrence of anal intercourse in the myths presents a more complicated problem. In two instances, its occurrence is purely symbolic. Impregnation takes place by blowing upon the anus. In other cases, however, a transvestite-homosexual theme appears. But the hero is not a human being but *Wísakedják,* the trickster-culture hero. He is reputed to be always doing things backwards. In the narrative *Wísakedják* disguises himself as a woman, marries, and anal intercourse takes place. *Wísakedják* poses as a stranger and tells "her" husband that this mode of intercourse is customary in the locality from which "she" comes. The mythologic dramatization of what is forbidden conduct in actual life is thought uproariously funny. I am reminded, in this connection, of a long conversation I once had with an old Indian about sexual vagaries. At one point he remarked that it was best to laugh at all such things.[22] The myth referred to affords just such an opportunity. Since anal humor of all kinds is quite characteristic of these Indians, the occurrence of anal intercourse in myth and the attitude towards it points to a strand in the personality structure of the Ojibwa that is deeply rooted. We also find in myth, an account of how sexual intercourse itself was accidentally discovered by *Wísakedják* and his extremely long penis is dramatized to humorous effect. But there are anecdotes from real life about men who had sex organs of unusual size that were instrumental in bringing grief to girls. It is also interesting to note the remarkable correlation between the kind of animal "wives" with whom men mate in myths and the animals with whom actual bestiality is reported. The porcupine is the most striking example.

Sexual themes in myth and tale and sexual behavior and attitudes in actual life are related. They are part of one culturally constituted behavioral world. The many connections that exist are complex but their full psychologic significance cannot be understood except by probing beneath the surface of overt behavioristic fact.

PERSONALITY STRUCTURE AND PSYCHOSEXUAL ADJUSTMENT

In this paper I have discussed the problem of psychosexual adjustment chiefly from the standpoint of the cultural evaluation of sexual conduct in relation to the social order and its sanctions. The actual dynamics of social organization is ill-conceived, however, if some account is not taken of the fact that the individuals who interact in particular ways, behave thus because they have been psychologically structured for living and acting as they do. Thus personality organization and actual behavior in society are part of a basic continuum, an integration of personal adjustment and organized social living. In conclusion, I wish briefly to point out what seem to be the most significant items in the personality organization of the Northern Ojibwa[23] that have a bearing upon their psychosexual adjustment.

The average Ojibwa is a highly controlled person. This is especially true of the men, for the women do not feel so vulnerable in their self-respect. All the early parental nurture and training of both boys and girls are in the direction of strengthening self-reliance, self-control, and developing skills. They are gradually weaned at an early age from parental help both literally and psychologically. But for the boy there is a further step: he is explicitly directed to seek the help of supernaturals. These actually become parent surrogates from puberty onward.

In this process of strengthening the individual to deal alone with the problems of survival, to rely upon his inner resources and "blessings," there is a general muting of any extensive development of emotional responsiveness, tender affective ties or social relations. Nor do advantages accrue from any social position. For men, in particular, self-esteem rests mainly upon their own powers and achievements reinforced by the inner support obtained from supernaturally derived blessings. So too, feelings of guilt come from a highly internalized conscience and often take the form of hypochondriacal fears of various kinds. There is no external rewarding and punishing agent to relieve one of such a strict conscience. As we might expect, such individuals are introverted, highly sensitive to others, are friendly only in a reserved way, for they are wary of others' powers that may be covertly exercised through sorcery. Any fancied rebuff may be taken as a slight. With so little real give and take or learning to know each other on an openly confident and genuinely friendly basis, there is a high degree of projection in interpersonal relations.

Among the women, however, there is more outgoingness and although they, too, do not develop extensive friendly relations and are shy; toward their children they are warm and affectionate. A woman's life being primarily domestic does not necessitate all the safeguards about her ego that men develop.

Between men and women whose personality structure is characterized by such an underdevelopment of deep and fully elaborated affective ties, sexuality functions primarily as a means of satisfying basic biologic urges, rather than an enriching factor in a mutual integration of their emotional lives at a more complex level of psychosexual development.

Notes

Published in Paul H. Hoch and Joseph Zubin, eds., *Psychosexual Development in Health and Disease* (New York: Grune and Stratton, 1949), 102–23.

1. Alfred C. Kinsey, Wardell B. Pomeroy and Clyde E. Martin, *Sexual Behavior in the Human Male* (Philadelphia: W. B. Saunders & Co., 1948).

2. If we wished to go farther it would be possible to show that in some societies, the cultural evaluation of dreams may be such that interpersonal relations in dream experiences are morally evaluated in the same way as overt acts and the individual may be held responsible for them.

3. Details may be found in A. Irving Hallowell, "Was Cross-Cousin Mar-

riage Practiced by the North-Central Algonkians?" Proceedings International Congress of Americanists, 23, 1928, 519–544; (2) "Cross-Cousin Marriage in the Lake Winnipeg Area" [chapter 5, this volume]. For comparable Ojibwa groups elsewhere see Ruth Landes, *Ojibwa Sociology*, 29, Columbia University Contributions to Anthropology (New York, 1937), and *The Ojibwa Woman* (New York, 1938).

4. Early inquiries I made led to the complete denial of masturbation. I was told that Indian boys knew nothing about it until they were segregated in boarding schools, away from the Reservation. Later, confessed cases of masturbation obtained from the "mental" notes of native doctors, along with other types of sexual transgression, proved the inadequacy of my original approach to the subject. Kinsey's data on the incidence and frequency of masturbation in the American population makes it appear reasonable that if we had quantitative data for these Indians it would be comparable in the premarital period at least to lower, rather than upper, level males. For in both groups there appear the common factors of a strong tabu on the one hand and the tolerance of heterosexual intercourse on the other.

5. Culturally defined *aggression* also falls into the category of "bad conduct" and is subject to the same sanction as sexual transgression. See A. Irving Hallowell, "The Social Function of Anxiety in a Primitive Society" [chapter 16, this volume] and "Aggression in Saulteaux Society" [chapter 15, this volume].

6. For a brief resume of the world view and religious beliefs of these people see A. Irving Hallowell (1) "Some Empirical Aspects of Northern Saulteaux Religion" [chapter 20, this volume] and (2) "The Role of Conjuring in Saulteaux Society" (Philadelphia, 1942).

7. For a few concrete examples see A. Irving Hallowell, "Sin, Sex and Sickness in Saulteaux Belief" [chapter 17, this volume.]

8. However, Ruth Landes, *Ojibwa Sociology*, refers (54–55) to a reported homosexual relationship between a girl and her aunt, both of them being married.

9. She was the daughter of his deceased first wife by a previous marriage.

10. Comparable in size and shape to a man's penis.

11. [Ed. note: See William Berens's telling of this dream in Berens, *Memories, Myths, and Dreams of an Ojibwe Leader* (2009), Part III.]

12. "Sin, Sex and Sickness" [chapter 17, this volume].

13. [Ed. note: See Berens, *Memories, Myths, and Dreams*, Part III, for William Berens's telling of this story. For another episode of this kind with a

bawdier touch see, A. Irving Hallowell, "Some Psychological Characteristics of the Northeastern Indians," chapter 25, this volume.]

14. Kinsey, *Sexual Behavior*, 371.

15. [Ed. note: this narrative can be found in American Philosophical Society (APS), Philadelphia, Alfred Irving Hallowell Papers, 1892–1981, Ms. Coll. 26, Series V, Saulteaux Indians, Myths and Tales, file 22.]

16. [Ed. note: See William Berens's telling of this experience in Berens, *Memories, Myths, and Dreams*, Part III.]

17. See A. Irving Hallowell, "The Incidence, Character and Decline of Polygyny among the Lake Winnipeg Cree and Saulteaux" [chapter 6, this volume].

18. Kinsey, *Sexual Behavior*, 751.

19. Kinsey, *Sexual Behavior*, 572.

20. Cf. A. Irving Hallowell, "Myth, Culture and Personality" *American Anthropologist*, 49, 1947, 544–556.

21. Such questions will be dealt with in a manuscript now in preparation entitled "*Myth, Tale and Behavior in Northern Ojibwa Society*." [Ed. note: this manuscript was never completed for publication, but drafts are preserved in Hallowell's papers in the APS, Philadelphia.]

22. [Ed. note: For this myth, "Wísakedják pretends to be a woman," and its two variations, see APS, Philadelphia, Alfred Irving Hallowell Papers, 1892–1981, Ms. Coll. 26, Series V, Saulteaux Indians, Myths and Tales, file 20.]

23. For data on the close relationship between the personality characteristics of the people described and Indians of the Eastern Woodlands of an earlier period see "Some Psychological Characteristics of the Northeastern Indians" [chapter 25, this volume].

NINETEEN

Values, Acculturation, and Mental Health

Anthropologists, like many other social scientists, have fought shy of dealing with one of the most characteristic features of the life of man. This is the plain and simple fact that implicit as well as explicit values of various kinds are one of the central and inescapable phenomena of a human existence. Diversity in systems of value is a concomitant of cultural variability in the development and functioning of the human species.

Consciously striving to be objective, tolerant, and sophisticated in the study of our own species, anthropologists usually have considered various classes of values as phenomena that must be considered primarily in their cultural context and thus relativistic in nature. They have been content to leave generic problems—such questions as intrinsic or universal human values—in the hands of the philosopher, moralist, or theologian. Anthropologists have felt that their major contribution lay in reporting the variations in value systems which came under their observation. Most of us have not had the temerity to attempt an evaluation of the value systems of different cultures because it is said we have no supercultural standard that can be used as a yardstick in making any such judgment.

In addition to recognizing the relativity of different value systems and the inherent difficulty in making any appraisal of them with reference to any absolute ethical or other standard, we should not close our minds to the possibility that, from the standpoint of the psychodynamics of human adjustment, the value systems of different societies may vary significantly as more or less efficient instruments in the molding of personalities that are fully capable of functioning at a level of mental health. If we adopt this as a hypothesis, we have indicated to us another angle of approach to the value systems of different human societies. We may ask: What is the role of different systems of value with reference to the general level of personality adjustment which is found in different groups? Or, in the phraseology of Dr. Henry in a recent article: "What are the *consequences* in terms of the physical and spiritual well-being of the population of the culture's attempt to live out in daily life this particular value system?"[1] (Italics ours.)

The crucial question remains: Are there, or are there not, any significant differences in personal adjustment to be observed if, by using an optimum concept of integrative behavior[2] as a measure, we examine the consequences of one set of culturally embedded value systems as compared with another?

It is possible, I believe, that some light may be thrown on this question by the anthropologist: first, by studying systems of value in different societies from the standpoint of total personality integration and functioning viewed in the perspective of our knowledge of mental health; secondly, by studying more closely the psychological aspects of acculturation, particularly the effects of the social readjustment involved with reference to personality structure and value systems. One of the questions that arises here is how far, and under what conditions, the value system of one culture is transferable to individuals of another in the process of acculturation in order for it to become an integral part of their life adjustment.

The purpose of this paper is to show how the modifications of the personality structure of the Ojibwa Indians under the very acute pressures and frustrations of acculturation highlight the integrative role of the value system of their native culture in relation to the functioning of the total personality.

In the course of acculturation their personality structure has been skewed in a nonintegrative direction, instead of being reconstituted. One of the reasons for this seems to lie in the fact that, despite many outward manifestations of acculturation, no substitute for the value system of the old culture has become psychologically functional. Consequently these people exhibit a psychological impasse. Their characteristic personality structure can no longer function at its optimum level, so that there are many signs of regression, withdrawal, and aggression to be observed. Individuals can no longer depend upon culturally constituted group support, since the old mode of life has disintegrated for the most part. The only positive avenue open for psychological readjustment is for the individual to struggle through alone as best he may. This, in turn, places an enormous burden upon him with highly variable consequences. On the whole, an optimum of mental health has not been maintained.

First, I shall give a brief sketch of the central values of the old culture of the Ojibwa with primary reference to their psychological implications.

Secondly, I shall summarize the steps taken in a series of investigations designed to discover the psychological consequences of various levels of acculturation. At least four of these levels are distinguishable. They are concretely represented by the following groups of Ojibwa: Level 1, The Ojibwa of certain parts of Western Ontario (Canada); level 2, The Inland Ojibwa (Saulteaux) of the Berens River (Manitoba); level 3, The Lakeside Indians of the Berens River; level 4, The Lac du Flambeau Ojibwa (northern Wisconsin). (For extended description see chaps. 18 and 19 [*Culture and Experience,* 1955].)

Thirdly, I shall make some concluding comments on the psychological impasse that appears to have been reached in the case of the most highly acculturated group mentioned, the Lac du Flambeau Ojibwa.

THE VALUE SYSTEMS OF OLD OJIBWA CULTURE AND MODAL PERSONALITY STRUCTURE

The central value of aboriginal Ojibwa culture was expressed by the term *pīmädazīwin,* life in the fullest sense, life in the sense of health, longevity, and well-being, not only for oneself but for one's family. The goal of living was a good life and the Good Life involved *pīmädazīwin.*

How was it possible to achieve *pīmädazīwin?* The answer to this question leads directly to the core of the world view of these people. (See chaps. 7 and 8) [in *Culture and Experience;* "Spirits of the Dead," "The Ojibwa Self," chapters 22, 26, this volume]. In the first place, *pīmädazīwin* could only be achieved by individuals who sought and obtained the help of superhuman entities and who conducted themselves in a socially approved manner. In the second place, the functioning of sexual dichotomy in this culture was such that, while *pīmädazīwin* was a central value for both sexes, it was absolutely imperative that males, rather than females, seek out and obtain superhuman aid. Women might obtain such help; men could not get along without it. Thus we find the institutionalized expression of this culturally constituted imperative in the so-called "dream fast" for boys as they approach puberty. Thirdly, it is important to note that superhuman help was sought in solitude, that the "blessing" or "gift" could not be compelled, but was bestowed because the superhuman entities took "pity" upon the suppliant who, in effect, asked for Life (i.e., *pīmädazīwin).* In the fourth place, it should be understood that the solitary faster usually obtained "blessings" from many "helpers" or guardian spirits, but that the nature of the gifts depended upon his own interpretation of the dreams or visions he experienced. For example, one dream might be interpreted as meaning that the individual would be invulnerable to bullets; another that, in due course of time, he would be able to cure people by certain classes of medicine or conjuring.[3] From a cultural point of view, the fasting experience was a sacred experience since direct contact with superhuman entities had been made. This was why the individual never referred to this experience lightly. Unless he were willing to lose his blessings he could not recount his dream in whole or even in part except under extraordinary circumstances.

It is fully characteristic of the highly introverted personality organization of these people, and the rudimentary cast of their social organization, that this direct contact with superhuman entities was made by each individual alone, that it necessitated the interpretation of a highly subjective experience, the details of which were not usually revealed to anyone else, except perhaps the boy's father. Thus the dream fast was the most highly treasured experience of every man. It was a psychological talisman of *pīmädazīwin*, if he did his part by conducting himself properly throughout the rest of his life. It was the foundation of all he was to be in the future. Every special aptitude, all his successes and failures, hinged upon the blessings of his supernatural helpers, rather than upon his own native or acquired endowments, or even the help of his fellow human beings.

From a psychological point of view the Ojibwa boy in his dream fast met the personified forces of his own unconscious, reified in culturally constituted images. And this occurred at a crucial period in his psychological maturation. The fast marked the transition from the infant and child state to adulthood. Formerly the boy had been dependent upon older *human* beings, who, in addition to teaching him necessary skills, had trained him to rely upon himself to the extent of his capacity. Henceforth he was to rely primarily upon *superhuman beings*, that is, upon *inner* promptings, derived from further dreams or the memories of his fasting experience. Culturally phrased, his objective security depended largely upon his contact with superhuman entities, a conviction which was the basis of the sense of inner personal security he now felt. At the same time the dream fast introduced the boy to new obligations. He must respect his blessings and use them carefully. In effect, the basic principle involved might be stated as the obligation to preserve the equilibrium of nature. Nature's bounty depends on his using his powers skillfully, being self-reliant, ready to endure hardship, even starvation. He may be aggressive, predatory, in relation to the flora and fauna of his habitat, for his was a food-gathering and hunting economy. But he must only take what he actually needed to provide food, clothing, and warmth for himself and his family. He must not be destructive or greedy, and he must never torture any animal. If he acts otherwise the animals will be withdrawn from him by the superhuman entities who directed them to him. In the end he will destroy himself since neither the material nor spiritual sources of life will be any longer available to him.

Thus the Ojibwa was far from considering himself the "lord of creation." He was only one of the "children" of nature, a suppliant *for pīmädazīwin*. Fundamentally, therefore, his relationship to nature expressed a passive attitude. He did not enter the creative process in order to control it for his own ends, as does the horticulturalist who plants seeds, tends them, and gathers in the harvest, thereby controlling his food supply.

From the standpoint of this characteristic attitude toward his place in the universe, it can be said that the main binding force of Ojibwa institutions was not so much to link individuals together through common cooperative aims as it was to permit individuals seeking a common central value to achieve it without too much human interference from without. Thus there was no institutionalized chieftainship in the old days nor any organized penal sanctions. In his relations with his fellows the extended use of kinship terms throughout the social world of the individual defined accompanying roles in what was, in effect, an extended family group. Thus, highly individuated relationships with people were not required, since basic attitudes and behavior patterns learned in childhood prepared the individual for dealing with kin of every traditional category. Departure from approved behavior, especially in the sexual sphere, provoked its own penalty automatically—disease or sometimes death—that is, withdrawal of *pīmädazīwin*. Thus no one could ultimately escape moral responsibility for his conduct. (chaps. 14 and 16) [*Culture and Experience*; "The Social Function of Anxiety"; "Psychosexual Adjustment," chapters 16, 18, this volume]. Other human beings, however, could interfere with the achievement of *pīmädazīwin* through sorcery. They could mobilize their "helpers" against one, and one's only recourse was to defend oneself in the same terms. This possibility was the source of much latent fear since no one, of course, could ever know the power of another person until it was demonstrated. Consequently, there was a general suppression of overt hostility accompanied by a surface amiability between people who were actually wary of one another. This was especially true among men, since women ordinarily did not practice sorcery. But covert hostility, especially in the form of gossip and slander, was rife (chap. 15) [*Culture and Experience*; "Aggression," chapter 15, this volume].

Thus, with so little real give-and-take on an open, confident, and genuine basis, and so few economic tasks where any but the very simplest kinds of cooperative efforts were necessary, there was no great emotional depth or security possible in personal relationships. Instead, all such relationships were fraught with a high degree of projection.

Although I have had to present the material in a highly condensed form, I hope that it has been possible to communicate the essential psychological characteristics of the Ojibwa viewed in relation to their central system of values. Theirs was a personality structure that was necessarily introverted and that functioned in terms of a highly internal conscience[4] that made the individual bear the full brunt of responsibility for his own acts. In the case of men in particular, ego support was intimately linked with a belief system and values that made it necessary for them to be firmly convinced of their own superhumanly derived power in order to feel psychologically secure. But this security was never absolute since they might fail to conduct themselves properly and their power could be challenged by other men. This latter possibility was a great source of potential anxiety. Women, on the other hand, were less sensitive in this respect since their life adjustment did not depend primarily upon direct contact with superhuman entities, so that their psychological security was more essentially a function of their human contacts.

ACCULTURATION LEVELS AND PSYCHOLOGICAL CONSEQUENCES

What have been the psychological effects of acculturation upon the Ojibwa? In what respects are they similar to, or different from, their aboriginal ancestors? Has there been a complete psychological break with the past at one of these levels of acculturation, or is there a demonstrable psychological continuity in personality structure? Is it possible that the psychological readjustments that the acculturation process implies, or certain stages of it, can take place without any radical change in the personality organization of the people involved? If there are modifications what is their nature? And how has the actual behavior of these people been affected?

Detailed studies of the Rorschach and TAT, along with the other data already cited, provided a body of evidence that all points in the same direction—a persistent core of psychological characteristics sufficient to identify an Ojibwa personality constellation, aboriginal in origin, that is clearly discernible through all levels of acculturation thus far studied. For this reason all the Ojibwa referred to, including the most highly accultur-ated group at Lac du Flambeau, are still Indians in a psychological sense, whatever the clothes they wear, whatever their occupation, whether they speak English or not, and regardless of race mixture. Although, culturally speaking, they appear more and more like whites at "higher" levels of acculturation, there is no evidence at all for a basic psychological shift in a parallel direction. Thus, familiar anthropological terms like "borrowing" and "diffusion," which are entirely appropriate to describe the acculturation process in a cultural frame of reference, are misleading and inappropriate if the acculturation process is viewed from the standpoint of a psychological frame of reference. At least in the situation described, no identifiable constellation of *psychological* "traits" has been "borrowed" by the Ojibwa or "diffused" to them as a result of their contacts with whites.

All the evidence points to far more complicated psychological processes than those which have led to the acquisition of the culture traits which I have used as objective empirical guides to different levels of acculturation. Consequently, descriptive facts of this order are no direct index to facts pertaining to personality adjustment and personality organization.

Perhaps I can best indicate the nature of this more complex psychological problem by clarifying another fundamental point in the data: While these show, as I have said, the persistence of an aboriginal character structure among the Ojibwa, this must not be interpreted to mean that no psychological modifications whatever have been produced in the acculturation process. Actually, quite the contrary is true. Personality structure is a dynamic construct, not a substantive one. When the data at hand are viewed in terms of the actual life adjustments which individuals have been making, the nature and dynamics of these modifications are fairly clear, although I have not yet assembled all the evidence. But it is a striking fact that all through the Rorschach data there are common trends. These are evident whether we compare the Lakeside Indians with the Inland Indians of the Berens River, or the Flambeau children is a whole with the Northern children, or the Flambeau adults with the Berens River adults. The impression one receives is of a personality structure which, under the varying pressures of acculturation in these localities, is being pushed to the limits of its functional adequacy at Lac du Flambeau. (See chap. 19 [*Culture and Experience*] for further details.)

What seems to have happened is that the acculturation process at Flambeau has reached a level which presents a situation in which we find the personality structure of the Ojibwa in the process of breaking down, rather than undergoing reintegration in any new or positive form. It is also at this level of acculturation that, along with the disappearance of language, old economic pursuits and customs, the native system of belief and values exhibits the most striking disintegration. Consequently there is little or nothing of genuine integrative value that the old culture can offer the individual.

THE PSYCHOLOGICAL IMPASSE AT LAC DU FLAMBEAU

There is a real psychological impasse at Flambeau for three reasons: (a) The functional support, in the form of a system of values, which was one of the factors that enabled the personality structure of the Ojibwa to function at an optimum level under aboriginal conditions, is no longer available. (b) On the other hand, contact with the version of Western culture available to these Indians has provided no substitute. (c) Furthermore, the objective economic and other conditions are not conducive to any constructive resolution of the psychological impasse that exists.

In conclusion I should like to make a few interpretative comments:

1. The disintegration of the old belief system and the substitution of a superficially acquired Christianity as the basis of a new world view have been particularly serious in the case of the men. Their inner life has been emptied of the deep convictions, motivations, and goals that were all integrated in terms of the older belief system and its concomitant stabilized values. Besides this, the men have been cut off from their traditional economic occupation, except as guides for white men, while at the same time, vocational opportunities are limited unless they leave the reservation. They have become apathetic, and drink all they can. Young men just out of the Armed Services in 1946 were sitting around idly, drawing their unemployment insurance until it became exhausted. The government had become the great provider. The old passive attitude of dependence on natural products and superhuman helpers which was so fruitful for their old adjustment has become a liability, like a dead weight that pushes them further into apathy. For it is unbalanced by the pressures of the old life in which daily efforts to wrest a living from a rigorous environment were a primary necessity. Many men are not even successful bread-winners, whereas in the old culture this task developed almost entirely upon them. There has been an accompanying impairment of self-regard, of any feeling of real security. The women, on the other hand, are becoming more and more important as a potential source of cash income. Quite a few of them, almost all married women, have taken jobs in a small local factory. But their children are running wild.

An unconscious sense of the keen loss of vital central values to these peoples is indicated by an attempt on the part of a few of them to retain the Midéwi·win. This aboriginal rite might be said to symbolize the old belief system, and the values inherent in it. But the psychological weakness of this kind of withdrawal was exposed to me by the question one of the leaders once asked me. He was an old man with whom I had become quite friendly, partly because of the interest I had shown in the old religion and no doubt because he was interested in what I could tell him about the less acculturated Ojibwa in Canada. One day he sent for me and asked me whether I thought the Indian religion was really true. This question, of course, clearly indicated the doubts that beset him and demonstrated to me the lack of vitality which the old belief system now had as any sort of psychological resource.

2. As indicated in the sketch of the aboriginal value system and personality organization, there was a great deal of suppressed hostility in the interpersonal relations of these people even under optimum conditions. In the stage of acculturation represented at Lac du Flambeau, overt aggression appears to have replaced the covert aggression that formerly existed in the form of sorcery.

While verbally expressed aggression remains, all white people getting a large share of it, in addition there has been a marked increase in crimes against property by boys and young men. Furthermore, overt hostility comes to the surface with remarkable rapidity as soon as these Indians start drinking, even though they may be otherwise very friendly. While inner control is still present, its threshold has been greatly lowered by the loosening of the psychological integration that has occurred under present conditions. And, of course, the only outer controls now are the institutionalized penal sanctions of the surrounding white community, since even in the old culture these were not developed among the Indians themselves. Aggression may also be interpreted as a sign of the terrific psychological struggle many individuals are experiencing in reacting to the apathy which the paucity of inner resources has produced. These Indians have been thrown back on their psychological heels, as it were. They are attempting to survive in a situation which offers them no culturally defined values and goals that they can really make their own, that have any vital psychological significance for them. Consequently, they lack the kind of cultural fulcrum which is necessary, it seems to me, for full psychological maturity and an optimum of mental health in any human society.

3. Finally, the inner core of their nonintegrative adjustment may be characterized as regression in the sense of a kind of primitivation.[5] That is to say, not literally falling back upon actual modes of earlier behavior, but what is perhaps even more serious, *a frustration of maturity*. From the Northern Rorschach data, for example, we can see what steps in the process of psychological maturation are. At Flambeau it is a striking fact that the protocols of adults are so much like those of the children. This means that these regressive trends in their personality structure make an optimum of mental health impossible under the conditions that now confront them. In this respect the Flambeau adults are the antithesis of the Berens River Ojibwa, who are quite well adjusted on the whole. Thus the Flambeau Indian represents what is, in effect, a *regressive version* of the personality structure of the Northern Ojibwa.

So far as I have been able to analyze the situation, it does not seem to me that there is any positive resolution of this psychological impasse in sight. While, externally viewed, these Indians are highly acculturated, their level of psychological adjustment falls far below the optimum that we know was possible with their type of personality structure, not only under aboriginal conditions but at lower levels of acculturation. At Flambeau a high level of acculturation conceals a psychological skeleton. *Pīmädazīwin* has become an empty word for these Ojibwa. To give it a vital content a new set of values will have to emerge that will either implement a reintegration of their old personality structure or serve as a catalyst for a reconstitution of their whole psychological orientation.

In this paper I have analyzed the role of certain values in relation to the functioning of personality among the Ojibwa, both in the aboriginal culture and under the conditions created by contact with Western culture. If I have analyzed the data adequately it would appear that the role of values as a factor in an integrative level of adjustment has implications beyond this particular instance. Values have an important significance with reference to the whole problem of mental health and the conditions necessary for its fulfillment.

Notes

First published in *American Journal of Orthopsychiatry* 20 (1950): 732–43; reprinted in *Culture and Experience* (1955), 358–66.

1. Jules Henry, "Anthropology in the General Social Science Course," *Journal of General Education*, 1949. Cf. also the remarks of Kluckhohn (*Mirror for Man*, New York, 1949, 285–86), on the necessity for studying values in relation to behavior.

2. O. H. Mowrer has suggested *integrative* as contrasted with *nonintegrative behavior*. Whereas the former is more psychologically rewarding than punishing, the latter is balanced in the opposite direction since adjustment is achieved "only at the expense of partial psychic self-destruction." O. H. Mowrer and A. D. Unman, "Time as a Determinant in Integrative Learning," *Psychological Review*, 52, 1945, 84, 86. Cf. O. H. Mowrer, "What Is Abnormal Behavior?" in L. A. Pennington and I. A. Berg (eds.), *An Introduction to Clinical Psychology* (New York, 1948).

3. [Ed. note: William Berens once dreamed about meeting a magical boy who wore a red tuque. The boy challenged Berens to several trials with bow and arrows. When Berens won the contest, the boy, who also took the form of a certain insect, told him he would not be hit by any bullet unless the shooter was skilled enough to hit a fly. Berens, *Memories, Myths, and Dreams of an Ojibwe Leader* (2009), Part III.]

4. Following a query from Dr. George Spindler, to avoid any confusion with the psychoanalytic "internalized superego" constituted in *social* interaction, the "highly *internalized* conscience" of the original paper has been changed to "highly *internal* conscience."

5. Cf. David Krech and Richard S. Crutchfield, *Theory and Problems of Social Psychology* (New York, 1948). "In general, his psychological field tends spontaneously in the direction of a lower level simplification, which is a reversal of the normal trend toward higher level complexity characteristic of the growth and maturation of the individual" (57).

6

RELIGION, DREAMS, AND THE SPIRITUAL LIFE

Introduction

Hallowell's most inspired and influential thinking and writing centered on his elucidation of what he called the Ojibwe world view. The four essays in this section reflect not only Hallowell's interest in Ojibwe cosmology, but also his ability to interpret the concepts that were explained to him, to build upon his field experiences in these communities. In the 1930s, Hallowell was already breaking new ground in Ojibwe studies. This is clear in chapter 20, "Some Empirical Aspects of Northern Saulteaux Religion" (1934). Hallowell's scholarship matured further over four decades. His early essays were rooted solidly in fieldwork, ethnographic and concrete. Over time Hallowell found his own voice as surely as he brought out the voices of his Ojibwe collaborators. As his ideas gained substance, he moved, for example, from discussing "spiritual entities" to realizing that what he was really writing about were "other-than-human persons," a term that was far more descriptive of the relationships that existed between these persons and human persons.

"Some Empirical Aspects of Northern Saulteaux Religion" is a shining glimpse of the expansive views that Hallowell later developed on this subject. It is curious that this article was not reprinted in either of the two previous collections of Hallowell's essays, for it is fundamental reading for those who are interested in learning about Ojibwe spiritual ideas. In an era when many scholars were still mired in notions of primitive mentality—that aboriginal peoples were credulous, childlike, and naïve, Hallowell demonstrated how the Ojibwe incorporated sophisticated empirical thought, soundly reasoned within their cultural frame of reference, into their understanding of their spiritual universe.

In this essay, published after only three summer sojourns along the Berens River, Hallowell presented what he called the "religious philosophy" of the Ojibwe Indians as "a living reality, as a relatively coherent and self-contained system of beliefs and customs." He concluded that Ojibwe people's experiences, coupled with their observations of the events of daily life, offered "recurrent proof" to them of the validity of their beliefs.

He also cautioned against assuming that Native beliefs were born of dogma and glibly passed down through mythology. William Berens showed how Ojibwe people continually tested their assumptions through experience and observation, and changed their views or tactics when changes seemed needed. Since the eighteenth century, Westerners had been fascinated with empiricism, enthusiastically bringing the methodology of critical questioning to the arenas of science, social science, and religion.[1] The idea that aboriginal people were also empiricists within their own cultural frameworks was nothing short of revolutionary in 1934.

One of Hallowell's talents was his ability to recognize the intellectual gold he had found in William Berens. Hallowell's reliance on Berens was manifest as early as his 1936 article, "The Passing of the Midewi·win in the Lake Winnipeg Region" (chapter 21), in which he credited Berens as not only his interpreter and mentor, but as the inspiration that propelled him to take on this subject in this depth. Berens "proved to be such a spontaneous and reliable source of information in regard to all events and personalities during his lifetime, and even before, that I felt impelled to record as much as I was able, of what he told me . . . owing above all to an exceedingly alert mind and a fine memory, I consider the facts obtained from him to be as reliable as any such information can humanly be."

Hallowell described this piece as "a postmortem record of a ceremony which was once of major importance in the native culture of the Lake Winnipeg Saulteaux." Where possible, he located the places where the Midewi·win ceremonies were held and recorded when the ceremony stopped being practiced. But some of his most interesting work focused on telling the life stories of the powerful and gifted men who led these ceremonies. Through Berens and other intelligent and informed Ojibwe men such as Kīwítc (Alec Keeper), Hallowell was able to tap into the rich personal biographies of the great leaders of the Midewi·win.[2]

Midewi·win ceremonies embodied concepts and symbols that lay at the heart of Ojibwe spiritual life. Although William's parents raised their children as Christians, his father ensured that he maintained rich contact with their non-Christian family and this meant that the children were part of both Methodist and Ojibwe rituals. William later told Hallowell that the impact of the Ojibwe ceremonies—especially those involving the Midewi·win—was so formidable that Christian ceremonies paled in comparison. "I had reason to believe that my grandfather [Bear, who died without converting to Christianity] knew what he was doing and that his beliefs were true. I used to hear my mother talk about God but. . . . I saw no power comparable to what I had seen my grandfather use. For I saw my grandfather in the Midewi·win once ... the last one ever held at the mouth of the [Berens] river."[3]

Hallowell's article brought to life some of these miracles. We read, for example, that one of Yellow Legs' great-grandsons "told me that on one occasion Yellow Legs was seen walking on the water, on a calm day, over to Jack Head Island in order to secure medicine (mackīkī). He was brought back by *memengwécīwak*,[4] semi-human creatures who live in the rocks and travel in canoes. All this happened in broad daylight while people were watching." In the same essay, Hallowell described another great Midewi·win leader, Arrow Legs, walking on the water of Lake Manitoba, again having received knowledge of the location of medicine through a dream.

Hallowell articulated the important connections between the Midewi·win leaders' ability to perform miracles and provide knowledge through dreams. Dreams could reveal instructions about the location and use of sacred rocks and stones. Yellow Legs, for example, was told in a dream about the location of a stone that proved to have magical qualities. These miracles spoke to the permeability of the line that separated the Ojibwe everyday world from the world of other-than-human persons—and of the line that separated the land of the living from the land of the dead.

Through dreams, and the gifts of magic powers bestowed on dreamers by other-than-humans, people could even visit the Land of the Dead. In "Spirits of the Dead in Saulteaux Life and Thought" (chapter 22) Hallowell examined Ojibwe ideas of life after death and the testimony of those who travelled to and returned from the *djībaiàking* (the Land of the Dead).

Djībaiyag (souls of the dead) often played important parts in the lives of the living. The centrality of spirits of the dead was embodied in Kīwítc's (Alec Keeper's) Drum Dance at Little Grand Rapids, for example, a dance where the *djībaiyag* were clearly his *bawaganag*. Ojibwe people often invoked the *djībaiyag* in conjuring lodges and in other ceremonies. Hallowell wrote of a particularly powerful event he observed in the drum dance of the great medicine man, Naamiwan (Fair Wind). As he watched Naamiwan and his son, Angus, it dawned on Hallowell that they were interacting with *djībaiyag*. This was yet another example of spirits of the dead comprising "an integral part of the Saulteaux universe ... [merging] intimately with other aspects of Saulteaux life and thought."

Another compelling story in chapter 22 tells of Jacob Berens's communication with his deceased father, Bear, in the conjuring tent. Jacob had been ailing for some time and no medicine seemed to work. Finally, he asked a conjuror to help. Berens was truly moved when the *djibai* of Bear came to the shaking tent, saying "(half to himself): 'I wonder if it can be so?'" Bear assured his son that he was in a good place and had lived a good life. Then he explained to Jacob why the sickness had taken such tenacious hold of him: "There was one time, my son, that I made a mistake. A man died and I dressed him for burial. I pulled his belt too tight. I pulled as hard as I could. That is what makes you sick now. That is the reason the medicine you have taken has not helped you. The medicine cannot work itself down into your body ... My son, I hope you will get well now. It's my fault that you have been so sick around your waist." After this confession, the *memengwéciwag* provided special curative medicine for him. Again, the permeability of the line that separated living from spirit and living from dead made that union possible. And the connective tissue that allowed such fluidity was dreaming.

Dreams were at the heart of the spiritual culture of Ojibwe people. It was mainly through dreams that they interacted with other-than-humans to receive blessings, warnings, and instructions. Through powers granted in dreams, people predicted the future, sought revenge, or saved their families' lives. Through dreaming, one cultivated strength of mind and, thus, strength of spirit and power.

Hallowell published the final article in this section, "The Role of Dreams in Ojibwa Culture" (chapter 23) in 1966, after more than thirty years of research, inquiry, and reflection. Espousing the view that myth provided the continuity of memory as well as the idea of the thinness of the veil that separates reality in myth from reality in wakefulness or dreams, this essay represents Hallowell at his mature best.

Underscoring Hallowell's examination of the interactions that occurred in dreams between Ojibwe people and other-than-human beings was his understanding that everything the Ojibwe people knew and understood about their spiritual universe had been conveyed to them through dreams. Hallowell here provides a broad discussion of Ojibwe socio-cultural life, closely examining the role of dreams in giving validity to conjuring, the dream quests embarked upon by young men who would have "a long and good life if [they] dreamed well," as well as other kinds of blessings such as the procurement of special medicine from the *memengwéciwag*—small other-than-human persons who lived in rocks,—to enable one to become a *mänáo*—a doctor who dispenses medicine from the *memengwéciwag*.

Hallowell's work was informed by the continuing quest of Ojibwe people to live a good life—to achieve *bimaadiziwin* (life in its fullest sense) through close relationships with beings on a greater-than-human stage. This was a concept that he articulated most clearly towards the end of his career. Dreaming, as he concluded in 1966 (chapter 23), was "a means to this end."

Notes

1. See Susan Elaine Gray, *"I Will Fear No Evil": Ojibwa-Missionary Encounters Along the Berens River, 1875–1930* (Calgary: University of Calgary Press, 2006), chapter 2.

2. Hallowell made only brief mention of reasons for the passing of the Midewi·win ceremonies. Beginning in 1885, the Canadian Government moved to ban aboriginal ceremonies as part of its efforts to "civilize" Indians, instituting compulsory education and seeking to put a stop to "heathen ceremonies" such as the Midewi·win. This ban was especially effective in communities that lay along major travel routes like Berens River, although some say these practices never stopped—that they simply went deep underground. Regardless, Hallowell was able to access knowledge of the Midewi·win in more remote communities like Little Grand Rapids. In her book, *Severing the Ties that Bind: Government Repression of Indigenous Ceremonies on the Prairies*, Katherine Pettipas notes that, "the last recorded interference in woodland ceremonies, such as the Midewi·win, resulted in the prosecution of George Gilbert of the Wabigoon Reserve, Ontario, in 1938" (Pettipas 1994, 157).

3. William Berens, *Memories, Myths, and Dreams of an Ojibwe Leader* (2009), Part II; see also Susan Elaine Gray, *"I Will Fear No Evil": Ojibwa-Missionary Encounters Along the Berens River, 1875–1940* (Calgary: University of Calgary Press, 2006), 26.

4. "The implication is that these were among the old man's guardian spirits. They are noted for the knowledge of medicines which they transmit to those human beings whom they bless." [AIH]

TWENTY

Some Empirical Aspects of
Northern Saulteaux Religion

One of the intrinsic difficulties involved in the presentation of the religions of so-called "primitive" peoples is to make them rationally convincing. Indeed a few decades ago when the theory of evolutionary stages in religious development was in full swing, perhaps no one expected them to be. Primitive religions lay jumbled in an unassorted heap at the bottom of a genetic series topped by the "historic" religions in general and Christianity in particular. Besides, not much could be expected of primitive religions when so little was expected of primitive man. As contrasted with the maturity, logical mentality, and well equilibrated personalities of civilized man, he was often conceived as childlike in character, pre-logical in mentality, and psychotic in personality. Today, however, with the total collapse of unilinear historical reconstructions, with the burden of proof on those who would demonstrate any but minor differences in racial mentality, whether quantitative or qualitative, to say nothing of the body blows which psychoanalytic theories have dealt the assumption of complete rationality in any man, the discussion of religious phenomena, it seems to me, cannot be profitably carried on except in terms applicable to all races, periods, and cultures. What I wish to do is to present the religious philosophy of the Pigeon River Indians as a living reality, as a relatively coherent and self-contained system of beliefs and customs and particularly to indicate in what measure the knowledge and personal experiences of individuals reared in this cultural milieu lend rational support to their religious beliefs and practices.

The Indians I have been studying in the past two summers [1932, 1933] inhabit the environs of the Berens River which rises in western Ontario and flows westward through the province of Manitoba into Lake Winnipeg at an approximate latitude of fifty-two degrees N. In native terminology it is called Omīmīsīpī, Pigeon River.[1] The Pigeon River Indians depend upon hunting and fishing for their living, supplemented by the limited resources which the wild plants of their environment afford. Linguistically they belong to the Ojibwa branch of the far flung Algonkian stock, although locally, in government records and in historical and ethnographic literature, these natives among others, have long received the generic designation Saulteaux, on the assumption that their ancestors were northwestern migrants from an old Ojibwa focal center near Sault Ste. Marie. The Pigeon River people were brought into treaty relations by the Canadian government, along with other Indians on the eastern periphery of Lake Winnipeg, in 1875, and today [1934] they constitute three distinct bands from the administrative point of view. The band farthest up the river, whose reserve is located on Lake Pekangikum, Ontario, at a distance of some 260 miles from the mouth of the river, is known as the Pekangikum band; while approximately midway between the latter and the band at the mouth, known as the Berens River band, is located the [Little] Grand Rapids group. Although the Hudson's Bay Company has had posts on the river for more than a century there were no Christian missionaries among these Indians until 1873. The mission established at this date was at the mouth of the river and while today all the Indians of the Berens River band are members of either the Catholic or Protestant church, Christianization has spread more slowly inland. Two of the three settlements of the Pekangikum band are entirely pagan and the remaining one has only had a native missionary in residence a few years. The Grand Rapids Indians are nominally Christian, but the fact remains that here certain aboriginal ceremony and practices are still actively carried on, which parallel those in the forthrightly pagan groups. I have visited all of the settlements on the river and collected information in regard to the topics discussed from the leaders of the pagans as well as from other individuals of the older generation who today consider themselves Christian.

According to Saulteaux belief the earth is flat. It is also an island, the present form of which is accounted for by reference to a myth in which Wísakedják survives a flood, and through the help of the muskrat who dives for earth, secures a sufficient quantity of it which, magically expanded, provides the familiar theatre of subsequent human activities.[2] The wider reaches of Saulteaux cosmographical conceptions embody the notion of a vertical stratification of "worlds" in which the one known phenomenally is more or less central in position. The daily course of sun and moon is conceived in terms of an orbit around the earth. It is daylight in the world directly beneath this one when it is night in ours and vice versa.

The Saulteaux world proper is also roughly stratified in terms of a hierarchy of powers, which parallel terrestrial, meteorological and celestial phenomena in an ascending series. The Winds and Thunder, e.g., are of a higher order of power and importance than most, if not all, terrestrial phenomena and Kadabéndjiget or K`tchi·mǎ'ni·tu, the "owner" of the world, is both the most remote (highest?) and powerful of all beings. The Saulteaux universe[3] is also quartered through the identification of cardinal points with the Winds. The latter, according to a myth which recounts their birth and characteristic relations to man, are under the control of four brothers.[4]

With this brief sketch of Saulteaux cosmogony and cosmography in mind we may turn to their interpretation of the nature of the universe. Here we find that two fundamental notions are entertained. (1) Everything in the universe is animate. Each phenomenal entity has an animating principle, a soul (òtcatcákwin), and a body (mi·yó). Man has a ghost (djí·bai), as well. This animistic conception is the fundamental dogma in their religious philosophy. (2) To this conception, however must be added a more specific and characteristic notion. For all the various natural entities or classes of entities, as well as certain kinds of human institutions, there exist corresponding spiritual "bosses" or "owners." In regard to animals and plants, e.g., these "owners" (kādɑbenī·míkuwat)[5] are the controllers of the individuals of different species, or what corresponds to this natural grouping, in native terminology. The bears have an "owner," as do the caribou, beavers, otters, etc. Certain giant animals like the great snake, the great beaver, etc., which are thought to inhabit the Saulteaux country even today, although seldom seen, are likewise under the control of the same spiritual entities as their smaller congeners. The "owners" of these natural species are never seen with the naked eye. In regard to the "owners" of other classes of natural phenomena, the four brothers who rule the winds may be cited; the Thunder Bird (pinèsï) who controls Thunder and Lightning, the Great Hare (Misábos), who is the "boss" of seismic phenomena, etc.

With respect to human institutions, it should be noted that those which are believed to have spiritual "owners" are those which require professional leadership for their maintenance and more particularly offer specialized forms of service or information with the layman desires to obtain from time to time (as, e.g., medicinal information, curative treatment, sorcery and magic, clairvoyance, etc). Some of the spiritual owners of institutions are entities associated with these particular institutions alone: midemǎ'ni·tu with the medicine lodge (midéwi·win), wábano mǎ'ni·tu with the wábano dance (wabanówīwin), kadɑbéndɑng with conjuring (djisáki·win or kosábɑndamowin), while others, such as the "owner" of the "skill" by which disease is removed by sucking (ni`bɑkíwin) is identified with the "owner" of the bears, as is pinèsï, the "owner" of the potáte dance, with Thunder and Lighting.

On the same conceptual level with these "bosses" or "owners" of natural phenomena and human institutions there also exist entities to which there are no phenomenal correspondents of the kinds described. Of these entities, the human characters in mythology may be cited as typical. Their very individuation and anthropomorphization in familiar narratives gives them a pseudo-reality which offers a convenient psychological foundation for their projection into the cosmos as contemporary living entities. But the most important independent entity of the entire cosmic scheme, totally divorced from any phenomenal manifestation whatsoever, is kadabéndjiget (or k`tci manitu), the Lord of the Universe, whose power and importance are in inverse ratio to any genuine trace of anthropomorphization.

We are now ready to inquire, what is the relation of the system of beliefs just outlined to the everyday life and habits of the Pigeon River Indians? The authority of tradition, elaborated most specifically in the *mythos* is, of course, the source from which native belief receives its primary sustenance. But it is a mistaken view, I believe, to assume that any body of religious beliefs is transmitted mechanically from generation to generation with nothing save dogmatic assertion and mythology to support it. Even "primitive" man can hardly be saddled with so naïve a faith. It is almost tantamount to the implication that religious beliefs are not taken with sufficient seriousness to make them a subject of reflective thinking and discussion. On the contrary, it may be assumed that any system of beliefs, insofar as it involves an interpretation of the phenomenal world, is recurrently and, in fact, inevitably, subject to challenge on empirical grounds. Granting for the moment that this is the case, how do beliefs react in the crucible of experience? In the case of the Pigeon River Indians, the men, e.g., are expert hunters. Their knowledge of the habits of animals would excite the envy of any naturalist. Their knowledge of the topography of their country is extremely accurate, and they are constantly observing meteorological conditions. A white man unfamiliar with the country might be subject to illusions regarding the identity of some strange object but dimly perceived in the bush, or he might be inclined to misidentify the source of some unfamiliar sound. But the native has spent his life in these surroundings. He has run the gamut of sights and sounds. Moreover, a man subject to delusions and hallucinations would make a poor hunter. His living actually depends upon accurate identifications. Consequently we must reckon with the fact that, although the weight of tradition always conditions the mind of the individual in favor of native belief, yet the daily round of life, the first hand knowledge of celestial, meteorological, physiographic, and biotic phenomena, cannot be dismissed as an unimportant factor in the total situation. Experience and belief must be harmonized if beliefs are to be believed. The Indian is no fool. He employs the same common sense reasoning processes as ourselves, so that if he firmly holds to certain beliefs, we may be sure that they are supported in some degree by an empirical foundation. Thus experience is obviously the crux of religious rationalization. But dogma furnishes the leverage which makes the reconciliation of experience with belief possible. This, indeed, is its sociological function, else a system of beliefs would constantly be subject to disintegration. Since the fundamental assumptions of any religious system are those usually least transparent to its adherents, they are able to retain a relative stability even when the more superficial beliefs of the superstructure are modified. It is in the toils of these implicit underlying tenets that the individual mind is caught. It cannot escape them through the ordinary processes of reasoning because it is uncritical of the assumptions they involve. And unconsciously, much of the experience itself is interpreted in terms of them. Thus it comes about that although experience is consciously recognized by the Indians as a means of verification of beliefs, experience itself is unconsciously interpreted in terms of traditional dogma so that in the end, specific beliefs receive a satisfying empirical support and dogma and experiences are reconciled.

What are the types of experience to which the Saulteaux appeal and how is knowledge derived from these sources interpreted in a manner which supports belief? For the purposes of our discussion three categories of experience have been selected.

1. Direct experience of natural phenomena, including (a) phenomena of the external (public) world as ordinarily perceived by normal individuals and (b) experience of extraordinary or unusual phenomena classified by the Saulteaux with (a) but which depend upon the testimony of a few individuals recounted to other persons.
2. Dreams. Although not usually related to other persons, certain portions of dream experience may be revealed under certain circumstances.
3. Observation of conjuring performances. This is a type of experience publicly shared by a number of persons.

These three categories are all of major importance when viewed from the standpoint of Saulteaux religious philosophy. The same categories would not, of course, receive a similar evaluation from the standpoint of some other system of beliefs, despite the fact that the first two of them are ubiquitous in human experience and the third, which in a more generalized form would include supernormal and psychic phenomena of all kinds, approaches the universal in one form or another. But whereas in Saulteaux culture, e.g., dreams are of central importance in securing direct knowledge of spiritual entities of various classes, in other cultures dreams are subordinated, if recognized at all, as the source of religious knowledge.

1. DIRECT EXPERIENCE OF NATURAL PHENOMENA

The belief that the earth is flat is supported by daily observation and experience. No Indian, in fact, can be convinced that the earth is round. Indeed, I should say that in our culture the prevailing belief that the earth is spherical is a scientific dogma which, so far as the common man is concerned, rests almost entirely upon authority. It by no means receives support in ordinary experience. The Indians are honest, even if naïve, empiricists.

The journey of the sun across the heavens is again a matter of direct observation and the inference that it must pass under the earth to reach the east is reasonable, as well as harmonious with the stratified conception of "worlds." In this case the nature of the scientific proof that the earth moves around the sun is even more remote from ordinary experience than the data which indicate the earth is round.

The Indian idea that the earth is an island, on the other hand, rests on dogma alone. But contacts with the whites have convinced them of the truth of it when they are told that the western hemisphere, in which they live, is surrounded by water.

The belief that Thunder and Lightning are the manifestations of a huge hawk-like bird (pinèsï) may at first sight seem a preposterous idea, without the slightest empirical evidence in its favor. But consider the following facts. In April, when pinèsï first appears, it inevitably comes from the south. This is likewise the month when the birds begin to arrive from the same direction. In the fall, thunderstorms move towards the south at the same time that the birds begin to disappear in this direction, following the Milky Way which stretches across the heavens almost north and south and [is] called the "summer birds' trail." And these birds, like pinèsï, have disappeared by the end of October, are absent all winter and only reappear the following spring.[6]

Here we have a perfectly rational inference made from the common observation of concomitant phenomena—summer birds and thunderstorms. They are not independent variables. They always occur together. Therefore, they are somehow related. Science develops hypotheses on the same rational basis but attempts to check observation by experiment. The question is raised whether concomitant phenomena are truly connected or whether A can, under certain conditions, occur without B and vice versa. But such a critical analysis of observed phenomena is not only a recent but a unique feature of European scientific tradition. The Pigeon River Indians infer that the relationship between birds and thunder, as observed in seasonal behavior, indicates that the animating agency of the latter must also be bird-like in nature. Their fundamental animistic assumption with respect to natural phenomena in general strengthens this analogy.

But the evidence that Thunder is a bird does not rest here. In addition to the authority of tradition, backed by the observation already referred to, there is the corroborative authority of personal testimony to be considered. There is a man now living who, when a boy of twelve years or so, saw pinèsï with his own eyes. During a severe thunderstorm he ran out of his tent and there on the rocks lay a strange bird. He ran back to get his parents, but when they arrived the bird had disappeared. He was sure that it was a pinèsï but his elders were skeptical because it is an almost unheard of thing to see pinèsï in such a fashion. It was not until later when testimony from another source was invoked that the boy's story was believed.

Unusual experiences of this sort also provide evidence for the existence of the giant animals, the Great Snake, the Great Beaver, the Great Lynx, etc.; beasts which were more plentiful in the past, but which still persist in small numbers today. The particular spot where one of these animals was seen is often commemorated in topographical nomenclature, as e.g., Wábamiko baùtik, White Beaver Rapids, Mi·cí·pi·jiu baùtik, Great Lynx rapids. And in folklore we have episodes, or even whole stories, which account for the disappearance of these giant creatures from the earth. Interestingly enough, it is not only the lone hunter who sometimes catches sight of these great beasts even today. Several individuals in the same party may see them. My interpreter [William Berens], e.g., and his two sons once saw the Great Snake. Multiple testimony of this sort is hard to contradict.

As among all unlettered peoples, first hand testimony in regard to observed "fact" ranks extremely high among these Indians, just as a generation or so ago many reputable captains helped to support the belief in the existence of Great Sea Serpents by their personal testimony. Oral testimony among the Saulteaux, in fact, parallels the exaggerated emphasis upon the authority of the written word among us as represented, e.g., in newspaper reports, "true story" magazines, etc. Unless a man, by general reputation belongs to the tall-story club, it is difficult to call him a liar. And the fact that so few persons in all have seen these great animals, gives the accounts of those who have far greater influence. Furthermore, a man who described a creature of his *own* imagination would be subject to ridicule. Only the animals which are known in tradition and mythology are seen. There can be discerned, in consequence, an extremely close correlation between personal experience and traditional beliefs.

As an extreme example of this kind of experience which, although judged to be extraordinary, is nevertheless accepted as fact, is the adventure of a boy who was befriended by the Great Trout.[7]

> This young man paddled eight or nine miles out to an island in God's Lake to collect some birds' eggs. While he was gathering the eggs his canoe got loose and drifted away. He remained on the island several days with very little food. As he was sitting on the shore one day he heard someone say "Nózis ([my] Grandson), come down here". The voice came from the water. So he went down to the water and there he saw the Great Trout. "Get in under my fin," the Fish said. So the boy did this. It was as comfortable there as if he were in a wigwam.

The story goes on to tell about the great distances which the boy traveled with the Fish, how the Trout obtained any kind of fish the boy wished to eat, and finally, how the Great Trout took him back to the island where later the boy's father found him.

From an objective point of view this story is indistinguishable in spirit and content from dream experiences or mythology. There is in fact a well known myth in which the hero, Tcɑkábec, is swallowed by a great fish.[8] Nevertheless the Indians classify it as tɑbätcɑmoin, which carries the meaning of news or tidings, as contrasted with ätsokan, the traditional formalized narratives of mythology. It is a "true" story then, and not myth. And it demonstrates the extremely close relationship which exists between reputed personal experience and the *mythos*. It likewise emphasizes the unitary character of the empirical universe as it must appear to the natives themselves.[9]

Lest we credit the Indian with excessive naïveté I cannot resist drawing the parallel here to the literal belief in Jonah's experience, dear to the hearts of many Christian believers. And still closer to the contemporary period there are the experiences of Swedenborg, who it will be recalled, attended the Last Judgment in the year 1757 and remarked, "to all this I can testify, because I saw it with my own eyes *in a state of full wakefulness*" (italics our own).

The subtle interrelations of belief and personal experience are not confined, of course, to this pseudo-mythological level. The following experience of an encounter with a bear, related to me by Wigwaswátik [Birchstick], chief of the Pekangikum band, shows how the notion that bears understand human speech received empirical support.

> One spring when I was out hunting I went up a little creek where I knew suckers were spawning. Before I came to the rapids I saw fresh bear tracks. I walked along the edge of the creek and when I reached the rapids I saw a bear coming towards me, along the same trail I was following. I stepped behind a tree and when the animal was about thirty yards from me I fired. I missed and before I could reload the bear made straight for me. He seemed mad, so I never moved. I just waited there by the tree. As soon as he came close to me and rose up on his hind feet, I put the butt end of my gun against his heart and held him there. I remembered what my father used to tell me when I was a boy. He said that a bear always understands what you tell him. The bear began to bite the stock of the gun. He even put his paws upon it something like a man would do if he were going to shoot. Still holding him off as well as I could I said to the bear, "If you want to live, go away," and he let go the gun and walked off. I didn't bother the bear anymore.

This anecdote illustrates how the generalized belief that bears understand what is said to them, emphasized in childhood by the narrator's father, influenced his behavior in a specific situation. It is a striking illustration because the narrator expressly refers to the influence of the belief upon his behavior. In other cases it would be more difficult to trace the precise influences at work. The repeated narration of personal experiences of this nature, and hunting experiences of all kinds are favorite subjects of conversation, indicates the matrix in which beliefs are disseminated and kept flourishing from generation to generation. And on what grounds, in view of such personal testimony can such a belief as the one cited be denied? The bear undoubtedly acted *as if* he understood what the hunter said and the inference that the spoken words were the efficient cause of this behavior was a rational interpretation. A sequence of events, that is to say, was judged to be a cause-effect relationship.

2. DREAMS

It is now time to return again for a moment to the Thunder Bird. As I pointed out, the Indians were skeptical of the personal testimony of the boy who claimed to have seen pinèsï. But the matter was clinched when a man who had *dreamed* of pinèsï verified the boy's description. This leads us to the second category of Saulteaux experience, one that is of paramount importance to them and characteristic of their religious culture. These Indians believe that they obtain direct personal knowledge of the spiritual entities of the cosmos, e.g., the "bosses" or "owners" of the phenomenal world, as well as other beings, through dreams.[10] Consequently dreams cannot be overemphasized as an empirical source of evidence in respect to the real existence of the genii of the cosmos, which on account of the importance of this avenue of knowledge are generically referred to as pawáganak, i.e., dream visitors.[11] Moreover, it is a dogma that most of these pawáganak are *only* seen in dreams (although, as we shall see later, they may be *heard* under certain special conditions). This is why the testimony of the man who *dreamed* of pinèsï was needed to verify the account of the boy who had *seen* pinèsï, instead of the other way about.

Dreaming is institutionalized in the puberty fast for boys, at which time the pawáganak (i.e., dream visitors who function as guardian spirits or protectors) are obtained which serve an individual throughout the rest of his life. A man would be practically helpless without them, particularly if he aspires to leadership in certain ceremonies, conjuring, curing, or to special prowess in hunting. But all men do not dream of all pawáganak, nor is it customary for a man to speak of his protectors to others or to narrate his dreams. If he does, his pawáganak may desert him. Thus while the acquisition of guardian spirits is democratic, there is, at the same time, an esoteric aspect to dream knowledge. Consequently it is next to impossible to obtain satisfactory data in regard to the details of dream experiences, or an adequate sampling of such experiences from a large series of individuals. But such data as I have obtained, although chiefly from one individual, is strikingly similar in character to myth. The following dream experience from another source is also myth-like. In general pattern it closely resembles the "true" story of the boy and the Fish. Attention may also be called to the fact that in this case and, as I understand the matter, in general, the spiritual "bosses" of natural phenomena, such as animals, for instance do not by any means assume the form of their earthly underlings in dreams.

When I was a boy I went out to an island to fast. For several nights I dreamed of an ógimă (chief, superior person, gentleman). Finally one night he said, "Nózis ([my] Grandson), I think you are now ready to go with me." Then ógimă began dancing around me as I sat there on a rock and when I happened to glance down at my body, I noticed that I had grown feathers. Soon I felt just like a bird, a kīnīu (golden eagle). Ógimă had turned into a bird also and off he flew towards the south. I spread my wings and flew after him in the same direction. After a while we arrived in a place where there were lots of tents and lots of people. We stayed there all winter. It was the home of the summer birds. I shot lots and lots of birds there; ducks, geese, and many other kinds. In the spring when the birds started to fly north, ógimă came too and guided me to the island from which we had set out. "Your relatives must wonder where you are," he said. "Do not be afraid. Remain here a day or two and your father will come for you and take you to your home. Any time that you want me, just mention my name and I will help you." The next day my father did come to the island. I knew that he was glad to see me again but he asked me no questions. I went home with him.

The ógimă of this dream was of course, the "boss" of the golden eagles, an extremely powerful pawágan. It is through dreams such as this that the individual becomes directly acquainted with the entities which he believes to be the active agencies of the universe about him. But he only sees them with the eyes of the "soul," not with the eyes of the body. To him, moreover, these spiritual entities of the cosmos represent a continuum with the ordinary world of sense perception. They are an integral part of reality and are not super-natural beings in any strict sense of the term. It is true that their powers are of a higher order than the entities they control such as the plants and animals or man himself, for that matter. But this is just the reason man requires their help. If a man wishes to hunt caribou or trap beaver, his gun and traps are not sufficient as means to this end. He must be in favor with the "boss" caribou and "boss" beaver. This does not mean that he must have them as spiritual protectors, although this is highly desirable. But negatively it means that he must not offend them and positively it requires that he treat the bones of the animals he shoots or traps, or the carcass, if it is a fur bearing animal the flesh of which is not eaten, in a respectful manner. If a man does have the bosses of the game or fur bearing animals as his pawáganak, they will, of course, constantly help him by sending their earthly congeners to his traps. Sometimes they will also offer him specific guidance in dreams. The following dream was narrated to me by a Christian Indian [William Berens]. Nevertheless, it illustrates concretely the nature of this dream guidance and it also shows how a dream of this sort is tested objectively.

> Once when I was out hunting I was discouraged. I had no luck at all. And I kept worrying all the time about my "debt." One night after I had finished making the rounds of my traps I lay down for a bit while my son was chopping wood. I fell fast asleep. I dreamed of a long trail running north. I was traveling on it. Then I saw a girl coming towards me. She was very pretty and dressed in white. She moved along as if she were skating, with very graceful motions. Then I saw another girl, closer to me, who was setting a table with lots of good things to eat. I started off towards the girls and first I came to the one who was setting the table. "This is all for you," she said. Then I woke up. Almost before I realized it I grabbed my hat and started off to visit a deadfall straight north of our camp.[12] It was about fifteen minutes walk and I began to think that it was rather foolish of me to go to this trap since I had set so many steel traps on my line. But I kept on and when I got there I found a fine fisher in the deadfall. It was a female. Then I knew what my dream meant.[13]

The comment that the narrator made when he had fished this anecdote is significant. He said, "If I had been a pagan I would have made a feast then and there and smoked to the 'boss' fisher." At any rate this Indian got his fisher[14] and we have a dream-story which conforms to the old aboriginal pattern. And of course he actually believed that the "boss" fisher had sent him the animal, even though his Christian conscience inhibited the overt ceremonial behavior which he would not have ventured to omit had he been a pagan.

To the Indians, then, the connection between hunting luck and spiritual controllers of the game which they pursue is perfectly plain. Everyone possesses practically the same knowledge of animal habits, everyone uses essentially the same kind of traps, and the fur bearing animals are more or less evenly distributed throughout the country. Why then should one man make an extremely good catch and another hunter find his traps empty? The answer is clear. The successful hunter has received the help and guidance of the animal "owners," the unsuccessful hunter has not. Something has gone wrong. Perhaps he has weak pawáganak. Perhaps he has failed to honor the "boss" of some animal, as my friend failed to do. Or perhaps he is just a poor hunter in a thoroughly objective sense. As I have previously pointed out the Indian is a practical man, regardless of what he may believe, so that he does not expect the animals to drop from the sky without effort on his part. But the differential in hunting luck, the departure from the mean, demands explanation. And the terms of this explanation are those of his basic beliefs.

Similarly, the Indian who becomes a conjurer, exercises mediumistic powers of clairvoyance and pre-cognition by virtue of the fact that in youth he has been "blessed" by certain kinds of pawáganak. These abilities are not interpreted as congenital traits of his personality, nor is it believed that they are learned in some conventional way, since there is no ostensible social mechanism for their transmission. These powers are mediated directly to the conjurer through dreams and are dependent upon the active help of his guardian spirits. In fact, if he abuses these powers his pawáganak may leave him and then his career as a professional conjurer is finished. Besides, men who have tried to develop similar manifestations without dreaming have failed to make good. Such cases, and there have been quite a few of them in recent years, obviously lend support to the dream origin of mediumistic powers.

Thus dreams are not only a direct means by which the individual can obtain knowledge of the unseen powers that surround him, but the overt behavior and the experiences of other persons, even if an account of their dreams as such is withheld, give further empirical support in behalf of the nature of dream revelation, as well as to the more fundamental dogmas regarding the cosmographical scheme.

3. THE CONJURING TENT

Finally, there is a third source of experience open to everyone which, through auditory channels, brings man into direct contact with a large range of pawáganak. This is the institution of conjuring (kosábandamowin or djisáki·win). From the standpoint of the means employed to obtain the manifestations observed, this institution may be characterized as "mediumistic," to borrow a term standardized in modern psychical research. In the presence of the conjurer, who is concealed within a small structure built of poles driven deep into the ground and covered with birchbark or canvas, various pawáganak manifest themselves. The structure is violently shaken by the controllers of the winds, and in fact, to a greater or less degree, this agitation continues throughout a performance which may last hours on end. One of the exhibitions I witnessed, e.g., continued for three hours. Voices of different pawáganak issued from the tent, songs were sung by them, the

"Boss" Turtle (Miki·nă´k) carried on a humorous repartee with members of the audience and Wemti·gózi[15] offered a prize of "spirit" tobacco to the Indian who could repeat his song correctly. This "tobacco" is not the commercial variety and is considered to be extremely mysterious in origin as well as empirical proof of the transcendent reality of Wemti·gózi.

From an objective standpoint we might characterize such a performance as the dramatic vocalization of the pawáganak. They sing songs peculiar to themselves, and Miki·nă´k, in the performance I saw, was characterized by a very distinctive vocal peculiarity. A conjuring performance is somewhat like visiting a "spiritual" zoo where one *hears* the "boss" animals—the moose, the caribou, the beaver, the porcupine, the sturgeon, etc., but does not see them. Mythological characters also manifest themselves. Theoretically, any of the spiritual entities of the cosmos, with one exception, may enter the conjuring tent. But since no conjurer has precisely the same helpers, although there is a nuclear group present in all performances, there is variety in the manifestations observable in the presence of different men. The spiritual "owner" of the institution itself (Kadabéndang), who is euphemistically called "the one that takes them out" (Ozági·zi·ì·we), is always present, as are Miki·nă´k, the Boss Snapping Turtle, and one or more of the Winds.

From the native point of view such performances are not primarily "mediumistic" demonstrations or entertainment, although I think it cannot be denied that these ends are incidentally served. The "real" purpose of conjuring is to obtain information in regard to persons or events at a distance, to recover lost or stolen articles, and formerly, if not now, to detect the sources of witchcraft, usually on the part of a sorcerer in another settlement. Empirically then, belief in the reality of pawáganak is not only based upon auditory perception, it depends upon the outcome of events. If the lost article is found, if the information regarding an absent person proves true, if pre-cognitions are subsequently verified, if the bewitched person recovers, there is no room for skepticism. In this way conjuring often offers startling evidence in support of fundamental beliefs. In the performance [I] witnessed three of the inquiries made were as follows:

I sought information in respect to the health of my father who was ill at the time. I was informed, after Miki·nă'k had been sent to Philadelphia, that my father was no worse. This was correct.

An Indian inquired about the condition of his brother who had been convicted of a minor offense some months before and was in jail several hundred miles away. The information given was to the effect that this man would be seen very soon. We met him on his way up the river a few days later.

Another Indian, who had left the mouth of the river a few days before, just when his brother was stricken with pneumonia, wanted to know how his brother was. The answer was that the man was better and would recover. When we arrived at the mouth of the river a week later, he was walking about.

The conjuring institution must be recognized, therefore, as one of the most important empirical sources which sustain belief. Even though there are relatively few *bona fide* conjurers on the river today and Christianity is spreading even to the outright pagan groups, all the Indians retain a firm belief in the authenticity of this institution. And why not? In our culture fortune telling and particularly spiritualism, supported in principle by the same sort of empirical evidence, are parallel phenomena which are anything but moribund.

There is one spiritual entity, however, which neither manifests itself in the conjuring tent, appears to man in dreams, nor has even been seen by the waking eyes of any human being. This is Kadabéndjiget or K'tchi·mă΄ni·tu, the supreme power in the universe. Perhaps the best English equivalent to the native term is Lord. Even from the standpoint of Saulteaux religious philosophy this spiritual entity is purely conceptual. Kadabéndjiget is not specifically anthropomorphized in respect to bodily form or sex, nor is there any trace of iconographic representation. Yet by implication this power possesses the faculties of sentience, omnipotence and presumably omniscience. Kadabéndjiget is the Creator and Ruler of all things, if I have fathomed the native mind sufficiently. In terms of the religious system itself, in short, he is the Boss of Bosses, the Owner of the Owners. And since the notion that everything has its boss is so fundamental to their beliefs, Kadabéndjiget is a logical necessity, if not logically prior in their whole scheme. Yet because the name of this supreme power is so seldom mentioned—I mean because of a positive tabu, which implies respect and veneration—the casual inquirer might mistakenly characterize this religious system as polytheistic. In my opinion this notion of a High God is indubitably aboriginal. And one intrinsic bit of evidence may be offered here. This is the modesty of knowledge which the Indians exhibit in respect to the positive characteristics of the Great Boss. If their concept was due to missionary influence I doubt whether this would be true. For Christians—and particularly missionaries—claim a much more intimate and positive knowledge of their Deity than any Pigeon River Indian. In this the natives remain more consistent empiricists. No one knows just what Kadabéndjiget is like because no human being has ever had sensible experience of "him," even in dreams.

In conclusion we may say that, while from our point of view the body of religious tradition of these Pigeon River Indians is the primary conditioning factor in the beliefs of successive generations of individuals, and that in this sense their beliefs are but the impingement upon human minds of an arbitrary pattern, the result of historical circumstance, yet in the experience of the believers themselves, the events of daily life and reflective thought offer recurrent proof of the objective truth of their beliefs. It is also apparent that the mental processes involved in this reconciliation of experience with belief are those of normal human reasoning, even though we may grant that this rationalization is naively applied. Yet even in this they are but following the mental procedure of common men. For how else may the truth of religion be demonstrated or belief upheld?

Notes

Read at the November, 1933, meeting of the Oriental Club of Philadelphia. Published in *American Anthropologist* 36(3) (1934): 389–404.

1. Referring to the once plentiful, but now extinct passenger pigeon (Ectopistes Migratorius). Berens was the surname of a Hudson's Bay Co. official for whom the river was renamed a century ago.

2. [Ed. note: William Berens in 1933 told Hallowell the myth of "Wísakedják and the Water Lions." See Berens, *Memories, Myths, and Dreams of an Ojibwe Leader* (2009), Part IV].

3. Here used synonymously with world.

4. [Ed. note: See William Berens's telling of "The Birth of the Winds, Flint and the Great Hare" in Berens, *Memories, Myths, and Dreams*, Part IV.]

5. A generic term applicable to the "owner" of any animal or plant species.

6. The consultation of a bird calendar compiled from the records of the Ornithological Secretary of the Natural History Society of Manitoba, showing the usual times of occurrence of 69 species in the vicinity of Winnipeg, indicates that the species wintering in the south begin to appear at this latitude in April and disappear for the most part not later than October. Comparison with meteorological observations, also taken in Winnipeg (Canada Year Book 1927–28, 59) shows that the average number of days

with thunder per month begins with one in April, increases almost arithmetically to a total of five in mid-summer (July) and then declines to one in October. Although these data are based on observations almost 200 miles south of the Berens River it is a striking objective corroboration of the correlation noticed by the Pigeon River Indians and I have no doubt that it would hold if similarly unbiased data were compiled at some point in their habitat.

7. [Ed. note: See Berens, *Memories, Myths, and Dreams*, Part III.]

8. [Ed. note: See APS, Hallowell Papers, Series V, Saulteaux Indians, Myths and Tales, files 20, 25; Berens, *Memories, Myths, and Dreams*, Part IV; Louis Bird and Susan Elaine Gray, *The Spirit Lives in the Mind: Omushkego Stories, Lives, and Dreams* (Montreal: McGill-Queen's University Press, 2007), 23–36.]

9. [Ed. note: For detailed discussion on these distinctions see Berens, *Memories, Myths, and Dreams*, Parts III and IV.]

10. Not all dreams, it may be noted in passing. But for the purposes of our discussion it is unnecessary to go into the details of this question.

11. More literally "that which is dreamed"(pawágan); ak=plural.

12. This deadfall was not in his regular trap line. He had made it near the camp in a spare moment.

13. [Ed. note: See also Berens, *Memories, Myths, and Dreams*, Part III.]

14. Worth $85 at the time.

15. A mythological character translated into English as "white man," although this is not the etymology of the word.

TWENTY-ONE

The Passing of the Midéwi·win
in the Lake Winnipeg Region

This study is a postmortem record of a ceremony which once was of major importance in the native culture of the Saulteaux[1] Indians of the Lake Winnipeg country. So far as I have been able to discover, through direct personal inquiry where possible and likewise by hearsay, the Midéwi·win is no longer being held at any of the localities discussed below and which are indicated on the map.[2] Undoubtedly a great deal of valuable information could still be obtained, however, by making inquiries on the spot, at places which I have never visited.[3] Most of the information recorded below was obtained more or less incidentally to an ethnological study of the Berens River Saulteaux: the detailed account of the Midéwi·win of the Indians of this river will be published elsewhere. But Chief William Berens, my interpreter and mentor during the course of my inquiries, proved to be such a spontaneous and reliable source of information in regard to all events and personalities during his lifetime,[4] and even before, that I felt impelled to record as much as I was able, of what he told me. Owing to family connections which will be brought out later, to an active life of varied occupations, which brought him into contact with Indians in one end of Lake Winnipeg to the other, as well as with the inland peoples to the east, and owing above all to an exceedingly alert mind and a fine memory, I consider the facts obtained from him to be as reliable as any such information can humanly be. I have attempted to correlate the oral information obtained from him, as well as from a few other informants, with the data extant in documentary sources in order to place on record (a) the places where the Midéwi·win was formerly held, (b) the approximate dates (whenever possible) when it was discontinued, (c) the names of headmen and such anecdotes about them as seem pertinent to the subject, and (d) facts concerning the connection between different localities, especially where these concern personnel in leadership.

So far as our information goes, the Midéwi·win or Grand Medicine

Lodge, as it is sometimes known, was confined to certain Algonkian and Siouan-speaking peoples: the central Algonkians in particular, Siouan tribes immediately in contact with these, and other Siouan tribes in contact with the latter. There are some indications that the ceremony was, in origin, an Algonkian rather than a Siouan institution[5] and the suggestion has been advanced more than once that among Algonkian peoples the Ojibwa may have represented the hearth from which it was originally spread.[6] If this be taken as an historical hypothesis, and to it be added the idea that it is not a ceremony of great antiquity, the provenience of the Midéwi·win in the nineteenth century, when we first have real knowledge of it, is fairly intelligible. From both earlier and later records we know that the extreme northeastern Algonkians (Montagnais-Naskapi) did not have it, nor the Wabanaki peoples of northern New England nor the Algonkians of the middle Atlantic States. Where it has been reported for the Cree[7] it is most likely a late acquisition, presumably from some Ojibwa group, but Skinner's assertion[8] that "the rite extended northward almost to the shores of Hudson Bay" is not borne out either by the intrinsic evidence offered in that author's "Eastern Cree and Northern Saulteaux"[9] or the later ethnographic work of J. M. Cooper in this region. Likewise, the absence of the Midéwi·win among the plains Algonkian (Blackfoot, Arapaho, Cheyenne) would make it appear that the ceremony must have had its rise and spread after these peoples had become detached from the main stock. Unfortunately the relative contemporaneity of all our records offers little, if any, opportunity for establishing chronological developments or even directions of spread in any detail. All that we can do is to infer for the most part that the Midéwi·win must have been spread by the movements of the peoples with whom in recent times we know it to have been associated most intimately or to have been borrowed, in certain cases, by peoples who came in contact with those who had it.

In the case of the Ojibwa speaking peoples it would appear that their northwestward expansion from the region of the Great Lakes carried the Midéwi·win into regions where it had been previously unknown. Its maximum distribution subsequently, if we could plot it, would be a direct reflection of this migratory movement. It will be unnecessary, of course, to review here the evidence for this expansion of the Ojibwa. That they were intruders in the Red River valley and farther west is referred to again and again by various classes of writers. Begg, for example, with the former region in mind, says that the Cree considered the Saulteaux as having encroached upon their territory, an instance of which was given when Lord Selkirk, in making his treaty with the Indians, committed the mistake of placing the Saulteaux first on the list. As will be remembered, the Crees were bitterly indignant at this and threatened not only to break the treaty, but also to demand back their lands, thus causing the Scotch settlers much anxiety, lest their farms should be taken from them by the savages.[10]

Since the date of Lord Selkirk's treaty was 1817, the movement from the east must have taken place much earlier. Both the diary of the younger [Alexander] Henry and [John] Tanner's account of his early life offer substantial testimony, at the very beginning of the nineteenth century, for the presence of Saulteaux in the Red River valley and in certain portions of the country west of it.[11] But just how early in the preceding century this westward movement of the Ojibwa began it is hard to say, since this country was totally unknown to white men before the explorations of La Verendrye, which did not begin until the fourth decade of the eighteenth century,[12] and documentary sources are almost nonexistent until much later in the same century. We do know positively, however, that Ojibwa speaking peoples had spread far beyond Lake Winnipeg by the end of the eighteenth century and that by 1794 some of them were to be found near the Pas and a considerable distance up the Saskatchewan River.[13]

Today there are a number of Saulteaux bands in the province of Saskatchewan which are often called "Plains Ojibwa," although the districts they inhabit are part of the "bluff" country intermediate between the wooded areas and the true prairie. The Sun Dance has become their major ceremony, but it is not unlikely that the Midéwi·win was formerly held by some, if not all, of these groups before they absorbed so much Plains culture. It is a problem which deserves inquiry and I have a single scrap of positive evidence which is perhaps worth recording here.

In the summer of 1931 when visiting the Fishing Lake Reserve (Indian Reserve 89, Saskatchewan) I was told[14] that the Midéwi·win had actually been performed there in the past. The last leader was mekwégi·zik, "amidst the sky," who died about 1919. He was the father-in-law of my informant. I also had an amusing personal experience on this Reserve which may be offered as evidence supporting the contention that the Midéwi·win was probably known, although I made no systematic inquiries.

Earlier in the summer I had obtained a few medicine bags and some other articles at Wanipigow River on Lake Winnipeg. I had these in my luggage and one day, while sitting in a tipi, some mention was made of the

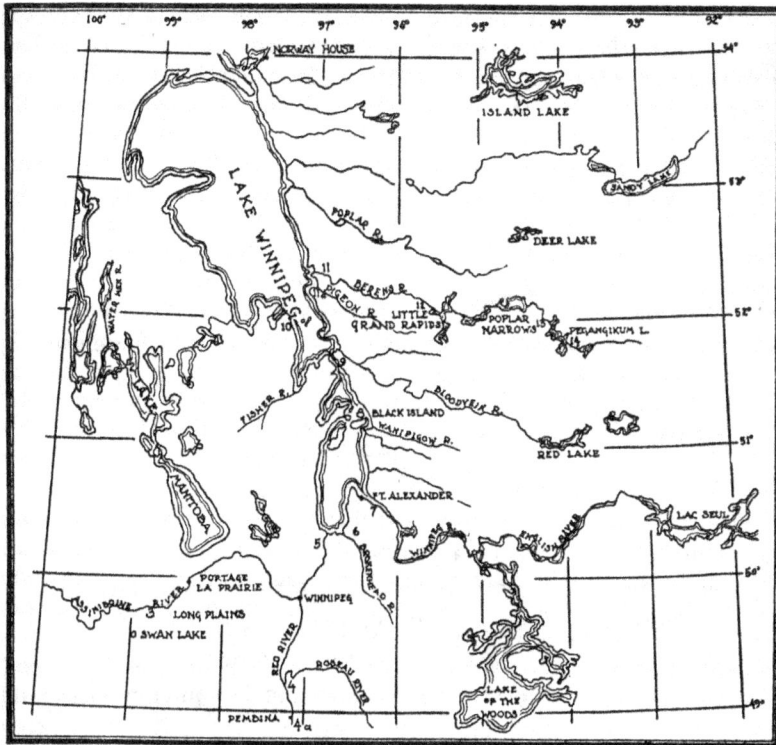

2. Lake Winnipeg Region

Midéwi·win and I casually remarked that I would bring one of the bags along with me the next day to show them. The words had no sooner left my lips than one of the older women present rose instantly to her feet and with considerable agitation pointed her finger at me and said, "Don't you bring that thing in here." And with that she left the tent. Later I did show a couple of the old men the bags, but at the farm house where I was staying. The old woman's behavior, however, seemed to me a sufficiently objective demonstration that the magical function of those articles was understood, even though the ceremony itself was extinct. I might as well have remarked that I planned to a loaded gun with a hair trigger into her tipi.

Returning now to the province of Manitoba and the Lake Winnipeg region, I will review the data I have been able to collect concerning the former occurrence of the Midéwi·win at various points, starting with the district west of Lake Winnipeg, then moving south of it, next proceeding up the eastern shore and finally ascending the Berens River to Lake Pekangikum, which is in Ontario.

1. In Manitoba, at some point west of the lake of the same name, there is casual mention by Tanner[15] that, in the spring, the Indians with whom he was staying at the time were "collected for the solemn ceremony of the meta or medicine dance, in which Net-no-kwa always bore a very conspicuous part."[16] From Tanner's subsequent reference[17] to descending the "Little Saskawjewun" as he started off for the Red River, as well as his previous peregrinations, it is at least plain that he had been hunting somewhere west of Lake Manitoba and probably south of the Riding Mountains. After returning from Red River he speaks of the "Naowaw-gunwudju, the hill of the buffaloe chase near the Saskawjewun" which can hardly refer to other than the Riding Mountains[18] and he further states that he did not follow the Indians to "Clear Water Lake," which is probably the present day Clear Lake. Broadly speaking then, Tanner had been living somewhere in the upper reaches of what is now called the Minnedosa River,[19] and it was here that the Indians must have held the Midéwi·win referred to. The period was the early nineteenth century (1801–1806) as we know from the contemporary events and persons referred to by both Henry and Tanner.[20] Furthermore, there was a small band of Riding Mountain Saulteaux which were included in Treaty No. 2 (1871). The name of their representative who signed it was "Mekis, the Eagle, or Giroux"[21] (migazï—bald-headed eagle).

2. In respect to what must have been formerly the territory of the Waterhen[22] and Crane River Saulteaux, who also were signers of the same treaty through their representative Broken Fingers or François,[23] I received oral information[24] that the Midéwi·win was formerly held on Garden Island[25] in northern Lake Manitoba. The last head man there was ăgásgogat, Arrow Legs,[26] who died before the treaty was signed. Years before, when a middle-aged man, he had said, "As long as I can lift my drum stick I shall not die." He revealed the fact that he had been told this by wísakedják[27] who was one of his strongest guardian spirits.[28] Like wísakedják, Arrow Legs constantly wore a woodchuck (aká 'kotci·s) skin bound around his head,[29] undoubtedly a command of this spiritual helper. People testified that they had seen Arrow Legs walk upon the water. On one occasion when the old man could be plainly seen ap-

proaching the shore, his son sneaked down to the point where he believed his father would reach the land. Arrow Legs, however, observed the young man, and at once began to sink into the water, but he managed to reach the shore. He chided his son for his impetuous curiosity. All the other observers were said to have remained at a discreet distance. In addition to being a great midé, Arrow Legs had obtained medical knowledge through a dream blessing.[30] He was mänáo.

3. South of Lake Manitoba, at the Long Plains Reserve (I. R. 6),[31] Skinner gathered some meager information on the Midéwi·win in 1913, at which time it was apparently a going concern. He also obtained some of the bark records used.[32] In 1925 Cadzow visited the same reserve and also Swan Lake to the southwest. He obtained more information and bark records and stated that the Dominion Government had forbidden the ceremony.[33]

4. South of the Forks[34] or Grand Fork of early writers, the site of the present city of Winnipeg, we know from Henry's diary that the Midéwi·win was being regularly held by the Saulteaux of this region at the beginning of the nineteenth century. In May, 1801, Henry was in process of establishing a fur trading post near the junction of the Pembina and Red Rivers.[35] On one of his trips to the "Forks" he camped at the mouth of Roseau River,[36] where on May 18, he "found the Indians busy making the grand medicine—a ceremony performed every spring, when they meet and there is some novice to be admitted into the mysteries of this solemn affair."[37] The following spring (May 20) Henry reports that the Indians were "performing their grand medicine, as usual"[38] and a similar entry is of May 23, 1803.[39] Since Henry is established by this time at Pembina one might suppose that the Midéwi·win was being held there, but, on the other hand, he may simply be referring to the ceremony without detailed reference to locale since he was trading with the Indians within a considerable radius and since the point referred to above was about fifteen miles to the north. At any rate, the information provided by Henry demonstrates the annual periodicity of the ceremony and the season of the year at which it was customarily held, even though more intimate details are lacking. Of course, it cannot be denied that it may have been held near Pembina too, at one time or another, but it seems unlikely that there would have been two of these ceremonies performed annually at points relatively so close to one another.

At a later date there is a bit of evidence that the Midéwi·win was being held some twenty miles up the Roseau River. Hind's party[40] made an attempt to attain the upper reaches of this river, but gave it up, because they were improperly equipped. For some twenty miles upstream the river is said to wind a tortuous course through prairie country. Then at a point called by Hind the "crossing place" and beyond for some distance, the banks rise fifty to fifty-five feet above the level of the river, and farther on the country changes to reedy flooded swamps. The point at which this change in topography occurs is identified as the rim of an old lake (Agassiz). Coming back they did not return to the mouth, but evidently cut across the prairie to the "Forks," diverging from the river at the "crossing place." Here it was that they observed the "skeletons" of dwellings, sweat lodges, and the "framework of a large medicine wigwam [which] measured twenty-five feet in length by fifteen feet in breadth." I suspect that this must have been a structure built the previous spring for the Midéwi·win. If it were, this identifies another point at which the ceremony was once held. A portion of the reserve belonging to the Roseau River Saulteaux of the present day is located at approximately this point. From still later sources we know that the Indians of the Roseau River Reserve remained outright pagans until the beginning of the present century[41] and even in 1934 only ninety-one individuals out of a total of 206 in the band were reported Christians.[42] Whether the Midéwi·win has been held here within recent years I do not know.

5. On the lower Red River,[43] after Lord Selkirk had established his colony (1811–12) the pure-blooded Indians, both Cree and Saulteaux, tended to congregate between St. Andrews Rapids[44] and Lake Winnipeg, although even prior to this period there is evidence that this point was an old rendezvous of Indians and traders.[45] It was in this district that the missionaries first began to labor when they actually went beyond the borders of the colony proper.[46] It was chiefly in the neighborhood of Netley Creek[47] that the Saulteaux of lower Red River periodically gathered in the spring and remained until autumn when they dispersed to their hunting grounds. It was here that the famous Pegwis [Peguis] made his headquarters, and in May 1832 when the Rev. Cockran paid a visit to the Indians encamped here, he was shocked to find that they were performing a heathen ceremony. Even from the meager description evidently paraphrased from Cockran's journal by Sarah Tucker,[48] it can hardly have been other than a Midéwi·win.

He found a large tent had been pitched, and was directed to the east end, where the chief was sitting, fanning himself with the skin of a muskrat. Pieces of riband and cloth were hanging all round the tent, the offerings of these poor people to the conjurer. . . . There were as many as 150 men, women and children crowded together in the tent, the top of which was open, and admitted the rays of a cloudless sun; and here the whole party was engaged in dancing, shouting, singing, and drumming, shaking their rattles, and running round and round the tent.

That this ceremony was likewise in full swing three decades later is evidenced by the remarks of Hargrave,[49] who did not come out to the colony until 1861 and wrote of contemporary events subsequent to this date. He refers to the "dog feasts" held each autumn [*sic*] near Lower Fort Garry in "an enclosure about forty feet long by twenty-five feet broad, fenced in with the branches of trees." This structure was oriented east and west and had two doors facing these directions.

The ceremony occupies two or three days, during which the ground in the interior of the enclosure is crowded with the savages, who sit along side each other drawn up close inside the fence. In a line running lengthways through the center are erected perpendicular poles with large stones at their bases, both stones and poles coloured red over different portions of their surfaces with the blood of the dog sacrifice. The animals are selected and killed, and after lying exposed on the stones beside the posts during the performance of certain ceremonies by the "medicine man," whose "medicine bags" composed of the entire skins of wild animals, form an important feature of the ceremony, are cooked and eaten by the company. The dog meat when prepared presents a very uncouth and repulsive appearance, as it is borne from man to man, in shapeless tin trenchers, that each may select the portion he means to devour.

Hargrave comments that it appears that the object of the affair is to eat dogs, but then he adds that a resident informed him that the natives were "assembled for what in their eyes is the celebration of a solemn act of communion with spirits."

Despite the inadequacy of Hargrave's account and the probable inaccuracy of certain statements, the ceremony he refers to must be the Midéwi·win.

In 1871 Red Eagle, miskógi·ni·u,[50] son of Pegwis (pi·gwaí·s) was one of the signers of Treaty No. 1 or the "Stone Fort"[51] Treaty, and these Saulteaux (along with some Cree) of lower Red River became known as the St. Peters band[52] and were domiciled upon a reserve seven miles square, located twenty-two miles north of Winnipeg, adjoining the town of Selkirk. Even as early as 1875 they were characterized in the report[53] of the Deputy Superintendent of Indian affairs as "the best settled and most progressive of all the Bands which have been a party to Treaty No. 1." In 1907 they surrendered their lands on Red River and were transferred to a reserve on Fisher River which was named after their famous chief.[54] No Midéwi·win has ever been held on the latter reserve and the last one held at St. Peters was probably not held much after the 1870s. Two brothers were probably the last leaders, äsini·bon and djakógwaiyo, short neck. The former was the father of sagatcí·weäs [Peter Stoney] who later became the chief of the "Island bands" and the leader of the Midéwi·win given at Dog Head. This man is no longer alive but his sister's daughter is the oldest woman of the Berens River band today [1936].

6. In contrast with the "progressive" character of the St. Peters band, the Saulteaux formerly known as the "heathen" or Fort Garry band[55] became domiciled after Treaty No. 1 on Broken Head River[56] (I. R. 4), a tributary of Lake Winnipeg east of Red River. They remained pagans for many years. In respect to the performance of the Midéwi·win here we are dependent upon oral information of relatively recent data secured by Skinner and the writer. The former[57] records the fact that a Long Plains Saulteaux (ogimauwinini) interviewed in 1913 was "taught the secrets of the four degrees in order that he might establish an accepted lodge at Long Plains,"[58] by an old mide at Broken Head, many years before. The name of this man was nénagi·s,[59] quivering, who was also remembered as a midé by my informant at Berens River. Although I could obtain no information in regard to the probable date of the last ceremony given on Broken Head River,[60] it can be stated that it was within the lifetime of my informant. Whether the Midéwi·win of the Long Plains group did actually stem from this man, as Skinner's statement implies, I do not know. But it may well have been the case and I suspect that if so, it also implies that nénagi·s may have been the best known midé south of Lake Winnipeg at the time, and that possibly the ceremonies on the St. Peters and Roseau River Reserves were already extinct. On the other hand, of course, there may have been other reasons

which guided the Long Plains Indian in his selection of a capable tutor.

7. Following the eastern shore of Lake Winnipeg, we soon reach Traverse Bay and the mouth of the Winnipeg River.[61] There is some dispute whether Fort Maurepas, the earliest post established in the Lake Winnipeg country by La Verendrye, was built here or on the Red River below Selkirk.[62] The present Fort Alexander was built by the Hudson's Bay Company in 1792 on the site of an old Northwest Company fort.[63] In the journal[64] of Peter Jacobs, a converted Ojibwa, who passed down the Winnipeg River in 1852, is found an exceedingly brief, but sufficiently explicit statement that establishes the fact that in the middle of June of this year a Midéwi·win was being held at Manitou Rapids, a short distance east of Fort Alexander, and the first rapids encountered going up the river. That this was an established locale of the ceremony we infer from the author's statement that this is the "place where they generally hold their manito feasts." About fifty years ago or more, it was given up, the last headman being ni·jotés, little twin, also known as Two Hearts.[65] Chief Berens recalls having seen him. The old man still retained the fashion of wearing his hair in two braids, a custom that at the time was not common among the other Indians. It may be remarked in passing that the acculturation of the Fort Alexander band proceeded very rapidly.

8. The next point to the north which was an old established locale of the Midéwi·win was the east end of what today is called Black Island;[66] the Saulteaux name for the island being kapïpïkwewi·k, a term referring to a curious reverberation or thumping sound, said to occur when walking near Drumming Point, its eastern extremity. The latter place name, apparently, is derived either from the Saulteaux name for the island or it has reference, perhaps, to the custom of holding the Midéwi·win there. The mysterious reverberations which are said to occur may have been a factor which led the Indians to choose this spot as one especially suited for the performance of the Midéwi·win. Sekanɑkwégabau, the one who reaches the sky when he stands up, was the earliest leader about whom information was obtained. He must have been born very early in the nineteenth century, for one of his sons was about the same age as Jacob Berens who died in 1916 when he was almost ninety. The latter, who was occasionally a visitor in the camp of the old midé, often commented upon the pet bear which the latter kept tied up in his wigwam. The animal was perhaps three years of

age. It was fed with pounded fish and berries, and its special feeding dish was a shallow wooden platter, stained or painted black. In those days the young men often used to play lacrosse in the early summer evenings. As soon as the bear saw them starting to play, he would begin to cry, and to strain at his tether. Then the old midé would say to the animal, "I'll let you go if you behave yourself. Now remember, don't hurt any of those young men." Then he would unloosen the bear which would run off and caper playfully about among those watching the game. As soon as the game was over, however, the bear would straightway return to the wigwam of the midé. It was believed by the Indians that the bear was controlled by the magic power which the midé possessed.

After the death of sekanakwégabau, leadership of the Midéwi·win was assumed by nódage, old woman (Cree). He was also mänáo. This man was living at the time Treaty No. 5 was made, but refused to have any dealings with the government, even relinquishing his per capita share of the annual payments. His successor was kagi·wébit,[67] one who turns. Since the latter's English name was Black, the contemporary name of the island where the Midéwi·win was held may have been derived from his connection with it. By this time the Saulteaux of the adjoining mainland were organized into the Hollow Water River[68] (wanapi·gáuwi·si·bi) band which was given a reserve (I. R. 10) at the mouth of the river.[69] Kagi·wébit was of the Moose sib and called my informant "younger brother." He died about 1919 and was said to have reached the age of ninety years.[70] From this date until 1925, or perhaps later, the Midéwi·win was conducted by Morning Star (wábanänang,[71] who died in 1932. So far as I know, he was the last leader of the Midéwi·win to survive, not only among the Saulteaux whose territory borders directly on Lake Winnipeg, but inland to the east for a distance of three hundred miles.

9. Another contemporary place name, Dog Head,[72] on the eastern side of the Narrows (wapăng), perpetuates a memory of an ancient locale of the Midéwi·win on Lake Winnipeg. On Bloodvein River[73] nearby, is the reserve (I.R. 12) of a contemporary Saulteaux band. An Indian called sagatcí·weäs, one who comes up over the mountain,[74] also known as Peter Stoney, was elected chief of the so-called "Island bands" as a result of the treaty negotiations (1876).[75] These bands comprised: (1) a few scattered families on what was formerly called the White Earth or White Mud River, since re-named Icelandic;[76] (2) the Indians on Big

Island (k`tcí·minis),[77] now Hecla, and on Wanipigow River, previously mentioned; (3) a group on Bloodvein River and at Dog Head; (4) another band on the west side of the lake at the mouth of Jackfish River (kinozéwi·si·bi).[78] It is interesting to note that the Indians gathered at Dog Head to receive their treaty money at this period, a fact which is probably connected with the annual performance of the Midéwi·win there. Sagatcí·weäs was the headman of the Midewiwin as well as chief. He wore his hair in long braids and was never converted to Christianity. He was the son of äsini·bon, one of the former leaders of the Midéwi·win at St. Peters Reserve on Red River, and his English surname, Stoney, as still happens among these Indians, was derived from his father's personal name.[79] Sagatcí·weäs was assisted in the Midéwi·win by two other leading men, wasbosékwan, rabbit robe, and wagi·békwan, crooked back, both of whom died before him. Evidently sagatcí·weäs sometimes participated in the Midéwi·win held at Jack Head, across the lake, because a Berens River man (François Felix) told me about a miracle (mămandawi·zi) which he had seen sagatcí·weäs perform during a Midéwi·win held there. He sharpened a stick into a point and then walked up to one of the other midé. The latter stuck out his tongue as far as he could. Sagatcí·weäs then spitted the man's tongue with the stick and cut it off with his knife. He then circled the Midéwi·win lodge, exhibiting the spitted tongue, after which he returned to the man whose tongue had been cut off, and replaced it. Another miracle witnessed by my informant was equally astonishing. A midé named makatcí·wewe, black (lesser) snow goose, took a gun in one hand and a cup of water in the other. He poured the water down the barrel of the gun (a muzzle loader), pulled the trigger and the gun went off.

10. At a previous period Yellow Legs, uzaúaskogat, the paternal great-grandfather of Chief W. Berens, had conducted the Midéwi·win on the east side of the lake near the mouth of what is now called Pigeon River[80] and at Jack Head on the western side. After the death of sagatcí·weäs the ceremony was no longer held at Dog Head, but the people of the Bloodvein band used to go across the lake to Jack Head each year where Wawásan, lightning,[81] had assumed leadership. This man had gone through the various degrees under Yellow Legs and was assisted by his three sons, one of whom, manzi·napkinegéwinini, the man who is painting the rock, may still be alive. But the Midéwi·win itself has not been given at Jack Head for perhaps forty years. Chief Berens remembers Lightning well, and was at Jack Head once when the ceremony was in

2. Morning Star. (*Courtesy of the American Philosophical Society.*)

progress. The sons of Lightning assisted in the Midéwi·win given at Hollow Water River after their father's death and its irregular performance at Jack Head.

11. The midé previously mentioned, called Yellow Legs, although born on the western side of Lake Winnipeg, and who was the head man at Jack Head early in the nineteenth century,[82] later took up his residence on Berens River, where his descendants are numerous and constitute

the contemporary members of the Moose sib at the mouth of the river. From the standpoint of the history of the Midéwi·win in this region Yellow Legs represents an important link between the Saulteaux on the eastern and western sides of Lake Winnipeg at this period. He appears to have been the most famous midé of his time whose reputation has survived. There is no one now living, of course, who ever saw him, but his widow was still alive when the oldest man of the Berens River band was a boy. This man,[83] who is one of Yellow Legs' great-grandsons, told me that on one occasion Yellow Legs was seen walking on the water, on a calm day, over to Jack Head Island in order to secure medicine (mɑckīkī). He was brought back by memengwécīwak,[84] semi-human creatures who live in the rocks and travel in canoes. All this happened in broad daylight while people were watching. He also brought back some gulls' eggs from the island, "in order to make the people believe in his power," my informant added.

On another occasion Yellow Legs dreamed of a large round stone on what is now called Egg Island, but which the Indians call wig-wasiminis, Birch Island.[85] He sent two men to fetch this stone for him: they were told to follow a bear's tracks to be found on the shore, which would lead them directly to it. But to make sure that they had found the right stone, a few branches would be broken directly above it. The men found the stone by following the directions given them by Yellow Legs, and it was brought to Berens River. It is now in the possession of Chief Berens. It was used in the Midéwi·win for many years, and exhibited certain animate properties, externally represented by what appear to be a mouth and eyes. In the course of the Midéwi·win, Yellow Legs used to tap the stone with a knife, whereupon the mouth would open and he would extract a deerskin packet of medicine. The latter would be made into a concoction, which was then shared by all present.

Another miraculous demonstration by Yellow Legs took place under the following circumstances. One day when a group of young men were idling near his wigwam, a golden eagle (kīnīu) was sighted, far up in the sky. As it was observed sailing aloft, the young men again and again kept expressing the wish that they might obtain some of the bird's feathers for their arrows. Finally Yellow Legs got tired of hearing them repeat their desires. From his medicine bag he took a small iron spear-head, with a hole in the butt. Placing the spearhead in the palm of one hand, he slapped it with the other. No sooner had he done this than the eagle began to fall towards the earth, turning over and over as it dropped. It fell to the ground not far from where they were sitting. "Now, go and get your feathers," the old man said to the young men. With shouts of pleasure, they did so. Then Yellow Legs said to his wife, "You go now and open the heart." Inside of it was the spear point.

After the death of Yellow Legs, one of his sons, Maskwa, Bear (Cree) [Makwa in Ojibwe], assisted by his brother, Caúwanäs [Zhaawanaash], the one who travels with the south wind, became leaders of the Midéwi·win. After the former died Caúwanäs became converted and joined the Protestant church. This was during the initial period of Christianization, when Rev E. R. Young was conducting the mission-ary work.[86] The last Midéwi·win must have taken place over fifty years ago. My informant pointed out the spot where the lodge had been erected.

Fortunately we have an extremely interesting, though superficial account of the ceremony as given at the mouth of this river. Although not published until 1905, the observer, James Stewart,[87] has unwittingly provided us with several clues which indicate the approximate period at which the ceremony described must have taken place. There is ref-erence, for example, to the fact that a Mr. Cummings acted as Stewart's interpreter. This man was in charge of the Hudson's Bay Company post when Peter Jacobs and Rev John Ryerson stopped there in the middle of the last century.[88] Stewart also mentions "the Indian called Bear," who is said to have explained the general meaning of the ceremony to him. This man can be no other than the grandfather of Chief Berens, referred to above.

Berens River, it may be mentioned in passing, not only represents the farthest point north on Lake Winnipeg at which the Midéwi·win was held, but it also marks the northern boundary of the ceremony to the east of the lake for at least three hundred miles. It was never given at Poplar River, at Island Lake,[89] Deer Lake, or Sandy Lake, ac-cording to unanimous testimony of my informants, although Saulteaux speaking people are found today in all of these localities.[90] In view of the western spread of the institution, even as far, apparently, as the Saskatchewan bluff country, its absence among these Saulteaux speak-ing bands of the wooded country north of 52° N. Lat. presents a striking contrast.

12. Proceeding eastward up Berens River we find the Little Grand Rapids band domiciled a little over one hundred miles from the mouth. This

was a less important center of the Midéwi·win than farther up the river or at the mouth. From the information I have been able to secure, it appears that a lodge was only opened up for a few years under the leadership of Flatstone (nαgagábek), assisted by Bluffhead (pi`kwάkwαsti·gan). The last ceremony was held about 1918.[91] Flatstone's son told me that the last few years the Midéwi·win was given, his father did not actually participate. Bluffhead acted as head man. The midéwigamik was built on a little rise of ground near the place where John Duck's wábano pavilion now stands.

13. The chief reason for the subsidiary character of the Midéwi·win at Little Grand Rapids was the dominance of tetαbaiyábin, daylight all around the sky, one hundred miles farther east at Poplar Narrows [Poplar Hill]. This man and his father (pαzαgwi·gabau) before him were indisputably the most influential and famous midés up the river. The son (otci·tcák, crane) of the former is the individual from whom the major portion of my information in respect to the ritual and significance of the ceremony has been obtained, and although he has never conducted a ceremony in the capacity of leader, he is the only man on the river who, at present, would be capable of doing so. Sαgαski, hiding by bending down, was the associate of tetαbaiyábin in the conduct of the ceremony. The lodge was erected on the north side of the river, on a level piece of ground near where I found some of the Poplar Narrows Indians[92] camped late in the summer of 1932. The last Midéwi·win was held here not later than 1922 and tetαbaiyábin died a couple of years after this. He was failing rapidly and probably was not physically able to conduct another ceremony. Flatstone was trained in Midéwi·win affairs by tetαbaiyábin's father and before opening a lodge at Little Grand Rapids, he was an active participant at Poplar Narrows, where other [Little] Grand Rapids Indians also went, either to see the ceremony or to go through it.

The relationship of all these men to each other is of interest. Every one of them, including those at Little Grand Rapids, belonged to the Sturgeon sib. Bluffhead and Flatstone were parallel cousins and the former was a half-brother of tetαbaiyábin. The father of pαzαgwí·gabau was likewise a head man of the Midéwi·win. Although unformalized, it is obvious that effective Midéwi·win leadership was here confined to a single family line for three generations.

14. At a still earlier period it is said that pαzαgwí·gabau used to hold the Midéwi·win farther up the river, where it enters Lake Pekangikum.

His chief assistant was pindă'ndɑkwɑn, stuffing something with brush, a son-in-law who conducted the ceremony at Pekangikum after the death of pazɑgwí·gabau. It was discontinued here about 1920 when pindă'ndɑkwɑn went to live at Lac Seul.[93] As late, therefore, as the second decade of the present century, the Midéwi·win was being given at three places on Berens River. Before the next decade had passed, every one of the leaders had died or, as in the case just cited, moved away. No one seemed prepared to assume the leadership and since missionary effort, governmental supervision of the Indians, and other acculturative influences are becoming stronger each year, it is not likely it will be given again unless revived under the leadership of Otci·tcák. Pazɑgwí·gabau himself was in close touch with the head man at Lac Seul and used to make trips there occasionally to obtain new medicine. The man who was his acknowledged master was sagɑtcí·weäs,[94] but as we have previously pointed out, his father was also a well known leader.

This link with the Lac Seul band makes it clear that the Berens River Saulteaux, so far as the Midéwi·win was concerned, were open to influences emanating from a point fairly close to the Ojibwa proper only a few generations ago. At the mouth of the river, on the other hand, there were connections across the lake mediated through Yellow Legs, and to the south there were also connections regarding which we have less specific information. These and other links, already mentioned, it is interesting to note, connect points which it would be impossible to infer were connected without specific reference to individuals, Long Plains and Brokenhead, St. Peter's Reserve and Bloodvein River Reserve, the latter with Berens and Jack Head, and Jack Head in turn with Hollow Water River and Berens River, to say nothing of Lake Pekangikum and Lac Seul. Furthermore, I was told that pazɑgwí·gabau sometimes came to the mouth of the Berens River and participated in the Midéwi·win there, so that in this case, through the mediation of a single individual information could have been disseminated all the may from the Lac Seul Ojibwa to the Saulteaux on the western shore of Lake Winnipeg and perhaps beyond.

Notes

Published in *American Anthropologist* 38 (1936): 32–51.

1. The local term for Ojibwa speaking Indians which has gained a place in historical and ethnographical literature and, except for pedantic reasons, can scarcely be discontinued at this late date.

2. The numbers placed at the beginning of certain paragraphs later in the text correspond to those on the map.

3. I have only had direct contact with the Indians of Norway House, Island Lake, Grand Rapids (mouth of the Saskatchewan River), Poplar River, Wanipigow River, and, on the Berens River, from the mouth to Lake Pekangikum (Ontario).

4. He was born not later than 1865. [Ed. note: For the texts that Hallowell collected from Berens, see William Berens (2009), *Memories, Myths, and Dreams of an Ojibwe Leader.*]

5. Alanson B. Skinner, "Medicine Ceremony of the Menomini Iowa, and Wahpeton Dakota, with Notes on the Ceremony among the Ponca, Bungi Ojibwa, and Potawatomi," *Indian Notes and Monographs*, vol. 4, 1920, 12; Paul Radin, "The Ritual and Significance of the Winnebago Medicine Dance," *Journal of American Folk-Lore*, 24, 1911, 168: "The songs of the Winnebago ceremonies are to a large extent in some central Algonkian dialect"; cf. also 179.

6. Skinner, "Medicine Ceremony," 13.

7. Skinner, "Medicine Ceremony," 9. The author says it was carried nearly to the foothills of the Rockies by the Plains Cree and Ojibwa. Rev. Henry Budd, e.g., who took up his residence at the Nepowewin mission on the north bank of the Saskatchewan River opposite Fort à la Corne in 1852, records in his Journal the following spring, that the Midéwi·win is to be omitted. He adds that "it is the first spring for a long time that that ceremony is not to he kept up here." It appears from a previous entry that he is speaking of the Thickwood Crees (cf. H.Y. Hind, *Narrative of the Canadian Red River Exploring Expedition of 1857 and the Assiniboine and Saskatchewan Expedition of 1858* [2 vols., London, 1860] vol. 1, 399, 402–403). But as indicated below there is good evidence that Ojibwa speaking groups had penetrated the Saskatchewan country by the end of the eighteenth century. Even farther west, in fact, but still later in the nineteenth century than the previous citation, Father Petitot, in a letter dated December 30, 1873, from Lac la Biche (Saskatchewan) and addressed to his Superior (cf. Missions de la Congregation des Missionnaires Oblats de Marie Immaculée [Paris, 1874], vol. 12, 462), says that between Lake Vert and Carlton he met many bands of Cree on their way to the Midéwi·win which was being held on the shores of Pelican Lake. Whether the leaders of this ceremony were Cree or Saulteaux (Ojibwa) is not stated. Today there is a small band of the latter on Indian Reserve 159 north of North Battleford. I am indebted to Dr. J. M. Cooper for calling my attention to this latter reference which also contains

a description of the ceremony narrated to Petitot, it may be emphasized, by a *half-breed Saulteaux* (464). I have not been able to consult the text but Dr. Cooper provided me with an extensive resumé.

8. Skinner, "Medicine Ceremony," 9.

9. Anthropological Papers, American Museum of Natural History, vol. 9, pt. 1, 60.

10. Alexander Begg, *The History of the Northwest* (3 vols., Toronto, 1894–95), vol. 1, 216.

11. To Henry we owe an explicit statement in regard to the triple synonomy for the Ojibwa of the old "Northwest" which allays any possible confusion. In 1808 he wrote, "the Ogeebois are commonly called by the English Algonquins, by the Canadians [i.e., the voyageurs and others from Quebec] Salteurs and by the Hudson Bay Co. servants Bungees" (Elliott Coues, *New Light on the Early History of the Greater Northwest* (3 vols., New York, 1897), vol. 1, 533).

12. He first reached the present site of the city of Winnipeg in 1738.

13. *The Journal of Duncan McGillivray of the Northwest Company at Fort George on the Saskatchewan, 1794–5* (Introduction by A. S. Morton, 1929). See Introduction, xxxvi, et seq., and 13,18,20, all of which contain references to Saulteaux met by the author en route to his post. The location of Nipawin (20) is approximately 53° 4' N. Lat., 104° W. Long.

14. By Ambroise Wolf of the Miscowequan Reserve (I. R. 85) near Lestock, who was visiting Fishing Lake at the time. His wife belonged to this band.

15. Edwin James, *Narrative of the Captivity and Adventures of John Tanner during Thirty Years Residence among the Indians in the Interior of North America* (New York, 1830), 106.

16. Net-no-kwa was the Indian woman who had adopted him. Interesting accounts of the praying, singing, and prognostic dreams of this old woman (51–53, 66–67, 72) whenever food was scarce is undoubtedly a corollary of her reputation as a mi·dékwe.

17. Page 107.

18. Cf. Coues, *New Light*, 305n. The same identification is suggested in *Place-Names of Manitoba* (Geographic Board of Canada, Ottawa, 1933). The meaning of the native term appears to be "backbone mountain" (nawáwi·ganewadji·wan) which may be reconciled to Tanner's "hill of the buffaloe chase" if the contour referred to suggested a bison's back to the Indians.

19. The name of the river had not been changed in Coues' time ("New Light"). Cf. *Place-Names of Manitoba*.

20. See Coues, *New Light*, vol. 1, 96.

21. See A. Morris, *The Treaties of Canada with the Indians of Manitoba and the Northwest* (Toronto, 1880), 317, 320.

22. The grebe, cing*a*bis.

23. Morris, *The Treaties of Canada*.

24. From Chief Berens of the Berens River band. When subsequently I speak of "my informant," without further specification, the information may be attributed to the same source.

25. K'tigani·minis, Lat. 51.5°N., Long. 99+° W.

26. From Cree ăg*a*s, arrow.

27. The equivalent of nanabójo, nä 'năbŭc.

28. Pawáganak.

29. pasi kwébi zon kaká'kotci sweyan [wearing a woodchuck skin around one's head].

30. Usually from memengwécī, a semi-human creature living in the rocks.

31. I. R. stands for Indian Reserve and the number in preceding and succeeding citations is the official numerical designation used on government maps, etc.

32. Skinner, *Medicine Cermony*, 309.

33. Donald A. Cadzow, "Bark Records of the Bungi Midewin Society" (*Indian Notes*, vol. 3, no. 2, 124–34, 1926). Mr. Cadzow writes me that there seems to be no immediate prospect of publishing the remainder of his notes.

34. The junction of the Red and Assiniboine Rivers.

35. Trading posts in this locality were built successively by the Northwest Company (Peter Grant's House, 1793; Chaboillez House, 1797, and Fort Pembina, 1801 by Henry), the XY Company, 1801, and the Hudson's Bay Company, 1793, 1801, 1821 (Fort Daer). See Coues, *New Light*, vol. 1, 79n., and E. Voorhis, *Historic Forts and Trading Posts* (Department of the Interior, Ottawa, 1930).

36. Called by him the Reed River, which joins the Red River from the east at about thirteen miles north of 49°. Coues (*New Light*, vol. I, 69) provides an excellent historical note. The Indian term for the river given by W. H. Keating (*Narrative of an Expedition to the Source of St. Peter's River, Lake Winnepeek, Lake of the Woods, etc.* [2 vols., London, 1825], vol. 2, 76) is Pekwioniusk, Reed-grass River, which corresponds with the contemporary

Saulteaux term, pebi·gwéwanaskosi'bi, hollow grass river. Near its mouth this river flows through I.R. 2 occupied today by the remnants of the Pembina band who remained within Canadian territory after the boundary line was established. They were brought into treaty in 1871.

37. Coues, *New Light*, vol. 1, 182.

38. Coues, *New Light*, 197.

39. Coues, *New Light*, 212. In his entry of October 31st of this year Henry (p.229) refers to an Indian of the name of Rats Liver camped at his post. Coues identifies this man with Tanner's "O-zhush-koo-koon (the muskrat's liver), a chief of the Metai" (115n.) who offered his granddaughter to Tanner as a wife.

40. Hind, *Narrative of the Canadian Red River*, vol. 1, 157, 163.

41. See *Annual Report*, Department of Indian Affairs, 1902, 89.

42. *Annual Report*, Department of Indian Affairs, 1934, 37.

43. That is between the "Forks" and Lake Winnipeg.

44. Formerly known as Elk or Red Deer Rapids, omaskósobautik, in modern Saulteaux. Cf. Coues, *New Light*, vol. 1, 42n.

45. Henry, e.g., remarks, "The Crees and Assiniboines formerly assembled here in large camps to await the arrival of the traders." This, of course, was prior to the days of the Red River Colony and it seems that Joseph Frobisher in 1774 had built a fort a short distance below the rapids (cf. McDonnell in L. R. Masson, *Les Bourgeois de la Compagnie dur Nord-Ouest* [2 vols., Quebec, 1890], vol. 1, 268), which Coues (*New Light*) thinks may have been the earliest on the Red River after the French establishments of the early eighteenth century. The last fort to be built in this district was the famous Lower Fort Garry in 1831.

46. See, e.g., Ross, *The Red River Settlement* (London, 1856), 278 *et seq.* on Archdeacon Cockran's unofficial attempt to Christianize the Cree and to teach them farming. The Saulteaux have always had the reputation of being more intractable.

47. Which joins Red River from the west at a point nine miles from the lake. It was formerly known as Dead River, oni·bówisi·bi, a term still perpetuated among the modern Saulteaux, and which refers to the slaughter by the Sioux of some Cree, Saulteaux, and perhaps Assiniboine families camped here on the late eighteenth century. See Coues, *New Light*, vol. 1, 21n.; McDonnell in Masson, *Les Bourgeois*, vol. 1, 268. Keating (*Narrative of an Expedition*, vol. 2, 78) speaks of one Indian village at the mouth of Red River and the other at Death River (1823). At the junction of Red River and Netley Creek the Northwest Company established a post in 1803.

See Voorhis, *Historic Forts*. The still earlier Fort aux Roseaux was near the mouth of the Red River.

48. *The Rainbow in the North; a Short Account of the First Settlement of Christians in Rupert's Land by the Church Missionary Society* (New York, 1852), 128. In the same volume verbatim quotations from Cockran's journal are given, but I have been unable to discover whether it was ever published.

49. J. J. Hargrave, *Red River* (Montreal, 1871), 197.

50. His English name was Henry Prince.

51. Referring to Lower Fort Garry, where the treaty negotiations were conducted.

52. From the name of the parish which was included within the reserve. The parish was an organized settlement prior to the "transfer" of these western lands to Canada or the date of the Indian treaties. See Annual Report, Department of Indian Afffairs, 1908, 79–80.

53. See Report for 1875, 38. It is also stated that more than half the band were of mixed blood.

54. But in 1932 there was a schism and under the leadership of Grey Eyes some of these Indians returned to the St. Peters Reserve and, despite the efforts of the government, refuse to be ousted (1934). [Ed. note: The 1907 removal was imposed under very dubious circumstances and has been severely criticized.]

55. *Annual Report*, Department of Indian Affairs, 1878, 51.

56. The Saulteaux term is paskandɑbéwi·si·bi, raw head (scalped?) river, from which the English form is no doubt derived.

57. *Medicine Ceremony*, 316–317.

58. Another stronghold of paganism.

59. Written as nänigis by Skinner and translated as "someone shaking." Descendants of the brother of this man are members of the Berens River band.

60. At present this band has almost completely disintegrated.

61. Saulteaux, sagi wi si bi; the initial element sagi—simply means the mouth of a river, or where it opens into a lake.

62. See articles "Ft. Maurepas" (*The Beaver*: A Magazine of the North, March and June, 1934).

63. See Voorhis, *Historic Forts*.

64. Peter Jacobs *Journal* (New York, 1857), 36

65. Which is the literal meaning of twin.

66. Cf. Coues, *New Light*, vol. 2, 453n., who says it was also sometimes

called Grand Island. It has always been famous for the abundance and quality of the blueberries which grow there.

67. His maternal grandfather was äsini·bon, a leader of the Midewi·win on Red River.

68. Locally known as "Hole" River. I do not understand the precise meaning of the name but it is reputed to refer to some peculiar characteristic of the local topography.

69. Which on the maps is spelled Wanipigow.

70. A photograph of his grave, made in the old-fashioned way, was obtained by the writer in 1931.

71. Chief Berens was making a trip south by sailboat in June, 1923, and put in at the Hollow Water Reserve. The Midéwi·win was in progress at this time.

72. The contemporary Saulteaux maintain that this place name was applied by the whites. It can be traced back to at least the beginning of the nineteenth century, as it is mentioned by the younger Henry.

73. Miskoósi·bi, a name which is said by the Indians to have reference to personal decoration with red paint and not to the "red veins in the granite of its bed." See *Place Names of Manitoba*, 16.

74. Said to imply reference to the Thunder Bird (pinèsï).

75. Morris, 155.

76. The Sandy Bar band. See Morris, 129.

77. As Coues says (*New Light*, vol. 2, 451n.) its name is warranted by the fact that it is the largest island in the southern portion of the lake. He believes it to be the Isle de Fer of La Verendrye.

78. The term, jackfish, is the local name of the pike, *Esox lucius.*

79. He was married to one of the granddaughters of Pegwis, a daughter of Henry Prince.

80. The native name for this river is pimitctígweasi·bi, obliquely running river. The next river to the north, known as Berens River, is the Pigeon River, omīmīsīpī, in Saulteaux parlance. The now extinct passenger pigeon is the bird referred to.

81. Who, like several of the other leaders, retained the old-fashioned style of hair dressing.

82. He probably died not later than 1830.

83. Jim MacDonald.

84. The implication is that these were among the old man's guardian spirits. They are noted for the knowledge of medicines which they transmit to those human beings whom they bless.

85. It is the larger of the pair of islands in the middle of the lake, east of Jack Head, of which Jack Head Island is the other member.

86. Started in 1873. [Ed. note: Egerton R. Young served as Methodist missionary at Berens River from 1874 to 1876; his successor, John Semmens, baptized Zhaawanash in 1877. For more on these personages, see Berens 2009 and Gray 2006.]

87. "Rupert's Land Indians in the Olden Times," *Annual Archaeological Report*, 1904, Appendix, Report, Minister of Education, Toronto, 1905.

88. Peter Jacobs stopped at Berens River in 1852 (see Journal, 42, 43). Cummings [HBC post master Robert Cumming] is referred to in 1854 by Rev. John Ryerson, *Hudson's Bay or a Missionary Tour in the Territory of the Hon. Hudson's Bay Company* (Toronto, 1855), 81.

89. My own inquiries yielded only negative statements.

90. Needless to say, perhaps, it also failed to spread to the Cree of Norway House, Cross Lake, Oxford House, God's Lake.

91. Chief Berens, who was the representative of one of the opposition fur traders at Grand Rapids in 1919 or 1920, was told at the time that the Midewi·win had been held only a couple of years previously.

92. Descendants, in fact, of tetabaiyábin. I have in my possession the leaders' "bark" (k'itci·wigwas) belonging to him as well as a number of "barks" obtained from descendents of other deceased leaders, and a large number of other articles connected with the Mide·wewin. [Poplar Hill has become the standard name for "Poplar Narrows."]

93. He belonged to the Pelican sib.

94. Who was chief of the Lac Seul band at the time Treaty No. 3 (Northwest Angle), 1873, was negotiated. See Morris, *The Treaties of Canada*, 321. His name is spelled sak-katch-eway in this document. [Ed. note: Morris's spelling here is Sah-katch-eway.]

TWENTY-TWO

Spirits of the Dead in Saulteaux Life and Thought

Aboriginal beliefs in the reality of a life beyond the grave cannot be viewed as simple dogmas that gain currency without any appeal to observation and experience.

In the case of the Berens River Saulteaux, they are supported by the testimony of individuals who are said to have traveled beyond the bourne and returned to tell their fellows about it; by the testimony of those who have approached the land of the dead in dreams; by the resurrection, or resuscitation, of persons reputed to be dead; by the invocation of the spirits of the dead in the conjuring lodge, and in other ways.

The individuals who are said to have visited *djībaiàking*, the spirit (ghost) land,[1] are usually persons believed to be dead, or thought to be fatally ill. To the outsider it seems more likely, of course, that the former were not actually dead, and we would be inclined to say that in both types of cases the individuals *dreamed* that they made the journey to *djībaiàking*. But the Saulteaux do not phrase things in this manner. Despite the fact that in native theory the soul (*òtcatcákwin*), detached from the body, makes the journey in any case, and that dream experiences are classified as "real" experiences, categorically continuous with those of the waking life, a purely empirical distinction is made. The experiences described by persons observed to be dead, or fatally ill, are not said to have been "dreamed," while the "experiences" described by healthy persons *are* said to have been dreamed. The distinction is based on the direct observation of the bodily condition of the persons involved. In the former cases it is coma, or illness, that lends support to their testimony. So far as I understand the matter, while healthy persons may *dream* of the dead, or even approach *djībaiàking*, their souls do not ordinarily *visit* this land of the dead. To do so is very dangerous, if one wishes to return to the land of the living; so only persons with extraordinary spiritual powers could achieve the journey. One such case will be referred to below.

3. Fair Wind (Naamiwan) and his wife, Koowin, seated in front of his Waabano pavilion at Pauingassi, Manitoba. Seated beside them is Joseph Owen; his older brother, Zaagajiwe (Charlie Moose Owen), stands behind them. In the pavilion, directly behind Fair Wind, is his eldest son, Aangish (Angus Owen), and on the right, Fair Wind's youngest son, Wejaanimaash. Note the drumstick and tin rattle that Fair Wind is holding, his water drum in the foreground, and the ceremonial staffs; also the carved bird alluding to Fair Wind's spirit helper (see Berens, *Memories, Myths, and Dreams,* 2009, Hallowell's essay, "Thunder Bird.") Photograph by Hallowell in the summer of 1933 (Koowin died the next year). (*Courtesy of the American Philosophical Society.*)

From the Saulteaux point of view, at any rate, Bevan[2] certainly errs when he unequivocally states that, with the exception of Saint Paul, "there is no single instance given us of a man visiting the spirit-world which is not either mythological or literary fiction" (62). It is also curious that he does not mention Swedenborg. Of course, he is thinking primarily of classical antiquity, of Odysseus, of Plato's Er the Pamphylian and, in later times, of Dante. Apparently Bevan thinks that the "widely diffused idea amongst primitive peoples that a man might go or be carried into the spirit world and come back to tell what he had found" belongs to the same general category. Among the Saulteaux, at least, it is otherwise. Specific individuals are referred to, whose historicity is not in question, however one may choose to evaluate their testimony. When I made inquiries about life after

4. Fair Wind's drum dance pavilion at Pauingassi in 1925. This photograph by Gerald W. Malaher appears in his book, *The North I Love* (Winnipeg: Hyperion Press, 1984), 56; his son, David Malaher, provided this reproduction and kindly granted permission to publish it here. Note the tall poles topped by wooden birds (cf. previous plate), and the wooden tower holding a bell that Fair Wind rang on Sundays when, according to descendants, he also read from a Cree syllabic bible (Brown and Matthews 1994, 68–69). Hallowell's images of the pavilion are from a distance and show the poles, but the bell tower was absent when he visited. (*Courtesy of David Malaher.*)

death, it was the alleged experiences of these individuals that were first mentioned. I was not given generalized statements. Consequently, there is often no categorical distinction that can be drawn between alleged personal experiences and the more highly formalized narrative on the same theme, ordinarily classified as a myth.[3]

Once it is recognized that such reputed experiences need not be true, in any absolute sense, but may yet be accepted as genuine by those who share the cultural tradition which gives them reality, it is possible to penetrate beneath the surface of native beliefs, and to understand how they function in Saulteaux life.

ACCOUNTS BY TRAVELERS RETURNED FROM THE LAND OF THE DEAD

The following narrative of a human being's visit to *djībaiàking* is said to have been repeated more than once by Nɑbagábek [Nɑgagábek] (Flatstone).

One of his hearers gave me the account the first time I inquired about life after death. According to him, Nɑgagábek had said:

I saw a man who died and lay dead for two days. He told me what had happened to him. He never felt any pain. He thought he was going to sleep. Then, "all of a sudden," he said, "I found myself walking on a good road. I followed this road (*djïbaiikana,* spirit [ghost] road). On it I came to a wigwam. I saw an old man there. He spoke to me. 'Where are you going?' he asked me. I told him, 'I'm going this way.' 'You better stop and have something to eat,' he said. I told him I was not hungry, and started off again. He came along with me. 'I'll show you where your parents are staying,' he said. While we were walking we came in sight of lots of wigwams. As far as I could see, there were wigwams. The old man pointed one of them out to me. 'You go there,' he said, 'that's where your mother and father live.'

"So I went there. I found my father in the wigwam. He shook hands with me and kissed me. My mother was not there. Soon she came in, and greeted me in the same way. My father called out, 'Our son is here!' After that a lot of people came in to see me. They asked about people on this earth. They wanted to know whether their friends were well. I told them that they were not sick. Then I was offered something to eat. But I could not eat.[4] Some of these people that came to visit me had moss growing on their foreheads, they died so long ago.

"While I was talking, I heard three or four beats of a drumstick. They were very faint, I just barely heard them, they were so far away. All of a sudden I thought about coming back. I thought of my children I had left behind. I went outside the wigwam without telling my parents. I started back along the same road I had followed before. When I came to the old man's wigwam he was not there. I kept on walking along the road. Then I thought I heard someone calling me. I could hardly hear the voice and I could not recognize who it was. Finally the voice became plainer. I knew that I was getting nearer then. When I got still closer, I could hear my wife and children crying. Then I lost my senses. I could not hear anything more.

"When I opened my eyes and came to my senses it was daylight. But even daylight here is not so bright as it is in the country I had visited. I had been lying for two days. But I had traveled a long distance in that length of time. It is not right to cry too much for our friends, because they are in a good place. They are well off there. So I'm going to tell everybody not to be scared about dying."

Another man, Caúwanäs [Zhaawanaash](One Who Travels with the South Wind), was once very ill, and was expected to die. But he recovered. Later he said to his brother's son [Jacob Berens]: "I got pretty close to *djïbaiàking*. I was on the road there." He said there were lots of strawberries on the way, and one enormous strawberry[5] just this side of the town (*ódena*[6]). He could see the chunks that had been scooped out of it by passers-by. As he approached the town he could hear the voices of people shouting and laughing. But someone met him on the road and ordered him back. "You're not wanted yet," he was told.

Caúwanäs said he got close enough to the town, however, to recognize one individual whom he knew. This was Pi`kotcīs (Sand-Fly) of the Poplar River Band, who had been talked about a great deal because he had once eaten human flesh.

APPROACH TO THE LAND OF THE DEAD IN A DREAM

In the following account of a dream experience, the soul of the narrator traveled an even shorter distance towards the land of the dead.

> I was sick. I dreamed that I saw a road-not a very good one—and I started to walk along it. I could see my body lying there as I left. When I had traveled along this road for some distance I came to a rocky hill. A voice said to me [indicating by a gesture that the voice came from near his head]: "Can you see beyond this hill?" "No," I said. "Well, I'll show you what is there." Then I could see a beautiful country beyond the hill with a road through it. The grass and trees were all green, there were lots of flowers and it seemed very bright there. Then the voice spoke to me again: "Can you go there?" I tried, but could not make it. The voice said: "You're not ready to go there yet. You must go back and prepare yourself" (that made me glad, I did not want to go yet). So the voice pointed out another road, that led back the way I had come, not the one I had traveled. I followed this road. Finally I reached the place where my body was. But in the place I lay was a big fire—I had to go through that.[7] Then I lost my senses, but woke up.

Since I obtained this account directly from the dreamer, and discussed it with no one else, I do not know how the other Indians would evaluate it; but I believe that the illness of the dreamer would be a substantial factor in its validation. However, this man did not actually reach *djïbaiàking*.

Although I have not obtained any personal accounts of the journey of the soul of a perfectly healthy man to the land of the dead while he was asleep, in the case of "resurrection," described below, this seems to be substantially what is supposed to have occurred.

> Long ago, there was a man called Miskwádesīwískījik (Mud-Turtle's Eye). After being buried, he took up his earthly life again. His wife had visited his grave one day, and hearing a noise, had the grave dug up. She found her husband was alive. But he often acted strangely after this, as if he had not entirely detached himself from the spirit world. Sometimes in the summer, when it was getting dark, Mud-Turtle's Eye would say: "It's just coming daylight. There is going to be a game of lacrosse." Then, instead of preparing for bed, he would dress himself and make ready to play the ball-game. As the night wore on and it got still darker he would make the motions of playing lacrosse, although he still remained in his wigwam. And he fell backwards all of a sudden and shouted, "the ball struck my forehead." He grabbed something and, sure enough, there in his hands was a rock, shaped like a ball.

The implication is, of course, that this man was actually playing lacrosse with the spirits of the dead.[8] The latter sleep during the day, and dance and play all night.[9] There is likewise the well-known association of the Northern Lights with the playing and dancing of the deceased in *djíbaiàking*. This is what makes their land so bright.

Mud-Turtle's Eye is so well remembered, I may add, that a contemporary Indian bearing the same name is occasionally teased about being a lacrosse player, although this game itself has never been played on the Berens River in the memory of living individuals.

RESUSCITATION

Closely allied to these cases are instances in which human intervention is said to have resulted in bringing the dead back to life. On account of the nature of the Saulteaux philosophy of the universe, and the acceptance of such testimony as that already cited, fetching the soul of a dead person from *djíbaiàking* is by no means an impossibility. The case cited below was narrated quite casually to me, at the same time as a number of other "cures," by the son of the "doctor" credited with the achievement, and no special emphasis was laid upon it at the time; yet it does fall in the miracle class. Tricks performed in the Midéwi·win, however, were equally celebrated. This is not to say, of course, that bringing a person back to life was a common occurrence. Only the most powerful doctors ever did it. The point is that it is *possible* to do so, according to the Saulteaux theory of the nature of things, and in this case the individual concerned was not a legendary figure.

> Tcetcebú[10] was very ill. Otcíbamasīs (Northern Barred Owl) was sent for. He found that it was too late to save her life. The day after he arrived where her father was encamped she died. Otcíbamasīs tied a piece of red yarn around the girl's wrist at once. Then she was dressed in her best clothes and laid out. "After this," said the narrator, "my father lay down alongside of her. He lay in this position for a long time. He kept very still; he did not move at all. Then he began to move ever so little. The girl began to move a little also. My father moved a little bit more. So did the girl. Finally my father raised himself into a sitting posture and at the same time the girl raised herself up in the same way."

The native explanation of this objectively simple procedure is this. In order to bring the girl back to life, it was necessary for Otcíbamasīs to follow her soul along the road to *djībaiàking* and bring it back. Only a very powerful man would even attempt such a thing, but Otcíbamasīs was notable for his extraordinary powers. The yarn he tied about the girl's wrist was to enable him to identify her quickly, for no time could be lost. The journey to *djībaiàking* does not take long. There are many, many people there, and if he had had to make a search for her, it might have been too late to bring her soul back. By lying down beside the girl, Otcíbamasīs symbolized the fact that he was making the journey with her. That is to say, his body lay there as hers did, but his *òtcatcákwin* [soul] traveled the road to *djībaiàking* too. Both returned to their "senses" together, since he found her soul easily and quickly in the land of the dead, thanks to the red yarn, and brought it back to animate her body. But, as the narrator commented, "he got her just in time."[11]

It can easily be seen, from such case material as this, how relatively unelaborated are Saulteaux conceptions of life after death. But there are a few additional details that should be mentioned.

THE LOCATION OF THE LAND OF THE DEAD

The general location of *djībaiàking* is said to be in the south,[12] and this may be the explanation of the north-south orientation of the body in the grave. The head is placed to the north, but the body is said to be "facing the south." One old man [Kiwitc, see below], in talking about his "Drum Dance," referred again and again to the "old people" *(keté änicinábek)* "down south," and how much they enjoyed hearing the Indians "up here" beating the drum. He did not refer, of course, to the people of the United States, but to the Indians of previous generations who had "gone away." A more sophisticated Indian once tried to explain that there were white people, and even "living" Indians, far to the south, but the old man did not find this account of things very intelligible.

According to the aboriginal view, at any rate, *djïbaiàking* was not conceived to be above the earth,[13] or below it, but in a distant region to the south. It was in this country that Indians whose souls left their bodies went on living, presumably forever; and it was a land presumably richer in game and bird-life than the northern country, a place where no one had any trouble in making a living, although life was in other respects a duplication of this one.[14]

THE ROAD TO THE LAND OF THE DEAD

The "spirit (ghost) road," *djïbai ikana,* led to the land of the dead, but before one reached the great town in which the *djïbaiyak* dwelt, there was a river to be crossed. This river is not mentioned in the accounts given above, but it is a common feature of Ojibwa belief,[15] and is also encountered among the Berens River Saulteaux. The current of this river is said to be very swift, and it has to be crossed on a bridge made of a single log. This log is very slippery, and sometimes people fall off. I was told by one man that the bones of such persons can be seen in the river.

I could find no one who knew about the dogs guarding the road near this river, or about the suspended line of shoulder blades that has to be passed, according to the beliefs of other Ojibwa-speaking peoples.[16] But the dog and shoulder blades do appear in the myth recounting the adventures of *Aásï.*[17]

Because of the necessity of traveling the *djïbai ikana* (a journey of which a very realistic concept prevails), some of the pagan Saulteaux have, from time to time, asked their relatives not to bury them in a coffin—a practice which began, of course, under the influence of the whites, but which is quite general now. These Indians believed that they would have to carry their coffin along the "spirit road" and across the river,[18] and they refused to be burdened with it. They were quite satisfied to be buried in their best clothes, so that they would not be ashamed of their appearance when they reached *djībaiàking* and to be provided (in their graves) with a small kettle, an axe, a knife, and perhaps a gun; for it was formerly the custom to wrap the body of the deceased in a new blanket, and also to leave a little food at the grave. These articles were all, they felt, that a person required.

GOD AND THE DEVIL IN THE AFTER LIFE

So far as I could discover, the Supreme Being is not associated in any way with *djībaiàking* in the minds of the pagan Saulteaux. But there is a "boss" *djí·bai*, regarding whom more will be said later. Moreover, though *mätci mänītu*[19] was attributed to the level of aboriginal beliefs by several individuals, there was no associated belief in a "hell." In fact, the notion that eternal happiness or misery in the life after death is in any way dependent upon the conduct of one's life "here," is derived from Christianity, even when held in a modified form.

Since all of these Indians, even when professed pagans, are superficially acquainted with the general outlines of Christian doctrine, it is extremely difficult to establish the complete *absence* of any particular concept in aboriginal theology. Even when a man of advanced years, whose own father was the headman of the Midéwi·win, maintains that, according to aboriginal beliefs, good people go to *k`tchi·mă´ni·tu* after death, and have plenty to eat and are well off, whereas "bad" people go to *mätci mänītu*, where they are forever poor and miserable[20] (although they do not suffer torment as in the orthodox Christian hell), I think that one can hardly accept his testimony at its face value. It must be taken, rather, as evidence of the partial assimilation of Christian ideas, and the unconscious attribution of them to an aboriginal pattern of thought.[21] On the other hand, I believe that the genuine skepticism in regard to the Christian notion of hell, which many contemporary Indians show, is to be accounted for, not only by the complete absence of this idea in their aboriginal culture, but by some persistence of the positive notion, traditional with them, that the life after death is a happy one for everybody.

Beliefs regarding the life after death, then, did not embody sanctions of any great importance with respect to man's daily conduct during life. Even today, fear of illness in this life is a controlling factor of much greater importance than any fear of unhappiness in the life after death. In former times, customs with a "disease-sanction" were undoubtedly those followed with maximum stringency.

With reference to the transitional character of the thought and customs of these Indians at the present day, I was told a "true" story which further documents aboriginal concepts, besides embodying the projection into the future life of the inferior social status the Indians occupy, with relation to the whites, in the present one, and their sensitiveness to it:

There was once an Indian boy, who lived at Lac Seul. He received a good education and became a teacher. After a while he became a preacher, a great preacher. Then he was taken ill. The doctors could not help him, and he died. He followed the "white man's road" to *djībaiàking,* and came to a house. He knocked. The door was opened, but only a crack, by the person inside. A man spoke to him and said, "You don't belong here on this road." So he found another road and followed that. He came to another house. The door was opened only a little. He could not see inside, but he was told that he had better go back. Now this Indian was feeling pretty bad by this time. So he retraced his steps by the way he had come. He came all the way back and regained his senses again. But he did not take back his job. Now all the Indians in that part of the country are turning to the old Indian ways again [the narrator concluded].

OFFERINGS AS A MEANS OF COMMUNICATION BETWEEN THE LIVING AND THE DEAD

It is apparent from the beliefs quoted above that those contemporary Indians who still adhere to the native concepts of life after death, or even approximate to them, must feel much less remote from the spirits of the dead than do those who have more completely capitulated to Christian notions. If human beings have visited *djībaiàking* and returned again, if a powerful doctor can follow the soul of a dead woman to the spirit world and bring it back to her dead body, and if Mud-Turtle's Eye could play lacrosse with the spirits of the dead, possible lines of communication are open, which more closely integrate the living with the dead than is conceivable from an orthodox Christian standpoint.

This more intimate communication is evidenced in a number of ways. Not only is food placed in the grave-house at the time of burial in order to provide the *djī·bai* with nourishment for his journey, but it was formerly the custom (and it sometimes happens up the River, even now) for relatives to place a little food at the grave from time to time, subsequent to burial. The graves of deceased Indians were much more scattered formerly than now, since when death occurred in the autumn and winter, individuals were buried wherever their relatives happened to be. Today there are cemeteries near every summer settlement, and if the settlement includes resident missionaries, these burial grounds are under Christian control. But when an Indian paddling along some lake or river in the bush notices a grave, he will usually go ashore, especially if he knew the person buried there. If he finds some tea, tobacco, and food in the grave-house, he will help himself to just enough tea to make a cupful or two, enough tobacco for a couple of pipefuls, and enough food for a single meal. To drink tea, eat, and smoke at a grave is equivalent to having a visit with the dead. As one informant put it: "If the person had been alive and well, he would have offered these things to you, if you had come to his wigwam. Even after he is dead, it makes him glad that you should stop and visit him." Thus by leaving food in the grave-house from time to time, the relatives of the deceased not only maintain a certain relationship with him, but they enable the spirit of the deceased to continue the tradition of hospitality and the sharing of food, drink, and tobacco with others that was customary to him during his life.[22]

Communication with the dead through the medium of food and tobacco is also carried out in another way. A little of both may be offered to the spirits of the dead by throwing them in the fire. This is often done, up the river, at the present day. It is unnecessary even to think of any particular person, nor need there be any special occasion for the food-offering. One informant said:

> Long ago there was an old man who went to *djībaiàking*. He found out that when a child died and its parents made a little birchbark dish and put some food in it and placed it in the fire, the fire carried the gift to *djībaiàking* and the child told the "boss"[23] about what had come from its parents. Something is sent back to the parents—perhaps they will live longer. But they are sure to receive some kind of "blessing." It is because of what this old man saw, that living people make offerings to *djībaiyak*.

GHOSTS

Since the spirits of the dead carry on their activities during the night, it is not surprising to find them occasionally wandering near their own graves, or in the bush. Sometimes one hears a whistle after dark, and it is most certainly a *djí·bai*. The Indians seldom whistle, except as a means of attracting the attention of a hunting partner to an animal, when the voice might frighten it away. This abstention seems to be connected with the association of whistling with the spirits of the dead. When Chief [William] Berens was a boy he used to whistle, but his grandmother [Amo] forbade him to do it after dark; and two of his children have been similarly cautioned by their mother. So far as tunes are concerned, such a practice would, indeed, be out of harmony with the way in which music functions in a conventional context, to say nothing of the personal property aspect of songs.

Since the Berens River Saulteaux live at a latitude where the days are relatively short during the autumn and winter months, thus necessitating the carrying on of some activities in darkness, an intense fear of moving about, because of the possible presence of some *djĭ·bai,* would be a severe handicap. (One informant specifically said: "There is no reason to fear the dead.") Graves and cemeteries are nevertheless avoided, if possible, after dark, but far out in the bush, it is not the spirits of the dead which occasion the most intense fear these Indians know, but possible encounters with *wíndĭgowak,* cannibalistic monsters.

Possibly the fact that when *djĭ·bai* have been seen, it has usually been in the neighborhood of a grave, accounts for the avoidance of such spots. A man of the Berens River Band once saw a *djĭ·bai* near the graveyard of the Protestant church. It was years ago, when he was a boy, and he was with five other lads. They had left a prayer meeting, and were on their way down to the river to skate. It was moonlight, and as they passed the cemetery they all noticed the figure of a man lurking there. They wondered who it could be, and it was suggested that perhaps he was after a girl. "Let's head him off," someone said. They scattered and then closed in on him. They met no one, nor did they even find any tracks on the snow; yet there was no way for him to avoid meeting some of them. So it must have been a *djĭ·bai.*

Certain it is that whatever apprehension may be felt in meeting the dead in spectral form, the *djĭbaiyak* are conceived to be interested in human affairs and benevolently disposed towards the living, especially their kinsmen.

METEMPSYCHOSIS OF THE DECEASED

Sometimes the spirits of the dead may visit their kinsmen in the form of a bird, according to one informant.

> An Indian may be grieving over a child. The *djĭ·bai* knows its parents are very sad, and will turn itself into a bird, and come back to pay them a visit. Often a person is almost able to touch one of these little birds, it is so tame. A bird seen hopping close to a camp may be a deceased relative. [Usually, however, the approach of any wild animal is considered an ill omen.]
>
> Once I lost a granddaughter. One day I went out to set my nets. I had a sail on the boat. While I was sailing, a bird came and sat on top of the

sail. I said to my boys: "Don't bother that bird. It means something." The bird sat there a long time, as if it were visiting us while we were sailing. I told people about this, and the ones who had good sense believed me.

THE DEAD AS GUARDIAN SPIRITS

Djībaiyak occasionally appear in dreams and even function as guardian spirits, that is, confer blessings. One instance is reputed to have occurred a long while ago, when native games were in full swing.

A moccasin game had been played, and on the losing side was a man named Kekekós (Little Duck Hawk). He had lost everything, even his shirt. Only his pants were left. He felt bad, he did not even move from the place where he was sitting after the game was over. He lay down there and finally dropped asleep. In his dream he heard someone speaking to him. The voice asked him why he was so sad. He replied that he had been playing a game and lost. He did not know to whom he was talking, but the one that had spoken to him said: "I am *djí·bai*. Now early tomorrow morning you must get the game started again," and the *djí·bai* told him exactly what to do.

So the next morning Kekekós got all the losers together to make up his side, and the game was started. Those who had been the winners before now became the losers. The men on the side of Kekekós got back all the goods they had lost, and more. This was because the *djí·bai* had taught him what to do. People found out about it, and some of the old *midéwak* said they could beat him, because they had medicine that would help them win. But Kekekós played against them and beat them, too.

The point to be noted here is the lack of identification of the *djí·bai* mentioned with any particular human being; and the fact of the matter is that the concept of "owners" or "bosses" of all phenomena likewise applies to the spirits of the dead. Consequently it is the *master* of the *djībaiyak* that is believed to function here as a guardian spirit. The implication is that Kekekós must have been blessed by this spirit in his youth. The same notion is the key to the role which the *djībaiyak* play in the Drum Dance of Kīwítc.[24] This dance, like other ceremonies of its class, was a dream gift, and its performance provocative of blessings from superhuman sources. Kīwítc was likewise the individual visited by a *djí·bai* in bird-like form, and the one who told me the story about Kekekós just related.

While I did not obtain full details of his dream revelation (which is strictly taboo), Kīwítc gave me sufficient information to permit certain conclusions

> One morning the old wife[25] spoke to me and said: "Do you know what I have been dreaming about?" "No," I replied. "I dreamed about a drum in *djībaiàking*. It seemed as if this drum was offered to us," she said.
>
> At the time I did not know what this dream of the old wife meant, but I was anxious to find out. Some time after this, I was lying on my bed when I heard someone speak to me. "Look!" the voice said. And right in front of me I saw two things. They were empty coffins. Then I heard the voice again. It seemed to come from somewhere between the earth and the sky. It commanded me to go to a certain point. "I will meet you there," it said. When I reached this place I saw four naked old men sitting there. (This place was between the earth and the sky.)

At this point in his narrative, Kīwítc unrolled a small piece of birchbark on which were drawn some animal figures, dots, and geometric devices, and indicated the point at which he had seen the empty coffins and met the old men. These were not drawn, however. "They came from the other end," he said, "through here"—pointing to the central line.

Who were these old men, and whose voice was it that Kīwítc heard? I think there can be no doubt that the latter was the voice of the Thunder Bird. The allusion to "between earth and sky" is in itself fairly conclusive, but even more so is the fact that, during part of the ceremony, two eagle skins are attached to the south posts of the dancing ground. These represent *pinèsï*, the Thunder Bird, and other allusions to this *pawágan* (guardian spirit, literally "dream visitor") are usually made during the course of the ceremony. Thus the dream revelation is, in part, a blessing from *pinèsï*.

But what of the old men? These, as I understand it, were representatives of what Kīwítc termed *keté änicinábek*, "old Indians" ("Ancients"). They are equivalent to *djībaiyak*. With this identification in mind, we are brought back to his wife's dream of a drum in *djībaiàking*, and the coffins in his own dream. The connection of the Thunder Bird and the spirits of the dead in a dream is not altogether an arbitrary one, since in the Saulteaux universe *pinèsï* comes from the south and the country of the dead lies in the same direction. This emphasis on the south is objectified, to a certain extent, on the dance ground itself, which is delimited by a series of stakes laid out in a square, with openings ("doors") left on the northern and southern sides. People enter the dance ground by the north "door," and thus must face south as they do so; moreover, the exit after the ceremony is through the south "door." This orientation is in contrast to the east-and-west orientation of the Wábano pavilions and, in former times, of the Midéwi·win.

The importance of the "old people down south," as Kīwítc sometimes called them, of the *keté änicinábek,* and of the *djíbaiyak,* becomes clearer by further reference to the bark. Pointing to the dots, Kīwítc said:

> These are the dwellings of human beings, but not those living today or yesterday. They lived long ago, when *wísakedják was* living here, too. In those days these Indians did not use the articles you see them using today. They made everything themselves. They got nothing from the white man. They lived just like the *ätisokának.*[26]

On the bark the dwellings of these ancients lay in the direction from which the old men came. One may infer, therefore, that these old men, whom Kīwítc saw in his dream, were actually the spirits of deceased Indians-*djíbaiyak.* He also saw the drum, which is likewise represented on the bark, and he said: "All the animals that you see drawn there spoke to me, even the flies."

Now it has already been mentioned that the drumming of human beings can be heard in *djíbaiàking,* and that the spirits of the dead themselves sing, dance, and drum. There is, then, a correspondence between human activities and those of the *djíbaiyak.* It is also believed that the latter are extremely pleased when they hear human beings drumming. Consequently the general setting, as well as the derivation and significance, of the Drum Dance of Kīwítc is intelligible. *Djíbaiyak* were among its spiritual sponsors; therefore, as Kīwítc remarked on another occasion about the drum he uses, "in a way the drum *belongs* to the old people down south." A line in one of the songs used in the ceremony may also be noted:[27] *djí·bai ígamegong kanímīting,* "spirits of the dead wigwam where dancing is held."

Finally, I believe that the importance of the spirits of the dead in the dream revelation of Kīwítc is supported by a conversation subsequent to his description of part of the revelation. He said:

> I went south in my dream. I was almost dead at the time I was telling you about. I saw all those people who died long ago and some that I knew myself. It was only when I came to my senses that I knew I was living in this part of the world. It was also at this time that I was told I would have gray hair. As long as I live, I'll hold to what those old men told me.

The drum used in the ceremony is called *kīmícómisanän,* meaning "our grandfather," a term which Kīwítc himself explained as due to the fact that it is one of the "oldest" things known to the Indians. But since "grandfather" is commonly used, not only as a term of respect for any old man, but also in addressing, or referring to, spiritual helpers of all types, it has probably a deeper significance in this context.

It is very striking that the *djībaiyak*, as conceived of in connection with this Drum Dance of Kīwítc, function as *pawáganak*. In the first place, they played an important role in his dream revelation; in the second place, there is the evidence of his own statement: "I ask in the wigwam [i.e., the ceremony] for blessings from our grandfathers down south for those of us here."

In 1934, when I first saw this ceremony, such a reference occurred in one of the first speeches that Kīwítc made. After the drum had been carried in and placed in the center of the dance ground, the singers had taken their places north, south, east, and west of it, and Kīwítc had circled the dance ground with his pipe, ceremonially pointing it in all the directions of the compass, he stopped southeast of the drum, and spoke. He referred to the beginning of the earth (*a`kī*) and the Indians (*änicinábek*). He said: "God (*mänītu*) was the creator and owner of everything, of all that we see growing. We must thank him for life (*pīmädazīwin*). He loves us and he will help us."

Kīwítc also spoke of children as "the gift of God" (*mänītu omīgīwewin*).[28] Then he went on to say:

> I'm thinking of the Ancients who sat in your places [referring to the singers] long, long ago, before any of us were born. Now I'm speaking to them, the old people down south, who gave this (the drum and the dance) to us to use. We expect blessings from them, and from all the *ätsokának* [= *pawáganak*] in the north, south, east, and west. No one knew the names of all these until the old people named them for us.[29] *Pinèsī* up there is watching us.[30] We were told how to name him. I open my hand for a blessing. We are pitiable. God knows what we need. He will bless us with Life.

After this speech, Kīwítc circled the dance ground once, and went to his seat on the east side. Later an equally definite grouping of the *djībaiyak* and the *pawáganak* occurred. Taking a beaded tobacco pouch in his hand, Kīwítc said: "This tobacco was handed to me, but it is not for my own use.[31] It is for those old people down south, *keté änicinábek*, and the *ätsokának*. After I fill my pipe, one of them will circle around in the sky above to bless us, and he will also do some smoking."

This latter reference, of course, is to the Thunder Bird. But "the Ancients" and the *pawáganak*, as already observed, are expected to reciprocate, and Kīwítc went on to say, "Some of the people here are not feeling well. But we have this great tree,[32] and we shall take this tobacco as medicine[33] and smoke it. Now you can go on and dance."

The allusion here is to curative powers validated by the nature of the ceremony itself, and mediated to the human beings participating in it. It would thus appear that, in connection with this ceremony at least, any sharp distinction between human beings long since dead and the superhuman *pawáganak* has been obliterated. Both are objectives of sacrifice, and are looked upon as potential sources of blessings. Although the emphasis noted here might be the product of individual interpretation on the part of Kīwítc, I doubt whether this was the case. Here and there among Algonkian-speaking peoples elsewhere, the *djībaiyak* are found occasionally playing a comparable role.[34] Perhaps the most striking generic parallel among an Ojibwa people is that reported by Alexander Henry[35] in a description of a "feast to the dead," at which the leader "called upon the names of his deceased relatives and friends, beseeching them to be present *to assist him in the chase* [my italics] and to partake of the food which he had prepared for them."

INVOCATION OF DECEASED PERSONS IN THE CONJURING LODGE

It is not so surprising, then, to find that, in the course of a conjuring performance, not only the master of the *djībaiyak* may appear, but the spirits of deceased relatives of persons present may be invoked. While I was told that this was exceptional, Arthur Felix, an eye-witness of one such séance, gave me the following account:

> In the early fall (October) of the year when the War started [1914], I was camping at Sandy Bar. There were several other families from Berens River, and a Poplar River man, William Franklin. We were fishing. One evening, when some of us were sitting in his tent, William said: "I'd like to try something. I want to conjure before the snow falls, but the kind of trees I need for the lodge don't grow here."
>
> "What kind of sticks do you want?" I asked. "I'm going to take my fish to Berens River tomorrow."
>
> "I want seven *cingubīwátigok* [generic term for evergreens], and one or two green birch sticks, straight ones," said William. So I agreed to cut the kind of trees he needed and bring them back with me.

After I had returned the next day, two other men and myself put up the conjuring lodge. We started before dark, and it took us an hour or a little more. The same day another man and his family arrived from the Berens River Reserve. This man, Jacob Berens, was sickly, and when he found that William was going to conjure, he went to his tent and asked him to try and find out why the medicine he had taken did him no good.[36]

After sunset William came out of his dwelling. He had his coat on, and carried a blanket and pillow. He used the pillow to sit on while in the conjuring lodge. He went into the conjuring tent, and at once it began to shake. All the people, of course, were seated around it. Before he went in William called me to him and handed me some tobacco wrapped in a handkerchief.[37] He said: "Give this to the people, give everyone a pipeful." I did as he told me, and after he was inside I called to him and said I had some left. At this William replied: "That tobacco does not belong to me. It belongs to our grandfathers. Pass it to anyone that wants a smoke."

By this tune the tent was shaking harder, and the *pawágañak* had started to come in. They named themselves and sang their songs. All the winds were there and, of course, *miki·nă´k* [the Great Turtle]. There were also present *memengwéciwak* [semi-human creatures living in the rocks], *pijíu* [Lynx], and many others.

After a couple of hours someone came in singing very, very strongly. I heard William saying to it: "One thing I was asked and I don't know the answer. You are one of those that sees many things. You can look around and tell me what I don't know."

Then this *pawágan* sang again, a very long song. It was the boss *djí·bai*. Then this *pawágan* spoke: "I saw something a long, long way back. It's the old people's fault this man here is sick." Then the boss *djí·bai* talked to Jacob Berens.

D: "How long have you been sick?"

J. B.: "Quite a long while."

D.: "Where are you sick?"

J. B.: "I'm always feeling pain around my waist. It is as if there were something drawing me together there."

D.: "Your father [Bear] has something to do with this. If you like, I'll call him, and ask him to come in here."

J. B. (half to himself): "I wonder if it can be so."

[The narrator commented here that it seemed as if Berens did not believe it could be true.] Then someone whispered to Jacob Berens: "It's all right. Go ahead." So Berens said: "I'd like to hear my father."

The boss *djí·bai* sang again. All at once, while this was going on, someone else came into the conjuring lodge. The singing stopped, and everyone sat very quiet. Then William spoke: "Here is the one you asked for. You can talk to him," he said to Berens. The tent was shaking very gently now.

J. B.: "Is that you, father?"

D.: "Yes, my son."

J. B.: "Who are you with?"

D.(1): "I'm with my grandchild. Ever since I left, I've always been happy. I've never been hungry. I've never been thirsty. I've never suffered any pain. It is a beautiful country where I am living. When I was alive, I always tried to do what was right. Try to do the same thing, my son; don't do any wrong to anyone. If there is ever anyone who says something bad to you, don't answer. That's the way I tried to act. If you act this way you will be glad. You'll see me someday, too. I see some people I know sitting outside. I see my oldest daughter."

Suddenly another voice, that of a child, came from the conjuring lodge.

D.(2): "I see my mother sitting there. Don't do that, Mother! I don't like to see you do that" (the woman whose father and adopted daughter had appeared in the conjuring tent was crying). "You hear my voice here. Well, I'll tell you something. I'm living in a good place. I'm happy. It is always bright like day where I live. It is never dark. I was very sick that time, but now I'm not sick any longer. There are pretty flowers where I live, it's like a great garden And there are lots of us. There are great singers there too. Don't forget what I am telling you. Live right and some day you'll find me."

Then the father of Jacob Berens spoke again.

D.(1): "Have you taken much medicine for your sickness, my son?"

J. B.: "Yes, but it has not helped me."

D.(1): "There was one time, my son, that I made a mistake. A man died and I dressed him for burial. I pulled his belt too tight. I pulled as hard as I could. That is what makes you sick now. That is the reason the medicine you have taken has not helped you. The medicine cannot work itself down into your body."

J. B.: "I hope I will get well now."

D.(1): "My son, I hope you will. It's my fault that you have been so sick around your waist."

Then William Franklin spoke again: "I don't know what kind of medicine to give this man tomorrow morning. Is there anyone here inside that has some medicine I can give this man?

At this point, the *memengwécī* spoke up: "I'll give him a little," he said.

W. F.: "You can give it to him tomorrow morning."

M.: "No, I'll go and get it now." So he went out.

J. B: "I wonder how far he has to go." A *pawágan* answered: "There is only one place to go." Someone in the audience: "Where is that?" *Pawágan*: "*Memengwécīwak* live at *kickábiskan* [high rock]."

Soon the *memengwécī* was back in the conjuring tent, and said to W.F.: "When morning comes, you give that Indian this medicine of mine I have brought you, and tell him how to use it."

DRUM DIVINATION AND THE SPIRITS OF THE DEAD

Another method of communication between the living and the dead, one which has sprung up in recent years among the Berens River Saulteaux at the Pauingessi [Pauingassi] settlement, is apparently unique. I know of no specific analogies to it anywhere among Algonkian peoples.

Despite the emphasis given to the role of the *djībaiyak* in the Drum Dance described above, when I mentioned to Kīwítc the ceremony I had witnessed at Pauingessi (in 1933), he said: "I have not gone *that* far." In the Pauingessi dance, the *drum* has become the medium of communication between the living and the spirits of the dead.

This dance was a dream revelation to Nämawin (Fair Wind), now blind, and one of the oldest men on the river. For many years he has dominated a sector of the [Little] Grand Rapids Band, which has its summer fishing settlement and winter houses about twelve miles north of the other Grand Rapids settlement. Fair Wind has four married sons and one married daughter living there, and all his sons assist their father in carrying on both the *Wabanówīwin* and the dance in question. He is the ostensible leader of both of these ceremonies.

The dance, like the one owned by Kīwítc, has no specific name; but my interpreter said that it might be called, simply, *Djībaisímowin*, "Ghost (or Spirit of the Dead) Dance." It differs from the dance of Kīwítc in that allusions to *pawáganak* are absent.

It is held within a pavilion, consisting of a circular structure made of poles,[38] which has four doors, facing north, south, east, and west. The northern door is used as entrance.

On the occasion when I witnessed it, the dance followed a three-day *Wabanówīwin.* It was cloudy and windy, and a little rain fell in the morning. Preparatory to the performance, the ground inside the pavilion was swept out, some broken poles were repaired, and spruce boughs were cut by the women and placed both around the periphery of the interior, and in the middle, where the drummers sit. There was a flagpole in the center, from which a British flag flapped in the wind.

The drum was brought in about noon, and a windbreak of canvas erected to one side of it. A fire was kindled outside the pavilion, to which the drum was later taken from time to time to stretch the drumskin. The drum was called "our grandfather."

The dance was opened by old Fair Wind, who with lighted pipe in hand (the stem pointing towards the drum), and his hat off, made some opening remarks. Then he circled the pavilion, took his place, and smoked for a while.

Before the actual drumming started, he made a speech, in a voice which expressed deep feeling, and was punctuated by many gestures. The gist of it was an explanation of how he had obtained the dance. He spoke about one of his grandsons, who grew up to be a good-sized boy, and then fell sick. He said:

> I tried to cure him, but I found I was unable to help him. Others tried, too, but they also failed. Finally, he was so weak that he had to be fed with a spoon. Then one day he slept away. After that, even in the daytime it was dark to me. I was full of grief.
>
> One day I was away in the bush by myself. The tears were running down my cheeks all the time, thinking about this boy. I put down my gun and my mittens. I made up my mind to die. I lay down on the point of a rock, where I could be found. When I closed my eyes, towards the sky I saw something like a nest.[39] When I looked towards the east, I heard something saying: "This is something that will stop you from crying. You'll not die. For this is one of the finest things to play with."

All this, of course, is typical of the situations in which many Eastern Woodland Indians have received a "blessing" from the superhuman powers.

They provoked pity, and they were given something to "amuse" themselves with.

Fair Wind then went on to a homely human analogy in his speech. He said: "If any of you heard one of your children crying, you would run to the child at once to find out what made him cry. He might have hurt himself, and you would try to give him something to amuse him, so he would stop crying."

After a few more remarks that are irrelevant here, the drumming started. There were four drummers, two of them sons of Fair Wind, and one of them his brother's son. Angus was the head drummer and sat on the south side of the drum. Not being aware at this time of the association of the *djībaiyak* with this dance, neither Chief Berens nor I paid any special attention to Angus, as he lightly tapped on the edge of the drum before they began to sing, and uttered a few words in a very low tone at the same time. We later discovered that these words were addressed to the *djībaiyak,* whose medium of communication was the drum.

After the drumming and dancing had been going on for some time, a new song was started, and a number of people, most of them women, appeared with dishes in their hands. These dishes were each covered with a handkerchief or small piece of cloth, and the women carried them into the pavilion, circled round the drum, and then deposited them beside the drum. Presently Fair Wind got up, and after some remarks about God as the creator, who had delegated a little of his power to the *ätsokának* said:

> I'm going to explain to the great visiting Chief the meaning of those dishes that have just been brought in here, and are lying there with a little food in them.[40] When a person has lost a brother, a child, or some other relative, we call upon them to look down upon us.[41] They have been on this earth once, and before that they were sent from above to come on this earth. Jesus, too, came from above to be the boss of the earth.

The food in the dishes, then, was offered to the *djībaiyak* and it is noteworthy that it was not "the Ancients" that the participants had in mind on this occasion, but the more recent dead, those that were still being mourned.

Towards the close of the dance, the dishes of food were placed on the ground, arranged roughly in a ring around the drum; then the persons who had brought them in, while dancing around the drum took their respective dishes, and after circling around the dance path once or twice, placed them on top of the drum. The dishes were now unwrapped by the drummers, and every person in the pavilion stepped forward and helped himself to the bannock.

At this point, Angus made a speech. He said:

> My beloved friends, when I was a boy, I never expected to be sitting here beating this drum. Even when I was a young man, I never thought of it. Later, when I was a full-grown man, I worked hard on the York boats, just like my father had done. Yet I knew nothing. Even when I got married, I was still ignorant. Recently one of my brother's sons slept away. He is sleeping over there [pointing in the direction of the grave]. I did not like to see his grave like that of an animal, all covered with snow. I went there and put my tent over the grave.[42]
>
> A few months later, I went north to hunt. I was crying, even while I was hunting. Finally, I made up my mind that I would rather sleep than live.[43] Then I heard a voice saying to me: "I'll give you something to ease your mind and that of others. But you must take care and carry things through as you are told."
>
> Even a minister's name was mentioned. But the minister did not tell me half of what he should have told me. He did not even know what *pinèsï* was. He is one of those that tries to make us believe that stones striking together makes the noise that we hear (thunder). I do not believe this. I mention it today because I know something different on account of what I have dreamed.

Shortly after this, during one of the intervals between songs, Angus talked to the *djïbaiyak* that were reputed to be speaking through the drum. This episode was not dramatized in any way. It seemed to occur quite spontaneously. Because of its unexpectedness, as well as its unique character, my interpreter, Chief Berens, did not at first understand to whom Angus was talking, or even what he was talking about. The words were uttered by Angus in a low tone, with his head partly bent over the drum, which he gave slowly timed blows with his drumstick at fairly regular intervals.

It appears that Angus, while listening carefully to the drum, was at the same time repeating certain questions which were being asked, and then answering them. One of the questions he heard, for example, was repeated by him as: "The master (*kadabéndang*) wants to know how we are getting along." The answer was given: "Just the same as before. We are very poor." The reply to another question was: "You're merciful to the Indians. You know what they want—more Life, and the things we need for our bodies on this earth."

Once Angus called to his father and asked: "Did you understand what was said?" "No," replied Fair Wind, "I was not listening closely enough."

Then Angus began to sing another song, but suddenly stopped. He evidently had heard something more, but did not quite catch it. At any rate he said: "I missed it. I didn't finish it." He asked his wife for some tobacco. She did not have any, so he told her to run and get some, and to be quick about it. This tobacco was then immediately thrown into the fire outside the pavilion, evidently as a sacrifice because of a mistake Angus had made. He said: "I've started singing now and I'll have to go on"; and he talked no more to the *djíbaiyak*.

Soon there was the last dance, led by the wife of Angus. After going clockwise, the direction was reversed and the participants went counterclockwise to the end of the dance. During this movement, Pīkwákīgan (Lump Breast), walking clockwise, wove in and out of the line of dancers. Then the drummers stood up, Fair Wind came forward, and the whole group sang a Christian hymn. Finally, Fair Wind lifted his hand in benediction, in the Christian manner, and Jesus was mentioned again. The exit was through the west door, where Fair Wind stood and shook hands with everyone as they went out. To some he said, "Good night," in English; to others, the women in particular, he said, *nīpá* (sleep well).

When I later inquired whether the dance was a gift of the *djíbaiyak*, or of some *pawágan*, I was answered in the negative. It came directly from God. In this it contradicts, of course, one of the fundamental principles of even contemporary Saulteaux dream revelation. But the mixed character of the elements of the ceremony is obvious even in a superficial description. Moreover, the songs used are similar to, if not identical with, those employed in the ordinary *potáte* dances, and these songs came from the Plains. Nevertheless this dance also illustrates extremely well how diverse strands of belief and practice can be welded together under the influence of a strong personality, and yet still kept within the framework of the Saulteaux interpretation of the universe. To my mind, the dance indicates the dynamic character of syncretic processes, and the fact that it is of fairly recent origin shows that there is still some religious vitality left in the non-Christian beliefs of the Indian population along the river. The unique features it embodies stamp it as a creative, rather than a decadent, product.

There was one other practice, said to be associated with this Drum Dance that should be mentioned. When a person dies, if his clothes or other belongings are sent to Pauingessi it can be determined, by consulting the drum, to whom they should go. This custom is certainly derived from an older one, which consisted in sending the clothes of the deceased to some other settlement in exchange for similar articles, in order to avoid being reminded of the loved one. But Fair Wind and his sons send nothing in exchange; the articles are reputed to go to those who loved the deceased most. The drum is the medium of this information; and only Fair Wind and Angus, I may add, understand the messages which come through the drum.

The fact should further be stressed that the curative function, associated with all the principal ceremonies of the Berens River people since the Midéwi·win has died out, is a feature of the Drum Dance also. This is the aspect of it which I heard about at the Poplar Narrows settlement. Their drum was made for them under the direction of Fair Wind and his sons, and by the purchase of it[44] they have been able to share the benefits of the dream blessings of Fair Wind and Angus.

OTHER CEREMONIAL INVOCATIONS OF THE DEAD

The only emphasis upon the spirits of the dead comparable to that in the two dances described above occurred in two ceremonies now extinct.

One was formerly held farther north on the Poplar River. This dance was once described to Chief Berens by his grandmother [Amo]; he was unable to recall all the details, but she called it Djí·baisímowin, and stated that it was held once a year. It began after nightfall, and continued until daybreak. Eight or more carved wooden figures, painted black, and looking like human beings, were attached to a string and hung up in a row inside the wigwam. When the old man who was the owner of the dance drummed and sang, these figures would dance. They represented *djībaiyak*. During the course of the dance a whistling noise would be heard outside the wigwam, and it was the *djībaiyak* who were in this way characteristically indicating their presence.

The second ceremony, held at Jack Head across the Lake, had become associated with the Wabanówīwin. It was called Djībai Wabanó, and was said to have continued during ten nights. On the last night, the *càbandawan* the multiple family dwelling of former days in which the ceremony was being held, was closed up tight. Only those who had dreamed of *djibaiyak*[45] were allowed in. As the drumming and singing went on, *djibaiyak* were seen to pass through the *càbandawan* from end to end and then disappear. They did not walk on the ground, but "floated" along some little distance above it. After passing through, they were heard calling outside. Their call sounded like that of gulls.

THE DJĪBAIMIDÉWI·WIN CEREMONY

There was, of course, formerly the Djībaimidéwi·win on the Berens River itself, but this was of a character entirely distinct from that of the ceremonies already described. A living person was conducted through the ceremony, in place of a deceased relative who had already accumulated goods, and for whom all arrangements had been made with the leaders, but who had died before the spring came and the Midéwi·win proper was given. Obviously these special circumstances in no way changed, indeed rather maintained, the emphasis of the fundamental ideology of the Midéwi·win as ordinarily held; it was merely believed that the soul of the deceased person would be present.

REINCARNATION

Finally, a few words may be said about the belief in reincarnation. In this connection it will be necessary to return to Kīwítc once more. When he was telling me about his early life, he said:

> Some people say that a child knows nothing when it is born. Four nights before I was born I knew that I would be born. My mind was clear when I was born as it is now. I saw my father and my mother, and I knew who they were. I knew the things an Indian uses, their names, and what they were good for—an axe, a gun, a knife, and even an ice-chisel. I used to tell this to my father and he replied: "Long ago the Indians used to be like that, but the ones that came after them were different." I have asked my own children about this, but there is only one of them that remembers when he was in his mother's womb. People said to me: "You are one of those old people who died long ago and were born a second time."

This last statement is certainly sufficient to indicate that a belief in the possibility of reincarnation is extant; but it remains almost wholly unelaborated. In the case of Kīwítc, it merges with the idea of *precognition,* the belief in which is stressed by making it one of the tokens of the possession of magical powers. It is this aspect of his account which is really significant. In terms of Saulteaux thought, the idea of reincarnation is in the nature of a secondary explanation of something remarkable. Thus Kīwítc, no doubt unconsciously, has invested himself with what, in Saulteaux opinion, is a sign of great spiritual power.

Reincarnation is also cited when a child is found to have a few gray hairs. People will say that it is some old man or woman who has been born again

5. The drum dance pavilion at Poplar Hill on the upper Berens River, from the water. Photograph by A. Irving Hallowell, probably in the summer of 1932. On the transmission of Fair Wind's drum dance from Pauingassi to Poplar Hill, see Brown and Matthews 1994, 70. Note the men coming forward to greet their visitors; as Hallowell noted, the women stayed discreetly back in the bushes. (*Courtesy of the American Philosophical Society.*)

(*keté änicinábe èändjīnictáuwige*) But no identification is made with any particular individual, and the linkage with the spirit of the dead therefore remains extremely vague.[46]

CONCLUSIONS

Despite the emphasis given to the spirits of the dead in the ceremonies described, and the intimate relations which they are supposed to have with the living in many other respects, it is obvious that there is nothing that can be specifically characterized as ancestor worship, or a cult of the dead. However, Saulteaux conceptions of the universe are of such a nature, and permit of so much flexibility in their concrete application as explanatory principles, that it is quite conceivable that discrete elements, now typically unelaborated, might, in the hands of some influential personality, be developed in that direction.

As it is, the spirits of the dead, instead of being central in the ideology of the Indians, are actually peripheral to other spiritual beings who are

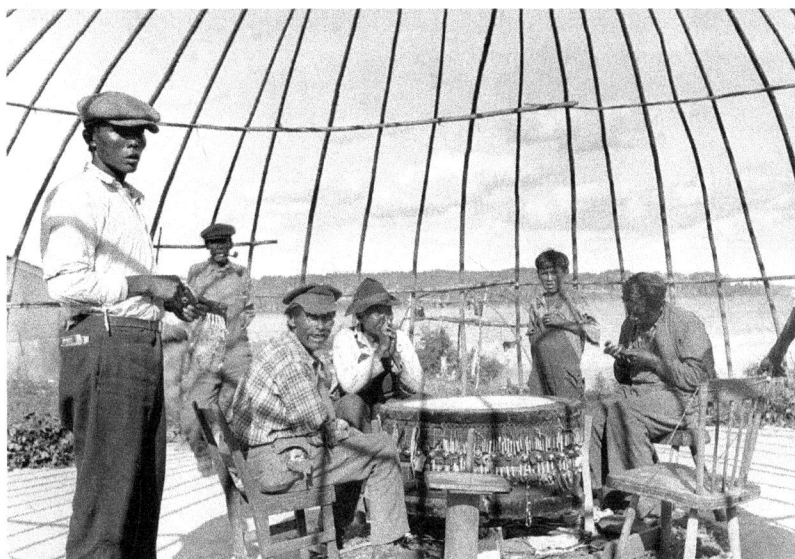

6. Drummers and Fair Wind's big drum in the pavilion at Poplar Hill. Photograph by A. Irving Hallowell. Note the drum decorations—the fur cuffs at top and bottom, the metal tinklers, and the leather strap with harness bells around the middle, all of which contributed to the impressive sound it produced. For details on the Poplar Hill man (a relative of Fair Wind) who purchased the drum and on the others who conducted the ceremony there, see Brown and Matthews 1994, 70. The drum, damaged and without its regalia, now resides in retirement in the Red Lake District Cultural Heritage Centre, Red Lake, Ontario. (*Courtesy of the American Philosophical Society.*)

conceptually the dynamic forces of the universe, helping men to achieve the ends for which they strive. This relationship is demonstrated by the fact that the spirits of the dead tend to coalesce, in certain instances, with the *pawáganak*, conceptually and functionally. The gap is easily bridged, indeed, if for no other reason than the presence in mythology of anthropomorphic characters who themselves function as spiritual helpers; typical of such is *wísakedják*. These anthropomorphic beings, while now immortal like the dead, once lived on earth like the Indians, so that they too are among the *keté änicinábek*.

Nor must it be forgotten how shadowy is the line, in Saulteaux thought, between "humanness" and the essentially animate qualities of other orders of being. No wonder, then, that the spirits of the dead are such an integral part of the Saulteaux universe, and that they merge so intimately with other aspects of Saulteaux life and thought.

Notes

First published in *Journal of the Royal Anthropological Institute* 70 (1940): 29–51; reprinted in *Culture and Experience* (1955), 151–71.

1. See E. L. M. Conrad, "Les Idées des Indiens Algonquins relatives à la Vie d'Outre-tombe," *Review of the History of Religion*, 42, 1900, 9–81, 220–74. P. 43 ff. where references to visits to the land of the dead, culled from the older sources, are given. See also William Jones, "The Youth Who Died and Came Back to Life," *Ojibwa Texts,* II (Publications of the American Ethnological Society 1919). [Ed. note: See also Louis Bird's story, "The Power of the Orphan—a Resurrection Story," in Louis Bird and Susan Elaine Gray, *The Spirit Lives in the Mind: Omushkego Stories, Lives, and Dreams* (Montreal: McGill-Queen's University Press, 2007), 64–66.]

2. Edwyn Bevan, *Sibyls and Seers: A Survey of Some Ancient Theories of Revelation and Inspiration* (London, 1928), 42 ff.

3. A. H. Gayton ("The Orpheus Myth in North America," *Journal of American Folk-Lore,* 48, 1935, 263–86) points out, for example, that such a journey is invariably described as an historic event among certain California tribes (269), and that there, as elsewhere, versions of this myth, or related tales about visits to the after-world by human beings, form the basis of tribal beliefs concerning life after death. A Fox account, for example, is "given as a personal experience of the informant's grandfather" (275); "supposed actual visits to the land of the dead are not uncommon or unnatural experiences in the Plains" (277); and "on the Northwest Coast tales which deal with pursuit or resuscitation of the dead are common. Beside these there are experiences described by persons who believed that they had visited the land of the dead while unconscious or 'dead'" (280). See Conrad, *Les Idées,* 48–49.

4. This point has a significance which I did not grasp at the time. In the Ojibwa account of a similar journey (Jones, *Ojibwa Texts,* 11), a youth visiting the land of the dead is offered their "supremely selected food"—decayed (i.e., phosphorescent) wood—by his grandmother. When he refused it she said: "Naturally you are not yet truly dead. . . . When the time is at hand for you also to come here, then will you also want to eat this food of ours."

5. See Conrad, *Les Idées,* 77.

6. A term used for a large unit of population, and applied to the settle-

ment occupied by the dead by Ojibwa-speaking peoples generally. See Jones, *Ojibwa Texts*, 9.

7. A similar incident is found in the personal account of an Ojibwa (Gitchegausiné) who dreamed he was journeying to the Land of the Dead (T.L. McKenney, *Sketches of a Tour to the Lakes, of the Character and Customs of the Chippeway Indians, and of the Incidents Connected with the Treaty of Fond du Lac* (Baltimore, 1827), 370–372.

8. Taking the account at its face value, one suspects a delusional state. That the man was suffering from some mental disorder is likewise suggested by another peculiarity in his behavior which was mentioned. When he had to evacuate his bowels, he would not always leave the place where he happened to be, but would throw the feces to one side with his hand. My interpreter commented that Mud-Turtle's Eye did not seem to have all his senses, after he "came back," but that half of his mind had remained in the spirit world.

9. See Jones, *Ojibwa Texts*, 11.

110. A nickname for which I could obtain no translation.

11. D. Jenness, *The Ojibwa Indians of Parry Island, Their Social and Religious Life* (Canada Dept. of Mines, Bulletin No. 78, 1935), 110, records three *unsuccessful* attempts to bring back the souls of deceased persons. Two of these attempts were made by his informant; one by the latter's father.

12. Other Ojibwa peoples locate it in the West; see Conrad, *Les Idées*, 71.

13. The Christianized Indians use the term *k'tcígijik*, lit. "great sky," for heaven, and *k'tcígijikodenawan*, lit. "great sky town (city)," for kingdom of heaven (or heavenly city).

14. The Indian referred to above, however, maintained that there were no trees, and said that he supposed the *djíbaiyak* needed no plants for medicine.

15. See Conrad, *Les Idées*, 77, and Jones, *Ojibwa Texts*, 7.

16. See Jones, *Ojibwa Texts*, 7. The word *odinigang*, translated as "wild cucumber," should, it seems to me, be translated "shoulder-blade."

17. [Ed. note: William Berens told this myth to Hallowell; see Berens, 2009, Part IV. Aásī, after complicated travels in which he encounters these elements, destroys the world in a great conflagration to avenge his abused mother, and then recreates it.]

18. Note the reference to the child who was buried in a cradle-board, and was laboriously making its way along the *djíbai ikana*, in Jones, *Ojibwa Texts*, 5.

19. "Bad spirit," the contemporary term for the devil.

20. "Bad" deeds, according to this informant, were those which injured other people without just cause: e.g. murder (including infanticide), sorcery, theft, and wife-beating ("if the woman does not deserve it").

21. I suspect that this process has been underestimated, particularly with reference to the moral and religious notions of people undergoing acculturation. I have the highest regard for the character and veracity of the man in question, and the statement quoted was of particular psychological interest because of the many details of aboriginal life and thought concerning which his statements were undoubtedly authoritative.

22. [Ed. note: Several decades later, in 1994, Fred Baptiste at Berens River told Susan Gray a story about a friend's funeral he had recently attended. Showing an interesting blend of Christian and Ojibwe ideas, Fred said that he put a piece of cake in Alec McKay's casket, explaining that he was influenced by his painting of the Last Supper and that he wanted to have a bite with Alec before he went on his journey. Fred's conviction was that Alec would surely tell others what Fred had done—a good thing for Fred. Gray, "I Will Fear No Evil": Ojibwa-Missionary Encounters Along the Berens River, 1875–1940 (Calgary: University of Calgary Press, 2006), 150–151.]

23. Kadabéndang, "the master" (of the spirits of the dead), i.e., not the Supreme Being; see Conrad, Les Idées, 81.

24. A nickname for which I have no translation. [Alec Keeper.]

25. A characteristic epithet, used regardless of age.

26. Anthropomorphic characters occurring in myths; of these wisakedják is the most important.

27. A number of other songs allude to the Thunder Bird.

28. Just how much these statements owe to Christian influence it is hard to say; but I would not wish to assert their complete aboriginality. Kīwítc also referred to "our friends who have come from such a long distance," and expressed the hope that we would be taken care of and be given "Life."

29. In a private conversation, Kīwítc once expressed naïve amazement that all the plants, animals, etc. had names.

30. A specific illustration of the belief that the pawáganak are always imminent at such times.

31. That is, it was a sacrifice, and therefore must be shared among the participants in the ceremony, and be smoked during the course of it.

32. This refers to an unpeeled, decorated birch tree, placed outside the southern boundary of the dance ground, on which sacrifices were hung. It is considered one of the "leading" trees, and it appeared in the dream

of Kīwítc. It symbolizes, in this case, the medicinal properties of the plant world. There is a dreamed song, a gift of the birch tree, that is sung when the sacrifices are hung up.

33. In another speech, Kīwítc also referred to the "medicine" he had asked me for, "to help us with a few mouthfuls." This was flour, of which bannocks were made and consumed by the participants. These commonplace things were sacramentalized through their use in the dance.

34. See Jenness, *The Ojibwa Indians,* for a reference to an annual Feast of the Dead, held in the autumn, before the Indians scattered to their hunting grounds; also Conrad, *Les Idées,* 64.

35. Alexander Henry [the Elder], *Travels and Adventures in Canada and the Indian Territories, 1760–76* (New York, 1809), 130–31.

36. The description of the conjuring performance is oriented with respect to this man's request, and is thus only a partial account of what took place. [Ed. note: Jacob Berens was William Berens's father; see Berens (2009), *Memories, Myths, and Dreams.*]

37. The narrator was acting as *skabéwis* (usher).

38. I saw a similar pavilion in use at Poplar Narrows, farther up the river. The dance in this settlement was purchased from Fair Wind, but when I witnessed a performance there in 1932, no reference was made to *djībaiyak*.

39. The allusion here is to a drum.

40. Sugared bannock.

41. This phraseology is significant because of subsequent references to Christian beliefs. Fair Wind was once a professing Christian, and had only obtained the revelation on which the dance is based a few years before this speech was made.

42. This indicates that no grave-house had been built, as was the custom in former times. Angus was unconsciously reviving this old custom.

43. This repetition of his father's experience not only repeats a cultural pattern but must have a personal significance. The same mode of identification was noted in another instance.

44. The price is reputed to have been so exorbitant that the payments are not yet finished.

45. This is further evidence, not only that the spirits of the dead functioned as guardian spirits, but that dream visits from the *djībaiyak* were not exceptional.

46. Subsequent investigation (1940) has revealed the belief that infants who cry constantly are trying to utter the name they bore in a previous existence, and that if this name is given, they stop crying.

TWENTY-THREE

The Role of Dreams in Ojibwa Culture

While dreaming has long been taken for granted as a commonplace human phenomenon, recent experimental observations in the laboratory have supplied firmer empirical evidence of its universality, particularly since objective quantitative measures of the frequency and amount of time consumed by dreaming in laboratory subjects are now available. Among other things, it has been demonstrated that the total amount of time devoted to dreaming during any single night is much greater than previously realized. Dreams reported following a night of sleep offer no precise measure of dreaming time since most of the dreams experienced of individuals are never recalled.[1] On the other hand, a high percentage of dream recall is possible when subjects under experimental observation are awakened. Dement, moreover, has advanced the hypothesis that since experimental curtailment produces such phenomena as anxiety, irritability, and so on, "a certain amount of dreaming each night is a necessity."[2] If this hypothesis is substantiated, it may turn out that we can assume that dreaming is not only a universal human experience but that it is vitally linked with man's psychobiological functioning and his distinctive level, perhaps, of behavioral adaptation.[3]

Since *Homo sapiens*, as contemporarily observed, is the end product of a long process of hominid evolution it may be possible in the future to consider the phenomenon of dreaming in this wider evolutionary perspective. Although direct observations of early hominids can never be made, it would be interesting to know whether systematic observations on living infrahuman primates would yield any of the objective indicators of dreaming which have been observed in man. I should like to suggest, speculative though it may be, that a consideration of dreams in an evolutionary frame of reference has important anthropological implications that are closely related to a revitalization of interest in man's behavioral evolution. For it is becoming increasingly clear that the problems presented by hominid evolution no longer can be focused exclusively in the area concerned with the study of the structural changes that occurred. It is necessary to take into account all the complex and interrelated variables that made possible not only the emergence of Homo sapiens considered as a zoological species, but concomitantly to consider the development of language and the cultural mode of adaptation which distinguish the behavior of the euhominids (i.e., the subfamily Hominidae) from earlier hominid species and other primates. Linguistic communication and cultural adaptation may be interpreted as the culminating stage of anciently established modes of organized social living in which protolinguistic and protocultural levels of social organization represent earlier evolutionary levels. A fact often overlooked is that structural changes, such as the erect posture that distinguishes the earliest hominids from related primate groups, and the expansion of the brain that characterizes the later hominids, occurred in animals typified by the fact that they lived in discretely organized social groups. Consequently the interplay and cumulative effects of such structural changes must have been fed back into the systems of social action that existed and, in time, modified social behavior and prepared the way for later developments.[4]

I have made this brief excursion into the behavioral evolution of man because it seems to me that the same condition that made possible the development of a new behavioral plateau, characterized by language and fully developed forms of cultural adaptation, was also that which enabled dreams, visions, and products of imaginative processes to be articulated, and thus to assume the social significance we find in Homo sapiens.[5] Dreaming may have occurred in the early hominids, but, without the psychological potentialities fully released only with the expansion of the hominid brain, it would not have been possible for the content of dreams or the products of imaginative processes to have been communicated to others. It will be recalled that Mrs. Hayes observed the homebred Viki playing with an imaginary pull toy. This was inferred from Viki's overt behavior. "Viki was at the pull-toy stage when a child is forever trailing some toy on a string . . . dragging wagons, shoes, dolls . . . [Viki's] body assumed just this angle." Viki herself had no means of representing and articulating the content of her imaginative processes and communicating them to Mrs. Hayes.[6]

The development and elaboration of cultural adaptation in the hominids implies a psychological restructuralization. It led to the development of a personality structure in which ego-centered processes and self-awareness became prime characteristics. Until this psychological level was reached memories of dreams could not be recalled and integrated with other self-related experiences. But, once in possession of psychological capacities, which made symbolic modes of personal expression and communication possible, the inner life of individuals could take on a new personal significance and be communicated to others through verbal and graphic means. The inner world of private experience and the outer world of publicly shared experience now became intricately meshed through symbolic representation. Unconscious psychological forces, hitherto latent in hominid evolution, but now mediated through dreams, visions, and other imaginative processes, intruded themselves upon man, because of his evolving capacity for self-awareness and the knowledge he could acquire of the inner life of other persons. Dream experiences could become the object of reflective thought and become socially significant. Varied interpretations of the meaning of dreams could become an integral part of the diversified world views that arose and became embedded in traditional cultural systems.

When we assume that contemporary individuals in our society are able to recall and report dreams, we are postulating psychological capacities and an evolutionary level of communication and cultural adaptation that did not exist at the earliest levels of hominid evolution. The capacity for recalling, communicating, and identifying "more or less coherent imagery sequences during sleep" as a "dream" not only implies complex psychological functions, but a culturally defined attitude toward a particular kind of subjective experience. We assume the existence of a sense of the continuity of a self in time and a capacity for objectifying self-related experience. We take it for granted that the subject associates memory images recalled from his period of sleep with a continuing self in the same way that memory images from past experience when awake can be recalled and self-related.

While dreams in our culture are recognized as self-related, the manifest content of dream experiences is not fully integrated with memories of past experiences while awake. Dream experiences are not considered to be of the same order. A dichotomy exists in our thinking. The world of dreams is considered to be a world of unreality, imagery, and fantasy, as compared with the "real" world of perception. The dreams I report are recognized as mine, but they are not considered the equivalent of other personal experiences. In the cognitive orientation of individuals in other cultures, however, such a sharp dichotomy may not exist, or may exist only to a lesser degree. Dream experiences may be interpreted, in some cases, as the literal equivalent of the experiences of individuals when fully awake. Indeed, the psychological depth of this attitude is attested by the fact that even in acculturated individuals, the "reality" of dreams may persist.

Devereux, for example, refers to the case of a highly educated Plains

Indian who was once a patient of his. When this man "realized that the flo-
rist's delivery wagon of which he had dreamed represented the counselor, he
quite spontaneously, though with an air of half-humorous shamefacedness,
asked the counselor where he went after he disappeared from the patient's
dream." Devereux also mentions a group of Papuan natives who, having
been converted to the Catholic faith, were "sufficiently well indoctrinated
to know that they were not 'morally' responsible for the content of their
dreams." Nevertheless, their priest discovered that when they frequently
confessed adultery, "the adultery occurred merely in dream." [7]

Dorothy Eggan has pointed out that, viewed in cross-cultural perspective, dreams "can be considered both a projection of the personality and a
reflection of the culture," so that in this frame of reference depth analysis of
dreams is only a single facet of the area of dream study. Dreams may "not only
[be] remembered and told," she says, but likewise may become "an active
force in cultural conditioning and personality expression." And, functioning
in response to varying cultural concepts, they "can operate in one direction
as a sanction for witchcraft, murder and cannibalism, and in the opposite
direction, to maintain group unity and individual equilibrium." [8]

What I wish to do here is to show how the dream experience of a group
of North American Indians, the Ojibwa, interpreted as actual experiences
of the self, functioned as a positive factor in the operation of their aboriginal
sociocultural system. In this case we have an interesting example of a mode of
cultural adaptation in which man's capacity for dreaming has been made an
integral part of the life adjustment of a people who faced the harsh realities
of a northern environment in which subsistence depended upon hunting,
fishing, and gathering. If dreaming may be considered to be a necessity at the
individual level of psychobiological adjustment, here, at the level of group
adaptation, the Ojibwa interpretation of dreams may be seen as a positive
and necessary factor in the maintenance of the sociocultural system that
gives meaning to their lives. Imaginative processes linked with traditional
values play a vital role in psychocultural adaptation.

The northern Ojibwa represent a regional branch of a widely distributed
group of Algonquian-speaking Indians in the United States and Canada,
perhaps numbering 50,000 in all. When first reported in the *Jesuit Relations* of 1640, they appear to have occupied a much more restricted area
in the region north of the Great Lakes. Their association with the Sault
Ste. Marie led to their designation as Saulteurs by the French fur-traders,
a name which, in its Anglicized form, Salteaux, is still applied to them in
Canada. A form of the term Ojibwa is an equally early name for them. In

the United States their designation as Chippewa is derived from the fact that the Bureau of American Ethnology officially adopted this term, a corruption of Ojibwa.

What I say here applies primarily to the northern group of Ojibwa I have studied at first hand. Located east of Lake Winnipeg along the Berens River in the eastern part of the province of Manitoba and western Ontario, at approximately 52° N. Lat., these Ojibwa retained much of their aboriginal system of beliefs until recent years. During the period of my fieldwork (1930–1940) for example, there was one band that had not yet become entirely Christianized. The relative conservatism of the Ojibwa east of Lake Winnipeg is partly the result of the fact that, unlike many other North American Indians, they were able to retain their native ecological adjustment as hunters and fishermen. The physical environment inhabited by them was not fitted for agriculture or settlement, and the white population has remained extremely sparse.

I shall not deal with the changing aspects of their culture here but endeavor rather to present the substantive aspects of their outlook upon the world as it was constituted for them by their aboriginal culture.[9]

Man's cultural adaptation everywhere embodies a cognitive orientation that makes life meaningful and establishes a blueprint for action. A psychological field, or behavioral environment, is structured for the individual. Traditional beliefs, knowledge, concepts, and values mediate personal adjustment to a culturally defined world.[10] It is in these terms that events become intelligible to human individuals. A world view is created which establishes the ultimate premises for all that is involved in any comprehensive explanation of the nature of events in the universe and man's relation to them. "Of all that is connoted by 'culture,'" says Redfield, "'world view' attends especially to the way a man, in a particular society, sees himself in relation to all else. It is the properties of existence as distinguished from and related to the self. It is, in short, a man's idea of the universe. It is that organization of ideas which answer to a man the questions: Where am I? Among whom do I move? What are my relations to things?"[11]

The culturally defined attitude toward dreams which we find among different peoples is often a direct clue to the basic premises of their world view. Among other things, it provides insight into how what we are accustomed to designate as "objective" and "subjective" phenomena are sharply differentiated, fused, or blurred. It will be recalled that Tylor, in his *Researches into the Early History of Mankind*, spoke of the life of primitive man as resembling "a long dream."[12] And, in his *Primitive Culture*, he referred to the "vivid and intense belief in the objective reality of the human spectres" which peoples at lower levels of culture "see in sickness, exhaustion, or excitement.... Even in healthy waking life," he says, "the savage or barbarian has never learned to make that rigid distinction between imagination and reality, to enforce which is one of the main results of scientific education."[13]

What I should like to emphasize here is the fact that it is inconceivable that man could have evolved without making *some* distinction between dreams, or visions, and the objective realities of his actual physical environment. Man could not have developed the tools and techniques for which we have ample evidence in the archaeological record if this were not so. What should not be overlooked is that the intrusion of dreams upon man's consciousness and the exercise of imaginative processes of all kinds did not overwhelm him or submerge him in a totally subjective world. Early man became endowed with capacities that enabled him to absorb such experiences and, through his creative imagination, to integrate them with an apprehension of the actual properties of the objects in his actual environment. This human capacity is reflected in the world view of different peoples when we examine and compare the cultural patterning of the polarity we characterize as "objective-subjective." Too often conceived as a simple linear continuum, I believe that the basic principle involved has been stated by MacLeod. He points out that "subjectivity and objectivity are properties of an organized perceptual field in which points of reference are selves (subjects) and objects, and the degree of articulation in this dimension may vary greatly."[14] This variation is a function, in part, of the outlook upon the world provided the individual by his culture. It is through concepts pertaining to the nature of the self, and to the nature of the objects in the universe other than self, that the individual receives his basic psychological orientation.

Ojibwa culture defines a psychological field of conduct for individuals in which their cognitive orientation—in the dimension of self to other—is elaborated with particular emphasis upon the interaction of "persons" in a "society" that is cosmic in scope. The participating individuals of this "great society" manifest differential personal characteristics and play various roles, but they are unified by traditionally established rights and obligations. There are two categories of the "person" class which can be differentiated: human beings and other-than-human persons. While animals, plants, and inanimate objects constitute other classes of being in the Ojibwa world, "persons" are the focal point of their ontology and the key to the psychological unity and dynamics of their outlook. This aspect of their metaphysics of being permeates the content of their cognitive processes; perceiving, remembering, imagining, conceiving, judging, and reasoning. Nor can the motivation of much of their conduct be thoroughly understood without taking into account the relation of their central values and goals to the constant awareness they have of the existence of other-than-human as well as human persons in their world. "Persons," too, are so inextricably associated with notions of causality that, in order to understand their appraisal of events and the kind of behavior demanded in situations as they define them, we are constantly confronted with the role of "persons" as loci of causality in the dynamics of their universe. For, by and large, the Ojibwa make no cardinal use of any of the concepts of impersonal forces as major determinants of events. Thus it is within an intricate web of social relations with other-than-human, as well as human persons, that the Ojibwa individual strives for *pīmädazīwin,* life in the fullest sense.[15]

Whereas social relations with human beings belong to the sphere of waking life, the most intimate social interaction with other-than-human persons is experienced chiefly, but not exclusively, by the self in dream. Social interaction in terms of the Ojibwa outlook involves no vital distinction between self-related experience when awake and experiences during sleep which are recalled and self-related. There is no sharply defined differentiation between subjectivity and objectivity here. The culturally accepted patterning overrides any such polarity. At the same time, dream experiences are not confused with events when awake. Qualitative differences are recognized as well as the fact that the kind of persons who play the major role in dreams are not those with whom the individual is most concerned in waking life. On the other hand, it should be noted that the Ojibwa are expert hunters whose reliable knowledge of the "real" properties of the fauna of their physical environment, as well as other resources, is highly impressive. Important as dreams are when considered with reference to their world view and the functioning of their sociocultural system, the Ojibwa cannot actually be said to live in a world of dreams.

What kind of entities, then, comprise the other-than-human class of persons of the Ojibwa world? I have used this somewhat awkward term in order to avoid applying the label "supernatural" to them. The concept of the "natural," ambiguous as it often is when used in Western culture,[16] is certainly not indigenous to Ojibwa thought. Consequently, the use of the term "supernatural" doubly distorts their outlook. Supernatural is an easily applied cliché but its descriptive accuracy, when introduced into discussion of the cognitive orientation of non-Western peoples, is highly questionable.[17] Bidney, among others, has pointed out that "the dichotomy of the natural and supernatural implies a scientific epistemology and critical, metaphysical sophistication which must not be assumed without reliable evidence."[18]

A few selected examples must suffice to illustrate the *types* of *other-than-human* objects or personified natural objects. They are thought of as persons; they may be addressed as such, and interaction with them is cast in a personal mode. In an anecdote I recorded, it is recounted how two old men at dawn vied with each other in influencing the sun's movements:

> The first old man said to his companion:
>
> "It is about sunrise now and there is a clear sky. You tell Sun to rise at once." So the other old man said to Sun: "My grandfather, come up quickly." As soon as he had said this, Sun came up into the sky like a shot. "Now you try something," he said to his companion. "See if you can send it down." So the other man said to Sun: "My grandfather, put your face down again." When he said this, Sun went down again. "I have more power than you," he said to his companion, "Sun never goes down once it comes up."

In a myth, an other-than-human person once set a snare in the path that Sun regularly traveled.[19] Sun was caught and could not move; darkness continued until Sun was released by an animal sent by human persons who could not carry on their daily activities in the darkness. In this myth, the movements of Sun are those of a person, not a natural object subject to impersonal forces. In the anecdote, the "natural" movement of the sun is reversed by the command of a human being. When Sun appears in the dream of a human person he addresses the dreamer by the reciprocal term used by the old men, that is, "my grandchild." These brief examples give the flavor of the Ojibwa outlook; they illustrate the occurrence of "social" interaction between the "persons" of the Ojibwa universe,[20] and they demonstrate the unity in thought which prevails in anecdote, myth, and dream.

The Winds are conceptualized as siblings, and there is a myth referring to their birth from an anthropomorphic mother.[21] The directions of the Ojibwa cosmos are defined by their dwelling places, that is, the homes of these other-than-human persons. Another typical subcategory of other-than-human person comprises the "owners" or "masters" of what we term natural species of plants and animals. There is a "master" of birch trees, and of bears. If animals, like the bear, are not treated properly after being killed, the master may take offense and retaliate by withholding members of the species from the hunter.

The Thunderbirds represent another type of personage. They live in a land above the flat earth that is the dwelling place of human persons, that is, *änicinábek* (the Ojibwa). The Thunderbirds are classified with the hawks, of which there are several natural species known to the Ojibwa. In a myth, a human being reaches Thunderbird Land where he immediately finds himself at home. These creatures hunt and talk and dance. Besides this, the young man is enabled to find his place in their kinship system at once because it is precisely the same as that of the Ojibwa. He marries a Thunderbird girl. Later she and her sisters return to earth with him and her sisters marry his brothers, a pattern that often occurs among the Ojibwa.[22] In one case in my genealogies six blood brothers were married to a sorority of six sisters.

Although the Thunderbirds are primarily conceived as avian in form, their outward appearance is not constant. In the myth, metamorphosis occurs as part of the plot. Some of them become anthropomorphic in appearance. Here we come close to the metaphysical core of the Ojibwa conception of being. Outward appearance is actually superficial. Although the Thunderbirds, like other entities of the other-than-human category, have distinctive attributes of their own, they have the same basic, enduring essence as do human persons. It is this vital core that is constant in both categories of persons. Human persons, too, have a constant and enduring essence (*òtcatcákwin*) and a bodily form (*mi·yó*) which, under most circumstances, is an identifying characteristic. But in neither category of the person class is the inner essence accessible to *visual* perception under any conditions. What can be perceived visually is only the aspect of being that has form. As we shall see later, metamorphosis, under certain conditions, is also possible for human beings. Change in outward appearance is potentially inherent in individuals belonging to both categories of persons. Consequently, the metamorphosis of the Thunderbird girls in the myth, and their marriage to human beings, can be accepted by the Ojibwa as an actual event in the kind of world to which they are culturally oriented. It is not a fanciful event attributable only to fictitious characters in an alien world of myth. I was once told of an Ojibwa woman (identifiable in my genealogies) who claimed that North Wind was the father of one of her children. My informant said he did not believe this; nevertheless, he thought it would have been accepted as a possibility in the past.[23]

The kind of social interaction possible between human and other-than-human persons in the context of daily life is illustrated by another anecdote. An informant told me that once on a summer afternoon during a storm he was sitting in a tent with a very old man [Naamiwan (Fair Wind) at Pauingassi] and his wife. There was one clap of thunder after another. Suddenly, the old man turned to his wife and asked, "Did you hear what was said?" "No," she replied, "I didn't catch it." My informant, an acculturated Indian, told me that at first he did not know what the old man and his wife referred to. It was, of course, the thunder. The old man thought that one of the Thunderbirds had said something to him. He was reacting to this sound in the same way as he would respond to a human being whose words he did not at once understand. The casualness of the remark demonstrates the psychological reality of the social relations with other-than-human persons that may become explicit in the behavior of the Ojibwa as a consequence of the cognitive "set" induced by their culture. I may add that, implicit in this anecdote is the assumption that the old man must have had previous contact with a Thunderbird in the dreams of his puberty fast. This explains why he thought he was addressed. By and large, the Ojibwa do not attune themselves to receiving messages every time a thunderstorm occurs!

Another occasion when social interaction becomes possible between human and other-than-human persons is at a conjuring performance (*kosábandamowin*). Its purpose is to secure help from other-than-human persons by invoking their presence and communicating human desires to them. A barrel-like framework of poles is built and covered with birchbark or canvas. The conjurer enters the structure after dark; the audience gathers outside. The conjurer invokes his particular benefactors among the host of other-than-human persons. They manifest themselves vocally, the voices issuing from the lodge being distinguishable from each other and from the voice of the conjurer who kneels within. These invoked entities may sometimes sing a song and name themselves. The Master of the moose may say: "Moose I am called:" The lodge is in almost constant movement from the time the conjurer enters it. The Winds are responsible for this. Direct communication sometimes takes place between members of the audience and some of the other-than-human persons present. At one performance I attended several members of the audience called for Miki·nă´k, the Great Turtle. Anyone may speak to Miki·nă´k and he always has a witty answer ready. He talks in a throaty nasal voice not unlike that of Donald Duck. His popularity with the audience was manifested throughout the evening by the intermittent stream of repartee that took place between Miki·nă´k and members of the audience. He strikes a note of levity in performances that are basically very serious in purpose.

One of the major sources of information about other-than-human persons, both to the Ojibwa themselves and to the investigator, are the myths. From the Ojibwa point of view they are not fiction. On the contrary, they narrate the past activities of well-known other-than-human persons who are their chief characters. The attitude toward myth exemplified in Ojibwa culture is essentially generalized by Eliade when he says that "it is the foundation of a structure of reality as well as a kind of human behavior. A myth always narrates something as having *really happened*, as an event that took place, in the plain sense of the term . . . Myths reveal the structure of reality, and the multiple modalities of being in the world . . . . They disclose the *true* stories, concern themselves with the *realities*."[24] In the context of their aboriginal culture, myths among the Ojibwa were only told during the long winter evenings by a narrator who dramatized them by gestures and other appropriate actions. These occasions were, in fact, a kind of invocation. The characters of myth, immortal living persons, were thought to come and listen to what was being said. In ancient times, one of these entities (Wisekedjak) is reputed to have said to the others: "We'll try to make everything to suit the *änicinábek* as long as any of them exist, so that they will never forget us and will always talk about us." Whereas we are inclined to think of myths as a special class of stories, the Ojibwa term for them—*ätisokának*—has no such connotation. It refers, rather, to the characters themselves, so that as William Jones said many years ago, "Myths are thought of as conscious beings, with powers of thought and action."[25] Consequently there is conclusive linguistic evidence of the category to which the characters in these belong. Along with other persons of the other-than-human category they are collectively referred to by the Ojibwa as "our grandfathers." This attests both to their psychological status as persons while, at the same time, it brings them within the boundaries of a social system in which everyone is given a kinship status. On account of the repeated recitation of myths winter after winter, children growing up in Ojibwa society became almost as familiar with their other-than-human grandfathers as they did with their human grandfathers.[26] They also heard the voices of the former at conjuring performances.[27] Furthermore, the individuality of other-than-human beings became reinforced by the fact that a character like Miki·nă´k always was heard to speak in the same characteristic manner whether in the narration of myths or in the shaking tent. Thus the reality of these characters did not depend upon conceptualization alone; their image was strongly reinforced by actual perceptual experience.

Any members of the other-than-human category of persons might appear in the dreams of Ojibwa individuals. In this context they were usually referred to as *pawáganak,* which may be rendered "dream visitors." Their appearance in the dreams was, of course, not as strangers or unfamiliar figures but as well-known living entities of the Ojibwa world. It is scarcely to be expected, then, that interpersonal relations with them in dreams could be dissociated from the knowledge of them which already existed in other contexts. Such relations could not be interpreted as other than experiences of the self. But dream experiences brought the individual into intimate personal contact with particular other-than-human persons. Besides this, the role that this category of persons played in those experiences was culturally defined as immensely vital to the welfare of the individual.

DREAMS, MOTIVATION, AND
THE SOCIOCULTURAL SYSTEM

Having considered the world view of the Ojibwa, I now analyze the relations between dreams, the motivation of individuals, and the functioning of their sociocultural system. I already have indicated that, for the Ojibwa, social relations with other-than-human persons are not metaphorical but intimately meshed in their thought and experience with interrelationships between human beings. I have referred to a few examples which show how social relations with other-than-human persons may enter the waking consciousness of human beings. Dreams, however, assume a special significance in any analysis of the functioning of the Ojibwa sociocultural system because the dream imagery that is interpreted as bringing the individual into direct face-to-face contact with other-than-human persons becomes so intimately linked with the motivation of individuals, traditional values, and social behavior. Contacts with other-than-human entities are highly motivated and sought by individuals as a means of achieving a personal life adjustment consonant with the characteristic values of the Ojibwa world. At the same time, dream experiences have significance with relation to the social system and community life because they are not only influential components of actual conduct but because they validate specialized services, like curing, which become available to other persons.

It must likewise be noted that interpersonal relations between human and other-than-human beings involve reciprocal rights and obligations, in the same way that social relations between human persons do. And these obligations are reinforced by the same sanctions that apply to social relations between human beings. Failure to fulfill them, in either case, is one variety of "bad conduct," bad conduct being culturally defined as any unpredictable or deviant conduct that fails to conform with the traditional normative standards of interpersonal relations. The penalty for bad conduct is illness. Any kind of bad conduct on my part is said to "follow me." I will inevitably become ill, or my children may get sick, or my wife may die. The fear of becoming ill and the anxiety engendered by any serious sickness is the major sanction of the Ojibwa sociocultural system. What is particularly characteristic is the fact that the bad conduct of human beings is believed to be the major source of illness. Consequently in every case of serious sickness an individual must reflect upon what kind of misdeeds he may have been responsible for in the past. Even in cases of sorcery the reputed act of the sorcerer is interpreted as retaliation for some previous bad conduct on the part of the *victim* in his interpersonal relations with the sorcerer.[28]

In this society no institutionalized means exist for the public adjudication of disputes or personal conflicts of any kind. There is no way in which publicly sanctioned punishments can be initiated in cases of incest, murder, or other offenses. For adults there are no superordinate modes of social control. Nor do other-than-human persons, any more than human beings, sit in judgment upon the acts of the latter and initiate punishment. Other-than-human entities exercise no punishing role; their relations to man are benevolent. If a human being fails to fulfill any obligation to them, sickness "follows him" as a matter of course. Social control in Ojibwa society conforms to the type that Whiting describes as operating through the mechanism of conscience or superego.[29] It involves a highly developed sense of personal responsibility for one's own conduct, sensitivity to guilt, and readiness to accept blame for one's actions. Consequently, it is necessary that the Ojibwa individual be groomed for independent action, associated with the capacity for bearing a heavy burden of moral responsibility, acquired through self-discipline. At the same time he needs to develop an inner sense of personal security in order to face the vicissitudes of life. This applies particularly to males who, being the hunters, are responsible for supplying the daily needs of their families.

A central value correlative with the Ojibwa food-gathering economy is the emphasis laid upon what may be called "equalitarian" values; these serve to equilibrate the distribution and consumption of goods in a system where purchase in a market is absent. They are expressed through sharing, borrowing, and mutual exchange. Dependence upon hunting, trapping, and fishing for a living is precarious at best and, even though the individual hunter may exercise his best skills, it is impossible to accumulate food for the inevitable rainy day. As a result, if I have more than I need today, I share it with you because I know that you, in turn, will share what you have with me tomorrow. In Ojibwa society there are no culturally structured incentives that induce individuals to surpass their fellows in the accumulation of material goods. No one is expected to have much more than anyone else, except temporarily.

It is particularly important to recognize that sharing what one has with others is a value that permeates the "great society" in which the Ojibwa live. This is the reason why the Ojibwa expect that powers possessed by other-than-human persons will be shared with them. Beings of the other-than-human category, considered as persons, are believed to be oriented to the same values and to be motivated like themselves. Other-than-human beings have more power than they need. From the Ojibwa point of view they may be said to have a surplus of power, so that it is legitimate to induce them to share it with human beings in order to meet the latter's needs.

The Ojibwa believe that a good life, free from illness, hunger, and misfortune (i.e., pīmädazīwin) cannot be achieved through relations with other human beings alone, cooperative as they may be. The help of powerful persons of the other-than-human category is a necessity, especially for men. Women may obtain such help but men cannot get along it. Since the Masters of the game animals, for instance, control the most vital source of food supply, a man needs contact with them. His own acquired skill as a hunter and trapper is not all that is required. With the help of powerful other-than-human persons a man can also defend himself against human beings hostile to him. Besides this, every special aptitude—such as curing and conjuring—exercised by men, depends upon the help of other-than-human entities, rather than upon their own individual talents or efforts. Furthermore, other-than-human persons of any functional significance were males, a fact correlative with patrilineal descent in Ojibwa culture and the subordinate role that women played in ceremonial life and in such specialized activities as conjuring and curing.

THE DREAM FAST

The help that men needed from males of the other-than-human category was primarily obtained in a lonely vigil through personal face-to-face contact with them in dreams. The grandfather of one of my informants said to him:

"You will have a long and good life if you dream well." In aboriginal days it was customary to send boys between the ages of ten and fifteen out to fast for six or seven nights. They became suppliants in need of help; they were said to provoke the "pity" of their other-than-human grandfathers.[30] Coming to their aid these *pawáganak* "blessed" them, as English-speaking informants phrase it, by offering to share their knowledge and power.

A boy undergoing a dream fast was called *kīgúsämo*. The essential condition for this experience was that he be *pékīze*, that is, pure, clean. He must never have had sexual intercourse. Even less intimate relations with women before, during, and immediately after fasting were considered contaminating and were to be avoided. If he had not met these conditions no other-than-human person would bless him or even approach him. Anecdotes are told to illustrate the importance of keeping such taboos. Boys were sent out in the spring to some distance from the camp. One informant said he was about thirteen years old at the time. A boy's clothes were carefully washed beforehand and he was provided with a new blanket. A moose or caribou skin, dyed with red ochre or sometimes painted with pictographs, was given him to lie on. Prior to his departure the boy slept in the "cleanest" place in the dwelling, that is, toward the rear, in the area reserved for the men. Before this he had slept nearer the front with his mother and other prepuberal children. This shift in sleeping quarters symbolized his segregation from the women and his approach to manhood.

When a boy is ready to depart for his dream fast he is accompanied into the bush by his father, grandfather, or other male relatives. When they arrive at a desirable spot a "nest" (*wázisan*) is built. In the case of the informant mentioned, an older brother built it. The *wázisan* is a platform made by laying poles across the branches of a tree, about fifteen feet from the ground. The *kīgúsämo* climbs the tree and seats himself, or stretches out, on this platform. It was forbidden to descend to the ground during the dream fast except to urinate and defecate. No food or drink must pass his lips. My informant said that his dream fast had lasted ten nights. "While I was there," he said, "I only thought of the good things I wanted for myself. I thought of nothing evil."

During the period when a boy was fasting alone in the forest, his father or grandfather might drum and sing continually in order to strengthen and help him. It may be mentioned in passing that many songs of the Ojibwa are not composed in the ordinary sense, but are the consequences of dream experiences.[31] Thus, older male relatives of the *kīgúsämo* may invoke, or communicate with, their own other-than-human tutelaries at the same

time that the boy is undergoing his first personal contacts with such entities. When the fast is ended the *kīgúsämo* usually returns to camp shortly
after daybreak. He hides in the bushes nearby and signals his presence by
a whistle, or call, his father knows. The latter goes immediately to him and
brings him to camp. The purpose of this procedure is to avoid being seen
by a woman first. This would endanger the boy's blessings.

Many years ago Paul Radin published a sample of dreams from the
dream fasts of Ojibwa boys. It should be emphasized, as Radin pointed
out, that all the dreams of this type which we have on record were told
by adults in later life, in some cases, filtered through another person. We
have no information whatever on dreams obtained immediately or even
a short time after the dream fast itself.[32] I believe, nevertheless, that the
general outlines of the basic cultural patterning of such dreams are known
to us. Since recounting experiences in a dream fast violated an obligation
to *pawáganak*, no investigator who had been present when aboriginal culture was flourishing could have obtained such material. Although I was
not able to add very much to the scanty corpus of published examples,
discussion with informants confirmed the general pattern exhibited by
Radin's sample. There are, however, a few points with regard to the content
of dream experience on which I wish to comment.

In one dream I collected, a *pawáganak* first appeared to a boy in anthropomorphic guise. Later, this being said, "Grandchild, I think you are strong
enough now to go with me." Then the *pawágan* began dancing and, as he
danced, he turned into what looked like a golden eagle, that is, the Master
of this species. Glancing down at his own body, the boy noticed that it
was covered with feathers. The Great Eagle spread its wings and flew off
toward the south. The *kīgúsämo* then spread his wings and followed.[33] In
this case we find the instability of outward form in both human and other-
than-human persons succinctly dramatized. Individuals of both categories
undergo metamorphosis. In later life the boy will recall that in his dream
fast he himself became transformed into a bird. This does not imply that
subsequent to his dream fast the boy can transform himself into a golden
eagle at will. But it does demonstrate by personal experience that such a
metamorphosis is possible for a human being. In this instance, the dream
itself does not inform us whether the boy's blessing included power to
transform himself. There are, however, many anecdotes told where it is
believed that a human individual has appeared in the guise of a bear.[34] The
assumption is that power to do this does exist in exceptional cases and
that it was obtained in a dream fast. In the dream cited what we do know

is that the Master of the Golden Eagles became one of the boy's tutelaries, or "guardian spirits," for life.

Even in the dreams of acculturated individuals who never underwent a dream fast, we find a manifest content that is interpreted as a great blessing, so that the significance of certain dream experiences remained the same for individuals long after the period when the aboriginal culture flourished. An example of this is a dream of my friend W. B. He entered a house and there he found a small boy wearing a red toque. This boy had a bow and two arrows, one red and the other black. "I'm going to find out how strong you are," he said to the dreamer. The latter took up a position in the middle of the room and when the boy shot his arrows he managed to dodge them. Then the boy exchanged places with the dreamer. My friend managed to hit the boy with the second (red) arrow, but it did not kill him. He said it was difficult because the boy seemed to be constantly moving, yet remaining in the same place, which was about a foot above the floor. The boy acknowledged that he had been beaten in the contest. The *pawágan* identified himself as an insect, "one of those which are so quick in their movements that they never seem to be at rest." The narrator called them "flies."[35] They have a yellow body and red marks on the head. The latter feature he associated with the red toque worn by the boy in his dream. Finally, this boy said to the dreamer: "If at any time in your life you are in a fight; think of me. Your body will always be quivering like mine." The dreamer was then directed to enter the next wigwam he came to on the trail. The moment he did so a man pointed a gun at him and fired. But W. B. felt no bullet enter his body. "This proved to me," he said, "how I had been blessed. Later I told my wife I would not be killed if I went to war. She asked me how I knew that, I told her it was none of her business." W. B. recognized this dream as a very special kind of dream. And it was. It falls within the type that is traditional in the dream fast. Other dreams of this man, of which I have more than a dozen, were not all of this type. W. B. was absolutely confident with respect to his invulnerability to bullets and if he had gone to war I am sure this would have given him unusual courage.

Another dream of this same man likewise illustrates the kind of manifest content associated with the dream fast. W. B. said it would have enabled him to become a *mänáo* if he had so desired. A *mänáo* is a doctor who dispenses medicine, which he obtains from the *memengwécīwak*. The latter look very much like human beings, but they belong to the other than-human category. They travel in canoes and make their home in the rocky escarpments that border some of the lakes. W. B. dreamed that he was out hunting and met one of the *memengwécīwak*. He asked W. B. to visit his home. "On the northwest side of the lake there was a very high steep rock. He headed directly for this rock. With one stroke of the paddle we were across the lake. The fellow threw his paddle down as we landed on a flat shelf of rock about level with the water. Behind this the rest of the rock rose steeply before us. But when his paddle touched the rock this part opened up. He pulled the canoe in and we entered a room in the rock." In this dream the geographical details are extremely precise. W. B. said that some time later, when *awake* and out hunting, he recognized the exact spot he had visited in his dream. He could go back any time in the future and obtain the special kind of medicine for which the *memengwécīwak* are famous.[36] The fact that W. B. said he could act this way in the future with reference to a dream experience of the past indicates clearly enough that in the Ojibwa world there is a unified spatiotemporal frame of reference for *all* self-related experience.

While the personal motivation of the boy who undergoes a dream fast is to secure "blessings" that will augment his limited human powers and enable him to achieve *pīmädazīwin*, exceptional powers can be obtained which may be exercised for the benefit of other human beings. If W. B. had been a pagan instead of a Christian, he would have become a *mänáo*. All specialized forms of curing, such as the ability to remove from the body lethal objects that have been projected there by sorcery,[37] depend upon dream revelation. The boy destined by his dream fast to become a conjurer is blessed by the Master of conjuring who lives in the West, but not on earth; he also must dream of the Winds, who are responsible for the movements exhibited by the conjuring lodge, and the Great Turtle, who acts as a messenger. I was told that four dreams are required before the instructions of the neophyte are completed. In the last dream he is told what kind of wood to select for the poles of the conjuring tent, which differs from conjurer to conjurer. The Master also designates the "moon" in which his initial performance must take place. The neophyte is told that he must not conjure too frequently, or to show off. There must be a real need for his services. In practice the occasions when there is a resort to conjuring are quite varied. If game is scarce and famine threatens, a conjurer, with the aid of his other-than-human helpers, may be able to direct hunters to the place where game can be found. By similar means it is possible for him to receive news about the health or circumstances of absent persons which will alleviate apprehension. A powerful conjurer is also able to protect a whole community for [from] malevolent influences, such as the approach of a cannibal monster (*wíndīgo*).

The knowledge and power acquired by human individuals in their dream experiences vary greatly. One man may acquire a great many more tutelaries than another, but only a relatively few individuals acquire exceptional powers. In these cases, there is no sharp line that divides human from other-than-human persons. Exceptional men may be able to make inanimate objects behave as if they were animate.[38] They are able to transform one substance into another, such as ashes into gunpowder, or a handful of goose feathers into birds or insects. In such manifestations they are elevated to the same level of power as that displayed by other-than-human persons. We can, in fact, find comparable episodes in the myths. It must also be observed, however, that despite wide variation in the powers obtained from other-than-human sources, "equalitarian" values prevail in this sphere, too. Although other-than-human persons are willing to share their knowledge and power with human persons, greediness is discountenanced, as is the hoarding of material goods among human beings. I was once told about the dream fast of a boy who was not satisfied with his initial blessing. He wanted to dream of all the leaves of all the trees in the world so that absolutely nothing would be hidden from him. This was considered greedy and, while the *pawágan* who appeared in his dream granted his desire, the boy was told that "as soon as the leaves start to fall you'll get sick and when all the leaves drop to the ground that is the end of your life." Overfasting is considered as greedy as hoarding. It violates a basic moral value of the Ojibwa world and is subject to a punitive sanction.

The knowledge and power that other-than-human persons share with the suppliant who seeks their help is not a free gift. The dream fast introduced a boy to a new set of moral obligations. The full benefit of the power and knowledge obtained was made contingent upon the fulfillment of obligations to other-than-human entities that assumed a primary moral force in his life. A reciprocal principle, equivalent to the basic patterning of social interaction between human persons, where rights and duties obtain, was operative. Besides this, the commands of *pawáganak* were considered absolute. The obligations they imposed took various forms. There might be a food taboo in the case of relations with the Masters of game animals. One man was forbidden to kill or eat porcupine by the Master of the porcupines.[39] In another case a man was commanded to wear the kind of headgear attributed to the mythical character who had blessed him in a dream. Another man was forbidden to speak to, or to have sexual intercourse with, his wife for a defined period after marriage.

Such obligations are never talked about because there is a general taboo directed against any reference to the relations of a man and his *pawáganak*, except in a highly allusive manner or under unusual circumstances. It is equivalent to the taboo against narrating myths in summer, which is not considered the proper time to talk about "our grandfather." All children are given a personal name by a human grandfather and this name contains an allusion to some dream event in the namer's experience. But no one is given further information. We can see, then, that the obligations imposed by the *pawáganak*, which individuals must fulfill in order to obtain great blessings, often involve firm self-discipline, because the behavior they involve cannot be explained to anyone. The man who was not permitted to sleep with his wife, or even talk to her, did not succeed in fulfilling his obligation. She did not understand his conduct and left him after one winter of married life. He married again and this time he broke the taboo. One of his children became sick and died; later his new wife died. He married a third time and the same thing happened. It was useless for him to expect *pīmädazīwin*. He had received a blessing, but had not been able to exercise sufficient self-control to benefit by it. Food taboos were interpreted so rigidly that inadvertent or unconscious violations did not modify the penalty for their infraction. The linguistic term for such infractions means "failure to observe an obligation earnestly entered into."

The seriousness of the failure to fulfill obligations to *pawáganak* is exemplified by the belief that the sickness that inevitably follows as a penalty cannot be cured. Other-than-human persons have done what they could for me; they have fulfilled their role. If I have been unable to fulfill my obligations to them it is my own fault, and I can only blame myself. The severity of the disease sanction in such cases is psychologically sound if it is interpreted as a means of strongly reinforcing self-discipline and personal independence among a people for whom life is fraught with objective hazards that are inescapable. At the same time the sanction lends support, in principle, to a readiness to accept personal responsibility for one's conduct in all interpersonal relations in a society where any organized superordinate forms of authority are absent.

The existence of the dream fast undertaken by boys in aboriginal days receives explanation as a necessary institution when considered in the perspective of the world view of the Ojibwa. It served to validate, through direct personal experience, the existence of other-than-human persons.

It served to engender, at an early age, self-confidence in meeting the vicissitudes of life as defined by Ojibwa values. The dream fast was the most crucial experience of a man's life: the personal relations he established with his *pawáganak* determined a great deal of his destiny as an individual. He met the "persons" on whom he could most firmly depend in the future. He also acquired knowledge of the specialized powers that would be of potential benefit to his fellow human beings. The dream fast was recognized as the ultimate source of their validation. If a doctor or a conjurer offered his services without dream validation, this was considered "deceit" and illness would surely follow. One such conjurer began to suffer from acute insomnia and a phobia. He found he could not go into the woods alone, not even for 200 yards. He confessed "deceit" and recovered from his phobia. Finally I believe we can say that the obligations, imposed in the dream fast, were the source of psychological effects which were of characterological importance. They reinforced a type of personality structure that, functioning primarily with emphasis upon inner control rather than outward coercion, was a necessary psychological component in the operation of the Ojibwa sociocultural system.

This system exploited a generic human experience—man's capacity for dreaming. Individuals, through appropriate socialization processes and institutions, were given a cognitive orientation toward the universe and themselves which required participation in a greater-than-human society in order to fulfill their personal needs. Dreaming was a means to this end. But dreaming was always linked to conduct. Thus, the role that dreaming played in the sociocultural system of the Ojibwa exemplifies the complex, coordinate, yet variable factors that may become structurally and functionally related in man's adjustment to a world in which his own imaginative interpretation of it is fed back into his adaptation to it.

Notes

First published in G. E. von Grunebaum and R. R. Caillois, eds., *The Dream and Human Societies* (Berkeley: University of California Press, 1966), 267–92; reprinted in the Hallowell essay collection, *Contributions to Anthropology: Selected Papers of A. Irving Hallowell* (Chicago: University of Chicago Press, 1976), 449–74.

1. See Dement and Kleitman, 1957; Kleitman, 1960; Wolpert and Trosman, 1958.

2. Dement, 1960.

3. In the course of the Fifth Conference on Problems of Consciousness, held in 1954, Kleitman said at one point in the discussion (1955, 114): "I am quite sure you need a cortex for dreaming." If this is so, the question may be asked whether the *expansion* of the cortex in the course of hominid evolution did not introduce a differential factor of importance with respect to the level of dream functioning that we find in the later and more evolved hominids. Early hominids, or other primates, may have experienced dreaming but, if the cortex is given special emphasis, it would be interesting to know how its expansion influenced dreaming.

4. For a more detailed discussion of the behavioral evolution of man, see Hallowell, 1960.

5. Beres (1960), departing from the everyday usage "which makes imagination a phenomenon associated with creativity and unreality, beyond the realm of ordinary thought processes," defines it as a "process whose products are images, symbols, fantasies, dreams, ideas, thoughts, and concepts." He considers imagination to be "a ubiquitous component of human psychic activity unique to man." He views it as "a complex psychic function, itself the resultant of a group of ego functions, that enters into all aspects of human psychic activity-normal mentation pathological processes, and artistic creativity.... Reality is a relative, indeterminate concept, influenced by the imaginative processes in man." Thus "imagination is not opposed to reality, but has as one of its most important applications, adaptation to reality."

6. See Hayes, 1951, chap. 11, 81, and comments in Hallowell, 1960, 354.

7. Devereux, 1951, 86.

8. Eggan, 1961, 552, 554.

9. See Hallowell, 1955, chap. 5, "The Northern Ojibwa." [Chapter 1, this volume.]

10. See Hallowell, 1955, chap. 4.

11. Redfield, 1952, 30.

12. Tylor, 1878, 137.

13. Tylor, 1874, 445.

14. MacLeod, 1947.

15. Cf. Hallowell, 1961. [Chapter 27, this volume.]

16. Many years ago Lovejoy observed that the "word 'nature' is probably the most equivocal in the vocabulary of the European peoples" (see Lovejoy and Boas, 1935, 12; Lovejoy, 1948, 69).

17. With respect to the general applicability of the natural-supernatural dichotomy to primitive culture see van der Leeuw, 1938, 544–545. Ackerknecht (1958, 53) says: "'Supernaturalistic,' though often used by the best

authorities, is quite obviously a misnomer for these primitive representations, as it presupposes the notion of the predictable natural which primitives characteristically do not have. This notion of natural is a much later invention. I have been as prone to use 'supernatural' in some of my earlier writings as others have."

18. Bidney, 1953, 166.

19. [Ed. note: Hallowell heard this story about the well known mythic character, Tcakabek, from Berens River Ojibwe. APS, Hallowell Papers, Series V, Saulteaux Indians, Myths and Tales, files 19, 25, 26. For a Cree rendition of this myth, see Louis Bird and Susan Elaine Gray, *The Spirit Lives in the Mind: Omushkego Stories, Lives, and Dreams* (Montreal: McGill-Queen's University Press, 2007), 29–36.]

20. Radin (1924, 518) records an anecdote that refers to a man who had dreamed of the "thunder-spirit." "When he wanted to make lightning he used to sing a song praising the thunder-spirit. Then when he had finished singing, he would cut up some tobacco, put some into the fire and some into his pipe. Then he would shout in the direction of the south, 'Let thunder come!' The next day there would be a tremendous thunder storm."

21. [William Berens told Hallowell this myth in 1933: "The Birth of the Winds, Flint and the Great Hare." See Berens, *Memories, Myths, and Dreams of an Ojibwe Leader* (2009), Part IV.]

22. [Ed. note: See "Mätcīkīwis," told to Hallowell by William Berens, in Berens, *Memories, Myths, and Dreams*, Part IV.]

23. This may have been a rationalization of mother-son incest. But, if so, the woman's "bad conduct" was never punished by sickness, nor did she ever confess her wrongdoing. These circumstances may have lent credence to her claim, when considered in the context of the Ojibwa world view.

24. Eliade, 1960, 14–15.

25. W. Jones, 1919, Part II, 574n.

26. I was told that on the winter evenings when myths were narrated children were encouraged to dream about their other-than-human grandfathers. That they may well have done so is suggested by the fact that C. W. Kimmis has called attention to the influence of stories read to children before going to sleep upon the content of their dreams. See quotations from Kimmis in Woods, 1947.

27. I once asked an informant who was about seventy years old to name all the other-than-human persons he had heard speak, or sing, in conjuring performances (see Hallowell, 1942 for the list). They included five characters

who play a prominent role in myth; four other personages semihuman in form; and almost two dozen of the "masters" of various animal species.

28. For a detailed discussion of Ojibwa world view and disease, see Hallowell, 1963.

29. On the basis of systematic cross-cultural sampling, Whiting (1959) has discriminated three types of social control, which he related to three independent motivational systems and the child-rearing practices and conditions required to produce and maintain them. Although he did not include the Ojibwa in his study, they would appear to conform to Whiting's Type 3.

30. Blumensohn, in his survey, points out that "the use of fasting in a personal relation with the supernatural was peculiar to the Central Algonkian" (1933, 468). "They believed that by fasting the suppliant underwent such suffering, made himself so weak, that the spirits were overcome with pity, and so granted him whatever he desired" (451). Kohl, visiting the Lake Superior Ojibwa over a century ago, was fascinated with the dream fast. "I found this subject most remarkable," he writes (1860, 228), "in fact, could it be possible to hear any thing stronger, or, I might say, more wonderful, than these stories of unheard of castigations and torments, to which young boys of thirteen or fourteen subject themselves, merely for the sake of an idea, a dream, or the fulfillment of a religious duty, or to ask a question of fate.... What courage! What self control! What power of enduring privation does this presuppose!"

31. Densmore, 1910, 118.

32. See Radin's discussion (1914, 7–10) regarding the transmission of the patterns of the dreams reported. Not all of the Ojibwa material in Radin (1936) is new. Dreams to be found in the earlier article are republished in a different wording but with no reference to previous publication. Lincoln (1935, 271–293) gives a selection from Radin's material.

33. For a fuller account of this dream see Hallowell, 1955, 178 [chapter 26, this volume].

34. For a more detailed discussion of this kind of metamorphosis see Hallowell, 1961, 36–38 ["Ojibwa Ontology," chapter 27, this volume]. Peter Jones, a converted Ojibwa, who became famous as a preacher and author says (1861, 145–146) that "sorcerers can turn themselves into bears, wolves, foxes owls, bats, and snakes.... Several of our people have informed me that they have seen and heard witches in the shape of these animals, especially the bear and the fox. They say that when a witch in the shape of a bear is being chased all at once she will run around a tree or hill, so as to

be lost sight of for a time. . . . Then, instead of seeing a bear they behold an old woman walking quietly along or digging up roots, and looking as innocent as a lamb."

35. He said they did not sting. But I never was able to make a positive identification of the species. [Ed. Note: For William Berens's telling of this dream, see Berens, *Memories, Myths, and Dreams*, Part III.]

36. [Ed. note: For fuller texts of this dream, see Hallowell, 1955, 97 (chapter 26, this volume), and Berens, *Memories, Myths, and Dreams*, Part III.]

37. See Densmore, 1910, 119ff., where the songs used by this type of doctor, as well as other details, are recorded.

38. For example, the animation of a string of wooden beads, or animal skins (Hoffman, 1891, 205–206).

39. This is an example of what was called "individual totemism" by older writers.

References

Ackerknecht, Erwin H. 1958. "Primitive medicine's social function," in *Miscellanea Paul Rivet Octogenario Diata*. Mexico City: Universidad Nacional Autónoma de México. I, 3–7.

Beres, David. 1960. "Perception, imagination, and reality," *International Journal of Psycho-Analysis*, 41:327–334.

Bidney, David. 1953. *Theoretical Anthropology*. New York: Columbia University Press.

Blumensohn, Jules. 1933, "The fast among North American Indians," *American Anthropologist*, 35: 451–469.

Dement, William. 1960. "The effect of dream deprivation," *Science*, 131: 1705–1707.

Dement, William, and Nathaniel Kleitman. 1957. "Cyclic variations in EEG during sleep and their relation to eye movements, body motility, and dreaming," *Electroencephalography and Clinical Neurophysiology* (Amsterdam), 9: 673–690.

———. 1957. "The relation of eye movements during sleep to dream activity: An objective method for the study of dreaming," *Journal of Experimental Psychology*, 53: 339–346.

Densmore, Frances. 1910. *Chippewa Music*. Bureau of American Ethnology. Bulletin 45. Washington.

Devereux, George, 1951. *Reality and Dream*. New York: International Universities Press.

Eggan, Dorothy. 1961. "Dream analysis," in Bert Kaplan, ed., *Studying Personality Cross-Culturally*. Evanston: Row, Peterson.

Eliade, Mircea. 1960. *Myths, Dreams and Mysteries*. Trans. Philip Mairet. London: Harvill.

English, Horace B., and Ava Champney. 1958. *A Comprehensive Dictionary of Psychological and Psychoanalytical Terms*. New York: Longmans, Green.

Hallowell, A. Irving. 1942. *The Role of Conjuring in Saulteaux Society*. Philadelphia: University of Pennsylvania Press.

———. 1955. *Culture and Experience*. Philadelphia: University of Pennsylvania Press.

———. 1960. "Self, society, and culture in phylogenetic perspective," in *Evolution after Darwin*, vol. 2 of *The Evolution of Man*, ed. Sol Tax. Chicago: University of Chicago Press.

———. 1961. "Ojibwa ontology, behavior, and world view," in *Culture in History: Essays in Honor of Paul Radin*. New York: Columbia University Press.

———. 1963. "Ojibwa world view and disease," in Iago Galdston, ed., *Man's Image in Medicine and Anthropology*. New York: International Universities Press.

Hayes, Cathy. 1951. *The Ape in Our House*. New York: Harper and Brothers.

Hoffman, W. J. 1891. *The Midēwiwin or "Grand Medicine Society" of the Ojibwa*. Bureau of American Ethnology. Seventh Annual Report. Washington.

Jones, Peter. 1861. *History of the Ojibwa Indians*. London.

Jones, William. 1919. *Ojibwa Texts*. Publication of the American Ethnological Society. Vol. 7, Part II. New York.

Kimmis, Charles W. 1920. *Children's Dreams*. New York: Longmans, Green.

Kleitman, Nathaniel. 1960. "Patterns of dreaming," *Scientific American*, 203: 82–88.

———. 1955. "The role of the cerebral cortex in the development and maintenance of consciousness," in *Problems of Consciousness*. Transactions of the Fifth Conference sponsored by Josiah Macy Jr., Foundation, 1950–1954. New York.

Kohl, J. G. 1860. *Kitchi-Gami: Wanderings Round Lake Superior*. London: Chapman and Hall.

Leeuw, G. van der. 1938. *Religion in Essence and Manifestation*. London: Allen and Unwin.

Lincoln, Jackson Steward. 1935. *The Dream in Primitive Cultures.* London: Cresset.

Lovejoy, Arthur O. 1948. *Essays in the History of Ideas.* Baltimore: Johns Hopkins Press.

Lovejoy, Arthur O., and George Boas. 1935. *Primitivism and Related Ideas in Antiquity,* vol. 1 of *A Documentary History of Primitivism and Related Ideas.* Baltimore: Johns Hopkins Press.

MacLeod, Robert B. 1947. "The phenomenological approach to social psychology," *Psychological Review,* 44: 193–210.

Radin, P. 1914. *Some Aspects of Puberty Fasting among the Ojibwa.* Canada Department Mines. Museum Bulletin no. 2, Ottawa.

———. 1924, "Ojibwa ethnological chit-chat," *American Anthropologist,* 26: 491–530.

———. 1936. "Ojibwa and Ottawa puberty dreams," in *Essays in Anthropology Presented to A. L. Kroeber . . . June 11.* Berkeley: University of California Press. Pp. 233–264.

Redfield, R, 1952. "The primitive world view," *Proceedings of the American Philosophical Society,* 96: 30–36.

Tylor, E. B. 1878. *Researches into the Early History of Mankind.* New York. (1st ed., 1865.)

———. 1874. *Primitive Culture.* 2 vols. New York. (1st ed., 1871.)

Whiting, John W. M. 1959. "Sorcery, sin and the superego: A cross-cultural study of some mechanisms of social control," in *Nebraska Symposium on Motivation.* Lincoln: University of Nebraska Press. VII, 174–195.

Wolpert, Edward A., and Harry Trosman. 1958. "Studies in the psychophysiology of dreams. I. Experimental evocation of sequential dream episodes," *American Medical Association Archives of Neurology and Psychiatry,* 79:603–606.

Woods, Ralph L. 1947. *The World of Dreams: An Anthology.* New York: Random House.

7

PERSONALITY, THE SELF, AND WORLD VIEW

Introduction

Part VII presents four articles that Hallowell published between 1941 and 1960. As a group, they reveal his evolving approaches to and thoughts about personality and the self. His work in this area culminated in two major essays: "The Self and its Behavioral Environment" (of which the "Ojibwa Self" portion appears in chapter 26), and "Ojibwa Ontology, Behavior, and World View" (chapter 27). In 1976, Raymond Fogelson presciently considered the latter to be perhaps Hallowell's most important work, and the one likely to have "the largest and most continuing impact."[1]

"The Rorschach Method as an Aid in the Study of Personalities in Primitive Societies" (1941) appears as chapter 24. Hallowell's engagement with the Rorschach inkblot test from the late 1930s to the early 1950s stirred much discussion, as has the Rorschach method itself over the years.[2] Beginning in 1941, he published several articles on Rorschach testing; the selection presented here is both concise and closely related to his Berens River work. He later recalled that he first heard Ruth Benedict utter "the strange word Rorschach" in Edward Sapir's Committee on Personality in Relation to Culture, sometime before 1938. Thinking this new psychological tool could have great potential use, he read all the literature he could find on it and "worked up a procedure for myself," which he applied at Berens River, Little Grand Rapids, and Pauingassi, Manitoba, in 1938 and 1940.[3] In the late 1940s, he and the graduate students who did summer fieldwork at Lac du Flambeau also used it there (see chapters 18 and 19 in Hallowell, *Culture and Experience*, 1955).

By the 1960s, Hallowell seldom referred to his Rorschach analyses. *The Ojibwa of Berens River, Manitoba*, written during that decade (though not published till 1992), made only one reference to the test; like his other late writings, it took a more humanistic than scientific approach. But writing in 1972, Hallowell still thought the test "had many advantages over other psychological tests . . . it was a subtle means of probing many of the complexities of personality and it was 'culture-free'" (prologue, this volume). It was not bound to a particular language and the images were non-representational, fostering free association. In 1956, Hallowell also emphasized its value cross-culturally: "at every level of technological and cultural development in which this test has been administered, subjects have attempted to offer 'meaningful' responses to what are, objectively, 'meaningless' inkblots"; people, even across cultural boundaries, proved insistent "on finding meaning [even] in what is for them an exotic task," pointing to "a universal need for meaning."[4] Given Hallowell's growing interest in Ojibwe cosmology and worldview, it is understandable that the test's power to elicit interpretive meaning had a strong appeal.

Hallowell's reference to the taking of the Rorschach test as an "exotic task" needs notice, however. In some respects, the test was not "culture-free." To be scientifically valid, it was supposed to be given under strict conditions in a standardized procedure, and the tester and the subject were to be alone in a quiet place. But as Hallowell noted in the article published here, the Berens River Ojibwe were "not accustomed to interviews, clinical examinations or tests of any kind"; nor were they used to such isolation. Women were shy and uncomfortable being alone with Hallowell, even with an interpreter present. Some people enjoyed the experience, however. At Berens River, one of William Berens's sons, Percy, was among the Rorschach subjects, and in the early 1990s, he still recalled being shown those "funny pictures." But he also had a grasp of their purpose; as he said one time, he supposed Hallowell was trying to figure out "how an Indian thinks."

The testing conditions in the small community of Pauingassi, near Little Grand Rapids, in the summer of 1938, would not have passed muster with Hallowell's psychologist colleagues back home, but his way of proceeding engaged the people's participation. While there, he stayed in the cabin of Naamiwan (Fair Wind), "a blind old man who was the acknowledged leader of the community." Naamiwan obviously could not take the test himself, but he was present as others took it, "and seemed to derive considerable entertainment from listening to the answers given to the cards." In the circumstance, Hallowell allowed the men who had finished the test to stay on while the next subjects took it. "As I was a guest in the house," he wrote, "I could hardly have ordered the old man's sons and other close relatives out." As a result, "the cooperation of this whole group of subjects was excellent. They appeared to enjoy the task and Namawin . . . expressed his appreciation when I left."[5]

On June 16, 1938, anthropologist Ruth Bunzel wrote to Hallowell about some pitfalls of the Rorschach test that she had experienced. In using it with the Chamula of Chiapas, Mexico, she saw the difficulties of trying to give the test in privacy and isolation. She also pointed out that one could not test the range of responses until one had a large number of cases with supporting case material: "And once you have that information," she added, "the question is already answered." Her colleague Jules Henry was enthusiastic about using the test with the Pilaga in South America, but, she cautioned: "that was a small group that he knew intimately, and I imagine that the test probably pointed up the things he had already found out in striking fashion." Her point evoked a problem that modern critics have identified: "confirmation bias," which "can mislead a clinician who attempts to evaluate the validity of a test through personal observation. If one begins with such a bias, evidence to support it can nearly always be found."[6] Hallowell may have come to recognize this problem, realizing that his understandings of Ojibwe personality and world view came essentially from long experience that already formed the intellectual context in which he administered the test. Rorschach testing proved to be only a supplement to his years of fieldwork with William Berens and others.

"Some Psychological Characteristics of the Northeastern Indians" (chapter 25), first published in 1946, delved into documentary sources from the 1600s on to assess what they could reveal about Native psychological characteristics, intelligence, and emotional structure in earlier times. Well aware of the cross-cultural limitations of modern intelligence and psychological tests (except for his favored Rorschachs), Hallowell looked at the writings of the missionaries, fur traders, and others to see how their various observations compared with his field and Rorschach results. He found that the comments of the Jesuit Le Jeune and others strongly paralleled his own observations of Ojibwe emotional restraint, avoidance of open criticism of others, and politeness. Similarly, older observers also cited fears of retaliatory sorcery and illness that could befall those who caused offense. Humor, joking, and teasing were ways of expressing feelings while avoiding and deflecting potential harm. If things went wrong, causation was personalized; someone must be responsible. Hallowell found that documentary sources seemed to support his Berens River findings as reported in Parts IV and V in this volume.

"Some Psychological Characteristics" was written a decade earlier than a somewhat parallel piece, "The Northern Ojibwa" (1955), the latter (chapter 1, this volume) being the broad historical introduction to the Ojibwe people that Hallowell wrote for *Culture and Experience*. These two chapters are the most ethnohistorical of Hallowell's works, showing his skilled use of published historical sources. As noted in the introduction to Part I,

Hallowell never got into using primary archival sources, but his command of published materials is impressive, and the references he gathered are still useful for scholars today.

"The Ojibwa Self and its Behavioral Environment" (chapter 26) has a distinctive history. It first appeared in April 1954, in an original and short-lived venue. *Explorations: Studies in Culture and Communication* was edited by anthropologist Edmund S. Carpenter and Marshall McLuhan, among others, at the University of Toronto. As its front matter announced, it was published "three times a year for two years." It was "designed, not as a permanent reference journal that embalms truth for posterity, but as a publication that explores and searches and questions," and as "a series that will cut across the humanities and social sciences by treating them as a continuum." *Explorations Two* included short essays by Carpenter, McLuhan, and others, and at the end, Hallowell's essay, "The Self and its Behavioural Environment," which at sixty-nine pages was by far the longest. When Hallowell selected it for inclusion in *Culture and Experience* (1955), he broke it into two parts. The first (thirty-five pages), which addressed the broad issue of self-awareness as a "psychological constant" and the nature of the self "as a culturally identifiable variable," bore the original title and appeared in Part I. The second, on "The Ojibwa Self and its Behavioral Environment" (ten pages) appeared in Part II. Only the latter is reprinted here because of its Ojibwe content, but the whole essay is well worth reading, as it sheds light on how Hallowell in 1954 was developing major ideas that informed his writing from then on.

Hallowell's discussion of the self reveals his working towards what he (and others) later called an "emic" or inside-oriented approach to understanding: "an excursion into ethnoscience—or ethnosemantics, if you will" (prologue, this volume). All peoples have concepts of the self (and of others), and of self-awareness. But the environments in which they live cannot simply be seen as external or "natural" or "cultural": rather, we all live in culturally constituted behavioral environments with which we constantly interact. It is not enough to achieve an objective description of "a culture." The question is how to approach more closely "an 'inside' view ... the kind of naïve orientation we unconsciously assume towards our own culture, but which is so difficult to achieve in the case of another." How, for example, do we come to understand a "greater society of selves," which encompasses "relations with dead ancestors or other-than-human selves" that may be "much more crucial for an understanding of the most vital needs and goals of the individual, than ... interpersonal relations with other human beings"? (Hallowell, *Explorations Two*, 124, 128; see also 145).

Occasionally, when Hallowell republished a text, he made small alterations in the reprint. In *Culture and Experience,* the paragraph that opened the Ojibwe section in *Explorations Two* has been omitted. In *Explorations* (153), the next paragraph begins: "In the Ojibwa language there is no term for 'self.' The equivalent opening sentence in *Culture and Experience* (172) reads: "Although there is no single term in Ojibwa speech that can be satisfactorily rendered into English as 'self,' nevertheless, by means of personal and possessive pronouns, the use of kinship terms, and so on, the Ojibwa Indian constantly identifies himself as a person." Working with original and reprinted texts for this volume, we have found almost no other instances of such changes from one version to another, but they are worth watching for.

The final article in this volume is "Ojibwa Ontology, Behavior, and World View" (chapter 27, first published 1960). It is perhaps the best known of Hallowell's essays, and one of the most appreciated. Anthropologist Tim Ingold recently cited it as "one of the great classics of northern circumpolar ethnography. I have turned to it over and over again for inspiration, and every reading has yielded some new insight."[7]

Many of the concepts, stories, and data mentioned in "Ojibwa Ontology" occur individually in various contexts in Hallowell's earlier works. What makes this piece special is its synthesizing of thoughts and data, its bringing together of insights and reflections in an organized way to achieve a higher level of qualitative and humanistic analysis, a tone that was already being set in the essay that Hallowell published in *Explorations* six years earlier. In regard to these qualities, it is of note that neither these texts nor "The Role of Dreams" (chapter 23) mention Rorschach testing, except in one anecdote recounted in the *Explorations* article (133).

It is also of interest that both this essay and the prologue to this volume ("On Being an Anthropologist," the last piece that Hallowell published in his lifetime in 1972), exhibit a positive tone about Ojibwe life that was not always present in his earlier writings. The articles in Parts IV and V often have a darker cast, partly owing to subject matter, and partly, as noted before, because they perhaps echo dark periods in Hallowell's own life. Hallowell's interpretations of the Ojibwes' individualism and what he occasionally called, after Ruth Landes, the "atomism" of their social life, were not as negative as those of Landes, but ostensibly good aspects of social behavior—hospitality, sharing, generosity, amiability—often appeared in his earlier analyses to be motivated essentially by fear, anxiety, and covert hostility.

In 1960, those elements were still there; they did after all, grow out of

Ojibwe testimony and careful field observation. But (as also in "The Role of Dreams") a stronger emphasis was placed on pīmädazīwin, "life in the fullest sense ... longevity, health, and freedom from misfortune. This goal cannot be achieved without the effective help and cooperation of *both* human and other-than-human persons." Hallowell went on to stress the need for mutual help and reciprocity, and the positive quality of sharing and avoiding greed; hunters shared their catch with their kin, and grandfathers shared their dreamed powers with their grandchildren. Fear and guilt entered in, but Hallowell concluded that "sanctioned moral values" guide relationships: "It is within this web of 'social relations' that the individual strives for pīmädazīwin."

A final passage from the prologue seems worth quoting here, as a summation of Hallowell's outlook in 1972:

> Dreams, fantasies, myth, art, and the world views of man, as articulated in cultural traditions, may be interpreted as making positive use of psychological resources in cultural adaptation and personal adjustment. Reliable knowledge of reality in any scientific sense need not be assumed to be a necessary condition for either biological adaptation or cultural adjustment to the actualities of human existence. Man ... has been able to survive by making cultural adaptations in which his own imaginative interpretations of the world have been fed back into his personal adjustment to it.

Again we see Hallowell's midlife scientism receding, and giving way to a humanistic emphasis on trying to understand how people interact with their "behavioral environments," how they engage with and create their worlds in their minds, adapting to the conditions of their existence through the mental powers of their imaginations. It might even be said that he here implicitly circles back to the earliest of his articles reprinted in this volume, "Some Empirical Aspects of Northern Saulteaux Religion" (1934, chapter 20), with its emphasis, almost forty years earlier, on how Ojibwe people both generate and relate to a spiritual universe arising from their deepest existential observations and experience.

Notes

1. Quoted in Melford E. Spiro, Introduction to Part V, "Ojibwa Culture and World View," in A. Irving Hallowell, *Contributions to Anthropology* (Chicago: University of Chicago Press, 1976), 355. See the preface to Berens,

Memories, Myths, and Dreams of an Ojibwe Leader (2009) for a discussion of Hallowell's work and for some recent scholars' appreciation of this essay in particular.

2. See, for example, James M. Wood, M. Teresa Nezworski, Scott O. Lilienfeld, and Howard N. Garb, *What's Wrong with the Rorschach? Science Confronts the Controversial Inkblot Test* (San Francisco: Jossey-Bass, 2003).

3. Stocking, "A. I. Hallowell's Boasian Evolutionism," 209. The test involves the subject being shown "a series of ten bilaterally symmetrical inkblots with no evident representative character, thereby presumably minimizing the imposition of [the investigator's] ethnocentric categories" (209 n6). Five were black-and-white; five were colored. The images are reproduced at the end of chapter 24, without the colors.

4. This quotation citing Hallowell's points is from Melford E. Spiro's 1966 essay, "Religion: Problems of Definition and Explanation," in Michael Banton, ed., *Anthropological Approaches to the Study of Religion* (London: Tavistock, 1966), 124 n6.

5. Hallowell, typescript on Berens River Rorschach analysis, n.d., 13. Hallowell papers, Rorschach files. The entertainment value of the Rorschach inkblots in this setting recalls the fact that Swiss psychologist Hermann Rorschach got his idea for the test in 1921 from a popular parlor game, Klexographie ["blot-writing"] at which he excelled in his youth (Dirk Olin, "Crash Course: The Rorschach Test" [*New York Times Magazine*, April 27, 2003], 32).

6. Bunzel to Hallowell, Hallowell correspondence, American Philosophical Society, Philadelphia; James M. Wood, et al., *What's Wrong with the Rorschach?* quoted in Olin, "Crash Course: The Rorschach Test," 31.

7. Ingold, "A Circumpolar Night's Dream." In Ingold, ed., *The Perception of the Environment: Essays in Livelihood, Dwelling, and Skill* (London: Routledge, 2000), 90–91.

TWENTY-FOUR

The Rorschach Method as an Aid in the Study of Personalities in Primitive Societies

The investigation of personality among the so-called primitive or nonliterate peoples presents a new and challenging problem. It offers the possibility of studying the effects upon individuals of a wider range of cultural and situational factors than is possible within occidental society. In fact, the relative constancy of many such factors within the ambit of our own culture, combined with an overemphasis upon organic determinants, for long obscured the importance of cultural variables in the genesis, structure, and functioning of personality. By enlarging the scope of our inquiries and taking mankind as a whole into account, a great scientific gain is indicated in so far as the social determinants of human personality and the problems which they raise are more and more clearly exposed to view.

But this extension of the area of investigation adds practical and methodological difficulties to those which confront us already in the study of personality in occidental society. It is obvious, for example, that factors of time and distance make it expensive to study nonliterate peoples with any degree of thoroughness, and to undertake the investigation of psychological and psychiatric problems in such groups does not simplify matters. Then there is always the linguistic barrier to be considered. Adequate communication between investigator and subjects is even more important in psychological than in ethnographical projects. There is likewise the problem of training. If the anthropologist is to undertake psychological as well as ethnographic research, the question of training in two disciplines is a matter of serious moment if the observations made are to be accepted as equivalent with those of psychologists, psychiatrists, or psychoanalysts upon individuals in our own society. Nor does it help matters much to ask the psychiatrist or psychologist to learn a native language and to familiarize himself with the field techniques of ethnography in addition to his own technical training. Of course these practical problems are not insuperable, but they are directly relevant to the quantity and quality of the data that can be expected from the pursuit of the study of personality in nonliterate societies.

Closely associated with these practical considerations are problems of a methodological nature. Up to the present time [1941] a great deal of our data on the personality and behavior of individuals in nonliterate societies are what may be labeled impressionistic. These observations, however astute, are of the same common-sense order that we all utilize in making psychological judgments about our fellow human beings. They involve no control of behavioral conditions and little or no use of theoretical concepts of a scientific order. To some extent the collection of biographical and autobiographical material has extended our factual range of data, but life-histories oriented in terms of systematic psychological concepts are yet to come. There are, however, an increasing number of observations—particularly on child behavior—that are guided by a definite selection of situations for detailed study and oriented in terms of problems that already have been investigated in occidental society. But as yet there are few observations that are controlled in the sense that the subject's responses under standard circumscribed conditions are studied. The reason for this is not far to seek. Most of the laboratory methods and methodological tools devised by psychologists for use in occidental culture are not adapted for use among primitive peoples. Deprived of many of his familiar techniques, handicapped in communication by the barrier of a strange language and by unfamiliar attitudes on the part of his subjects, the trained psychologist or psychiatrist, even were he to be set down in the midst of a primitive community, might feel somewhat at a disadvantage in approaching his usual tasks with satisfying efficiency and in a scientific manner.

In meeting this situation and as an important aid in advancing one of the new frontiers in the study of personality, I believe that the Rorschach has both methodological and practical advantages. It is a well-tested means of obtaining responses from individuals under controlled conditions that can be compared, analyzed, and interpreted according to well-recognized principles. Rorschach protocols, moreover, furnish objective data on personality that can be utilized by those who have not seen the individuals whose responses are recorded in them.

From a practical point of view the Rorschach method recommends itself because of the simple equipment needed, the minimum verbal instruction required, the fact that the literacy of the subject is not involved in any way, and the applicability of the method to all age groups. A further advantage must not be overlooked, although it should not be overstressed.

The Rorschach can be administered with a fair degree of success by those who are not fully expert in interpreting the results. A relatively short period of intensive training enables the individual to obtain protocols of value, even though they may not be equivalent in all respects to those secured by the expert.

Up to the present time, however, there are not to my knowledge more than 300 Rorschach protocols extant which have been obtained from individuals belonging to nonliterate cultures. Of these, the overwhelming majority (perhaps 250) have been secured from four American Indian groups by Jules Henry, Irving Goldman, Ruth Bunzel, and myself. In addition, twenty-nine protocols were collected in North Africa (Morocco) by the Bleulers,[1] and I obtained one protocol in native text from an Ibo in this country. I likewise have ten records obtained in Fiji by one of my students, Dr. Dorothy Spencer, and in Indonesia Dr. Cora Du Bois obtained some thirty-five records in Alor. It should be noted that, with the exception of the protocols obtained by the Bleulers, these Rorschach data from primitive societies have not been collected by professional psychologists or psychiatrists. And since none of this material has been analyzed or published in full detail, it is impossible as yet to estimate its value from a technical standpoint, or its significance with respect to the investigation of specific problems among nonliterate peoples. In fact, certain crucial questions arise which must be satisfactorily answered even before the use of the Rorschach method may be assumed to be an effective instrument in the study of personality in primitive societies.

Among these questions are the following:

1. What adaptations in administration, if any, are necessary to secure the best results?
2. Can natives be induced to associate freely to the blots so that in productivity their responses will be comparable with those of European and American subjects?
3. Are the qualitative aspects of the responses obtained comparable with those of whites? In terms of the scoring system of the Rorschach Research Exchange, for example, do we find all the categories used?
4. Do the responses given point to determinants with the same significance? Can they be utilized as indices to the same facets of personality organization?
5. Do differences in the frequency of certain categories of responses suggest that the significance of these for individual diagnosis requires refer-

ence to local group norms as a standard rather than to universal norms?

These questions cannot be satisfactorily answered for nonliterate peoples at large without more data than is now at hand. But I shall attempt to give tentative answers on the basis of my own experience in utilizing the Rorschach method in an American Indian society. After a brief discussion of some of these technical and practical considerations, I shall indicate a couple of specific problems that have arisen in the course of my own work on which I believe the Rorschach can throw important light, and suggest some larger questions that might be approached by extending its usage to the investigation of primitive peoples.

The Indians I used as subjects were members of four Saulteaux bands that inhabit the wooded region east of Lake Winnipeg in the province of Manitoba, Canada. Three of the bands are located on the Berens River and one on the Poplar River to the north. These Indians are hunters and fishermen and they speak Ojibwa, a language of the Algonkian stock. I have been engaged in ethnographic work among them since 1932.

Altogether I obtained Rorschach protocols from 100 individuals,[2] a sample representing approximately 10 percent of the native population. Their ages ranged from thirteen to eighty years; 18 percent were between the ages of thirteen and nineteen; 43 between twenty and thirty-nine; 26 percent between forty and fifty-nine, and 13 percent were sixty or more. Sixty-eight percent were males and 32 percent females.

Only twelve subjects were of mixed white and Indian blood. According to my genealogies, the rest were of unmixed Indian ancestry. Although there are those who[3] have envisaged the Rorschach test as another instrument for investigating that perennial and elusive problem—racial psychology— any such idea is not only a delusion, but demonstrably erroneous from a methodological point of view. For it would have to be assumed that the personality structure inferred from the Rorschach protocols was a direct reflection of biological determinants. At a time when those who use the standard intelligence tests no longer claim that these measure purely innate and biologically determined factors, it would be a pity if those who employ the Rorschach method should be led to assume that a biologically rooted personality structure is discernible that in any way can be related to so-called racial characteristics.

In administering the Rorschach, what I tried to bear in mind throughout was the spontaneous interpretations of the blots that it is designed to elicit. In so far as I departed from the standard procedure my aim was to facilitate this end.

In the first place, it was necessary to motivate individuals to look at the cards. This did not prove to be such a simple task, since these Indians are not accustomed to interviews, clinical examinations, or tests of any sort. Besides, they are not used to being isolated in order to perform any task, and isolation was a difficult practical problem to be solved. What I did was to tell my prospective subjects that I had something to show them, and I let it be known that each individual would receive a package of tobacco or a chocolate bar. I presented them with either one as a preliminary to the presentation of the cards. Nevertheless, some of the Indians refused point blank to look at the cards at all; others said that they would do so at some future time, and never showed up. On the other hand, some individuals apparently enjoyed the experience and even thanked me for letting them see the cards.

To many of these Indians I am sure there seemed something "phony" about sitting quietly and looking at the blots one after the other. It was not only a totally unfamiliar task—as it is with everyone—but in terms of their experience it was particularly strange because there is not even the vague analogy of looking at pictures and of course they do not read. At any rate, they often appeared apprehensive and tense at first, on the defensive, and fearful of making a mistake. Because I sensed this situation after a little initial experimentation, and also because I discovered that they did not always understand the task, I decided to use a trial blot and to amplify the initial instructions. This afforded an opportunity to make the subject feel at ease as well as to make sure that he understood what was required of him. In my instructions, therefore, I told the subjects that they could turn the cards and demonstrated this with a trial blot. Many of them handled the cards so cautiously that obviously they were not at ease and consequently not in a state of mind to associate freely to the blots. During the course of the examination I also gave verbal encouragement from time to time when it seemed that the subject was bored and ready to give up a task that seemed to require unnecessary concentration for dubious ends.

The most radical departure from the standard administration procedure was the use of an interpreter in the large majority of cases. But since these Indians are habitually deliberate in all their reactions, they were extremely slow in giving their responses to the Rorschach cards, and there was ample time for the interpreter to repeat their answers. Although there were some exceptions, on the average their reaction time was very much slower than that of whites. The average time of the first response to card V, for instance, was one minute. There were only four individuals in the entire series who responded to this card in five seconds and there were just as many who delayed for a couple of minutes or more. If their reaction time had not been so slow, it would have complicated the use of an interpreter, and this, I believe, is a practical problem of vital importance that might arise in other native groups. In looking over some of my records, however, Dr. Bruno Klopfer saw no significant differences in the protocols of individuals with whom I had used an interpreter and those cases in which the examination had been conducted in English. As a matter of fact, I used an interpreter in several instances when it was not absolutely necessary because in these cases I felt that the subject could express himself more spontaneously in his own language than in English.

So far as the productivity of responses is concerned, my data show that on the whole the Saulteaux had no real difficulty in associating to the blots. The number of responses given exhibit a range from five to 129. There was a slight sexual difference, however, the range for men being greater than that for women. But the mean group for both sexes was 20–30 responses. The next frequency group was 10–20 responses and the third in rank 30–40 responses. While some white groups have been found to average considerably higher, Gardner's nurses averaged only 22 responses, as did 25 Yale students.[4] Beck estimates a frequency of 20–30 responses as median.[5] Quantitatively, therefore, these Indians were sufficiently productive to make the collection of Rorschach data worthwhile.

So far as the qualitative aspects of the responses obtained are concerned, in my series of protocols these are fully comparable with those obtained from European and American populations. All the categories of determinants utilized in the refined scoring system of the Exchange are exhibited, although it may turn out that there is a quantitative difference in the frequency of certain categories in this Indian group as compared with others. I have not yet investigated this problem, but if there is any such difference I suspect that it may be reducible to a cultural variable of some sort.

In the content of the responses given, the cultural background of these Indians is often reflected in specific ways but not to the preponderant degree that I should have expected. This may be partly explained by the degree of acculturation to which the Saulteaux have been subjected. In a few cases it would be almost impossible to distinguish the protocol of an Indian from that of a white person in occidental civilization. On the other hand, there are other protocols in which reference is made to mythological figures and in quite a few instances reference is made to dream material. This reflects a characteristic preoccupation, since dreams mediate direct communication between man and supernatural beings. But in Rorschach terms it is interesting to note what the propensities of the cards elicit from the cultural background of the natives. *Pagak*, for instance, is a semihuman creature, skeleton-like. This was the association to card III in a few instances, and several individuals expressed amusement that the figures on the cards were of creatures that they had seen only in dreams. To be presented with their own dream images by a white man was particularly startling. But it gave me an interesting objective clue to the actual character of their dream figures. Card IX, for example, was interpreted by one man as a fantastic kind of supernatural entity that he had once dreamed of.

In the individual records there is not only a great variety in the number and quality of the responses, but some records are as rich and as interesting as any obtained among whites. There are also plenty of indications of a high intellectual level in a number of cases as well as of emotional difficulties. Despite the fact that the total series of protocols has not yet been scored and analyzed in detail so that no group norms are available, it appears that excellent personality pictures can be built up by taking a protocol as it stands and by applying the general principles of interpretation that have already been established. Dr. Klopfer has made a few blind diagnoses that correlate with my own impressions of the individuals concerned.

It was very interesting to discover, moreover, that in this group of Indians some of *their* popular responses were identical with those universal among Europeans and Americans. As might be expected, this applies to the animal figures on card VIII. One of the few Indians who did not see these figures was a man who exhibited marked color shock. He rejected the last three cards saying that they were the ugliest things he had ever seen and that he did not want to see anything like them again. Although I have not studied the popular responses in my total series, an analysis of all the responses to card V (which was rejected 7 times) indicates that butterfly was given twenty-three times and bat fourteen times, which provides a satisfactory quantitative basis for rating these answers "popular" among the Saulteaux.

On the other hand, the response "animal skin" to card VI cannot be rated a popular answer among the Saulteaux. It was only given four times, whereas "turtle" was given seventeen times. Adopting the criterion of one in six as the quantitative basis for a popular rating, "turtle" rather than "animal skin" is a popular answer to card VI among the Saulteaux. I think we can partly explain this difference in terms of a culturally derived *Einstellung.* While two species of turtle occur in the habitat of the Saulteaux, the larger variety (*Miki·nă′k*) is the one seldom seen, and yet this is the popular association to card VI. The point is that this variety of turtle has strong mythological and supernatural associations. It is the "boss" of all the turtles and is familiar to everyone in the conjuring lodge, where it plays the role of messenger and interlocutor. In this situation *Miki·nă′k* even carries on a witty repartee with members of the audience, so it is not surprising to find associations to the Great Turtle emerging as a popular response.

Since the scoring of popular answers and original responses, too, involve an evaluation of content, a category which is bound to reflect the cultural background of the individual as well as his particular interests, it seems necessary in this case to establish provincial norms as frames of reference. On the whole, however, I am convinced from my own experience in working with the Rorschach data from the Saulteaux that tentatively we can interpret individual records in terms of established criteria. Whether this will hold true for the protocols of other nonliterate peoples remains to be seen. But the positive conclusions reached in one primitive group suggest that further experiment would be worthwhile.

On the assumption, then, that all the questions we raised earlier in this paper about the adaptability of the Rorschach for work among nonliterate peoples have been answered positively, how can this method aid us specifically in studying personality in primitive societies?

One of the basic contributions of cultural anthropology to the study of personality has been the demonstration of a functional relation between certain traditional patterns of culture and what may be called the "ideal-typical" personality traits of individuals. It has been shown that the values and goals set up in different societies are directly related to the motivations, the affective life and the organization of habit patterns found in individuals in these societies. Nevertheless, we know practically nothing yet about *intrasocietal* variations in personality under different cultural set-ups since the inferences made usually have been deducted from the cultural patterns themselves, supplemented only by impressionistic observations of individuals. The study of actual individuals by means of the Rorschach should enable us to penetrate to a still deeper level and to check the culturally derived inferences.

In "Aggression in Saulteaux Society"[6] I have examined the relation between ambivalence in the interpersonal relations of the Saulteaux and their belief in witchcraft and magic. On the surface they are an extremely patient, placid, and peace-loving people, but at the same time there are strong currents of hostility that exist on a covert level of expression. Individuals greatly fear the exercise of witchcraft against them; consequently, they present a placid and cooperative outward demeanor, although they may seethe with hate within and even make accusations against their neighbors which have no foundation in fact. It will be interesting to discover from the Rorschach data the range of and quality of the personality structures of individuals that function in such a social order.

Another interesting problem is suggested by the fact that the "strong" men in this society are those believed to possess the greatest magic power. This power can be used for good or evil—to cure or to kill. In this class of individuals are those who conjure by invoking supernatural spirits in a structure set up at night. The voices of the spirits issue from this lodge, which is constantly agitated during the entire performance. The conjurer exercises clairvoyant functions in relation to all sorts of problems and under the old regime was one of the most powerful leaders in the society—highly respected, yet greatly feared. Despite the fact that this institution has been recorded among the Algonkian peoples as far back as the seventeenth century, there is practically nothing in the literature about the personality of the conjurers. I have Rorschach records of a dozen men of this class and I hope to determine whether they exhibit any common features of personality organization or individual peculiarities as compared with a control group of men of the same age.

These are merely samples from my own work of the way in which the Rorschach can be of supplementary aid in a program of combined ethnographic and psychological research. In conclusion, I should like to suggest some broader applications.

In recent years one of the angles from which the study of personality in primitive societies has been approached has been through the collection of biographies and autobiographies. I believe that the psychological value of this class of data would be greatly enhanced if Rorschach protocols were also obtained from these individuals.

Another use of the Rorschach on a much larger scale in primitive societies would be in connection with a psychiatric survey. Again and again the question of the relative incidence of mental disorders and psychopathic symptoms in societies with different cultural traditions has arisen. It has been both asserted and denied, for example, that mental disorder increases with civilization. And it is true that, so far as our data goes, certain types of mental disturbance appear to be infrequent or absent in some nonliterate

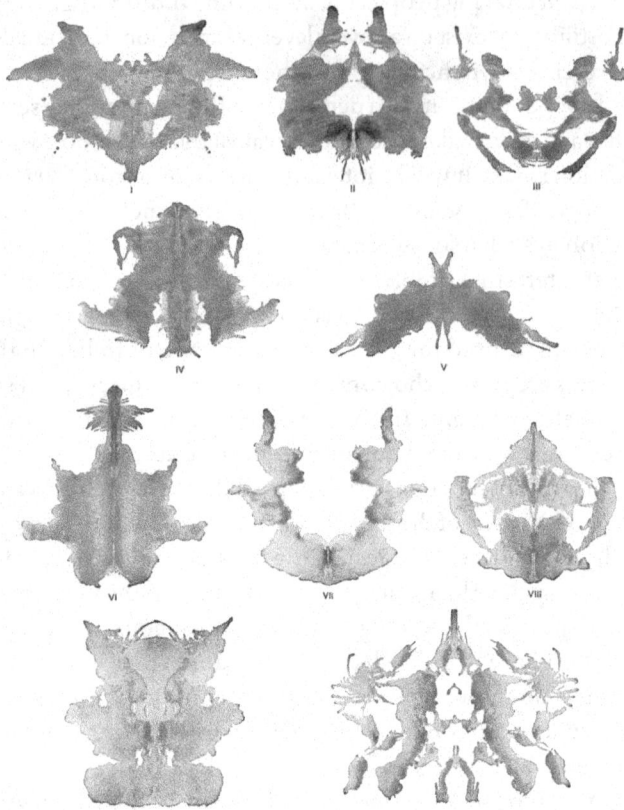

7. Rorschach Inkblots.

societies. The problem is particularly difficult because the symptomatology of certain mental diseases familiar in occidental society may be obscured in primitive communities by a culturally determined facade. At any rate, we know practically nothing about the quantitative aspects of mental disorder in primitive societies. Even if we were determined to collect such information, how could we secure it? In our own society we secure statistics on the incidence of psychoses from hospitalized cases. Since neither hospitals nor clinics exist among nonliterate peoples, there is no obvious way in which to secure comparable data. But I believe that a Rorschach survey of a primitive community—and some of them are not very large—might provide very interesting and perhaps significant data on the actual incidence of psychotic and neurotic traits in such a population. A survey of this kind might also provide a better picture of the variability in intellectual level exhibited by these individuals than has hitherto been obtained by means of intelligence tests, which offer greater difficulty in administration with dubious results.

Of course it may not be worth while to investigate such problems, but I believe that they would provide some surprises if actually carried out. Since many generalizations involving intelligence and even the reputed psychotic traits of primitive peoples have been made from time to time without any adequate data, it seems to me that we had better confess our ignorance or make a frontal attack on such questions by using the best practical means at our disposal.

Notes

Published in *Character and Personality: An International Psychological Quarterly* 9 (3) (1941): 235–45. The Rorschach images referred to in the text are illustrated on page 484.

1. M. Bleuler and R. Bleuler, "Rorschach's ink-blot test and racial psychology: mental peculiarities of Moroccans." *Character and Personality,* 1935, 4, 97–114.

2. In the summer of 1940 [mainly at the two mission schools at Little Grand Rapids] an additional series of fifty protocols was secured from children between the ages of six and sixteen years. [Ed. note: The three Berens River bands involved were Berens River, Little Grand Rapids, and Pauingassi, a smaller community several miles north of Little Grand Rapids. Hallowell's description of the testing situation in 1938 at Pauingassi, quoted in the introduction to this section, shows how conditions there, even more than elsewhere, departed from the "strict isolation" prescribed for test subjects.]

3. P. E. Vernon, "Recent work on the Rorschach test." *Journal of Mental Science,* 1935, 81, 915. Cf. Bleuler and Bleuler, "Rorschach's ink-blot test."

4. Helen H. Davidson and Bruno Klopfer, "Rorschach statistics." Part I, "Mentally retarded, normal and superior adults." *Rorschach Research Exchange,* 1937–38, 2, 166.

5. S. J. Beck, *Introduction to the Rorschach method: A Manual of Personality Study.* American Orthopsychiatric Association, 1937.

6. Hallowell, *Psychiatry,* 1940, 3, 395–407 [chapter 15, this volume].

TWENTY-FIVE

Some Psychological Characteristics
of the Northeastern Indians

In the history of anthropology the biological and cultural attributes of human populations in their group aspects have been the major focus of attention. The questions which anthropologists most frequently have set out to answer have been of the following kinds: What are the physical characteristics of the population of a given region? What languages are spoken? What are the beliefs and customs? What kind of artifacts are used?

Questions of quite a different order arise if one approaches a human population as people; that is, as personalities in social interaction with one another. From this point of view such questions arise as: At what level of intelligence do these individuals function? What are the characteristic attitudes they display? What characteristic patterns of emotional expression are found? What are the personality traits exhibited by individuals? Which of these appear to be typical for the entire population? What is the range of idiosyncratic variation in personality? More searching questions lead to an investigation of the conditions that have given rise to specific constellations of personality traits, and, in terms of the deeper layers of the personality, the kind of character structure that underlies the behavior of individuals.

In short, the study of people as functioning personalities inevitably leads to a consideration of sociopsychological problems, central to which is the relation between personality organization and the cultural matrix in which it is formed. Instead of highlighting the folkways, the mores, and institutions of a given population, and subordinating individuals as undifferentiated *bearers* of a culture, we accent human beings as differentiated personalities for whom the culture specifies the values of life, defines situations in a meaningful way, and provides patterns of social interaction for achieving traditional goals. Furthermore, if we assume that there are intimate connections between personality and culture, it follows that individuals in societies with different cultural backgrounds will reflect this fact and that changes in culture will be accompanied by changes in personality organization.

So far as the Woodland Indians are concerned this latter point was demonstrated in an investigation I made of the Berens River Saulteaux, which was based upon data obtained by the Rorschach method. A comparison was made between two groups of Indians with the same cultural background, and living on the same river, but acculturated to different degrees at the present time [1946]. While all these Indians exhibited tendencies towards the same basic type of character structure, the sample representing those who had come into closest contacts with whites departed significantly from the sample whose culture was most heavily weighted in the aboriginal direction. (See Part IV) ["The Psychological Dimension in Culture Change," in *Culture and Experience.*]

The results of this investigation suggest a general inference. Since none of the Northeastern Indians have entirely escaped the impact of Western culture we cannot assume that their psychological characteristics today, any more than their culture patterns, are equivalent to those of the aborigines who inhabited this area in the seventeenth century. We cannot expect the remnants of the Micmac living in the Maritime Provinces today to manifest the psychological characteristics of their forebears described by Biard, Le Clercq, and Denys. Nor can we expect the highly acculturated Iroquois flourishing in New York State to exhibit the personality traits of those described by the Jesuits since, unlike the Algonkians among whom acculturation has been stimulated chiefly from without, the Iroquois have in addition been subjected to the influence of their native reformer, Handsome Lake, and his followers.[1] On the other hand, Algonkian groups like the Montagnais-Naskapi and, farther west, the Cree and Saulteaux-Ojibwa-speaking peoples, who have remained culturally conservative even under modern conditions, might be expected to approximate in some respects the psychological characteristics of their congeners of earlier times. And since the Iroquois on the Six Nations Reserve in Ontario are not only very numerous, but retain certain aboriginal institutions, it is possible that a systematic investigation might expose some differences in personality organization if they were compared with the Iroquois of certain reservations in New York State. Whatever the answer may be to such questions, the fact remains that whereas we know a great deal about the culture of the Indians of the Northeast, we know very little about the Iroquois and Algonkians as people.[2]

Since the native population of the entire Eastern Woodland area, as compared with other regions of North America, had a certain community of culture traits in aboriginal times we might expect the people of the Northeast to share *some* basic psychological features in common. On the other hand, the differences between Algonkian and Iroquois cultures possibly imply some psychological differences.

Instead of initiating our discussion with the living peoples who have all been influenced to a greater or less extent by contact with whites, I should like to raise the question whether it is possible to secure any data of psychological value from our earliest sources of information on the Northeastern Indians. Although this way of attacking the problem has never been systematically exploited, and I do not intend to do more than sample the possibilities here, these old sources do offer some interesting data for investigation. Besides, if any conclusions of positive value can be established, we shall then have a base line from which to chart later developments.

While the early missionaries, traders, and explorers were neither trained anthropologists nor psychologists, they had one decided advantage over later investigators. They were able to observe the Indians under purely aboriginal conditions. Consequently, in building up a picture of native culture in the seventeenth and eighteenth centuries we have profited greatly by their observations. Is it not possible that their statements about the Indians as people also are worth considering? Missionaries and traders, we should remember, unlike modern anthropologists, were not primarily interested in the Indians as informants from whom a generalized picture of the culture was to be built up, nor as subjects in a sample of a population whose physical traits were to be measured. These early observers were forced to deal with the Indians much more as differentiated personalities. Part of their task was to obtain insight into the character of the Indians in order to devise ways and means for influencing them toward certain ends. It is not surprising, then, that the missionary, the trader, and the explorer reflected upon what we would now call the psychological characteristics of the Indians. Consequently, we find statements here and there that refer to the character of particular individuals or to whole tribal groups. While many of these observations are crudely stated generalizations that lack the psychological sophistication to which we have become accustomed in the present century, nevertheless one often wishes that such remarks had received further elaboration and documentation.

Of course it is true that if one takes some of these generalizations at their face value, without evaluating the relation of the particular observer to the natives he was describing, all we may have is a prejudiced view.

As Kinietz has said, "In considering all of their characterizations of the Indians, it should be borne in mind that most of the Europeans wanted something: the missionaries sought converts, the traders were after furs, and the military men wanted warriors. To those who got what they desired, the Indians were sensible, brave, and upright people; but if the overtures of the Europeans were not favorably received, the tribe was composed of thieves, liars, dissemblers, and even traitors."[3] The margin of error involved can be controlled, however, in several ways: (1) In most cases we have the observations of more than one person in which case we may have corroborative testimony by independent witnesses at our disposal; (2) we can ask ourselves whether the observations make psychological sense when put side by side with other remarks and with any concrete behavioral data cited; (3) we can evaluate the older observations in terms of our knowledge of contemporary peoples who are culturally the most conservative.

What I propose to do is to examine some of the early accounts of the Northeastern Indians in the light of our contemporary knowledge of the psychodynamics of human behavior to see whether the psychological characteristics depicted for an earlier period present an intelligible picture. The two major topics I have selected for discussion are (1) the general level of intelligence and (2) the emotional structure of the Indians.

INTELLIGENCE LEVEL

In view of the heated debate in modern times about the differential mental capacities of the various races of Man, the almost complete unanimity with which seventeenth-century observers equate the Indians with Europeans is striking. Apparently the idea never arose in the minds of those who had first-hand knowledge of them that the Indians were in any way mentally inferior to whites. Bressani, for example, who had been a missionary in Huronia from 1645 until 1649, and later wrote a general account of the New World natives, points out that they "are hardly Barbarians, save in name. There is no occasion to think of them as half beasts, shaggy, black and hideous" (*The Jesuit Relations*, 38, 257 ff., hereafter cited as J. R.).[4] He goes on to remark the acuteness of their senses and their tenacious memory. He is particularly impressed by their "marvellous faculty for remembering places, and for describing them to one another," for finding their way about and for recalling details that whites "could not rehearse without writing." Bressani even goes so far as to say that, "they have often persuaded us in affairs of importance, and made us change the resolution which, after mature deliberation, we had taken for the weal of the country. I doubt not that they are capable of the sciences."

Other Jesuits who, being intellectually trained men themselves, may be accepted as good common-sense judges of intellectual functioning, give similar reports. Du Peron (J. R., 15 [1639], 157) writes of the Huron, and Ragueneau (J. R., 29, 281) corroborates him: "They nearly all show more intelligence in their business, speeches, courtesies, intercourse, tricks and subtleties, than do the shrewdest citizens and merchants in France." Jerome Lalemant writes, "for I can say in truth that, as regards Intelligence, they are in no wise inferior to Europeans and to those who dwell in France. I would never have believed that, without instruction, nature could have supplied a most ready and vigorous eloquence, which I have admired in many Hurons; or more clear-sightedness in affairs, or a more discreet management in things to which they are accustomed" (J. R., 28, 63).

The Micmac were said by Le Clercq not only to "have naturally a sound mind and a common sense beyond that which is supposed in France,"[5] but "they conduct their affairs cleverly." The editor of Le Clerq remarks, "indeed they were able to outwit the French captains in trade, as Denys makes very plain," for which there is likewise evidence in Father Biard's account.

It is worth noting, too, that Father Le Jeune, that sage Jesuit, appears to have sensed the importance of training in relation to the full exercise of native capacities. For he observes that, "Those who cross over here from your France are almost all mistaken on one point,—they have a very low opinion of our Savages, thinking them dull and slow-witted; but as soon as they have associated with them they confess that only education, and not intelligence, is lacking in these peoples" (J. R., 19 [1640], 39). In another *Relation*, after remarking that the "mind of the Savages" is of good quality, he goes on to write, "Education and instruction alone are lacking. . . . I naturally compare our Savages with certain villagers, because both are usually without education; though our Peasants are superior in this regard; and yet I have not seen any one thus far, of those who have come to this country, who does not confess and frankly admit that the Savages are more intelligent than our ordinary peasants" (J. R., 6, 231). Cadillac, referring to the Ottawa at Mackinac (1695), makes this general statement, "We may say without flattery, that all the Indians are naturally intelligent."[6]

These are extremely interesting appraisals and, so far as we know, as honest as could be desired. While other citations, supporting the high level of intelligence attributed to the Indians in their native state, could be given,[7] those referred to must suffice as an index of the general impression created upon the early observers.

Is this impression supported by the more refined methods and observational techniques we now have at our disposal? It is impossible to answer this question specifically for the Northeastern Indians since no attempt has ever been made to rate their level of intelligence in terms of the results of a systematic application of standard intelligence tests. When such studies have been made the same questions arise that have plagued all the investigators who have used such tests on other American Indians or native peoples on other continents. For example, a study was made of children of the Six Nations Reserve (Iroquois). They all spoke English, but on the whole their command of the language was not that of white children, a fact that adversely affected their scores in the verbal tests. In non-verbal tests they approximated white norms.[8] While test results, when taken at their face value, may show the subjects to be "retarded" in terms of the average I.Q. (the majority of I.Q.'s obtained from studies of Indians at large fall between seventy and ninety),[9] sophisticated students are now aware that differences in language facility, schooling, speed in performance, motivation, and other factors related to the cultural background of the subject, all affect the results. Anne Anastasi writes,

> Thus it would seem that intelligence tests measure only the ability to succeed in our particular culture. Each culture, partly through the physical conditions of its environment and partly through social tradition, "selects" certain activities as the most significant. These it encourages and stimulates; others it neglects or definitely suppresses. The relative standing of different cultural groups in "intelligence" is a function of the traits included under the concept of intelligence, or, to state the same point differently, it is a function of the particular culture in which the test was constructed.[10]

Consequently, until intra-cultural variables are properly weighed in inter-cultural comparisons, the results of intelligence tests may be highly misleading in the conclusions they suggest. Anastasi elaborates this point for primitive peoples:

> Tests of abstract abilities, for example, are considered more diagnostic of "intelligence" than those dealing with the manipulation of concrete objects or with the perception of spatial relationships. The aptitude for dealing with symbolic materials, especially of a verbal or numerical

nature, is regarded as the acme of intellectual attainment. The "primitive" man's skill in responding to very slight sensory cues, his talents in the construction of objects, or the powers of sustained attention and muscular control which he may display in his hunting behavior, are regarded as interesting anthropological curios which have, however, little or no intellectual worth. As a result, such activities have not usually been incorporated in intelligence scales but have been relegated to a relatively minor position in mental testing.[11]

The difference in the criteria used for evaluating superiority or inferiority of intelligence is strikingly brought out by the reports of the Indians' opinion of whites compared to themselves. They did not accept naively the white man's evaluation of himself as superior; actually, they considered themselves to be superior to whites. Europeans were sometimes perplexed by such an odd notion. Biard, for example, writes: "You will see these poor barbarians, notwithstanding their great lack of government, power, letters, art and riches, yet holding their heads so high that they greatly underrate us, regarding themselves as our superiors" (J. R., 3, 73). Peter Grant, referring to the Saulteaux of a much later date, indicates quite clearly the nature of some of the criteria employed in judging the whites. After observing that, "Though they acknowledge the superiority of our arts and manufactures and their own incapacity to imitate us, yet, as a people, they think us far inferior to themselves," he adds, "They pity our want of skill in hunting and our incapacity for travelling through their immense forests without guides or food."[12] It is evident that the qualities of mind required for success in such pursuits are quite different from those exercised in abstract thinking or the manipulation of quantitative concepts.

The Standard Intelligence Tests, however, are not the only tool now at our disposal for gaining information about the intelligence level of nonliterate peoples. While designed as a technique for arriving at a more inclusive picture of personality structure and functioning, the Rorschach test permits judgments of general intelligence level that the expert, also familiar with intelligence tests, can translate into I.Q. points with a fair degree of accuracy. "Form level rating," as a means of arriving at a more precise appraisal of the intellectual functioning of the subject, has been recently discussed by Bruno Klopfer.[13] The advantage of this technique is that the subject's intellectual approach to things is evaluated as only one facet of the personality picture the Rorschach protocol reveals. This means that the *qualitative* aspects of intelligence can be judged in relation to the functioning of the personality as a whole and not as something abstracted from it. The range of the individual's intellectual aptitudes can be evaluated, for the test material itself is not weighted in any particular direction. Thus, it is possible to discern whether the subject shows capacities for intellectual functioning on an abstract or concrete level; how far either type of functioning predominates, and the quality of such functioning. When the group results from an adequate sample of a population are considered, it is possible to see how far the intellectual functioning of an individual is typical of the general trend of the group. Furthermore, since verbal facility, speed, and other factors that have complicated the interpretation of the results of intelligence tests among primitive peoples play quite a different role in the Rorschach, it can be used with very little difficulty among native peoples, and the results obtained are comparable with those obtained on white subjects. (See chap. 3) [*Culture and Experience.*]

The results of an analysis of the Rorschach records of 102 adult Saulteaux and forty-nine children, so far as general level of intelligence is concerned, are interesting to compare with the evaluation of the intelligence of the Northeastern Indians given by early observers, and the somewhat equivocal results obtained when Indians have been given intelligence tests. Of course, the contemporary Saulteaux cannot be fully equated with the Indians of the Northeast in the seventeenth century, yet there are basic cultural and linguistic connections and the inland Saulteaux of the Berens River still maintain today a modicum of their aboriginal life. Like the Indians of an earlier day the chief problems they have to solve are the practical ones that face them daily in order to make a living. There are no large ventures to be planned by anyone, nor has the individual any responsibilities that extend beyond the members of his family group. (Even a chief has very little more.) There was nothing in the aboriginal culture to stimulate abstract thinking and the very elementary schooling some individuals have received is not directed toward this end. Furthermore, there is nothing in the culture to call forth any imaginative powers of a highly creative sort. Myths and tales are *recounted,* not invented, and the same situation holds true for most of their music. The only art that seems to call out any inventiveness is beadwork. It is not strange to find, then, that the results of the Rorschach technique indicate that the intelligence of the Saulteaux functions at a concrete, practical, common-sense level and that their characteristic intellectual approach to things is very cautious and precise. Many of them add to this a capacity for observing acutely fine details that might escape other observers, but they show little interest in organizing such details into wholes with a significant meaning. The details are of interest for their own sake rather than as part of some larger pattern. Related to this concrete approach to things is the passive fantasy, a kind of idling imaginative activity, without boldness or genuine creativeness, which is also shown in the Rorschach protocols.

From this brief resumé we can readily see that the Saulteaux, on the average, could hardly be expected to rate as high as educated whites on any intelligence test which stressed a qualitatively different type of intellectual functioning. They are not an intellectual people; abstract concepts of the order of those developed in Western culture are tools that are lacking for the development of their theoretical or artistic thinking. Saulteaux culture has encouraged intelligence to concentrate on such capacities as sharpness of perception and detailed memory. A few individuals do show tendencies toward more abstract and combinatorial thinking. One of these men is a conjurer whose personal history shows him to be ill-adapted to the practical exigencies that the life of a hunter and trapper demands. His Rorschach record shows him to have superior intelligence and a genuine capacity for abstract thought. His lack of social adjustment may be due to the fact that he has found no adequate scope for the exercise of his abilities in Saulteaux society.

Turning again to the statements of the early observers, we see that their estimates of the intelligence of the Indians were based on some of the same intellectual qualities that emerge from the picture which the Rorschach presents of Saulteaux intelligence. They were highly appreciative of the "practical intelligence" of the Indian as evinced in judgment about everyday affairs, a detailed knowledge of place and events, and so on. It was probably for this reason, too, that the Indians were compared to the peasantry of Europe rather than to the educated classes. The comparison was an apt one, since it is not unlikely that the qualitative aspects of the intelligence of both groups are rooted in comparable modes of meeting the problems of life.

EMOTIONAL STRUCTURE

The structure of the emotional life of human beings has proved to be of such major importance for an understanding of the foundations of personality development and functioning that I have sampled the statements of early observers for cues that provide some insight into the affective life of the Indians of the Northeast.

One thing which seems to have impressed all Europeans alike is what may be characterized as a multifaceted pattern of emotional restraint or inhibition. All observers do not document every aspect of this pattern but there is little doubt that it is all of a piece psychologically. One receives the impression that it probably applied quite generally to all the Woodland peoples, irrespective of tribal or linguistic affiliation, and that it reflects an important aspect of their personality organization.

The most familiar facet of this pattern of emotional restraint is the basis for the stereotype of the Indian as a stoical type of human being. He is pictured as displaying the greatest fortitude and patience in the face of all the vicissitudes of life—hunger and hardships of all kinds, disease, losses in gambling, torture, childbirth, and so on. Jouvency, for example, in his general account of the Indians of Canada (1710) writes,

> Whatever misfortune may befall them they never allow themselves to lose their calm composure of mind, in which they think that happiness especially consists. They endure many days fasting; also diseases and trials with the greatest cheerfulness and patience. Even the pangs of childbirth, although most bitter, are so concealed or conquered by the women that they do not even groan; and if a tear or a groan should escape any one of them, she would be stigmatized by everlasting disgrace, nor could she find a man thereafter who would marry her (J. R., 1, 277). [An exaggeration, no doubt, but the behavior expected of a woman is clearly indicated.]

During the winter Le Jeune camped with the Montagnais some of them said to him:

> We shall be sometimes two days, sometimes three, without eating, for lack of food; take courage, *chichiné*, let thy soul be strong to endure suffering and hardship; keep thyself from being sad, otherwise thou wilt be sick; see how we do not cease to laugh, although we have little to eat (J. R., 6, 231). [And later, generalizing, he says,] The Savages, although passionately fond of gambling, show themselves superior to our Europeans. They hardly ever evince either joy in winning or sadness in losing, playing with most remarkable external tranquility,—as honorably as possible, never cheating one another (J. R., 16, 201). [On the Micmac Le Clercq makes similar observations.] They have the fortitude and the resolution to bear bravely the misfortunes which are usual and common to all men. . . . They have patience enough in their sickness to put Christians to confusion.[14]

So far as torture is concerned, the fortitude of those subjected to this torment is almost too well known to need documentation. Jouvency says,

> The prisoner who has beheld and endured stake, knives and wounds with an unchanging countenance, who has not groaned, who with laughter and song has ridiculed his tormenters, is praised; for they think that to sing amid so many deaths is great and noble. So they themselves compose songs long beforehand, in order that they may repeat them if they should by chance be captured (J. R., 1, 273).

A somewhat less celebrated aspect of the pattern of emotional restraint that seems to have characterized the Woodland Indians is the inhibition of any expression of anger in interpersonal relations. An amiable attitude was even maintained towards prisoners at the stake. According to the account of one eye-witness of the gruesome torture of an Iroquois captive by some Hurons,

> Anger and rage did not appear upon the faces of those who were tormenting him, but rather gentleness and humanity, their words expressing only raillery or tokens of friendship and good will. There was no strife as to who should burn him—each one took his turn; thus they gave themselves leisure to meditate some new device to make him feel the fire more keenly. (J. R., 13 [1637], 67).

A cold-blooded affair, indeed, which the observer thought increased the victim's suffering, but nevertheless noteworthy because of the absence of any expression of anger.

The emotional structure of the situation just referred to becomes more intelligible when we consider the larger pattern with which it is connected. The early observers frequently comment on the amiability and mildness exhibited in all face-to-face relations in so far as these were *in-group* relations. This is merely a corollary of the fact that any overt expression of anger was characteristically inhibited. Of course, this impressed the missionaries in particular since it approximated a Christian ideal. Jouvency goes so far as to say that "they (the Indians) know nothing of anger" (J. R., 1, 275), and Bruyas writing from the Oneida Mission observes, "I have never seen them become angry, even on occasions when our Frenchmen would have uttered a hundred oaths" (J. R., 51 [1666–67], 129). Le Jeune, speaking in particular of the Montagnais, phrases the matter with greater psychological subtlety. He says,

They make a pretence of never getting angry, not because of the beauty of this virtue, for which they have not even a name, but for their own contentment and happiness; I mean, to avoid the bitterness caused by anger. The Sorcerer said to me one day, speaking of one of our Frenchmen, "He has no sense, he gets angry; as for me, nothing can disturb me; let hunger oppress me, let my nearest relation pass to the other life, let the Hiroquois, our enemies, massacre our people, I never get angry." What he says is not an article of faith; for, as he is more haughty than any other Savage, so I have seen him oftener out of humor than any of them; it is true also that he often restrains and governs himself by force, especially when I expose his foolishness (J.R., 6, 231).[15]

This last statement leads us directly to another facet of the pattern since in dealing with such matters we must always take account of interpersonal relations. Le Jeune used to argue with the sorcerer about native beliefs in a provocative manner and evidently the old man did his best to hold his temper. But Le Jeune in this situation, as is clear from other evidence, was not following the Indian pattern. For the pattern of emotional restraint not only implies that the individual restrain his *own* anger, it also requires that he suppress open criticism of his fellows in face-to-face relations and avoid disputation of a personal kind in order to avoid arousing *their* anger. This is why Jouvency remarks

[that at first the Indians] were greatly surprised when the Fathers censured their faults before the assembly: they thought that the Fathers were madmen, because among peaceful hearers and friends they displayed such vehemence. [Later he goes on to say that] friends never indulge in complaint or expostulation to friends, wives to their husbands, or husbands to their wives (J. R., 1, 275, 277).

In other words, individuals avoid arousing emotions of displeasure or anger in others by the suppression of verbal criticism in face-to-face situations. (See "Aggression in Saulteaux Society" [chapter 15, this volume], for details.)

All of this fits in with the reputed independence and individualism of the Indians, with the absence of much, if any, real political authority vested in so-called chiefs or leaders. Writing of the Micmac, Le Clercq says:

In a word, they hold it as a maxim that each one is free: that one can do whatever he wishes: and that it is not sensible to put constraint upon men. It is necessary, they say, to live without annoyance and disquiet, to be content with that which one has, and to endure with constancy the misfortunes of nature, because the sun, or he who has made and governs all, orders it thus.[16]

For the Delaware we have the statement of Loskiel:

[A *chief*] dare not venture to command, compel, or punish anyone, as in that case he would immediately be forsaken by the whole tribe. Every word that looks like a command is immediately rejected with contempt by an Indian, proud of his liberty. The chief must endeavour to rule over his people merely by calm reasoning and friendly exhortation."[17]

Zeisberger making the same point says: "They may not be prevailed on in any matter that does not please them, much less forced. If they cannot be persuaded with gentle words, further effort is in vain."[18] Even among the Huron, according to Baron de Lahontan, the leaders had no more power. Speaking through Adario, the Huron chief, he remarks that,

our Generals and Presidents of the Council have not more Power than any other Huron; that Detraction and Quarrelling were never heard among us; and in fine, that everyone is his own Master, and does what he pleases, without being accountable to another, or censur'd by his Neighbour.[19]

In short, no one was in a position to order anyone else around. Tailhan, in an editorial footnote to Nicholas Perrot's elaboration of this same point ("the savage does not know what it is to obey") extends the generalization to all "the savages of New France."[20] How even the semblance of what to us would be a very trivial kind of social pressure was avoided is illustrated by an anecdote related by Father Laure. Once he was descending the Saguenay River by night in a canoe. He had two Montagnais with him and when they both dropped off to sleep the father continued paddling. "Some time afterward, one of my men awoke, and took his paddle; and, as it is the custom of the Savages, who are exceedingly independent among themselves, never to say anything to one another about work, for fear of giving offense, he begged me to rouse the other" (J. R., 68, 35).

This suppression of any impulse to tell someone else what to do if viewed as a generalized pattern of interpersonal relations partly accounts for the reputed lack of restraint exercised by parents upon their children. Le Clercq says that the Micmac "never contradict anyone, and that they let everyone do as he pleases, even to the extent that the fathers and the mothers do not dare correct their children, but permit their misbehavior for fear of vexing them by chastising them."[21] Jouvency comments on this same fact immediately following his reference to the restraint exercised between spouses and between friends: "They treat their children with wonderful affection, but they preserve no discipline, for they neither themselves correct them nor allow others to do so. Hence the impudence and savageness of the boys, which, after they have reached a vigorous age, breaks forth in all sorts of wickedness" (J. R., 43, 271).

These statements must be taken in a purely relative sense unless methods of child care observed among contemporary Indians are a revolutionary departure from those of aboriginal days. What early observers probably had in mind, although they did not say so, was the absence of the kind of *corporal* punishment known to Europeans. A more balanced statement is found in a passage of the *Relation* of 1656–57. Dablon, referring primarily to the Onondaga whom he knew best, says: "There is nothing for which these people have a greater horror than restraint. The very children cannot endure it, and live as they please in the houses of their parents, without fear of reprimand or of chastisement." But he also observes that they are sometimes punished "by having their lips and their tongues rubbed with a very bitter root." With reference to the general pattern we have been describing, it is of psychological interest that Dablon says this punishment is seldom administered for "fear that vexation might lead the children to cause their own death by eating certain noxious plants." In other words, parents are said to avoid certain disciplinary measures because their children may resent it and take retaliatory measures. Fenton, in his study of Iroquois suicide,[22] records only five cases in which the alleged motivation was rebellion against parental restraint, so that actually child suicide was scarcely a serious social problem among the Iroquois. What is psychologically significant is the anxiety-laden attitude of parents toward severe disciplinary measures and its persistence down to the present day. For Fenton says that even the modern Seneca have a stock excuse for not disciplining their children too much—they say that children might grow up to mistreat their parents! The anxiety that such a rationalization reveals points to the operation of the same underlying psychological pattern that we have been discussing. This pattern has its roots in the demand that individuals learn to suppress overt expression of aggression in interpersonal relations of all kinds. When any impulses which can be so interpreted are expressed, retaliation in some form is expected. This expectation, in turn, arouses anxiety. Thus the only way to avoid anxiety is to restrain *oneself* and to comply with the demands of others. The Iroquois seem to have been more self-conscious of the pattern as applied to the relations of parents and children than was the case in Algonkian groups.

Still another facet of the basic pattern we have described was the reluctance on the part of the Indians to refuse a favor outright. That is, they maintained a surface amiability in this respect, even though they did not wish to do what was asked. Biard, referring to the Micmac, says that "no one would dare refuse the request of another" (J. R., 3, 95). (But he gives a very neat instance of how some Indians avoided sharing *too much* on one occasion.) Peter Grant, writing of the Saulteaux, states the matter more fully: "Such is their notion of politeness that they seldom give a square refusal to any favor that is required from them; should they not be inclined to oblige, they know perfectly well how to give a plausible reason for their refusal."[23] Here again we can discern the obverse of the expression of displeasure, that is, a desire, motivated by anxiety, to avoid arousing displeasure or anger in others.

The same motivation undoubtedly was involved in what often seemed to be an intellectual assent to the teachings of the missionaries, when in fact this was not the case. Le Clercq[24] remarks that the Micmac "never contradict anyone." For the Montagnais we have the same observation recorded. Le Jeune says, "The Savages agree very readily with what you say, but do not, for all that, cease to act upon their own ideas" (J. R., 5, 151), while Le Caron describing the people at Tadoussac, P. Q., remarks that one of the obstacles to their conversion "is the opinion they have that you must never contradict anyone, and that everyone must be left to his own way of thinking. They will believe all you please, or, at least will not contradict you, and they will let you, too, believe what you will."[25] All this was extremely disconcerting to the Jesuits, as Jouvency points out. "From the same desire for harmony," he says, "comes their ready assent to whatever one teaches them, nevertheless they hold tenaciously to their native beliefs or superstition, and on that account are the more difficult to instruct. For what can one do with those who in word give agreement and assent to everything, but in reality give none?" (J. R., 1, 275). Undoubtedly this explains why the Indians sometimes were accused of deceit and dissimulation.

It can now readily be seen that with this strong weighting on the side of restraint not only in enduring the fortuitous circumstances of life, but in all the daily face-to-face relations with others that inevitably must have aroused emotions of annoyance, anger, or a desire to criticize or correct, all of which had to be suppressed for fear of arousing resentment in others, that individuals must have developed an extreme sensitivity to overtones of anger or the overt expression of it. The whole psychological picture is one that suggests underlying anxiety[26]—anxiety lest one fail to maintain the standard of fortitude required no matter what the hardship one must endure; anxiety lest one give way to one's hostile impulses; anxiety lest one provoke resentment or anger in others. As Willoughby says, "In the field of the aggressive impulses, there is little anxiety in groups accustomed to settling differences immediately and definitely, as by a passing exchange of blows; it arises most characteristically in individuals overtrained to a standard of forbearance which makes any expression of resentment impossible."[27] No wonder then that the Indians were taken aback by the openly expressed criticism of the Jesuits referred to by Jouvency, and no wonder that Le Jeune reports that only on one occasion did he hear an Indian say, "I am angry," and he adds that this man only said it once. "But I noticed," says Le Jeune, "that they kept their eyes on him, for when these Barbarians are angry, they are dangerous and unrestrained" (J. R., 6, 231). This is precisely what one would expect; it is the true psychological explanation of the apprehension felt both by the individual and his fellows. The suppression of all semblance of anger can be accompanied by a surface amiability in interpersonal relations, but at the same time open expressions of aggressive impulses become so markedly accented in this sort of affective balance that they become the symbols of the most violent intentions.

Of course, open fights and quarrels did sometimes occur, but it is interesting to note that after mentioning these Biard says they were usually adjusted easily. He then goes on to picture the same amity described by other observers:

> we have never seen anything except always great respect and love among them, which was a great grief to us when we turned our eyes upon our own shortcomings. For to see an assembly of French people without reproaches, slights, envy, and quarrels with each other, is as difficult as to see the sea without waves, except in Monasteries and Convents where grace triumphs over nature (J. R., 3, 93 [Micmac]).

Assuming the actual operation of the characteristic pattern of emotional inhibition described, we can be quite sure that the affects generated in daily social life presented a genuine problem to the individual. How was he to deal with the emotions he experienced but could not always spontaneously express?

One procedure would be to maintain a certain emotional indifference to things, to avoid investing too much emotion in anything, and when deep feelings were aroused to put them consciously aside as quickly as possible. This attitude is well expressed by the sorcerer to Le Jeune. Perhaps it was a factor in the so-called haughtiness of the Indian. It represents an extension of the idea of fortitude to all aspects of the affective life. The whole philosophy of this manner of dealing with the emotions is beautifully expressed in a passage of Le Clercq:

> If some one among them laments, grieves, or is angry, this is the only reasoning with which they console him. "Tell me, my brother, wilt thou always weep? Wilt thou always be angry? Wilt thou come nevermore to the dances and the feasts of the Gaspesians? Wilt thou die, indeed, in weeping and in the anger in which thou are at present?" If he who laments and grieves answers him no and says that after some days he will recover his good humor and his usual amiability,—"Well, my brother," will be said to him, "thou hast no sense; since thou hast no intention to weep nor to be angry always, why dost thou not commence immediately to banish all bitterness from thy heart, and rejoice thyself with thy fellow-countrymen?" This is enough to restore his usual repose and tranquility to the most affected of our Gaspesians. In a word, *they rely upon liking nothing, and upon not becoming attached to the goods of the earth, in order not to be grieved or sad when they lose them"* [italics ours].[28]

Applied to one's relations with people such a philosophy would preclude any development of profound emotional ties.

If emotion could not be successfully handled by a stern indifference, and, particularly in cases of anger, face-to-face encounters were precluded, the individual had to discharge his affect in some less direct fashion. Jouvency clearly describes what happened. "If any person has injured another by means of a rude jest (for they are commonly very talkative and are ready jesters) the latter carefully conceals it, or lays it up, and in retaliation injures his detractor behind his back" (J. R., 1, 277). In other words, the affect generated in such cases might be nursed and turned into a deep and burning resentment. This is one possible result of so deeply anchored and ramified a pattern of emotional restraint. The individual was compelled to be devious instead of direct and spontaneous. No wonder, then, that the Indians were sometimes characterized as incalculable, as "naturally fickle, mockers, slanderers and dissimulators,"[29] and why humorous sallies and often nicknames took the form of semidisguised attacks upon other persons.

Biard, for example, says of the Micmac, "they are droll fellows, and have a word and a nickname very readily at command, if they think they have any occasion to look down upon us" (J. R., 3, 75 [1616]). Humor was one way of combining an amiable exterior with the necessity of expressing one's actual feelings. Besides, anything and everything that provoked laughter was thoroughly approved. Mirth seems to have been one expression of emotion that was relatively unrestrained. It provided a healthy psychological balance to all the other inhibitions demanded. Yet even laughter, as I have observed it, is muted among these people rather than boisterous.

Le Jeune gives the most vivid picture presented by any observer of the interplay of surface amiability and laughter combined with covert slander. While Le Jeune is referring to the Montagnais in particular, his remarks fit the general pattern analyzed so well that I believe his statement lends itself to a wider generalization.

> I do not believe that there is a nation under heaven more given to sneering and bantering than that of the Montagnais. Their life is passed in eating, laughing, and making sport of each other, and of all the people they know. There is nothing serious about them, except occasionally when they make a pretense among us of being grave and dignified; but among themselves they are real buffoons and genuine children, who ask nothing only to laugh (J. R., 6, 243). The Savages are slanderous beyond all belief; I say, also among themselves, for they do not even spare their nearest relations, and with it all they are deceitful. For, if one speaks ill of another, they all jeer with loud laughter; if the other appears upon the scene, the first one will show him as much affection and treat him with as much love, as if he had elevated him to the third heaven by his praise (J. R., 6, 247).

One day Le Jeune was left alone in the wigwam with the women after the hunters had departed. The women, unaware that he could understand what they were saying, began talking about a certain man who had failed to carry anything home to his wife from a feast he had attended.

> [The women] spoke aloud and freely, tearing this poor apostate to pieces. "Oh, the glutton," they said, "who gives his wife nothing to eat. If he could only kill something! He has no sense; he eats everything like a dog." [While all this was going on the man suddenly appeared.] They knew very well how to put a good face on the matter, showing countenances as smiling as usual, even to such an extent that the one who had said

the worst things about him gave him a bit of tobacco, which was then a great present (J. R., 7, 175).

Le Jeune goes on at this point to remark that "they are not troubled even if they are told that others are making sport of them, or have injured their reputation," because he believes "that their slanders and derisions do not come from malicious hearts or from infected mouths, but from a mind which says what it thinks in order to give itself free scope, and which seeks gratification from everything, even from slander and mockery." This interpretation does not coincide with that of other observers, for instance, Raudot[30] who, referring to the Indians in general, says, "They are very polite and patient when one insults them, but they retain their resentment and do not lose any occasion to get vengeance." But it will be noted that Le Jeune himself stresses the fact that this raillery takes place behind a person's back and he says the Indians are "deceitful." Furthermore, he says that "at the first opportunity they will pay their slanderer in the same coin, returning him the like." It is to be presumed that this retaliation will also not be in a face-to-face situation. So we are bound to suspect that there is a more genuine aggressive component in all this raillery than Le Jeune says. He must have given considerable thought to this matter because in a later *Relation* (12 [1637], 13) he comes to the conclusion that there is a very real undercurrent of hostility involved despite all the surface amiability. "It is strange," he writes, "to see how these people agree so well outwardly, and how they hate each other within. They do not often get angry and fight with one another, but in the depths of their hearts they intend a great deal of harm. I do not understand how this can be consistent with the kindness and assistance they offer one another." This is an extremely astute psychological observation, thoroughly realistic and entirely consistent with the emotional structure I have tried to sketch. It highlights the psychological effects of suppressed affects and suggests that verbal raillery by no means disposed of all the animosity generated. It also suggests that the reputed indifference referred to by Le Jeune himself was not altogether genuine in all cases. Much undischarged hostility probably remained. In fact, Le Jeune himself in one of his early *Relations* (1632) had written: "So enraged are they against everyone who does them an injury, that they eat the lice and other vermin that they find upon themselves—not because they like them, but only, they say, to avenge themselves and to eat those that eat them" (J. R., 5, 31). This remark is appended at the end of a description of the cruelty and torture meted out to enemies. In another place he again refers to this vindictiveness toward enemies (J. R., 6, 245) and says the women even surpass the men in this respect.

In connection with retaliation it may be recalled that there was a highly institutionalized means of *covert* aggression at the disposal of the Indians. This was sorcery. ["Aggression in Saulteaux Society," chapter 15, this volume.] So far as the Montagnais are concerned, Le Jeune himself remarks that belief in sorcery was so prevalent among them that "I hardly ever see any of them die who does not think he has been bewitched" (J. R., 12, 7). This is sufficient evidence that from the standpoint of the Indians, retaliation by this covert means was a stark reality. From a psychological point of view, of course, it can be said that this belief was supported by a large component of projection. Slander, backbiting, humor and witchcraft among the Indians all give evidence of the actual discharge of aggressively motivated affects that sought these indirect outlets because direct ones were not culturally approved. Because these other channels were approved the character traits of the Indians are found to be consistent with them. It could hardly be otherwise in view of what we know about the interplay of culture and personality.

Additional evidence is supplied by the data we have on what happened when the Indians got drunk. Liquor was supplied them from the beginning of their contact with Europeans and so even the earliest sources comment on how it affected them. Le Clercq was among the first to protest against its use in the fur trade because oƒ its demoralizing effects.[31]

Alcohol, as we know, often releases inhibitions so that impulses are revealed which usually are kept in check when the individual is sober. Since there also appears to be a connection between personality organization, culture pattern, and behavior under the influence of alcohol,[32] the conduct of the Indian when drunk was, in a sense, a natural experiment, a cue to his character.[33] If his basic emotional structure was one that led to the suppression of a great deal of affect, in particular aggressive impulses, then we would expect that these might be released in a notably violent form under the influence of alcohol. This seems to have been what happened. In fact, it is a commonplace that the Indians became exceedingly dangerous when drunk so that Europeans stood in great fear of them and traders who used alcohol in the fur trade barred the gates of their forts when the Indians were in their cups. MacKay says, "Precautions for the defense of themselves and the Company property were the only positive reactions of the English to the bestiality and murderous fury roused in the Indians by alcohol. The exclusion of Indians from the stockaded enclosures of the forts and the conduct of trading through a small wicket were practices which survived many years and arose from the necessity of protection from drunken natives."[34]

Here we are more concerned with the possible direction of aggression toward in-group, rather than out-group, members. No better testimony is available than a statement on this point by Le Clercq:

> Injuries, quarrels, homicides, murders, parricides are to this day the sad consequences of the trade in brandy; and one sees with grief Indians dying in their drunkenness: strangling themselves: the brother cutting the throat of the sister: the husband breaking the head of his wife: a mother throwing her child into the fire or the river: and fathers cruelly choking little innocent children whom they cherish and love as much as, and more than, themselves when they are not deprived of their reason. They consider it sport to break and shatter everything in the wigwams, and to brawl for hours together, repeating always the same word. They beat themselves and tear themselves to pieces, something which happens never, or at least very rarely, when they are sober. The French themselves are not exempt from the drunken fury of these barbarians, who, through a manifestation of the anger of God justly irritated against a conduct so little Christian, sometimes rob, ravage, and burn the French houses and stores, and very often descend to the saddest extremes.[35]

The homicidal aspect of drunken behavior becomes still more significant when we recall that however implacable and cruel the Indian may have proved as a foe, in-group behavior was not only amicable, but, by and large, it was characterized by a remarkable absence of murder. This, of course, is a corollary to what has already been said. Thus, while individuals, projecting their own aggressive fantasies, often believed that they were the victims of witchcraft, in actual fact physical violence among in-group members was a rarity. Drunkenness, however, leading as it did to release from the pattern of emotional restraint, permitted the discharge of suppressed hostility in the form of overt physical aggression which in the sober state was inhibited and overlaid by an effective facade of amiability. Although he refers specifically to the Saulteaux of Ontario in the early nineteenth century, Duncan Cameron expresses the point I have been emphasizing with such precision that his statement lends itself to wider generalization: "When sober they are of very gentle and amiable disposition towards their friends, but as implacable in their enmity, their revenge being complete only by the entire destruction of those against whom they have a spite. They very seldom take that revenge when sober, as few people disguise their minds with more art than they do, but, when in the least inebriate all they have in their mind is revealed and the most bloody revenge taken."[36]

Duncan Cameron's statement that "few people disguise their minds with more art than they do" epitomizes to a large extent the impression which the Indian pattern of emotional restraint must have made on many white observers. Emotional expression provides the most direct cues to the inner life of other human beings, and when the spontaneous play of emotion is concealed we are deprived of one of our chief guides to an understanding of others. Since the data assembled point very clearly to the fact that the emotional structure of the Indian was such that a great deal of emotional expression familiar to whites was inhibited, naturally it would appear to white observers that it was a matter of artful disguise rather than an integral part of the personality of the Indians. Their "persona" did seem to offer evidence of concealment, dissimulation, lack of candor, and deceit. In psychological terms, this inhibitory pattern suggests the characteristics of a defense mechanism against anxieties. And the inference would be that, since the manifestations of this psychic mechanism are typified in the behavior of groups of individuals, the determining factors must lie in the culturally constituted world in which these individuals live. If this is true, and I believe it is, the emotional structure attributed to the Indians of the seventeenth and early eighteenth centuries should have persisted into later periods in so far as the cultural conditions that gave rise to it were not reconstituted through acculturation processes.

Evidence of the actual persistence of the old pattern is attested by the essential similarity between the psychological characterization reconstructed from the early sources and that written by Schoolcraft in the nineteenth century, which, to a large extent, was based upon first-hand knowledge of the Indians of the Woodlands. Schoolcraft's characterization is also interesting because he phrases part of it with reference to certain conditions that he believes to be of determinative significance. These conditions, moreover, are those which are anxiety-provoking.

What are the facts that the Indian mind has had to guard against? Physical suffering of the intensest character! This has made him to exhibit the most hardened and stoical qualities. Sometimes deception of a deep dye. This made him eminently suspicious of everyone and everything, even things without life; for, being a believer in necromancy and witchcraft, he has had to suspect all forms of life and matter. It became a prime object, in all classes, to suppress the exhibition of the feeling of nervousness, susceptibility, and emotion. He was originally eminently a man of concealments. He always anticipated harm, never good. Fear and suspicion put double guards upon him. A look or a word might betray him, and he therefore often had not a look or a word to bestow. This severe mental discipline made him a stoic of the highest character to his enemies, and to all whom he had reason to fear or suspect. It is the aged, the sedate, the experienced, to whom these traits peculiarly apply. If such men are dignified and reserved before strangers and councils, it is the dignity of Indian philosophy. No wonder the French missionaries and officers of the crown admired such a man, and made strong efforts to convert him, and transmitted enthusiastic reports of him to the Court of France. Imperturbability, in all situations, is one of the most striking and general traits of the Indian character. To steel his muscles to resist the expression of all emotion, seems to be the point of attainment; and this is particularly observed on public occasions. Neither fear nor joy are permitted to break this trained equanimity. The newest and most ingenious contrivance placed before him, is not allowed to produce the least expression of wonder. And, although his language has provided him with many exclamations of surprise, he cannot, when placed in the gaze of public observation, be induced to utter any, even the slightest of them, to mark emotion. The mind and nerves are schooled to this from the earliest hours, and it is deemed to be a mark of timidity or cowardice to permit his countenance to denote surprise. [Even among relatives] it is not customary to indulge in warm greetings. The pride and stoicism of the hunter and warrior forbid it. The pride of the wife, who has been made the creature of rough endurance, also forbids it.[37]

While it is true that this characterization of Schoolcraft's is discerning enough on the descriptive level, and while he does hint at links between emotional restraint and the culturally constituted world of the Indian (e.g., the suspicion and anxiety aroused by sorcery), nevertheless his statement is marred by over-generalization. For, to Schoolcraft, this "stern discipline of the mind and nerves," as he called it, was typical of the Indians as a whole, in South America as well as North America. This, of course, is not the case; the "stoical stereotype" is not applicable to the Indians as a race.[38] As a matter of fact, Schoolcraft himself was most familiar, by marriage and experience, with the Indians of the Eastern Woodlands. This enhances his character portrait of the Indians of this area while weakening it as a racial portrait of the Indian at large.

The same emotional structure remains characteristic of some of the Indians of the Eastern Woodlands at the present time. My own observations of the Berens River Saulteaux and the Rorschach records that I obtained from them corroborate the older descriptions. Among the less acculturated Indians of the upper reaches of the river in particular, the emotional structure to be observed is almost identical with that of the Northeastern Indians of an earlier period. Furthermore, the connection between this psychological pattern and the cultural conditions of which it is a function are fairly clear.

There are no parallels, of course, to some of the conditions which existed in earlier centuries. The modern Saulteaux have no tradition of the warpath, nor any experience of native war or torture. Native games have completely disappeared so that we have no direct knowledge of how individuals acted when gambling. Yet the hardiness which women display in childbirth conforms to the traditional pattern. And since the Saulteaux still depend mainly upon hunting and fishing for a living, hunger and the hardships accompanying a low standard of living must be faced. Chief Berens has commented more than once that Indians, as compared to whites, do not mind going hungry. They do not worry about it; in fact they continue to laugh and joke even when hunger is gnawing at their vitals. I believe that this attitude is typical, but I also believe that we must interpret it as an excellent defense against the real anxiety which the threat of hunger, or the experience of it, actually imposes upon the Saulteaux. As a matter of fact, the latent anxiety aroused is much more serious than is apparent and for this reason requires more suppression or emotional displacement than is obvious on the surface. What I have in mind is the belief among the Saulteaux that one may fail to find animals because some sorcerer is exerting a malevolent influence, or because one has offended the "masters" of the game animals or fish. In other words, according to native theory one *should* be able to make a living unless something goes wrong, and, if something does go wrong, it is *somebody's* fault. Since the aboriginal backgrounds of belief largely persists, it can only be concluded that fortitude in the face of hunger and hardship is a defense against latent anxiety derived from this source as well as from the objective conditions imposed by a food-gathering economy.

Illness among the present-day Saulteaux is also met with great patience, and this thoroughly coincides with what is reported for the Indians of earlier centuries. But here, again, while some anxiety naturally is intrinsic to such situations, there is a distinctive psychological attitude to be noted which is a function of the prevailing beliefs about the causes of sickness. Any kind of serious illness is a consequence of wrong-doing on the part of some individual or the result of sorcery ["The Social Function of Anxiety" and "Sin, Sex and Sickness in Saulteaux Belief," chapters 16, 17, this volume].

So far as interpersonal relations go, there is a great deal of restraint among the Saulteaux upon the expression in public of all categories of emotion—joy, irritation, anger, etc. The most outstanding exception is laughter. In fact, the very positive emphasis upon the expression of amusement, in contrast to the inhibitions imposed upon the expression of other forms of emotion is highly characteristic. What Gilfillan says about the Minnesota Ojibwa of the nineteenth century completely accords with my observation among the Manitoba Saulteaux in the twentieth century.

> There is continual laughter, and jests flying all around the wigwam from the time they wake in the morning till the last one goes to sleep. As long as they have anything to eat, and if no one is very sick, they are as cheerful and happy as can be. The laughter and droll remarks pass from one to the other, a continual fusillade all round. The old woman says something funny; the children take it up, and laugh at it; all the others repeat it, each with some embellishment, or adding some ludicrous feature, and thus there is continual merriment all day and all evening long.[39]

Consequently anyone, Indian or white, who can tickle the risibilities of the Saulteaux is socially popular. The psychological importance of laughter among them is also evidenced by the institutionalization of humor. Despite the fact that their myths are sacred stories, many of them are characterized by a Rabelaisian humor that never fails to provoke a laugh. "Tear jerking" or tragic stories of any kind would, in fact, be unthinkable among the Saulteaux. Laughter seems to be the catharsis they need for their resolution of tensions. Then, too, there is the joking relationship between cross-cousins of opposite sex. The bawdy exchanges between persons of this category are not only permissible; they are actually demanded. Since cross-cousins are found in every camp and in practically all social situations, laughter may be said to be one of the psychological functions of Saulteaux social organization.

The characteristic balance maintained between the expression and inhibition of emotion among the Saulteaux and that which prevails among ourselves can be epitomized by a few concrete illustrations. Once when I was preparing to photograph an old man, several Indians gathered around. Among them was a very dignified old woman, a Christian and a pillar of the Church, the mother of a large family of grown children. The old man had assumed a position in which it happened that his legs were spread widely apart. Just before I was ready to snap the shutter of my camera, the old lady suddenly reached towards the old man's fly as if to unbutton it. Everyone went into peals of laughter. The old man was her cross-cousin. But on other occasions I have seen this same old woman watch the departure of her husband without a gesture or change of expression and accept his return home after weeks of absence with a similar nonchalance.[40] And once, when her favorite son returned from boarding school after three years' absence, I saw him step off the boat and walk past his mother with scarcely a greeting, while she stood there impassively. Since I was living with this family, however, I knew about the excited talk that anticipated that homecoming and continued long after we were all finally settled in the kitchen. Yet one would have gained no clue to the emotion that seethed beneath the surface from the behavior observed on the dock. In public the pattern is always one of severe restraint under such circumstances.[41] Peter Grant observed a similar pattern of restraint among the Saulteaux over a century ago. He says,

> Their manner of salutation is most ridiculous: when strangers or long absent friends meet, they remain like statues for a considerable time with their faces hid or inclined to one side and without exchanging one word. After a long pause, they smile or grin at each other, this is understood to be the prelude to asking news, and the conversation becomes general after they have smoken a pipe.[42]

I once witnessed the arrival of a group of inland Indians from Lake Pekangikum who had paddled 250 miles to the mouth of the Berens River to receive their Treaty Money. They acted very much as the Saulteaux described by Peter Grant. After beaching their canoes they stood at the foot of the bank staring at the local Indians who had gathered at the top of the bank and were staring at them. Everyone seemed frozen by embarrassment. These Indians were not total strangers to each other, either. While there is not much social intercourse on account of the distance involved, there are blood connections and relationships through marriage. At the same time there are always latent suspicions between Indians of different communities, possibly very much greater in the past,[43] mainly due to the possibilities of sorcery, so that moving from one settlement to another even now stirs up a certain amount of anxiety. I found, for example, that some men of the Berens River Band at the mouth of the river were very loath to have their hair cut when up the river for fear that someone might obtain strands of it and do them harm. They hardly thought of this when at home. Hence a cautious and restrained manner of approach is adopted.

But sorcery may also emanate from individuals of one's own community and even from one's own relatives. Even the Christianized Indians believe this. In the summer of 1940 I learned of the death during the previous winter of a man whom I knew fairly well. Later I heard a rumor that he had been killed by his father's brother. Consequently, I believe that it is reasonable to assert that the major factor which was at the root of the latent suspicion and distrust that colored the interpersonal relations of the Indians of earlier periods operates today. In the last analysis, almost every Saulteaux believes that it is possible for another person to harm him by covert means. This idea is supported by the fact that some individuals have confessed to killing dozens of persons by sorcery. From the viewpoint of the Indians no better proof is needed that such things do happen. Even today it is literally true, as Schoolcraft says, that harm rather than good is anticipated from others. The same is true in other Ojibwa communities. Jenness, for instance, speaking of the present day Indians of Parry Island says,

> Every man suspects his neighbor of practicing the nefarious art to avenge some fancied grievance, and the older and more conservative the Indian, the more he is held in suspicion. Probably there is not a single adult on the island who has not been accused of sorcery at some time or other, and who has not himself suffered some misfortune which he attributes to the same cause.[44]

This is the psychological explanation, it seems to me, of the "atomism," or individualism, of Ojibwa society and of Indians with comparable cultures in the past. It is impossible for people to get together when their outlook is colored by the possibility of malevolence, particularly when there are no social institutions that demand a high degree of cooperation. Since covert malevolence is always potentially present in one's dealings with others and the only defense against it is one's own supernaturally augmented powers, psychological security can only be achieved by the enhancement of "confidence in one's power to stand alone. Close kin are important because identification with them is possible. Religion is a system of obtaining individual power for individual ends, originally dependent upon the individual's ability to attain it."[45] Consequently, the better part of wisdom is to avoid offending others. In practice this means that an amiable front, the suppression of one's own feelings or opinions, and even positive helpfulness, is the best policy to pursue. Naturally this policy leads to a certain amount of dissimulation and the inhibition of many spontaneous impulses because its foundation is anxiety. One is even led to mistrust the sincerity of those who *do* appear to be genuinely pleasant, amiable, and helpful people. When I heard that the old man mentioned above was reputed to have killed his nephew, I said to my informant, "But he was such a nice old man!" "That's just the reason I really believe he did it," was the reply. [See "Aggression in Saulteaux Society," chapter 15, this volume.]

Thus, the latent mistrust engendered by a belief in sorcery has the widest ramifications in Saulteaux society. I think it explains the suppression of criticism in face-to-face relations, also mentioned in the older sources, the hesitancy to command others, and the ready assent to requests even though the individual may not carry them out. Hospitality, lending, sharing, likewise may be motivated by anxiety, since a guest, a borrower or a neighbor may become piqued and seek retaliation by covert means. As Jenness says of the Parry Islanders, "He sets food before chance visitors of his own race, whatever the hour of the day or night, lest they resent any semblance of inhospitality and later cast a spell on himself and his household." A case is also cited in which a loan was refused. The man who requested it left in an angry mood. Later when the man who refused the loan was taken ill, he believed that he had been bewitched by the man he had turned down.[46] A Saulteaux whom I know sold some brown sugar, at a considerable loss, to one of the sons of the "nice" old man who was said to have killed his nephew. My friend, who really wanted to keep the sugar for his own use, was warned that it was best not to deny the old man's sons anything, so he let one of them have the sugar cheap. On the surface it looked like a very neighborly gesture; actually the loss that he took was a kind of "life insurance" for himself and his family. The whole transaction was carried out in what would have appeared to any outside observer as the friendliest spirit. But I know that it was not a generous act and that my friend suppressed his genuine feelings in the matter.

It can readily be understood that if such care is taken to avoid offending others in such small matters of daily life, that the Saulteaux are even more careful to avoid any open expression of anger in face-to-face relationships.[47] An overt expression of anger or aggression of any sort in this society is tantamount to a challenge to a duel by sorcery, since there is no institutionalized form for settling such matters in any other way. Consequently, individuals maintain their taciturnity in face-to-face relations even though they may simmer with suppressed emotion. If retaliation is sought it is always by some covert means. It is obvious that the deflection of emotion that is demanded not only requires a great deal of restraint; anxiety is also generated because no one knows when, how, or even if, retaliation will take place. Hence, the amiable demeanor adopted by the Saulteaux cannot be separated from the suppressed aggression that is experienced. This means that there is a deep-seated ambivalence in their emotional structure.

Turning now to the Rorschach protocols, which furnish us with direct evidence of the manner in which the personality of individuals is functioning, we find corroboration for the inferences drawn from Saulteaux culture, firsthand observation of the behavior of individuals, and other case material. (For further details see chapters 3 and 19 [in *Culture and Experience*].

The most prominent feature in the great majority of records is the emphasis on strong restraint and control. From the Rorschach evidence alone one would be bound to infer that the Saulteaux were a people whose personal lives were organized within the ambit of formalized habit patterns and that very little of their emotional and imaginative life escapes these bonds. Another inference would be that behind the facade represented by this severe control is wariness and caution. There is meager evidence of spontaneous emotional expression or testing other people's emotional reactions realistically in face-to-face relations. The sort of social roles the individual conceptualizes are on the whole very passive—standing, sitting, looking, sometimes talking. However, almost half of the individuals tested (over half of the inland women), in spite of their introverted personalities and their lack of spontaneous emotional reactions, were sensitive, in some cases hypersensitive, to outer emotional stimuli. Among the inland men who showed this sensitivity, only one showed a tendency to adjust to it and act upon it, but his protocol revealed that tension and fear restrained him. Not able to adjust in his extraversial way, neither has he been able to adopt in any great measure the general pattern of reactions, so that he is a very maladjusted person. Of the two inland women with a tendency to act upon their extraversial tendencies, one rigidly controls her hypersensitivity, and the other, not quite so rigidly controlled, has anxiety that interferes with her adjustment. In the group at the mouth of the river there are many evidences in the Rorschach records that changes are taking place in the basic personality structure. Many more of those who show sensitivity to outer emotional stimuli are attempting to adjust in an extraversial manner under the pressure of contacts with white people and their culture. These men and women, while on the whole less rigidly controlled and restrained, all show anxieties coming to the surface. The women, however, appear to be much more successful in their attempts at social adjustment. On the other hand the two persons who have broken most completely away from the old pattern are also women. One is a girl who has gone wild, losing all restraint, and the other is a very egocentric, hot-tempered individual by any Indian standards, who, however, retains a large measure of control.

The imaginative life also shows evidence of repression although this is less repressed than outward emotional reactions. Evidently, unless the individual feels strong enough through acquired magic powers, all fantasy is dangerous, more especially aggressive fantasy of which there is little evidence. Where aggression is mainly covert, hostile thoughts must be inhibited in the individual himself for fear of inviting the evil thoughts of others to attack him. The greater development, relatively speaking, of fantasy over social and emotional rapport exposes the individual to the development of convictions divorced from any testing of their objective reality. There is thus a danger that he will act upon some distorted idea of what another intends.

The typical Saulteaux character structure as revealed by the Rorschach is largely built upon the basis of defense mechanisms against anxieties. This is understandable in view of the great lack of other developed technics for mastering the economic and social environment. The best defense against all these threats is, as Mead has pointed out, a rigid self-discipline to stand alone and to acquire as much personal magic power as possible. For so rigidly patterned a personality it is not surprising that the missionaries found these Indians resistant to any change of beliefs. It is not stubbornness, nor obstinacy, but an incapacity for change in the habitual ways of thinking and feeling.

It should be understood that without a knowledge of the cultural background and actual behavior of individuals it would be impossible to infer from the Rorschach data alone the *specific conditions* which produced the typical personality picture. On the other hand, any deductions one makes about the personality of individuals from a knowledge of the cultural background of these people and their external behavior needs to be checked by some method of controlled observation on the individuals themselves. The Rorschach technique provides such a method since it offers an integral picture of the personality as it functions under given conditions. It enables us to approach people directly as people.

Notes

Published in Frederick Johnson, ed., *Man in Northeastern North America,* Papers of the R.S. Peabody Foundation for Archeology, III (1946) 195–225. Reprinted as chapter 6 in Hallowell, *Culture and Experience* (1955), 125–50.

1. Morris Wolf, *Iroquois Religion and Its Relation to Their Morals* (New York, 1919).

2. Since this paper was published Anthony F. C. Wallace has published *The Modal Personality Structure of the Tuscarora Indians* (Bureau of American Ethnology, Bulletin 150 [1952]).

3. W. Vernon Kinietz, *The Indians of the Western Great Lakes, 1615–1760* (Occasional Contributions from the Museum of Anthropology of the University of Michigan, No. 10 [1940]), 167.

4. Reuben Gold Thwaites (ed.), *The Jesuit Relations and Allied Documents* (73 vols.; Cleveland, 1896–1901).

5. Chretien Le Clercq, *New Relation of Gaspesia*, trans. and ed. with a reprint of the original by W. F. Ganong (Toronto, 1910), 241.

6. Kinietz, *Indians*, 232.

7. Cf. Duncan Cameron (on the Saulteaux) in R. L. Masson, ed. *Les bourgeois de la compagnie du Nord-Ouest* (2 vols.; Quebec 1890), II, 238.

8. E. Jamieson and P. Sandiford, "The Mental Capacity of the Southern Ontario Indians," *Journal of Educational Psychology*, 19 (1929), 536–51. See also T. R. Garth, *Race Psychology: A Study of Racial Mental Differences* (New York, 1931); Beatrice Blackwood, *A Study of Mental Testing in Relation to Anthropology* (Mental Measurement Monographs, No. 4 [1927]); Otto Klineberg, *Race Differences* (New York, 1935), chap. 8; Cecil Mann, "Mental Measurements in Primitive Communities," *Psychological Bulletin*, 37 (1940), 366–95; Ann Anastasi, *Differential Psychology* (New York, 1937), chap. 7.

9. See Klineberg, *Race Differences*, 153.

10. Anastasi, *Differential Psychology*, 511.

11. Anastasi, *Differential Psychology*, 510–11.

12. Masson, ed., *Les bourgeois*, II, 325.

13. Bruno Klopfer, "Form Level Rating," *Rorschach Research Exchange*, VIII (1944), 164–77.

14. Le Clercq, *New Relation*, 243.

15. Le Clercq, *New Relation*, 242. Le Clercq phrases a parallel statement in a manner which may indicate that he had Le Jeune's *Relation* of 1634 at hand. (See editor's remarks.) But he undoubtedly intended the observation to apply to the Micmac.

16. Le Clercq, *New Relation*, 243.

17. H. G. Loskiel, *History of the Mission of the United Brethren among the Indians in North America* (London, 1794), Part I, 132.

18. David Zeisberger, "History of the North American Indians etc.," Ohio *Archeological and Historical Society Quarterly*, 19 (1910), Nos. 1 and 2; 90.

19. Louis Armand, Baron de Lahontan, *New Voyages in North America,* reprinted from the English edition of 1703, Reuben G. Thwaites (ed.), (2 vols.; Chicago, 1905), II, 579.

20. E. H. Blair, *Indian Tribes of the Upper Mississippi and Region of the Great Lakes* (2 vols.; Cleveland, 1911), I, 195.

21. Le Clercq, *New Relation,* 242.

22. W. N. Fenton, "Iroquois Suicide: A Study in the Stability of a Culture Pattern," *Anthropological Papers,* No. 14 *(Bureau of American Ethnology Bulletin,* 129 [1941]), 80–137.

23. Masson, ed., *Les bourgeois,* II, 327.

24. Le Clercq, *New Relation,* 242.

25. Quoted by Chretien Le Clercq, *First Establishment of the New Faith in New France,* translated with notes by J. G. Shea (2 vols.; New York, 1881), II, 222. (First printing Paris, 1691.)

26. The original text [1946] read "a suffusion in anxiety," but since this suggests "free-floating anxiety" which is not at all the case, I have substituted "underlying anxiety." [Ed. note: Hallowell made occasional small textual changes in the articles reprinted in *Culture and Experience,* 1955.]

27. Cf. R. R. Willoughby, "Magic and Cognate Phenomena: A Hypothesis," in C. Murchison (ed.), *Handbook of Social Psychology* (2nd ed.; Worcester 1933), 504.

28. Le Clercq, *New Relation,* 243.

29. Le Clercq, *New Relation,* 252.

30. Letter 25, in Kinietz, *Indians,* 344.

31. For references to the sources and a general discussion see A. G. Bailey, *The Conflict of European and Eastern Algonkian Cultures, 1504–1700* (Monograph Series, no. 2, New Brunswick Museum, St. John, New Brunswick, 1937), chap. 6.

32. Cf. Ruth Bunzel, "The Role of Alcoholism in Two Central American Cultures," *Psychiatry,* 3 (1940), 361–87.

33. For an analysis of the interrelated psychological and cultural variables that characterize several distinctive patterns of drinking behavior in a sample of seventy-seven societies, see the significant pioneer study of Donald Horton, "The Function of Alcohol in Primitive Societies: A Cross-cultural Study," *Quarterly Journal of Studies on Alcohol,* 4 (1943), 199–320.

34. Douglas MacKay, *The Honourable Company: A History of the Hudson's Bay Company* (New York, 1936), 220. [Ed. note: MacKay's statement is simplistic. The company had other concerns—for protection of property,

privacy, and control of its men's relations with women. Actual violence was rare.]

35. Le Clercq, *New Relation*, 255. For nineteenth-century Ojibwa parallels see, for example, J. A. Gilfillan, *The Ojibways of Minnesota* (Minnesota Historical Society Collections, 10 [1901]); Peter Jones, *History of the Ojibway Indians; With Special Reference to Their Conversion to Christianity* (London, 1861), 167; John Tanner, *A Narrative of the Captivity and Adventures of John Tanner During Thirty Years Residence among the Indians in the Interior of North America*, Edwin James, ed. (New York, 1830), 163–65.

36. Masson, ed., *Les bourgeois*, II, 248; also the statement of James, the editor of Tanner, 1830.

37. Henry R. Schoolcraft, *Information Respecting the History, Conditions and Prospects of the Indian Tribes of the United States* (Philadelphia, 1851–57), Part III, 58.

38. Klineberg, *Race Differences*, 280.

39. Gilfillan, *The Ojibways*, 64; cf. 114.

40. Gilfillan, *The Ojibways*, 86, writes, "I have never seen the slightest endearment pass between husband and wife, not the slightest outward token of affection. Yet there is no doubt that they are as much attached to each other, especially in middle and later life, as those of our own race." [Ed. note: Hallowell was staying at Berens River with the family of Chief William Berens and his wife, Nancy.]

41. Egerton R. Young, *Stories from Indian Wigwams and Northern Camp-Fires* (New York, 1892). Young, who spent a long period as a missionary among the Cree and Saulteaux of the Lake Winnipeg region [1868–76 at Norway House and Berens River], comments (19) on the emotional restraint in domestic life.

42. Masson, *Les bourgeois*, II, 328; cf. J. G. Kohl, *Kitchi-gami; Life among the Lake Superior Ojibway* (London, 1860), 35.

43. This ever recurrent suspiciousness has been frequently commented upon. Cf. Ruth Landes, "The Ojibwa of Canada," in Margaret Mead (ed.), *Cooperation and Competition among Primitive Peoples* (New York, 1937), 102; and Gilfillan, *The Ojibways*, 92.

44. Diamond Jenness, *The Ojibwa Indians of Parry Island, Their Social and Religious Life* (Canadian Department of Mines, Bulletin 78, Anthropological Series No. 17 [Ottawa, 1935]).

45. Cf. Margaret Mead's analysis of the Ojibwa, "Interpretive Statement," in *Cooperation and Competition*, 489, 491, 498–99.

46. Cf. Jenness, *The Ojibwa Indians of Parry Island*, 87, 88.

47. Jenness, *The Ojibwa Indians of Parry Island*, 88, says that the Parry Islander "strives to avoid malice and ill-will by hiding his emotions, and by carefully weighing his words lest he give vent to some angry or ill-timed remark." Timolean Ducatel ("A Fortnight among the Chippewa," *United States Catholic Magazine*, 5 [1846]), a casual observer of the La Pointe Ojibwa in 1846, writes (28), "A very remarkable trait of character in the Indians is, that they never quarrel, nor address insulting epithets to each other."

TWENTY-SIX

The Ojibwa Self and Its Behavioral Environment

Although there is no single term in Ojibwa speech that can be satisfactorily rendered into English as "self," nevertheless, by means of personal and possessive pronouns, the use of kinship terms, and so on, the Ojibwa Indian constantly identifies himself as a person. Every individual knows who he is, where he is, and what kind of being he is; he entertains definite beliefs and concepts that relate to his own nature. Besides this, his language enables him to express such concepts as self-defense, self-glorification, self-deceit, self-command. Large areas of his most characteristic thinking, his affective experience, his needs, motivations, and goals are not thoroughly intelligible unless we take the content of his self-image into account.

I believe that the essential features of the self-image of the Ojibwa, in their full psychological reality, can best be communicated by indicating how they function as an integral part of the experience of an individual. To present the material in this form I have let an Indian, long deceased, speak in the first person, rather than attempt an abstract exposition. In order to cover as many aspects of the topic as possible and yet remain as close as possible to data collected in the field, I have attributed to my Indian speaker knowledge and experience derived from the statements of a number of different informants. Furthermore, the statements of my Indian speaker, which all appear between quotation marks, may be taken as a free translation of a possible Ojibwa text, since I have not used any English words that do not have a fairly good equivalent in Ojibwa. Beside this, Ojibwa terms for key concepts are cited. In brackets I have added my comments on particular points in order to highlight significant concepts and have sometimes gone into further elaboration. In the footnotes are references to published articles or books where fuller data or case material highly abbreviated in the account given by my Indian speaker, will be found.

When I was born I had a body, *mi·yó* and I had a soul, *òtcatcákwin*. My body came out of my mother's womb and when I was an old man it was buried in the earth [the body has a definitive existence in time]. I was not one of those people who knew what was happening before he was born.[1] But my father did. (See "Spirits of the Dead," *Reincarnation*) [chapter 22, this volume].

I have heard some other old people say that they had heard babies crying constantly until someone recognized the name they were trying to say. When they were given this name they stopped crying. This shows that someone who had once lived on the earth came back to live again. [Reincarnation is possible, even if occasional. There are special cues in such cases: the recall of prenatal memories; crying and babbling that only stops when the name of a deceased person is mentioned,[2] which indicates the importance of the personal name in self-identification. Another cue is the presence of a few gray hairs on the infant's head. In cases like this no personal identification may be made. Certain inferences are clear: the soul is independent of a particular body; it transcends the body in time; an implicit concept of the self is intimately connected with the idea of the soul. Self-objectification is clearly implied since self-awareness is even attributed to the fetus. The informant says that his father knew when he was going to be born. To the Ojibwa to know what is going to happen ahead of time is one of the signs of a "great" man, i.e., a man with unusual powers.]

When I was living on the earth I had to be careful that nobody got hold of any part of my body. When my hair was cut I always burnt the part that was cut off. I was afraid that someone with power [magic] might get hold of it. If he wanted to, such a person could make me sick or even kill me. I didn't want to die before I had to. I wanted life, *pīmädazīwin*. But someone did manage to kill me by sending something towards me that penetrated my body. That's when you need a *nībakīwininī* [an Indian doctor who tries to remove the object by sucking as part of his ritual]. Sometimes he will suck out a shell, a piece of metal, or a dog's tooth and show it to you. Then you can live. But he couldn't cure me. He didn't have enough power. The person who killed me had more. [The body is intimately connected with the self, so intimately that physical possession of even a part of it is considered as endangering the self. The self can also be attacked by magically potent material substances projected into the body. In general, it may be said that bodily illness of any kind arouses great anxiety. The Ojibwa tend to be hypochondriacal. There are two points of interpretation that are relevant in this connection: Since serious illness, in many instances, is thought to be due to sorcery, it becomes a direct personal attack upon the self by an enemy. At the same time since illness, viewed from the standpoint of experience, involves the dysfunctioning of bodily processes, the bodily aspect of the self assumes great importance. The further implication is that an attack on the body destroys the balance that should exist between soul and body in order to realize the Good Life, that is, life in terms of longevity, health, and absence of misfortune. Since self-awareness is given content in terms of a self-image defined by this dichotomy, anxiety may be aroused if either soul or body is endangered. In a positive sense this is why *pimädazïwin* expresses a very central goal for the self—a level of aspiration towards which the self is motivated.[3]]

When I died and my body was buried that was not the end of me. I still exist[4] in *djïbaiàking*, Ghost land or the Land of the Dead. [Existence of self is not coordinate with bodily existence in the ordinary human sense.] When I was dead people called me a *djï·bai*, ghost. Some Indians have seen *djïbaiyak* (plural) or heard them whistle. [In other words, a dead person has a form, a ghostly appearance that can be seen by the living and, without being visually perceived, may occasionally be heard by the living. Death involves metamorphosis because the body formerly associated with the soul has become detached from it and lies in the ground. On the other hand "I" *know* when "I" am a *djï·bai*; self-awareness, personal identity, personal memories persist; there is a continuity of the self maintained.]

It is a long hard journey to the Land of the Dead. To reach it you travel south.[5] [There are cases known in the past in which pagan Indians begged their Christianized relatives not to bury them in a coffin. They believed that they would have to carry it with them on the journey to the Land of the Dead, and they did not wish to be burdened with it. This journey is not conceived in "spiritual" terms at all; the "living" self can become emotionally disturbed by the anticipation of difficulties to be encountered by the "dead" self. It is plain that, psychologically, the behavioral environment of the self is all of one piece.]

When I got there I found it to be a very fine place. The Indians who had died before me were glad to see me. Some of them had moss growing on their foreheads [like old rocks] they had died so long ago. I sang and danced with them. A few Indians have reached the Land of the Dead and then gone back to tell those who were alive what they saw there. [The dead in appearance are thought of anthropomorphically, not as disembodied spirits. They live in wigwams. But there are differences. In one account a youth visiting the land of the dead was offered food by his grandmother. It was decayed (i.e., phosphorescent) wood. When he refused, she said: "Naturally you are not truly dead." An essential point for emphasis is the continuation of a fundamental duality of essence. *Djībaiyak* like *änicinábek* have souls, and some kind of *form*. As will became more apparent later, this duality holds for *all* orders of animate beings.]

If an Indian dies and a good medicine man starts after him quickly enough he may be brought back [i.e., his soul may be captured and returned to his body]. Then he can go on living as before. Once I saw Owl do this.[6] Tcètcebú was very ill. By the time Owl arrived where her father was encamped, she died. Owl tied a piece of red yarn around the girl's wrist at once [to enable him to identify her quickly in a crowd] and lay down beside her body. He lay in this position a long, long time. He was still; he did not move at all. Then I saw him move ever so little. The girl began to move a little also. Owl moved more. So did the girl. Owl raised himself up into a sitting posture. At the same moment the girl did the same. He had followed her to the Land of the Dead and caught her soul just in time. Everything has to have a soul in order to exist (as an animate being). I'm in the Land of the Dead now but I have a soul just as I had one before I came here. [Death involves the departure of the soul from the body; the soul takes up its residence in a new locale. There is metamorphosis. The body becomes inanimate and "selfless." The persistence of the self in conjunction with the soul in its new form is implied in the self-awareness attributed to ghosts.]

If a conjurer, *djisáki·wininī*, has power enough, he can bring a soul back from the Land of the Dead into his 'shaking tent.' I was called by a conjurer once because my son was ill and this man was trying to cure him. My grandchild went with me. When her mother, who was sitting with the other Indians outside the conjuring tent, heard her speak, she cried.[7] I had to tell about something wrong I had done when I was living. This helped my son to get well.[8] [Under these circumstances the ghost has no usually perceptible form; only the soul is there. But functionally, a self continuous with a "living" existence is implied because personal memories of an earlier period in life are recalled.]

When a person is sleeping anyone can see where his body is, but you can't tell whether his soul is there or not. Some conjurer may have enough power to draw your soul into his shaking tent while you are asleep. If he has the power you can't resist. Perhaps he only wants to have you talk to the people in his camp and tell them the latest news. But he may want to kill you. If your soul doesn't get back to your body then you'll be a *djí·bai* by the next morning and have to start off to the Land of the Dead. I had a lucky escape once. I was only sixteen years old. A conjurer drew my soul into his conjuring lodge and I knew at once that he wanted to kill me, because I had made fun of his son who was a 'humpy' [hunchback]. I said 'I'm going out.' But the old man said, 'No! You can't go.' Then I saw my own head rolling about and the people in the lodge were trying to catch it. [The "people" were the guardian spirits, *pawáganak*, of the conjurer—superhuman entities.] I thought to myself that if only I could catch my head everything would be all right. So I tried to grab it when it rolled near me and finally I caught it.[9] As soon as I got hold of it I could see my way out and I left. Then I woke up but I could not move my legs or arms. Only my fingers I could move, but finally I managed to speak. I called out to my mother. I told her I was sick. I was sick for a couple of days. No one saw my soul go to and fro but I knew where I had been. I told my father about it and he agreed with me.

[It is quite clear from all this that the soul is detachable from the body and may occupy a different position in space. This is true both with respect to a dead person and a person asleep. It is also possible to infer with reasonable certainty that the soul cannot be conceptually dissociated from the self. Where a functioning self exists, there must be a soul. Where a soul exists there must be a self. In terms of an assumed dependent relationship the self-soul relation in Ojibwa thought logically parallels the self-body relation in our sophisticated thinking. We emphasize a certain kind of *physical* body or form as a necessary substratum for a functioning self. We are skeptics so far as any other kind of a structural substratum is concerned. On the other hand, the Ojibwa take it for granted that the soul is the only necessary substratum. Any particular form or appearance is incidental. Thus, various kinds of metamorphosis can be accepted so long as it is assumed that a soul continues to exist. What is particularly interesting to note, it seems to me, is that once we accept this assumption, it becomes more and more apparent that *functionally* the same generic attributes of the self as we understand it—and that we assume can only be manifested where a human bodily structure is present—are constant functions of the soul as thought of by the Ojibwa. The soul of the living or the dead knows who it is, what it is, where it is in space and time; it is conscious of past experiences, it has a capacity for volition, etc., irrespective of the form or appearance it may present to others at the moment. This interpretation is further illustrated by what follows.]

There was a *djí·bai* here who paid a visit to her grandfather. He was so very sad after she died. She visited him one day when he had put a mast up in his canoe and with a blanket for a sail was crossing a lake. She appeared to him as a little bird that alighted on the top of the mast. She didn't say anything but he knew who it was because he was a wise old man.[10] [The deceased—one of the very old people, *keté änicinábek*—may be seen by a living person, not as a ghost but in the form of a bird. Metamorphosis is possible for a *djí·bai*; in this case from ghost to bird.]

The soul of a living person, too, after it leaves the body can look like an animal. A powerful medicine man can do a lot of harm because he can go about secretly at night. But you can see his body lying there in his wigwam all the time. A long time ago a friend of mine told me what he had seen.[11] He and his wife were living with an old man suspected of being a sorcerer. One night he thought the sorcerer was up to something. The latter lit his pipe and covered himself up completely with his blanket. My friend kept watch. After a long, long time had gone by, all of a sudden the sorcerer threw off the blanket and fell over towards the fire. Blood was running from his mouth; he was dead. My friend found out what killed him. At the very same time that the sorcerer was lying under his blanket so quietly, in another part of the camp Pindǎ`ndɑkwɑn was waiting with a gun in the dark beside the body of his son who had been killed by sorcery. A kind of 'fire' had appeared around the camp several times before the boy died. This night Pindǎ`ndɑkwɑn saw the 'fire' coming again. It[12] made a circle around the corpse, which was covered by birchbark. He heard a voice saying, 'This is finished.' Then he saw a bear trying to lift the bark near the head of his son; he was going to take what he wanted.[13] Pindǎ`ndɑkwɑn shot the bear and he heard a man's voice crying out. Both the sorcerer and the boy were buried the next day. Everyone thought the old man was a bad one. No one blamed Pindǎ`ndɑkwɑn.

[This anecdote requires some lengthy comment, since it will enable us to penetrate further into Ojibwa thought and the basic premises involved. (a) It is obvious that there is not metamorphosis of the body of the sorcerer. The *mi·yó* remains in the wigwam in its usual form. (b) Unlike the previous case where the soul was drawn from the body by the power of another person, here the soul leaves the body behind through a volitional act of the conjurer himself. In fact the Ojibwa would say that *he* left his body and point out that this was not the first time, since his reputation for wickedness implies this kind of behavior. And the "fire" had been seen at Pindă`ndɑkwan's camp before. (c) It is likewise obvious that, in this case, the conjurer was not understood to be prowling around *dressed up* in a bear skin. This was John Tanner's interpretation, over a century ago, of similar stories. He writes: "by some composition of gunpowder, or other means [they] contrive to give the appearance of fire to the mouth and eyes of the bear skin, in which they go about the village late at night, bent on deeds of mischief, oftentimes of blood."[14] This is simply Tanner's effort at an explanation intelligible to him. (d) I believe that all we need to say is that the self of the sorcerer was in Pindă'ndɑkwan's camp. To say that *he* was there is the meaningful core of the whole situation; it was Pindă`ndɑkwan's assumption that *he* would be there and he acted on this premise. In these terms the situation is as humanly intelligible to us as it is to the Ojibwa. What is always difficult for them is to explain what we would call the *mechanism* of events, exactly *how* they occur. To them, this line of thought seems "pedantic." Explanation is never pursued in much detail at this level (which is actually the level of science). But to say that *he* (the sorcerer) had visited Pindă`ndɑkwan 's camp on several occasions, that *he* had killed Pindă`ndɑkwan's son, that he was caught there on a particular night and killed by Pindă`ndɑkwan in revenge is thoroughly meaningful to them. All they take for granted (as an implicit metaphysical principle) is that *multiform appearance is* an inherent potential of all animate beings. What is uniform, constant, visually imperceptible and vital is the soul. A sorcerer being a person of unusual power is able to leave his human body in one place and appear in another perceptible manifestation elsewhere. (e) There is an additional point to be noted. Inquiry revealed that Pindă`ndɑkwan was known to have considerable power himself. Since he assumed it was a sorcerer prowling around and not an ordinary bear, he did not load his gun with an ordinary bullet. He mixed "medicine," *mackīkī* (having magical potency), with his gunpowder. Just as it is thought possible to attack a person's ordinary body with intent to kill by projecting a material object with magical properties into it, in the same way the sorcerer, in the bodily appearance of a bear, could be directly attacked through his body, although something more than an ordinary bullet was required. (Under the circumstances there was no way of focusing the attack on his soul). In both instances the body is assumed to be a vulnerable point of attack. Since it is fairly clear that what death implies for the Ojibwa is the *separation* of the soul from its humanly-formed body,

I believe they would agree that the soul of the sorcerer did not succeed in getting back to his human body. This explains why his body was seen to collapse. It could not resume its normal functioning without a soul. This is why Owl was in such a hurry to capture the soul of Tcètcebú. Not being able to reach his body in time to resume living (which was, no doubt, part of the magic employed by Pindǎ`ndɑkwɑn), the sorcerer's soul was compelled to assume the form of a *ghost*. In a brief account of his puberty fast, to which our Indian speaker now refers, the reader will note another situation in which the *temporary* separation of the soul from the body occurs. To the Ojibwa there is nothing particularly unusual in such a personal experience. We lack autobiographical anecdotes, however, because there is a traditional taboo upon references to personal experiences during the puberty fast.]

Long ago, when every boy used to go out alone into the woods to obtain his helpers his body remained in the *wázisan* (nest) his father built for him.[15] If you had been there you could have seen his body for yourself. But his soul might have been elsewhere. One of his helpers might have taken him somewhere. That is what happened to me.

When I was a boy I went out to an island to fast. My father paddled me there. For several nights I dreamed of an *ógimǎ* (chief, superior person). Finally he said to me, "Grandson, I think you are now ready to go with me." Then *ógimǎ* began dancing around me as I sat there on a rock and when I happened to glance down at my body I noticed that I had grown feathers. Soon I felt just like a bird, a golden eagle (*kĩnĩu*). *Ógimǎ* had turned into an eagle also and off he flew towards the south. I spread my wings and flew after him in the same direction. After a while we arrived at a place where there were lots of tents and lots of 'people.' It was the home of the Summer Birds." [After returning north again the boy was left at their starting point after his guardian spirit had promised help whenever he wanted it. The boy's father came for him and took him home again.][16]

From this account it can be inferred that in addition to living Indians and deceased Indians, there are other classes of animate beings in the behavioral environment of the Ojibwa self with whom the individual comes into direct contact under certain circumstances. For it is apparent that the dreams of the puberty fast are interpreted as experiences of the self. The being that first appears as a human being and then is transformed into a bird is representative of a large class of other-than-human entities that maintain an existence independently of *änicinábek* and are more powerful than man.

The eagle-man is not the bird one ordinarily perceives but belongs to the class of "owners" or "bosses." All animal species, such as the golden eagle, are thought to have a *kādabenīmíkuwat*. These "owners" are only perceived, however, in dreams or visions.

If we assume that dream experiences are interpreted by the Ojibwa as experiences of the self, we then arrive at a very important deduction. The *pawáganak* are experienced as appearing in a specific form, that is, as having a bodily aspect, whether human or animal. Years ago I wrote in my notebook that Chief Berens, my most intelligent informant, said flatly that the *pawáganak* had "bodies" and "souls," but no "ghosts." Since *my* natural bias was to think of these *pawáganak* as "spiritual beings," I did not at first see the implications of the statement he had made. In our present discussion its full import is clarifying. The soul is the essential and persisting attribute of *all* classes of animate beings, human or nonhuman. But the soul is never a direct object of *visual* perception under any conditions. What can be perceived visually is only the aspect of being that has some form or structure. Consequently, it is not surprising to find that when the *pawáganak* appear in dreams they are identifiable in a tangible visual form. This *experiential* fact taken at its face value indicates, of course, that they, too, have a body as well as a soul. Structurally, they are the counterpart of man. On the other hand, it is *not* assumed that they have a uniform or stable appearance. Metamorphosis is always possible, as in the dream reported. It may be inferred, therefore, that there are inherent attributes which remain constant for different classes of beings. In the dream referred to, the *being* that appeared was a *pawágan* of a certain kind and not a human being, even though he first appeared in a human form. This is just the reverse of the bad old sorcerer who was essentially human even though he appeared as a bear on certain occasions. This means, of course, that in the behavioral world of the Ojibwa, no sharp line can be drawn between animals, *pawáganak*, men, or the spirits of the dead on the basis of outward bodily aspect or appearance alone. Myths illustrate this, too, and unless we are aware of the point I have just made it is utterly impossible to apprehend their veridical nature from the Ojibwa point of view. Myths are sacred stories because they rehearse actual events in which the superhuman *pawáganak* are the main characters. These *pawáganak* are specially adept at metamorphosis. This is part of the dramatic interest of the myths. The Ojibwa are quite prepared to have the *pawáganak* manifest the same characteristic attribute in dreams. It is one of their essential attributes because metamorphosis, especially when volitionally induced, has the implication of "power." It is thought that the human being who is capable of metamorphosis has derived his power through the help of *pawáganak*. This is the only source of it. When he possesses it he, therefore, becomes superior to his fellow men in this regard. They have to respect him even though they fear him. The only metamorphosis of *all änicinábek* is brought about by death. The dead, however, have more power than the living; consequently they are more like *pawáganak*, including the power of metamorphosis. But the *pawáganak*, who are eternal, do not die; they never become *djíbaiyak*.

The only sensory mode under which it is possible for human beings to directly perceive the presence of souls of *any* category, and then under certain conditions only, is the auditory one. The chief context of this kind of experience is the conjuring tent where, as I have already pointed out, the souls of *djíbaiyak* may be present and speak.[17] It is only infrequently that ghosts may be heard to whistle, perhaps in the neighborhood of a grave, where it is sometimes said they have been seen. It is from the conjuring tent, too, that the voices of *pawáganak* may be heard to issue. They cannot be seen. Thus from the standpoint of our central problem it is difficult not to draw the conclusion that, while according to Ojibwa dogma it is a soul that is present, even to them it is always an identifiable self—*pawágan* or ghost—that speaks. For them *òtcatcákwin* defines the conceptual substratum of beings with self-awareness and other related attributes (speech, memory, volition, etc.) that we associate only with a stabilized anthropomorphic structure. When Ojibwa speak of their own dream experiences or those of others, when they refer to what has been heard in conjuring performances, it is assumed that one's own soul or that of some other being was present and not the body. But this fact does not have to be explicitly stated any more than we have to be explicit about the presence of the body in referring to self-related experience or to social interaction with other selves. What is implied by the Ojibwa and by ourselves is an indication of the differences between their self-orientation and ours. What is held in common is a self-concept that assumes certain generic human attributes, despite conceptual differences in the nature of the substratum of a functioning self.

Returning once again to the puberty dream I should like to stress the fact that once dreams, on this occasion or any other, are construed as experiences of the self, we can only conclude that metamorphosis can be *personally* experienced. It follows from this, too, that to anyone who has had such a dream, episodes in myth, or anecdotes like those in which the sorcerer figured, cannot appear as strange or fantastic occurrences. In a dream, too, the self may experience the separation of the soul from the body and mobility over large distances. Accounts of such mobility also occur in myth and in anecdotes connected with conjuring. I was told by one informant that he once attended a conjuring performance to which another conjurer, from two hundred miles away, was called. He said, "I was sleeping, but I heard you calling me." People in the audience asked for news and received replies to questions. Then the soul of the visiting conjurer sang a song and departed for home.[18]

In addition to metamorphosis and spatial mobility, the self may likewise experience events in its dream phase that transcend the temporal schema of waking existence. Our autobiographer, for instance, not only made the long journey to the Land of the Summer Birds during his puberty fast; he stayed there all winter and flew north with the other birds under the guidance of his *ógimă* in the spring. It is self-related experiences of this nature that coordinate the world as dramatized in myth with the world as experienced by the self in certain phases of its existence. Myths are understood as past experiences of superhuman selves—the *pawáganak*. Dreams are among the past experiences of the self. Thus the world of the self is not essentially different from the world of the *pawáganak*. The cultural emphasis given to dream experience helps to unify the world of the self through *experience*. For anthropomorphic entities such as Wísakedják may appear in both myth and dream as may the Winds, Snow, Thunder Birds, and so on, in personified form. No wonder that certain "natural" objects belong to an animate rather than an inanimate gender in linguistic expression. Furthermore, all classes of *pawáganak* are linguistically integrated in the kinship terminology since, collectively, they are spoken of as "our grandfathers." And in the dream reported by our autobiographer the *pawágan* calls him *nozis,* "[my] grandson."

The Ojibwa self is not oriented to a behavioral environment in which a distinction between human beings and supernatural beings is stressed. The fundamental differentiation of primary concern to the self is how other selves rank in order of *power*. "Is he more powerful than I, or am I more powerful than he?" This is a crucial question applying to all human beings as well as to the *pawáganak*. But the fundamental distinction is that while other Indians may be more powerful than I, any *pawágan* is more powerful than any Indian. The power ranking of different classes of entities is so important because events only become intelligible in terms of their activities. All the effective agents of events throughout the entire behavioral environment of the Ojibwa are selves—my own self or other selves. *Impersonal* forces are never the causes of events. *Somebody* is always responsible. This is just as true for past events as the myths demonstrate. For example, Wísakedják, the "culture hero" was responsible for certain events in the past that led, among other things, to the distinguishing characteristics of certain animals as known today.

A further assumption is this: While power may be used for good or evil ends, most of the *pawáganak,* but not all, are beneficent. Human beings, too, for the most part use their power for beneficent ends. This is exemplified by all those who specialize in curative functions. They have received their power to cure from the *pawáganak* and, in turn, they help their fellow men. At the same time superhumanly acquired power may be used for malevolent ends.

Since "magic" power, as we have seen, is the ultimate source of successful adaptation in every sphere of life—from hunting to defense against sorcery—and the ultimate source of this power rests in the hands of the *pawáganak,* the fundamental relationship of the Ojibwa self to the *pawáganak is* clearly defined. It is one of dependence and is the root of their deep motivational orientation toward these powerful beings. But there is a normative aspect of this relationship as well. I must fulfill certain obligations that my guardian spirits impose upon me. I may have to make certain sacrifices, perhaps material ones (*pagitcigan*). In the dream visit of W. B[erens] to the *memengwécīwak* these were mentioned. There is a story told about a man who, after he was married, went off hunting all winter. He never spoke to his wife or had sexual intercourse with her. She left him in the spring. It turned out that he had been observing taboos imposed upon him in his puberty fast as a condition of a long and healthy life. "If she could only have held out three more moons," he said, "it would have been all right." He married again but did not follow the taboos. One of his children died, then his wife. A third wife died, too. This was all the result of his failure to live up to his side of the bargain with his *pawáganak.* Since all the relations between an individual and his *pawáganak* are based on dreams, their psychological reality is fundamental. It is what makes the puberty fast so important. The conceptual reality of all these beings the

Ojibwa boy has been acquainted with from babyhood by listening to the myths recited on long winter nights becomes in the course of the fast a *personal* experience. If the puberty fast of the Ojibwa is crucial to them for living in their world, this same experience, viewed psychologically, is equally crucial for making their world a reality for the self.

Notes

Published as the second section (153–65) of "The Self and Its Behavioral Environment," *Explorations* 2 (April 1954); reprinted as chapter 8 in Hallowell, *Culture and Experience* (Philadelphia: University of Pennsylvania Press, 1955). The 1955 text appears here. As noted in the introduction to this section, Hallowell slightly revised its opening text from that appearing in *Explorations*.

1. Victor Barnouw, "The Phantasy World of a Chippewa Woman," *Psychiatry*, 12 (1949), 67–76, cites verbatim the intra-uterine reminiscences of a Wisconsin Chippewa (Ojibwa) man and refers to specific examples of memories from early infancy on the part of other individuals.

2. I discovered that the occurrences of identical personal names, sometimes more than a generation apart in my genealogies, could be explained in every case by reincarnation. None of these people were living at the time of my inquiries.

3. See "Values, Acculturation, and Mental Health" [chapter 19, this volume], where this goal is discussed with reference to what has happened to the Ojibwa as a consequence of acculturation.

4. There is a term for existence that is applicable to any class of animate beings.

5. For details about the Land of the Dead and stories of visits there, see "Spirits of the Dead" [chapter 22, this volume].

6. For this case, and a reputed case of resurrection, see "Spirits of the Dead" [chapter 22, this volume].

7. For details and a full account of this episode see Hallowell, *The Role of Conjuring in Saulteaux Society* (Publications of the Philadelphia Anthropological Society, vol. 2, 1942) [also "Spirits of the Dead," chapter 22, this volume, on Jacob Berens's father's help to his son].

8. For the role of confession in relation to illness see "The Social Function of Anxiety," "Psychosexual Adjustment, Personality, and the Good Life in a Nonliterate Culture," and "Sin, Sex, and Sickness in Saulteaux Belief" [chapters 16, 18, 17, this volume].

9. Even in this "dream" a *bodily* part of himself—his head—assumes vital importance. The dreamer gives himself "form." [Ed. note: For William Berens's telling of this episode, see Berens, *Memories, Myths, and Dreams of an Ojibwe Leader* 2009), Part III.]

10. See "Spirits of the Dead in Saulteaux Life and Thought" [chapter 22, this volume].

11. What I have given here is a highly abbreviated version of a longer text (unpublished).

12. This reference to "fire" illustrates the allusive manner of Indian narration. The listener is supposed to know what is meant. What is referred to here is made explicit in another anecdote. "One night when I was asleep, I was suddenly awakened. My strength came to me and I managed to get on my feet and walk outside" [the narrator had been very ill and thought he knew who had sorcerized him]. "Right in front of me I saw something. It was a bear lying right outside the tent." [Wild animals do not ordinarily come so close to any human habitation.] "I saw the flame when he breathed. I said to my wife very quietly: 'Hand me the axe.' She could not find it. The bear started to go. I tried to follow but I could not walk fast enough. I spoke to the bear. I said, "I know who you are and I want you to quit. I'm good natured but if you come here again I won't spare you.' He never came back and after that I gradually got better."

13. It is said that a sorcerer who kills a person in this way is bound to visit the grave. He cuts off the fingertips of the corpse, the tip of the tongue, and gouges out the eyes, and stores them in a little box for magical use. This is why Pindă`ndɑkwɑn made a pseudo-grave for his son outside the wigwam. It was a deliberate "trap" for the sorcerer. Pindă`ndɑkwɑn was an actual person who appears in my genealogies.

14. *Narrative of the Captivity and Adventures of John Tanner, etc.,* E. James (ed.), 1830, 343 [text written by Edwin James]. Tanner was a white man captured by Indians as a boy. He lived with Ojibwa and Ottawa, learned their language and published his reminiscences in later life. For further information on bear walking and the attitude of contemporary Indians toward it, see R. M. Dorson, *Bloodstoppers, and Bearwalkers: Folk Traditions of the Upper Peninsula* (Cambridge, 1952), 26–29 and Notes, 278.

15. The Ojibwa boy, at puberty or before, sought tutelaries or guardian spirits: without their help no man could be expected to get much out of life or amount to anything. The "nest" referred to was a sort of stage constructed by laying poles across the branches of a tree about fifteen feet from the ground. The boy was expected to remain on this stage for several days and

nights without food or drink. He was only allowed to descend to the ground to urinate and defecate. This fast was the most crucial event in a man's life and to undertake it he had to be *pekize*, pure (without sexual experience). Failure to observe all preliminary conditions and the fasting regulations destroyed his chances of blessings from other-than-human entities—the *pawáganak* (literally, "dream visitors")—who were more powerful than human beings. The situation is often described by the Ojibwa by saying that the *pawáganak* took "pity" upon the *kīgúsämo*, the faster. It was through dreams or visions, while the body lay inert, that direct experience of these entities occurred.

16. This account was repeated to me by a man who said he had heard the dreamer narrate it when he was an old man.

17. The conjuring tent consists of a barrel-like structure, covered with bark or canvas, that conceals the conjurer who kneels within. Those who witness the performance are *outside* this structure. Since the *pawáganak* reputedly are *inside* they, like the conjurer himself, are invisible to the audience without. On the other hand, it is said that the *pawáganak* do have a visible aspect from inside the tent. They look like tiny stars or minute sparks. It is only under very exceptional circumstances, however, that any person except the conjurer ever has an opportunity to even peep inside the structure during the performance. [Ed. note: A Cree conjuror at Lac la Ronge (sk) gave fur trader George Nelson this privilege in 1823, and Nelson reported seeing such a light. (*The Orders of the Dreamed: George Nelson on Cree and Northern Ojibwa Religion and Myth, 1823*, Jennifer S. H. Brown and Robert Brightman, Winnipeg: University of Manitoba Press, 1988, 106.] Consequently, the sensory manifestation of the spirits is typically auditory, not visual. See Hallowell, *The Role of Conjuring*, 50–51.

18. See Hallowell, *The Role of Conjuring*, 59, where other similar cases are given.

TWENTY-SEVEN

Ojibwa Ontology, Behavior, and World View

"It is, I believe, a fact that future investigations will thoroughly confirm, that the Indian does not make the separation into personal as contrasted with impersonal, corporeal with impersonal, in our sense at all. What he seems to be interested in is the question of existence, of reality; and everything that is perceived by the sense, thought of, felt and dreamt of, exists."—Paul Radin, 1914

INTRODUCTION

It has become increasingly apparent in recent years that the potential significance of the data collected by cultural anthropologists far transcends in interest the level of simple, objective, ethnographic description of the peoples they have studied. New perspectives have arisen; fresh interpretations of old data have been offered; investigation and analysis have been pointed in novel directions. The study of culture and personality, national character, and the special attention now being paid to values are illustrations that come to mind. Robert Redfield's concept of world view, "that outlook upon the universe that is characteristic of a people," which emphasizes a perspective that is not equivalent to the study of religion in the conventional sense, is a further example.

"World view," he says, "differs from culture, ethos, mode of thought, and national character. It is the picture the members of a society have of the properties and characters upon their stage of action. While "national character" refers to the way these people look to the outsider looking in on them, "world view" refers to the way the world looks to that people looking out. Of all that is connoted by "culture," "world view" attends especially to the way a man, in a particular society, sees himself in relation to all else. It is the properties of existence as distinguished from and relate to the self. It is, in short, a man's idea of the universe. It is that organization of ideas which answers to a man the questions: Where am I? Among what do I move? What are my relations to these things? . . . Self is the axis of "world view."[1]

In an essay entitled "The Self and Its Behavioral Environment" [*Culture and Experience* 1955, chapter 4] I have pointed out that self-identification and culturally constituted notions of the nature of the self are essential to the operation of human societies and that a functional corollary is the cognitive orientation of the self to a world of objects other than self. Since the nature of these objects is likewise culturally constituted, a unified phenomenal field of thought, values, and action which is integral with the kind of world view that characterizes a society is provided for members. The behavioral environment of the self thus becomes structured in terms of a diversified world of objects other than self, "discriminated, classified, and conceptualized with respect to attributes which are culturally constituted and symbolically mediated through language. . . . Object orientation likewise provides the ground for an intelligible interpretation of events in the behavioral environment on the basis of traditional assumptions regarding the nature and attributes of the objects involved and implicit or explicit dogmas regarding the 'causes' of events."[2] Human beings in whatever culture are provided with cognitive orientation in a cosmos; there is "order" and "reason" rather than chaos. There are basic premises and principles implied, even if these do not happen to be consciously formulated and articulated by the people themselves. We are confronted with the philosophical implications of their thought, the nature of the world of being as they conceive it. If we pursue the problem deeply enough we soon come face to face with a relatively unexplored territory—ethno-metaphysics. Can we penetrate this realm in other cultures? What kind of evidence is at our disposal? The forms of speech as Benjamin Whorf and the neo-Humboldtians have thought?[3] The manifest content of myth? Observed behavior and attitudes? And what order of reliability can our inferences have? The problem is a complex and difficult one, but this should not preclude its exploration.

In this paper I have assembled evidence, chiefly from my own field work on a branch of the Northern Ojibwa,[4] which supports the inference that in the metaphysics of being found among these Indians, the action of persons provides the major key to their world view.

While in all cultures "persons" comprise one of the major classes of objects to which the self must become oriented, this category of being is by no means limited to *human* beings. In Western culture, as in others, "supernatural" beings are recognized as "persons," although belonging, at the same time, to, an other-than-human category.[5] But in the social sciences and psychology, "persons" and human beings are categorically identified. This identification is inherent in the concept of "society" and "social relations."

In Warren's *Dictionary of Psychology* "person" is defined as "a human organism regarded as having distinctive characteristics and social relations." The same identification is implicit in the conceptualization and investigation of social organization by anthropologists. Yet this obviously involves a radical abstraction if, from the standpoint of the people being studied, the concept of "person" is not, in fact, synonymous with human being but transcends it. The significance of the abstraction only becomes apparent when we stop to consider the perspective adopted. The study of social organization, defined as human relations of a certain kind, is perfectly intelligible as an objective approach to the study of this subject in any culture. But if, in the world view of a people, "persons" as a class include entities other than human beings, then our objective approach is not adequate for presenting an accurate description of "the way a man, in a particular society, sees himself in relation to all else." A different perspective is required for this purpose. It may be argued, in fact, that a thoroughgoing "objective" approach to the study of cultures cannot be achieved solely by projecting upon those cultures categorical abstractions derived from Western thought. For, in a broad sense, the latter are a reflection of *our* cultural subjectivity. A higher order of objectivity may be sought by adopting a perspective which includes an analysis of the outlook of the people themselves as a complementary procedure. It is in a world view perspective, too, that we can likewise obtain the best insight into how cultures function as wholes.

The significance of these differences in perspective may be illustrated in the case of the Ojibwa by the manner in which the kinship term "grandfather" is used. It is not only applied to human persons but to spiritual beings who are persons of a category other than human. In fact, when the collective plural "our grandfathers" is used, the reference is primarily to persons of this latter class. Thus if we study Ojibwa social organization in the usual manner, we take account of only one set of "grandfathers." When we study their religion we discover other "grandfathers." But if we adopt a world view perspective no dichotomization appears. In this perspective "grandfather" is a term applicable to certain "person objects," without any distinction between human persons and those of an other-than-human class. Furthermore, both sets of grandfathers can be said to be functionally as well as terminologically equivalent in certain respects. The other-than-human grandfathers are sources of power to human beings through the "blessings" they bestow, i.e., a sharing of their power which enhances the "power" of human beings. A child is always given a name by an old man, i.e., a terminological grandfather. It is a matter of indifference whether he is a blood relative or not. This name carries with it a special blessing because it has reference to a dream of the human grandfather in which he obtained power from one or more of the other-than-human grandfathers. In other words, the relation between a human child and a human grandfather is functionally patterned in the same way as the relation between human beings and grandfathers of an other-than-human class. And, just as the latter type of grandfather may impose personal taboos as a condition of a blessing, in the same way a human grandfather may impose a taboo on a "grandchild" he has named.

Another direct linguistic clue to the inclusiveness of the "person" category in Ojibwa thinking is the term *wíndǐgo*. Baraga defines it in his *Dictionary* as "fabulous giant that lives on human flesh; a man that eats human flesh, cannibal." From the Ojibwa standpoint all *wíndǐgowak* are conceptually unified as terrifying, anthropomorphic beings who, since they threaten one's very existence, must be killed. The central theme of a rich body of anecdotal material shows how this threat was met in particular instances. It ranges from cases in which it was necessary to kill the closest of kin because it was thought an individual was becoming a *wíndǐgo,* through accounts of heroic fights between human beings and these fabulous giant monsters, to a first-hand report of a personal encounter with one of them.[6]

The more deeply we penetrate the world view of the Ojibwa the more apparent it is that "social relations" between human beings (*ǎnicinábek*) and other-than-human "persons" are of cardinal significance. These relations are correlative with their more comprehensive categorization of "persons." Recognition must be given to the culturally constituted meaning of "social" and "social relations" if we are to understand the nature of the Ojibwa world and the living entities in it.[7]

LINGUISTIC CATEGORIES AND COGNITIVE ORIENTATION

Any discussion of "persons" in the world view of the Ojibwa must take cognizance of the well known fact that the grammatical structure of the language of these people, like all their Algonkian relatives, formally expresses a distinction between "animate" and "inanimate" nouns. These particular labels, of course, were imposed upon Algonkian languages by Europeans;[8] it appeared to outsiders that the Algonkian differentiation of objects approximated the animate-inanimate dichotomy of Western thought. Superficially this seems to be the case. Yet a closer examination indicates that, as in the gender categories of other languages, the distinction in some cases appears to be arbitrary, if not extremely puzzling, from the standpoint of common sense or in a naturalistic frame of reference. Thus substantives for some, but not all—trees, sun-moon (gízis), thunder, stones, and objects of material culture like kettle and pipe—are classified as "animate."

If we wish to understand the cognitive orientation of the Ojibwa, there is an ethno-linguistic problem to be considered: What is the meaning of animate in Ojibwa thinking? Are such generic properties of objects as responsiveness to outer stimulation—sentience, mobility, self-movement, or even reproduction—primary characteristics attributed to all objects of the animate class irrespective of their categories as physical objects in our thinking? Is there evidence to substantiate such properties of objects independent of their formal linguistic classification? It must not be forgotten that no Ojibwa is consciously aware of, or can abstractly articulate the animate-inanimate category of his language, despite the fact that this dichotomy is implicit in his speech. Consequently, the grammatical distinction as such does not emerge as a subject for reflective thought or bear the kind of relation to individual thinking that would be present if there were some formulated dogma about the generic properties of these two classes of objects.

Commenting on the analogous grammatical categories of the Central Algonkian languages with reference to linguistic and nonlinguistic orders of meaning, Greenberg writes: "Since all persons and animals are in Class I (animate), we have at least one ethnoseme, but most of the other meanings can be defined only by a linguiseme." In Greenberg's opinion, "unless the actual behavior of Algonquian speakers shows some mode of conduct common to all these instances such that, given this information, we could predict the membership of Class I, we must resort to purely linguistic characterization."[9]

In the case of the Ojibwa, I believe that when evidence from beliefs, attitudes, conduct, and linguistic characterization are all considered together the psychological basis for their unified cognitive outlook can be appreciated, even when there is a radical departure from the framework of our thinking. In certain instances, behavioral predictions can be made. Behavior, however, is a function of a complex set of factors—including actual experience. More important than the linguistic classification of objects is the kind of vital functions attributed to them in the belief system and the conditions under which these functions are observed or tested in experience. This accounts, I think, for the fact that what we view as material, inanimate objects—such as shells and stones—are placed in an "animate" category along with "persons" which have no physical existence in our world view. The shells, for example, called *mīgis* on account of the manner in which they function in the Midéwi·win, could not be linguistically categorized as "inanimate." "Thunder," as we shall see, is not only reified as an "animate" entity, but has the attributes of a "person" and may be referred to as such. An "inanimate" categorization would be unthinkable from the Ojibwa point of view. When Greenberg refers to "persons" as clearly members of the animate grammatical category he is, by implication, identifying person and human being. Since in the Ojibwa universe there are many kinds of reified person-objects which are other than human but have the same ontological status, these, of course, fall into the same ethnoseme as human beings and into the "animate" linguistic class.

Since stones are grammatically animate, I once asked an old man: "Are *all* the stones we see about us here alive?" He reflected a long while and then replied, "No! But *some* are."[10] This qualified answer made a lasting impression on me. And it is thoroughly consistent with other data that indicate that the Ojibwa are not animists in the sense that they dogmatically attribute living souls to inanimate objects such as stones. The hypothesis which suggests itself to me is that the allocation of stones to an animate grammatical category is part of a culturally constituted cognitive "set." It does not involve a consciously formulated theory about the nature of stones. It leaves a door open that our orientation on dogmatic grounds keeps shut tight. Whereas we should never expect a stone to manifest animate properties of any kind under any circumstances, the Ojibwa recognize, *a priori*, potentialities for animation in certain classes of objects under certain circumstances.[11] The Ojibwa do not perceive stones, in general, as animate, any more than we do. The crucial test is experience. Is there any personal testimony available? In answer to this question we can say that it is asserted by informants that stones have been seen to move, that some stones manifest other animate properties, and, as we shall see, Flint is represented as a living personage in their mythology.

The old man to whom I addressed the general question about the animate character of stones was the same informant who told me that during a Midéwi·win ceremony, when his father was the leader of it, he had seen a "big round stone move." He said his father got up and walked around the path once or twice. Coming back to his place he began to sing. The stone began to move "following the trail of the old man around the tent, rolling over and over, I saw it happen several times and others saw it also."[12] The animate behavior of a stone under these circumstances was considered to be a demonstration of magic power on the part of the Midé. It was not a voluntary act initiated by the stone considered as a living entity. Associated with the Midéwi·win in the past there were other types of large boulders with animate properties. My friend Chief Berens had one of these, but it no longer possessed these attributes. It had contours that suggested eyes and mouth. When Yellow Legs, Chief Berens's great-grandfather, was a leader of the Midéwi·win he used to tap this stone with a new knife. It would then open its mouth, Yellow Legs would insert his fingers and take out a small leather sack with medicine in it. Mixing some of this medicine with water, he would pass the decoction around. A small sip was taken by those present.[13]

If, then, stones are not only grammatically animate, but, in particular cases, have been observed to manifest animate properties, such as movement in space and opening of a mouth, why should they not on occasion be conceived as possessing animate properties of a "higher" order? The actualization of this possibility is illustrated by the following anecdote:

A white trader, digging in his potato patch, unearthed a large stone similar to the one just referred to. He sent for John Duck, an Indian who was the leader of the *wábano*, a contemporary ceremony that is held in a structure something like that used for the Midéwi·win. The trader called his attention to the stone, saying that it must belong to his pavilion. John Duck did not seem pleased at this. He bent down and spoke to the boulder in a low voice, inquiring whether it had ever been in his pavilion. According to John the stone replied in the negative. [See also "Rocks and Stones," chap. 3, this volume.]

It is obvious that John Duck spontaneously structured the situation in terms that are intelligible within the context of Ojibwa language and culture. Speaking to a stone dramatizes the depth of the categorical difference in cognitive orientation between the Ojibwa and ourselves. I regret that my field notes contain no information about the use of direct verbal address in the other cases mentioned. But it may well have taken place. In the anecdote describing John Duck's behavior, however, his use of speech as a mode of communication raises the animate status of the boulder to the level of social interaction common to human beings. Simply as a matter of observation we can say that the stone was treated *as if* it were a "person," not a "thing," without inferring that objects of this class are, for the Ojibwa, necessarily conceptualized as persons.

Further exploration might be made of the relations between Ojibwa thinking, observation, and behavior and their grammatical classification of objects but enough has been said, I hope, to indicate that not only animate properties but even "person" attributes may be projected upon objects which to us clearly belong to a physical inanimate category.

THE "PERSONS" OF OJIBWA MYTHOLOGY

The Ojibwa distinguish two general types of traditional oral narratives: 1. "News or tidings" (*tabätcamoin*), i.e., anecdotes or stories, referring to events in the lives of human beings (*änicinábek*). In content, narratives of this class range from everyday occurrences, through more exceptional experiences, to those which verge on the legendary. (The anecdotes already referred to, although informal, may be said to belong to this general class.) 2. Myths (*ätisokának*)[14] i.e., sacred stories, which are not only traditional and formalized; their narration is seasonally restricted and is somewhat ritualized. The significant thing about these stories is that the characters in them are regarded as living entities who have existed from time immemorial. While there is genesis through birth and temporary or permanent form-shifting through transformation, there is no outright creation. Whether human or animal in form or name, the major characters in the myths behave like people, though many of their activities are depicted in a spatio-temporal framework of cosmic, rather than mundane, dimensions. There is "social interaction" among them and between them and *änicinábek*.

A striking fact furnishes a direct linguistic cue to the attitude of the Ojibwa towards these personages. When they use the term *ätisokának*, they are not referring to what I have called a "body of narratives." The term refers to what we would call the characters in these stories; to the Ojibwa they are living "persons" of an other-than-human class. As William Jones said many years ago, "Myths are thought of as conscious beings, with powers of thought and action."[15] A synonym for this class of persons is "our grandfathers."

The *ätisokának*, or "our grandfathers," are never "talked about" casually by the Ojibwa. But when the myths are narrated on long winter nights, the occasion is a kind of invocation. "Our grandfathers" like it and often come to listen to what is being said. In ancient times one of these entities (*Wísakedják*) is reputed to have said to the others: "We'll try to make everything to suit the *änicinábek* as long as any of them exist, so that they will never forget us and will always talk about us."

It is clear, therefore, that to the Ojibwa, their "talk" about these entities, although expressed in formal narrative, is not about fictitious characters. On the contrary, what we call myth is accepted by them as a true account of events in the past lives of living "persons."[16] It is for this reason that narratives of this class are significant for an understanding of the manner in which their phenomenal field is culturally structured and cognitively apprehended. As David Bidney has pointed out, "The concept of 'myth' is relative to one's accepted beliefs and convictions, so that what is gospel truth for the believer is sheer 'myth' and 'fiction' for the non-believer or skeptic. . . . Myths and magical tales and practices are accepted precisely because pre-scientific folk do not consider them as merely 'myths' or 'magic,' since once the distinction between myth and science is consciously accepted, the acquired critical insight precludes the belief in and acceptance of magic and myth."[17] When taken at their face value, myths provide a reliable source of prime value for making inferences about Ojibwa world outlook. They offer basic data about unarticulated, unformalized, and unanalyzed concepts regarding which informants cannot be expected to generalize. From this point of view, myths are broadly analogous to the concrete material of the texts on which the linguist depends for his derivation, by analysis and abstraction, of the grammatical categories and principles of a language.

In formal definitions of myth (e.g., *Concise Oxford Dictionary* and Warren's *Dictionary of Psychology*) the subject matter of such narrative often has been said to involve not only fictitious characters but "supernatural persons." This latter appellation, if applied to the Ojibwa characters, is completely misleading, if for no other reason than the fact that the concept of "supernatural" presupposes a concept of the "natural." The latter is not present in Ojibwa thought. It is unfortunate that the natural-supernatural dichotomy has been so persistently invoked by many anthropologists in describing the outlook of peoples in cultures other than our own. Linguists learned long ago that it was impossible to write grammars of the languages of nonliterate peoples by using as a framework Indo-European speech forms. Lovejoy has pointed out that "The sacred word 'nature' is probably the most equivocal in the vocabulary of the European peoples,"[18] and the natural-supernatural antithesis has had its own complex history in Western thought.[19]

To the Ojibwa, for example, *gízis* (day luminary, the sun) is not a natural object in our sense at all. Not only does their conception differ; the sun is a "person" of the other-than-human class. But more important still is the absence of the notion of the ordered regularity in movement that is inherent in our scientific outlook. The Ojibwa entertain no reasonable certainty that, in accordance with natural law, the sun will "rise" day after day. In fact, *Tcakabec*, a mythical personage, once set a snare in the trail of the sun and caught it. Darkness continued until a mouse was sent by human beings to release the sun and provide daylight again.[20] And in another story (not a myth) it is recounted how two old men at dawn vied with each other in influencing the sun's movements.

> The first old man said to his companion: "It is about sunrise now and there is a clear sky. You tell the sun to rise at once." So the other old man said to the sun: "My grandfather, come up quickly." As soon as he had said this, the sun came up into the sky like a shot. "Now you try something," he said to his companion. "See if you can send it down." So the other man said to the sun: "My grandfather, put your face down again." When he said this, the sun went down again. "I have more power than you," he said to the other old man, "The sun never goes down once it comes up."

We may infer that to the Ojibwa, any regularity in the movements of the sun is of the same order as the habitual activities of human beings. There are certain expectations, of course, but, on occasion, there may be temporary deviations in behavior "caused" by other persons. Above all, any concept of *impersonal* "natural" forces is totally foreign to Ojibwa thought.

Since their cognitive orientation is culturally constituted and thus given a psychological "set," we cannot assume that objects, like the sun, are perceived as natural objects in our sense. If this were so, the anecdote about the old men could not be accepted as an actual event involving a case of "social interaction" between human beings and an other-than-human person. Consequently, it would be an error to say that the Ojibwa "personify" natural objects. This would imply that, at some point, the sun was first perceived as an inanimate, material thing. There is, of course, no evidence for this. The same conclusion applies over the whole area of their cognitive orientation towards the objects of their world.

The Four Winds and Flint, for instance, are quintuplets. They were born of a mother (unnamed) who, while given human characteristics, lived in the very distant past. As will be more apparent later, this character, like others in the myths, may have anthropomorphic characteristics without being conceived as a human being. In the context she, like the others, is an *ätísòkán*. The Winds were born first, then Flint "jumped out," tearing her to pieces. This, of course, is a direct allusion to his inanimate, stony properties. Later he was penalized for his hurried exit. He fought with *Misábos* (Great Hare) and pieces were chipped off his body and his size reduced. "Those pieces broken from your body may be of some use to human beings some day," *Misábos* said to him. "But you will not be any larger so long as the earth shall last. You'll never harm anyone again."[21]

Against the background of this "historic" event, it would be strange indeed if flint were allocated to an inanimate grammatical category. There is a special term for each of the four winds that are differentiated, but no plural for "winds." They are all animate beings, whose "homes" define the four directions.

The conceptual reification of Flint, the Winds, and the Sun as other-than-human persons exemplifies a world view in which a natural-supernatural dichotomy has no place. And the representation of these beings as characters in "true" stories reinforces their reality by means of a cultural device which at the same time depicts their vital roles in interaction with other persons as integral forces in the functioning of a unified cosmos.

ANTHROPOMORPHIC TRAITS AND
OTHER-THAN-HUMAN PERSONS

In action and motivations the characters in the myths are indistinguishable from human persons. In this respect, human and other-than-human persons may be set off, in life as well as in myth, from animate beings such as ordinary animals (*awésiak*, pl.) and objects belonging to the inanimate grammatical category. But, at the same time, it must be noted that "persons" of the other-than-human class do not always present a human appearance in the myths. Consequently, we may ask: What constant attributes do unify the concept of "person"? What is the essential meaningful core of the concept of person in Ojibwa thinking? It can be stated at once that anthropomorphic traits in outward appearance are not the crucial attributes.

It is true that some extremely prominent characters in the myths are given explicit human form. *Wísakedják* and *Tcakabec* are examples. Besides this they have distinctive characteristics of their own. The former has an exceptionally long penis and the latter is very small in size, yet extremely powerful. There are no equivalent female figures. By comparison, Flint and the Winds have human attributes by implication; they were born of a "woman" as human beings are born; they speak, and so on. On the other hand, the High God of the Ojibwa, a very remote figure who does not appear in the mythology at all, but is spoken of as a "person," is not even given sexual characteristics. This is possible because there is no sex gender in Ojibwa speech.

Consequently an animate being of the person category may function in their thinking without having explicitly sexual or other anthropomorphic characteristics. Entities "seen" in dreams (*pawáganak*) are "persons"; whether they have anthropomorphic attributes or not is incidental. Other entities of the person category, whose anthropomorphic character is undefined or ambiguous, are what have been called the "masters" or "owners" of animals or plant species. Besides these, certain curing procedures and conjuring are said to have other-than-human personal entities as patrons.

If we now examine the cognitive orientation of the Ojibwa towards the Thunder Birds it will become apparent why anthropomorphism is not a constant feature of the Ojibwa concept of "person." These beings likewise demonstrate the autonomous nature of Ojibwa reification. For we find here a creative synthesis of objective "naturalistic" observation integrated with the subjectivity of dream experiences and traditional mythical narrative which, assuming the character of a living image, is neither the personification of a natural phenomenon nor an altogether animal-like or human-like being. Yet it is impossible to deny that, in the universe of the Ojibwa, Thunder Birds are "persons."

My Ojibwa friends, I discovered, were as puzzled by the white man's conception of thunder and lightning as natural phenomena as they were by the idea that the earth is round and not flat. I was pressed on more than one occasion to explain thunder and lightning, but I doubt whether my somewhat feeble efforts made much sense to them. Of one thing I am sure: my explanations left their own beliefs completely unshaken. This is not strange when we consider that, even in our naturalistic frame of reference, thunder and lightning as perceived do not exhibit the lifeless properties of inanimate objects. On the contrary, it has been said that thunder and lightning are among the natural phenomena which exhibit some of the properties of "person objects."[22] Underlying the Ojibwa view there may be a level of naive perceptual experience that should be taken into account. But their actual construct departs from this level in a most explicit direction: why is an avian image central in their conception of a being whose manifestations are thunder and lightning? Among the Ojibwa with whom I worked, the linguistic stem for bird is the same as that for Thunder Bird (pinèsï; pl. pinèsïwak). Besides this, the avian characteristics of Thunder Birds are still more explicit. Conceptually they are grouped with the hawks, of which there are several natural species in their habitat.

What is particularly interesting is that the avian nature of the Thunder Birds does not rest solely on an arbitrary image. Phenomenally, thunder does exhibit "behavioral" characteristics that are analogous to avian phenomena in this region.[23] According to meteorological observations, the average number of days with thunder begins with one in April, increases to a total of five in midsummer (July) and then declines to one in October. And if a bird calendar is consulted, the facts show that species wintering in the south begin to appear in April and disappear for the most part not later than October, being, of course, a familiar sight during the summer months. The avian character of the Thunder Birds can be rationalized to some degree with reference to natural facts and their observation.

But the evidence for the existence of Thunder Birds does not rest only on the association of the occurrence of thunder with the migration of the summer birds projected into an avian image. When I visited the Ojibwa [in the 1930s] an Indian [Peter Berens] was living who, when a boy of twelve or so, saw *pinèsï* with his own eyes. During a severe thunderstorm he ran out of his tent and there on the rocks lay a strange bird. He ran back to call his parents, but when they arrived the bird had disappeared. He was sure it was a Thunder Bird, but his elders were skeptical because it is almost unheard of to see *pinèsï* in such a fashion. But the matter was clinched and the boy's account accepted when a man who had *dreamed* of *pinèsï* verified the boy's description. It will be apparent later why a dream experience was decisive. It should be added at this point, however, that many Indians say they have seen the nests of the Thunder Birds; these are usually described as collections of large stones in the form of shallow bowls located in high and inaccessible parts of the country.

If we now turn to the myths, we find that one of them deals in considerable detail with Thunder Birds. Ten unmarried brothers live together. The oldest is called *Mätckïwis*. A mysterious housekeeper cuts wood and builds a fire for them which they find burning when they return from a long day's hunt, but she never appears in person. One day the youngest brother discovers and marries her. *Mätckïwis* is jealous and kills her. She would have revived if her husband had not broken a taboo she imposed. It turns out, however, that she is not actually a human being but a Thunder Bird and, thus, one of the *ätisokának* and immortal. She flies away to the land above this earth inhabited by the Thunder Birds. Her husband, after many difficulties, follows her there. He finds himself brother-in-law to beings who are the "masters" of the duck hawks, sparrow hawks, and other species of this category of birds he has known on earth. He cannot relish the food eaten, since what the Thunder Birds call "beaver" are to him like the frogs and snakes on this earth (a genuinely naturalistic touch since the sparrow hawk, for example, feeds on batrachians [frogs and toads] and reptiles). He goes hunting gigantic snakes with his male Thunder Bird relatives. Snakes of this class also exist on this earth, and the Thunder Birds are their inveterate enemies. (When there is lightning and thunder this is the prey the Thunder Birds are after.) One day the great Thunder Bird says to his son-in-law, "I know you are getting lonely; you must want to see your people. I'll let you go back to earth now. You have nine brothers at home and I have nine girls left. You can take them with you as wives for your brothers. I'll be related to the people on earth now and I'll be merciful towards them. I'll not hurt any of them if I can possibly help it." So he tells his daughters to get ready. There is a big dance that night and the next morning the whole party starts off. When they come to the edge of Thunder Bird land the lad's wife said to him, "Sit on my back. Hang on tight to my neck and keep your eyes shut." Then the thunder crashes and the young man knows that they are off through the air. Having reached this earth they make their way to the brothers' camp. The Thunder Bird women, who have become transformed into human form, are enthusiastically received. There is another celebration and the nine brothers marry the nine sisters of their youngest brother's wife.[24]

This is the end of the myth but a few comments are necessary. It is obvious that the Thunder Birds are conceived to act like human beings. They hunt and talk and dance. But the analogy can be pressed further. Their social organization and kinship terminology are precisely the same as the Ojibwa. The marriage of a series of female siblings (classificatory or otherwise) to a series of male siblings often occurs among the Ojibwa themselves. This is, in fact, considered a kind of ideal pattern. In one case that I know of six blood brothers were married to a sorority of six sisters. There is a conceptual continuity, therefore, between the social life of human beings and that of the Thunder Birds which is independent of the avian form given to the latter. But we must infer from the myth that this avian form is not constant. Appearance cannot then be taken as a permanent and distinguishable trait of the Thunder Birds. They are capable of metamorphosis; hence, the human attributes with which they are endowed transcend a human outward form. Their conceptualization as "persons" is not associated with a permanent human form any more than it is associated with a birdlike form. And the fact that they belong to the category of *ätisokának* is no barrier to their descending to earth and mating with human beings. I was told of a woman who claimed that North Wind was the father of one of her children. My informant said he did not believe this; nevertheless, he thought it would have been accepted as a possibility in the past.[25] We can only infer that in the universe of the Ojibwa the conception of "person" as a living, functioning social being is not only one which transcends the notion of person in the naturalistic sense; it likewise transcends a human appearance as a constant attribute of this category of being.

The relevance of such a concept to actual behavior may be illustrated by one simple anecdote. An informant told me that many years before he was sitting in a tent one summer afternoon during a storm, together with an old man [Fair Wind (Nämɑwin) at Pauingassi] and his wife. There was one clap of thunder after another. Suddenly the old man turned to his wife and asked, "Did you hear what was said?" "No," she replied, "I didn't catch it." My informant, an acculturated Indian, told me he did not at first know what the old man and his wife referred to. It was, of course, the thunder. The old man thought that one of the Thunder Birds had said something to him. He was reacting to this sound in the same way as he would respond to a human being, whose words he did not understand. The casualness of the remark and even the trivial character of the anecdote demonstrate the psychological depth of the "social relations" with other-than-human beings that becomes explicit in the behavior of the Ojibwa as a consequence of the cognitive "set" induced by their culture.

METAMORPHOSIS AS AN ATTRIBUTE OF PERSONS

The conceptualization in myth and belief of Thunder Birds as animate beings who, while maintaining their identity, may change their outward appearance and exhibit either an avian or a human form exemplifies an attribute of "persons" which, although unarticulated abstractly, is basic in the cognitive orientation of the Ojibwa.

Metamorphosis occurs with considerable frequency in the myths where other-than-human persons change their form. *Wísakedják,* whose primary characteristics are anthropomorphic, becomes transformed and flies with the geese in one story, assumes the form of a snake in another, and once turns himself into a stump. Men marry "animal" wives who are not "really" animals. And *Miki·nä´k,* the Great Turtle, marries a human being. It is only by breaking a taboo that his wife discovers she is married to a being who is able to assume the form of a handsome young man.

The senselessness and ambiguities which may puzzle the outsider when reading these myths are resolved when it is understood that, to the Ojibwa, "persons" of this class are capable of metamorphosis by their very nature. Outward appearance is only an incidental attribute of being. And the names by which some of these entities are commonly known, even if they identify the character as an "animal," do not imply unchangeableness in form.

Stith Thompson has pointed out that the possibility of transformation is a "commonplace assumption in folk tales everywhere. Many of such motifs are frankly fictitious, but a large number represent persistent beliefs and living tradition."[26] The case of the Ojibwa is in the latter category. The world of myth is not categorically distinct from the world as experienced by human beings in everyday life. In the latter, as well as the former, no sharp lines can be drawn dividing living beings of the animate class because metamorphosis is possible. In outward manifestation neither animal nor human characteristics define categorical differences in the core of being. And, even aside from metamorphosis, we find that in everyday life, interactions with nonhuman entities of the animate class are only intelligible on the assumption that they possess some of the attributes of "persons."

So far as animals are concerned, when bears were sought out in their dens in the spring they were addressed, asked to come out so that they could be killed, and an apology was offered to them.[27] The following encounter with a bear, related to me by a pagan Ojibwa named Birchstick, shows what happened in this case when an animal is treated as a person:

> One spring when I was out hunting I went up a little creek where I knew suckers were spawning. Before I came to the rapids I saw fresh bear tracks. I walked along the edge of the creek and when I reached the rapids I saw a bear coming towards me, along the same trail I was following. I stepped behind a tree and when the animal was about thirty yards from me I fired. I missed and before I could reload the bear made straight for me. He seemed mad, so I never moved. I just waited there by the tree. As soon as he came close to me and rose up on his hind feet, I put the butt end of my gun against his heart and held him there. I remembered what my father used to tell me when I was a boy. He said that a bear always understands what you tell him. The bear began to bite the stock of the gun. He even put his paws upon it something like a man would do if he were going to shoot. Still holding him off as well as I could I said to the bear, "If you want to live, go away," and he let go the gun and walked off. I didn't bother the bear anymore. [28]

These instances suffice to demonstrate that, at the level of individual behavior, the interaction of the Ojibwa with certain kinds of plants and animals in everyday life is so structured culturally that individuals act as if they were dealing with "persons" who both understand what is being said to them and have volitional capacities as well. From the standpoint of perceptual experience if we only take account of autochthonous factors in Birchstick's encounter with the bear his behavior appears idiosyncratic and is not fully explained. On the other hand, if we invoke Ojibwa concepts of the nature of animate beings, his behavior becomes intelligible to us. We can understand the determining factors in his definition of the situation, and the functional relations between perception and conduct are meaningful. This Indian was not confronted with an animal with "objective" ursine properties, but rather with an animate being who had ursine attributes and *also* "person attributes." These, we may infer, were perceived as an integral whole. I am sure, however, that in narrating this episode to another Indian, he would not have referred to what his father had told him about bears. That was for my benefit!

Since bears, then, are assumed to possess "person attributes," it is not surprising to find that there is a very old, widespread, and persistent belief that sorcerers may become transformed into bears in order better to pursue their nefarious work.[29] Consequently some of the best documentation of the metamorphosis of human beings into animals comes from anecdotal material referring to cases of this sort. Even contemporary, acculturated Ojibwa have a term for this. They all know what a "bearwalk" is, and Dorson's recent collection of folk traditions, including those of the Indian populations of the Upper Peninsula of Michigan, bears the title *Bloodstoppers and Bearwalkers*. One of Dorson's informants gave him this account of what he had seen:

> When I was a kid, 'bout seventeen, before they build the highway, there was just an old tote road from Bark River to Harris. There was three of us, one a couple years older, coming back from Bark River at nighttime. We saw a flash coming from behind us. The older fellow said, "It's a bearwalk, let's get it. I'll stand on the other side of the road (it was just a wagon rut) and you stand on this side." We stood there and waited. I saw it 'bout fifty feet away from us—close as your car is now. It looked like a bear, but every time he breathe your could see a fire gust. My chum he fall over in a faint. That brave feller on the other side, he faint. When the bear walk, all the ground wave, like when you walk on soft mud or on moss. He was goin' where he was goin'. [30]

It is clear from this example, and others that might be added, that the Indian and his companions did not perceive an ordinary bear. But in another anecdote given by Dorson, which is not told in the first person, it is said that an Indian "grabbed hold of the bear and it wasn't there—it was the old woman. She had buckskin bags all over her, tied on to her body, and she had a bearskin hide on."[31] I also have been told that the "bearwalk" is dressed up in a bearskin. All such statements, of course, imply a skeptical attitude towards metamorphosis. They are rationalizations advanced by individuals who are attempting to reconcile Ojibwa beliefs and observation with the disbelief encountered in their relations with the whites.

An old-fashioned informant of mine told me how he had once fallen sick, and, although he took various kinds of medicine these did him no good. Because of this, and for other reasons, he believed he had been bewitched by a certain man. Then he noticed that a bear kept coming to his camp almost every night after dark. This is most unusual because wild animals do not ordinarily come anywhere near a human habitation. Once the bear would have entered his wigwam if he had not been warned in a dream. His anxiety increased because he knew, of course, that sorcerers often transformed themselves into bears. So when the bear appeared one night he got up, went outdoors, and shouted to the animal that he knew what it was trying to do. He threatened retaliation in kind if the bear ever returned. The animal ran off and never came back.

In this case there are psychological parallels to Birchstick's encounter with a bear: In both cases the bear is directly addressed as a person might be, and it is only through a knowledge of the cultural background that it is possible fully to understand the behavior of the individuals involved. In the present case, however, we can definitely say that the "animal" was perceived as a human being in the form of a bear; the Indian was threatening a human person with retaliation, not an animal.

A question that I have discussed in *Culture and Experience* in connection with another "bearwalk" anecdote, also arises in this case.[32] Briefly, the Ojibwa believe that a human being consists of a vital part, or *soul*, which, under certain circumstances may become detached from the body, so that it is not necessary to assume that the body part, in all cases, literally undergoes transformation into an animal form. The body of the sorcerer may remain in his wigwam while his soul journeys elsewhere and appears to another person in the form of an animal.

This interpretation is supported by an account which an informant gave me of a visit his deceased grandchild had paid him. One day he was traveling in a canoe across a lake. He had put up an improvised mast and used a blanket for a sail. A little bird alighted on the mast. This was a most unusual thing for a bird to do. He was convinced that it was not a bird but his dead grandchild. The child, of course, had left her body behind in a grave; nevertheless she visited him in animal form. [See "Spirits of the Dead," chapter 22, this volume.]

Thus, both living and dead human beings may assume the form of animals. So far as appearance is concerned, there is no hard and fast line that can be drawn between an animal form and a human form because metamorphosis is possible. In perceptual experience what looks like a bear may sometimes *be* an animal and, on other occasions, a human being. What persists and gives continuity to being is the vital part, or soul. Dorson goes to the heart of the matter when he stresses the fact that the whole socialization process in Ojibwa culture "impresses the young with the concepts of transformation and of 'power', malign or benevolent, human or demonic. These concepts underlie the entire Indian mythology, and make sensible the otherwise childish stories of culture heroes, animal husbands, friendly thunders, and malicious serpents. The bearwalk idea fits at once into this dream world— literally a dream world, for Ojibwa go to school in dreams."[33]

We must conclude, I believe, that the capacity for metamorphosis is one of the features which links human beings with the other-than-human persons in their behavioral environment. It is one of the generic properties manifested by beings of the person class. But is it a ubiquitous capacity of all members of this class equally? I do not think so. Metamorphosis to the Ojibwa mind is an earmark of "power." Within the category of persons there is a graduation of power. Other-than-human persons occupy the top rank in the power hierarchy of animate being. Human beings do not differ from them in kind, but in power. Hence, it is taken for granted that all the *ätíso'kának* can assume a variety of forms. In the case of human beings, while the potentiality for metamorphosis exists and may even be experienced, any outward manifestation is inextricably associated with unusual power, for good or evil. And power of this degree can only be acquired by human beings through the help of other-than-human persons. Sorcerers can transform themselves only because they have acquired a high order of power from this source.

Powerful men, in the Ojibwa sense, are also those who can make inanimate objects behave as if they were animate. The *Midé* who made a stone roll over and over has been mentioned earlier. Other examples, such as the animation of a string of wooden beads, or animal skins, could be cited.[34] Such individuals also have been observed to transform one object into another, such as charcoal into bullets and ashes into gunpowder, or a handful of goose feathers into birds or insects.[35] In these manifestations, too, they are elevated to the same level of power as that displayed by other-than-human persons. We can, in fact, find comparable episodes in the myths.

The notion of animate being itself does not presume a capacity for manifesting the highest level of power any more than it implies person-attributes in every case. Power manifestations vary within the animate class of being as does the possession of person-attributes. A human being may possess little, if any, more power than a mole. No one would have been more surprised than Birchstick if the bear he faced had suddenly become human in form. On the other hand, the spiritual "masters" of the various species of animals are inherently powerful and, quite generally, they possess the power of metamorphosis. These entities, like the *ätisokának*, are among the sources from which human beings may seek to enhance their own power. My Ojibwa friends often cautioned me against judging by appearances. A poor forlorn Indian dressed in rags might have great power; a smiling, amiable woman, or a pleasant old man, might be a sorcerer.[36] You never can tell until a situation arises in which their power for good or ill becomes manifest. I have since concluded that the advice given me in a common sense fashion provides one of the major clues to a generalized attitude towards the objects of their behavioral environment—particularly people. It makes them cautious and suspicious in interpersonal relations of all kinds. The possibility of metamorphosis must be one of the determining factors in this attitude; it is a concrete manifestation of the deceptiveness of appearances. What looks like an animal, without great power, may be a transformed person with evil intent. Even in dream experiences, where a human being comes into direct contact with other-than-human persons, it is possible to be deceived. Caution is necessary in "social" relations with all classes of persons.

DREAMS, METAMORPHOSIS, AND THE SELF

The Ojibwa are a dream-conscious people. For an understanding of their cognitive orientation it is as necessary to appreciate their attitude towards dreams as it is to understand their attitude towards the characters in the myths. For them, there is an inner connection which is as integral to their outlook as it is foreign to ours.

The basic assumption which links the *ätisokának* with dreams is this: Self-related experience of the most personal and vital kind includes what is seen, heard, and felt in dreams. Although there is no lack of discrimination between the experiences of the self when awake and when dreaming, both sets of experiences are equally self-related. Dream experiences function integrally with other recalled memory images in so far as these, too, enter the field of self-awareness. When we think autobiographically we only include events that happened to us when awake; the Ojibwa include remembered events that have occurred in dreams. And, far from being of subordinate importance, such experiences are for them often of more vital importance than the events of daily waking life. Why is this so? Because it is in dreams that the individual comes into direct communication with the *ätíso'kának*, the powerful "persons" of the other-than-human class.

In the long winter evenings, as I have said, the *ätisokának* are talked about; the past events in their lives are recalled again and again by *änicinábek*. When a conjuring performance occurs, the voices of some of the same beings are heard issuing from within the conjuring lodge. Here is actual perceptual experience of the "grandfathers" during a waking state. In dreams, the same other-than-human persons are both "seen" and "heard." They address human beings as "grandchild." These "dream visitors" (i.e., *pawáganak*) interact with the dreamer much as human persons do. But, on account of the nature of these beings there are differences, too. It is in the context of this face-to-face personal interaction of the self with the "grandfathers" (i.e., synonymously *ätisokának, pawáganak*) that human beings receive important revelations that are the source of assistance to them in the daily round of life, and, besides this, of "blessings" that enable them to exercise exceptional powers of various kinds.

But dream experiences are not ordinarily recounted save under special circumstances. There is a taboo against this, just as there is a taboo against myth narration except in the proper seasonal context. The consequence is that we know relatively little about the manifest content of dreams. All our data come from acculturated Ojibwa. We do know enough to say, however, that the Ojibwa recognize quite as much as we do that dream experiences are often qualitatively different from our waking experiences. This fact, moreover, is turned to positive account. Since their dream visitors are other-than-human "persons" possessing great power, it is to be expected that the experiences of the self in interaction with them will differ from those with human beings in daily life. Besides this, another assumption must be taken into account: When a human being is asleep and dreaming, his *òtcatcákwin* (vital part, soul), which is the core of the self, may become detached from the body (*mí·yó*). Viewed by another human being, a person's body may be easily located and observed in space. But his vital part may be somewhere else. Thus, the self has greater mobility in space and even in time while sleeping. This is another illustration of the deceptiveness of appearances. The body of a sorcerer may be within sight in a wigwam, while "he" may be bearwalking. Yet the space in which the self is mobile is continuous with the earthly and cosmic space of waking life. A dream of one of my informants [William Berens] documents this specifically. After having a dream in which he met some (mythical) anthropomorphic beings (*mémengwécīwak*) who live in rocky escarpments and are famous for their medicine, he told me that he had later identified precisely the rocky place he had visited and entered in his dream. Thus the behavioral environment of the self is all of a piece. This is why experiences undergone when awake or asleep can be interpreted as experiences of self. Memory images, as recalled, become integrated with a sense of self-continuity in time and space.

Metamorphosis may be *experienced* by the self in dreams. One example will suffice to illustrate this. The dreamer in this case had been paddled out to an island by his father to undergo his puberty fast. For several nights he dreamed of an anthropomorphic figure. Finally, this being said, "[My] Grandchild, I think you are strong enough now to go with me." Then the *pawágan* began dancing and as he danced he turned into what looked like a golden eagle. (This being must be understood as the "master" of this species.) Glancing down at his own body as he sat there on a rock, the boy noticed it was covered with feathers. The "eagle" spread its wings and flew off to the south. The boy then spread his wings and followed.

Here we find the instability of outward form in both human and other-than-human persons succinctly dramatized. Individuals of both categories undergo metamorphosis. In later life the boy will recall how he first saw the "master" of the golden eagles in his anthropomorphic guise, followed by his transformation into avian form; at the same time he will recall his own metamorphosis into a bird. But this experience, considered in context, does not imply that subsequently the boy can transform himself into a golden eagle at will. He might or might not be sufficiently "blessed." The dream itself does not inform us about this.

This example, besides showing how dream experiences may reinforce the belief in metamorphosis, illustrates an additional point: the *pawáganak*, whenever "seen," are always experienced as appearing in a specific form. They have a "bodily" aspect, whether human-like, animal-like, or ambiguous. But this is not their most persistent, enduring and vital attribute any more than in the case of human beings. We must conclude that all animate beings of the person class are unified conceptually in Ojibwa thinking because they have a similar structure—an inner vital part that is enduring, and an outward form which can change. Vital personal attributes such as sentience, volition, memory, and speech are not dependent upon outward appearance but upon the inner vital essence of being. If this be true, human beings and other-than-human persons are alike in another way. The human self does not die; it continues its existence in another place, after the body is buried in the grave. In this way *änicinábek* are as immortal as *ätisokának*. This may be why we find human beings associated with the latter in the myths where it is sometimes difficult for an outsider to distinguish between them.

Thus the world of personal relations in which the Ojibwa live is a world in which vital social relations transcend those which are maintained with human beings. Their culturally constituted cognitive orientation prepares the individual for life in this world and for a life after death. The self-image that he acquires makes intelligible the nature of other selves. Speaking as an Ojibwa, one might say: all other "persons"—human or other-than-human—are structured the same as I am. There is a vital part which is enduring and an outward appearance that may be transformed under certain conditions. All other "persons," too, have such attributes as self-awareness and understanding. I can talk with them. Like myself, they have personal identity, autonomy, and volition. I cannot always predict exactly how they will act, although most of the time their behavior meets my expectations. In relation to myself, other "persons" vary in power. Many of them have more power than I have, but some have less. They may be friendly and help me when I need them but, at the same time, I have to be prepared for hostile acts, too. I must be cautious in my relations with other "persons" because appearances may be deceptive.

THE PSYCHOLOGICAL UNITY OF THE OJIBWA WORLD

Although not formally abstracted and articulated philosophically, the nature of "persons" is the focal point of Ojibwa ontology and the key to the psychological unity and dynamics of their world outlook. This aspect of their metaphysics of being permeates the content of their cognitive processes: perceiving, remembering, imagining, conceiving, judging, and reasoning. Nor can the motivation of much of their conduct be thoroughly understood without taking into account the relation of their central values and goals to the awareness they have of the existence of other-than-human, as well as human, persons in their world. "Persons," in fact, are so inextricably associated with notions of causality that, in order to understand their appraisal of events and the kind of behavior demanded in situations as they define them, we are confronted over and over again with the roles of "persons" as *loci* of causality in the dynamics of their universe. For the Ojibwa make no cardinal use of any concept of impersonal forces as major determinants of events. In the context of my exposition the meaning of the term *mänîtu*, which has become so generally known, may be considered as a synonym for a person of the other-than-human class ("grandfather," ätisokan, pawá-gan). Among the Ojibwa I worked with it is now quite generally confined to the God of Christianity, when combined with an augmentative prefix (k`tchi·mä´ni·tu). There is no evidence to suggest, however, that the term ever did connote an impersonal, magical, or supernatural force. [37]

In an essay on the "Religion of the North American Indians" published over forty years ago, Radin asserted "that from an examination of the data customarily relied upon as proof and from individual data obtained, there is nothing to justify the postulation of a belief in a universal force in North America. Magical power as an 'essence' existing apart and separate from a definite spirit, is, we believe, an unjustified assumption, an abstraction created by investigators."[38] This opinion, at the time, was advanced in op-position to the one expressed by those who, stimulated by the writings of R. R. Marett in particular, interpreted the term mänītu among the Algonkians (W. Jones), orenda among the Iroquois (Hewitt), and wakanda among the Siouan peoples (Fletcher) as having reference to a belief in a magical force of some kind. But Radin pointed out that in his own field work among both the Winnebago and the Ojibwa, the terms in question "always referred to definite spirits, not necessarily definite in shape. If at a vapor-bath the steam is regarded as wakanda or mänītu, it is because it is a spirit transformed into steam for the time being; if an arrow is possessed of specific virtues, it is because a spirit has either transformed himself into the arrow or because he is temporarily dwelling in it; and finally, if tobacco is offered to a peculiarly-shaped object it is because either this object belongs to a spirit, or a spirit is residing in it." Mänītu, he said, in addition to its substantive usage, may have such connotations as "sacred," "strange," "remarkable" or "powerful" without "having the slightest suggestion of 'inherent power', but having the ordinary sense of these adjectives."[39]

With respect to the Ojibwa conception of causality, all my own observa-tions suggest that a culturally constituted psychological set operates which inevitably directs the reasoning of individuals towards an explanation of events in personalistic terms. Who did it, who is responsible, is always the crucial question to be answered. Personalistic explanation of past events is found in the myths. It was Wísakedják who, through the exercise of his personal power, expanded the tiny bit of mud retrieved by Muskrat from the depths of the inundating waters of the great deluge into the inhabitable island-earth of Ojibwa cosmography.[40] Personalistic explanation is central in theories of disease causation. Illness may be due to sorcery; the victim, in turn, may be "responsible" because he has offended the sorcerer—even unwittingly. Besides this, I may be responsible for my own illness, even without the intervention of a sorcerer. I may have committed some wrongful act in the past, which is the "cause" of my sickness. My child's illness, too, may be the consequence of my past transgressions or those of my wife.[41] The personalistic theory of causation even emerges today among acculturated Ojibwa. In 1940, when a severe forest fire broke out at the mouth of the Berens River, no Indian would believe that lightning or any impersonal or accidental determinants were involved. *Somebody* must have been responsible. The German spy theory soon became popular. "Evidence" began to accumulate; strangers had been seen in the bush, and so on. The personalistic type of explanation satisfies the Ojibwa because it is rooted in a basic metaphysical assumption; its terms are ultimate and incapable of further analysis within the framework of their cognitive orientation and experience.

Since the dynamics of events in the Ojibwa universe find their most ready explanation in a personalistic theory of causation, the qualitative aspects of interpersonal relations become affectively charged with a characteristic sensitivity.[42] The psychological importance of the range and depth of this sensitive area may be overlooked if the inclusiveness of the concept of "person" and "social relations" that is inherent in their outlook is not borne in mind. The reason for this becomes apparent when we consider the pragmatic relations between behavior, values, and the role of "persons" in their world view.

The central goal of life for the Ojibwa is expressed by the term *pīmädäzīwin*, life in the fullest sense, life in the sense of longevity, health and freedom from misfortune. This goal cannot be achieved without the effective help and cooperation of *both* human and other-than-human "persons," as well as by one's own personal efforts. The help of other-than-human "grandfathers" is particularly important for men. This is why all Ojibwa boys, in aboriginal days, were motivated to undergo the so-called "puberty fast" or "dreaming" experience. This was the means by which it was possible to enter into direct "social interaction" with "persons" of the other-than-human class for the first time. It was the opportunity of a lifetime. Every special aptitude, all a man's subsequent successes and the explanation of many of his failures, hinged upon the help of the "guardian spirits" he obtained at this time, rather than upon his own native endowments or the help of his fellow *änicinábek*. If a boy received "blessings" during his puberty fast and, as a man, could call upon the help of other-than-human persons when he needed them he was well prepared for meeting the vicissitudes of life. Among other things, he could defend himself against the hostile actions of human persons which might threaten him and thus interfere with the achievement of *pīmädäzīwin*. The grandfather of one of my informants said to him: "you will have a long and good life if you dream well." The help of human beings, however, was also vital, especially the services of those who had acquired the kind of power which permitted them to exercise effective curative functions in cases of illness. At the same time there were moral responsibilities which had to be assumed by an individual if he strove for *pīmädäzīwin*. It was as essential to maintain approved standards of personal and social conduct as it was to obtain power from the "grandfathers" because, in the nature of things, one's own conduct, as well as that of other "persons," was always a potential threat to the achievement of *pīmädäzīwin*. Thus we find that the same values are implied throughout the entire range of "social interaction" that characterizes the Ojibwa world; the same standards which apply to mutual obligations between human beings are likewise implied in the reciprocal relations between human and other-than-human "persons." In his relations with "the grandfathers" the individual does not expect to receive a "blessing" for nothing. It is not a free gift; on his part there are obligations to be met. There is a principle of reciprocity implied. There is a general taboo imposed upon the human being which forbids him to recount his dream experiences in full detail, except under certain circumstances. Specific taboos may likewise be imposed upon the suppliant. If these taboos are violated he will lose his power; he can no longer count on the help of his "grandfathers."

The same principle of mutual obligations applies in other spheres of life. The Ojibwa are hunters and food gatherers. Since the various species of animals on which they depend for a living are believed to be under the control of "masters" or "owners" who belong to the category of other-than-human persons, the hunter must always be careful to treat the animals he kills for food or fur in the proper manner. It may be necessary, for example, to throw their bones in the water or to perform a ritual in the case of bears. Otherwise he will offend the "masters" and be threatened with starvation because no animals will be made available to him. Cruelty to animals is likewise an offense that will provoke the same kind of retaliation. And, according to one anecdote, a man suffered illness because he tortured a fabulous *wíndīgo* after [while] killing him. A moral distinction is drawn between the kind of conduct demanded by the primary necessities of securing a livelihood, or defending oneself against aggression, and unnecessary acts of cruelty. The moral values implied document the consistency of the principle of mutual obligations which is inherent in all interactions with "persons" throughout the Ojibwa world.

One of the prime values of Ojibwa culture is exemplified by the great stress laid upon sharing what one has with others. A balance, a sense of proportion must be maintained in all interpersonal relations and activities. Hoarding, or any manifestation of greed, is discountenanced. The central importance of this moral value in their world outlook is illustrated by the fact that other-than-human persons share their power with human beings. This is only a particular instance of the obligations which human beings feel towards one another. A man's catch of fish or meat is distributed among his kin. Human grandfathers share the power acquired in their dreams from other-than-human persons with their classificatory grandchildren. An informant whose wife had borrowed his pipe for the morning asked to borrow one of mine while we worked together. When my friend Chief Berens once fell ill he could not explain it. Then he recalled that he had overlooked one man when he had passed around a bottle of whiskey. He believed this man was offended and had bewitched him. Since there was no objective evidence of this, it illustrates the extreme sensitivity of an individual to the principle of sharing, operating through feelings of guilt. I was once told about the puberty fast of a boy who was not satisfied with his initial "blessing." He demanded that he dream of all the leaves of all the trees in the world so that absolutely nothing would be hidden from him. This was considered greedy and, while the *pawágan* who appeared in his dream granted his desire, the boy was told that "as soon as the leaves start to fall you'll get sick and when all the leaves drop to the ground that is the end of your life." And this is what happened.[43] "Overfasting" is as greedy as hoarding. It violates a basic moral value and is subject to a punitive sanction. The unity of the Ojibwa outlook is likewise apparent here.

The entire psychological field in which they live and act is not only unified through their conception of the nature and role of "persons" in their universe, but by the sanctioned moral values which guide the relations of "persons." It is within this web of "social relations" that the individual strives for *pīmädäzīwin*.

Notes

Published in *Culture in History: Essays in Honor of Paul Radin*, ed. Stanley Diamond (New York: Columbia University Press, 1960), 19–52, and in Diamond, ed., *Primitive Views of the World: Essays from Culture in History*

(Columbia University Press, 1964), 49–82. Reprinted in Hallowell, *Contributions to Anthropology* (Chicago: University of Chicago Press, 1976), 357–90.

1. Redfield 1952, 30; cf. *African Worlds.*

2. Hallowell 1955, 91; for a more extended discussion of the culturally constituted behavioral environment of man see also 86–89 and note 33. The term "self" is not used as a synonym for ego in the psychoanalytic sense: ibid., 80.

3. See Basilius 1952; Carroll in Whorf, 1956; Hoijer, 1954; Feuer, 1953.

4. Hallowell 1955, chap. 5 ["The Northern Ojibwa," chapter 1, this volume].

5. Bruno de Jesus-Marie 1952, xvii: "The studies which make up this book fall into two main groups, of which the first deals with the theological Satan. Here the analysis of exegesis, of philosophy, of theology, treat of the devil under his aspect of a personal being whose history—his fall, his desire for vengeance—can be written as such." One of the most startling characteristics of the devil "is his agelessness" (4). He is immune to "injury, to pain, to sickness, to death . . . . Like God, and unlike man, he has no body. There are in him, then, no parts to be dismembered, no possibilities of corruption and decay, no threat of a separation of parts that will result in death. He is incorruptible, immune to the vagaries, the pains, the limitations of the flesh, immortal" (5). "Angels have no bodies, yet they have appeared to men in physical form, have talked with them, journeyed the roads with them fulfilling all the pleasant tasks of companionship" (6).

6. Hallowell 1934b, 7–9; 1936, 1308–9 ["Psychic Stresses and Culture Patterns," chapter 11, this volume]; 1951, 182–83; 1955, 256–58 ["Fear and Anxiety," chapter 12, this volume]. [Ed. note: See also William Berens, *Memories, Myths, and Dreams of an Ojibwe Leader* (2009), Part III, 15–17.]

7. Kelsen 1943, chapter 2, discusses the "social" or "personalistic interpretation of nature" which he considers the nucleus of what has been called animism.

8. In a prefatory note to *Ojibwa Texts,* Part I, Jones says (xiii) that, "'Being' or 'creature' would be a general rendering of the animate while 'thing' would express the inanimate." Cf. Schoolcraft's pioneer analysis of the animate and inanimate categories in Ojibwa speech, 1834, 171–72. [In the reprint ed. by Philip P. Mason (East Lansing: Michigan State University Press, 1993), Schoolcraft's analysis appears on 61–62.]

9. Greenberg 1954, 15–16.

10. [Ed. note: This was Alec Keeper (Kīwítc) at Little Grand Rapids in the early 1930s. See "Rocks and Stones," chapter 3, this volume.]

11. I believe that Jenness grossly overgeneralizes when he says (21): "To the Ojibwa . . . all objects have life." If this were true, their *inanimate* grammatical category would indeed be puzzling. Within the more sophisticated framework of modern biological thought, the Ojibwa attitude is not altogether naive. N.W. Pirie points out (184–85) that the words "life" and "living" have been borrowed by science from lay usage and are no longer serviceable. "Life is not a thing, a philosophical entity: it is an attitude of mind towards what is being observed."

12. Field notes. From this same Indian I obtained a smoothly rounded pebble, about two inches long and one and a half inches broad, which his father had given him. He told me that I had better keep it enclosed in a tin box or it might "go." Another man, Ketegas, gave me an account of the circumstances under which he obtained a stone with animate properties and of great medicinal value. This stone was egg shaped. It had some dark amorphous markings on it which he interpreted as representing his three children and himself. "You may not think this stone is alive," he said, "but it is. I can make it move." (He did not demonstrate this to me.) He went on to say that on two occasions he had loaned the stone to sick people to keep during the night. Both times he found it in his pocket in the morning. Ketegas kept it in a little leather case he had made for it.

13. Yellow Legs had obtained information about this remarkable stone in a dream. Its precise location was revealed to him. He sent two other Indians to get it. These men, following directions, found the stone on Birch Island, located in the middle of Lake Winnipeg, some thirty miles south of the mouth of the Berens River.

14. Cognate forms are found in Chamberlain's compilation of Cree and Ojibwa "literary" terms.

15. Jones, Texts, Part II, 574n.

16. The attitude manifested is by no means peculiar to the Ojibwa. Almost half a century ago (1910), Swanton remarked that, "one of the most widespread errors, and one of those most unfortunate for folk-lore and comparative mythology, is the offhand classification of myth with fiction." On the contrary, as he says, "It is safe to say that most of the myths found spread over considerable areas were regarded by the tribes among which they were collected as narratives of real occurrences."

17. Bidney 1953, 166.

18. Lovejoy and Boas 1935, 12; Lovejoy 1948, 69.

19. See, e.g., Collingwood 1945, also the remarks in Randall 1944, 355–56. With respect to the applicability of the natural-supernatural dichotomy to primitive cultures see Van Der Leeuw 1938, 544–45; Kelsen 1943, 44; Bidney 1953, 166.

20. [Ed. note: See Berens (2009), *Memories, Myths, and Dreams*, Part IV. See also stories in Louis Bird and Susan Elaine Gray, *The Spirit Lives in the Mind: Omushkego Stories, Lives, and Dreams* (Montreal: McGill-Queen's University Press, 2007), 23–27.]

21. [Ed. note: See Berens, *Memories, Myths, and Dreams*, Part IV.]

22. Krech and Crutchfield 1948 write (10): "clouds and storms and winds are excellent examples of objects in the psychological field that carry the perceived properties of mobility, capriciousness, causation, power of threat and reward."

23. Cf. Hallowell 1934a ["Some Empirical Aspects of Northern Saulteaux Religion," chapter 20, this volume].

24. [Ed. note: See Berens, *Memories, Myths, and Dreams*, Part IV.]

25. Actually, this was probably a rationalization of mother-son incest. But the woman was never punished by sickness, nor did she confess. Since the violation of the incest prohibition is reputed to be followed by dire consequences, the absence of both may have operated to support the possibility of her claim when considered in the context of the Ojibwa world view.

26. Thompson 1946, 258.

27. Hallowell 1926.

28. Hallowell 1934a, 397 ["Some Empirical Aspects of Northern Saulteaux Religion," chapter 20, this volume].

29. Sorcerers may assume the form of other animals as well. Peter Jones, a converted Ojibwa who became famous as a preacher and author, says that "they can turn themselves into bears, wolves, foxes, owls, bats, and snakes. . . . Several of our people have informed me that they have seen and heard witches in the shape of these animals, especially the bear and the fox. They say that when a witch in the shape of a bear is being chased all at once she will run around a tree or hill, so as to be lost sight of for a time by her pursuers, and then, instead of seeing a bear they behold an old woman walking quietly along or digging up roots, and looking as innocent as a lamb" (Jones 1861, 145–46).

30. Dorson 1952, 31.

31. Dorson, 29. This rationalization dates back over a century. John Tanner, an Indianized white man who was captured as a boy in the late eighteenth century and lived with the Ottawa and Ojibwa many years, refers to it. So does Peter Jones.

32. Hallowell 1955, 176–77 ["The Ojibwa Self and its Behavioral Environment," chapter 26, this volume].

33. Dorson 1952, 31.

34. Hoffman 1891, 205–6

35. Unpublished field notes.

36. See Hallowell 1955, chapter 15 ["Aggression in Saulteaux Society," chapter 15, this volume].

37. Cf. Skinner 1915, 261. Cooper 1933 (75) writes: "The Manitu was clearly personal in the minds of my informants, and not identified with impersonal supernatural force. In fact, nowhere among the Albany River Otchipwe, among the Eastern Cree, or among the Montagnais have I been able thus far to find the word Manitu used to denote such force in connection with the Supreme Being belief, with conjuring, or with any other phase of magico-religious culture. *Manitu*, so far as I can discover, always denotes a supernatural personal being. . . . The word *Manitu* is, my informants say, not used to denote magical or conjuring power among the coastal Cree, nor so I was told in 1927, among the Fort Hope Otchipwe of the upper Albany River."

38. Radin 1914a, 350.

39. Radin 1914a, 349–50.

40. [Ed. note: See Berens, *Memories, Myths, and Dreams*, Part IV.]

41. "Because a person does bad things, that is where sickness starts," is the way one of my informants phrased it. For a fuller discussion of the relations between unsanctioned sexual behavior and disease, see Hallowell 1955, 294–95; 303–4 ["Psychosexual Adjustment, Personality, and the Good Life in a Nonliterate Culture," chapter 18, this volume]. For case material, see Hallowell 1939. ["Sin, Sex, and Sickness in Saulteaux Belief," chapter 17, this volume.]

42. Cf. Hallowell 1955, 305 ["Psychosexual Adjustment," chapter 18, this volume].

43. Radin 1927, 177, points out that "throughout the area inhabited by the woodland tribes of Canada and the United States, overfasting entails death." Jones, *Texts*, Part II, 307–11, gives two cases of overfasting. In one of them the bones of the boy were later found by his father.

References

African Worlds: Studies in the Cosmological Ideas and Social Values of African Peoples. 1954. Published for the International African Institute. London, Oxford University Press.

Baraga, R. R. Bishop. 1878. *A Theoretical and Practical Grammar of the Otchipwe Language.* Montreal, Beauchemin, and Valois.

———. 1880. *A Dictionary of the Otchipwe Language Explained in English.* Montreal, Beauchemin and Valois.

Basilius, H. 1952. "Neo-Humboldtian Ethnolinguistics," *Word,* vol. 8.

Bidney, David. 1953. *Theoretical Anthropology.* New York, Columbia University Press.

Bruno de Jésus-Marie, père, ed. 1952. *Satan.* New York, Sheed and Ward.

Chamberlain, A. F. 1906. "Cree and Ojibwa Literary Terms," *Journal of American Folklore,* 19:346–47.

Collingwood, R. G. 1945. *The Idea of Nature.* Oxford, Clarendon Press.

Cooper, John M. 1933. "The Northern Algonquian Supreme Being," *Primitive Man,* 6:41–112.

Dorson, Richard M. 1952. *Bloodstoppers and Bearwalkers: Folk Traditions of the Upper Peninsula.* Cambridge, MA: Harvard University Press.

Feuer, Lewis S. 1953. "Sociological Aspects of the Relation between Language and Philosophy," *Philosophy of Science,* 20:85–100.

Fletcher, Alice C. 1910. "Wakonda," in *Handbook of American Indians.* WashingtonDC: Bureau of American Ethnology, Bull. 30.

Greenberg, Joseph H. 1954. "Concerning Inferences from Linguistic to Nonlinguistic Data," in *Language in Culture,* ed. by Harry Hoijer. Chicago, University of Chicago Press.

Hallowell, A. Irving. 1926. "Bear Ceremonialism in the Northern Hemisphere," *American Anthropologist,* 28:1–175.

———. 1934a. "Some Empirical Aspects of Northern Saulteaux Religion," *American Anthropologist,* 36:389–404.

———. 1934b. "Culture and Mental Disorder," *Journal of Abnormal and Social Psychology,* 29:1–9.

———. 1936. "Psychic Stresses and Culture Patterns," *American Journal of Psychiatry,* 92:1291–1310.

———. 1939. "Sin, Sex and Sickness in Saulteaux Belief," *British Journal of Medical Psychology,* 18:191–97.

———. 1951. "Cultural Factors in the Structuralization of Perception," in John H. Rohver and Muzafer Sherif, *Social Psychology at the Crossroads.* New York, Harper.

———. 1955. *Culture and Experience*. Philadelphia, University of Pennsylvania Press.

Hewitt, J. N. B. 1902. "Orenda and a Definition of Religion," *American Anthropologist*, 4:33–46.

Hoffman, W. J. 1891. "The Mide-wiwin or 'Grand Medicine Society' of the Ojibwa." Washington DC, Bureau of American Ethnology 7th Annual Report.

Hoijer, Harry, ed. 1954. *Language in Culture*. Memoir 79, American Anthropological Association.

Jenness, Diamond. 1935. *The Ojibwa Indians of Parry Island, their social and religious life*. Ottawa, Canada Department of Mines, National Museum of Canada Bull, 78. Anthropological Series 12.

Jones, Peter. 1861. *History of the Ojibway Indians*. London.

Jones, William. 1905. "The Algonkin Manitu," *Journal of American Folklore*, 18:183–90.

———. 1917, 1919. *Ojibwa Texts*. Publications of the American Ethnological Society, Vol. 7, Parts I and II. Leyden:1917; New York:1919.

Kelsen, Hans. 1943. *Society and Nature: A Sociological Inquiry*. Chicago, University of Chicago Press.

Krech, David, and Richard S. Crutchfield. 1948. *Theory and Problems of Social Psychology*. New York, McGraw-Hill.

Lovejoy, Arthur O. 1948. *Essays in the History of Ideas*. Baltimore, Johns Hopkins University Press.

———, and George Boas. 1935. *Primitivism and Related Ideas in Antiquity*. Baltimore, Johns Hopkins University Press. Vol. I of *A Documentary History of Primitivism and Related Ideas*.

Pirie, N. W. 1937. "The Meaninglessness of the Terms 'Life' and 'Living'," in *Perspectives in Biochemistry*, ed. by J. Needham and D. Green. New York, Macmillan.

Radin, Paul. 1914a. "Religion of the North American Indians," *Journal of American Folklore*, 27:335–73.

———. 1914b. "Some Aspects of Puberty Fasting among the Ojibwa." Geological Survey of Canada, Department of Mines, Museum Bull. No. 2, Anthropological Series, No. 2, 1–10.

———. 1927. *Primitive Man as Philosopher*. New York, D. Appleton & Co.

Randall, John Herman Jr. 1944. "The Nature of Naturalism," in *Naturalism and the Human Spirit*, ed. by H. Krikorian. New York, Columbia University Press.

Redfield, Robert. 1952. "The Primitive World View," *Proceedings of the American Philosophical Society,* 96:30–36.

Schoolcraft, Henry R. 1834. *Narrative of an Expedition through the Upper Mississippi to Itasca Lake, the Actual Source of the River . . .* New York, Harper.

Skinner, Alanson. 1915. "The Menomini Word 'Hawatuk'," *Journal of American Folklore,* 28:258–61.

Swanton, John R. 1910. "Some Practical Aspects of the Study of Myths," *Journal of American Folklore,* 23:1–7.

Tanner, John. 1830. *Narrative of the Captivity and Adventures of John Tanner,* ed. by Edwin James. New York, Carvill.

Thompson, Stith. 1946. *The Folktale.* New York, Dryden Press.

Van Der Leeuw, G. 1938. *Religion in Essence and Manifestation.* London, Allen and Unwin.

Whorf, Benjamin Lee. 1956. *Language, Thought, and Reality: Selected Writings of Benjamin L. Whorf,* ed. with an introduction by J. B. Carroll; Foreword by Stuart Chase. New York, Wiley.

GLOSSARY OF OJIBWE WORDS AND NAMES USED BY HALLOWELL

Compiled by Susan Elaine Gray

This glossary presents a compilation of the Ojibwe words and names that appear in Hallowell's writings. In his essays, Hallowell rendered the many Ojibwe words he used in a distinctive orthography which is no longer in use, and was perhaps never used by anyone else documenting Ojibwe. A great linguistic challenge for us has been the issue of Hallowell's spelling. In both his published articles and (especially) his handwritten research notes, he often spelled the same word in different ways, sometimes within the same document. Some of his handwritten texts were typed by a secretary not familiar with the words and symbols, and he did not always proofread them if they were not developed for publication. Below is a phonetic key that Hallowell published in his collection of essays, *Culture and Experience*; it is presented here in the form in which he published it. The key yields some clues about Hallowell's linguistic assumptions and is his only published description of his orthography.

For consistency, we have silently adopted the spelling he most frequently used for each word, and provided the definitions that he gave beside these words. With the generous help of Roger Roulette, a fluent speaker and teacher of Ojibwe, and Rand Valentine, a scholar of Algonquian languages, we have, where possible, accompanied these usages with modern orthography written directly under the word and have given supplementary translations where needed, and their comments are indicated by their initials, R. R. or R. V. If either Roulette or Valentine provided any speculative remark regarding usage or meaning, we have inserted a question mark beside the comment. Beside each word is also the name of one of the essays in which it occurs. Often these words appeared in several different essays, and the index will help in locating other instances of their use.

The Glossary of Personal Names is a listing of Ojibwe people whom Hallowell mentioned. Each name is spelled in Hallowell's orthography and accompanied by a short biography. Again, we include the name of one article in which the reader can locate the subject. Proper names also appear in the index.

In the rendering of native Ojibwa words which appear in this book [*Culture and Experience*, 1955], I have approximated the *Phonetic Transcription of Indian Languages* (Smithsonian Miscellaneous Collections [61], no. 6, 1916), recommended by a committee of the American Anthropological Association. I have not, however, followed all the refinements indicated. For the general reader it is hoped that the symbols used for the following sounds will make the Indian words sufficiently pronounceable:

VOWELS CONSONANTS AND ACCENT MARKS

a, as in *father*
ä, as in *hat*
c, approximates *sh* in *ship*
dj, approximates *j* in *judge*
e, as *a* in *fate*
ī, as in *pique*
j, approximates *z* in *azure*
o, as in *not*
tc, approximates *ch* in *church*
u, as in *rule*
ɑ, as *u* in *but*
' breathing, concluding syllable after a vowel
´ (acute) and ` (grave) indicate major and secondary stress accents, respectively

KEY TO GRAMMATICAL CODES
by Rand Valentine

comp (short for complementizer): a preverb that subordinates a verb
expra: multi-word expression
nanoun: animate
na-namenoun: animate, name
na-ptnoun: animate, participle (a nominalized verb)
nadnoun: animate dependent
ninoun: inanimate
ni-locnoun: inanimate, locative form
ni-placenoun: inanimate, place name

nidnoun: inanimate dependent
pc: particle
pren: prenoun
prev: preverb
vaiverb: animate intransitive
viiverb: inanimate intransitive
vtaverb: transitive animate
vtiverb: transitive inanimate

LIST OF OJIBWE WORDS

aadisookaanag. See **ätisokának** below

aásī   crow (Berens, Part IV)

aa'aasi na

ăgɑs   Cree, arrow ("The Passing of the Midewi·win")

akask na (Swampy Cree) /acosis ni (Plains Cree)

aiyamɑyegījigɑn   praying day—the Sabbath ("Temporal Orientation in Western Civilization and in a Preliterate Society").

Usually in Ojibwe: anama'e-giizhigan/anami'e-giizhigan—vii: it is Sunday, lit. it is praying day, Sunday

Oji-Cree and Cree: ayamihaa vai prays

aká 'kotci·s   woodchuck ("The Passing of the Midewi·win")

akakojiish na-ag

a`kī   the earth ("Spirits of the Dead in Saulteaux Life and Thought")

aki ni -in   land, earth

ákīwezi   old man ("Temporal Orientation in Western Civilization and in a Preliterate Society")

akiwenzi -wag

akiwenzi na -wag

äkwáwänakŭn   poles ("Notes on the Material Culture of the Island Lake Saulteaux")

akwaakwanak -oon

akwaakwanaak (?) ni. -oon

ákwazīwin   sickness ("Fear and Anxiety as Cultural and Individual Variables in a Primitive Society")

aakoziwin an ni

ämanozówīgīzis   (September) "Rutting Moon" [Pikangikum] ("Temporal Orientation in Western Civilization and in a Preliterate Society")

aamanoozowi -giizis -oog

aamanozoowi? -giizis na

ämi`kwán   wooden spoon ("Notes on the Material Culture of the Island Lake Saulteaux")

emikwaan   na -ag

'emikwaan' is the name given to the back of the small, red turtle {miskwaadesi(wag)}. The small shell was originally used as a spoon by the Anishinaabeg, according to Charlie George Owen, Pauingassi, Manitoba. (R.R.)

Amo   bee (Berens, Introduction)

aamoo   na -g

änämatikèpī ágotcing gizis   the point when the rising sun is still behind the tree tops: "beneath trees when hangs (the) sun" ("Temporal Orientation in Western Civilization and in a Preliterate Society")

anaamaatigebii agoojing giizis?

anaamaatige/bii to sit, be placed behind trees

agoojing to hang, be aloft (animate)

änicinábe   man ("The Northern Ojibwa")

anishinaabe(g) human, man, aboriginal person

anishinaabe(g) na

änicinábek   men ("Ojibwa World View and Disease")

änishinábek Ojibwas

anishinaabe(g) na   human, man

anishinaabe(g)   human, man

änicinábewápine   "Indian sickness" brought on by sorcery ("Aggression in Saulteaux Society")

anishinaabewaapine vai   has an Indian/aboriginal sickness

anishinaabewaapine(win). Anishinaabe sickness attributed to moral infractions by individuals, moral infractions by association (bad karma), sorcery. (R. R.)

animɑkï   thunder (Berens, Appendix)

animikii

anwïpémondɑk   bullet carrier (Berens, Part IV)

anwi-bimoondag(?)

anwi ni -in   bullet

bimoojigan ni   carrier (in southern dialects)

änziän   breech cloth ("Notes on the Material Culture of the Island Lake Saulteaux")

aanziyaan ni-an   breech cloth, diaper

apīnondjī   child—term includes the viable fetus ("Temporal Orientation in Western Civilization and in a Preliterate Society") abinoonjii na -yag

abinoozhiish(ag)   child, fetus

ɑpiˈtapïbungïzis   (February) "Half—Winter Moon" [Berens River]
("Temporal Orientation in Western Civilization and in a Preliterate
Society")

aabitaa-biiboon giizis-lit. aabitaa-biboon giizis na, lit. half-winter moon

aabita half

apiˈtaúwɑse   (Wednesday) "half (week) gone" ("Temporal
Orientation in Western Civilization and in a Preliterate Society")

aabitawise aabitawise   vii is Wednesday, lit. half way in the process of the
week

Asatiwïsïbï   Poplar River

Azaadiwiziibi

äsígwan   spring season ("Temporal Orientation in Western
Civilization and in a Preliterate Society")

ziigwan -vii   is spring

aziigwan   (ziigwan—is the universal term; 'a' in front of the term is
only a particle).

askïbibun   the first part of winter: "new, fresh, winter" ("Temporal
Orientation in Western Civilization and in a Preliterate Society")

oshki-biboon -vii   it is the beginning of winter, lit. new winter, etc.

oshki   new, fresh

biboon   winter

atawágani·ogimakan   a barter chief ("The Incidence and Decline of
Polygyny among the Lake Winnipeg Cree and Saulteaux")

adaawaaganiadaawaagani-ogimaakaan (ag)-na barter leader ("chief" is a
Western interpretation)

atik   (Berens)

adik na -wag   caribou

atiˈkteminiˈkawïgïzis   (July) Ripe-berries gathering Moon [Berens
River] ("Temporal Orientation in Western Civilization and in a
Preliterate Society")

aditeminikaawi-giizis na   moon of ripe berries

aditeminikaawi-giizis -oog)   ripe pin cherries moon

atis   sinew ("Notes on the Material Culture of the Island Lake
Saulteaux")

atis(?) ni -iin   sinew

ätsokan   myths (Berens)

aadizookaan na -ag

ätisokának   other-than-human persons: the Four Winds, Sun,

Moon, Thunderbirds, "owners" or "masters"of species of plants and animals and the characters in myths—collectively spoken of as "our grandfathers" (Berens, Part IV)

aadizookaan (ag) na   ancestors, characters in stories and myths, etc.

ätsokának pawáganak   ("Spirits of the Dead in Saulteaux Life and Thought")

aadizookaan (ag)   ancestors, etc.

bawaagan (ag)   dream visitor

bībún   winter ("Temporal Orientation in Western Civilization and in a Preliterate Society")

baboon -vii   is winter; or biboon ni winter

càbandawan   a multiple family dwelling ("Notes on the Material Culture of the Island Lake Saulteaux")

zhaabandawaan(?) ni -an   lodge with doors at opposite ends (east—west)

cacagīs   young pelican ("Spirits of the Dead in Saulteaux Life and Thought")

zhashagiins (ag) na

cīcīgwan   rattle (Berens, Part IV)

zhiishiigwan ni-an

cinautcíganɛs   little bell (Berens, Part IV)

zhinaachiganens(?) ni -an

cingabis   duck (Berens, Part IV)

zhingibis na -ag grebe,   hell-diver

cingúbigan   brush tent (Berens)

zhingobiigan ni -an   'shelter or hut made of fir branches or boughs' (Baraga 1853:169)

cingubīwátigok   evergreens (generic term) (Berens)
  zhingobiiwaatig na -oog

dibaajimowinan   see tabätcamoin (Berens)

dibaajimowin ni -an   story, narrative

djí·bai   a person's ghost ("Spirits of the Dead in Saulteaux Life and Thought")

djībaiyak   souls of the dead—spirits of the dead

jiibay na -ag   ghosts, spirits

jiibay (ag)   ghosts, spirits

djībaiàking   the spirit (ghost) land ("Spirits of the Dead in Saulteaux Life and Thought")

jiibekiing (var.)

jiibayakiing ni -loc (jiibayaki)—the spirit (ghost) land

jiibekamigong   land of the dead, dreamscape, dreamland (R. V.)

djībai ikana   spirit (ghost) road ("Spirits of the Dead in Saulteaux Life and Thought")

jiibekana   spirit (ghost) road

jiibayikana ni   road of the spirits (associated with Milky Way)

djībaisímowin   Ghost (or Spirit of the Dead) Dance ("Spirits of the Dead in Saulteaux Life and Thought")

djisáki·win   conjuring ("Some Empirical Aspects of Northern Saulteaux Religion")

jiisakiiwin -ni   conjuring, divination (esp. in the shaking tent) (usually the southern Ojibwe term, gosaabanjigewin being the northern Ojibwe term)

djisáki·wininī   conjuror ("The Ojibwa Self and Its Behavioral Environment")

djïsdahótowin   tattooing ("Notes on the Material Culture of the Island Lake Saulteaux")

jiista'oodowin

jiishta'oodowin   tattooing (lit. pierce something, e.g., skin)

eagasabikizit   "getting small"(moon) ("Temporal Orientation in Western Civilization and in a Preliterate Society")

e-agaasaabiigizid ('e' in front of verb is in conjunct form, only in speech)

agaasaabiigizid something small, thin, rope-like

e-agaasaabikizid giizis na   (getting) small moon

eànīkketcī skīobakwit   "as high as the sun goes during the day"("as high as it goes up") ("Temporal Orientation in Western Civilization and in a Preliterate Society")

e-ani-gichi-[ishpaakwiid]

e-ani-gichi-ishpaakwiid   when the sun is its highest (lit. at its most highest, with reference to the trees)

ishpagoojing giizis—lit. when the sun is high

eanimitcapikizazit   "bigger" (moon) ("Temporal Orientation in Western Civilization and in a Preliterate Society")

e-ani-michaabiigizid 'e' (conjunct), 'ani-' (pv) michaabiigizid

ani-michaabiigizid lit. something large, rope-like

e-ani-michaabikizid -vai   expression 'when the moon gets big'

michaabikizi -vai   be big [of stone, glass, metal objects]

eàptagīzigak   (midday) "half day" ("Temporal Orientation in Western Civilization and in a Preliterate Society")

e-aabitaagiizhig   half day

aabitaagiizhig   midday

e-aabitaa-giizhigak -vai expr. "when it's the middle of the 'day'"

aabitaa-giizhigan-vii   the middle of the day

eàptawàbkizit   ["half (-gone)"] (moon) ("Temporal Orientation in
　　Western Civilization and in a Preliterate Society")

e-aabitaawaabiigizid(?)

aabitawaabiigizid   half something rope-like

e-aabitawaabikizid -vai expr. when the moon is half

aabitawaabizi -vai   is half [of stone, glass, metal objects]

eàptawīnazit   the sun "half-way to setting" ("Temporal Orientation in
　　Western Civilization and in a Preliterate Society")

e-aabitaawinaazhiid 'e-' conjunct

aabitaawinaazhiid   the sun is half-way to setting (this would be the
　　proper form) (R. R.)

ékwanákak épī`ágotcinggizis   the point when the rising sun reaches
　　the tops of the trees: "tops of trees when hangs (the) sun" ("Temporal
　　Orientation in Western Civilization and in a Preliterate Society")

ekwanagak api agoojing giizis   the point when sun reaches the tops of
　　the trees

ekwaanaakwak e-bi-agoojing giizis   when the sun comes to hang at the
　　extent of the trees

akwaanaakwan -vii   be the extent of the trees

e-prev complementizer; bi-prev   hither, come to be; agoojin vai hang

emetasīget   "it is going" (moon) ("Temporal Orientation in Western
　　Civilization and in a Preliterate Society")

e-mitaasiged 'e-' conjunct.

mitaasiged giizis   moonlight, when the moon shines

e-mitaasiged -vai expr.   'as it just shines' (total speculation, Rand
　　Valentine)

enīogijigan   (Friday) "approaching day" ("Temporal Orientation in
　　Western Civilization and in a Preliterate Society")

e-niiyogiizhigan

niiyo-giizhigan   Fourth day, Thursday

e-niiwi-giizhigang -vii expr when it's the fourth day; expected for is
　　e-niiyo-giizhigak (R. V.)

eoskagotcing   "newly hanging" (moon) ("Temporal Orientation in
　　Western Civilization and in a Preliterate Society")

e-oshkagoojing -vai expr. 'when it hangs anew'

e-comp; oshkagoojin -vai   hang anew

oshkagoojing giizis   new moon (lit. newly hanging)

epákwezit "going" (moon) ("Temporal Orientation in Western Civilization and in a Preliterate Society")

e-bakwezid?

e-prev comp?; bakwezi vai be broken off?

bakwezid giizis lit. part of moon is gone

èskin ice-chisel (Berens)

eshkan ni -an

èwáwīezit "round" (moon) ("Temporal Orientation in Western Civilization and in a Preliterate Society")

e-wawiiyezid

e-waawiyezid -vai expr. when it's round

e-prev comp; waawiyezi vai is round

waawiyezid giizis round moon

i`kwézes little girl (under puberty) ("Temporal Orientation in Western Civilization and in a Preliterate Society")

ikwezens na -ag girl

inïnagim a type of shoe ("Notes on the Material Culture of the Island Lake Saulteaux")

ininaagim? na -ag type of snowshoe

Kadabéndang a spiritual "owner" associated with djisáki·win or kosábandamowin [conjuring]—euphemistically called "the one who takes them out"—ozá gi·zi·i·we ("Some Empirical Aspects of Northern Saulteaux Religion")

Gaa-dibendang (Ozaagizi'iwe—One who takes others out)

gaa-dibendang na -pt one who owns, one who possesses, owner, Lord

gaa-prev comp; dibendan vti own it

The Christian god (lit. one who owns)

gaa-dibenimigoowaad? na -pt plural—the ones who are owned by an individual, the ones who are subject to another

gaa-prev comp; dibenim vta own s.o., be the lord of s.o.

Kadabéndjiget the "owner" of the world—the most remote (highest?) and powerful of beings (R. R.), ("Some Empirical Aspects of Northern Saulteaux Religion")

Gaa-dibenjiged na -pt the owner (God)

gaa-prev comp; dibenjige vai own (things)

Kādabenī·míkuwat a spiritual "owner" perceived through dreams ("The Ojibwa Self and its Behavioral Environment")

Gaa-dibenimigoowaad the ones who are owned by someone (see above)

kagïgebak   Labrador tea ("Notes on the Material Culture of the Island Lake Saulteaux")

gaagigebag(oon)   Labrador tea

gaagigebag ni   Labrador tea

kagīnwasīgetgīzis   (January) Long Moon [Little Grand Rapids] ("Temporal Orientation in Western Civilization and in a Preliterate Society")

gaa-ginwaasiged giizis lit.   lengthy sunshine

kamini`tgŭtci wang   water running on both sides of rock ("Rocks and Stones")

kapǐpǐkwewi·k   Black Island—the name refers to something reverberating (The Passing of the Midewi·win in the Lake Winnipeg Region)

gaa-prev comp; ginwaasige -vai   shine long (NB physically, not temporally) (R. V.)

kaskipītagan   a skin bag with magical properties similar to those used in the mīdewi·win (Berens, Part IV)

gashkibidaagan na/ni(varies by dialect)   pouch

kegáeapi`tatabíkak   (midnight) "nearly half (the) night" ("Temporal Orientation in Western Civilization and in a Preliterate Society")

gegaa aabitaadibikag—e-aabitaa-dibikak expr. it is nearly midnight

gegaa pc almost; e-prev comp; aabitaa-dibikan -vii   is midnight

kegáewáwīezit   "nearly round" (moon) ("Temporal Orientation in Western Civilization and in a Preliterate Society")

gegaa waawiyezid   expr. (when) it (anim.) is nearly round

gegaa pc almost; waawiyezi -vai   is round

kekek   the fastest-flying of all hawks (Berens, Part IV)

gekek na -wag   hawk

keté   prefix meaning "old" ("Temporal Orientation in Western Civilization and in a Preliterate Society")

gete-pren old

keté änicinábek   old people ("The Ojibwa Self and its Behavioral Environment")

gete-anishinaabe na -g   ancient people, people of long ago (usually in plural)

keté änicinábe èändjīnictáuwige   an old man or woman who has been born again—term used when a child has some grey hairs ("Spirits of the Dead in Saulteaux Life and Thought")

gete-anishinaabe e-aanji-nitaawigi(d)   expr. an ancient person who changes birth (i.e., reincarnates) e-prev comp; aanji-prev change; nitaawigi -vai is born; aanji-nitaawigi is reincarnated? (R. V.)

reincarnation (lit. the ancient anishinaabe is reborn)

ketéockīnīga old young man (bachelor) ("Temporal Orientation in Western Civilization and in a Preliterate Society")

gete-oshkiniigi na -wag lit. old young man, where young man has a conventional meaning of bachelor? (R. R.)

gete-oshkiniigi(wag) young man with wisdom

moozhaabe(g) bachelor

ketéockīnīkwe old young woman (spinster) ("Temporal Orientation in Western Civilization and in a Preliterate Society")

gete-oshkiniigikwe na -g old young woman, where young woman has a conventional meaning of unmarried (R. R.)

gete-oshkiniigikwe(g) young woman with wisdom

moozhaabekwe(g) unmarried woman

kictcopabīwatakinam (January) Long Moon [Berens River] ("Temporal Orientation in Western Civilization and in a Preliterate Society")

gichi-bapiiwaatakiinam lit. the final big step to see survival

kīgúsämo a boy undergoing a dream fast ("The Role of Dreams in Saulteaux Life and Thought")

gii'igoshimo -vai fasts for a vision or dream fast

kījégīzis (February) Kind Moon [Pekangikum] ("Temporal Orientation in Western Civilization and in a Preliterate Society")

gizhe-giizis kind, gracious moon

kīmändauzī a kind of wizard (Berens, Part IV)

kīmícómisanän our grandfather (Berens, Part IV)

kimi comissab kunan our grandfather's rock ("Rocks and Stones")

gimishoomisaabikonaan lit. 'our (inclusive) grandfather-rock'

kīneganīsī the boss of Thunder Bird Land (Berens, Part IV)

gii-niigaanizi -vai expr. it stood in front, it led (R. V.)

kinim cross-cousin (Berens, Part III). See also **nīnam** below.

giinim niinim nad -ag my sister, my female cross-cousin [man speaking]; my brother-in-law [woman speaking]

kīnïu Golden Eagle (Berens, Part IV)

giniw

kinozε͵εak small fish (Berens, Part IV)

ginoozhe na -g fish(at Pikangikum), northern pike, jackfish (more generally, including Pikangikum)

Kinozéwi·si·bi   Jackfish River ("The Passing of the Midewi·win in the Lake Winnipeg Region")

ginoozhewiziiibi ni

kinozïäp   belt ("Notes on the Material Culture of the Island Lake Saulteaux")

ginoozheyaab ni -iin

kïstäsïnän   our (inclusive) older brother (Berens, Part IV)

gistesinaan nistes nad my older brother Oji-Cree; probably from e.g., Swampy Cree, nistes (R. V.)

ki·tim   Cree word meaning marry ("Cross-Cousin Marriage in the Lake Winnipeg" Area)

kïjégïzis   (February) Kind Moon [Pekangikum] ("Temporal Orientation in Western Civilization and in a Preliterate Society")

gizhe-giizis na kind, gracious moon

kinebik   small snake (Berens, Part IV)

ginebig na -oog snake

kïnïu   golden eagle ("The Ojibwa Self and its Behavioral Environment")

giniw na -ag

kïsagwas   father's sister; also the term for mother-in-law ("Fear and Anxiety as Cultural and Individual Variables in a Primitive Society")

gizigos nizigos nad -ag   my cross-aunt, my mother-in-law

kitai ndakiwamik   your dog's biting me (Berens, Part IV)

kïwaskwe   an insane or demented person ("Shabwan: A Dissocial Indian Girl")

giiwashkwe lit.   senseless

giiwashkwe -vai   is crazy

kiwatin   north wind (Berens, Part IV)

giiwedin ni   north wind, north

kizasïpi'tam   failure to observe an obligation earnestly entered into ("Ojibwa World View and Disease")

kosábandamowin   conjuring (See for example, "Some Empirical Aspects of Northern Saulteaux Religion")

gosaabandamowin the noun ni -an shaking tent (for the shaking tent conjuring)

k'tcēkinébik   monster snake (Berens, Part IV)

gichi-ginebig na -oog; gichi-pren   big, giant, great

k'tci anang   a great star (Berens, Appendix)

gichi anang

k'tcimakokik   frogs (Berens, Part IV)

K`tchi·mǎ´ni·tu   the "owner" of the world—the most remote
   (highest?) and powerful of beings ("Some Empirical Aspects of
   Northern Saulteaux Religion")
Gichi-manidoo—Christian god na -g   great spirit
k`tcíapi`taúwase   (Thursday) "great half gone" ("Temporal
   Orientation in Western Civilization and in a Preliterate Society")
gichi-aabitawise -vii   it is greatly halfway; day after mid-week
k`tcígijik   great sky—a term used by Christianized Ojibwe for heaven
   ("Temporal Orientation in Western Civilization and in a Preliterate
   Society")
k`tcígijikodenawan   great sky town (city)—kingdom of heaven
   ("Temporal Orientation in Western Civilization and in a Preliterate
   Society")
K`tcí·minis   Big Island, now Hecla ("The Passing of the Midewi·win
   in the Lake Winnipeg Region")
Gichi-minis ni -an   Big Island
ktciogima   the big boss (Berens, Part III)
gichi-ogimaa na -g
K`tcīotcīganang   (Ursa Major) Great Fisher ("Temporal Orientation
   in Western Civilization and in a Preliterate Society")
Gichi-oojiig Anangojiiganang na -oog Great Fisher Star
k`tcizagimé   big mosquito (Berens, Part IV)
gichi-zagime na -g   big mosquito
K`tigani·minis   Garden Island in northern Lake Manitoba ("The
   Passing of the Midewi·win in the Lake Winnipeg Region")
gitigaani-minis -ni   place (lit. garden island)
kwabawhán   ice scoop ("Notes on the Material Culture of the Island
   Lake Saulteaux")
gwaaba'awaan (gwaaba'igan)   any scoop
gwaaba'waan? ni   ice scoop
kwawanatik   meat or fish drying rack (Berens, Part IV)
agwaawaanaatig
kwingwan   earthquake (Berens, Part IV)
gwiingwan ni -an   comet
kwīwīzes   little boy (under puberty) ("Temporal Orientation in
   Western Civilization and in a Preliterate Society")
gwiiwizens na -ag
mackīkī   having magical potency ("The Ojibwa Self and its Behavioral
   Environment")
mashkiki ni -in   medicine (healing property)

mɑckĭkī medicine ("The Ojibwa Self and its Behavioral
  Environment")
mashkiki
madjĭijĭwébɑzīwin bad conduct ("Fear and Anxiety as Cultural and
  Individual Variables in a Primitive Society")
maji-izhiwebiziwin ni be in a bad way, dilemma, misfortune
mɑkīkomin moss berry ("Notes on the Material Culture of the Island
  Lake Saulteaux")
mashkiigomin ni -an swamp cranberry
makwa bear ("Notes on the Material Culture of the Island Lake
  Saulteaux")
makwa na -g
makwátum the "bear-paw" snow shoe ("Notes on the Material
  Culture of the Island Lake Saulteaux")
makwadam? in south, makwasaagim na 'bear paw snowshoe'
mämändä'wis witch or wizard ("The Passing of the Midewi·win in the
  Lake Winnipeg Region")
mamaandaawis? -vai mamaandaawizi has extraordinary powers
mămandawi·zi a miracle ("The Passing of the Midewi·win in the Lake
  Winnipeg Region")
mamaandaawizi one is endowed with extraordinary power
mamaandaawizi -vai has extraordinary powers
mänáo a doctor who dispenses medicine from the memengwécīwak
  ("The Passing of the Midewi·win in the Lake Winnipeg Region")
mina'o one who gives a drink
mina'iwe one who gives a drink (i.e. medicine, etc.)
mändáitīwin the give-away dance ("Temporal Orientation in Western
  Civilization and in a Preliterate Society")
manda'idiwin
mada'idiwin (var.)
mändáuwīzī magic power ("Aggression in Saulteaux Society")
maandaawizi one is endowed with extraordinary power
mamaandaawizi -vai has supernatural powers
mángogīzis (May) Loon Moon ("Temporal Orientation in Western
  Civilization and in a Preliterate Society")
maangoogiizis -giizis na loon moon
mänītu God—the creator and owner of everything ("Spirits of the
  Dead in Saulteaux Life and Thought")
manidoo na -g spirits, ones with extraordinary abilities
mänītu omīgīwewin the gift of God ("Spirits of the Dead in Saulteaux
  Life and Thought")

manidoo omiigiwewin lit. gloss, (it would be odd to say term in it of itself unless it was contextualized) (R. V.)

miigiwewin ni   gift, something given omiigiwewin his/her/its (anim.) gift

mänómini`kawīgīzis   (September) Wild-rice-gathering Moon [Berens River] ("Temporal Orientation in Western Civilization and in a Preliterate Society")

manoominikaawi-giizis na   abundance of rice moon—lit. plenty of wild rice moon

mɑski`kwatikopi`kwakwɑt   tamarack cones (Berens, Part IV)

mashkiigwaatigo-bikwaakwad na/ni(uncertain, probably inanimate) lit. tamarack ball

Mätci mänītu   Bad Spirit—the contemporary term for the Devil ("Spirits of the Dead in Saulteaux Life and Thought")

maji-manidoo recent term to make a contrast between 'good and evil'

maji-manidoo na -g   devil, evil spirit

mätutzwán   sweat lodge ("Notes on the Material Culture of the Island Lake Saulteaux")

madoodiswaan

madoodoswaan ni -an   sweat-lodge

madoodiswan (madoodison, var.)

megwábībun   the latter, most severe half of winter ("Temporal Orientation in Western Civilization and in a Preliterate Society")

megwe-biboon?   mid-winter

megwe pre in the midst of biboon ni winter?

megwaa baboon?

mekis   eagle (Berens, Part IV)

mek wégi·zik   amidst the sky ("The Passing of the Midewi·win in the Lake Winnipeg Region")

megwe-giizhig?

awas-megwe-giizhig? pc   beyond the midst of the sky

memengwécīwak   small other-than-human persons who live in rocks—guardian spirits ("The Passing of the Midewi·win in the Lake Winnipeg Region")

memengweshi na -wag

memegweshiwag (memegwesiwag, var.) small other-than-human persons who live in rocks and caves (underground dens)

Mīcīpījìu   Great Lynx—a superhuman entity with malevolent character ("Psychosexual Adjustment, Personality and the Good Life in a Non-literate Culture") mishibizhiw cougar (mountain lion), water spirit resembling panther. Although these beings are understood to be enemies of the Thunderbirds, they are not necessarily malevolent or evil since they may be guardians of anishinaabeg.

Mishibizhiw na -ag

Mi·cí·pi·jiu baùtik Great Lynx Rapids ("Some Empirical Aspects of Northern Saulteaux Religion")

Mishibizhiw-Baawitig ni Great Lynx Rapids

Bizhiw here is complicated; mishibizhiw means 'large catlike creature,' so might be a cougar, etc. (R. V.)

mictigwewébɑzin wooden swing (Berens, Part IV)

mitig-wewebizon ni -an

mi·dékwe medicine woman ("The Passing of the Midewi·win in the Lake Winnipeg Region")

midekwe? na -g woman belonging to the Midewi·win

mide·mǎ´ni·tu a spiritual "owner" associated with the midéwi·win (medicine lodge) ("The Passing of the Midewi·win in the Lake Winnipeg Region")

mide-manidoo na -g any spirit involved with the Midewi·win (unattested elsewhere) (R. V.)

midé medicine man ("Some Empirical Aspects of Northern Saulteaux Religion")

midéwi·win medicine lodge ("Some Empirical Aspects of Northern Saulteaux Religion")

midewiwin ni

migazï bald eagle (Berens, Part IV)

migizi na -wag

migɑzīwīgīzis (March) Eagle Moon ("Temporal Orientation in Western Civilization and in a Preliterate Society")

migizigiizis—giizis na Bald Eagle Moon

mīgis a shell associated with the midéwi·win—their projection into a person usually causes death—these deadly shells are also used by midé men to show power and are thus sometimes part of sorcery duals ("Aggression in Saulteaux Society")

miiigis na -ag

migós awl (Berens, Part IV)

migoos na -ag

mīgwétc thank you ("Shabwan: A Dissocial Indian Girl")

miigwech pc

Miki·nǎ´k the "Boss" Turtle ("Some Empirical Aspects of Northern Saulteaux Religion")

Mikinaak na -wag   snapping turtle

mï'kitáigan   one-handed ("Notes on the Material Culture of the Island Lake Saulteaux")

mikita'igan?

nabenik   one handed, lit. hand on one side

minεsatagok   thorn bushes (Berens, Part IV)

mintímoye   old woman ("Temporal Orientation in Western Civilization and in a Preliterate Society")

mindimooye na -yag

Misábos   the Great Hare—a spiritual "owner" who is "boss" of seismic phenomena, etc. ("Some Empirical Aspects of Northern Saulteaux Religion")

Misaabooz na -oog   Jackrabbit; also Trickster was once a hare, so probably related (R. V.)

Misaziwak   Great eagles (Berens, Part IV)

Misinaméok   Great sturgeons (Berens, Part IV)

misinamewag [rather odd; expected form is misiname na -g, instead of misiname na -wag, unless AIH misheard] (R. V.)

misinigäp   portage ("Notes on the Material Culture of the Island Lake Saulteaux")

gakiiwe -vai

miskwabó   blood soup (Berens, Part IV)

miskwaaboo ni   blood soup

miskwanagáte   the point in the new day when the rising sun reddens the treetops—"red shining (reflected) light" ("Temporal Orientation in Western Civilization and in a Preliterate Society")

miskwaanagaate

miskwaanaakaate -vii   the trees shine red?

mistikwagim   A Cree word referring to a type of shoe ("Notes on the Material Culture of the Island Lake Saulteaux")
Looks like mitigwaagim which would mean 'wooden snowshoe'; not attested; mistik is the Cree word for wood/tree, cognate with Ojibwe mitig. But Pikangikumers often fiercely pre-aspirate, so it could sound like mistik. The Cree word for snowshoe is asaam-this could be a Cree partial borrowing from Ojibwe. (R. V.)

mi·yó   a body ("Some Empirical Aspects of Northern Saulteaux Religion")

miiyaw a body

miiyaw   one's body   niiyaw nid   my body

mizisak   dog fly (Berens, Part IV)

mizisaak na -wag   deer fly

mizizak   bulldog (Berens, Part IV).

Looks like same word as above, but unattested with this meaning. (R. V.)

muzwano   moose tail (Berens, Part IV)

moozwanow? ni   moosetail (spelling somewhat uncertain due to
     dialect variation)

namekwen   glue ("Notes on the Material Culture of the Island Lake
     Saulteaux")

Baraga 1853:263 has namekwan, probably namekwaan ni glue

namisómis   my paternal uncle, my step-father.

Looks like word nimishoomis nad my grandfather; the word with this
     meaning is usually nimishoomenzh nad -ag (Berens, Part IV) (R. V.)

nänītaga   dusk ("Temporal Orientation in Western Civilization and in
     a Preliterate Society")

neniitagaa?

bangishimon   dusk, sundown

näpäwan   ring and pin game ("Notes on the Material Culture of the
     Island Lake Saulteaux")

naabawaan

ndindawa   a term adopted between the respective parents of a married
     couple

nindindawaa(g)   in-laws ("Cross-Cousin Marriage in the Lake
     Winnipeg Area")

ni`bakíwin   the "owner" of the skill of sucking out disease from the
     body ("Sin, Sex, and Sickness in Saulteaux Belief")

nibikiiwin   the act of sucking out a disease (harmful agent) from a body

nībakīwininï? nibikiiwin ni   sucking cure (Baraga 1853:280)

nībakīwininï   a doctor who tries to remove an object in the body
     by sucking it out as part of his treatment ("The Ojibwa Self and its
     Behavioral Environment")

nibikiiwinini   the person who sucks out disease (harmful agent) from
     a body.

nibikiiwinini na -wag?   sucking cure doctor (Baraga 1853:280)

nibakīwin   use of sucking tubes to draw illness from the body ("The
     Ojibwa Self and its Behavioral Environment")

nibikiiwin

nībín   summer ("Temporal Orientation in Western Civilization and in
     a Preliterate Society")

niibin -vii   is summer

nïpin

nījogíjigɑn (Tuesday) two days "after" ("Temporal Orientation in Western Civilization and in a Preliterate Society")

Niizho-giizhigan -vii is Tuesday (lit., is day two)

ni`kīgīzis (April) Goose Moon ("Temporal Orientation in Western Civilization and in a Preliterate Society")

niki-giizis na Canada goose moon

nimama my mother ("Cross-Cousin Marriage in the Lake Winnipeg Area") A late, Anglicized term.

nimaamaa nad -g (in the north, in the south,-yag)

nimīcomis my grandfather ("Cross-Cousin Marriage in the Lake Winnipeg Area")

nimishoomis nad -ag my grandfather

nīnɑm cross-cousin, "sweetheart" ("Cross-Cousin Marriage in the Lake Winnipeg Area")

niinim (female) my brother-in-law

niinim nad my sister/female cousin (man speaking), brother-in-law (woman speaking) pl. niinimag stem /iinim/ dial.

nīnɑmɑk sweethearts? ("Ojibwa World View and Disease")

niinimag?

nīoníndjépī`tɑgotcing the rising sun hanging in the sky "the breadth of my hand" above the trees ("Temporal Orientation in Western Civilization and in a Preliterate Society")

niiyoninj epiitagoojing lit. it hangs four fingers

niiyoninj pc four fingers, hands; apiitagoojin vai hang from such height

nīpá sleep well (Berens, Part IV)

nipapa my father An Anglicized term. ("Cross-Cousin Marriage in the Lake Winnipeg Area")

nimbaabaa (anishinaabe southern pronunciation) (plural variable by dialect -g or -yag) (R. V.)

nīsɑgwas her hair ("Fear and Anxiety as Cultural and Individual Variables in a Primitive Society")

ninzagwaaz I am entangled

nitci brother ("Notes on the Material Culture of the Island Lake Saulteaux")

niijii nad vocative my fellow (usually male to male) (R. V.)

ningikskwezis otter-girl (Berens, Part IV)

nigigikwezis? nigig-ikwezens? (expected form is nigigokwezens) (R. V.)

no`kahïgɑnɑk pounded fish ("Notes on the Material Culture of the Island Lake Saulteaux")

nooka'iganag

nooka'igan na -ag flaked dried fish or meat

nokam my grandmother ("Some Empirical Aspects of Northern Saulteaux Religion")

nookom nad -ag my grandmother

nózis grandson ("Some Empirical Aspects of Northern Saulteaux Religion")

noozis (ag) my grandchild

noozhis nad my grandchild; pl.-ag stem /oozhis/

ockapīnondjī "fresh (new, young) child"—the infant before it can walk ("Temporal Orientation in Western Civilization and in a Preliterate Society")

oshkabinoonjii na -yag (unattested elsewhere but makes sense; cf oshkabinoonjiizhens -ag na newborn baby) (R. V.)

ockīnīge male after puberty and before marriage ("Temporal Orientation in Western Civilization and in a Preliterate Society")

oshkiniigi (na-wag) young man, youth

ockinīgi`kwe female after puberty and before marriage ("Temporal Orientation in Western Civilization and in a Preliterate Society")

oshkiniigikwe na -g young woman, youth

Odádawaämok Orion's Belt Constellation—three young men ("Temporal Orientation in Western Civilization and in a Preliterate Society")

odaadawaamoog?
A verb aadawa'am vta, signifies go with s.o. in a boat; this seems to have been made into a noun odaadawa'amoo 'one who goes in a boat with others. The plural, odaadawa'amoog, is one traditional term for the constellation comprised of the three stars of Orion's Belt. Also: odaadwaa'amoog na-pl constellation (six stars in a V-shape)stem /odaadwaa'amoo/ (R. V.)

ódena term used for a large unit of population (a town), and applied to the settlement occupied by the dead ("Spirits of the Dead in Saulteaux Life and Thought")

oodena settlement with largely the same clan members, contemporary usage 'town'

oodena ni -wan town

odjīneaúwaso illness caused by bad conduct of one's parents ("Fear and Anxiety as Cultural and Individual Variables in a Primitive Society")

onjine'aawaso illness, misfortune caused by one's parents or caregivers

onjine'aawaso -vai causes one's child to be ill with a sickness caused by her/her caregiver (R. V.)

ógimă   chief, superior person, gentleman ("Some Empirical Aspects of
    Northern Saulteaux Religion")
ogimaa   a person of wealth (having surplus of something)
ogimaa na -g
ogimaakanag   made up chiefs ("Some Empirical Aspects of Northern
    Saulteaux Religion")
ogimaakaan na -ag
okickicgtäsin   (his) leggings (Berens, Part IV)
ogishkidaasin noun, but its gender and whether dependent or not are
    uncertain (R. V.)
omαkαkï   toad, frog (Berens, Part IV)
omakakii na -g, omagakii na-g
Omaskóso bautik   Elk or Red Deer Rapids ("The Passing of the
    Midewi·win in the Lake Winnipeg Region")
Omīmīsīpī   Pigeon River (See for example "The Northern Ojibwa")
Omiimii-ziibi   Pigeon River (In some Ojibwe varieties, there is an
    'ii' and 'e' correspondence in certain positions. Contemporary
    pronunciation of Omiimiiziibi is Omemewiziibi.) (R. V.)
omiimii-ziibi   place Pigeon River (omiimii na pigeon)
onabemīmä   married man ("Temporal Orientation in Western
    Civilization and in a Preliterate Society")
onaabemimaa na -g   the husband
Onαpαkistαkwanisαnowin   Flathead Point (Berens, Appendix)
On·bówisi·bi   Dead River
onótcïkinèbikwesï   snake hunting bird (Berens, Appendix)
opa`piwatcαgenazis   (December) Early Winter Moon [Berens
    River]? ("Temporal Orientation in Western Civilization and in a
    Preliterate Society")
òtcatcákwin   a soul ("Some Empirical Aspects of Northern Saulteaux
    Religion")
εojajaakowin
ojachaakwan   his/her soul (perhaps a variant) achaak na -wag soul
Otcībamasīs   Northern Barred Owl (Berens, Part IV)
otci·tcák   crane (Berens, Part IV)
Ozági·zi·ì·we   "the one that takes them out"—a euphemism for
    kadαbéndαng ("Some Empirical Aspects of Northern Saulteaux
    Religion")
Ozaagizi'iwe lit. the one who takes others out, fig. the one who pulls you
    out of something, e.g. a dilemma.
o-zhush-koo-koon   the muskrat's liver ("The Passing of the
    Midewi·win in the Lake Winnipeg Region")

ozhashkookon

wazhashkookon (proper)

wazhashkokon?

pagitcigan sacrificing ("The Ojibwa Self and its Behavioral Environment")

bagijigan? ni -an a sacrifice, offering (R. V.)

pɑkwatcigɑn two-headed scraper ("Notes on the Material Culture of the Island Lake Saulteaux")

pakwéjigɑngījigan (Saturday) "flour (bread) day" ("Temporal Orientation in Western Civilization and in a Preliterate Society")

Bakwezhigan Giizhigan Saturday (northern Ojibwe term) (R. R.) [Friday in Oji-Cree]

pangi a little ("Psychic Stresses and Culture Patterns") In English, Bungi-an alternate term for Ojibwe.

pɑngīcimɑn gīzis (sunset)—"falling (out of sight) the sun" ("Temporal Orientation in Western Civilization and in a Preliterate Society")

bangishimon giizis expr. the sun sets—sundown (the addition of 'giizis' is redundant (R. V.)

pasi kwébi zon kaká`kotci sweyan wearing a woodchuck skin around one's head ("The Passing of the Midewi·win in the Lake Winnipeg Region")

basikwepizon gakakojiishwayaan this is two nouns put together in a somewhat odd way: basikwepizon ni headband (R. V.)

gakakojiishiwayaan? na woodchuck skin

Paskandɑbéwi·si·bi Broken Head River—raw head (scalped?) river (R. V.) ("The Passing of the Midewi·win in the Lake Winnipeg Region")

Baaskaandibewiziibi, place (contemporary name for Brokenhead, Manitoba)

baaskaandibe broken head

päskwátcïgɑn two-handed ("Notes on the Material Culture of the Island Lake Saulteaux")

bashkwaazhigan scraper (scrape fur off)

bashkwaajigan?

pɑskwégɑn partition (Berens, Part IV)

pawáganak guardian spirits—dream visitors—a synonym for "our grandfathers" ("Fear and Anxiety as Cultural and Individual Variables in a Primitive Society") bawaagan na -ag this may refer to guardian spirits; however, it also refers to anything that is dreamed

Pebi·gwéwanaskosi`bi Hollow Grass River ("The Passing of the Midewi·win in the Lake Winnipeg Region")

pejīgonik one arm-stretch—a fathom ("Some Psychological Aspects of Measurement among the Saulteaux")

bezhigoonik

bezhigonik pc (only in Baraga 1853:292, so length of /o/ uncertain) (R. V.)

pejiwákwagan one finger stretch ("Some Psychological Aspects of Measurement among the Saulteaux")

bezhigwaakwagan? Baraga 1853:292 has Ningotwakwoagan 'a span'

pékīze pure ("Psychosexual Adjustment, Personality and the Good Life in a Non-literate Culture")

bekizi -vai is clean, pure

pezagógījik term meaning "one day" ("Temporal Orientation in Western Civilization and in a Preliterate Society")

bezhigo-giizhig? pc

pezagwátabik term meaning "one night" ("Temporal Orientation in Western Civilization and in a Preliterate Society")

bezhigo-dibik? pc

pezagwákwagan èpīápi`tagotcing refers to the sun hanging in the sky "a thumb -middle -finger stretch" above the tree tops (See for example "Temporal Orientation in Western Civilization and in a Preliterate Society")

bezhigwaakwagan apii apiitagoojing

bezhigwaakwagan? e-bi-apiitagoojing exp 'it (anim.) comes to hang at the height of one measure'

e-prev complementizer; bi-prev come to, hither; apiitagoojin vai hang at such height

pezígoa`ki one year—"one earth" ("Temporal Orientation in Western Civilization and in a Preliterate Society")

bezhigo-aki or bezhigwaki pc? one year, lit., one earth

pezīgonik one arm-stretch (fathom) ("Some Psychological Aspects of Measurement among the Saulteaux")

bezhigonik?

pīgi`kánaan time between the loss of leaves and the start of winter ("Temporal Orientation in Western Civilization and in a Preliterate Society")

pījíu lynx (Berens, Part IV)

piˋkogàn tent (Berens)

bikogaan ni -an traditional shelter, traditional tipi

pīmädazīwin life in the fullest sense ("Fear and Anxiety as Cultural and Individual Variables in a Primitive Society")

bimaadiziwin ni life

pimitctígweasi·bi obliquely running river ("The Passing of the Midewi·win in the Lake Winnipeg Region")

pindabawádjïgan enema syringe ("Notes on the Material Culture of the Island Lake Saulteaux")

biindaabaawajigan

biindaabaawajigan ni enema. pl.-an

pinewītis kágotik and so the gizzard of the ruffed grouse now hangs aloft (Berens, Part IV)

binewidis ge-agoodeg expr. (common in various forms at the end of stories in the William Jones compilation, seemingly archaic now); binewidis as 'ruffed grouse gizzard' is not found elsewhere. ge-prev changed form of ga-future tense; agoode vii hang (R. V.)

pinèsï Thunder Bird—a spiritual "owner" who controls thunder and lightning—also the owner of the potáte dance ("Some Empirical Aspects of Northern Saulteaux Religion")

binesi na -wag

Pinèsïwàbikusagahïgan Thunder Bird Lake (Berens, Appendix)

Pinèsïwakotakïwaspīming Thunder Bird Land (Berens, Part IV)

binesiwag odakiiwaa ishpiming, lit. "thunder birds, their land, above, in the heavens," with thanks to John Nichols

binesiwag odakiiwaang in the Thunderbird's land; aki ni land

pïpïkïwasɛs American sparrow hawk (Berens, Part IV)

biipiigiwizens na -ag

pītában dawn ("Temporal Orientation in Western Civilization and in a Preliterate Society")

biidaaban -vii dawn

pitcībabunwīgīzis (December) Early Winter Moon [Grand Rapids] ("Temporal Orientation in Western Civilization and in a Preliterate Society")

biijibibooniwi-giizis na

pitawákamik the world that lies just below Earth

piwának flint (Berens, Part IV)

biiwaanag na -oog

pónïaiyàmayegíjigan (Monday) "cease praying day" ("Temporal Orientation in Western Civilization and in a Preliterate Society")

Booni-anami'eayama'e-giizhigan vii   is the cease-praying day; this
form seems to use the Cree word for pray, since Ojibwe word is
anama'aa (R. V.)

poni`animīgījigan   the point after the sunset when a band of light still
rims the horizon after the sun itself has disappeared—"disappearing
underneath day" ("Temporal Orientation in Western Civilization
and in a Preliterate Society")

booni-animigiizhigan?

potáte   a dance held after dark ("Temporal Orientation in Western
Civilization and in a Preliterate Society")

boodaade   something is blown (A reference to the gift or breath of
life.)[1] (R. R.)

sägatagan   tinder (Berens, Appendix)

zagataagan

sagi   the mouth of a river, or where a river opens into a lake ("The
Passing of the Midewi·win in the Lake Winnipeg Region")

zaagii expect: zaagiing (loc.) pc at, from, to the opening of the river (R. V.)

sagībagauwīgīzis   Leaves-coming-forth moon (June moon)
("Temporal Orientation in Western Civilization and in a Preliterate
Society")

Sagi·wi·si·bi   Winnipeg River ("The Passing of the Midewi·win in the
Lake Winnipeg Region")

Zaagiiwi-ziibi

sakīgīzik   standing up and reaching the sky ("The Passing of the
Midewi·win in the Lake Winnipeg Region")

Zaagi-giizhig?

skabéwis   usher or servant (Berens, Appendix)

oshkaabewisag   was the term at Pauingassi, Manitoba, for the religious
apprentices who helped Fair Wind (Naamiwan) with his ceremonies.
(R. R.)[2]

sósïman   snow snake game (Berens, Part II)

zoosiman

zoosoman

sóskŭtciwanak   swift currents English derivative: Saskatchewan

zhooshkojiwan? -vii   the current slides? (R. V.)

tabätcamoin   news or tidings ("Some Empirical Aspects of Northern
Saulteaux Religion")

dibaajimowin ni—an   news, narrative, as opposed to aadksookaan

tawanange   thunderbird skins (Berens, Part IV)

tcagatecizg   shadow (Berens, Part IV)

jaagaateshin?

tcangakwïwagim   man's shoe ("Notes on the Material Culture of the Island Lake Saulteaux")

jaangaakwiwaagim   shoes where toes are turned up? (R. V.)

tcïbwaságàtik   the moment before the sun has risen above the tree tops ("Temporal Orientation in Western Civilization and in a Preliterate Society")

jibwaa zaagaateg expr. jibwaa prev before; zaagaate vii the sun shines—lit. before the sun shines

te`te`pictigwan   rolling head (Berens, Part IV)

ditibishtigwaan? ni   rolling head

tikïnágan   cradle board ("Notes on the Material Culture of the Island Lake Saulteaux")

dikinaagan ni -an

wabagwanïwïgïzis   (July) Blossom Moon [Little Grand Rapids] ("Temporal Orientation in Western Civilization and in a Preliterate Society")

waabigwani-giizis na

Wábamiko baùtik   White Beaver Rapids ("Some Empirical Aspects of Northern Saulteaux Religion")

Waabamikoo-baawitig ni

wábano   medicine lodge. The Waabano ceremony usually lasted all night until dawn; *waabano* refers to dawn or "what is represented by the east."[3] ("Fear and Anxiety as Cultural and Individual Variables in a Primitive Society")

   waabano what is represented by the east (dawn) (R. R.) Also the name of a ceremony that Hallowell saw at Little Grand Rapids and Pauingassi.

wábano mă'ni·tu   a spiritual "owner" associated with the wabanówïwin [wabano dance] ("Some Empirical Aspects of Northern Saulteaux Religion")

Waabanoo-manidoo   spirits—spirit involved with the waabanowin

Waabanoo-manidoo na -g

wábanänang   the morning star ("Temporal Orientation in Western Civilization and in a Preliterate Society")

Waabanang

waaban-anang na   morning star, lit. dawn star

wabanasi   east wind (Berens, Part IV)

wabanówïwin   a dance where individuals are sometimes given therapeutic attention—it is held only once a year and lasts several days ("The Passing of the Midewi·win in the Lake Winnipeg Region")

waabanoowiwin ni?

wabatcïtcak white crane—whooping crane (Berens, Part IV)

waabajijaak? na -wag

wabïzi swan (Berens, Appendix)

waabizii

wágīnogan a dome-shaped house

waaginogaan ni -an wigwam, any dome-shaped lodge

wagï 'kuman crooked knife ("Notes on the Material Culture of the Island Lake Saulteaux")

waagikomaan ni -an

walacip crow-duck, cormorant

wanakwaian otter skin sleeves (Berens, Part IV)

wanagwayaan?

onagwayaan seems a combination of onagway 'sleeve' and wayaan 'hide' No mention of otter (nigig); onagwayaan na sleeve of hide? (R. V.)

wanáman a reddish substance usually found on "dead" water, ocherous in origin (Berens, Part IV)

wanaman na red ochre

Wanapi·gáuwi·si·bi Hollow Water River ("The Passing of the Midewi·win in the Lake Winnipeg Region")

Waanibiigaawi-ziibi place

Wapăng Narrows ("The Passing of the Midewi·win in the Lake Winnipeg Region")

waabang tomorrow

wasi medicine woman

Wasigamak Waasagomach Bay ("Notes on the Material Culture of the Island Lake Saulteaux")

Waasaagamaag

Waasaagamaag? -vii conjunct (when) the waves froth white on the lake

watap spruce roots ("Notes on the Material Culture of the Island Lake Saulteaux")

wadab ni -iin spruce root

wawásan lightning

waasamowin

wázisan a nest built for a dream quest ("The Role of Dreams in Ojibwa Culture") waziswan   nest, dream quest nest

wazason ni a   nest

wemti·gózi   a mythological character translated into English as "white man," although this is not the etymology of the word ("Some Empirical Aspects of Northern Saulteaux Religion")

wemitigoozhi na -wag   white man; perhaps earlier, Frenchman. Related to the James Bay Cree, wemsti—person with a wooden boat, applied to the English who came by ship.

wewsähïgan   a birchbark fan to keep oneself free of mosquitoes ("Notes on the Material Culture of the Island Lake Saulteaux")

wewese`igan (ag)

wïgóbe`äp   willow ("Notes on the Material Culture of the Island Lake Saulteaux")

wiigobeyaab   willow twine

wïkwemút`   a fairly large storage box ("Notes on the Material Culture of the Island Lake Saulteaux")

wiikwemod

wiikwemod? ni -an   storage box? from /wiikwe/ encircling + mod ending for bag? (R. V.)

wíndïgo   cannibal giant ("Some Psychological Aspects of Measurement among the Saulteaux")

wiindigoo na -g

Wísakedják   a mythical culture hero ("Notes on the Material Culture of the Island Lake Saulteaux")

Wiisakejaak—Southern Ojibwe variations are Nenabozho or Waynabooz-ho na name (R. V.)

wïwïmän   married woman ("Temporal Orientation in Western Civilization and in a Preliterate Society")

wiiwiman wife

GLOSSARY OF OJIBWE PERSONAL NAMES USED BY HALLOWELL

Traditional Anishinaabe names are neither literal nor conventional in that the names may be a part of a larger phrase or they may be shortened versions of complex words. Because some personal names seem to derive from other-than-human sources, it is sometimes difficult to verbalize them and they were rarely used in ordinary speech. They were ceremonially conferred on a child by an elder who stood in a grandfather role and had received the name in a dream.

Abïtanɑkwɛp (One Sitting On Cloud From End To End Of The Sky) (Berens, Appendix)

Ăgásgogat (Arrow Legs) was the last headman at Garden Island in northern Lake Manitoba where he held the midéwi·win. He died before the treaty was signed. Years before, as a middle-aged man, he had said, "As long as I can lift my drum stick I shall not die." He revealed the fact that he had been told this by Wísɑkedják who was one of his strongest guardian spirits. Like Wísɑkedják, Ăgásgogat always wore a woodchuck skin (aká 'kotci·s) bound around his head, likely a command of this spiritual helper. People testified that they had seen Ăgásgogat walk on the water. One day, when he could be clearly seen approaching the shore, his son stole down to the point where he believed his father would reach the land. On detecting the young man, however, Ăgásgogat immediately began to sink into the water, just managing to reach dry land. He upbraided his son for his rash curiosity—the other observers had remained at a respectful distance. In addition to being a great midé, Ăgásgogat obtained medical knowledge through a dream blessing to become a mänáo (a doctor who dispenses medicine from the memengwécīwak). ("The Passing of the Midewi·win in the Lake Winnipeg Region")

Aiïtabï'tazk (The One That Sits Firmly) (Berens, Appendix)

Amo (Bee) (English name listed in her burial record of 1890: Victoria) was an Ojibwe woman from the Pelican clan. Amo was from the Cumberland House (Saskatchewan) area and was William Berens's paternal grandmother. (Berens, Introduction)

Asagesi met Hallowell at Little Duck (Barton) Lake, which connects with the upper Berens River near Poplar Hill. It must have been on that occasion that they had the conversation about religious matters and the Waabano, which Hallowell recorded in his research notes on Saulteaux religion. Asagesi told him of k'tci anang [gichi anang] or a great star, implied to be a source of his powers: "When Asagesi dreamed of his wabanowigamik there was a brilliant star above the tent which flooded it with light. This is why the young people who dance in the wabano can conceal nothing from him. Everything is (to him) always flooded with light." He also told Hallowell that k'tci anang was "seen only in dreams" and "was 'beyond' the 'real' stars and much brighter than any of them." The celestial symbolism of the great star, of the pole reaching to the sky, and of the Thunder Bird made for a powerful combination.[4] (Berens, Appendix)

Äsini·bon with his brother, **Djakógwaiyo (Short Neck)** was the last leader of the midéwi·win at St. Peters reserve near Selkirk, Manitoba. He was the father of Sagatcí·weäs. ("The Passing of the Midewi·win in the Lake Winnipeg Region")

Cääbakamägok (Going Right Through From One End Of The World To The Other) a name (that carries a blessing) sometimes given to girls. See also: **Nèwadànakwap** below. ("Ojibwa World View and Disease") Zhayaabakamigook (we) na name

Caúwanäs See **Zhaawanaash** below.

Cɛnawágwaskang Shenawakoshkank (making a rattling noise by stepping on a twig) was the father of the medicine man **Naamiwaan** (Fair Wind). When he was collecting data on men with multiple wives, Hallowell recorded a single instance of a man having six wives—this was Cɛnawágwaskang, who appeared in the 1876 treaty records with four wives, two of his spouses having already died. Cɛnawágwaskang was also known as Kihchi Omoosoni (Great Moose) and, like Jacob and William Berens, was a member of the Moose clan. ("The Incidence, Character and Decline of Polygyny among the Lake Winnipeg Cree and Saulteaux")

Djakógwaiyo (Short Neck) See **Sagatcí·weäs** below.

Eguidänakwïäs (Counting The Clouds While Sailing) (Berens, Appendix)

Kagi·wébit (One Who Turns) succeeded **Nódage** at Drumming Point (Black Island). Since his English name was Black, Hallowell conjectured that the contemporary name of the island where the midéwi·win was held was derived from his connection with it. By this time the Saulteaux of the adjoining mainland were organized into the Hollow Water River (Wanɑpi·gáuwi·si·bi) Band which was given a reserve (I.R. 10) at the mouth of the river. Kagi·wébit was of the Moose clan. He died about 1919 at the age of about ninety years. His successor was Wábanänang (see below). ("The Passing of the Midewi·win in the Lake Winnipeg Region")

Kapīmoiweäs (You Can Hear The Sound When He Passes) (Berens, Appendix)

Katebweyasïk (Something Sounding in the Sky) (Berens, Appendix)

Kekekós (Little Duck Hawk) was coached by a djí·bai (dead person's soul) to win an important moccasin game. ("Spirits of the Dead in Saulteaux Life and Thought")

Kepeäs (Going Straight Through The Air) was a member of the Pelican clan and one of the first men to settle at Poplar River. He arrived from the western side of Lake Winnipeg, seemingly from the predominantly Cree area of Cumberland House. Kepeäs's daughter was Amo. ("Ojibwa World View and Disease")

Kepekïzïkweäs (Sailing Through The Sky From End To End Forever) (Berens, Appendix)

Ketagas was the son of Kīwítc. He told Hallowell of being cured of illness by **Miki·nä'k**. ("Rocks and Stones")

Kiwetin (North) was a midéwi·win leader who possessed a great understanding of magic of various kinds. ("Aggression in Saulteaux Society")

Kīwítc (English name Alec Keeper) was a son of **Pazagwí·gabo** (see below). Kīwítc was once visited by a djí·bai (dead person's soul) who appeared to him in the form of a bird when his granddaughter died. He created a Drum Dance in which the djībaiyak (souls of the dead) played the key role. The drum used in the ceremony was called kīmícómisanän, meaning "our grandfather." Kīwítc was over seventy years old in 1932 when Hallowell met him at Little Grand Rapids. He shared several myths with Hallowell and offered a wealth of information. In his field notes, Hallowell wrote that Kīwítc, a member of the Sturgeon sib, was "a sweet tempered old man—liked and respected by everyone—partly blind." ("Spirits of the Dead in Saulteaux Life and Thought")

Machkajence (English name John Duck) was a powerful mide at Little Grand Rapids who conducted wábano and shaking tent ceremonies. He practiced his ceremonies until he gave his big drum to United Church missionary Luther Schuetze in 1938. He may have suffered from mental illness; on August 22, 1936, William Berens told Hallowell in a letter that Machkajence was "very sick" and that there was talk of sending him to "the hospital or to the asylum." Berens was clear that, although some feared him, he did not think he was crazy: "I don't think that the poor man was looked after right," he wrote.[5] ("Fear and Anxiety as Cultural and Individual Variables in a Primitive Society")

Makatcí·wewe (Black [lesser] Snow Goose) once participated in a miracle performed by **Sagatcí·weäs**. ("The Passing of the Midewi·win in the Lake Winnipeg Region")

Makwa (Bear, known as Makwa in Ojibwe and Maskwa in Cree) was Yellow Legs's eldest son, born in about 1790. Bear was William Berens's paternal grandfather. He married **Amo**. Together with Bear's younger brother, **Cauwanäs** (Zhaawanaash), they later moved to the east side of Lake Winnipeg, Bear bringing with him his father's magical stone. Sometime around 1870 he and **Zhaawanaash** conducted the last midéwi·win ceremonies recorded at the mouth of the Berens River. He died at Berens River circa 1873-74 without converting to Christianity, although he adopted the Christian surname Berens. (Berens, Introduction)

Manzi·napkinegéwinini (The Man Who Is Painting The Rock) was one of three sons of **Wawásan**. He and his brothers assisted their father with Mide ceremonies at Jack Head, Manitoba. ("The Passing of the Midewi·win in the Lake Winnipeg Region")

McKaye [McKay], Mary (1836-1908) was the granddaughter of Donald McKay, a Scottish fur trader employed by the Hudson's Bay Company. Her father was William McKay, the Hudson's Bay Company trader at Trout Lake in Ontario's Severn River drainage. Her mother was Julia Chalifoux of Cree and French Canadian descent. The Berens River Ojibwe classification of Mary Berens as white was influenced by her fair complexion and cultural attributes. (The term Mètis did not exist among Berens River Ojibwe at this time.) She married Jacob Berens around the time of his conversion. She was **William Berens**'s paternal grandmother. (Berens, Introduction)

Mekis (The Eagle), or Giroux (migazï-bald eagle), was a leader who represented a small band of Riding Mountain Ojibwe in Treaty 2 (1871) ("The Passing of the Midewi·win in the Lake Winnipeg Region")

Mekwégi·zik (Amidst The Sky) was the last leader to perform the midéwi·win on the Fishing Lake Reserve, Saskatchewan. Mekwégi·zik died about 1919. ("The Passing of the Midewi·win in the Lake Winnipeg Region")

Miki·nă´k The "Boss" Turtle ("Some Empirical Aspects of Northern Saulteaux Religion")

Misábos The Great Hare was a spiritual "owner" who is "boss" of seismic phenomena, etc. ("Some Empirical Aspects of Northern Saulteaux Religion")

Miskógi·ni·u (Red Eagle) (English name: Henry Prince) was the son of **Peguis** and one of the signers of Treaty No. 1 or the "Stone Fort" Treaty in 1871(at Lower Fort Garry. These Ojibwe people (along with with some Cree) of lower Red River were known as the St. Peters band. Their reserve, seven miles square, adjoining the town of Selkirk, was terminated in 1907, and a new, less favourable location was assigned to them on the Fisher River, west of Lake Winnipeg. Miskógi·ni·u was married to a daughter of English-born Frederick Disbrowe, Hudson's Bay Company post manager at Berens River, for many years. ("The Passing of the Midewi·win in the Lake Winnipeg Region")

Miskwádesīwískïjik (Mud-Turtle's Eye) was resurrected from his grave by his wife and went on to play lacrosse with the spirits of the dead. ("Spirits of the Dead in Saulteaux Life and Thought")

Mistamut was the wife of Uzaúaskogat (Yellow Legs) and great-grand-mother of William Berens.

Mízakï (The Thing That Comes From Above) a name (that carries a blessing) sometimes given to boys ("Ojibwa World View and Disease")

mizhakii—verb, to make contact with the ground?

Mizäkïäsïk (Hits Ground When Flying) (Berens, Appendix)

Munias, Richard was a bilingual member of the Sturgeon clan and Hallowell's main informant at Island Lake. ("Notes on the Material Culture of the Island Lake Saulteaux")

Nagagábek (Flatstone) was a leader of a midéwi·win lodge at Little Grand Rapids, Nagagábek was assisted by Pi'kwákwasti·gan (Bluffhead, the half-brother of Tetabaiyábin). The midéwigamik was built on a little rise of ground near the place where Machkajence (John Duck) later built. Nagagábek once killed a wíndīgo. Bluffhead was the half-brother of Tetabaiyábin. ("The Passing of the Midewi·win in the Lake Winnipeg Region")

Nämawin (Fair Wind) was a greatly respected and feared healer and leader who carried out an important drum dance and the wabanówīwin. The drum dance came from a dream revelation that was given to Nämawin. ("Spirits of the Dead in Saulteaux Life and Thought")

Naamiwan

Nanákaweweyäs (Making Different Sounds While Flying) (Berens, Appendix)

Nauwigizigweas (Aloft In The Centre Of The Sky) (English name: Jacob Berens) (Naawigiizhigweyaash-translation from Roger Roulette) was born in about 1832 and was the father of William Berens. He married Mary McKaye [McKay], whose father, William, was a Hudson's Bay Company trader at Trout Lake in the Severn River drainage. In 1861, during a visit to the Methodist mission at Norway House at the north end of Lake Winnipeg, he was baptized by the Reverend George McDougall, becoming the first Berens River Ojibwe to convert to Christianity. Berens died in 1916. (Berens)

Nawekïzïkwɛp (Sitting In The Center Of The Sky) (Berens, Appendix)

Nénagi·s (Quivering) was a Long Plains Saulteaux who may have been the best known midé south of Lake Winnipeg in 1913. ("The Passing of the Midewi·win in the Lake Winnipeg Region")

Nèwadànakwap (Between the Clouds) a name (that carries a blessing) sometimes given to boys. See also **Cäàbakamägok.** above.

naawadaanakwab lit. to sit in the midst of the clouds

naawadaanakwan? in the middle of the clouds (R. V.) ("Ojibwa World View and Disease")

Nïbïtceasïk (Passes Everything Between Earth and Sky) (Berens, Appendix)

Ni·jotés (Little Twin) (also known as Two Hearts) was the headman when the last midéwi·win in the Fort Alexander area was held in the late 1800s. ("The Passing of the Midewi·win in the Lake Winnipeg Region")

Nïskatwewïtang (When He Calls It Rains) (Naaskaatwewitank) was a Long Plains Saulteaux who brought the potáte dance [boodaade] to Pigeon River around the turn of the twentieth century. (Berens, Appendix)

Nódage (Old Woman [Cree]) took over leadership of the midéwi·win at Drumming Point (Black Island) after **Sekanakwégabau** died. Nódage was a mänáo (a doctor who dispenses medicine from the memengwécïwak). Although he lived at the time Treaty No. 5 was made, Nódage refused to have any dealings with the government, even relinquishing his annuity payments. ("The Passing of the Midewi·win in the Lake Winnipeg Region")

Otcïbamasïs (Northern Barred Owl) was a powerful midé who once brought a girl's soul back from djïbaiàking (the land of the dead). Only a very powerful person would attempt such a thing. ("Spirits of the Dead in Saulteaux Life and Thought")

Otci·tcák (Crane). See **Tetabaiyábin** below.

Pawanagwebïk (Somebody You Can See Behind A Cloud) (Berens, Appendix)

Pazagwí·gabau was a famous headman of the midéwi·win at Poplar Narrows (Poplar Hill). His son, Ki·wí·tc (Alec Keeper) related numerous myths and tales to Hallowell between 1932 and 1936 (see above). Pazagwí·gabau was also the father of **Tetabaiyábin.** His chief assistant was **Pindä'ndakwan,** a "son-in-law who conducted the ceremony at Pikangikum after the death of Pazagwí·gabau." In his essay, "Rocks and Stones" (Chapter 3) Hallowell discussed a boulder located near the western end of one of the portages between Poplar Narrows and Pikangikum. Gimishoomisaabikonaan (our grandfather's rock) it was revealed in a dream to Pazagwí·gabau, who placed it there. In Hallowell's time, passers-by often left sacrifices of tobacco and other objects.

Pazagwí·gabau had two wives, from different families and different sibs. ("The Passing of the Midewi·win in the Lake Winnipeg Region.")

Pegwis (Peguis) In 1817 Peguis signed a treaty with Lord Selkirk ceding lands along the Red and Assiniboine rivers for settlement. In association with the Reverend William Cockran he helped to establish the first Anglican mission at St. Peter's, Dynevor. He died in 1864. ("The Passing of the Midewi·win in the Lake Winnipeg Region.")

Pɛmagïzïkwewatazk (The One That Calls in the Sky) (Berens, Appendix)

Pi'kotcīs (Sand-Fly) was a member of the Poplar River Band who caused a sensation because he had once eaten human flesh. **Zhaawanaash** encountered him while traveling on the road of the dead. ("Spirits of the Dead in Saulteaux Life and Thought")

Pīkwákīgan (Lump Breast), one of the dancers in **Naamiwan**'s drum ceremony ("Spirits of the Dead in Saulteaux Life and Thought")

Pi'kwákwasti·gan (Bluffhead). See **Nagagábek** above.

Pïmänakwɛp (The One That Sits On The Long Narrow Cloud) (Berens, Appendix)

Pindă'ndakwan (Stuffing Something With Brush) was a powerful Mide leader and son-in-law of **Pazagwí·gabau** (above). ("The Passing of the Midewi·win in the Lake Winnipeg Region.")

Pinesïwas (Thunder Bird Woman) (Berens, Appendix)

Sagaskī (Hiding By Bending Down) obtained great magical power from other-than-human persons. In a dream the "master of the Beavers" commanded him to mate with his sister, as the beavers do. Sagaaski's sister-wife predeceased him as did all his children but one daughter by this marriage. She never married and neither did two daughters by a second marriage. Sagaaski trained his daughters to do many of the tasks men usually perform and guarded them much more closely than Ojibwe fathers ordinarily do, keeping all young men at bay. Sagaskī was the associate of **Tetabaiyábin** in the conduct of the midéwi·win. ("Ojibwa World View and Disease")

Sagatcí·weäs (One Who Comes Up Over The Mountain) (English name Peter Stoney) was the son of **Äsini·bon**. He became chief of the "Island bands" in Lake Winnipeg in 1875 and a leader of the midéwi·win at Dog Head. Sagatcí·weäs competed unsuccessfully with Jacob Berens for the position of first elected chief of Berens River in 1875. He was assisted in the midéwi·win by two other leading men, **Wasbosékwan**, and **Wagi·békwan**. ("The Passing of the Midewi·win in the Lake Winnipeg Region")

Sekanɑkwégabau (The One Who Reaches The Sky When He Stands Up) was likely born early in the nineteenth century since he had a son who was about the same age as **Jacob Berens**. Sekanɑkwégabau was the earliest leader of the midéwi·win at Drumming Point (Black Island) on whom Hallowell had information. Berens, who sometimes visited Sekanɑkwégabau often commented on the three-year-old pet bear which Sekanɑkwégabau kept tied up in his wigwam. It was believed that he controlled the bear by his magic power. ("The Passing of the Midewi·win in the Lake Winnipeg Region")

Sekanɑkwébines (Touching The Clouds Above While Standing Straight Up) (Berens, Appendix)

Shabwan was a young girl at Little Grand Rapids. Hallowell was asked to help in treating her apparent mental distress, and was thanked for his help. ("Shabwan: A Dissocial Indian Girl")

Souwanas. See Caúwanäs, Zhaawanaash

Tabasigizikweas (Sailing Low In The Air After Thunder) (English name: William Berens) (dabasi-giizhigweyaash? (missing final/i/)-drifts low in the sky) was the son of **Jacob Berens** and **Mary McKay**. Born in 1866, Berens served as chief of the Berens River band from 1917 until his death in 1947. Berens was the chief collaborator and friend of Hallowell. (Berens)

Täpästä'nɑm became the first treaty chief of the Cross Lake band under Treaty 5 in 1875. Täpästä`nɑm was a gifted medicine man who was recognized as leader because of his powers. Unlike numerous others in that position, he had only one wife. ("The Incidence, Character and Decline of Polygyny among the Lake Winnipeg Cree and Saulteaux")

Tcɑkábεc was a tiny magical man who possessed great powers and about whom there are many important myths in Ojibwe and Cree cultures. Tcɑkábεc lived with his wise older sister after their parents were murdered. He got into many scrapes because he failed to heed his sister's advice— once, for example, she had to rescue him from the belly of a great fish. In some versions, because of his tendency to disobey her instructions, he winds up living permanently on the moon. ("Temporal Orientation in Western Civilization and in a Preliterate Society")

Tetɑbaiyábin (Daylight All Around The Sky) was an influential midé. Tetɑbaiyábin and his famous father, **Pazɑgwí·gabau**, practiced east of Little Grand Rapids at Poplar Narrows (Poplar Hill). Hallowell attributed the weaker standing of the Little Grand Rapids midéwi·win to the dominance of this leader. His son, **Otci·tcák**, shared information about his father with Hallowell. Tetɑbaiyábin died around 1924. ("The Passing of the Midewi·win in the Lake Winnipeg Region")

Tetcakawäs (The One That Sails Straight From Point To Point) (Berens, Appendix)

Tcɑsämän (Brimmed Hat) was involved in a raid on a fur trade outpost in the 1830s. He was taken into custody, but escaped on the way to York Factory, and made his way back to the Berens River through unfamiliar country, with no gun or knife—a sign that he must have had spiritual helpers. ("The Size of Algonkian Hunting Territories. A Function of Ecological Adjustment")

Uzaúaskogat (Yellow Legs) (Ozaawashkogaad—translation from Roger Roulette) was the paternal grandfather of William Berens and the husband of Mistamut. He lived on the west side of Lake Winnipeg in the 1790s and was likely one of the first Ojibwe to move into the Lake Winnipeg area between the 1780s and 1790s when Montreal-based fur traders were expending their territory westward. Uzaúaskogat led the midéwi·win on the east side of the lake near the mouth of Pigeon River near Berens River, and at Jack Head on the western side. He was the headman at Jack Head early in the nineteenth century and later lived at Berens River, where, Hallowell said, "his descendants are numerous and constitute the contemporary members of the Moose sib at the mouth of the river." Yellow Legs was a famous mide, and an important link between midéwi·win practitioners on the eastern and western sides of Lake Winnipeg. A great-grandson of Yellow Legs told Hallowell that on one occasion, when Yellow Legs was on his way to find medicine, he walked on the water. Uzaúaskogat died before 1830. ("The Passing of the Midewi·win in the Lake Winnipeg Region")

Wabɑdjesi was a powerful shaman from Deer Lake. ("Aggression in Saulteaux Society")

Wábanänɑng (Morning Star) took over the leadership of the midéwi·win at Black Island after the death of **Kagi·wébit** in 1919, conducting the ceremonies until at least 1925. Hallowell's information indicated that he was the the last surviving leader of the midéwi·win in the region east of Lake Winnipeg. Wábanänɑng died in 1932 at the Hollow Water reserve. ("The Passing of the Midewi·win in the Lake Winnipeg Region")

Wagi·békwɑn (Crooked Back) was one of **Sagɑtcí·weäs**'s assistants in the midéwi·win. He had three wives. His first two wives were sisters and, when one fell ill, his parents-in-law promised Wagi·békwɑn another of their daughters if he was successful in curing the one who was ill. He cured his sick wife and married the third sister. ("The Passing of the Midewi·win in the Lake Winnipeg Region.")

Wasbosékwan (Rabbit Robe). See **Sagatcí·weäs.**

Waskeändjabis (Bald Head) (Berens, Appendix)

Wawásan (Lightning) assumed the leadership of the midéwi·win at Jack Head after having passed through various degrees under **Yellow Legs.** He was assisted by his sons, one being **Manzi·napkinegéwinini.** ("The Passing of the Midewi·win in the Lake Winnipeg Region")

Waasamowin lightning

Wigwaswátik (Birchstick) was an important chief of the Pikangikum band. To illustrate the point that bears always understand what a human says to them, Wigwaswátik told Hallowell about an encounter he had with a bear. ("Some Empirical Aspects of Northern Saulteaux Religion")

Wísakedják was a mythical culture hero featured in many stories. (Berens, Part IV)

Zhaawanaash (The One Who Soars Or Is Blown On The South Wind) (referred to by Hallowell as Caúwanäs, sometimes also referred to as Souwanas)was a son of **Yellow Legs.** Zhaawanaash and his brother, Bear (Makwa) became leaders of the midéwi·win after their father's death. He later converted to Methodism. ("The Passing of the Midewi·win in the Lake Winnipeg Region")

Notes

1. Jennifer S. H. Brown and Elizabeth Vibert eds., *Reading beyond Words: Contexts for Native History* (Peterborough: Broadview Press, 2003), 265n5.

2. Brown and Vibert 2003, 269, caption.

3. Matthews and Roulette ("Fair Wind's Dream," 330) note that Ojibwe people held it "in the spring and summer to celebrate rebirth and revitalization or healing." See Brown and Vibert (2003).

4. Series V, Research, Saulteaux Indians, Religion.

5. See Susan Elaine Gray, *"I Will Fear No Evil": Ojibwa-Missionary Encounters Along the Berens River, 1875–1940* (Calgary: University of Calgary Press, 2006), 111–12. See also Alfred Irving Hallowell Papers, 1892–1981, Ms.Coll. 26, box 14, Letters to A. I. Hallowell by William Berens, July 11, 1935; August 22, 1936; July 10, 1941; July 31, 1945; January 3, 1947.

SOURCE ACKNOWLEDGMENTS

PROLOGUE

"On Being an Anthropologist" was first published in Solon T. Kimball and James B. Watson, eds., *Crossing Cultural Boundaries* (New York: Chandler, 1972), 51–62, and is here reprinted from Hallowell, *Contributions to Anthropology* (Chicago: University of Chicago Press, 1976), 3–14.

1. THE NORTHERN OJIBWA

A. Irving Hallowell, "The Northern Ojibwa," in *Culture and Experience* (Philadelphia: University of Pennsylvania Press, 1955), 112–24. Reprinted with the permission of the University of Pennsylvania Press.

2. NOTES ON THE NORTHERN RANGE OF *ZIZANIA* IN MANITOBA

Published in *Rhodora*, Journal of the New England Botanical Club 37, no. 440 (August 1935): 302–4.

3. ROCKS AND STONES

American Philosophical Society Library, Philadelphia. Alfred Irving Hallowell Papers, 1892–1981, Ms. Coll. 26. Unpublished typescript, written ca. 1935–36 to judge by internal evidence.

4. NOTES ON THE MATERIAL CULTURE OF THE ISLAND LAKE SAULTEAUX

First published in 1938 in *Journal de la Société des Américanistes de Paris*, new series, 30: 129–40. Hallowell's detailed diary account of his trip to Island Lake is in his field notebook of July-August 1930, in the Hallowell Papers, Ms. Coll. 26, American Philosophical Society, Philadelphia.

5. CROSS-COUSIN MARRIAGE IN THE LAKE WINNIPEG
AREA

Published in 1937 in D. S. Davidson, ed., *Twenty-fifth Anniversary Studies*, 95–110 (Philadelphia Anthropological Society); reprinted in Hallowell, *Contributions to Anthropology* (Chicago: University of Chicago Press, 1976.)

6. THE INCIDENCE, CHARACTER, AND DECLINE OF
POLYGNY AMONG THE LAKE WINNIPEG CREE AND
SAULTEAUX

Published in *American Anthropologist* 40 (1938): 235–56.

7. TEMPORAL ORIENTATION IN WESTERN CIVILIZATION
AND IN A PRELITERATE SOCIETY

Published in *American Anthropologist* 39 (1937): 647–70. Reprinted in Hallowell, *Culture and Experience* (Philadelphia: University of Pennsylvania Press, 1955), 216–35.

8. SOME PSYCHOLOGICAL ASPECTS OF MEASUREMENT
AMONG THE SAULTEAUX

Published in *American Anthropologist* 44 (1942): 62–77; reprinted in Hallowell, *Culture and Experience* (Philadelphia: University of Pennsylvania Press, 1955).

9. THE SIZE OF ALGONKIAN HUNTING TERRITORIES:
A FUNCTION OF ECOLOGICAL ADJUSTMENT

Paper read at American Anthropological Association meetings, Albuquerque NM, December, 1947. Reprinted from *American Anthropologist* 51 (1949): 35–45.

10. CULTURAL FACTORS IN SPATIAL ORIENTATION

A. Irving Hallowell, *Culture and Experience* (Philadelphia: University of Pennsylvania Press, 1955). Reprinted with permission of the University of Pennsylvania Press.

11. PSYCHIC STRESSES AND CULTURE PATTERNS

Reprinted with permission from the *American Journal of Psychiatry* 92 (1936): 1291–1310. American Psychiatric Association.

12. FEAR AND ANXIETY AS CULTURAL AND INDIVIDUAL VARIABLES IN A PRIMITIVE SOCIETY

First published in *Journal of Social Psychology* 9 (1938): 25–47, and reprinted in Hallowell, *Culture and Experience* (Philadelphia: University of Pennsylvania Press, 1955).

13. FREUDIAN SYMBOLISM IN THE DREAM OF A SAULTEAUX INDIAN

A. Irving Hallowell, "Freudian Symbolism in the Dream of a Salteaux Indian," *Journal of the Royal Anthropological Society*, published by Wiley-Blackwell.

14. SHABWÀN: A DISSOCIAL INDIAN GIRL

Published in *American Journal of Orthopsychiatry* 8 (1938): 329–40.

15. AGGRESSION IN SAULTEAUX SOCIETY

Published in *Psychiatry: Interpersonal and Biological Processes* 3 (1940): 395–407. Reprinted with permission of Guilford Press.

16. THE SOCIAL FUNCTION OF ANXIETY IN A PRIMITIVE SOCIETY

Published in *American Sociological Review* 7 (1941): 869–81, reprinted in *Culture and Experience*, 1955. The essay in this volume is the second version; Hallowell made some minor editorial changes to the earlier article in preparation for its republication in *Culture and Experience*.

17. SIN, SEX, AND SICKNESS IN SAULTEAUX BELIEF

A. Irving Hallowell, The British Journal of Psychology Medical Section 3 (1939): 21–29. Reproduced with permission from the *British Journal of Medical Psychology*, © The British Psychological Society.

18. PSYCHOSEXUAL ADJUSTMENT, PERSONALITY, AND THE GOOD LIFE

Published in Paul H. Hoch and Joseph Zubin, eds., *Psychosexual Development in Health and Disease* (New York, 1949), 102–23.

19. VALUES, ACCULTURATION, AND MENTAL HEALTH

First published in *American Journal of Orthopsychiatry* 20 (1950): 732–43; reprinted in *Culture and Experience* (1955), chapter 20.

20. SOME EMPIRICAL ASPECTS OF SAULTEAUX RELIGION

Read at the November, 1933, meeting of the Oriental Club of Philadelphia. Published in *American Anthropologist* 36(3) (1934): 389–404.

21. THE PASSING OF THE MIDEWI·WIN IN THE LAKE WINNIPEG AREA

Published in *American Anthropologist* 38 (1936): 32–51.

22. SPIRITS OF THE DEAD IN SAULTEAUX LIFE AND THOUGHT

Published in *Journal of the Royal Anthropological Institute*, published by Wiley-Blackwell. reprinted in *Culture and Experience* (1955).

23. THE ROLE OF DREAMS IN OJIBWA CULTURE

First published in G. E. von Grunebaum and R. R. Caillois, eds., *The Dream and Human Societies* (Berkeley: University of California Press, 1966), 267–92. © 1966 by the Regents of the University of California. Reprinted in the Hallowell essay collection, *Contributions to Anthropology: Selected Papers of A. Irving Hallowell* (Chicago: University of Chicago Press, 1976).

24. THE RORSCHACH METHOD AS AN AID IN THE STUDY OF PERSONALITIES IN PRIMITIVE SOCIETIES

Published in *Character and Personality: An International Psychological Quarterly* 9(3) (1941): 235–45. Published by Wiley-Blackwell.

25. SOME PSYCHOLOGICAL CHARACTERISTICS OF THE NORTHEASTERN INDIANS

© 1955, 184–202. Reprinted with permission of the University of Pennsylvania Press.

26. THE OJIBWA SELF AND ITS BEHAVIORAL ENVIRONMENT

Published as the second section (153–65) of "The Self and Its Behavioral Environment," *Explorations* 2 (April 1954); reprinted as chapter 8 in Hallowell, *Culture and Experience* (Philadelphia: University of Pennsylvania Press, 1955). The 1955 text appears here. As noted in the introduction to this section, Hallowell slightly revised its opening text from that appearing in *Explorations*.

27. OJIBWE ONTOLOGY, BEHAVIOR, AND WORLD VIEW

Published in *Culture in History: Essays in Honor of Paul Radin*, ed. Stanley Diamond. © 1960. Columbia University Press. Reprinted with permission of the publisher. Reprinted in Hallowell, *Contributions to Anthropology* (Chicago: University of Chicago Press, 1976), 357–90.

ancestors of, 29–30; as *änicinábe*, 27, 572; beliefs and thought about spiritual universe, 359–63, 365–81; characteristic cultural patterns of, 215–29; Christianity in population of, 25; cross-cousin marriage practices of, 6, 78, 223; dreams and contacting spiritual beings, 203; ecological adjustment by, 30–31, 442; fear and anxiety as cultural variables, 230–49; hunting territories of, 31–32, 112, 158–63, *163*, 164–70; incest taboos, 223–25; interactions with white populations, 9, 23; kinship pattern and social organization, 6; Lake Winnipeg community of, *xii*, xiii; as local Saulteaux variant, 23; Midé·wiwin practices, xvi, 46, 394–95, 396, 398; migration into remote region, 23, 26, 30; ninam, 6; old belief system and acculturation, 311; patrilineage, 30; personality organization of, 341–42, 349, 350; polygyny practices, 90; psychological characteristics of, 487–515; psychosexual adjustment of, 326–42; Rorschach testing of, 487, 493–94; self and behavioral environment of, 10, 520–34; as southern Ojibwe, xvi; temporal orientation of, 120–36; theory of disease, 215–16; trading posts and, 24; Winnipeg Treaty of 1875 and, 32, 39n20

Beres, David, 11, 459n5
Bergson, Henri, 117
bestiality, 237, 293, 316, 320, 324nn13–14, 328, 329, 341
Bevan, Edwyn, 407
Biard, Father, 487, 490, 492, 500, 501, 503
Bidney, David, 445, 543
Biennial Review of Anthropology, 8
Big Island, 392–93
Bigmouth, Adam, 316, 323n4
birchbark: canoes, 4, 57, 147; dishes, 416; drawings on, 419; fans (wewsähïgɑn), 57; records, 387; tipis, 35, 36, 53
Birch Island (Wigwasiminis), 395, 405n85
Birchstick, 373, 550, 552, 554

birch trees, 445
birds: as agents of sorcerers, 234; as deceased visiting kin, 417–18, 525–26, 552; pinèsï (hawk-like bird), 370, 371, 374; seasonal, 370, 380–81n6
Black Hawk, 28
Black Island, *385*, 391–92, 403–4n66
Bleuler, M., 477
Bleuler, R., 477
Bloodstoppers and Bearwalkers (Dorson), 551
Bloodvein River, *385*
Bloodvein River Ojibwe, 42; marriage practices of, 88, 99; Midé·wiwin practices, 392, 393, 398, 404n73
Bluffhead (Pi`kwákwɑsti·gɑn), 397
Boas, Franz, xiii, 2, 3–4
botany, xiii
braids, 391, 393, 404n81
breech cloth (änzïän), 54
Bressani, Father, 489
Brill, A. A., 2, 7
Brimmed Hat (Tcɑsämän), 188, 198n38
Broken Fingers (François), 386
Broken Head River, *385*, 390, 398, 403n56
Brown, Jennifer, xxi
Bruyas, Father, 496
Bunzel, Ruth, 467–68, 477
butterfly, 481

cà`bandawan (multiple family dwelling), 54, 107n54, 430, 574
Cadillac, 490
Cadzow, Donald A., 387
Cameron, Duncan, 92, 93, 273, 506–7
Canada: acculturation of Indian populations, 9; American anthropologists' studies in, xiii; ban of ceremonies, 363n2; Barren Ground band of Naskapi, 6; Department of Indian Affairs, 52, 80; Dominion Census, 25; education of Indians, 35; First Nations, xiv, xvi; Laurentian area or Canadian Shield, 33; Ojibwe populations, 27; Pre-Cambrian Shield, 44; racial issues, 9; reservation system of, 32; Royal

Canada (*continued*)
Canadian Mounted Police, 34,
238; Selkirk Treaty, 112; St. Francis
Abenaki, 4, 12n4; Treaty No. 1, 80,
390; Treaty No. 5, 68, 87, 393; United
Church of, 51, 52; Winnipeg Treaty of,
32, 34, 39n20, 87, 236
Canada Research Chair, xxi
Canadian Shield, 33, 34
cannibals, 225–27, 410, 538; destruction
and disposal of, 238, 272; fears of
encounters with, 237–41; gastric symptoms of, 238; giant, 238; as wíndĩgo,
207n3, 237, 238, 242
canoes, 4, 57–58, 147
caribou, 55, 150, 317, 330, 367, 375
Caribou Eskimo, 57
Carpenter, Edmund C., 470
Carver, Jonathan, 100
Caúwanäs [Zhaawanaash] (One Who
Travels with the South Wind), 396,
410
Cɛnawágwaskang, 93, 94, 598; as barter
chief, 99; as conjurer, 98; polygynous
practices of, 97, 98, 102
ceremonialism, directional orientation
and, 190–91, 198–99n43
Chaboillez House, 401n35
Chamula of Chiapas, Mexico, 467–68
Chippewa Indians: Canadian popula-
tions, 92; designation of, 26, 27; mar-
riage practices, 92
Christianity: attitudes toward polygyny,
101, 102–3; impact on Indian cultures
and practices, 23, 24–25, 51–52, 68–69,
89; medical aid by, 34–35; missionary
activities of, 9, 88–89, 489; teaching
Sabbath as praying day, 124
cingubīwátigok (evergreens), 422
Civilization in the United States (Stearns),
3, 12n2
Cockran, Rev., 388
Cole, Sally, 69
Collio, J. Martin, 5
Columbus, Christopher, 175
Commissioner's Island, 185

A Concise Dictionary of Minnesota Ojibwe
(Nichols and Nyholm), xxii
"Concordance of Ojibwa Narratives in the
Published Works of Henry R. Schoolcraft" (Hallowell), 28
confession: balance between instinctual
forces and cultural tradition, 322–23;
as cure for illness, 237, 298, 305n20,
315–23, 362, 523, 532n8; individual
motivations, 301, 306n27; public, 203;
relieving psychic stress, 215–18, 228n11,
321–22
conjuring: after dark, 123; as blessed with
abilities, 377; bringing soul back from
Land of the Dead, 523–24, 527; deference to conjurers, 282, 289nn19–20;
discovering causes of illness, 36, 256,
299, 305n22; false powers of, 203; four
dream blessing requirement, 455;
kadabéndang (spiritual owners), 367,
378; pawáganak or guardian spirits of,
216–17, 228n12, 524; performances of,
369, 377–80; purposes of, 378; as social
interaction between human and other-
than-humans, 377–78, 406, 422–25,
447–49; supernatural validation of,
216, 242; tent or lodge, 36, 49, 216–17,
256, 265n9, 447, 448, 523, 529, 534n17;
voices heard in performances, 448,
460–61n27
Contributions to Anthropology, xv, xxiii,
112, 309
Cooper, J. M., 72, 82–83n14, 158, 167–
68nn11–12, 226, 383
Cope, L., 130, 131
Copway, George, 28
co-wife, 78
Crane (Otci·tcák), 397, 398
Crane River Saulteaux, 386
"crazy" (kīwaskwe), 255–69
Cree Indians: anthropometric studies of,
72; artifacts collected by Hallowell, 21;
cannibalistic desires, 225; Christian
influences, 52; Island Lake community, 22; Lake Winnipeg regional
bands, 22, 25, 26, 88; late acquisition

of Midé·wiwin, 383; Nelson House band, 73; Norway House band, 52, 72, 73, 88, 102; Ojibwe utilization of language terms, xxii, 52; polygyny in Lake Winnipeg region, 87; psychological characteristics of, 487; Swampy Cree, 26, 72; trade with Ojibwe, 52; Woods Cree, 26, 72

Creek Indian wars, 28

Crooked Back (Wagi·békwan), 99

cross-cousin marriages, 4, 6, 67–68, 73, 223, 510–11

Cross Lake, 21, 51

Cross Lake Cree, 72, 73, 88, 90

Crow Indians, acculturation patterns, 81

crows, 55

cultural relativism, ix

Culture and Experience (Hallowell), xxiii, 19, 111, 311, 469, 470, 471, 552

Cumberland House Cree, 88, 93

Cummings, Mr., 396, 405n88

Curtis, E. S., 72

Dablon, Claude, 499

dances and dancing: directional orientation of, 190; drum dances, 361, 418–22, 427–30, 432, 433, 436nn28–29, 437n41; entering dance area, 419; food offerings during, 427–28, 437n40; giveaway dance (mändáitīwin), 123; great tree, 422, 436–37n32; multiple family dwellings and, 54, 430; potáte, 123, 261–62, 268n32, 268n32368, 428; temporal patterning of, 123; wabanówīwin, 36, 123, 246, 247, 258, 261, 267n21, 268n34

Darnell, Regna, ix, x

Davidson, D. S., 162, 164, 165, 166

dead: Christian influences and, 414–15; clothes and belongings of, 429–30; djĭbaiàking (the spirit, ghost land), 406, 522; Djĭbaimidéwi·win ceremony, 431; Djĭbaisímowin ceremony, 430; Djĭbai Wabanó ceremony, 430; dream approach, 406; drum divination of spirits, 425–30; "feast of the dead," 422, 437n34; food, tea and tobacco

at grave, 415, 416; ghosts, 416–17; as guardian spirits, 418–22; inconsiderate behavior toward, 293, 362, 424; invoking spirits in conjuring lodge, 406, 422–25; journey to Land of the Dead, 413, 435n18; keté änicinábek (old Indians, Ancients), 419, 420, 421, 525; life beyond the grave, 406–37, 414–15; mätci mänitu (bad spirit), 414, 436nn19–20; naming infants and, 432, 437n46, 521; offerings as communication, 415–16; Ojibwe burial practices, 413–14; reincarnation, 431–32; resuscitation of, 406, 411–12, 435n11; scattered and organized grave sites, 415–16; soul (òtcatcákwin), 406, 412, 520, 529; spirit activities at night, 416–17; visiting kin in form of bird, 417–18, 525–26, 552; whistling by spirits of, 416–17, 430, 522. *See also* Land of the Dead (djĭbaiàking); Ojibwe universe

deception, 216, 237, 315

Deer Lake, 53, 278, *385*, 396

Delaware Indians, 498

Delusion and Dream (Freud), 7

Dement, William, 438

Densmore, Frances, 92

Denys, Nicolas, 487, 490

Devereux, George, 440, 441

Dewey, John, 3, 230

The Dial, 7

Disbrowe, Frederick, 85n39

dissociative psychic states, 214

Djakógwaiyo (Short Neck), 390, 597–98

Djĭbaimidéwi·win ceremony, 431

Dobzhansky, T., 10

Dog Head, 390, 392, 393, 404n72

Dog Head Indians, 88, 100, 108n65

dogs: in camps, 55, 56, 320, 330, 389, 413; guarding road to Land of the Dead, 413; hunting with, 54; teeth as disease causing, 237, 521

dog sleds, 57

Dorson, Richard, 551, 553

Drage, T. S., 92, 95

The Dream in Primitive Cultures (Lincoln), 250

dreams: animating inanimate objects, 456, 462n39; as contact with spiritual beings, 203, 441, 554–57; cultivating strength of spirit and power, 32, 362; dream faster (kīgúsämo), 452, 453; dream gifts, 418–22; Freudian symbolism in, 250–52; giving self form, 524, 533n9; greedy practices, 456; as guidance, 376; hominid capability of, 438–41, 459n3; identifying stories as animate, 44; interpreting, 211; intruding on man's consciousness, 443; knowledge of spiritual entities through, 374, 375, 381n10; metamorphosis in, 453–54, 461–62n34, 524–29, 552–53, 554–57; obligations imposed by pawáganak, 456–57, 531, 560; ógimä (chief, superior person), 375; patterns of, 453, 461n32; pawáganak or dream visitors, 32, 371n11, 374, 524, 528–29, 530, 531, 545, 591; puberty fast for boys, 282, 284, 347–48, 451–58, 527–28, 529–30, 531, 556, 559–60; receiving knowledge of medicine, 361; roles in Ojibwe culture, 362, 438–64, 449–50, 458; soul abduction and, 219–21; as supernatural blessings, 216, 243, 249n12; as symbolic modes of expression, 440; taboos against recounting of, 555; traditional beliefs in experiences of, 369, 374–77; visiting Land of the Dead, 361, 410–11, 435n7

Drumming Point, 391

drums, 54; divination of spirits with, 425–30; as medium of communication with the dead, 425–30; as sacred objects, 245

Du Bois, Cora, 477

Duck, John (Machkajence): as conjurer, 46–47, 49, 50n6, 148, 204, 206, 244; guardian spirits of, 245; phobias of, 243–47; as Wábano leader, 244, 541; wábano pavilion of, 397

duck hawks, 547

Duck Lake, 46–47

Duck Lake Ojibwe, 124

ducks, 55, 124, 375

Dung-man, 335

Du Peron, Father, 490

eagle (kinïu), 127, 527

Eagle Lake, 317

Eagle Moon, 126–27, 219

Eggan, Dorothy, 441

Eggan, Fred, 81

Egg Island, 395

Eiseley, Loren C., 158

enemies and prisoners, treatment of, 496, 505

ethnohistory, 19

Ethnohistory, 19

ethnonyms, xvi, xxiii

ethnosemantics, 10

Evans, James, 25, 88

Evans, Thomas, 51

Explorations (Carpenter and McLuhan), 470

Explorations Two (Carpenter and McLuhan), 471

Fair Wind (Nämɑwin), 407; Christian influences on, 428; dance pavilion of, 407, 408, 426, 433, 437n38; Djïbaisímowin, Ghost (or Spirit of the Dead) Dance of, 425–30; drum dance of, 361, 427–30, 437n41; drum of, 407, 407, 426, 433; home of, 468; as medicine man, xxiii, 46, 47, 50n8, 361, 601; rattles of, 407, 407; sons of, 361, 407; spirit helper, Thunder Bird, 407, 408, 447, 549; wife of, 407

Family Society, 2

Farrington, E., 51

fear: of covert aggression, 274–75, 287n10; creating inner tensions, 220; as cultural and individual variables, 230–43; of disease, 293, 294; of disorientation, 187–88, 198n37; encounters with cannibals, 237–41; traditional dogma and, 239, 249n9. *See also* aggression; anxiety

Great Beaver, 371

Great Eagle, 453

Great Fisher (K`tcīotcīganang), 121

Great Hare (Misábos), 45, 367, 544, 600

Great Lakes, 57

Great Lynx, 204, 222, 223, 335–36, 371

Great Snake, 371

Great Trout, 372

Greenberg, Joseph, 539, 540

Grey Eyes, 403n54

guardian spirits: conferring blessings, 245, 298, 418–22; dead as, 418–522; owners or bosses of, 31, 418, 528. *See also* dreams

guilt, 220

gulls, 55

Haeckel, Ernst, 176

Hallowell, A. Irving, *xiv*; anthropological studies and career of, ix–x, 2–3, 11; behavioral evolution studies by, 10–11; Berens River Ojibwe fieldwork visits by, xiii, xxiii; Cree studies, 9; cross-cousin marriage studies, 6, 71–85; education of, 1–8; essays and writings as historical documents, xv, xvi, xxi–xxiv; ethnographic and ethnoscience methods of, x, xi, 10; as ethnohistorian, 19; genealogical data collected, 73, 74, 76–81, 84n30; kinship studies by, 4, 5–6, 71–85; Ojibwa field experiences, xiii, xxiii, 9–10; personal tragedies of, xv, 206, 207n4, 471; photographs taken by, xxiii, 258, 267n28; relationship with Chief Berens, xiii, xvi–xviin1, xix, xxiii, 21, 22; Rorschach tests of Ojibwe, xxiii, 8, 311, 350, 467–68; social work studies, 1–2; working with informants, 81, 85n39; writings and essays of: "Concordance of Ojibwa Narratives in the Published Works of Henry R. Schoolcraft," 28; *Culture and Experience*, xxiii, 19, 111, 311, 469, 470, 471, 552; "Northern Ojibwa Ecological Adaptation and Social Organization," 112–13; *The Ojibwa of Berens River, Manitoba*,

xv, 112–13, 467; "Ojibwa World View and Disease," xiv, 309, 312; *The Role of Conjuring in Saulteaux Society*, xxiii

Handbook of North American Indians, vol. 6, Subarctic (Helm and Sturtevant), xvi

Handsome Lake, 487

hare, 55

Hargrave, J. J., 389

hawks, 546

Hayes River, 51, 188

health: as positive value, 294. *See also* illness

Hecla Island, 393

Henry, Alexander (elder), 26, 91, 92, 422

Henry, Alexander (younger), 26–27, 90, 384, 386, 387, 400n11

Henry, Jules, 345–46, 468, 477

Herskovits, Melville, 3, 4

Hewitt, J. N. B., 558

Hiebert, Weldon, xix

Hind, H. Y., 387–88

historicism, ix

History of Human Marriage (Westermarck), 3

Hole River, 404n68

Hollow Water River Saulteaux, 42, 393, 394, 404n68

Horney, Karen, 240, 241

horses, 144–45

Hudson Bay, ix, 25, 57; Canadian Shield, 33; canoe routes, 30; native knowledge of, 182

Hudson's Bay Company: barter chiefs in, 99, 108n59; fur trade, 23–24, 36n2; missionary activities and, 25; paydays, 126; trading posts of, 9, 23–24, 36n2, 51, 52, 132, 187–88, 253, 366, 391, 396, 401n35

Hudson's Bay Company Archives (HBCA), 20

Human Nature and Conduct (Dewey), 3

hunting: active hunters in, 160, 163, *163*, *164*, 168n18; beliefs about animals and, 31–32, 375, 376, 560; dreams as guidance, 331, 376; ecological adjustment in, 158–59, 161, 442; game scarcity and,

land, 235; Bloodvein River, 24; canoe
routes, 34, 41, 44, 51, 52, 57; Christian
missions in region of, 21, 25; Dog
Head, 88; exploration by white popu-
lations, 25; fur trade expansion, 21, 24,
25; geologic origin, 85n33; Jack Head
Island, 88, 361; Ojibwe migration into,
23, 26, 30; Pigeon River, 23, 24; Poplar
River, 24; reserves in region on, 366;
wild rice cultivation areas, 41–42;
Winnipeg River, 24. *See also* Berens
River
Lalemant, Jerome, 490
La Marte blanche, 92
Landes, Ruth, Ojibwe studies by, xiii, 69,
70n1, 72, 99, 269n37, 285n3, 286–87n5,
288n11, 343n8, 471
Landis, C., 231
Land of the Dead (djïbaiàking): accounts
of travelers returning from, 408–10;
djïbaiikana (spirit, ghost road), 409,
522; dreams as visits to, 361, 410,
522–23; food offered by the dead, 409,
434n4, 523; healthy and ill visits to,
406, 434n1; invoking and interacting
with souls of dead, 361; journey to, 188,
521–22, 532n4; location of, 188, 190,
412–13, 435nn13–14; road (djïbaiikana)
to, 413–14; visits to, 188
language: loan words, xxii, 4; self-image
and, 520–34; Siouan-speaking peoples,
26
Laufer, Bertold, 5
Laure, Father, 498
La Verendrye, Pierre Gaultier de, 25, 92,
100, 384, 391
Leach, Frederic, xxiii–xxiv
Le Caron, Father, 500
Le Clercq, Chretien, 487, 490, 495, 497–
98, 500, 502, 505–6, 516n15, 518n35
Le Jeune, Father, 270, 273, 277, 285n2,
288nn13–14, 469, 490, 495, 496–97,
502, 503–4
Lesser, A., 5
Lewis, Wyndham, 117
life cycle: ákïwezi (old man), 132;

apïnondjï (child), 132; i`kwézes (little
girl), 132; ketéockïnïga (old young
man), 132; ketéockïnïkwe (old young
woman), 132; kwïwïzes (little boy),
132; mintímoye (old woman), 132;
ockapïnondjï (new, young), 132;
ockïnïge (male before marriage),
132; ockinïgi`kwe (female before
marriage), 132; onabemïmä (married
man), 132; pïmädazïwin (life in the
fullest sense), 285, 301, 322, 328–29, 338,
340, 347, 348, 349, 363, 421, 444, 451,
455; wïwïmän (married woman), 132
lightning, 367, 370, 371, 546
Lightning (Wawásan), 393, 394
Lincoln, J. S., 250
lithic animation, 44–50, 361, 540–41
Little Grand Rapids, 385
Little Grand Rapids Ojibwe: activities
of post-pubertal boys and girls, 256,
266n14; animate stones of, 46–47;
canoe routes, 44; cross-cousin marriages, 75; Hallowell's observations
of, 204–5; impact of Christianity, 243;
leader of, 100–101; location of, 366;
material culture of, 35; Midé·wiwin
practices of, 397; parenting, 262,
268n33; reservation of, 33; Shabwán,
dissocial adolescent in, 124, 253–65,
265nn4–6, 266–69; treaty location of,
88; wabanó pavilion of, 46, 50n6, 261,
268n30; wild rice gathering by, 40,
41, 42
Longfellow, Henry Wadsworth, 27, 28, 29
Long Plains Saulteaux, 387, 390, 398,
403n58
loon, 127
Loskiel, H. G., 498
Lovejoy, Arthur, 543
love magic, 218–19, 335
Lower Fort Garry, 389, 403n51
Lowie, Robert H., 3
lunar changes: adding thirteenth
moon, 127, 139n33; ämanozówïgïzis
(Rutting Moon), 128; api`tapïbungizis
(Half-winter Moon), 128;

mink, 323n11, 330, 337
Minnedosa River, 386, 401n19
miracle (mămandawi·zi), 393
Misábos (Great Hare), 45, 367, 544, 600
misínigäp. See "Maria" Portage
Miskógi·ni·u (Red Eagle), 389–90, 403n50
Miskwádesīwískījik (Mud-Turtle's Eye),
    411, 416, 435n8
mistikwagim (snowshoe), 57, 585
Miwok Indians, 79
moccasin games, 418
moccasins, 55, 56, 62nn34–35
Montagnais Indians, 500, 503; cross-cous-
    in marriages, 72; emotional structure
    of, 495, 496; Mistassini band of, 71
Montagnais-Naskapi Indians, 270, 277,
    487
moon. See lunar changes
moose, 55, 320, 330, 447
Moose clan, 80, 392, 395
Moose Lake Cree, 88, 89, 98, 101
moral transgressions, 216, 217–18, 237
Morning Star (Wábanänang), 392, 394
Morris, Alexander, 89, 104n8
mosquitos, 55
Mossy Portage, 51, 59n2
Mowrer, O. H., 292, 303–4n8
Mud-Turtle's Eye (Miskwádesīwískījik),
    411, 416, 435n8
Munias, Richard, 53, 76
murder, 216, 237, 275, 315
Murdock, G. P., 6
Museum of the American Indian, Heye
    Foundation, 4, 21–22, 53, 60n18
muskeg, 51
muskrats, 55, 134, 150, 239, 558
Muskrat's Liver, 402n39
myths and tales: Aásī, 135, 571; animal
    wives, 341; contemporary living enti-
    ties, 133, 368; as continuity of memory,
    362; distortion of, 28; earth as an is-
    land, 52, 189, 366–67, 370; Flint, 44–45,
    540, 544, 545; as formalized narratives
    (ätsokanak), 28, 372; giant animals,
    233, 235, 367, 371–72; Great Beaver,
    134; Great Hare (Misábos), 45, 600;

Great Mosquito, 134; Great Snake, 134;
    Great Trout, 134; hierarchy of pow-
    ers, 367; human beings and previous
    forms, 134; Kaiánwe, 135; Land of the
    Dead, 408, 413, 434n3; Manabozho, 29;
    metamorphosis in, 446–47, 524–29,
    549–57; news or tidings oral narra-
    tives, 372, 542; other-than-human class
    of beings, 311, 444–49, 459–60nn16–17,
    536, 542–49, 564n19; owners and boss-
    es of spirits, 445, 528, 546; as past real
    events, 340, 528, 530, 542–43, 563n16;
    as recounted and not invented, 493;
    as sacred stories, 528, 542; sexual be-
    havior in, 339–41; Snow, 530; of sun
    movements, 445, 543–44; Tcakábɛc,
    133, 139–40n44, 543–44, 545, 604; tell-
    ing in winters, 204, 448, 460n26, 542;
    temporal clues, 133–34; Thunder, 367;
    Thunder Bird, 246, 446, 530, 546–49,
    547–48; Winds, 44, 134–35, 178, 190,
    367, 378, 445, 447, 455, 530, 544, 545,
    548, 564n25; Wísakedják, 134, 135,
    530, 531, 542, 545, 558. See also Ojibwe
    universe

Nagagábek (Flatstone), 397
Nämawin (Fair Wind). See Fair Wind
    (Nämawin)
Naowawgunwudju, 386
Naskapi Indians, 6, 56, 71
National Topographic Series maps, 162,
    182
Natural History of Creation (Haeckel), 176
Navajo Indians, 212
Nearing, Scott, 1
Nelson House Cree, 73
Nénagi·s (Quivering), 390, 403n59
Netley Creek, 388
Net-no-kwa, 386, 400n16
New England Botanical Club, 20
Newfoundland, Micmac hunting territo-
    ries, 159–60
ni`bakīwin (use of sucking tubes), 98,
    236–37, 277, 316, 317, 323n5, 521
Nichols, John D., xxii

polygyny, 336
Pomeroy, Wardell, 310
Poplar Narrows [Poplar Hills], 47, *385,*
397, 432, 433
Poplar River, 238, *385, 396*
Poplar River Ojibwe, 41, 72; invocation of
deceased persons in conjuring lodge,
422–25; marriage practices, 75, 78, 93,
94, 98, 99; in treaty books, 88
porcupines, 330
portages, 51, 52, 59n2, 59n4
potáte dance: held after dark, 123; pinèsï
as spiritual owner, 368; social activity
of, 261–62, 268n32, 268n34, 428
primitive, defining, xxiii, 9
Primitive Culture (Tylor), 442
Prince, A. E., 85n39
Prince, Henry, 85n39
prisoners, treatment of, 496, 505
privacy, 257, 266n17
pseudosurgical techniques, 236–37
psychiatry, xiii
psychic stress: adjusting to tension of, 225;
confession as relieving, 215–18, 228n11,
321–22; creation and resolution,
215–29; culture patterns and, 209–29,
322; intra-psychic conflicts, 225–27;
love magic and, 218–19; role of dreams
in resolving, 219–25
psychoanalysis, influences of in American
thought, 2
The Psychoanalytic Method (Pfister), 7
psychological anthropology, 7
psychological characteristics of Northeastern Indians, 486–519; alcohol and
behavior, 505–6, 517n33; described
by traders, explorers and missionaries, 488–515; emotional structure,
494–515; gossip and slander as covert
aggression, 502–3, 505; humor and
laughing, 503, 510; individualism and,
512; intelligence level, 489–94; Ojibwe
self and behavioral environment,
520–34; personalities, 486; restraint in
public faces, 512–14, 519n47

psychological testing, 117, 137n11. *See also*
Rorschach inkblot test
Psychological Types (Jung), 7
psychology, xiii; affective experiences in,
231; articulating cultural traditions, 11;
ego processes, 10; imaginative processes, 11; learning and, 231; nature versus
nurture, 231; self-objectification, 10;
socialization of symbolic forms, 10;
stimulus-response concept, 230
psychosexual adjustment: factors in,
326–41; in nonliterate culture, 325–44;
personality structure and, 326, 341–42,
349, 350. *See also* sexual behavior
puberty fasts: gaining guardian spirits and
power, 527, 530, 533–34nn15–16, 556;
for Ojibwe boys, 282, 284, 347–48,
451–58, 527–28, 529–30, 531, 556, 559–
60; as temporary separation of soul
from body, 527
Pueblo Indians, 190
pygmy owl, 279

Quebec, Grand Lake Victoria band,
161–63, *163,* 164–70

rabbits, 55
Radcliffe-Brown, A. R., 76–77, 119,
204nn14–15, 294
Radin, Paul, 453, 461n32, 535, 558
Rank, Otto, 291, 303n6
Rat's Liver, 402n39
rattles, 262, 407, *407*
Raudot, Antoine Denis, 504
Raup, Hugh M., 41
Raw Head River [Broken Head River],
403n56
Red Eagle (Miskógi·ni·u), 85n39, 389–90,
403n50
Redfield, R., 442
red fox, 55
Red Lake, mining operations, 33
Red River Colony, 27, 155n4, 402n45
Red River, 25, 27, 144, 182, 384, *385,* 386,
387, 388, 401–2n36
Red Sucker Lake, 53

337, 340–41; artificial phallus, 316, 317, 318, 330, 337; autoeroticism, 316, 317; avoidance practices, 327, 328; bestiality, 237, 293, 316, 320, 324nn13–14, 328, 329; cultural context of, 310, 325–44; extramarital affairs, 337–38; fellatio, 237, 299–300, 316, 320, 330, 337; heterosexual transgressions, 316, 318–20; homosexuality in, 316, 317–18, 329–30, 343n8; incest, 216, 218, 223–25, 237, 293, 300–301, 316, 319, 323–24n12, 328, 329–30, 446, 460n23, 548, 564n25; living the Good Life (pimädαziwin), 328–29, 338, 340; love magic and, 335; marital intercourse in, 335–36; masturbation, 237, 316, 318, 319, 328, 330, 343n4; modal patterns of, 330–39; moral evaluations of, 325, 326, 327, 342n2; in myths and tales, 339–41; play and rendezvous of unmarried, 332–34; psychosexual adjustment in nonliterate culture, 325–44, 349; rejection and aggressive responses, 335; sexual transgressions causing illness, 316–22; stimulation and gratification, 328; verbal references and banter, 331–32

shaman, plural marriages by, 69

shells, illness caused by, 237, 284, 290n22, 521, 539–40

Sherif, M., 119

Sioux Indians: aggression in social behavior, 270; displacement by Ojibwe, 29; hunting territories, 161; wakanda, 558

skabéwis (usher), 423, 437n37

Skinner, Alanson, 9, 53, 92, 93, 387, 390, 399nn5–8

sleep or sleeps: as distance, 122; as temporal length, 115

Smooth Rock, 52, 53

snakes, 204, 232–33, 367, 371, 547

snowshoes, 34, 56–57

snow snake game (sósïman), 58, 593

sociology, xiii, 2

The Song of Hiawatha (Longfellow), 27, 28, 29, 38nn15–16

sorcery and sorcerers: covert aggression by, 274–75, 287n10, 505; duels by, 283–84; interfering with pīmädαzīwin, 349; projecting objects into victims, 49, 236–37; suspicions of, 511–12, 513, 518n43; taking forms of animals, 525–26, 551, 553, 564nn29, 31; using hair, 521

soul abduction, 219–21

South Africa, Bushmen of, 212

South America: Araucanian Indians, 5–6; kinship and social organization, 6; Pilaga, 468

sparrow hawks, 547

spatial orientation: in animals, 177, 195n21; cosmic space and, 188–90; cultural factors in, 171–99; defining, 171, 173, 192n1; directional orientation in ceremonialism, 190–91, 198–99n43; fear of disorientation, 187–88, 198n37; of graves, 190; as intersensory, 172, 192n6; knowledge of terrain, 180–82, 195n26; mental maps, 174, 193n10; as native or acquired, 172, 192n5; psychological aspects of measurement, 141–52, 152, 153–58; spatial schema, 173; travel and, 184–87, 197n33; of urban populations, 180, 195n24. *See also* temporal and time orientation

Speck, Frank G.: fieldwork in Canada, xiii; as Hallowell's mentor, xv, 2–3, 5, 21; hunting territory studies by, 158, 159–60, 167n3, 167n10, 169n20; as proto-ethnohistorian, 19; on salvage ethnography, 3, 12n1, 21; studies of Montagnais-Naskapi, 71, 270

Spencer, Dorothy, 151, 477

Spengler, Oswald, 117

sphagnum moss, 36

Split Lake Cree, 73

Standard Intelligence Tests, 492

St. Andrews Rapids, 388

St. Peter's Reserve, 68, 80, 85n35, 398

stars: Belt of Orion (Odádawaämok, three young men), 121; K`tcïotcïganαng (Great Fisher), 121; Milky Way as path of summer birds, 179, 370, 380–81n6; Ursa Major, 121; wábanänαng (morning star), 121

Thompson, Stith, 549
thunder, 367, 460n20, 540, 546, 547
Thunder Bird, 189, 246, 374, 419, 421,
    436n27, 446, 530, 546–49
Thunderbird Land, 446
tikínágan (cradleboard), 36, 56, 594
time. *See* temporal and time orientation
Time Cult, 117
tipis, 35, 36, 53, 60–61n20
toads, 204, 232, 234, 241, 248n6, 547
tobacco, 35, 49, 247, 378, 421, 423, 436n31,
    558
trading posts, 9, 23–24, 36n2, 51, 52, 132,
    187–88, 253, 366, 391, 396, 401n35
trait complexes, 4
traps and trapping: defilement of, 221, 274;
    dreams as guidance, 331, 376, 381n12;
    spiritual owners of animals, 221
travel: spatial orientation and, 184–87,
    197n33; by water, 34, 41, 44, 51, 52, 57–
    58, 185, 197n35; during winter, 185–86
Traverse Bay, 391
treaties: Selkirk Treaty, 112; Stone Fort
    Treaty, 390; Treaty No. 1, 80, 390;
    Treaty No. 5, 68, 87, 393; Winnipeg
    Treaty of 1875, 32, 34, 39n20, 87, 101–3,
    144, 236, 366
Tucker, Sarah, 388, 403n48
turtles, 481–82
Two Hearts, 391
Tylor, E. B., 442–43

United States, xvi; Armed Services, 352;
    Bureau of American Ethnology, 26,
    442; Indian Affairs, 28; National
    Research Council, 7, 203; Navaho
    populations, 27; Ojibwe populations,
    27; reservation system of, 9, 29; Sioux
    populations, 27; social interaction of
    black and white populations, 9; War
    of 1812, 29
Uzaúaskogat. *See* Yellow Legs
    (Uzaúaskogat)

Valentine, Rand, xix, xxii
value systems: diversity of, 345–46; inte-

grative behavior as measure, 346, 354,
    355n2; mental health and, 345–46;
    pīmädazīwin (life in the fullest sense),
    347, 348, 354, 363, 421, 444, 451, 455,
    472, 521, 522, 559–61

Waasagomach Bay, 52
Wabadjesi, 278–80
wabanówīwin: animate stones associated
    with, 46, 47, 48–49, 451; as curative
    dancing ceremony, 258, 261, 267n21,
    268n34; lodge or pavilion for, 45, 148,
    261, 268n30, 407, 426; Midé·wiwin
    features in, 246, 247; wábano mă'ni·tu
    as spiritual owner, 367
Wagi·békwan (Crooked Back), 99, 393
Wanipigow River, 384, 385
Wanipigow River Ojibwe, 72, 75, 393,
    404n69
Wasbosékwan (Rabbit Robe), 393
Waterhen Saulteaux, 386, 401n22
Wawásan (Lightning), 393–94
weasel, 134
Wejaanimaash, 407
wemti·gózi (mythological white man),
    378
West Africa, 250
Westermarck, Edward, 3
White, William A., 210
White Earth (White Mud) River, 88, 392
White Mud Falls, 188
Whiting, John W. M., 450, 461n29
Whorf, Benjamin, 536
Wigwaswátik (Birchstick), 373
wild rice, 20, 40–43, 128
"Wild-Rice Gatherers of the Upper
    Lakes" (Jenks), 40
Wild Rice Lake, 42
Wild Rice River, 42
Willoughby, R. R., 501
Wilson, Maggie, 69
wíndīgo: as cannibal monster, 142, 147,
    237, 238, 242, 456, 538; destruction
    and disposal of, 272, 560; nighttime
    encounters, 417
wíndīgo psychosis, 207n3, 225–27

Winnebago Indians, 558

Winnipeg, 387

Winnipeg River, 24, 25, 30, 87, 385, 391, 403n61

Winnipeg Treaty of 1875, 32, 34, 39n20, 87, 101–3, 144, 236, 366

Winston, Ella, 210

Winter, Ella, 118

Wísakedják: as culture hero in myth and tales, 52, 134, 135, 340–41, 344n22, 366, 386, 401n27, 530, 531, 542, 545, 549, 558, 606; head encased in bear skull, 186; as spiritual helper, 133, 150, 420, 433, 436n26, 606

Wissler, Clark, 90

witches: covert aggression by, 506; detecting work of, 378; illness caused by, 236, 295, 296; projecting objects into bodies, 258, 267n23

Wolf, Ambrose, 400n14

woodchuck (aká`kotci·s), 386, 401n29

Woods Cree, 26, 72, 91

world views, x; cognitive orientation in, 538–42; defining, 535–36; Hallowell's writings on, 359; linguistic categories,

538–42; psychological unity of, 557–61; sophisticated thought about spiritual universe, 359

World War I, anthropological practices during, 1, 2, 3, 12n2, 132

World War II, scholarly research during, 20

xy Company, 401n35

Yellow Legs (Uzaúaskogat): ancestors of, 80; animate stone of, 45–46, 395, 541, 563n13; guardian spirits of, 361, 363n4, 395, 404–5n84; as Midé·wiwin leader, 361, 393–96, 398, 541; walking on water, 395

Young, Egerton R., 102, 125, 396, 405n86, 518n41

Zaagajiwe (Charlie Moose Owen), 407

Zeisberger, David, 498

Zhaawanaash (The One Who Soars Or Is Blown On The South Wind), 396, 410

Zizania, cultivation in Manitoba, 40–43

IN THE CRITICAL STUDIES IN THE HISTORY OF ANTHROPOLOGY SERIES

Contributions to Ojibwe Studies:
Essays, 1934–1972
A. Irving Hallowell
Edited and with introductions
by Jennifer S. H. Brown
and Susan Elaine Gray

Excavating Nauvoo: The
Mormons and the Rise of Historical
Archaeology in America
Benjamin C. Pykles
Foreword by Robert L. Schuyler

Cultural Negotiations: The Role
of Women in the Founding of
Americanist Archaeology
David L. Browman

Homo Imperii: A History of
Physical Anthropology in Russia
Marina Mogilner

American Anthropology and
Company: Historical Explorations
Stephen O. Murray

Racial Science in Hitler's
New Europe, 1938–1945
Edited by Anton Weiss-
Wendt and Rory Yeomans

Cora Du Bois: Anthropologist,
Diplomat, Agent
Susan C. Seymour

Before Boas: The Genesis of
Ethnography and Ethnology in
the German Enlightenment
Han F. Vermeulen

American Antiquities: Revisiting the
Origins of American Archaeology
Terry A. Barnhart

An Asian Frontier: American
Anthropology and Korea, 1882–1945
Robert Oppenheim

Theodore E. White and the Development
of Zooarchaeology in North America
R. Lee Lyman

To order or obtain more information on these or other University of Nebraska
Press titles, visit nebraskapress.unl.edu.